D0927081

Encyclopedia of Prehistory

Volume 7: South America

Encyclopedia of Prehistory

General Editors: Peter N. Peregrine and Melvin Ember

Encyclopedia of Prehistory
Volume 7: South America

Edited by

Peter N. Peregrine
Lawrence University
Appleton, Wisconsin

and

Melvin Ember
Human Relations Area Files/Yale University
New Haven, Connecticut

Published in conjunction with the Human Relations Area Files
at Yale University

Kluwer Academic/Plenum Publishers
New York Boston Dordrecht London Moscow

Library of Congress Cataloging-in-Publication Data

Encyclopedia of prehistory/edited by Peter N. Peregrine and Melvin Ember
    p. cm.
    Includes bibliographical references and index.
    Contents: v. 7. South America
    ISBN 0-306-46261-3 (v. 7)
      1. Prehistoric peoples—Encyclopedias.   2. Antiquities, Prehistoric—Encyclopedias.   I.
Human Relations Area Files, Inc.

GN710 .E53 2000
960′.1′03—dc21

99-049489

ISBN 0-306-46264-8 (set)
ISBN 0-306-46261-3 (vol. 7)

©2002 Human Relations Area Files, Inc.

http://www.wkap.nl/

10 9 8 7 6 5 4 3 2 1

The Encyclopedia of Prehistory was prepared under the auspices and with the support of the Human Relations Area Files (HRAF) at Yale University. The foremost international research organization in the field of cultural anthropology, HRAF is a nonprofit consortium of 19 Sponsoring Member institutions and more than 400 active and inactive Associate Member institutions in nearly 40 countries. The mission of HRAF is to provide information that facilitates the cross-cultural study of human behavior, society, and culture. The HRAF Collection of Ethnography, which has been building since 1949, contains nearly one million pages of information, indexed according to more than 700 subject categories, on the cultures of the world. An increasing portion of the Collection of Ethnography, which now covers more than 365 cultures, is accessible electronically each year to member institutions. The HRAF Collection of Archaeology, the first installment of which appeared in 1999, is accessible electronically each year to those member institutions opting to receiving it. Each year the Collection of Archaeology adds indexed full-text materials on a random sample of the major traditions in the *Encyclopedia of Prehistory*. After a tradition has been included in the Collection of Archaeology, HRAF plans to add materials on the complete archaeological sequence relevant to the tradition.

Contributors

Mark Aldenderfer
Department of Anthropology
University of California
Santa Barbara, California
United States

Daniel Aresenault
Départment d'histoire
Université Laval
Québec
Canada

Tamara L. Bray
Department of Anthropology
Wayne State University
Detroit, Michigan
United States

Jose Proenza Brochado
CEPA, IFCH
Pontificia Universidade Catolica do RGS
Rio Grande do Sul
Brazil

David Browman
Department of Anthropology
Washington University
St.Louis, Missouri
United States

Warren B. Church
Department of Environmental Sciences
Columbus State University
Columbus, Georgia
United States

Tom Dillehay
Department of Anthropology
University of Kentucky
Lexington, Kentucky
United States

Timothy Earle
Department of Anthropology
Northwestern University
Evanston, Illinois
United States

Paul Goldstein
Department of Anthropology
University of California, San Diego
San Diego, California
United States

Wesley Hurt (deceased)

William Isbell
Department of Anthropology
State University of New York
Binghampton, New York
United States

vii

Patricia J. Knobloch
La Mesa, California
United States

Lawrence Kuznar
Department of Sociology and Anthropology
Indiana-Purdue University
Fort Wayne, Indiana
United States

Jerry Moore
Department of Anthropology
California State University, Domniguez Hills
Carson, California
United States

Peter N. Peregrine
Department of Anthropology
Lawrence University
Appleton, Wisconsin
United States

Ernesto Luis Piana
CADIC-CONICET
Malvinas Argentinas s/n
Tierra del Fuego
Argentina

Thomas Pozorski
Department of Psychology and Anthropology
University of Texas–Pan American
Edinburg, Texas
United States

Shelia Pozorski
Department of Psychology and Anthropology
University of Texas–Pan American
Edinburg, Texas
United States

Donald Proulx
Department of Anthropology
University of Massachusetts
Amherst, Massachusetts
United States

John Rick
Department of Anthropological Science
Stanford University
Stanford, California
United States

Anna Roosevelt
Department of Anthropology
The Field Museum
and
Department of Anthropology
University of Illinois
Chicago, Illinois
United States

Charles Stanish
Department of Anthropology
University of California
Los Angeles, California
United States

Preface

The *Encyclopedia of Prehistory* represents an attempt to provide basic information on all archaeologically known cultures, covering the entire globe and the entire prehistory of humankind. It is designed as a tool to assist in doing comparative research on the peoples of the past. Most of the entries are written by the world's foremost experts on the particular areas and time periods.

The *Encyclopedia* is organized according to major traditions. A major tradition is defined as *a group of populations sharing similar subsistence practices, technology, and forms of sociopolitical organization, which are spatially contiguous over a relatively large area and which endure temporally for a relatively long period.* Minimal areal coverage for a major tradition can be thought of as something like 100,000 square kilometers, while minimal temporal duration can be thought of as something like five centuries. Major traditions are not quite like cultures in an ethnological sense because, in addition to socioculturally defining characteristics, major traditions generally have a more extended temporal dimension. Major traditions are also defined by a somewhat different set of sociocultural characteristics than are ethnological cultures. Major traditions are defined based on common subsistence practices, sociopolitical organization, and material industries, but language, ideology, and kinship ties play little or no part in their definition because they are virtually unrecoverable from archaeological contexts. In contrast, language, ideology, and kinship ties are central to defining ethnological cultures.

There are three types of entries in the *Encyclopedia:* the major tradition entry, the regional subtradition entry, and the site entry. Each contains different types of information, and each is intended to be used in a different way. The major tradition entry is a general summary of information about a single major tradition; it provides descriptive information about the environment and culture of the people whose lifeways comprised the tradition. The major tradition entry lacks formal references but provides a list of suggested readings. Although the geographical and temporal range of the major tradition entry was stipulated for the authors, they were given the freedom to define regional subtraditions and sites on the basis of their own interpretations of the archaeological record. Regional subtradition and site entries, then, focus on archaeological areas and locales that are conventionally distinguished in the archaeological record for a given major tradition. The regional subtradition and site entries provide specific information on the unique archaeological record of a particular region or a particular archaeological site and are fully referenced.

How to Use the *Encyclopedia of Prehistory*

How you use the *Encyclopedia* will differ depending on the type of research you are doing. For most projects, you will want to begin with the maps at the front of the volume. Each map shows the geographical range of the major traditions in the volume at a given point in time. You may consult these maps and find the name(s) of major traditions in an area or time period of interest. The major tradition entries are organized alphabetically, with associated regional subtradition and site entries following immediately after the major tradition entry. It is important to note that although all major traditions have entries in the *Encyclopedia*, not all major traditions have regional subtradition or site entries associated with them. As noted above, in compiling the *Encyclopedia*, we allowed the authors to decide whether there is enough information in the archaeological record to warrant distinguishing regional subtraditions. Similarly, we allowed authors to determine which (if any) archaeological sites are important enough to warrant individual entries.

If you have a particular topic of interest, you will want to scan the major tradition entries and use the topical headings to determine which of the major traditions have information on that particular topic. Not all major tradition entries have information on all topics, but the following is a complete listing of the topics for which information may be presented:

Absolute Time Period
Relative Time Period
Location
Diagnostic Material Attributes
Regional Subtraditions
Important Sites
Environment
  Climate
  Topography
  Geology
  Biota
Settlements
  Settlement system
  Community organization
  Housing
  Population, health, and disease
Economy
  Subsistence
    Wild foods
    Domestic foods
  Industrial arts
  Utensils
  Ornaments
  Trade
  Division of labor
  Differential access or control of
    resources
Sociopolitical Organization
  Social organization
  Political organization
  Social control
  Conflict
Religion and Expressive Culture
  Religious beliefs
  Religious practitioners
  Ceremonies
  Arts
  Death and afterlife
Suggested Readings

Preparing the *Encyclopedia of Prehistory*

To develop the *Encyclopedia*, we first had to develop a comprehensive list of major traditions. To do this, we divided the world into eight regions: Africa, the Arctic and Subarctic, East Asia and Oceania, Europe, Middle America, North America, South America, and Southwest Asia. We then consulted basic, summary literature on the prehistory of each region and drew up a preliminary catalogue of the major traditions of the world. We sent this preliminary catalogue to our advisory board for comment and critique and revised the catalogue according to their suggestions. The revised catalogue was then sent to the advisory board for a final review and critique.

Once the complete list of major traditions was assembled, we invited recognized experts on the region and time period of each major tradition to contribute entries. Solicitations continued until we found authors for virtually all the major traditions. In extending these invitations, we tried whenever possible to first invite archaeologists from the region of the major tradition. We are pleased that scholars from more than 20 nations agreed to contribute to the *Encyclopedia*. We invited authors to comment on the definition of their major tradition and made numerous substantive changes based on their input. We also invited authors to contribute additional entries on important regional subtraditions and sites for their major traditions; many, although not all, did so. We reviewed all completed entries, and, if there were substantive questions or concerns about a particular entry, we asked appropriate members of the advisory board for adjudication.

We have used a fairly light hand in editing the entries that comprise the *Encyclopedia*. Our reasons were twofold: first, we wanted to maintain the authors' individual styles, despite the outline we required them to follow; second, interpreting the archaeological record is often not as empirical and scientific as many of us would like to believe. Experience with and knowledge of local variation in the archaeological record are often critical to interpretation. Thus we thought it important to allow the experts working in a particular area to advance interpretations of the archaeological record with which they are comfortable. We never forced authors to provide information on a topic for which they thought there were no data; nor did we remove statements that seemed to stretch the available data. In short, we have let the experts speak in their own voices.

Acknowledgments

Many people helped in preparing the *Encyclopedia of Prehistory*: Carol R. Ember, Executive Director of the Human Relations Area Files; Eliot Werner, Executive Editor for the Behavioral and Social Sciences at Kluwer Academic/Plenum Publishers; the copyeditor and Herman Makler and the rest of the production staff at Kluwer Academic/Plenum Publishers; and the members of our advisory board. We thank all of them, and of course the authors of the entries, for their help in creating this unique work.

Contents

Introduction

South America is a continent of amazing diversity. On the west coast the Andes rise abruptly from the Pacific Ocean and climb rapidly to more than 6000 m, then decend into the broad Amazon and Pampas basins. The Amazon is an equatorial rainforest, while the Pampas is a rich grassland. On the east coast the land rises again to a broad upland known as the Brazilian Highlands. These uplands are situated above 2000 m and stretch from the north coast of Brazil south of Uruguay. I find that South America can be usefully divided into four major regions: the Andes, the Amazon, the Pampas, and the eastern highlands. One other region of South America—the northwestern lowlands of Colombia, Venezuela, and the Intermediate Area—is covered in the *Encyclopedia of Prehistory, Volume 5: Middle America*, as are the coastal and highland regions of Ecuador. While there is great diversity (both cultural and environmental) in each of these regions and none of them has clear boundaries, I find this division provides a useful framework for looking at the prehistory of South America. In this brief introduction I hope to provide an overview of South American prehistory as a way to give context to the more specific entries that follow in this volume of the *Encyclopedia of Prehistory*.

The Andes

The earliest archaeological tradition in the Andes is the Old South American Hunting-Collecting (c. 13,000–10,000 B.P.) tradition; it may be the oldest established archaeological tradition in the New World, currently predating all other recognized traditions. People of the Old South American Hunting-Collecting tradition were, as the name implies, nomadic hunters and gatherers of Pleistocene megafauna and plant species. They were followed by peoples of the Late Andean Hunting-Collecting (c. 8000–6000 B.P.) tradition, who were also nomadic hunters and gatherers. By the time period of this traditon, Pleistocene fauna had disappeared, and peoples were hunting and gathering a wider variety of plant and animal species. This "broad spectrum" foraging was also true for peoples of the Early Highland Andean Archaic (7000–4500 B.P.) tradition, but these peoples also started experimenting with plant cultivation, particularly *Chenopodium*, perhaps some root crops including potato, and there is some evidence that alpacas were beginning to be kept.

Plant and animal domestication was in place by the time of the Late Highland Andean Archaic (4500–3500 B.P.) and Coastal Andean Archaic (c. 7000–4100 B.P.) traditions. Coastal Andean Archaic peoples raised a wide variety of plants, including squash, maize, potatoes, and beans, and kept llama and guinea pig. They supplemented these domestic foods with resources from the sea, and lived in large coastal villages near fresh water sources. Late Highland Andean Archaic peoples appear to have been seasonally sedentary and maintained a fairly high reliance on wild foods. However,

Late Highland Andean Archaic peoples did cultivate potatoes, beans, peppers, and other crops, and may have kept llama or alpaca. Ceramics were first made by peoples of the Highland Andean Formative (3500–2200 B.P.) tradition, who moved seasonally and lived in small villages of adobe houses. Llama and alpaca were kept, and potatoes and other root and grain crops were grown in summer villages. By the end of the tradition it appears that the highlands had become segregated into a series of perhaps a dozen regional polities.

Political development occurred somewhat more rapidly on the Andean coast. During the Early Coastal Andean Formative (4100–3000 B.P.) tradition, a settlement hierarchy emerged with large regional centers containing groups of carefully arranged platform mounds. Irrigation agriculture was established, and fish and shellfish were intensively harvested from the sea. This pattern continued through the Late Coastal Andean Formative (3000–2200 B.P.) tradition, with regional centers growing into true urban communities and the appearance fortified military sites. In the highlands, however, people of the Chavín (2800–2200 B.P.) tradition also developed a powerful centralized polity, focused at the large temple center of Chavín de Huantar. During the Andean Regional Development (2200–1300 B.P.) tradition, temple centers spread throughout the highlands as the foci of numerous regional polities.

The first Andean states appeared along the northern Peruvian coast. Peoples of the Moche (1950–1200 B.P.) tradition created true urban centers with several thousand residents and supported by a complex system of irrigation agriculture. On the southern coast, people of the Nasca (2200–1300 B.P.) tradition built large ceremonial centers, but these do not appear to have had large resident populations. Most people lived in agricultural villages in river valleys, some of which grew quite large over time. While a state may have been present, it is more likely that the Nasca peoples lived in regional chiefdoms. The Tiwanaku (1600–900 B.P.) tradition marks the first appearance of states in the highlands. People of the Tiwanaku tradition developed what appears to be a powerful centralized state in the area around Lake Titicaca. The state was supported by large-scale herding of llama and alpaca, and coordinated raised-field agriculture.

Peoples of the Huari (1200–950 B.P.) tradition developed in the northern highlands of Peru what may be the first Andean empire. Communities appear to have been planned, and common forms of dress and iconography suggest that Huari leaders were integrated into a complex, multiregional political system. This widespread integration appears to have dissolved into regionally distinct polities in the Andean Regional States (900–530 B.P.) and Aymara Kingdoms (900–530 B.P.) traditions, but reappeared during the Inca (c. 800–468 B.P.) tradition. It is clear that in all three traditions powerful elites ruled large agricultural population from urban centers. On the north coast of peru, the Chimu (1050–480 B.P.) tradition followed a similar pattern. The political center of Chan Chan had perhaps 50,000 residents, while agricultural hamlets may have had only a few families. These communities were integrated into a single polity through a king and a group of provincial and local elites. Finally, along the southern Andean coasts, peoples of the South Andean Ceramic (c. 2500–500 B.P.) tradition appear to have been influenced by political developments to the north and began coalescing into large communities and regional polities that persisted until the Spanish conquest.

The Amazon

Until recently it was thought that the Amazon basin was the last area of South America to be inhabited by humans. Today we know that the Amazon was inhabited from the time the first humans entered the continent. Peoples of the Old Amazonian Collecting-Hunting (11,000–7000 B.P.) tradition entered the region as nomadic collectors of forest nuts and fruits, fishers, and hunters of small game. By the time of the Early Amazonian (7000–2000 B.P.) tradition, peoples living in the Amazon basin appear to have begun settling in small villages, making ceramics, and experimenting with plant cultivation. They also hunted, fished, and collected extensively. Peoples of the Late Amazonian (2000–50 B.P.) tradition were village-dwelling horticulturalists who both planted domestic crops and cultivated wild trees and other plants. There is evidence that some villages were led by elites, and there is even evidence of regional site hierarchies in some areas.

The Pampas

The vast grasslands and arid flatlands of the Pampas and Patagonia have been home to humans for more than 10,000 years. Unfortunately, the material record of their lives has proved difficult to find and recover, and archaeological knowledge of the region is in a comparatively unsophisticated state. The earliest distinct tradition is the Early Parana-Pampean (7000–1500 B.P.) tradition. Peoples of this tradition were nomadic hunter gatherers who focused hunting on guanaco, rhea, and deer. They also fished and gathered a wide variety of plant foods. They were followed by peoples of the Late Parana-Pampean (1500–500 B.P.) tradition. These peoples were also hunters and gatherers, but some groups, particularly in the larger river valleys, also practiced agriculture and lived in sedentary villages, sometimes quite large. To the far south, peoples of the Magellan-Fuegian (6300–50 B.P.) tradition lived on the rugged Patagonian coasts in small nomadic groups. They hunted, gathered, and fished, with a particular emphasis on sea mammals and shellfish.

The Eastern Highlands

The first archeological tradition in the Eastern Highlands is the Early East Brazilian Uplands (11,000–5000 B.P.) tradition. Peoples of this tradition were hunters and gatherers who lived in rockshelters or small open-air sites. Most sites were probably occupied by individual families. Early in the tradition they hunted the last of the Pleistocene megafauna, but changed to hunting peccarys, tapir, capybara, and similar animal as the megafauna became extinct. They were followed by peoples of the Late East Brazilian Uplands (5000–50 B.P.) tradition, who continued to hunt and gather, but supplemented those wild foods with domesticated horticultural products. They also constructed villages of up to dozen pit houses and produced ceramics. Peoples of the Sambaqui (7000–500 B.P.) tradition lived during the same time as both the Early and the Late East Brazilian Uplands peoples, but occupied the coastal areas and focused subsistence on marine resources. They built distinctive mounds of shells, some of which were apparently used to support houses. Finally, peoples of the Tupi (1500–150 B.P.) tradition lived in small villages along the Brazilian coast and the interior region of the Parana, Paraguay, and Uruguay rivers. They fished, hunted, and raised a variety of domestic plants. In the historic period, village chiefs were present and village warfare was endemic, but it is unclear whether either was common in the prehistoric period.

Summary

The prehistory of South America seems one of disparate regional evolution, with Andean populations rapidly evolving village life and political centralization, and other populations maintaining a fairly stable way of life for thousands of years. The lifeways of peoples in the interior of the continent and on the eastern coasts seem to have remained largely unchanged after the adoption of agriculture, and all seem to have followed similar hunting and gathering way of life before agricultural crops were introduced. Perhaps this picture is biased because of the relative paucity of information for areas outside of the Andes, but it does appear that the Andes

were a particularly vibrant region for sociopolitical evolution. Why? What accounts for the dynamic nature of Andean cultural evolution when compared to the rest of the continent and, indeed, to much of the rest of the New World? Why didn't sociopolitical complexity appear, for example, in fertile and populous areas in the eastern highlands? Why was it the central Andes that saw the most dramatic changes, not the southern Andes? Questions such as these are at the center of most current archaeological research, and yet our answers are far from adequate. One purpose of the *Encyclopedia of Prehistory* is to offer a broad range of cases in order to examine such questions and test hypotheses about cultural evolution. Perhaps through a comparative perspective we will gain a better understanding of cultural evolution in South America and throughout the world.

A Word about the Entries

While the above summary may suggest a uniform knowledge of the archaeological record across South America, nothing could be farther from the truth. Some traditions have been the focus of intensive research, while others have gained the interest of only a few scholars. For example, we know considerably more about the Andes, even its very early prehistory, than we do about the Amazon or Pampas. The reasons for this variation are often difficult to ascertain, but have to do with physical accessibility, the personal interests of the researchers, as well as larger questions being asked by the community of archaeologists. As you use the *Encyclopedia*, bear in mind that some traditions have more and better information than others.

The above summary may also make it appear that the prehistory of South America can be easily cut up into discrete chunks. It cannot. As we discuss in the Preface to this volume, the units designed to organize the *Encyclopedia of Prehistory*—major archaeological traditions—are to some extent arbitrary, and they are most certainly meaningless in the context of the lives of the prehistoric peoples themselves. They are devices of our creation, in the present day, to make possible the comparative analysis of the peoples of the past. Thus, when I say, for example, that the Early Coastal Andean Formative tradition was followed by the Late Coastal Andean Formative tradition, it should not be taken to imply that the break between the two is clear and discrete, or that all people changed in exactly the same ways at precisely the same time. Nor should such a statement imply that there was a population replacement between the two traditions. More importantly, such a statement should not be taken to imply that the peoples of either tradition knew they were living in any sort of unity with other people who we, from our perspective today, suggest shared a common archaeological tradition.

Any undertaking this massive will face goals that cannot be met. While we attempted to have each entry written by a noted scholar on the given tradition, conflicting schedules, miscommunication, and unforeseen circumstances forced a number of scholars to miss our deadlines or withdraw from contributing to the *Encyclopedia*. In those cases I produced (often with generous assistance from other scholars and members of the editorial board) what I call "minimalist" entries which provide basic information on major traditions and bibliographical source material for further research. These entries, while checked and approved by regional experts, were not written by an expert, and should, perhaps, be taken less seriously than other entries in the volume.

PETER N. PEREGRINE

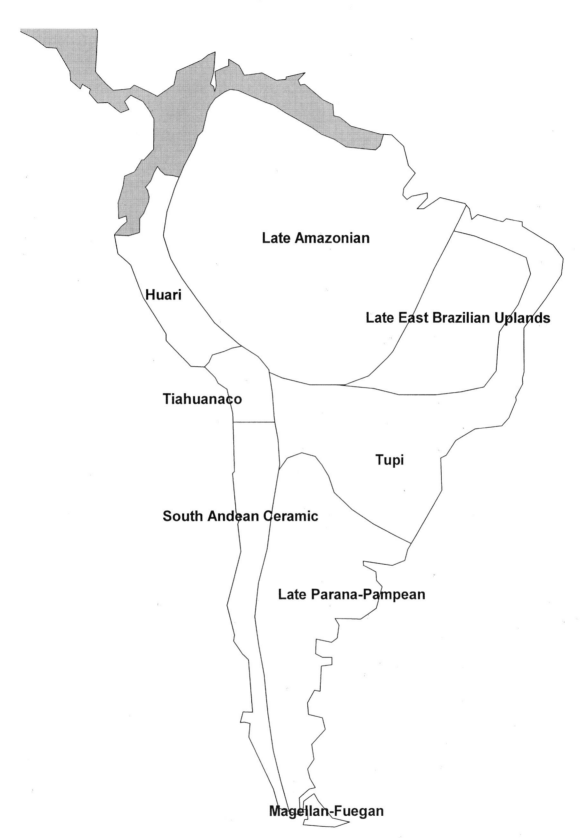

Late Amazonian

Huari

Late East Brazilian Uplands

Tiahuanaco

Tupi

South Andean Ceramic

Late Parana-Pampean

Magellan-Fuegan

(1) South America showing major traditions at 1000 B.P.

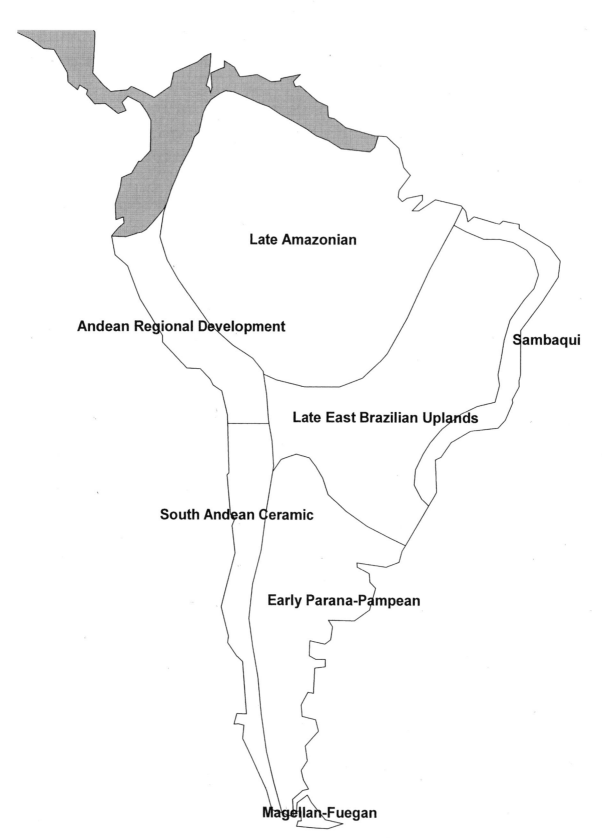

Late Amazonian

Andean Regional Development

Sambaqui

Late East Brazilian Uplands

South Andean Ceramic

Early Parana-Pampean

Magellan-Fuegan

(2) South America showing major traditions at 2000 B.P.

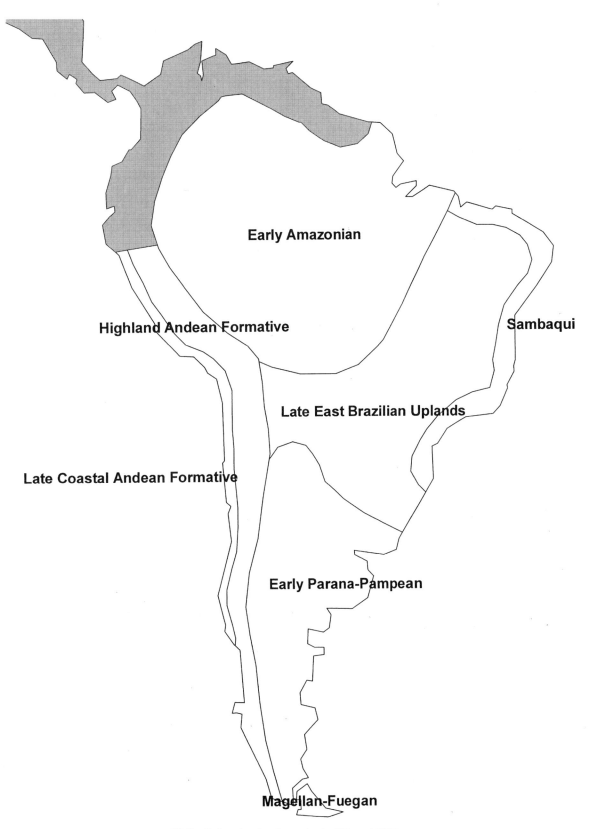

Early Amazonian

Highland Andean Formative

Sambaqui

Late East Brazilian Uplands

Late Coastal Andean Formative

Early Parana-Pampean

Magellan-Fuegan

(3) South America showing major traditions at 3000 B.P.

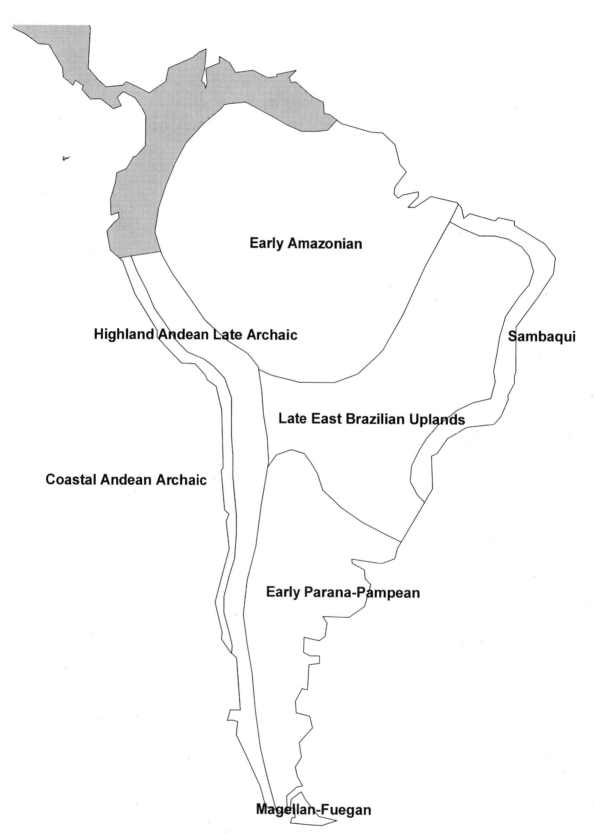

Early Amazonian

Highland Andean Late Archaic

Sambaqui

Late East Brazilian Uplands

Coastal Andean Archaic

Early Parana-Pampean

Magellan-Fuegan

(4) South America showing major traditions at 4000 B.P.

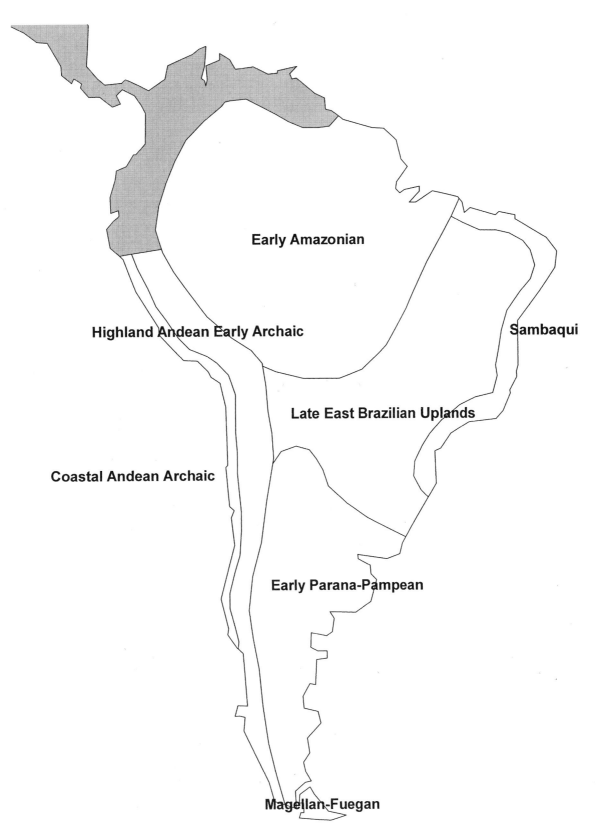

Early Amazonian

Highland Andean Early Archaic

Sambaqui

Late East Brazilian Uplands

Coastal Andean Archaic

Early Parana-Pampean

Magellan-Fuegan

(5) South America showing major traditions at 5000 B.P.

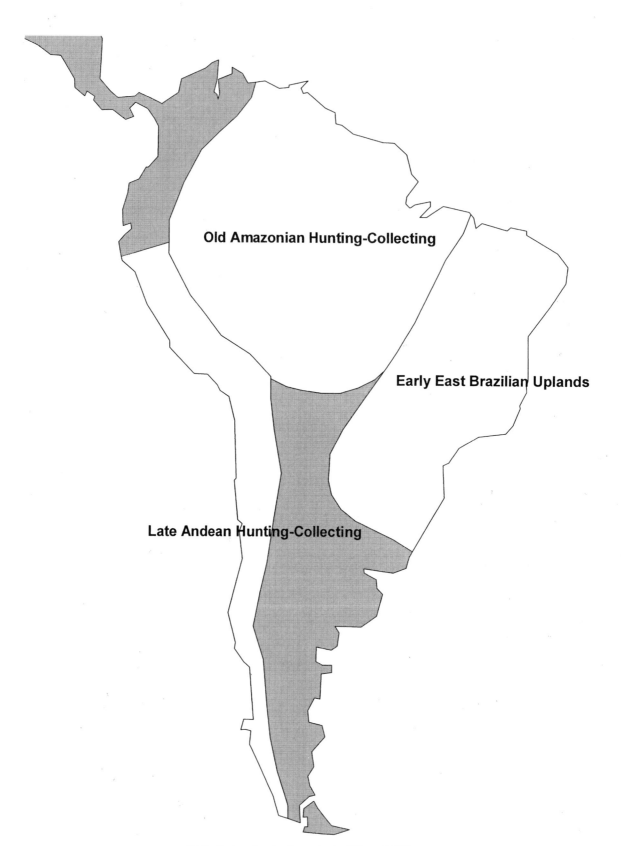

Old Amazonian Hunting-Collecting

Early East Brazilian Uplands

Late Andean Hunting-Collecting

(6) South America showing major traditions at 8000 B.P.

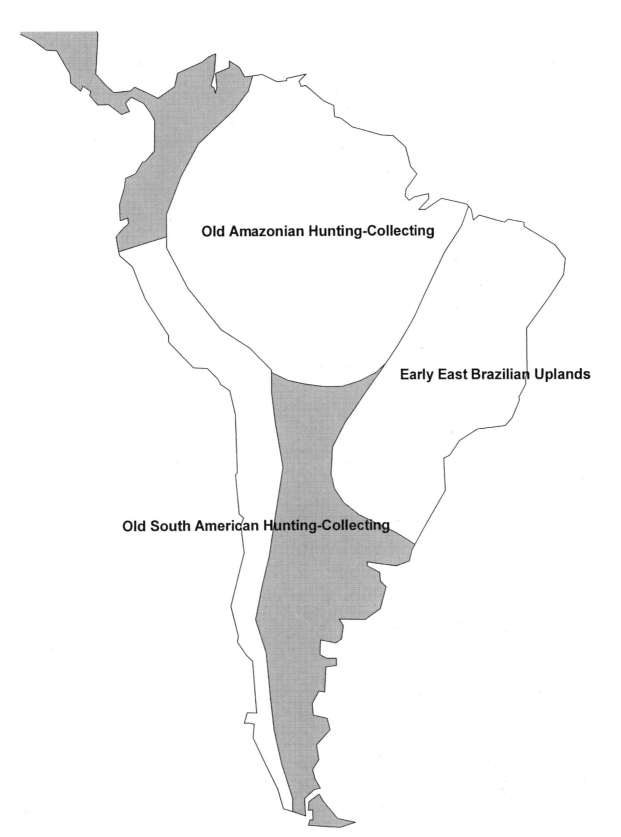

Old Amazonian Hunting-Collecting

Early East Brazilian Uplands

Old South American Hunting-Collecting

(7) South America showing major traditions at 10,000 B.P.

Andean Regional Development

ABSOLUTE TIME PERIOD: 2200–1300 B.P.

RELATIVE TIME PERIOD: Follows the end of the Upper Formative manifestations; in the northern and central highlands, after the fall of Chavin.

LOCATION: Andes region from Ecuador to northern Chile.

DIAGNOSTIC MATERIAL ATTRIBUTES: Localized but interacting states with complex ideologies, symbol systems, and social forms. Highly developed ceramics, metallurgy, and weaving.

REGIONAL SUBTRADITIONS: Huarpa phase of Wari or Huari, Qeya phase of Tiwanaku or Tiahuanaco, Recuay, Usupukio, Cajamarca, Huamachuco, Pucara.

CULTURAL SUMMARY

Environment

Topography. The highland area includes occupation areas between roughly 2500–4500 m. For the most part, this is characterized by a treeless high-altitude grassland, including roughly 25 percent of the area of Peru and Bolivia. Some areas, in the vicinity of lake Titicaca, are characterized by large expanses of tablelands, bounded on the east and west by two parallel sierra ranges. Farther north in Peru, the two ranges are closer, resulting in fractured expanses, with grasslands along long meandering ridges and mesas separated by deep valleys. Valley slopes may have growths of the native Andean trees in small copses; valley areas are also characterized by various shrubby vegetation. Grassland environment, however, dominates the zone, changing from the "dry *puna*" in the south, to the "wet *puna*" in midcountry, to the much more temperate "*paramo*" in the north.

Climate. Climatic details are very sketchy, but it appears that this was a period of slightly warmer temperatures than the preceding phase. Upper limits of cultivation were 100–300 m higher than today. On one hand, the high elevation means significantly less atmospheric insulation, so that temperatures warm up and cool down rapidly diurnally. But on the other hand, the proximity to the equator means that the permanent snowline is often over 4800–5000 m.

Geology. The uplifted strata of the Andes provided access to a variety of mineral resources: metal ores (gold, silver, copper, lead, tin, platinum); good-quality cryptocrystallines (obsidian and various cherts); gemstone minerals (turquoise, sodalite, lapis lazuli, fossil amber), which were exploited locally and traded long distances.

1

Biota. The *puna* grasslands were ideal environment for the deer and wild camelids (the vicuña and the guanaco) and also at this time supported significant herds of domestic camelids, the alpaca and the llama. This zone was the home for a large number of root varieties, many of which were domesticated by this time (multiple varieties of potatoes, *oca*, *papa lisa*, *olluco*, and *arracacha*) as well as several varieties of chenopods and other seeds.

Settlements

Settlement System. Topography resulted in a series of relatively geographically circumscribed areas, with a series of regional polities thus developing. Local competition for control affected many of these polities. Thus village settlements were often located on a defensible knoll or ridgetop location, immediately above the agricultural lands of the community. The larger controlling political settlements usually were defined by some sort of public architecture (temples, platform mounds, and, in the north, impressive burial architecture).

Community Organization. Clan-like *ayllu* organization is now in place. In the northern half, specific architecture of an open sepulcher nature begins, which would allow access to the fictional or real apical *ayllu* ancestor, for important integrating religious ceremonies. The *ayllu* controlled access to grazing areas and stock-watering holes, as well as to distribution and access to agricultural fields. Political development is envisioned as in a segmentary state, with villages at minor *ayllu* level, towns at major *ayllu* levels, and even larger population concentrations at the maximal *ayllu* level. Housing is irregularly clustered around major public architecture in the large centers, usually religious architecture of some nature. In the southern highlands, regularized town planning, in terms of discrete compounds situated along grid networks, is suggested to have begun. Community location at this period usually was situated so as to secure access to both good pasture lands (often at slightly higher elevations) for the llama and alpaca herds and also agricultural lands where the various root and seed crops could be grown. Villages at higher elevations, above the climatic limits allowing agriculture, were situated near springs, lakes, or marshy areas, which provided both water for the herds and rich fodder. In the southern highlands, various raised field systems were employed to help extend the upper limits of secure cultivation. Throughout the region, the first major systems of agricultural terraces were constructed to enlarge the available agricultural surfaces in the more topographically abrupt areas characteristic of the central and northern sectors.

Housing. Principal housing construction materials were adobe and fieldstone. Although there is a tendency to have round houses in areas that employ fieldstone and rectangular houses where adobes were employed, the reverse also occurs. There are regional patterns, but no clear area or temporal preferred style. Structures of individuals of greater economic resources may include outbuildings and small courtyards. Principal residences for the average inhabitant tend to be small, usually with a maximum dimension of no more than 4–5 m, thus providing primarily dormitory/sleeping space and storage space in the rafters, with many daily activities taking place outside the structure. Storage structures are common in villages in agricultural zones, usually internal to or attached to the house, rather than separate. The political elites of the villages now regularly have larger occupation structures.

Population, Health, and Disease. Most villages continue to be small, with population estimates usually in the 200–300 range. There are now more emerging political and religious centers with larger populations, but size estimates vary widely. The agropastoral regime characteristic of the last two millennia is firmly in place, with more secure diets. Nevertheless, at such high elevations, minor climatic variations produce much greater impacts on the productive systems, and we can identify population cycles that are intimately integrated into regional climatic cycles. Bioanthropological markers indicate elites experience less nutritional stress. The recurrent warfare of the period leaves some demographic profiles with gaps in the 15–35-year-old male interval. Trace element analyses indicate that males of this age range had more access to high-quality foodstuffs. Blunt trauma injuries led to successful procedures for amputation. Trepanning of skulls was not uncommon for higher status individuals, with evidence of multiple surgical events and survival of patients often decades after the first surgery. There is a high correlation between individuals with artificially deformed skulls and individuals involved in skull surgery. The brain is a plastic organ, readily accommodating itself to the various geometries resulting from deformations, but there is some suggestion that the impact on other cranial features, such as the sinuses, may have resulted in increased discomfort, possibly alleviated by surgical procedures.

Economy

Subsistence. The basic format is an agropastoral based economy. Herding of llamas and alpacas continues to be important throughout the region. Herders generally followed an annual cycle: moving the herds up to higher elevations in the austral winter/dry season and down to the village area or lower agricultural fields in the austral summer/wet season. Because of the high elevations involved, extensive cloud cover can drop the temperature enough that snow can fall in the austral summer in the southern highland area. The late austral summer is the time of birth of young llamas and alpacas; they need to be kept lower to avoid thermal stress from such unseasonable weather, as well as to take advantage of the rich grasses that grow in the rainy season. The agropastoral herders also have major labor demands in the local fields, harvesting the various grain and tuber crops at the end of the rainy season. By the time of the austral winter/dry season, plant agricultural labor demands are mainly over, the young camelids are strong enough to handle major diurnal temperature variations, and the previously less exploited grasslands at higher elevations now provide ideal grazing. As agropastoral communities, the villagers were required to integrate the labor demands of both agriculture and herding. The agricultural labor demands are those rather typical worldwide: sowing at the first rains, weeding the young plants, protecting the ripening fields from predators, and harvesting mature crops during a short but intense period.

Wild Foods. Herders particularly had opportunities to take guanaco, vicuña, and deer, as well as small rodents (vizcacha, wild guinea pigs), land birds (a partridge-size bird and smaller species) and waterbirds (sierra flamingoes, geese, ducks, grebes, and coots). Communities near larger streams and lakes also engaged in fishing. A wide variety of wild plants from the grasslands and marshy area was also collected.

Domestic Foods. Llamas, alpacas, and guinea pigs provided the major domestic meat resources. Maize continued to increase in importance, being particularly important in the fabrication of a corn beer, *chicha*. Primary agriculture in the highland remained focused on the various native seed plants (the chenopod *quinoa* and *caniwa* grains, amaranth grain, and *tarwi* seeds) and on the tubers (a wide range of white potato varieties, as well as other tubers such as *oca, ulluco, papa lisas, arracacha,* and the like). Root crops typically have short "shelf life." By this period, in the southern highlands where climatic conditions were appropriate, various "freeze-drying" techniques were now in place. These procedures had double rewards: not only did they modify the tubers into products that could be stored and retain reconstituted edibility for up to a decade or longer, but the freeze-drying process also destroyed most of the phytotoxins in the tubers. Most of the agricultural plants in this zone have significant levels of phytotoxins (which prevent or inhibit predation as well as human consumption). Thus until a technique was developed to detoxify the grains and roots, plant agriculture in the highlands was not a reasonable mechanism for production of food surpluses.

Industrial Arts. This time period represents the apogee in terms of experimentation with metallurgical technology. Techniques build on the earlier hammering, tempering, and annealing, to include embossing, repoussé, acid pickling, smelting, plating, gilding, soldering, casting (both simple and lost wax), and sintering. Ceramic technology also experiences a boom, with mass production of certain forms through molds and precision making of ceramic panpipes using slip-casting. Loom-made textiles include warp- and weft-faced weaves, double cloth, tie-dyed, gauze fabrics, brocades, tapestry, finely woven fabrics with thread count of 500 per inch, and feather cloth. Textiles were made both of native Peruvian cotton and of camelid (llama, alpaca, vicuña) wool. These fabrics were employed for sewn and tailored clothing, as well as for decorative elements. Fishing nets, sandals, mats, suspension bridges, and other ruder woven goods were made of bast fibers of a wide variety of plants.

Utensils. Primary materials employed in utensils were ceramics, bone, and wood. Cooking and eating utensils were primarily of ceramic and included spoons, plates, and cooking, serving, and storage bowls and jars. Decoration is typically polychrome prefired geometric designs on secular wares, with fancy religious symbols not infrequent on religious wares. Tools for hunting wild animals and for butchering both wild and domesticated animals were of obsidian, cherts, and other local stone. Sewing utensils were primarily bone and wood.

Ornaments. Ornaments were fabricated from marine shell, various metals, gemstones (such as turquoise, lapis lazuli, and sodalite), and textiles. Occupation and ethnic origin were represented in ornamentation as was socioeconomic status. Often associated with upper class individuals is also evidence of body piercing (labrets or ear ornaments), cranial deformation, and facial tattooing. Certain items of ornamentation, such as gold jewelry, *Spondylus* shell items, and feather cloth, seem limited to those of elite status.

Trade. Llama caravans provided a means of moving substantial amounts of goods over long distances, linking the highlands with the coast to the west and the jungle to the east. The first improved road networks developed around some of the larger centers. Both staple goods (such as maize, potatoes, and textile fibers) and well as status-validating items were moved by llama trains. There is a variable pattern of elite control of distribution of certain items such as metal, shell, textiles, gemstones, and the like.

Division of Labor. There is an artisan class focusing on craft specialization, but whether they are specialists attached to elite households or a separate social group is not clear. Primary public architecture at this time is limited to temples and platform mounds. To what extent there was a separate secular authority is not yet clear, although we have evidence of defended territories, conquest, and other activities of a magnitude usually associated with incipient state-level polities.

Differential Access or Control of Resources. Secular and religious elites appear to have controlled the distribution and trade of prestige goods and also most likely their production. This included access to desirable raw materials (such as obsidian or maize) as well as manufactured goods (such as textiles and metallurgical items).

Sociopolitical Organization

Social Organization. Most scholars believe that the modern clan-like *ayllu* organization was in place by this time period and have seen the villages as residence locations of single *ayllus*. These are generally viewed as groups emphasizing resource control (whether herding or agricultural lands), through real or fictive descent linkages.

Political Organization. The period is characterized by the coalescing and aggrandizing of local political groups into larger and larger units, such that by the end of the temporal period, this long linear tract of high Andean lands is subdivided into perhaps half a dozen larger polities. Except for payment of tribute to the larger centers, a good deal of local autonomy appears to have prevailed.

Social Control. Political and religious elites exist, but the precise mechanisms by which they secured and maintained political control are much debated.

Conflict. The preferred method of warfare continues to be based on man-to-man direct contact, using clubs. Other potential weapons include slings and spears, but these do not seem to have been employed often. The bow and arrow do not appear in this area until the very end of the period, and when they do appear, seem to be limited to hunting rather than warfare. Blunt trauma injuries from conflict are frequent in males 15–35 years of age. The taking or exhibition of "trophy heads" is frequent in the southern portion of the area.

Religion and Expressive Culture

Religious Beliefs. Much of what we think we know of this period is extrapolated from the two states that flourish next—the Wari and Tiwanaku. The assumption is that the religious traditions that are so well exemplified in the relics from these two states derive from practices developed in the Andean Regional Tradition. There is a strong emphasis on dualism, of male versus female, sky versus earth, wet versus dry, left versus right, or for example, in the case of Pucara ceremonial ceramics, Camelid Woman versus Feline Man. Coastal influences are more prominent; thus while the Sacrificer deity is particularly prevalent in the southern areas, the various manifestation of the Moon deity are found in the northern area.

Religious Practitioners. There are full-time religious specialists in the larger political centers like Pucara or Marcahuamachuco. In the southern area influenced by Tiwanaku, the importance of religious practitioners seems nearly paramount, with political authority deriving from religious power. In the northern areas, evidence suggests a greater importance of secular authorities, with possibly more separation of power of economic versus religious elites.

Ceremonies. Veneration of ancestor mummies is practiced. These mummies are believed to represent the real or fictional founders of the clan-like *ayllu*. The presence of "trophy heads" along with the Sacrificer god who holds an ax in one hand and a trophy head in the other hand suggests the possibility of several religious cults. That is, ceremonies may involve the veneration of the ancestor mummy for some groups. Importance may attach to the Viracocha-like sun god or feline god cult for others. Still others, or at other seasons, the Sacrificer god cult may be most important.

Arts. A wide variety of media was employed, including stone, metal, textile, pottery, and adobe. Important deities were carved on large stone stela; various religious and secular images were inscribed on more portable items of stone jewelry and ceremonial objects (from ear spools to stone cups). Metal objects were mainly limited to elite usages; because of the linkage between religion and political power, most of the images on metal items were of religious themes. Textiles and ceramics display a wide variety of both religious images and secular decorations, depending on their intended use for everyday life or for ceremonial occasions. The adobe walls of elite residences as well as of public buildings were decorated with painted murals of both religious themes and geometric designs. Remnants of pigment suggest that some of the stone buildings may have been similarly decorated.

Death and Afterlife. The principal ancestor mummies of the *ayllu* were taken out at scheduled periods; such mummies were thought not only to confer legitimacy, but also to provide guidance for the kin group elites. Burial patterns indicate a belief in an afterlife for all levels of society, but whether this belief involves recycling or rebirth of one of the souls is still a matter of speculation.

Suggested Readings

Albarracin-Jordan, J. (1996). *Tiwanaku: Arqueologia regional y dinamica segmentaria.* La Paz: Plural Editores.

Bermann, M. (1994). *Lukurmata: Household Archaeology in Prehispanic Bolivia.* Princeton: Princeton University Press.

Chavez, S. J. (1992). "The Conventionalized Rules in Pucara Pottery Technology and Iconography: Implications for Socio-Political Development in the Northern Lake Titicaca Basin." Ph.D. diss., Michigan State University. Lansing.

Conklin, W. J., and M. E. Moseley (1988). "The Patterns of Art and Power in the Early Intermediate Period." In *Peruvian Prehistory: An Overview of Pre-Inca and Inca Society,* ed. R. W. Keatinge. Cambridge: Cambridge University Press, 145–163.

Julien, D. G. (1988). "Ancient Cuismancu: Settlement and Cultural Dynamics in the Cajamarca Region of the North Highlands of Peru, 200 B.C.–A.D. 1532. Ph.D. diss., University of Texas. Austin.

Kidder, A., 2d (1943). *Some Early Sites in the Northern Lake Titicaca Basin.* Papers of the Peabody Museum of American Archaeology and Ethnology, vol. 27, no. 1. Cambridge, MA: Harvard University.

Knoblock, P. J. (1983). "A Study of the Andes: Huari Ceramics from the Early Intermediate Period to the Middle Horizon Epoch 1." Ph.D. diss., State University of New York, Binghamton.

Kolata, A. (1993). *The Tiwanaku: Portrait of an Andean Civilization.* Cambridge, MA: Basil Blackwell.

Isbell, W. H. (1997). *Mummies and Mortuary Monuments: A Postprocessual Prehistory of Central Andean Social Organization.* Austin: University of Texas Press.

Loten, H. S. (1987). *Burial Tower 2 and Fort A, Marcahuamachuco.* Peterborough, ONT: Trent University Occasional Papers in Anthropology, no. 3.

Lumbreras, L. G. (1974). *The Peoples and Culture of Ancient Peru,* trans. by B. J. Meggers. Washington, D.C.: Smithsonian Institution.

McCown, T. D. (1945). "Pre-Incaic Huamachuco: Survey and Excavations in the Region of Huamachuco and Cajabamba." *University of California Publications in American Archaeology and Ethnology* 29, 3: 223–399.

McNeish, R. S., T. C. Patterson, and D. L. Browman (1975). *The Central Peruvian Prehistoric Interaction Sphere.* Andover, MA: Papers of the R. S. Peabody Foundation for Archaeology.

Moseley, M. E. (2001). *The Incas and Their Ancestors: The Archaeology of Peru,* 2nd ed. London: Thames and Hudson.

Smith, J. W. (1978). "The Recuay Culture." Ph.D. diss., University of Texas, Austin.

Stanish, C., E. de la Vega, L. Steadman, C. Chavez Justo, K. L. Frye, L. Onofre Mamani, M. T. Seddon, and P. Calisaya Chuquimia (1997). *Archaeological Survey of the Juli-Desaguadero Region of the Lake Titicaca Basin, Southern Peru.* Fieldiana, Anthropology (n.s.), no. 29. Chicago: Field Museum of Natural History.

Topic, J. R., and T. L. Topic (1983). *Huamachuco Archaeological Project: Preliminary Report on the Second Season, June–August 1982.* Peterborough, ONT: Trent University Department of Anthropology.

Topic, T. L., and J. R. Topic (1984). *Huamachuco Archaeological Project: Preliminary Report on the Third Season, June–August 1983.* Peterborough, ONT: Trent University Occasional Papers in Anthropology, no. 1.

Topic, T. L., and J. R. Topic (1987). *Huamachuco Archaeological Project: Preliminary Report of the 1986 Field Season.* Peterborough, ONT: Trent University Occasional Papers in Anthropology, no. 4.

SUBTRADITIONS

Cajamarca

TIME PERIOD: 3000–1500 B.P.

LOCATION: Cajamarca valley in the northern half of the Cajamarca–Condebamba macrobasin, between the eastern and western cordillera, which join and become the Crisnejas River, a major tributary of the Rio Maranon of the Amazonian basin. Sites from 2500 to over 4000 m.

DIAGNOSTIC MATERIAL ATTRIBUTES: Beginning in the Formative, but particularly dominant during the Regional Development and subsequent Wari periods, the kaolin-clay based painted ceramics, which in the later periods become a prestige ware widely traded along the Andes.

CULTURAL SUMMARY

Environment

The highland area includes occupation areas between roughly 2500 and 4500 m. For the most part, this is characterized by a treeless high altitude grassland, mainly wet puna in nature, bounded on the east and west by two parallel sierra ranges. The two ranges vary in distances, resulting in fractured expanses, with grasslands along long meandering ridges and mesas separated by deep valleys. Valley slopes may have growths of the native Andean trees is small copses; valley areas are also characterized by various shrubby vegetation. Climatic details are very sketchy, but it appears that this was a period of slightly warmer temperatures than the preceding phase, allowing plant agriculture at elevations 100–300 m higher than today. The puna grasslands were ideal environment for the deer and the wild camelids (the vicuna and the guanaco), and also at this time supported significant herds of domestic camelids, the alpaca and the llama. This zone was the home for a large number of domesticated tubers, including multiple varieties of potatoes, *oca*, *isanu*, *ullucu*, *maca*, *arracacha*, and the like, as well as several varieties of chenopods, amaranths, lupines, and other seed-producing plants. Maize, which was introduced into the highland in the previous period, is grown at the lower elevation sites, but while markedly increasing in importance, does not yet seem to have attained the importance that characterizes it during the Wari and Inca periods.

Settlements

The Highland Andean Formative, as well as the Regional Development, period, settlements are generally composed of round or rectangular fieldstone single-room dwellings (mainly for storage and sleeping purposes) in the rural agropastoral communities. Rural villages are often on hilltops. Habitations are often in single or double rows on terraces or residential platforms. These sites generally lack defensive features. There are some larger centers, which appear to have political dominion over specific areas, which, in addition to larger size, also include rectangular structures of more than one room, presumed to be the residences of elites. Some of the communities are at such a high elevation (generally above 3900–4000 m) that agriculture is not possible, and seem to be likely specialized herding hamlets; some of the settlements are in lower 2500–3000 m) elevations, contain large numbers of agricultural tools, and may have been primarily agriculturally based hamlets, but most of the settlements include evidence of both herding and plant agriculture. Hamlet sizes seem to run from an estimated 6–8 households (perhaps a population of 50–75) up to

somewhat larger concentrations, perhaps 200–300 persons in size.

Ceremonial or public architecture from the Formative period is linked and influenced by the Chavin tradition. The Formative ceremonial structures at Huacaloma and Layzon, within 10 km, of modern Cajamarca, as well as Kuntur Wasi, have rectangular and circular fieldstone buildings with plastered walls and plastered floors on multitiered platforms, accessed by stone-lined staircases. Walls contain murals of black, white, yellow, green, brown and gray pigments. Interior rooms contain central hearths for burnt offerings. The structures are associated with underground stone-lined canals and ceremonial drains for the manipulation of water, similar to those seen at places like Pacopampa, Chavin de Huantar, and Kotosh. During the Regional Development tradition (locally portions of late Early Cajamarca, early Middle Cajamarca, or Cajamarca II and Cajamarca III phases), the high hilltop sites are abandoned, and sites move to lower hilltops and terraces. By the end of the period, bigger villages now contain rectangular compounds, thought to be derived from the Huamachuco region to the south.

Economy

The economy was agropastoral: subsistence was based on cultivation of chenopod grains such as quinoa, various cucurbits and tubers, beans, and other native Andean plants, with meat coming from domestic herd animals (llama and alpaca), guinea pig, and wild-hunted game, such as deer and various birds and rodents. Maize was first introduced into this area in the Formative period. By the Development period, irrigated, terrace agriculture had been developed, thought particularly suitable or necessary for maize cultivation, and stone hoes were now ubiquitous at habitation sites as well as on the agricultural terraces.

During the Formative period, the exploitation of kaolin clays for ceramics was characteristic, and these kaolin-based wares, especially the tripods and pedestal-based bowls, developed into major prestige trade items in later periods. Metal items first appear in the Formative sites, but for the most part seem to be of imported rather than local manufacture, until late in the Developmental tradition. There was an elaborate bone industry, including such items as clothing tupus, atlatl hooks, spoons, decorative pendant, flutes needles, spatulas, pins, and awls. The number of bone-weaving tools found at the sites indicates that textile manufacture was of increasingly significantly importance. There is a concomitant shift from the importance of the llama as a meat source to its importance as a caravan and wool animal during this period. This time frame marks a period of increasing external trade and contacts.

While there are only sporadic contacts between Cajamarca and coast polities, and no Cajamarca presence in Huamachuco at the early part of the phase, by the later phases of this period, there are strong linkages between Cajamarca and Recuay, and the Cajamarca traditional has expanded out of the area into the Crisnejas drainage area of Huamachuco at Marcahuamachuco. Huamachuco appears to be the principal regional prestige center for architecture, with late Andean Regional Period Huamachuco architecture being borrowed by Cajamarca; however, in terms of ceramics, Cajamarca ceramics appear to be the principal prestige ware, with Cajamarca kaolin ware now being typical of sites in Huamachuco; and with strong linkage established between Cajamarca and Recuay styles. As well, Cajamarca ceramics are found in significant numbers in the cis-Andean areas to the west, in amounts up to 15% of the assemblages in some coastal up-valley sites in the Moche area, sites usually associated with significant corral features relating to the llama caravan trade.

Sociopolitical Organization

During the Formative tradition, there is little evidence of social differentiation, except at places associated with the Chavin expansion, such as Kunturwasi and Huacaloma, which had burials with high-status items such as gold jewelry and Strombus seashells. With the collapse of Chavin, the area is characterized by a series of small feuding and warring polities. Defensive features such as fortified hilltop sites are common.

Toward the end of the Developmental tradition, the area appears to become united under a single paramount chiefdom at Cerro Coyor. The Coyor site has several large rectangular compounds of an architectural style believed to have been borrowed from Huamachuco, which now house new elites. Coyor displays a significant degree of sociocultural integration, seen by the local archaeologists as representative of a paramount chiefdom. The Coyor ascendancy corresponds with important new linkages outside of the region to adjacent highland areas such as Huamachuco and coastal area polities such as Moche and Recuay, with widespread distribution of the kaolin-based Cajamarca Classic Cursive and Cajamarca Floral Cursive prestige wares. Local social organization seems to

likely be based upon the *ayllu* of a similar or perhaps identical nature as described for the Inca empire.

Religion and Expressive Culture

Ceremonial or public architecture from the Formative period is linked and influenced by the Chavin tradition. The Formative ceremonial centers such as Kuntur Wasi, Huacaloma, and Layzon, have rectangular and circular fieldstone buildings with plastered walls and plastered floors, on multitiered platforms, accessed by stone-lined staircases. Walls contain murals of black, white, yellow, green, brown, and gray pigments. Interior rooms contain central hearths for burnt offerings, from the Kotosh tradition Kuntur Wasi even exhibits the typical Chavinoid U-shaped temple configuration. The structures are associated with underground stone-lined canals and ceremonial drains for the manipulation of water, similar to those seen at places like Pacopampa, Chavin de Huantar, and Kotosh. The high ratio of bowls at the temple sites suggest specific ceremonial feasting. Concentration of weaving tools indicates that the temple compounds were locales of textile production, possible of special textiles reserved only for religious elites, somewhat akin to the later Acllawasi structures associated with Inca religious compounds.

During late Formative, with the collapse of Chavin, public religious construction is reduced; for example, the stepped platform complex at Huacaloma destroyed and turned into a residential area, while they continued at Layzon, where a new square platform mound was constructed. The roots of the religious ceremonialism associated with *ayllu* founder ceremonies seems to have been established during this period. Each *ayllu* (usually a land-holding corporate group) has a real or fictional apical founder, and in later times in the Andes, access to the mummy of the founding member, to be displayed and incorporated into various processions and rituals, was a critical component of the *ayllu*.

The ancestral mummy would have been kept in open sepulchers, which allowed easy access. Such tomb architecture is first identified in the Chota-Cutervo, Huamachuco, Recuay, and Cajamarca areas during the Regional Developmental tradition, leading some authorities to speculate on whether this was the region of initial development of such rituals associated with the *ayllu*. Supporting this argument, in addition to the open sepulcher tombs, is the associated decorative iconography; crested felines, including the so-called Recuay "Moon Animal," are reported as decorative features of several of the proposed ancestor mummy sepulchers in this same region.

References

Carrion Cachot, R. (1948). "La cultura Chavin: dos nuevas colonias—Kuntur Wasi y Ancon." *Revista del Museo Nacional* 2, 1: 99–172.

Isbell, W. H. (1997). *Mummies and Mortuary Monuments: a Postprocessual Prehistory of Central Andean Social Organization.* Austin: University of Texas Press.

Julien, D. G. (1988). *Ancient Cuismancu: Settlement and Cultural Dynamics in the Cajamarca Region of the North Highlands of Peru, 200 B.C.–A.D. 1532.* Ph.D. diss., University of Texas. Austin.

Lumbreras, L. G. (1974). *The Peoples and Culture or Ancient Peru,* trans. B. J. Meggers. Washington D.C.: Smithsonian Institution.

Moseley, M. E. (2001). *The Incas and Their Ancestors: the Archaeology of Peru.* 2nd, revised ed. New York: Thames and Hudson.

Reichlen, P and H. Reichlen (1949). Recherches archeologiques dans les Andes de Cajamarca: Premier repport de la Mission Ethnologique Francaise au Perou.

Terada, K. (1985). "Early Ceremonial Architecture in the Cajamarca Valley." In *Early Ceremonial Architecture in the Andes,* edited by C. B. Donnan, pp. 191–208. Washington D.C.: Dumbarton Oaks Research Library and Collection.

Terada, K. and Y. Onuki, ed. (1982). *Excavations at Huacaloma in the Cajamarca Valley, Peru, 1979.* Report 2 of the Japanese Scientific Expedition to Nuclear America. Tokyo: University of Tokyo Press.

Terada, K. and Y. Onuki, ed. (1985). *The Formative Period in the Cajamarca Basin, Peru: Excavations at Huacaloma and Layzon, 1982.* Report 3 of the Japanese Scientific Expedition to Nuclear America. Tokyo: University of Tokyo Press.

Huarpa

TIME PERIOD: 1900–1500 B.P.

LOCATION: Middle Mantaro valley region, from 2300–3900 m, Ayacucho and Huancavelica departments, Peru.

DIAGNOSTIC MATERIAL ATTRIBUTES: Bichrome and polychrome ceramics in association with settlement systems that include elite rectangular structures as part of the developmental basis for the subsequent Wari empire.

CULTURAL SUMMARY

Environment

The Middle Mantaro sector from 2300–3900 m includes the subtropical ecological zones of the riverine thorny forest and the scrub thorny forest in the lower elevations, grading into the dry mountain parkland and *puna* grasslands at upper elevations. Below about 3400 m, lands are almost exclusively employed for farming purposes, based upon irrigation agriculture, as rainfall is seasonal and is 600 mm a year or less. Crops include maize, beans, cucurbits, and a variety of local fruits. Above 3,400 m, the crops shift to the chenopod grains and various tubers, with llama and alpaca pastoralism. Animals hunted included deer, guanaco, vicuña, a number of rodents, and birds.

Settlements

The early part of the Early Intermediate Period or Andean Regional Development tradition in this area was essentially a continuation of the previous Wichqana subtradition, with a shift in ceramic styles as the major distinguishing feature. Thus small hamlets characterized the early portion of this period. However, there appears to have been a rapid population growth occurring, with concomitant changes in settlement patterning, so that by the later half of the Early Intermediate Period or the Andean Regional Development tradition, larger settlements are not uncommon, with a shift to agglutination. Temple compounds develop, as well as residential-block patio groups, with exterior walls defining walled streets. The peripheries of larger centers, as well as many of the rural hamlets, were dominated by circular or elliptical fieldstone housing units, often but not always on artificially constructed housing terraces. The cores of the larger centers had rectangular temples, platform mounds, spacious courts, and patios. Ñawimpukio is typical of one of the probably multiple political centers at this time. Originally archaeologists treated Ñawimpukio as the single political entity in the region at this time, but subsequent surveys have suggested that there were probably other similar centers; we know Ñawimpukio best simply because of the historical accident of its being located on the outskirts of Ayacucho, easily accessible to investigations by scholars from the university in that modern city. Ñawimpukio is situated on a defensible hilltop, with its periphery packed with round and elliptical houses on habitation terraces. The core of the site has rectangular elite structures on occupation terraces, with streets, associated with granaries, small canals and water-control devices, and public architecture. It coalesces into a major urban center by the beginning of the following Wari tradition.

Economy

The Huarpa period marks a major period of construction of agricultural terraces in the Ayacucho region. Water was delivered to these agricultural terraces by an expanding massive system of clay-lined canals. Associated with the development of irrigated, terrace-based agriculture was a major increase in the importance of corn or maize for both basic food and production of the fermented maize beer or *chicha*, which subsequently became one of the necessary rations of the expansionist Wari state. Whereas earlier agriculture had been primarily based on tubers and local grains, the new pattern marks a significant shift in agricultural productivity. Analysis of the manufactured goods such as ceramics and stone tools indicates that these were probably still "cottage industries"; the manufactured goods were being produced at the local household level for the most part, not by a specialist class. However, there is some evidence for the increasing importance of inter-regional trade, which is seen as part of the basis of the secular mercantilism of the subsequent Wari state. There is evidence of increasing trade via llama caravans, securing significant quantities of coastal goods such as cochineal dyes, blocks of dried seaweed, and elite coastal ceramics from the Nasca peoples, as well as increased quantities of goods from cis-Andean and sierra locations, such as turquoise and copper for decorative purposes, obsidian for tools, and the like. The first preserved quipus or *kipus*, the strings best-known as mechanisms for production and census recording in the late Inca empire, are found in Wari-period tombs. Fragments of strings similar to the Wari *kipus* have been recovered from Huarpa-period associations, suggesting that this system of recording was likely in place or being developed in the rapidly expanding late Huarpa ceremonial centers. Textiles (of both wool and cotton) are a major industry of this time period, with essentially all of the known Andean techniques appearing by this time or earlier. Arsenic bronze artifacts were fabricated, as well as those of copper, gold, and silver, but the major developments in sierra metallurgical techniques do not occur until the Wari and later periods.

Sociopolitical Organization

Huarpa is conceptualized as having kin-based, non-hierarchical authority, a regional form of the *ayllu*, as its social basis. This organization provided the self-contained units of local production, which are seen as the basis of the secular economic power of the subsequent Wari state. *Ayllu* organization units were to become the later basis of the Wari and Inca empires, in part because of the facility by which they could be moved as integral units for economic production or military power. During the Huarpa period, however, hierarchy and centrality were emphasized only in the order of form and plan. In contrast to later polities, there is a lack of central public space for assembly and ritual in Huarpa sites. Thus although Huarpa is seen as the critical period for the

development of the ideas basic to Wari military and economic organization and fundamental organization of Wari urban life, these institutions apparently fully emerge only in subsequent periods. Social and political status is now marked by a number of devices. Cranial deformation (which must be effected in the first few years of life) is primarily limited to elites, as is also cranial trepanation. Labrets and ear ornaments define males of high economic and social status. Facial scarification and tattooing also seem to denote special social, economic, and probably geographic information, but damp climate in the highlands leaves us but few examples to extrapolate from. Woven textiles are a major indication of economic and social status, and as in later times, certain weaves, materials, and decorative motifs are limited to only high-status individuals. The increasing centralization of political power is believed to be supported by a new level of military organization, which is evident at the end of this period.

Religion and Expressive Culture

The majority, if not all, of the musical instruments employed in later pre-Columbian times are in use by this time period, including drums, panpipes, flutes, ocarinas (whistles), as well as various other idiophones. Tattooing (especially on the face and arms and hands) appears to have identified individuals not only by place of origin, but also by possible religious as well as secular office position. Religious traditions are poorly identified or exhibited during this time period, leading to the current archaeological reconstruction of the Huarpa as a period of development of secular rather than religious fluorescence. Huarpa is characterized as the period of the fundamental idea of sierra urban life as later exemplified by the Wari, with secularly administered, probably multiethnic larger town communities, as well as smaller special-resource communities, with the first major expansion of religious motifs being those borrowed from the Nasca Pacific coastal area as well as the Tiwanaku tradition at the end of this period. Secular economic militarism is believed to have been merged with the Tiwanaku and Nasca religious contributions to ultimately emerge as the subsequent Wari state.

References

Bennett, W. C. (1953). *Excavations at Wari, Ayacucho, Peru.* New Haven: Yale University Publications in Anthropology, no. 49.

Bonavia, D. (1970). "Investigaciones arqueologicaas en el Mantaro Medio." *Revista del Museo Nacional* 35: 211–294.

Conklin, W. J., and M. E. Moseley (1988). "The Patterns of Art and Power in the Early Intermediate Period." In *Peruvian Prehistory: An*

Overview of Pre-Inca and Inca Society, ed. R. W. Keatinge. Cambridge: Cambridge University Press, 145–163.

Gonzalez Carre, J. E. (1972). "Exploraciones en Nawinpukio, Ayacucho." *Arqueologia y Sociedad* 7/8: 30–46.

Gonzalez Carre, J. E. (1981). "La antigua ciudad de Wari en Ayacucho." *Boletin de Lima* 16/17/18: 83–97.

Gonzalez Carre, J. E. (1982). *Historia Prehispanica de Ayacucho*. Ayacucho: Universidad Nacional de San Cristobal de Huamanga.

Isbell, W. H. (1985). "El origen del estado en el Valle de Ayacucho." *Revista Andina* 5: 57–100.

Isbell, W. H. (1997). *Mummies and Mortuary Monuments: A Postprocessual Prehistory of Central Andean Social Organization*. Austin: University of Texas Press.

Knobloch, P. J. (1976). "A Study of the Huarpa Ceramic Style of the Andean Early Intermediate Period." M.A. thesis, State University of New York, Binghamton.

Knobloch, P. J. (1983). "A Study of the Andes: Huari Ceramics from the Early Intermediate Period to the Middle Horizon Epoch 1." Ph.D. diss., State University of New York, Binghamton.

Lumbreras, L. G. (1960a). "La cultura de Wari, Ayacucho." *Ethologia y Arqueologia* 1, 1: 130–227.

Lumbreras, L. G. (1960b). "Esquema arqueologico de la sierra central del Peru." *Revista del Museo Nacional* 28: 64–117.

Lumbreras, L. G. (1974a). *The Peoples and Culture of Ancient Peru*, trans. B. J. Meggers. Washington, D.C.: Smithsonian Institution.

Lumbreras, L. G. (1974b). *Las Fundacion de Huamanga*. Lima: Editorial Nueva Edicion.

Lumbreras, L. G. (1981). "The Stratigraphy of the Open Sites." In *Prehistory of the Ayacucho Basin*, ed. R. S. MacNeish, A. Garcia Cook, L. G. Lumbreras, R. K. Vierra, and A. Nelken-Terner. Ann Arbor: University of Michigan Press, 2: 167–198.

MacNeish, R. S. (1981). "Synthesis and Conclusions." In *Prehistory of the Ayacucho Basin*, 1 ed. R. S. MacNeish, A. Garcia Cook, L. G. Lumbreras, R. K. Vierra, and A. Nelken-Terner. Ann Arbor: University of Michigan Press, 199–252.

MacNeish, R. S., T. C. Patterson, and D. L. Browman (1975). *The Central Peruvian Prehistoric Interaction Sphere*. Andover, MA: Papers of the R. S. Peabody Foundation for Archaeology No. 7.

Moseley, M. E. (2001). *The Incas and Their Ancestors: The Archaeology of Peru*, 2nd ed. London: Thames and Hudson.

Ochatoma Paravicino, J. A. (1992). "Acerca de Formativa en Ayacucho." In *Estudios de Arqueologia Peruana*, ed. D. Bonavia. Lima: Fomciencias, 193–214.

Qeya

TIME PERIOD: 2000–1500 B.P.

LOCATION: Qeya materials have been recovered from a number of sites around lake Titicaca, and in altiplano and *puna* sites as far north as Cuzco.

DIAGNOSTIC MATERIAL ATTRIBUTES: The identification of Qeya as a subtradition is in large part based on its ceramic style, and the definition of the ceramic style is primarily based upon the definition of ceremonial wares, particularly *incensarios* (incense burners).

CULTURAL SUMMARY

Environment

The Lake Titicaca basin and adjacent Puno department areas to the north are characterized by a dry *puna* ecotype environment, mainly high grasslands with little associated stunted native shrubs or trees in protected enclaves. Thus the Qeya communities are basically agropastoral economies, but are also much influenced by the presence of Lake Titicaca. Herding of llamas and alpacas and planting of various tubers and seed plants dominate the economy along both the sites closer to the lake shore and thus further inland. Sites appear to be preferentially located near to the lake shore, however, for two reasons. On one hand, the lake provided additional resources, in terms of fisheries and waterbirds. But more important, the lake as a large heat sink provided ameliorating conditions for agricultural production, and the shores beginning in this period are dense with raised field complexes, which capitalized on the environmental conditions. Evidence from pollen profiles, lake cores, glacial ice cores, and other environmental proxies suggests century-long periods of milder climate, which may correlate with the Roman Warm period of Europe. Raised field systems capitalizing on improved farming conditions expand within the basin, and there is evidence at the end of the period of limited maize cultivation in favored locales (a crop that usually had to be imported from lower elevations). Regional mineral resources, such as locations of copper ores or of high-quality building stone, are now regularly exploited.

Settlements

Domestic housing stock is predominantly of rectangular structures, with round or oval varieties less common, constructed of fieldstone or adobe. Houses often had prepared clay floors; structures of adobe frequently had clay washes or "stucco," which display remnants of red, yellow, green, and/or white paint. Habitation terraces were constructed where necessary to provide flat residential-use areas. The Qeya subtradition is perceived as the foundation or roots of the subsequent Tiwanaku tradition, the second round of empire in the Andes. Tiwanaku itself is much studied, but we know relatively little of the diagnostics of the immediately preceding Qeya period, sometimes also known as Tiwanaku III. Excavations at the site of Tiwanaku in the early part of this century first recovered some ceramics that were different from the "classic" wares associated with the later empire. The most readily identifiable were a series of incense burners, which had rather abstract depictions of birds and felines and geometric designs, particularly the checkered cross. These designs occur in incised and painted variations. Sites that produced these sherds were then viewed as components of the Qeya tradition. Only recently has research reached the point where that archaeologists began doing site distributions of locations that produced Qeya ceramics, so that only a few very large ceremonial centers were identified in the immediate vicinity of the later Tiwanku capital, along with isolated high-status trade vessels at centers in the region involved with trade interchange with the south end of the Titicaca basin. Hence it became clear that although examples of high-status religious wares had been identified, the associated everyday ceramics were not clearly defined. Much debate is on-going about what they may include, but currently in addition to some geometrically painted wares also found in association with the *incensarios*, it is believed that the ceramic assemblage previously identified in Bolivia as "Tiwanaku I" is most likely one of the variants of the everyday ceramic assemblages. Thus if the definition of the subtradition is based on specifically associated ceremonially defined ceramics, the settlement pattern of the Qeya phase would be limited to temples and elite centers. On the other hand, there are now some "100 percent" settlement surveys of at least half a dozen different zones in the southern and western areas of the Titicaca basin. These surveys indicate a hierarchical, nested pattern of settlement organization, beginning in the Formative, and in a sense, culminating in the Tiwanaku tradition, with smaller villages and hamlets linked to larger population centers with platform mounds and temples (often semisubterranean in nature), and the gradual coalescing of these elite centers with ceremonial architecture under the domain of increasing hierarchical order. By the end of the period, there is a substantial level of standardization of theme and style; such standardization is often viewed in archaeology as indicative of more intense centralization of sociopolitical control. During this phase, there are trends toward coalescing into two supralocal regional centers, one centered at Pucara at the north end of the Titicaca basin, and one represented by the Qeya phase of the site of Tiwanaku at the south end of the basin. There appears to be a hierarchical nested organization in place; secondary centers include examples of artificial mounds, stone enclosures, and sunken temples or courts, which link to the larger complexes at Pucara and Tiwanaku.

Economy

The economic focus reflects increasing emphasis on extracting surpluses to be mobilized by elites. Raised field complexes were initially developed at the hamlet or village level. By the Qeya period, in some (but not all) zones around the lake, there is evidence of probable elite interference in order to establish larger field complexes for larger agricultural surpluses. Some climatic proxies indicate a period of milder climate may have existed, which would have encouraged plant agriculture. One of the continuing issues revolves around the problem of precisely dating raised field construction: such fields were often constructed as early as 3500–3000 B.P. and were used, either continuously or intermittently, until about 500 B.P. Thus identifying which field complexes were employed at 2000–1500 B.P. creates a challenge. The increasing occurrence of textiles, ceramics, and other goods manufactured in the Titicaca basin and southern Puno department, in Pacific coast sites indicates an increasing tempo of trade interactions via llama caravans. There is evidence of some specialization among communities, specialization not only in terms of focus on a specific subsistence resource, such as herding, fishing, or farming, but specialization in terms of production of metal goods, lithic items, textiles, ceramics, and other manufactured goods, including a series of artifacts associated with highland religious practices. Llama trade caravans traversed regular routes: north and south between communities in the *puna* and altiplano, trading different specialties; and east and west to the Amazonian jungle and Pacific coastal lowlands, to secure products not available in the highlands.

Sociopolitical Organization

Based on the imperfect linkages between the understanding of ceramic styles and political organization, this period appears to represent the coalescing of political authority in the southern part of the Titicaca basin into the Qeya phase manifestation at the site of Tiwanaku and in the northern part of the basin and southern Puno department, at the site of Pucara. Although there is no recovered indication of organized warfare, the rather sharp boundaries of ceramic style that are found during this period, linked with the subsequent demise of Pucara at the end of the period, suggest a significant level of coercive power being employed. There appears to be a tendency toward increasing nested hierarchical organization. The current interpretation of sociopolitical organization in the

Titicaca basin links it tightly with the emerging religious traditions. Most of the larger presumed centers are defined by religious architecture, in terms of a semisubterranean temple or artificial mounds, or both. The organizing principles, as intuited from the available evidence, seem to be around a kind of religious theater, of religious and political elites controlling the performance of required religious ceremony at large open mound and temple locations, where it is assumed that large numbers of residents from nearby communities assembled to partake in these rituals.

Religion and Expressive Culture

The religious themes derived from the ceramics include use of the ceramic *incensarios* among other items. Many descriptions conflate these artifacts with later Tiwanaku items, making reconstruction more tentative. Focusing on those of purely Qeya ceramic typologies, the themes include use of symbols representing the origin of life (including nested checkered crosses, infinity symbol-like lazy-eights, concentric circles), and feline and raptorial avian imagery, which in addition to occurring on the incense burner shape, are also found on a tube-shaped object usually called a trumpet. Identification of specific themes in the painted style is complicated by the fact that it begins as a very stylized, abstract assemblage, and only later, with the increasing popularity of an archaizing style sometimes known as the "second coming of Chavin", do the motifs become more naturalistic. The "hallucinogenic complex," which involves a series of artifacts employed by religious personnel in communicating with the spirits of other worlds, has its developmental stages at this time. Later "Classic" Tiwanaku manifestations of artifacts associated with the hallucinogenic complex include tubes for snuffing powder hallucinogens from flat wooden tablets and other items, with the derivatives of *Anadenathera*, *Banisteriopsis*, *Datura*, *Ilex*, and other plants being derived from contacts with *selva* or "eyebrow of the jungle" populations living in the Amazonian basin to the east of the Titicaca basin. This appears to be the beginning of the "religious theater" that is seen for Tiwanaku, where principal public buildings were situated so that large public religious presentations could be conducted on behalf of the citizenry. What we define as Pucara-style religious deities now widely appear on stone stelae at secondary hierarchical centers at the north end of the basin; while the Early Tiwanaku (or Derived Pajano) series of religious representations characterizes the religious art on stone monuments at the south end of the basin.

References

Albarracin-Jordan, J. (1992). "Prehispanic and Early Colonial Settlement Patterns in the Lower Tiwanaku Valley, Bolivia. Ph.D. diss., Southern Methodist University, Dallas.

Albarracin-Jordan, J. (1996). *Tiwanaku: Arqueologia regional y dinamica segmentaria*. La Paz: Plural Editores.

Bennett, W. C. (1934). "Excavations at Tiahuanaco." *Anthropological Papers of the American Museum of Natural History* 34, 3: 359–494.

Bennett, W. C. (1936). "Excavations in Bolivia." *Anthropological Papers of the American Museum of Natural History* 35, 4: 329–507.

Bermann, M. (1993). "Continuity and Change in Household Life at Lukurmata." In *Domestic Architecture, Ethnicity, and Complementarity in the South-Central Andes*, ed. by M. S. Aldenderfer. Iowa City: University of Iowa Press, 114–135.

Bermann, M. (1994). *Lukurmata: Household Archaeology in Prehispanic Bolivia*. Princeton: Princeton University Press.

Browman, D. L. (1978). "Toward the Development of the Tiahuanaco (Tiwanaku) State." In *Advances in Andean Archaeology*, ed. D. L. Browman. The Hague: Mouton, 327–349.

Browman, D. L. (1980). "Tiwanaku Expansion and Altiplano Economic Patterns." *Estudios Arqueologicos* 5: 107–120.

Browman, D. L. (1981). "New Light on Andean Tiwanaku." *American Scientist* 69, 4: 408–419.

Browman, D. L. (1994). "Titicaca Basin Archaeolinguistics: Uru, Pukina and Aymara A.D. 750–1450." *World Archaeology* 26, 2: 234–250.

Browman, D. L. (1996). "South Andean Federations and the Origins of Tiwanaku." In *Debating Complexity*, ed. D. A. Meyer, P. C. Dawson, and D. T. Hanna. Calgary: University of Calgary Press, 607–613.

Chavez, S. J. (1976). "The Arapa and Thunderbolt Stelae: A Case of Stylistic Identity with Implications for Pucara Influences in the Area of Tiahuanaco." *Nawpa Pacha* 13: 3–24.

Conklin, W. J. (1985). "Pucara and Tiahuanaco Tapestry: Time and Style in a Sierra Weaving Tradition." *Nawpa Pacha* 21: 1–44.

Cook, A. G. (1985). "Art and Time in the Evolution of Andean State Expansionism." Ph.D. diss., State University of New York, Binghamton.

Erickson, C. L. (1988). "An Archaeological Investigation of Raised Field Agriculture in the Lake Titicaca Basin of Peru. Ph.D. diss., University of Illinois, Urbana.

Girault, L. (1990). "*La ceramica del templete semisubterraneo de Tiwanaku*." La Paz: CERES.

Graffam, G. C. (1990). "Raised Fields Without Bureaucracy: An Archaeological Examination of Intensive Wetland Cultivation in the Pampa Koani Zone, Lake Titicaca Bolivia." Ph.D. diss., Toronto: University of Toronto.

Janusek, J. W. (1994). "State and Local Power in a Prehispanic Andean Polity: Changing Patterns of Urban Residence in Tiwanaku and Lukurmata, Bolivia." Ph.D. diss., University of Chicago, Chicago.

Kidder, A., 2d (1943). *Some Early Sites in the Northern Lake Titicaca Basin*. Papers of the Peabody Museum of American Archaeology and Ethnology, vol. 27, no. 1. Cambridge, MA: Harvard University.

Kidder, A., 2d (1964). "South American High Cultures." In *Prehistoric Man in the New World*, ed. by J. D. Jennings and E. Norbeck. Chicago: University of Chicago Press, 451–486.

Kolata, A. L. (1986). "The Agricultural Foundations of the Tiwanaku State: A View from the Heartland." *American Antiquity* 51, 4: 748–762.

Kolata, A. L., ed. (1989). *Arqueologia de Lukurmata*, vol. 2. La Paz: Producciones Pumapunku.

Kolata, A. L. (1991). "The Technology and Organization of Agricultural Production in the Tiwanaku State." *Latin American Antiquity* 2, 1: 99–125.

Kolata, A. L., ed. (1996). *Tiwanaku and Its Hinterland: Archaeology and Paleoecology of an Andean Civilization, vol. 1: Agroecology.* Washington, D.C.: Smithsonian Institution Press.

Kolata, A. L., and C. Ortloff (1989). "Thermal Analysis of Tiwanaku Raised Field Systems in the Lake Titicaca Basin of Bolivia." *Journal of Archaeological Science* 16: 233–263.

Mathews, J. E. (1992). "Prehispanic Settlement and Agriculture in the Middle Tiwanaku valley, Bolivia." Ph.D. diss., University of Chicago.

Mathews, J. E. (1997). "Population and Agriculture in the Emergence of Complex Society in the Bolivian Altiplano: The Case of Tiwanaku." In *Emergence and Change in Early Urban Societies*, ed. L. Manzanilla. New York: Plenum, 245–271.

Mohr-Chavez, K. L. (1985). "Early Tiahuanaco-related Ceremonial Burners from Cuzco, Peru." *Dialogo Andino* 4: 137–178.

Moseley, M. E. (2001). *The Incas and Their Ancestors: The Archaeology of Peru*, 2nd ed. London: Thames and Hudson.

Mujica Barreda, E. (1978). "Nueva hipotesis sobre el desarrollo temprano del altiplano, del Titicaca y de sus areas de interaccion." *Arte y Arqueologia* 5/6: 285–308.

Ortloff, C., and A. L. Kolata (1989). "Hydraulic Analysis of Tiwanaku Aqueduct Structures at Lukurmata and Pajchiri, Bolivia." *Journal of Archaeological Science* 16: 513–535.

Ponce Sangines, C. (1961). *Informe de labores.* La Paz: Centro de Investigaciones Arqueologicas en Tiwanaku, Publicacion, no. 1.

Ponce Sangines, C. (1964). *Descripcion sumaria del Templete Semisubterraneo.* Centro de Investigacion Arqueologia en Tiwanaku Pub 2. La Paz: Libreria Los Amigos del Libro.

Ponce Sangines, C. (1971). "La ceramica de la Epoca I de Tiwanaku." *Pumapunku* 2: 7–28.

Ponce Sangines, C. (1972). *Espacio, Tiempo y Cultura: Ensayo de sintesis arqueologica.* La Paz: Academia de Ciencias de Bolivia, Publicacion 30.

Ponce Sangines, C. (1989). *Arqueologia de Lukurmata*, vol. 1. La Paz: Producciones Pumapunku.

Portugal Ortiz, M, and M. Portugal Zamora (1977). "Investigaciones arqueologicas en el valle de Tiwanaku." In *Arqueologia en Bolivia y Peru* (Jornadas Peruano-Bolivianas de Estudio Cientifico del Altiplano Boliviano y del Sur del Peru), vol. 2. La Paz: Editorial Casa Municipal de La Cultura Franz Tamayo, 243–284.

Portugal Zamora, M., and M. Portugal Ortiz (1975). "Qallamarka, nuevo yacimeinto arqueologico descubierto cerca a Tiwanaku." *Arte y Arqueologia* 3/4: 193–216.

Posnansky, A. (1945). *Tihuanacu: The Cradle of American Man*, vols. 1 and 2. New York: J. J. Augustin.

Posnansky, A. (1957). *Tihuanacu: The Cradle of American Man*, vols. 3 and 4. La Paz: Ministerio de Educacion.

Smith, C. T., W. M. Denevan, and P. Hamilton (1968). "Ancient Ridged Fields in the Region of Lake Titicaca." *Geographical Journal* 134: 353–367.

Stanish, C., and L. Steadman (1994). *Archaeological Research at Tumatumani, Juli, Peru.* Fieldiana, Anthropology (n.s.), no. 23. Chicago: Field Museum of Natural History.

Stanish, C., E de la Vega, L. Steadman, C. Chavez Justo, K. L. Frye, L Onofre Mamani, M. T. Seddon, and P Calisaya Chuquimia (1996). "Archaeological Survey in the Southwestern Lake Titicaca Basin." *Dialogo Andino* 14/15: 97–143.

Stanish, C., E de la Vega, L. Steadman, C. Chavez Justo, K. L. Frye, L Onofre Mamani, M. T. Seddon, and P Calisaya Chuquimia (1997). *Archaeological Survey of the Juli-Desaguadero Region of Lake Titicaca.* Fieldiana, Anthropology (n.s.), no. 29. Chicago: Field Museum of Natural History.

Steadman, L. H. (1995). "Excavations at Camata: An Early Ceramic Chronology for the Western Titicaca Basin, Peru." Ph.D. diss., University of California, Berkeley.

Wallace, D. T. (1957). "The Tiahuanaco Horizon Styles in the Peruvian and Bolivian Highlands." Ph.D. diss., University of California, Berkeley.

Wassen, S. H. (1972). "A Medicine-Man's Implements and Plants in a Tiahuanacoid Tomb in Highland Bolivia." *Etnologiska Studier* 32: 8–114.

Webster, A. D. (1993). "The Role of the South American Camelid in the Development of the Tiwanaku State." Ph.D. diss., University of Chicago.

Recuay (Huaylas)

TIME PERIOD: 1900–1500 B.P.

LOCATION: Recuay occurs along the Upper Santa (or Huaras) river drainage and tributaries, running north-south in the Callejon de Huaylas, in Ancash, bordered by the Cordillera Negra on the west and the Cordillera Blanca to the east, roughly between 2800 and 3500 m. The valley bottom varies for the most part between 0.5 and 1 km in width from its origin at lake Conococha in the south, to roughly 200 km north, where the river turns west and rapidly drops toward the Pacific. The location is somewhat unique, in that the physical location is like the Andean valleys to the east, but the Santa river connects it directly to the Pacific coast areas.

DIAGNOSTIC MATERIAL ATTRIBUTES: Recuay is known for its easily recognized artistic style as exhibited on ceramics and stone. The ceramics are a kaolin paste ware, usually polychrome designs, often with resist or negative painting, among the most complex in the Americas, and also with modeled decoration. The designs are highly stylized and include a feline creator god, the *sacrificador* god, isolated human heads, arachniform figures, rampant felines, condors, raptors, serpents, double-headed serpents, feline-serpents, interlocking serpent or fish, two-headed animals, dragonlike creatures, and geometric motifs. Some vessels are elaborately modeled; examples include vessels depicting dignitaries and retainers, dwellings, and warriors. Recuay stone sculpture (sometimes known as the Aija style) is found on the jambs of tombs as well as on carved panels, boulders, and free-standing stela, and frequently includes low-relief warriors with clubs and shields; human and animal heads, as well as some of the mythological themes seen on the ceramics.

CULTURAL SUMMARY

Environment

The Recuay cultural tradition occurs along the Upper Santa river drainage, running roughly 200 km north-south in the Callejon de Huaylas, in Ancash, bordered by the Cordillera Negra on the west and the Cordillera Blanca to the east, roughly between 2800–3500 m. The valley bottom varies for the most part between 0.5 and 1 km in width. The location is somewhat unique, in that the physical location is like the high inter-Andean valleys in the upper sierra to the east, but the Santa river connects it directly to the Pacific coast. Unlike the inter-Andean sierra valleys, which are isolated by the massifs on either side and which drain to the east to Amazonia, the Callejon de Huaylas is continuous with the lower coastal reaches of the Santa river draining to the Pacific and thus much more closely integrated with Pacific coastal polities. The two ranges are close, resulting in fractured expanses, with grasslands along long meandering ridges running up from the valley. Valley slopes may have growths of native Andean trees in small copses; valley areas are also characterized by various shrubby vegetation and, in the lower portions of the valley, low-precipitation areas with cacti and xerophytic shrubs. Relatively open grassland-type environments, however, dominate the bulk of the zone. The lower elevation means that the valley is somewhat more temperate than the inter-Andean valley to the east. Sufficient rainfall is captured at the upper end of the drainage to feed irrigation-based agriculture along the valley bottom; the upper reaches are within the rainfall patterns of the sierra and have higher precipitation amounts, but as the elevation decreases, the rain-shadow effect of the Andes is noticed, and lower elevations have a more semiarid vegetational pattern. The *puna* grasslands were ideal environment for the deer and the wild camelids (vicuña and guanaco) and also at this time supported significant herds of domestic camelids, alpaca and llama. The valley bottom and associated terraces were low enough to grow corn, beans, cucurbits, and a number of other plant species of the lower elevations, while the upper sectors yielded potatoes, *maca*, and other tubers, as well as chenopod and amaranth grains and other more typical sierra cultigens.

Settlements

Settlements of the early part of the Recuay period show a shift in location from the valley bottom location of the earlier Formative period, to nearby defensible knolls and ridge-top locations. Most investigation has focused on the monumental architecture and burials associated with Recuay. Ordinary habitations are often built of dry fieldstone (including double-faced walls, with rubble fill, but nothing more than mud mortar), apparently of primarily rectangular configuration, and one-room surface structures, although some circular subterranean houses also have been reported to date to this time period. The overall settlement pattern is perceived as a hierarchical system, ceremonially based, with defensive control of access being emphasized. Public structures appear to exhibit a taste for massive stone building and include rectangular gallery-like rooms roofed with large slabs, sometimes on platform mound bases of one or more levels, subterranean stone-lined galleries, and underground chambers. Wall niches are features of both the habitation structures and the public architecture.

Economy

Evidence recovered to date indicates extensive agricultural production along the valley bottom, with maize, squash, beans, and other mid-elevation cultigens from the lower end of the valley, and with tubers and highland grains apparently being grown along the higher slopes. Because of the rapid vertical change up the slopes, upper-elevation hamlets associated with valley bottom centers seem to have agropastoral economics much like surrounding sierra regions. Preliminary paleoethnobotanical studies from sites like Pashash suggest that the highland tuber and pastoral economy was the major subsistence base for the Recuay culture. The negative- and resist-painted ceramics from Recuay become a significant prestige trade ware late during the Developmental tradition. Tripod forms, stirrup spout and bridge vessels, miniature vessels, trumpets, and other forms are traded to lower elevation coastal peoples and extensively exchanged with the Cajamarca region. At the end of the period, Recuay wares also occur in the Huamachuco area in the highlands. Metal items appear to be traded in from other locales; as yet there is no evidence of any metallurgical fabrication centers in the Callejon de Huaylas, although copper *tupu* clothing pins, gold sumptuary items, and the like do occur with elite Recuay burials in deep stone-lined tombs as well as in more elaborate above-ground gallery burial chambers.

Sociopolitical Organization

The settlement pattern and ceramic distribution appear to indicate a possible hierarchical social organization during the greater part of the Developmental tradition. Defense and defensive site locations, however, seem strongly emphasized, with strong emphasis on warfare seen at sites such as Pashash and in the depictions of warriors and other evidence in the ceramics. The Aija stone sculpture style seems to be dominated by warriors displaying shields, clubs, and other military paraphernalia and often displaying trophy heads in one hand. The occurrence of "priest-warrior" motifs in the ceramic and stone styles is presumed to imply a theocratic political hierarchy where secular and sacred powers are interdigitated. The commonalities of religious themes shared with areas such as Chota-Cutervo, Huamachuco, and Cajamarca in the adjacent sierra regions to the east, coupled with the first good occurrences of the kind of open sepulchers wherein ancestral mummies could readily be taken out for ritual events and returned for appropriate safekeeping, indicate that the material cultural aspects of this kind of apical ancestral ayllu recognition developed in the northern highland during this time frame. Nested social ranking of *ayllus* is thus reconstructed for the Callejon de Huaylas and is seen as supported by the evidence for public feasting rituals associated with these mausoleums and open sepulchers.

Religion and Expressive Culture

The Recuay religion seems to be represented by an exuberance of mythical images, such as two-headed serpents, other two-headed animals, the feline-creator god, the so called Moon Animal, the *sacrificador* deity, and many as yet less known images, which are associated with the primary public or ceremonial architecture of the area, the many variations of burial themes, from stone box graves and other subterranean galleries to massive above-ground multistory burial chambers. Among the major foci are clusters of images related to a presentation theme, to a pastoral complex, and to propagation and fertility. Gameboards, of stone, ceramic, and wood, have presumed religious importance as well as linkages to those known from Inca periods. The major sepulchers often have incised images on portions of the stone construction, in addition to major offerings of ceramic and stone vessels, stone and metal jewelry, figurines, ear spools, and the like. The mausoleum of Wilkawain, thought to have been first constructed at the end of the development period, is a stepped temple burial chamber with multiple rooms, surrounded by walls and a terrace. Each floor of the three levels has seven rooms with burial niches in their

walls, and the top level is covered by a barrel vault form. The roots of the religious ceremonialism associated with *ayllu* founder ceremonies seems to have been established during this period. Each *ayllu* (usually a landholding corporate group) has a real or fictional apical founder, and in later times in the Andes, access to the mummy of the founding member, to be displayed and incorporated into various processions and rituals, was a critical component of the *ayllu*. The ancestral mummy would have been kept in open sepulchers, which allowed easy access. Such tomb architecture is first identified in the Chota-Cutervo, Huamachuco, Recuay, and Cajamarca areas during the Regional Development tradition, leading some authorities to speculate on whether this was the region of initial development of such rituals associated with the *ayllu*. Supporting this argument, in addition to the open sepulcher tombs, is the associated decorative iconography; crested felines, including the so-called Recuay moon animal are reported as decorative features of several of the proposed ancestor mummy sepulchers in this same region.

References

Bennett, W. C. (1944). "The North Highlands of Peru: Excavations in the Callejon de Huaylas and at Chavin de Huantar." *Anthropological Papers of the American Museum of Natural History* 39, 1: 1–114.

Bennett, W. C. (1946). "The Archaeology of the Central Andes." In *Handbook of South American Indians*, ed. J. H. Steward. Washington, D.C.: Bureau of American Ethnology, Bulletin 143, 61–148.

Grieder, T. (1974). "Pashash: The Art of a Highland Refuge." *Special Publication of the Museum of Texas Technical University* 7: 159–169.

Grieder, T. (1978). *The Art and Archaeology of Pashash*. Austin: University of Texas Press.

Isbell, W. H. (1997). *Mummies and Mortuary Monuments: A Postprocessual Prehistory of Central Andean Social Organization*. Austin: University of Texas Press.

Lumbreras, L. G. (1974). *The Peoples and Culture of Ancient Peru*, trans. B. J. Meggers. Washington, D.C.: Smithsonian Institution.

Moseley, M. E. (1992). *The Incas and Their Ancestors: The Archaeology of Peru*. London: Thames and Hudson.

Smith, J. W. (1978). "The Recuay Culture." Ph.D. diss., University of Texas, Austin.

Usupukio

TIME PERIOD: 1900–1500 B.P.

LOCATION: Upper Mantaro river basin, from c. 2900–3800 m, in Junin, Lima, and Huancavelica departments.

DIAGNOSTIC MATERIAL ATTRIBUTES: The Usupukio painted geometric ceramic style, called Caja in Huancavelica. Usually bichrome ware, with common designs including stylized camelids and various linear geometric patterns.

CULTURAL SUMMARY

Environment

The zone is defined by the drainage of the Upper Mantaro river, as it runs north to south between the western and eastern cordillera ranges, creating a kind of highland valley basin. The Usupukio culture is an agropastoral group, with a strong emphasis on herding. Although the groups practice seasonal agriculture, it appears that access to herding areas is critical. The sites relating to this subtradition appear to be scattered along the slopes of the dry mountain woods and mountain grassland zones of the inter Andean valleys and uplands in this sector. Rainfall runs 600–800 mm on the average, so that the sheltered *quebradas* have a number of native trees and shrubby brushy species, but the open areas are mainly covered with grassland species. Although the valley bottom of the southern part of the Mantaro basin is generally low enough for typical corn, bean, and squash agriculture, these plants do not seem to be significant in the diet until the subsequent Wari conquest and reorganization of the valley.

Settlements

The settlements appear to reflect the "double domicile" pattern of some recent agropastoralists in the Andes. Along the hillslopes and upper valley rims are herding villages, which seem to be occupied during the dry season; along the river floodplain first and second terraces, there are larger sites, which are believed to represent the loci of coalescing of herding groups seasonally into wet-season settlements, with concomitant attention to agriculture. There appears to be a clustering of sites with circumscription zones of about 10-km radius, based on the initial evidence. Herding villages suggest habitations with prepared clay floors, for temporary or perishable superstructures. The larger valley villages have remains of fieldstone and adobe structures, apparently mainly round to oval in nature. Settlement location at this period is dramatically shifted to a new valley bottom pattern, emphasizing the agricultural lands at the southern end of the valley near Huancayo, during the subsequent Wari conquest. A few

pastoral groups maintain herding strategies at the northern end near Jauja at this period, but in general the Wari conquest is a dramatic reorganization of settlement patterning as well as productive activities.

Economy

The economy strongly emphasizes pastoral production, with agriculture apparently emphasizing the native Andean tubers and grains, rather than the more lowland maize, cucurbits, and beans. Ceramic production is local, with sufficient regional variation, to suggest that the local social clusters of roughly 10-km radius may have been self-sufficient. Metal items, such as clothing pins, seem to be accessible to all levels of the group, although evidence indicates they are not locally fabricated, but imported. Metal objects, obsidian, jewelry stone, and other items indicate a fairly extensive north-south trade, presumably along the Mantaro river corridor, as well as east-west into the upper reaches of the Pacific coastal valleys. Camelid pastoralism is particularly important in this region during this time period. Emphasis on maize agriculture and agricultural production to produce economic surpluses, is well known in other Andean zones to the north and south of the Usupukio zone at this period. Thus the Usupukio subtradition is significant as an example of an ethnic group that deliberately opted to focus on pastoral production, instead of plant agricultural production, not because of any ecological limitations, but because of cultural preferences. Productive mechanisms during this period are dominated by pastoral features; a sharp contrasted is noted with the conquest of the region by the Wari empire to the south, which within a single generation reconfigured the economic system of the southern end of the valley from pastoralism into major field systems of maize, among other plants.

Sociopolitical Organization

The Usupukio subtradition is employed here as typical of a number of closely related groups that inhabited areas of Huancavelica, Lima, Junin, and Pasco departments. These appeared to be relatively independent agropastoral groups, that emphasized pastoralism as a way of life. There are small herding villages that are posited to be the seasonal winter or day season dispersal of larger village populations, which returned to villages of populations estimated to be several hundred during the summer or wet season. There is little evidence of economic or political inequality, suggesting largely egalitarian, seasonally nomadic folk. If herds represent wealth, as they often do among modern pastoralists, economic inequality may have been represented primarily by significant differences in herd sizes, something difficult to recover archaeologically.

Religion and Expressive Culture

Ceramic figurines of both humans and camelids are common and are assumed to represent some kind of religious items. The camelid figurines most often emphasize female animals and animals with rich fleece, similar in fact to some of the *illa* ritual objects employed by modern Andean herders. The human figurines appear to emphasize females, suggesting a widespread interest in the fertility of both humans and livestock involved in the ritual organization. "Boot-shaped" tombs are the principal burial mode. These involve vertical access entries, from 1 m to up to 4–5 m deep. They are usually cut directly through the soil, although rarely they may be stone-lined at the top. The base of the vertical shaft opens up into a tomb—a tomb that may have only a single chamber or that may also have multiple side alcoves and additional rooms. Burials were placed in these chambers and alcoves in flexed position, wrapped in textiles (there is nearly always at least one or more clothing *tupu* pins at the neck of the bundle), and accompanied by most typically a ceramic bottle or jar and a serving plate or shallow bowl, suggesting that food and drink for the journey to the next world accompanied the burials.

Note: Huamachuco and Pucava substraditions are covered in the Highland Andean Formative tradition, pp. 123–137.

References

Bonavia, D. (1970). "Investigaciones arqueologicaas en el Mantaro Medio." *Revista del Museo Nacional* 35: 211–294.

Browman, D. L. (1970). "Early Peruvian Peasants: The Culture History of a Central Highlands Valley." Ph.D. diss., Harvard University.

Browman, D. L. (1976). "Demographic Correlations of the Wari Conquest of Junin." *American Antiquity* 41, 4: 465–477.

Conklin, W. J., and M. E. Moseley (1988). "The Patterns of Art and Power in the Early Intermediate Period." In *Peruvian Prehistory: An Overview of Pre-Inca and Inca Society*, ed. R. W. Keatinge. Cambridge: Cambridge University Press, 145–163.

Earle, T. K, T. N. D'Altroy, C. J. LeBlanc, C. A. Hastorf, and T. Y. LeVine (1980). "Changing Settlement Patterns in the Upper Mantaro Valley, Peru." *Journal of New World Archaeology* 4, 1: 1–49.

Hastorf, C. A. (1991). "The Ecosystem Model and Long-term Prehistoric Change: An Example from the Andes." In *The Ecosytem Apppoach in Anthropology: From Concept to Practice*, ed. E. Moran. Ann Arbor: University of Michigan Press, 131–152.

Hastorf, C. A. (1993). *Agriculture and The Onset of Political Inequality Before The Inka*. New York: Cambridge University Press.

Isbell, W. H. (1997). *Mummies and Mortuary Monuments: A Postprocessual Prehistory of Central Andean Social Organization*. Austin: University of Texas Press.

Lumbreras, L. G. (1960). "Esquema arqueologico de la sierra central del Peru." *Revista del Museo Nacional*. 28: 64–117.

Lumbreras, L. G. (1974). *The Peoples and Culture of Ancient Peru*, trans. B. J. Meggers. Washington, D.C.: Smithsonian Institution.

MacNeish, R. S., T. C. Patterson, and D. L. Browman (1975). *The Central Peruvian Prehistoric Interaction Sphere*. Andover, MA: Papers of the R. S. Peabody Foundation for Archaeology, no. 7.

Mallma Cortez, A. (1996). *Introduccion a la arqueologia e historia de los Xauxa Wankas*. Lima: University Nacional Mayor de San Marcos.

Matos Mendieta, R. (1971). "El periodo formativo en el Valle del Mantaro." *Cienca Social* 1, 1: 18–34.

Moseley, M. E. (1992). *The Incas and Their Ancestors: The Archaeology of Peru*. London: Thames and Hudson.

DAVID BROWMAN
Department of Anthropology
Washington University
St. Louis, Missouri
United States

Andean Regional States

Late Intermediate Period (LIP)

ABSOLUTE TIME PERIOD: 900–530 B.P.

RELATIVE TIME PERIOD: Follows the collapse of the Middle Horizon empires of Wari and Tiahuanaco, precedes the expansion of the Late Horizon Inka empire.

LOCATION: Coastal, high, and eastern slopes of the Andes from Ecuador to northern Chile and Argentina.

DIAGNOSTIC MATERIAL ATTRIBUTES: Stylistically highly variable. Handmade and mold-made ceramics, bronze-copper-silver-gold metallurgy, fine cotton and camelid-wool textiles, elaborate irrigation and terracing, camelid herding, some cities and fortified settlements, burial monuments.

REGIONAL SUBTRADITIONS: Highland Chiefdoms, Coastal Valley States and Chiefdoms, Chimu, Aymara Kingdoms.

IMPORTANT SITES: Cerro Azul, Chiribaya Alta, Punchaumarca, Tunanmarca, Chan Chan.

CULTURAL SUMMARY

The primary division within the archaeological tradition is between the coastal valley in which states developed based on irrigated floodplain agriculture supplemented by marine resources and the Andean highlands where diverse chiefdoms existed based on dry and irrigated terrace agriculture and pastoralism.

Environment

Climate. Within the region, climatic differences are largely determined by elevation. At sea level, average daily temperature is about 20° C, dropping to perhaps 12° C by 3400 m. The Andean Regional States tradition started during a period of interglacial warming similar to today, followed after 650 B.P. by a cooling of approximately 0.6° C that shifted vegetation zones down by about 70 m. On the coast, annual rainfall is nearly zero, except with heavy rains of El Niño; rainfall increases at higher elevations to perhaps 600 mm at 3400 m. Titicaca lake cores indicate a 10–15 percent drought between 850 and 500 B.P. that may have caused coastal abandonment of some large irrigation systems. Snow is rare below 4000 m, but hail and frost are a significant hazard down to about 3300 m. Heavy El Niño rains on the south coast caused major settlement abandonment late in the period.

Topography. The broken topography of the Andean mountains, resulting from the collision of the Nazca and south American plates, is among the most varied and dramatic in the world. The coast is a sandy desert, interspersed with many non-navigable streams and

18

alluvial valleys. The western sloping highlands are steep valleys and ridges of these streams. The mountains consist of uplifted limestone ridges with some volcanic cones. Between parallel ridges lie northwest-southeast trending intermontane valleys with fertile alluvial and moraine soils. Above 4000 m, glacial grassland terrain exists with gentle slopes, rounded hills, small ponds, and some large lakes. Glacial topped peaks rise above 6500 m. East of the mountains, sharp gradient streams have dissected the mountain walls, descending rapidly into the Amazon basin. Localized resources include volcanic stones (basalt and obsidian), alluvial and moraine clays, cherts, semiprecious stones (lapis, malachite, chrysocolla, and onyx), and metals (especially gold, silver, copper, tin, and lead).

Biota. The Andean biota varies greatly with elevation, rainfall, and local conditions. Offshore, nutrient-rich upwelling from the Peru-Chile trench enriches a bountiful marine habitat with diverse fishes from anchovy and sardines to drum and bonito, many mollusks and crustaceans, sea and shore birds, and sea mammals. Inland, the desert vegetation and fauna are sparse except for the *lomas*, watered by mist, and stream beds. As rainfall increases with altitude, species of cactus, grasses, scrubs, and bushes increase in density, deer become more abundant, and small pockets of tropical habitat were present especially in the uplands of some north-coast valleys. Above about 3000 m, some of the region would originally have been forested (part of the *quechua* zone), but already by this period human use had probably transformed the zone to open fields, grass, and shrubs. Deer were found, and locally cactus supported the cochineal beetle used for a brilliant red dye. Above 4000 m was the *puna* grasslands, home to the Andean camelids. The wild guanaco ranged more widely, even to the coast. The ponds and lakes would have had an abundance of migratory and nonmigratory waterfowl, shore birds, and fish. As the terrain drops rapidly and rainfall increases toward the east, forests increase with an extraordinary diversity of plants, birds (including brightly colored macaws, parrots, trogons, toucans, and harpy eagles), and mammals (including various monkeys and jaguars) that were important iconographically.

Settlements

Settlement System. A sharp divide existed in settlement systems of the coastal valleys versus the highlands.

Along the coasts, the primary settlement region was the lower and middle sections of the major valleys. In the more complex cases, a strong site hierarchy existed with two or more levels of political/religious centers, some with habitation for populations in the thousands and with varying amounts of special-purpose architecture such as elite compounds, burial and ceremonial monuments, storage, and administrative facilities; and with undifferentiated habitational settlements for populations in the low thousands down to less than one hundred. Some defensive sites existed with small habitation areas, and major cemeteries were common. In the more complex examples, the impression is of a valley-wide settlement system with significant urbanism and special-function facilities. Road systems organized the settlements of individual valleys and can connect several valleys. In the highlands, settlement systems were less differentiated and complex. Although settlement hierarchies existed, the size of the largest settlements and the scale of organized settlement systems were mostly much smaller. The hierarchy was based on the size of the habitation, only secondarily on architectural differentiation. Fortified settlements were typical, some as refuges for unfortified settlements. Burials were often dispersed in special structures, caves, or habitations; usually not in large cemeteries. Monumental construction and storage were less noted.

Community Organization. On the coast, settlements were characteristically placed along the valley sides or near its mouth, adjacent to the irrigation systems. Most communities were fairly undifferentiated architecturally with expanses of pathways and habitation wards that in the north have been called SIAR (small irregularly agglutinated rooms). In addition to SIAR, centers had special elite religious/administrative areas that were set off architecturally as with the walled compounds of the Chimu. In the more complex examples, site layouts are somewhat irregular, relying on focal-point monuments and dendritic pathways. Within wards, alleys provided local movement between housing areas. There is little evidence of open and accessible plaza or market areas. In upper valleys, settlements were often placed on hillslopes. In the highlands, settlements were typically organized by an enclosing wall that defined the settlement, although unfortified settlements were also used. Settlements typically sat on hills and ridge tops as well as on terraced hillslopes. Most settlements had little internal organization, although the relative elevations for household compounds indicate visibility and often status. A few examples exist for a dual organization of the settlement, perhaps indicative of a moiety system known historically. Special facilities, such as tombs, small central plazas, or towers provide focal points.

Housing. On the coast, house forms were varied. In some situations, quite simple domestic housing is placed on terraces with outer stone or cane walls. Larger structures were internally divided. In the larger settlements, especially in the lower valley sectors, housing can be organized into rectilinear compounds, sometimes built on impressive platforms; these contain an arrangement of rooms and open areas used for habitation and special activities including weaving, metallurgy, fish processing, and the like. The elite compounds at Chan Chan are distinctive, including organized facilities for elite housing, burials, ceremonies, administration, and considerable storage. Compounds probably housed a suprafamily, economic and social group. The differentiation in scale, decorative elaboration, and related activities documents strong social stratification in many situations. In the highlands, in marked contrast, most housing is domestic, usually circular in the north and rectangular in the south, perhaps 4–5 m across. An individual house stands singly with an entrance opening on an enclosed patio or terraced space with limited access. The number of structures on a patio varies according to social status, perhaps indicating polygynous or extended families for elites. Where the land slopes, houses stand on terraces. Most structures are domestic, although towers, burial monuments, and storage units are also described.

House construction is variable. On the coast, cane, adobe brick, and *tapia* were used. *Tapia* consists of large adobe blocks, sun-dried in frames to create thick earthen walls sometimes of monumental proportions. Cane was especially common for commoner housing. In elite compounds, the elaborate plaster frieze decorations at Chan Chan are famous. As one moves inland, stone walls, laid with a mud mortar, became more common. Rough stone walls were apparently plastered. In some highland sites, walls have elaborate decorative chinking. Cut stone was used for corners and door lintels, and in the southern highlands cut stone was sometimes used decoratively especially for fortifications and burial monuments. Through the Andes, plastered surfaces were probably often painted.

Population, Health, and Disease. There is no typical community size. On the coast, the Chimu capital of Chan Chan with a size of over 20 km^2 and an estimated population of 25,000–30,000 or more was the largest city of the period. More typical perhaps, in the lower Santa valley, two centers of 11 ha and 33 ha had estimated

populations of 2700 and 3300, and other sites were often only 1–2 ha, with populations below 100. Coastal valleys probably had populations typically in the low tens of thousands; Santa, for example, had an estimated 12,000. The Chimu state, controlling at its peak 12 valleys, ruled perhaps 200,000 or more subjects. Other coastal polities of a valley or two would have been only 10,000–30,000 in size. In the highlands, some settlements and polities reached this scale. In the Mantaro, the largest settlements is the center Tunanmarca (24 ha, 10,000 people). The chiefdom controlled eight settlements with a total estimated population of 24,000. Most polities would have been much smaller with a typical settlement of a few hectares and perhaps a hundred residents; chiefly centers were larger, and chiefdoms were perhaps 1000 or so persons. Anemia has been described in both coastal and highland populations. Periodontal disease, perhaps aggravated by coca chewing, caused considerable tooth loss. In the highlands, cramped fortified settlements and warfare resulted in a very short life span. On the south coast, evidence of tuberculosis suggests that virtually the whole population may have been infected. Culturally specific forms of cranial deformation have been commonly noted. Skeletal evidence suggests that coastal and highland populations had distinct genetic histories.

Economy

Subsistence. The dominant subsistence was intensive agriculture, with seasonal cycles according to water availability. On the coast, very large-scale irrigation systems were built with substantial facilities including dams, canals, aqueducts, and field systems. Total area under cultivation reached a maximum during the Late Intermediate Period (LIP), supporting a substantial urban population and providing the basis for staple financed states. Up the valleys, irrigation systems were shorter, sometimes associated with extensive terracing. In the highlands, uplands were farmed, sometimes using ridged fields to help cold-air drainage; hillslopes were terraced both for rainfall and irrigation farming. Irrigation systems tapped both springs and streams, but the extent of these systems was usually modest. Small-scale irrigation was practiced on the eastern slope, along with both terraced and shifting rainfall cultivation. Above 3800 m, camelid herding of llama (pack animals, meat, wool) and alpaca (wool) required corrals. Corrals for camelids were found down to the coast. Seasonal transhumance was probable: to high pasture in the summer, to lower pastures and harvested fields down to the coast in winter. At the coast, large-scale fishing, shellfish collecting, and sea-mammal hunting were practiced. Some fishing and hunting took place inland where resources were available. Trade in subsistence goods was limited. Specialized fishing communities on the coast traded with neighboring farming communities, but fish products were not traded in volume to the highlands. Highland pastoralists maintained symbiotic relationships with neighboring agriculturalists and probably provided animal products to the coast. Coca, grown in specialized mid-elevation fields on both sides of the Andes, was traded to the highlands and to the coast.

Wild Foods. Wild plants were probably important for medical uses. On the north coast and probably elsewhere, commoners differentially used wild plants that grew along the irrigation ditches. Deer, camelids, sea mammals, and some birds were hunted, but dietary contributions were minor. On the coast, much more important were anchovy, sardine, and other fishes. Shellfish were collected as supplemental foods. Seasonal exploitation was likely.

Domestic Foods. Primary domesticates included maize, potatoes, manioc, quinoa, and legumes. Secondary crops include the other Andean tubers, lupines, squash, and chili pepper. Tree crops included *pacay*, *lucuma*, guava, and avocado. Tubers and quinoa were more important at higher elevations. Domesticated animals used for food included llama, guinea pig, Muscovy duck, and occasionally dog. Llama and maize, preferred foods, were eaten more commonly by elites. Cannibalism is not documented.

Industrial Arts. In agriculture, tools included hoes and foot plows that were made of locally available stone and wood. No nonhuman power was employed. For hunting, bolas, slings, nets, and stone-tipped arrows and atlatl points were used. Fishing employed small, hand-paddled reed and log boats, a variety of throw and larger nets, line, sinkers, and hooks. Ropes and sturdy bags were used.

Utensils. Large rocker-based grinding stones served for food preparation. An opportunistic inventory of flakes and blades were utilized for cutting and scraping. Locally manufactured ceramic vessels were for household cooking, liquid transport and storage, dry storage, and serving. Most ceramics were handmade and little decorated, although more elaborate decorated pieces are known, especially on the coast. Other utensils included gourds, baskets, mats, wooden cups, spoons, and boxes. Both cotton and wool were spun and woven for everyday clothing that especially included ponchos,

hats, shawls, shirts, bags, and belts. Some highly elaborated examples are known. Sandals were worn. Most materials for household use were obtained locally.

Ornaments. An elaborate array of objects for personal decoration included head ornaments, pins, pendants, bead strings, hanging disks and pendants sown on clothing, and highly elaborated textiles. Materials included metals (gold, silver, copper, bronze), shells of marine and land mollusks, semiprecious stones including lapis and copper-related blue and green stones, mica, bird feathers, bone, and teeth, and fibers dyed with vibrant colors. Elaborate hair styles included braiding and plaiting. Most personal decorations were regionally specific in style.

Trade. Despite the level of complexity of human society, the extent and volume of trade were limited and specific. Within polities, trade existed between communities specialized in fishing or agriculture (on the coast) and between communities producing ceramics, occasionally lithics, pastoral products, and agriculture (in the highlands). Regional and long-distance trade between polities focused primarily on highly valued materials, ornaments, certain ceremonial objects including special ceramics (highly decorated or using special clays), dyes, and coca. Special ceramics were traded both along the coast and in more limited amounts between coast and highlands. Along the coast, trade probably used balsa rafts with sails, and llama caravans were used in the interior. In the far north, "money axes" have been recorded, but no other primitive currency is known. For the Chimu, redistribution of wealth can be inferred by extensive storage in elite compounds. In the highlands, no evidence exists for market exchange; plazas were small and restricted in access, and no exchange media have been described. Some central storage in the highlands may indicate small-scale redistribution. Throughout, most trade probably involved direct or down-the-line reciprocal relationships; specialized traders were documented ethnohistorically on the coast.

Division of Labor. The primary division of labor, documented historically, was within the household; high environmental variability allowed households access to most needed materials. Based in part on locally variable resources, however, craft specialization was organized at the community level for ceramics, occasionally for lithics, and for large-scale fishing on the coast. Between regions there was little specialization and exchange, exceptions being pastoralist communities in the *puna* and coca farms limited to specific microenvironments at mid-elevations. Evidence for attached specialization in special crafts can be inferred by the elaboration of metallurgy, weaving, and feather work, and some distinctive ceramics.

Differential Access or Control of Resources. The development of irrigation, especially on the coast, provided the basis for ownership of the productive facilities by an elite or by state institutions. Trade and fishing technologies offered alternative possibilities for control by specialized traders or fishermen. Although raw material sources, such as metal ores and clays, were localized, many alternatives offered little opportunities for control except through highly skilled or labor-intensive crafts associated with specialists producing for elite patrons.

Sociopolitical Organization

Social Organization. On the coast, major residential compounds suggest a different organizational form. As seen especially at Chan Chan, large elite compounds with elaborate burials and distinct consumption and productive activities indicate class divisions. The organization of the commoner housing into special compounds suggests a strong suprafamily organizational structure that may in the more complex situations have been imposed from above. That this organization was economically based is suggested by the industrial scale of fishing communities and special housing for corvée labor. In the highlands, the basic unit of organization was the household. An enclosed space with residential buildings and work space defines a small generalized production unit focused probably on a family unit. Differentiation between elite and commoner households was based on size, placement within the settlement, labor investment in stone work, and the frequency of prestige goods and feasting activities. Multiple residential buildings in elite patio groups may indicate polygynous or extended families (or alternatively co-residential specialists). On some larger sites, a bilateral division may correspond to the historical division of communities into moieties.

Political Organization. Along the central and southern coast, small states and chiefdoms organized populations in the low tens of thousands, and the successful conquest state of Chimu controlled 12 valleys on the north coast. The irrigation systems may well map on a hierarchy of political groups—lords of the local *señorios* controlling the smaller valley irrigation systems and overlords coordinating the larger ones. Leadership included elements of economic control, military domination, and

religious authority. The elaborate burial monuments within the elite compounds and their large ceremonial space documents, for the more complex examples, the use of a legitimizing ideology probably linked to an organized religion. In the highlands, the political organization appears to have been mostly smaller-scale, integrating populations in the low thousands; a few cases of larger-scale chiefdoms existed with populations greater than 10,000. The Cuzco region may have been an emergent state. Political leadership emphasized military prowess; feasting took place within a chief's compound.

Social Control. On the coast, large-scale irrigation systems were probably owned by the local lords and overlords, and the ownership effectively caged the agricultural population for whom few alternatives existed. In contrast to earlier periods, the importance of ceremonial constructions with an assumed ideological content was evidently of secondary importance. In the highlands, social control seems often based on military might and protection from external threat. The social groups are defined by walled enclosures. Ownership of some more intensive agricultural facilities was probably important, but less so than on the coast.

Conflict. On the coast, warfare was clearly important, and a few fortified settlements are described; the impression is that warfare was largely conquest based, as one valley state would try to expand laterally and incorporate other valleys or upvalley areas against highland groups. In some situations, extensive conquest was successful, as in the Chimu state, but in others the scale of polities seem to have been small. The stylistic integration of regions, like the central coast Chancay "culture," may indicate confederacies bridging neighboring valley polities. In the highlands, the scope of political integration was relatively limited spatially such that conflict within valleys, between neighboring chiefdoms, was evident from the fortified settlement pattern suggesting constant threat. Some suprachiefdom confederacies may well have been based on economic and ceremonial structures across broader regions. In the Cuzco region, warfare was apparently controlled by an emergent state organization.

Religion and Expressive Culture

Religious Beliefs. On the coast, complex religious institutions are suggested by elaborate iconography and ceremonial constructions. Figurines were typical. In the highlands, religious paraphernalia were household oriented, and monumental constructions were rare except for the *chullpa* tombs and the fortifications. Throughout, special caches of animals and valuables probably represented ritual offerings.

Death and Afterlife. On the coast, burial practice documents a clear relationship between the living and the dead. Most dramatic were the burial complexes in the Chimu compounds that may suggest the continuing role of a dead ruler in affairs of state, perhaps similar to what has been described historically for the Inca. Large cemeteries probably materialized the organization and continuity of communities. Some sites were apparently cemetery areas for large regions. In the highlands, tombs were often quite visible within or associated with settlements; the relatively small number of tombs suggests that only a portion of the population deserved a special treatment, which suggests continuing involvement of the dead individuals with the living. In some situations, burials were placed inconspicuously in caves or in the floors below residential buildings. Burial goods suggest a recognition of the continuing association of dead with objects of life, which define status and role. Food was buried with the dead. Strong differentiation of burials by richness of their contents suggests marked social stratification on the coast, but not in the highlands. Special burials of llama, dog, and guinea pig, often in houses, suggest a ritual significance for these domesticated animals.

Suggested Readings

Aldenderfer, Mark, ed. (1993). *Domestic Architecture, Ethnicity, and Complementarity in the South-central Andes.* Iowa City: University of Iowa Press.
Bauer, Brian (1992). *The Development of the Inca State.* Austin: University of Texas Press.
Billman, Brian (1997). "Population Pressure and the Origins of Warfare in the Moche Valley, Peru." In *Integrating Archaeological Demography: Multidisciplinary Approaches to Prehistoric Population*, ed. R. R. Paine. Carbondale: Center for Archaeological Publications, Southern Illinois University, 285–310.
Earle, Timothy (1997). *How Chiefs Come to Power.* Stanford: Stanford University Press.
Gumerman, George (1997). "Food and Complex Societies." *Journal of Archaeological Method and Theory* 4: 105–138.
Gumerman, George (1991). "Subsistence and Complex Societies: Diet between Diverse Socio-economic Groups at Pacatnamu, Peru." Ph.D. diss., Department of Anthropology, University of California, Los Angeles.
Haas, Jonathan, Shelia Pozorski, and Thomas Pozorski, eds. (1987). *The Origins and Development of Andean States.* Cambridge: Cambridge University Press.
Hastorf, Christine A. (1993). *Agriculture and the Onset of Political Inequality before the Inka.* Cambridge: Cambridge University Press.
Lavallée, Daniele (1973). "Estructura y organización del habitat en los Andes centrales durante el período intermedio tardío." *Revista del Museo National* 39: 91–116.
Marcus, Joyce (1987). *Late Intermediate Occupation at Cerro Azul, Perú.* Ann Arbor: University of Michigan Museum of Anthropology Technical Report 20.
Masuda, Shozo, Izumi Shimada, and Craig Morris, eds. (1985). *Andean Ecology and Civilization.* Tokyo: University of Tokyo Press.
Moseley, Michael (1992). *The Inca and Their Ancestors.* London: Thames and Hudson.
Moseley, Michael (1997). "Climate, Culture, and Punctuated Change: New Data, New Challenges." *Review of Archaeology* 17, 6: 19–27.
Moseley, Michael E., and Kent C. Day, eds. (1982). *Chan Chan: Andean Desert City.* Albuquerque: University of New Mexico Press.
Netherly, Patricia (1984). "The Management of Late Andean Irrigation Systems on the North Coast of Peru." *American Antiquity* 49: 227–254.
Ortloff, Charles, Michael Moseley, and Robert Feldman (1982). "Hydraulic Engineering Aspects of the Chimu Chicama-Moche Intervalley Canal." *American Antiquity* 47: 572–595.
Parsons, Jeffrey R., and Charles M. Hastings (1988). "The Late Intermediate Period." In *Peruvian Prehistory*, ed. R. K. Keatinge. Cambridge: Cambridge University Press, 190–229.
Stanish, Charles, Edmundo de la Vega M., Lee Steadman, Cecilia Chávez Justo, Kirk L. Frye, Luperio Onofre M., Matthew T. Seddon, and Percy Calisaya C. (1997). *Archaeological Survey in the Juli-Desaguadero Region of Lake Titicaca Basin, Southern Peru.* Chicago: Fieldiana 29.
Wilson, David A. (1988). *Prehistoric Settlement Patterns in the Lower Santa Valley, Peru.* Washington, D.C.: Smithsonian Institution Press.

SUBTRADITIONS

Andean Chiefdoms of the Central and Northern Highlands (Late Intermediate Period)

TIME PERIOD: 900–530 B.P.

LOCATION: High Andes from Ecuador to southern Peru.

DIAGNOSTIC MATERIAL ATTRIBUTES: Handmade ceramics of variable styles, stone hoes, copper-silver-gold metallurgy, camelid-wool textiles, terracing and modest irrigation, camelid herding, fortified settlements, and above-ground tombs.

CULTURAL SUMMARY

Environment

The topography of the Andean mountains is broken. The underlying geology consists of uplifted sedimentary Cretaceous limestone, metamorphosed rock, and intrusive volcanic formations. Parallel mountain ridges border intermontane valleys with fertile alluvial and moraine soils. Above 3800 m, glacial terrain includes gentle slopes, rounded hills, clay and gravel deposits, small ponds, and some large lakes. Glacial-topped peaks rise above 6500 m. East and west of the mountains, steep-gradient streams dissect the mountain walls. Localized resources include intrusive obsidian, Pleistocene gravel and clay, cherts, and metal ores (gold, silver, copper, and lead). Austral summer rainfall of around 600 mm at 3400 m allows for dry-land farming; increasing evapotransparation at lower elevations made irrigation necessary except to the east where rainfall is higher. Titicaca lake cores indicate a 10–15 percent drought between 850–500 B.P. Snow is rare below 4000 m, but hail and frost are a significant hazard down to 3200 m.

Above 3000 m, the central and northern parts of the region were originally forested (part of the *quechua* zone), but had probably been transformed well before the LIP to open fields, grass, and shrubs. Deer were present, and locally cactus supported the cochineal beetle used for a brilliant red dye. Above 4000 m was the *puna* grasslands, home to the Andean camelids including the wild vicuña. The guanaco ranged more widely. The ponds and lakes would have had an abundance of migratory and nonmigratory waterfowl, shore birds, and fish.

Settlements

Settlement hierarchies were typically not strongly differentiated. Some larger settlements, greater than 5 ha and with estimated populations above 500, dominated surrounding smaller settlements. The differentiation of settlements within the hierarchy was based primarily on size, with few architectural differences. In some locations, such as the Mantaro Valley in the central highlands, large town-size settlements, such as the center Tunanmarca (24 ha, 10,000 people), dominated a hierarchy of midsize settlements. Typically settlements were much smaller, only a few hectares with perhaps a hundred residents. Fortifications were ubiquitous, surrounding and defining habitation areas. In contrast, around Cuzco, which was to become the capital of the Inca state, LIP sites were smaller and apparently unfortified.

Settlements typically sit on hills and ridges, but also on terraced hillslopes and unfortified flats. Within most settlements, little formal organization is apparent, except for the surrounding walls that frame the settlement area. Larger settlements may have small central plazas with modest special buildings and can be divided by open zones that straddle the ridge to focus attention on the settlement's center and divide the settlement bilaterally, perhaps into moieties. The relative elevation of household compounds, their proximity to the settlement's center, their size, and masonry quality can indicate social status. Above-ground tombs, *chullpas*, were often located along settlement walls, near gateways or other access routes; the tombs may have provided focal points that organized social subgroups. Most architecture was domestic, usually circular in the north and rectangular in the south, perhaps 12–14 m^2. An individual house stood separately with an entrance opening on an enclosed patio or terraced space with limited access. On sloping ground, compounds stood on terraces, sometimes divided into multiple residential units. Houses were typically of stone construction. Masonry used local stone that was roughly faced on both sides of the wall, with a rubble core and mud mortar. Rough stone walls were probably plastered. Elaborate decorative chinking can mark elite houses, and roughly dressed stone was used for some corners and door lintels.

Economy

Mixed agriculture was the base of the highland economy. The upland glacial tills were farmed extensively, sometimes using ridged fields to facilitate cold-air drainage; hillslopes were terraced both for rainfall and irrigation farming. Irrigation systems tapped both springs and streams; the extent of these systems was usually modest, occasionally up to several square kilometers in area. Smaller-scale irrigation was also practiced on the steep eastern and western valleys. Primary domesticates included maize, potatoes, quinoa, and legumes. Secondary crops include the other Andean tubers, lupines, and chili peppers. Tubers and quinoa were especially important at elevations too high for maize. Below 2200 m, coca, *molle*, *pacay*, and avocado were grown. Above 3800 m, camelid herding of llama (pack animals, meat, wool) and alpaca (wool) required corrals. Domesticated guinea pig and occasionally dog provided additional meat sources. Trade in subsistence goods was limited, but pastoralists maintained symbiotic relationships with neighboring agriculturalists. Coca was traded to the highlands and coast. Wild plants were probably important for medical uses, but did not contribute significantly to the diet. Wild animals including deer and guanaco were seasonally hunted, but their dietary contribution was minor; vicuña was used as a special wool resource.

In agriculture, tools included hoes, foot plows, clod breakers, and prismatic bladed sickles that were made of locally available stone. No nonhuman power was employed, except for the use of llama as pack animals. For hunting, bolas (sometimes of lead), slings, perhaps nets, and rarely stone-tipped projectiles were used. Large rocker-based grinding stones served for food preparation. An opportunistic inventory of flakes and blades was utilized for cutting, scraping, and drilling. Locally manufactured ceramic vessels were used for household cooking, liquid transport and storage, dry storage, and serving. Ceramics were regionally distinctive in style. They were handmade, using a turning stone; the amount of decoration varied, but was generally not carefully executed. Wool was spun using recycled ceramic whorls and woven using various bone tools. Needles of bone, copper, and even gold are recovered; metal needles had pierced eyes to the south and looped to the north. Most materials for household use were obtained locally.

An array of fairly simple objects for personal decoration included pendants, bead strings, and hanging disks and pendants sown onto clothing. Materials included metals (gold, silver, copper, bronze), marine shells (including a few pieces of *Spondylus* from Ecuador), bone and teeth, and semiprecious stones such as lapis, turquoise, and quartz crystals. Metallurgy was relatively simple, including oxide-ore smelting, hammering, and casting. The availability of raw materials was quite localized; small amounts of wealth objects were traded regionally and over longer distances.

Despite the organization into chiefdoms and chiefly confederacies, the extent and volume of trade were limited and specific, dealing primarily with the special materials for ornaments. Within locales (<10 km), trade existed between communities partly specialized in ceramic and lithic production and in pastoral herding. Thus within a chiefdom's territory, villages specialized in the manufacture of ceramics or in the manufacture of stone tools from the best available local material; products were distributed probably through simple reciprocal exchanges within the polity. Regional and long-distance trade (>10 km), across polity boundaries, focused primarily on ceremonial important objects. These included large, elaborately decorated ollas probably used for *chicha*, special materials such as metals, mica, and marine shells used for ornaments, and ceremonially important plants such as coca, hallucinogens, and chili peppers. No evidence exists for market exchange; plazas were small and redistricted in access, and exchange media have not been described. Limited trade probably involved direct or down-the-line recipro-

cal relationships, especially among elites. In addition to gender and age divisions with the household, some division of labor was based on the irregular distribution of material resources including clay, stone, and metal ores. Between regions, community specialization could be based on agricultural zonation, the *puna* for camelid herding and lower humid pockets for coca fields. Evidence for attached specialization is minimal, and the technologies of wealth production, involving bead manufacture, simple metallurgy, and weaving, were not so esoteric or involved as to allow for control. Little evidence exists for differential access or control of resources. Agricultural facilities were generally not highly elaborated. Although most valued resources for the manufacture of wealth objects were localized, many alternative sources existed, thus making exclusive control unfeasible.

Sociopolitical Organization

The household, living within a walled residential compound, was the generalized production unit of society. It varied in size, probably representing variation among nuclear, extended, and polygynous families. Differentiation between elite and commoner households has been described, but these differences were not highly marked, being based on degree (not kind) of labor investment in stone work, the quantities of prestige goods, and feasting activities. Multiple residential buildings in elite patio groups may indicate polygynous marriages or extended families. Social stratification is indicated by richer remains in elite households (for example, more silver); although burial contents were not greatly differentiated, burial treatment could be distinctive in the labor investment in tombs. The political organization appears to have been mostly small-scale or simple chiefdoms integrating populations in the low thousands; a few cases of larger-scale chiefdoms existed with populations greater than 10,000. The Tunanmarca chiefdom, for example, controlled eight settlements with a total estimated population of 24,000. In areas with multiple small polities, sometimes economically differentiated, an integrating ceremonial structure has been described. Around Cuzco during the LIP, the settlement pattern of small, unfortified sites suggests an overarching political organization, perhaps an emergent state that was precursor to the Inca empire. In general, highland political leadership apparently relied on military prowess; feasting took place within a chief's compound. Within highland valleys, warfare typically existed between neighboring chiefdoms, although actual conflict was probably mediated by crosscutting economic and ceremonial relationships.

Religion and Expressive Culture

Religious paraphernalia and monumental constructions were comparatively few. The central plazas of the larger settlements and occasional impressive terraces probably define ceremonial spaces, but these constructions were modest and represent little labor expenditure in their construction. The settlements' fortification walls were the culture's primary monuments. Additionally the *chullpa* were often placed prominently along these walls, and these ancestral monuments may indicate the ceremonial importance of kin groups. Other burials were commonly placed in closed contexts, such as caves or below residential buildings. Goods buried with the dead suggest a recognition of the continuing association of dead with objects of life, but burial furnishings were not elaborate or well patterned. Burial of isolated body parts includes crania, feet, and pelvic sections; no evidence of cannibalism is reported. Modest special caches, including crystals or pieces of metal, probably represent offerings. Llama, dog, and guinea pig were given special burials, suggesting sacrifices described ethnohistorically.

References

Bauer, Brian (1992). *The Development of the Inca State*. Austin: University of Texas Press.

Browman, David (1970). "Early Peruvian Peasants: The Culture History of a Central Highland Valley." Ph.D. diss., Department of Anthropology, Harvard University.

Costin, Cathy (1986). "From Chiefdom to Empire State: Ceramic Economy and the Prehispanic Wanka of Highland Peru." Ph.D. diss., Department of Anthropology, University of California, Los Angeles.

Costin, Cathy (1991). "Craft Specialization: Issues in Defining, Documenting, and Explaining the Organization of Production." *Archaeological Method and Theory* 3: 1–56.

Costin, Cathy, and Timothy Earle (1989). "Status Distinction and Legitimation of Power as Reflected in Changing Patterns of Consumption in Late Prehispanic Peru." *American Antiquity* 54: 691–714.

DeMarrais, Elizabeth (n.d.). "The Architecture of Wanka Communities." In *Empire and Domestic Economy*, ed. T. D'Altroy and C. Hastorf. Unpublished manuscript.

Dillehay, Tom (1979). "Pre-hispanic Resource Sharing in the Central Andes." *Science* 204: 24–31.

Earle, Timothy (1985). "Commodity Exchange and Markets in the Inca State: Recent Archaeological Evidence." In *Markets and Exchange*, ed. S. Plattner. Latham, MD: University Press of America, 369–397.

Earle, Timothy (1997). *How Chiefs Come to Power*. Stanford: Stanford University Press.

Hastorf, Christine A. (1990). "The Effect of the Inka State on Sausa Agricultural Production and Crop Consumption." *American Antiquity* 55: 262–290.

Hastorf, Christine A. (1991). "Food, Space, and Gender in Prehistory." In *Engendering Archaeology: Women in Prehistory*, ed. J. Gero and M. Conkey. Oxford: Basil Blackwell, 132–159.

Hastorf, Christine A. (1993). *Agriculture and the Onset of Political Inequality before the Inka*. Cambridge: Cambridge University Press.

Lavallée, Daniele (1973). "Estructura y organización del habitat en los Andes centrales durante el período intermedio tardío." *Revista del Museo National* 39: 91–116.

Krzanowski, Andrzej (1977). "Yuramarca, the Settlement Complex in the Alto Chicama Region (Northwestern Peru)." In *Polish Contributions in New World Archaeology*, ed. J. K. Kozolowski. Krakow: Zaklad Narodowy im Ossolinkich, 29–58.

Owen, Bruce (1986). "The role of Common Metal Objects in the Inka State." M.A. thesis, Department of Anthropology, University of California, Los Angeles.

Parsons, Jeffrey R., and Charles M. Hastings (1988). "The Late Intermediate Period." In *Peruvian Prehistory*, ed. R. K. Keatinge. Cambridge: Cambridge University Press, 190–229.

Parsons, Jeffrey R., Charles M. Hastings, and Ramiro Matos M. (1997). "Rebuilding the State in Highland Peru: Herder-Cultivator Interaction During the Late Intermediate Period in the Tarma-Chinchaycocha Region." *Archaeological Method and Theory* 8: 317–341.

Andean Coastal Valley States and Chiefdoms (Late Intermediate Period)

ABSOLUTE TIME PERIOD: 900–530 B.P.

LOCATION: Central and south coastal region of Peru from Chancay to Arica.

DIAGNOSTIC MATERIAL ATTRIBUTES: Stylistically highly variable by region. Elaborately decorated, handmade ceramics, copper-silver-gold metallurgy, fine cotton and wool textiles, irrigation agriculture, adobe and *tapia* architecture, cemeteries, and urban settlements and monumental construction in the most complex examples.

CULTURAL SUMMARY

Environment

At sea level, average daily temperature is about 20° C, with extremes limited by the sea and coastal fog. Along the coast, annual rainfall approaches zero, except when El Niño conditions, documented for the later part of the LIP, produced heavy rains and mud flows that destroyed irrigation systems. Normal rainfall begins at higher elevations, but increasing temperatures above the coastal fog create high evapotranspiration with resulting deserts. The coast is a sandy desert with dunes, interspersed with many non-navigable streams and alluvial plains. The western sloping highlands are divided by streams, valleys, and ridges. Localized resources include alluvial clays and metals (especially gold and copper). During the time period, drought probably resulted in reduced stream flows and the abandonment of some irrigation systems. Offshore, nutrient-rich upwelling from the Peru-Chile trench feeds bountiful, but locally quite variable, coastal and marine habitats with diverse fishes from anchovy and sardines to drum and bonito, many mollusks and crustaceans, sea and shore birds, and sea mammals. Inland, the desert vegetation and fauna are sparse except for the fog-misted *lomas* and for the well-watered stream bottoms. As rainfall increases with elevation, species of cactus, grasses, scrubs, and bushes increase in density, and deer were found.

Settlements

Distinctive settlement systems existed in the lower and middle sections of some major valleys. Site types of the more complex polities included political/religious centers with habitation for populations sometimes in the thousands or more and with varying amounts of special-purpose architecture such as elite compounds, burial and ceremonial monuments, storage, and administrative facilities; undifferentiated settlements for populations in the low thousands down to less than one hundred; some defensive sites with habitation areas; and major cemeteries. Settlements were placed along the valley sides or near its mouth, adjacent to the irrigation systems; on valley slopes and ridges, especially in the upper valleys; and in small coastal spring drainages. In the lower valleys, at larger sites, focus was kept visually on impressive monuments (such as the central temple and subsidiary shrines at Pachacamac or at La Centinela) and on elite compounds. Distinctive rectilinear compounds were sometimes built on impressive platforms; these could contain a warren of rooms and open areas used for habitation and special-activity areas including weaving, fish processing, and the like. Both elite and common compounds portray an image of suprafamily economic and social organization. The differentiation in scale, decorative elaboration, and related activities documents strong social stratification. Settlements were often without evident formal organization, fitting into the natural topography. Monumental construction on the central coast used *tapia*—large adobe blocks, sun-dried in frames to create thick earthen walls. Commoner housing on terraces was often with cane walls and post supports. Alleys provided local movement between housing areas. There is little evidence of open and accessible plaza or market areas. Major cemeteries may be associated with the residential and ceremonial sectors or set apart.

In the upper valleys, settlements appear often to be of highland cultural traditions. They were generally smaller, irregular in layout, and often placed on hills or slopes. Late in the LIP, as in the Estuquiña culture, up-valley communities were fortified by encircling walls and ditches. As in the highlands, these settlements were relatively undifferentiated architecturally with perhaps 100 or fewer habitation terraces, only some of which supported structures. Terraces were apparently organized into household compounds. Individual houses were often of rectangular form, varying in size (20–450 m^2) depending on the number of rooms and perhaps the family size and structure. Outer stone walls, perhaps plastered, defined the structure that could be internally subdivided by stone or cane partitions. Roofing was probably of cane mats. Considerable variation suggests cultural differences. Burials could be in *chullpas* as found in the highlands. In some situations, such as in the Osmore area, multiple ethnic groups (Chiribaya and Tumilaca) resided within the same locality, but more commonly a uniform stylistic group in the lower valley contrasted to an up-valley grouping that was related in style of ceramics, housing, and burial and in biology to highland populations. Road systems connected settlements in the lower valley and interconnected some valleys.

Economy

The dominant subsistence was intensive agriculture, with seasonality according to water availability for irrigation. Fairly large-scale irrigation systems, limited always to a single valley system, were built. Up the valleys, irrigation systems were smaller, but often associated with impressive canals and extensive terracing near habitation sites. Important domesticates included maize, beans, squash, peanuts, manioc, *lucuma*, *achira*, *camote*, *molle*, *pacay*, chili pepper, and cotton. Guinea pigs were raised, and llama corrals suggest that they were routinely kept and probably bred on the coast. Agricultural tools include digging implements with stone or bone blades; small grinding stones were used for food processing. Mollusks and crustacea from salt and freshwater and some wild plants were eaten and may have increased the dietary quality.

Specialized and culturally distinctive communities fished on a large scale, hunted marine mammals, and collected shellfish. Most substantial were anchovy, sardine, and other fishes. Fishing probably employed hand-paddled reed or log boats and a wide variety of nets and line gear that included circular cast nets and larger nets, stone weights, and wood or gourd floats, used for cooperative and individual fishing. Large-scale processing and storage, as at Cerro Azul, suggest possible control over production. Hunting used slings, three-stone bolas, bows and arrows, and atlatls and darts. Trade in fish products was with neighboring valley communities, not substantially with the highlands. Some crawfish collecting and deer hunting took place up valley. Through the LIP, marine foods increased in the diet of mid-valley groups. Highland pastoralists may have maintained relationships with up-valley agriculturalists whom they could have visited during the winter. Highlanders, or up-valley intermediaries, probably traded animals to coastal states. Coca, grown in mid-elevation fields, was traded to both the highlands and coast.

Locally manufactured ceramic vessels were for household cooking, liquid transport and storage, dry storage, and serving. Most ceramics were handmade, occasionally molded, sometimes elaborately polychrome decorated using standardized geometric elements, and not infrequently traded between valleys. Execution was often not unusually careful, and decorated objects were generally available in all households. Styles tended to be localized to a number of neighboring valleys and distinguished between the lower and upper valleys. Various contemporary styles within the Osmore region indicate multiethnic regional populations. Cotton and wool were spun, dyed, and woven for everyday and special uses for shirts, belts, bags, hats, and loincloths. An impressive array of techniques included plain weave, warp stripe and weft-stripe plain weave, extrawarp float single-face weave, eccentric slit tapestry, gauze weave, painted textiles, embroidery, and brocade. Dyes were of various colors, especially red from the cochineal and a local *lomas* plant and blue from indigo. Some highly elaborated cloth examples with geometric and figural designs are known and have been associated with elite burials as at Chiribaya Alta. Cloth production implements include wooden spindles, spindle whorls (manufactured pottery, stone, and metal), needles (looped-eye metal and cactus thorns), acacia-thorn bobbins, cane looms, and a variety of camelid-bone weaving tools. Some materials, such as wool and dyes, were likely traded, but most materials probably derived from local sources. The elaboration in manufacturing techniques suggest some control over attached weaving specialists.

An elaborate array of special objects for personal decoration and use has been recovered especially from burial contexts. Materials included metals (gold, silver, and copper), marine shells (including *Spondylus* traded from Ecuador), semiprecious stone (turquoise, lapis, malachite, azurite, *chrysocolla*), and bird feathers (including some traded from the tropical forest). Metal forms that have been best studied include ear spools, rare finger rings, beads, bangles and disks sewn on clothing, *tupu* pins, axes, chisels, bowls, tweezers, lime spoons. Most ornamental types were quite regional in style. Manufacturing included sheet metal, cast objects, and silver- or gold-enriched surfaces on mostly copper cores. The availability of materials for special objects was often localized. Despite the complexity of coastal Andean society, the extent and volume of trade were quite limited and specific, dealing primarily with ornaments and some special ceramics. Along the coast, trade probably used balsa rafts with sails. Ethnohistorically specialized traders were documented on the coast, especially for *Spondylus* traded through Chincha.

The elaboration and dependence on irrigation provided the basis for ownership of the productive facilities by local lords and the basis for a staple finance political economy. Fishing for and trade in anchovy and sardines could also be centrally controlled. Trade technologies, involving large rafts, offered more limited alternative possibilities for control by specialized traders. Although raw materials resources, such as metal ores and clays, were localized, many alternatives offered little opportunities for control except by supporting highly skilled or labor-intensive crafts, as with weavers and metal smiths working for elite patrons.

Sociopolitical Organization

Major residential compounds, such as at Cerro Azul, suggest an organization of housing into special regularly laid-out compounds with a strong suprafamily organization. On top of platforms, rectangular rooms, work spaces, and open plazas suggest that a complex arrangement of personnel and activities organized residential life; such an organization suggests a strong overarching structure determining interpersonal relationships. Such community compounds may have been economically specialized as suggested by the industrial scale of fish processing at Cerro Azul and by ethnohistorical documents. Up valley, the more irregular arrangement of residential structures suggests a grouping of individual households, probably in a kin-based unit.

Leadership included elements of economic control over irrigation and fishing, military domination, and religious authority. The extensive irrigation systems were probably owned and managed by the ruling elite and related institutions, and the ownership effectively caged the agricultural workers for whom few alternatives existed in Peru's coastal desert. Cemeteries, such as those at Chiribaya Alta, in coastal polities show dramatic variability in the richness of burials, suggesting considerable social stratification and differentiation on the coast, but less so up valley. In contrast to the Early Intermediate Period on the central coast of Peru, ceremonial constructions represented a reduced scale and less labor investment, although some complexes like Pachacamac and La Centinela are still impressive. Small valley states organized populations in the tens of thousands. These were what Rostworowski calls *señorios*; they were organized by local lords and community specializations of fishermen, merchants, and farmers. The stylistic integration of regions, like the central coast Chancay culture or the south coast Ica culture, suggests an interacting set of neighboring polities that may represented a somewhat larger state or confederacy of neighboring valley polities.

Religion and Expressive Culture

Complex religious institutions are suggested by fairly elaborate ceremonial constructions, burial practice, and iconography. For example, at Pachacamac and at La Centinela, major temple pyramids visually dominated the centers and their lower valley settlements. In the Chicama valley, La Centinela consisted of a broad-based terrace with virtually vertical walls rising 13 m above the agricultural plain and topped by a 20-m-tall pyramid. Four straight roads radiated from the impressive monument, most probably organizing major ceremonies with the cardinal directions. Burial ritual was quite elaborated: corpses were wrapped in textiles, sometimes highly decorated and capped with elaborate headgear, and accompanied by decorated ceramics, metals, special toolkits like spinning and weaving tools, baskets, gourds, sandals, model boats, and food offerings such as fruit, tubers, maize, *chicha*, whole guinea pigs, and camelid parts. A few individuals were accompanied by human companions. High-status Chiribaya burials can contain weapons, sometimes not functional. Large cemeteries probably materialized the organization of communities and their connection with the ancestors. Burials (often quite common in domestic contexts) of llama and guinea pig suggest a ritual significance for these domesticated animals. Animal burials may include offerings of turquoise, silver, and feathers. Anthropomorphic figurines (sometimes still dressed) and anthropomorphic vessels are typical.

References

Aldenderfer, Mark, ed. (1993). *Domestic Architecture, Ethnicity, and Complementarity in the South-Central Andes.* Iowa City: University of Iowa Press.

Lozada C., María Cecilia (1998). "The Señorío of Chiribaya: A Bioarchaeological Study in the Osmore Drainage of Southern Perú." Ph.D. diss., Department of Anthropology, University of Chicago.

Marcus, Joyce (1987). *Late Intermediate Occupation at Cerro Azul, Perú.* Ann Arbor: University of Michigan Museum of Anthropology Technical Report 20.

Moseley, Michael (1992). *The Inca and Their Ancestors.* London: Thames and Hudson.

Owen, Bruce (1986). "The Role of Common Metal Objects in the Inka State." M.A. thesis, Department of Anthropology, University of California, Los Angeles.

Owen, Bruce (1993). "A Model of Multiethnicity: State Collapse. Competition, and Social Complexity from Tiwanaku to Chiribaya in the Osmore Valley, Perú." Ph.D. diss., Department of Anthropology, University of California, Los Angeles.

Owen, Bruce (1995). "Warfare and Engineering, Ostentation and Social Status in the Late Intermediate Period Osmore Drainage." Paper presented at Society for American Archaeology 60th annual meeting.

Owen, Bruce (1997). "The Prehistory of the Valley of Moquegua." In *Contisuyu: Memories of the Civilizations of the South of Perú.* ed. Moquegua, Perú: Moquegua Museum, 30–55.

Rostworoski D. C., Maria (1970). "Mercaderes del Valle de Chincha en la epoca prehispanica: Un documento y unos comentarios." *Revista Española de Antropología Americana* 5: 135–177.

Rostworoski D. C., Maria (1978). *Señorios indígenas de Lima y Canta* Lima: Instituto de Estudios Peruanos.

Rostworoski D. C., Maria (1992). *Pachacamac y el señor de los Milagros: Una tryectoria milenaria.* Lima: Instituto de Estudios Peruanos.

Stannish, Chip (1992). *Ancient Andean Political Economy.* Austin: University of Texas Press.

Wallert, Arie, and Ran Boytner (1996). "Dyes from the Tumilaca and Chiribaya Cultures, South Coast Peru." *Journal of Archaeological Science* 23: 853–861.

SITES

Cerro Azul

TIME PERIOD: 850–400 B.P.

DESCRIPTIVE SUMMARY

Local Environment

Cerro Azul is located above 10 m above sea level in the Cañete valley, Peru. The central section of the site is positioned just above the rocky sea cliffs on a protected saddle between two coastal hills. Terraces extend upward to around 80 m above sea level on the larger hill. Immediately to the west is the open sea and to the north is the sandy beach of the Cerro Azul bay. Nearby is the irrigated and agriculturally productive valley alluvium. The site receives no measurable annual rainfall and is bare of vegetation.

Physical Features

Cerro Azul is about 24 ha in total area, divided into two sectors. Along c. 8 ha of the saddle, an architectural core of the settlement consisted of 10 monumental constructions and many smaller buildings. Eight of the largest constructions define a large main plaza. Each major construction was built on an artificial platform and contains many internal walls that divided it into a complicated multiroom structure. The terraces, outer walls, and buttresses of these buildings were monumental in scale. Structure D, for example, was a massive *tapia* and adobe construction of 1640 m². It was divided into four large open patios, each associated with several habitation and storage rooms and other features. Entrance was highly restricted, being funneled through one large patio that contained llama dung indicating that caravans entered there. Special facilities and spaces existed for massive storage of dried fish, *chicha* preparation, and weaving. Construction was largely of *tapia*, large adobe blocks, sun-dried in frames to create thick earthen walls. Although buildings date primarily to the LIP, one Inca stone building and an adobe building with Inca-style trapezoidal niches were also described. Much fishing gear and fish remains (especially anchovies and sardines) were recovered during excavations. Domesticated llama were used, and guinea pigs were raised. Many crop remains were also found. Ceramics are dominated by LIP Pingüino and Camacho styles of the Cañete culture in addition to some imitation Inca pieces. Above the monumental core of the site, the rest of the site consisted of the steep talus slopes and *quebradas* of Cerro Camacho on which were built irregular rough stone terraces with midden fill. Cane structures were built on these terraces, and burial cysts were dug into them.

Cultural Aspects

Cerro Azul is a Late Intermediate Period Cañete central settlement. The compounds in the settlement's core probably each housed an elite's lineage and its associated productive and ceremonial activities. Commoner retainers may have also lived in the compounds and on the site's hill terraces. The settlement was apparently economically specialized in fishing with large-scale procurement of anchovies and sardines, processing, controlled storage, and caravan shipment to neighboring agricultural communities. The settlement would have been one of several in the *señorío* of Huarco, about 140 km² in the lower section of the Cañete valley. This political unit was a small valley state divided internally into agricultural and fishing communities and socially stratified with a ruling lord and other elite personnel. Although a fishing community, Cerro Azul had a strong elite religious-political presence.

References

Kroeber, A. (1937). "Archaeological Excavations in Peru, part IV: Cañete Valley." *Field Museum of Natural History, Anthropological Memoir* 2: 220–273.

Marcus, J. (1987). *Late Intermediate Occupation at Cerro Azul, Perú: A Preliminary Report.* Ann Arbor: University of Michigan, Museum of Anthropology, Technical Report 20.

Marcus, J., R. Matos, and M. Rostworowski (1985). "Arquitectura Inca de Cerro Azul, Valle de Cañete." *Revista del Museo National* 47: 125–138.

Marcus, J., J. Sommer, and C. Glew (1999). "Fish and Mammals in the Economy of an Ancient Peruvian Kingdom." *Proceedings of the National Academy* 96: 6564–6570.

Chiribaya Alta

TIME PERIOD: 1000–600 B.P.

DESCRIPTIVE SUMMARY

Local Environment

Chiribaya Alta is located just above 200 m above sea level, less than 5 km from the sea. The site is perched on the southern rim of the Osmore valley in southern Peru. It is outside of the valley proper, on the northern edge of a dry and level *pampa* that stretches southward. A steep slope drops 150 m from the site to the arable floodplain of the Osmore, and to the south is an area of desiccated *lomas* vegetation. The site receives no measurable annual rainfall and has no vegetation.

Physical Features

Chiribaya Alta is just over 7 ha in its primary site area. A 5.5-ha residential section occupies a projection of the *pampa* and the uppermost slopes of the valley.

This sector is enclosed on the *pampa* side by a 2-m-tall linear mound and parallel ditch and a second, partial (unfinished?) mound and ditch. Within the enclosure, large artificial terraces were constructed on which multiroom houses were built with cane walls. Residential midden includes shell, animal and fish bone, and various crop remains. The high density of manos and metates here may indicate *chicha* production for ceremonial occasions. Five delimited LIP cemeteries are outside the enclosure and four within. Burials were primarily of the Chiribaya culture, but also of the contemporary Ilo-Tumilaca culture. Some individual burials of late Chiribaya were very rich, containing quantities of elaborately decorated textiles, ceramics, baskets, and metal objects. Many burials contained whole camelid parts (heads, limbs, ears, and feet) and whole guinea pigs indicating sacrificial offerings and perhaps ritual feasting.

Cultural Aspects

Chiribaya Alta is a Late Intermediate period central settlement. It is unique. It is the only "fortified" Chiribaya site, located prominently and enclosed by large mounds and ditches. The enclosures may not have been literal defenses, but they certainly defined symbolically a powerful central place with special residential compounds, feasting activities, and burial areas. The size and number of cemeteries suggest that the site may have served as burial location for a broader regional population. The location may also have strategically controlled camelid movement between the *lomas* to the south and the river, but the settlement's location seems to have been chosen more for its physical dominance than for any direct economic significance. All other Chiribaya and Ilo-Tumilaca settlements were unfortified and without monumental construction, fringing the agricultural lands of the valley below. Conspicuously, the inhabitants of Chiribaya Alta were removed from daily needs of water and food, positioned above the commoner settlements of two ethnic groups. The cemeteries document a socially stratified population characteristic of a regional chiefdom. Unusually, the chiefdom apparently consisted of several ethnicities, one of which became increasingly dominant.

References

Buikstra, J. (1995). "Tombs for the Living... or... for the Dead: The Osmore Ancestors." In *Tombs for the Living*: *Andean Mortuary Practices*, ed. T. Dillehay. Washington, D.C.: Dumbarton Oaks, 229–280.

Ghersi B., H. (1956). "Informe sobre las Excavaciones en Chiribaya." *Revista del Museo Nacional* 25: 89–119.
Jessup, D. (1991). "General Trends in the Development of the Chiribaya Culture, South-coastal Peru." Paper Presented at the annual meeting of the Society for American Archaeology, New Orleans.
Lozada C., M. C. (1998). The Señorío of Chiribaya: A Bio-archaeological Study in the Osmore Drainage of Southern Peru. Ph.D. diss., Department of Anthropology, University of Chicago.
Owen, B. (1993). "A Model of Multiethnicity: State Collapse, Competition, and Social Complexity from Tiwanaku to Chiribaya in the Osmore Valley, Peru." Ph.D. diss., Department of Anthropology, University of California, Los Angeles.

Punchaumarca (Tarma Site 292)

TIME PERIOD: 900–530 B.P.

DESCRIPTIVE SUMMARY

Local Environment

Punchaumarca is located at 3920–3970 m above sea level in the upper Tarma drainage of the central Andes of Peru. It is in the lower *puna* zone where streams drop steeply eastward toward lower elevations and the tropical forest of the Amazon basin. The site sits in an area of broken topography atop a prominent hill that rises 30 m from the crest of a steep-sided ridge. Grass and bushes cover the hill. Below the site are the upper reaches of numerous *quebradas* and lower slopes where cereals and tubers are cultivated in small fields.

Physical Features

The site is 0.6 ha in area. Architectural features include at least 32 circular buildings that are probably residences, 10 rectangular buildings that may be storehouses, an unusual large, square structure in the middle of the site, stone-faced terraces that support the buildings, and two defensive ditches and wall across the ridge. Just outside the site are a small cemetery, a distinct pathway worn into the bedrock along the uppermost reaches of a *quebrada* below the site, and stone-faced agricultural terracing. The circular residential structures average about 6 m in diameter, with one large structure with a 10-m diameter. Each structure has one large doorway, c. 70 cm wide. The rectangular storehouses are clustered on and around the top of the hill;

individual structures are multistoried, averaging 4.5 × 2.5 m and up to 3.5 m high. Each story has one chamber with one entrance. The large square structure that may have had a public function is positioned near the highest point on the hilltop; it measures about 7 m on a side with walls preserved up to c. 1.7 m high. The fortification walls blocked the only easy access to the site along the ridge.

Cultural Aspects

Site 292 is a typical Late Intermediate period *kichwa* agricultural settlement of 20–50 households. Surface pottery occurs generally in very light concentrations, mainly LIP, with a trace of Inka-style ceramics. The site is one of three principal settlements and four smaller sites that form a cluster on the tops and upper slopes of Cerro Punchaumarca. The overall size of the cluster may have approached 100 households. The close spacing (600 m) of the two main settlements (Sites 291 and 292) could reflect a dual moiety organization. No sites in this settlement cluster had corrals, and the extensive ancient terracing suggests an agricultural base. The settlement cluster may have been linked socioeconomically with herders living in settlements a few kilometers away on the eastern edge of the main Junin *puna*. The defensive location and fortifications suggest active warfare (disputed by Parsons et al.). The pattern of social and economic organization documents a fairly simple regional organization that probably characterized much of the highland Andes during this period.

References

Parsons, J. R., C. M. Hastings, and R. Matos M. (1997). "Rebuilding the State in Highland Peru: Herder-Cultivator Interaction during the Late Intermediate Period in the Tarma-Chichaycocha Region." *Latin American Antiquity* 8: 317–341.

Tunanmarca

TIME PERIOD: 600–500 B.P.

DESCRIPTIVE SUMMARY

Local Environment

Tunanmarca is located at 3850–3900 m above sea level on the northwestern side of the Yanamarca valley, east of the Mantaro river in the central Andes of Peru. The site sits atop a prominent limestone ridge that rises 200 m or more above the surrounding terrain. It is in the lower *puna* zone with grasses and a few low bushes covering the hill. Below the site are a rolling moraine landscape and valleys that now support extensive cereal and tuber agriculture.

Physical Features

The site's outer walls enclose about 35 ha with 24 ha of densely packed habitation spread 2 km along the ridge. Architectural features include an estimated 3800 residential buildings, central plazas, and defensive walls. The residential structures were organized into patio groups; one to six circular structures faced on a common patio defined by the buildings, terraces, and/or enclosing walls. Entrance to a patio was restricted. The circular buildings average about 4.5 m in diameter. Each structure had one doorway, c. 65 cm wide, and no windows. Although commoner patios typically had one or two residential structures, elite patios contained more structures. The masonry was *pirka*— rough limestone pieces that were faced and irregularly coursed with a rubble core set in mud mortar. Larger, roughly dressed stones were used to frame the doors. Masonry of the elite patio residences was carefully chinked, creating a decorative surface. Within the houses were hearths. Burials were placed in the house subfloors and along the walls of the patios. The difference between elite and commoner burials was not great. Patios provided work spaces, and trash was swept against the walls. The dense residential area was organized haphazardly by interconnecting paths that meandered among the patio groups. At the center of the site, at its highest elevation, was the settlement's public sector. It consisted of two conjoined plazas, one larger (1800 m^2) and the other smaller (400 m^2) with two distinctive rectangular buildings that probably had public functions and/or housed the paramount. An avenue, bounded by converging walls, created an open band that divided the site into two residential areas and focused external attention and movement on the central plazas. A single stone fortification wall encircled the entire settlement; the wall was pierced by narrow, defended entrances. The northern residential area was surrounded by a second defensive wall that created a large open area 50–75 m across between the walls. A circular tower stood isolated in this area, overlooking one of the settlement's entrances. Below the settlement was a prehistoric, branching irrigation system that likely provided water both for upland agricultural fields and domestic uses. A stairway of steps for an ancient road led past the base of the hill.

Cultural Aspects

Tunanmarca is an unusually large Late Intermediate Period settlement with perhaps 2500 households. The patio arrangement of residences suggests the importance of the family unit; polygynous or extended families were apparently typical of elites. The dual division of Tunanmarca may reflect a moiety system. The defensive location and fortifications indicate active warfare. The irrigation system and catchment analysis suggest an agricultural base. Quinoa, potatoes, other Andean tubers, legumes, and traces of maize were recovered. Bones of the Andean camelid, guinea pig, and dog were also found. Pottery is local LIP Wanka red, micaceous self-slip, and Base Clara. An impressive ceramic dump may indicate a production site. Tunanmarca is the center of an eight settlement cluster (75 km^2) that probably defined a prehistoric chiefdom. The overall size of the cluster may have approached 5700 households, 44 percent living in Tunanmarca. Sites in this settlement cluster did not have corrals, but the open space between the defensive walls could have served this function. Village specialization and exchange in ceramic and lithics existed within the chiefdom. The population may have been linked socioeconomically with herders living to the north in the Junin *puna*. The pattern of social and economic organization documents a fairly complex regional organization that represents a complex political form found occasionally in the central highland Andes during this period.

References

Costin, C. (1986). "From Chiefdom to Empire State: Ceramic Economy and the Prehispanic Wanka of Highland Peru." Ph.D. diss., Department of Anthropology, University of California, Los Angeles.

Costin, C., and T. Earle. (1989). "Status Distinction and Legitimation of Power as Reflected in Changing Patterns of Consumption in Late Prehispanic Peru." *American Antiquity* 54: 691–714.

DeMarrais, Elizabeth (in press). "The Architecture of Wanka Communities." In *Empire and Domestic Economy*, ed. T. D'Altroy and C. Hastorf. New York: Plenum.

Earle, T. (1997). *How Chiefs Come to Power*. Stanford: Stanford University Press.

Earle, T., T. D'Altroy, C. Hastorf, C. Scott, C. Costin, G. Russell, and E. Sandefur (1987). *The Impact of Inka Conquest on the Wanka Domestic Economy*. Los Angeles: Institute of Archaeology, University of California, Los Angeles.

Guttierez N., C. (1937). "Ciudadelas Chullparias de los Wankas." *Revista del Museo National* 6: 43–51.

Hastorf, C. (1990). "The Effect of the Inka state on Sausa Agricultural Production and Crop Consumption." *American Antiquity* 55: 262–290.

Hastorf, C. (1993). *Agriculture and the Onset of Political Inequality before the Inka*. Cambridge: Cambridge University Press.

Hastorf, C., and T. Earle (1985). "Intensive Agriculture and the Geography of Political Change in the Upper Mantaro Region of Central Peru." In *Prehistoric Intensive Agriculture in the Tropics*, ed. I. Farrington. Oxford: British Archaeological Reports, International Series 232, 569–595.

LeBlanc, C. (1981). "Late Prehispanic Huanca Settlement Patterns in the Yanamarca Valley, Peru." Ph.D. diss., Department of Anthropology, University of California, Los Angeles.

Parsons, J. (1978). "El Complejo Hidraulico de Tunanmarca: Canales, Acueductos y Reservios." In *III Congreso Peruano: El Hombre y la Cultural Andina*, ed. R. Matos. Lima: Universidad Nacional Mayor de San Marcos, 556–566.

Russell, G. (1988). "The Effect of Inka Administrative Policy on the Domestic Economy of the Wanka Peru: The Production and Use of Stone Tools." Ph.D. diss., Department of Anthropology, University of California, Los Angeles.

TIMOTHY EARLE
Department of Anthropology
Northwestern University
Evanston, Illinois
United States

Aymara Kingdoms

ABSOLUTE TIME PERIOD: 900–530 B.P.

RELATIVE TIME PERIOD: Follows collapse of the Tiahuanaco state and precedes the expansion of the Inca empire in the 14th or 15th century.

LOCATION: The circum-lake Titicaca region in the south-central Andean highlands. A number of politically autonomous Aymara kingdoms were located around the lake.

DIAGNOSTIC MATERIAL ATTRIBUTES: Fortified settlements known as *pukaras*, burial towers called *chulpas*, Sillustani and Collao pottery types.

REGIONAL SUBTRADITIONS: Lupaqa, Colla, Pacajes, Omasuyus, Canas, Canchis, Carangas.

IMPORTANT SITES: Ale, Esturi, Cerro Carajuana, Huichajaja, Llaquepa, Pucara Chucuito, Pukara Juli, Cutimbo, Sillustani, Tanka Tanka.

CULTURAL SUMMARY

Environment

The Titicaca basin is classified as an intertropical climatic zone, based on its geographical location and high solar radiation. However, its high altitude and concomitant montane qualities such as low ambient temperatures and low humidity alter its tropical character toward typical alpine conditions, according to Dejoux and Iltis (Dejoux and Iltis 1991:11).

Paleoclimatic research suggests that there was a significant drought around A.D. 1100, the time in which the Aymara kingdoms developed in the wake of Tiwanaku collapse. This drought gave way to greater precipitation during the Little Ice Age that began in the 15th century A.D.

Topography. Lake Titicaca sits at 3810 m above sea level, making it the highest major lake in the world where complex society developed. Aymara kingdoms settled a several kilometer-wide strip along the lake edge and the edges of the rivers that flowed in and out of lake Titicaca. The higher grasslands above the water sources were also utilized and settled, but sites are much more dispersed and far less densely occupied.

Biota. The classic work of Javier Pulgar Vidal divides the Titicaca basin into two broad agricultural and ecological regions called the *suni* and *puna*. The *suni* is located between 3500 and 4000 m above sea level (m.a.s.l.). The *suni* represents the upper limit of plant agriculture, while the *puna* is a grazing zone for the extensive camelid herds owned by many Titicaca basin peoples. The *puna* is located between 4000 and 4800 m.a.s.l. According to Pulgar Vidal, the *suni* includes the lake shore area plus a few kilometers away from the lake up to 4000 m.a.s.l. The *suni* is the richest area, where most modern and pre-hispanic settlement is located. Pulgar Vidal notes the rich variety of agricultural products that grow in the *suni*, including many varieties of tubers, legumes, and chenopods.

The early Holocene vegetation of the Titicaca region was significantly altered well before the advent of the Aymara kingdoms. In some areas of the region today, aboriginal stands of stunted trees in protected areas are found. The existence of these trees indicates that the climax vegetation is not the vast, treeless grasslands that dominate the region today. Rather, the impact of human agricultural and pastoralism has resulted in a largely treeless landscape.

Settlements

The most significant settlement change during the ascendance of the Aymara kingdoms was the development of fortified hilltop sites or *pukaras*. In all cases, major *pukaras* have at least three large defensive walls reaching up to 3 m in height and 1–2 m wide. Some *pukaras* are huge, with walls encircling several square kilometers of area. The area covered by the fortification walls is so large, in fact, that there is little doubt that the walls were built to withstand a sustained siege by protecting agricultural fields, pasture land, and springs.

Contemporary with these large centers were numerous undefended villages and hamlets that surrounded these refuge sites. Most of the population, in fact, lived in these smaller settlements around the *pukaras*. It is likely that most of the residential areas in the fortified sites were not permanently occupied. Recent data, in fact, indicate that many of the *pukaras* were temporary "refuge" sites utilized in times of danger. The settlement pattern for the Aymara kingdoms prior to the Inca occupation was one characterized by a single large *pukaras* surrounded by smaller, associated settlements. At least a dozen large *pukaras* that conform to this pattern have been located in the Titicaca basin. In at least one area, the Tiwanaku valley, population densities were so high that fortified sites were not built.

Housing. Available evidence suggests that the normative household type for the Aymara kingdoms consisted of a series of small (2–4 m in diameter), round or oval structures built on artificial domestic terraces. The houses had stone foundations and uncut stone and adobe walls. In some cases, structures can still be found with intact doors and lintels from this period. Some of these houses were larger and had carvings of animals or reptiles on door stones. These may have housed elites or may have functioned as ritual areas. Apart from these minor differences, little differentiation in house type is evident for the pre-Inca Aymara kingdoms period.

Population, Health, and Disease. Settlement evidence indicates that the collapse of the Tiwanaku state did not entail a concomitant demographic collapse. Populations maintained or slightly increased the Tiwanaku levels although there was a massive shift from nucleated to dispersed settlements. In areas where we have 100 percent settlement survey coverage, mean site sizes decreased by a factor of three, while the number of sites increased by factors of three or more.

Economy

Aymara kingdom period populations shifted from intensive agricultural strategies of the preceding Tiwanaku period to extensive agropastoral ones. The Aymara kingdoms relied heavily on camelid pastoralism and small-scale household-level agriculture. Inter-regional trade was reduced as well. Most agriculture was rain-fed on terraces. The principal cultigens were the many varieties of potatoes famous in the Andes as well as other tubers and chenopods. In spite of the altitude of the Titicaca basin, some maize was probably grown in restricted areas as well, although it was not a major component of the diet. In some areas near the rivers, an intensive form of agriculture, known as raised fields, were probably utilized as well.

In areas where we have 100 percent archaeological survey data, the land use ratios indicate a major shift away from raised field agriculture and an increase in the relative importance of rain-fed terrace agriculture and pastoralism in the period after Tiahuanaco collapse. During the Aymara kingdom period, land-use patterns reverted to pre-Tiwanaku configurations. The settlement patterns represent site distributions characteristic of low-risk, labor, and resource optimization strategies utilized by farmers in an ecological context characterized by increasing drought conditions. This settlement pattern can be explained as one aimed at minimizing risk by diversifying economic activities.

Industrial Arts. Most technological items were manufactured by the individuals or households who utilized them, although there was possibly specialized production of some pottery and rare metal objects were most likely imported. Items manufactured locally include domestic pottery, stone tools, cloth, and the like. Reed boats were manufactured for use in fishing and transport around the lake, a tradition that goes back millennia. Copper and bronze tools were rare, but were occasionally imported.

Utensils. Primary utensils included sand-tempered pottery, manufactured from locally available clays. Unlike the subsequent and previous periods, there is little evidence of extensive regional exchange of fine-ware pottery. Some slightly decorated pottery was manufactured, and there is evidence that its distribution broadly correlates to different subtraditions in the circum-Titicaca area. In the north Titicaca basin, for instance, pottery styles known as Collao and Sillustani are associated with the Colla subtradition. In the southwest basin, the pottery style is called Pucarani, and in the south the tradition is called Pacajes. The majority of the vessels are well-burnished serving bowls that most likely were used for feasting.

Stone tools were manufactured out of locally available basalt and andesite. Projectile points essentially disappear with the emergence of the Aymara kingdoms. Andesite hoes were the most common agricultural tool found on sites. Basalt scrapers were also commonly utilized. Obsidian, a common raw material in early periods that was not locally available in the region, is virtually absent from Aymara kingdom sites. This confirms that there was a cessation of extensive exchange networks in the area, or it may have been a result of the importation of some metal objects.

Excavations in dry caves reveal that textiles were produced for domestic everyday purposes. The few recovered fragments are all made of camelid wool and are decorated with muted, parallel stripe designs. Wood and bone objects, including needles, awls, possible spoons used for ritual purposes, and knife shafts, have been found. A leather sandal was discovered as well.

Sociopolitical Organization

Social Organization. The Aymara kingdoms developed in the wake of the collapse of the great expansive archaic state of Tiwanaku. The collapse of the complex sociopolitical organization of Tiwanaku resulted in a dispersal of population and an emphasis on extensive agropastoral economies. Settlements of the Aymara kingdom are largely small villages and hamlets scattered over the landscape. These small settlements appear to be sociopolitically linked to the large *pukaras* that dot the landscape.

There is little to no evidence of marked social ranking in Aymara kingdom society prior to the expansion of the Inca state. Burials in above-ground mausoleums called *chulpas* were once thought to be rare. We now know that pre-Inca *chulpas* dotted the landscape and were a common form of burial. There appear to be little material differences in burial mortuary goods, domestic house construction, access to high-valued goods, and so forth. The current model of Aymara sociopolitical organization in the 12th–15th centuries is one of little to no class differentiation in a largely agropastoral society.

Political Organization. The nature of Aymara kingdom political organization is highly debated. Historic documents suggest that the post-Tiwanaku kingdoms were indeed kingdoms, state-level societies with a social and political hierarchy. Archaeological evidence, however, provides an entirely different view of pre-Inca Aymara society as one with only moderately ranked, perhaps segmentary, political organization. The large *pukaras* appear to have been the primary settlements, with villages and hamlets politically linked to centers. By these criteria, there were perhaps a dozen or so major *pukaras* in the region during the 15th century. These would correspond to a similar number of autonomous or semiautonomous polities in the region that would include the Colla, the Lupaqa, the Pacajes, and Omasuyus peoples.

Conflict. Inter- and intraethnic conflict was present in the Titicaca region well before the emergence of the Aymara kingdoms. From at least the 3rd century B.C., trophy head taking and military subjugation of neighbors were common. However, the rise of the kingdoms after the 12th century correlates with the development of a new style of conflict that necessitated the building of the large hilltop fortresses or *pukaras*. These *pukaras* were most likely designed to protect against large-scale aggression by others with tactics that included sieges. Siege warfare was common in Inca military strategy. The data suggest that it was present in the Titicaca region prior to Inca incursions, and that it first developed with the rise of the Aymara kingdoms.

Religion and Expressive Culture

Religious Beliefs. We possess virtually no data on Aymara kingdom religious beliefs prior to the 16th century. Historic documents indicate that hilltops, springs, rock outcrops, and other outstanding natural features were considered *huacas* or sacred places by

Aymara peoples. The lack of any iconographic or material expression of overt ideological beliefs suggests that formal ritual organizations disappeared with the collapse of Tiwanaku. In its place, there appear to have been informal village and household level rituals conducted by religious specialists common in historic Aymara society.

Arts. The media for artistic expression in the Aymara kingdoms were primarily textiles and pottery. Decorated pottery is rare and is generally characterized by red-slipped bowls with black and occasionally orange decoration. Virtually no textiles from the Titicaca basin proper have been discovered intact. However, textiles from contemporary cultures on the dry Pacific coast indicate that they were the medium of art in the period.

Suggested Readings

Browman, David (1994). "Titicaca Basin Archaeolinguistics: Uru, Pukina and Aymara A.D. 750–1450." *World Archaeology* 26, 2: 235–251.

Dejoux, C., and A. Iltis, eds. (1992). *Lake Titicaca: A Synthesis of Limnological Knowledge.* Dordrecht and Boston: Kluwer Academic.

Hickman, John M., and William T. Stuart (1977). "Descent, Alliance, and Moiety in Chucuito, Peru: An Explanatory Sketch of Aymara Social Organization." In *Andean Kinship and Marriage*, ed. R. Bolton and E. Mayer. Special Publication # 7. Washington, D.C.: American Anthropological Association, 43–59.

Hyslop, John Jr. (1977). "Chulpas of the Lupaca Zone of the Peruvian High Plateau." *Journal of Field Archaeology* 4: 149–170.

La Barre, Weston (1948). *The Aymara Indians of the Lake Titicaca Plateau, Bolivia.* Memoir #68, American Anthropological Association.

Thompson, L. G., E. Mosely-Thompson, and K-b Liu (1988). "Pre-Incan Agricultural Activity Recorded in Dust Layers in Two Tropical Ice Cores." *Nature* 336: 763–765.

Tschopik, Harry (1947). "The Aymara." In *Handbook of South American Indians*, 2. ed. J. Steward. Washington, D.C.: Smithsonian Institution Press, 501–574.

Wachtel, Nathan (1986). "Men of the Water: The Uru Problem (Sixteenth and Seventeenth Centuries)." In *Anthropological History of Andean Polities*, ed. J. Murra, N. Wachtel, and J. Revel. Cambridge: Cambridge University Press, 283–310.

CHARLES STANISH
Department of Anthropology
University of California, Los Angeles
Los Angeles, California
United States

Chavín

ABSOLUTE TIME PERIOD: 2800–2200 B.P.

RELATIVE TIME PERIOD: Overlaps with the Highland Andean Formative tradition and precedes the Andean Regional Development Period. In the chronological framework used by most Andean archaeologists, the Chavín tradition coresponds to the Early Horizon, which follows the Initial Period and preceds the Early Intermediate Period.

LOCATION: The center of the Chavín tradition is Chavín de Huantar located in central highland Peru, between the Andean Cordillera Blanca and Cordillera Oriental. The ancient ceremonial center and surrounding settlement sit on the bank of the Mosna river at its confluence with the Huacheqsa. The Mosna continues north to empty into the Marañon river. In essence, the Chavin tradition represents the peaceful spread of a religious ideology with its attendant art and iconography north to south through the modern Peruvian departments of Cajamarca and Ayacucho in the highlands, and from the Lambeyeque valley to the Ica valley on the coast.

DIAGNOSTIC MATERIAL ATTRIBUTES: Monumental stone and adobe temple mounds with plazas. Stone and adobe sculpture, painted textiles, metalwork, and decorated pottery expressing religious ideology through a complex symbolic system. These frequently depict a paramount supernatural and secondary deities. Ceramics are typically fired black, polished, and embellished with standardized sets of incised, stamped, textured, and molded design elements and motifs. Abundant exotic pottery, shells, and precious stones are often found in both ritual and domestic contexts.

REGIONAL SUBTRADITIONS: Highland Chavín, Coastal Chavín.

IMPORTANT SITES: Ataura, Cerro Blanco, Chongoyape, Karwa, Kotosh, Kuntur Wasi, Pacopampa, Pallka.

CULTURAL SUMMARY

Environment

Climate. The climate at Chavín de Huantar features seasonal rains averaging 856 mm annually and rare frosts. The Early Horizon climate in the central Andes was cooler and drier than at present. Snowlines on surrounding peaks that were depressed as much as 100 m would have constrained high-elevation agriculture and mountain travel.

Topography. The settlement at Chavín de Huantar lies at 3150 m within the narrow intermontane Mosna river valley, which forms a western branch of the upper

Marañon river drainage. The Cordillera Blanca bordering the Mosna to the west reaches elevations over 5000 m and bears glaciers and permanent snow. The Mosna valley and Chavín de Huantar are situated midway between the Pacific coast to the west and the Amazon rainforests to the east. Ultimately, the Chavín tradition extended across the coastal plains, through the humid northern Andean highlands, across expansive central highland 'punas,' to the edge of the upper Amazon basin rainforests.

Geology. The site of Chavín de Huantar lies atop Mosna river terrace alluvium covering Cretaceous age sedimentary formations that have been uplifted into the Cordillera Blanca and Cordillera Oriental ranges. Seismic activity and landslides are frequent.

Biota. Chavín de Huantar is surrounded by midelevation grasslands and remnants of deforested woodlands that may have been largely intact at the beginning of the Early Horizon. Forest genera likely included *Alnus*, *Escallonia*, *Gynoxys*, *Polylepis* and *Weinmannia*. High subalpine and alpine grasslands can be reached in less than 2-hours walk upslope. Fauna of the higher elevations included deer, the camelids vicuña and guanaco, spectacled bear, and partridge.

Settlements

Settlement System. Two kinds of settlements that can be inferred from the available archaeological data became increasingly integrated into a single regional economic system during the 600-year span of Chavín de Huantar's Early horizon occupation. The first kind consists of the temple and surrounding settlement at the site of Chavín de Huantar. At the beginning of the Urubarriu phase (2800–2500 B.P.), Chavín's Old Temple was strategically constructed at the convergence of inter-regional travel and trade routes, which connected Early Horizon population centers in distant coastal, highland Andean and Amazonian tropical forest regions. The residential area surrounding the temple at this time occupied approximately 6 ha of the valley bottom. Residents were dedicated chiefly to maintenance of the temple and its functions, as well as to subsistence cultivation and hunting in the valley. The second type of settlement is made up of dispersed villages surrounding Chavín de Huantar on mountainsides above 3200 m. In villages such as Waman Wain, Pojoc, Gotush, Runtu, and Yurayaku lived a large rural population engaged in high-altitude agriculture, hunting and, increasingly, to herding of domesticated llamas and alpacas. A new ceremo-

nial focus at Chavín de Huantar, the New Temple, was likely constructed by the beginning of the Chakinani phase (2500–2400 B.P.), and the surrounding settlement grew to approximately 15 ha. By the Janabarriu phase (2400–2200), the integrated settlement system featured an urban population spread over 42 ha at Chavín de Huantar, which specialized in maintenance of the temple and collection and redistribution of goods and services. The agricultural hinterland provided the system's subsistence base of agricultural produce and camelid meat.

Community Organization. Like many living Andean communities, the Chavín de Huantar settlement may have been divided into dual "upper" and "lower" moiety-like social segments separated by the Huacheqsa river. Specialists dedicated to maintenance of temple activities resided at the community's core. Evidence from the surrounding sites of Pojoc, Waman Wain, and Gotush suggests that the hinterland communities each organized around central precincts devoted to Chavín cult rituals.

Housing. The scant information from excavations indicates that rectangular houses were made of either adobe or stone. Stone houses proximate to the temple housed higher ranking residents. Ethnohistorical and ethnographic analogies suggest that such houses in the Andean highlands sheltered nuclear families of four to six individuals.

Population, Health, and Disease. The population of the Chavín de Huantar settlement grew from an estimated 500 during the Urabarriu phase, to 1000 during the Chakinani phase, to between 2000 and 3000 residents during the Janabarriu phase. Because no Chavín tradition tombs have been excavated at Chavín de Huantar, no additional demographic information is available. The regional population dynamics have yet to be assessed through systematic regional survey of the Mosna and Huacheqsa drainages.

Economy

Subsistence. The Chavín subsistence economy was based on agriculture in the valley bottom and food production in a variety of ecological zones on the surrounding slopes. A broad mix of crops was cultivated with an emphasis on high-elevation tubers, grains, and lupines as staples. Deer, camelids, and guinea pigs provided most of the meat protein.

Wild Foods. There is no direct evidence of wild plant foods exploited at Chavín. Faunal remains from excavations attest to the exploitation of whitetailed deer, vicuñas, birds, skunks, viscacha, canids (fox or dog), fish, and marine shellfish.

Domestic Foods. There is scant direct evidence of the Chavín diet. A variety of lowland tropical cultigens are depicted in Chavín art and iconography, specifically on the Tello Obelisk. However, Chavín de Huantar's highland setting and its considerable distance to lowland environments presuppose a reliance on high-altitude tubers such as potatoes, *oca*, *ollucu*, and *mashua*; the grains quinoa and *achis*; and lupines like *tarwi*. Isotopic evidence from bone collagen shows that maize was only a minor component in Chavín diet. By Chavín's Janabarriu phase climax, domesticated llamas and alpacas had replaced wild camelids and deer as principal sources of meat. Domesticated dogs and guinea pigs provided smaller amounts of meat from earliest times.

Industrial Arts. Chavín is known for the production of distinctive cut ashlar temple masonry; elaborate stone sculpture; and fine incised and polished pottery. Industrial arts show increased sophistication through time, and access to items symbolic of status was restricted to fewer households. Increased cultural interaction resulting from the peaceful expansion of the Chavín religious cult stimulated technological and stylistic innovations in crafts such as weaving and metallurgy at Chavín de Huantar and throughout the central Andes.

Utensils. Urabarriu phase finds include bone needles and implements that served for weaving. Stone tools such as projectile points were fashioned from slate and quartzite. Early ceramics featured plain jars and finely decorated cups and bottles. Janabarriu-phase workshops identified at Chavín de Huantar provide evidence for full-time specialization in the production of increasingly elaborate pottery and processing of animal meat and hides.

Ornaments. Ornaments consisted of portable sculpture and jewelry rendered in precious stone, bone, shell, gold, and silver. These include ear spools, mirrors, beads, and pendants.

Trade. Participation in long-distance trade was the salient economic activity at Chavín de Huantar, where many traded items were subsequently redistributed to the surrounding villages. Trade is evidenced by large quantities of decorated pottery found in Chavín's ceremonial and household contexts, which were imported from distant Andean regions. Mineralogical sourcing studies of "exotic" Chakinani and Janabarriu sherds

recovered from Chavín de Huantar indicate sources in the Casma and Nepeña coastal valleys to the west. Thorny oyster (*Spondylus*) and conch shells utilized for ornamentation and ritual activities originated in warm waters off the coast of modern Ecuador, while marine resources consumed at Chavín arrived from the central coast. Chlorite ear spools and anthracite mirrors are among artifacts crafted from rare and exotic materials. Chemical analysis of obsidian artifacts indicates distant southern Andean sources in Peru's Huancavelica region. The spread of the Chavín cult during the mid-Early Horizon apparently served to diffuse the innovation of long-distance commodity transport by llama caravan into the north-central Andes.

Division of Labor. Archaeological work at Chavín de Huantar has not yet produced direct evidence for sex- or gender-based divisions of labor. However, occupational specialization is evident in household remains. From Chavín de Huantar's Urabarriu-phase beginnings, specialists were engaged in at least part-time production of stone tools, textiles, and other crafts. Excavations in later Janabarriu-phase deposits have revealed clearly differentiated production areas. Individual households engaged in the specialized crafting of *Spondylus* beads, worked animal hides, and items destined for long-distance trade. Specialists likely oversaw construction of Chavín de Huantar's elaborate system of subterranean galleries and drainage canals, and it is likely that a full-time priesthood conducted ritual performances and the controlled production of public architecture, stone sculpture, and portable religious paraphernalia.

Differential Access or Control of Resources. Differential access and control of resources is most evident during the Janabarriu phase. A comparison of archaeological remains from domestic refuse at Chavín de Huantar shows that exotic materials like marine fish, shell, and imported pottery are more prevalent in excavated localities near the temple than at more distant localities. Houses proximate to the New Temple show more elaborate stone construction, and families within these households enjoyed access to meat from tender llamas typically less than 3 years of age. In contrast, household remains excavated at a distance from the temple had access only to meat from animals over 4 years of age.

Sociopolitical Organization

Social Organization. The households excavated at Chavín de Huantar pertained to nuclear families that likely belonged to larger unidentified kin-based social units.

By the Janabarriu phase, these larger kin groups were ranked in accord with their familial ties to the active priesthood. In a manner analogous to modern Andean communities, the largest social groupings at Chavín de Huantar probably consisted of dual, moiety-like "halves." These would have occupied opposite banks of the Huacheqsa river and intercommunicated by means of a stone bridge wiped out by a 1945 landslide.

Political Organization. Political organization took the form of a theocratic ranking led by a select group of priests that controlled calendrical rituals and other temple activities. The Janabarriu-phase political organization has been described as a "fragile state" showing incipient urbanization at Chavín de Huantar. The basis of power seems to have been the exclusive access to sacred knowledge restricted to temple leaders.

Social Control. Because indications of military and administrative bureaucratic armature are absent, archaeological evidence suggests that social control was achieved by a shared, pancommunity commitment to the ideology represented by the Chavín temple and priesthood. All individuals would have been bound to the community by strict and frequent ritual obligations. Behaviors deviating from ideologically accepted norms would have been deterred by both the fear of expulsion from the community and by supernatural sanctions.

Conflict. Direct evidence for conflict is absent at the site of Chavín de Huantar. However, the stratigraphic superposition of domestic structures directly on top of Chavín de Huantar's most sacred precincts at the end of the Early Horizon appears to indicate an abrupt demise and resounding rejection of the preexisting Chavín social, political, and ideological orders.

Religion and Expressive Culture

Religious Beliefs. Chavín de Huantar's religious cosmology is most clearly expressed through stone sculpture and its deployment throughout the Old and New Temple complexes. Both temple constructions exhibit U-shaped configurations that enclose central courts where public rituals presumably took place. Beneath the temples is a complex network of subterranean tunnels and drains described as "galleries." The low rumble of water surging through the underground drainage system would have instilled awe in spectators. In the core of the Old Temple, the supreme supernatural is represented by the 'Lanzón,' a fanged male deity carved in relief on a 4.5-m-high stone resembling an inverted lance, or more likely, a foot plow. This stone

idol most likely portrays a founding ancestor imbued with oracular powers. The same deity is represented at the New Temple by the Raimondi Stone, which exhibits many of the same expressive conventions as the *Lanzón*. Secondary deities are rendered in New Temple sculpture as crested eagles, hawks, serpents, caymans, and jaguars, frequently with human aspects. Conventions such as bilateral symmetry and the manipulation of paired symbols reflect the dual division of the cosmos into such opposing yet complementary counterparts as males/females, sun/moon, sky/water, and gold/silver. The intricate "Tello Obelisk" sculpture apparently portrays the bestowal of important cultigens like manioc, chili peppers, and peanuts by a pair of cayman deities pertaining to realms of water and sky. Symbols of fertility featured in Chavín art include food crops, marine shells, and aquatic animals. The transformation of shamans into animal "alter egos" is depicted along with hallucinogenic plants, human-feline composite creatures, jaguars, and raptorial birds.

Religious Practitioners. By the Janabarriu phase, full-time religious practitioners not only managed temple activities, but they exerted indirect yet unbending control over Chavín de Huantar's day-to-day secular functioning. Leadership likely corresponded to a small group of specialists rather than to a paramount individual, and positions of authority were achieved through demonstrated skills in manipulating the supernatural world, rather than ascribed by kin-group ranking. These specialists probably resided in the households closest to the temple.

Ceremonies. Rituals performed by the Chavín de Huantar priesthood included divination, celestial observation, and calendrical calculations, as well as health maintenance and healing. Ceremonies within the Old Temple apparently focused on the *Lanzón*, but the gallery's small size would have limited access to very few individuals at a time. During the Janabarriu phase, the New Temple's platforms and hidden entrances provided an elaborate "stage" for public ceremonies. The growing community observed these ritual performances from the large rectangular plaza facing the "Black and White Portal," the New Temple's main facade. The ritual use of hallucinogenic snuffs is attested by sculpted stone tenoned heads arrayed on the temple's outer walls sequentially in order to portray the transformation of the sober human into an animal alter ego, thus depicting the priest's "shamanic" entry to the supernatural world. Elaborate stone mortars sculpted in the Chavín style were probably used to grind hallucinogenic snuffs for such rituals.

Arts. Historically, scholars have regarded Chavín as one of the world's "great art styles" and the highest expression of prehistoric South American art. Chavín art is renowned for its fine, polished stone sculptures fabricated both in-the-round and in flat relief from limestone and granite. Stone sculpture articulated closely with the temple architecture, often embellishing the dressed ashlar masonry as panels, pillars, and tenoned heads. Supernatural beings with flared nostrils, bared fangs, and upward-looking pupils are most frequently represented in profile, utilizing modular design elements that are combined and recombined to create optical illusions. Many images can be rotated 180° to reveal other meaningful images. Especially common is the use of visual metaphorical substitutes such as snakes for hair or rows of teeth and fangs for vertebral columns. The same representational style evident in the stone sculpture is expressed on modeled stirrup-spout ceramic bottles, incised shell beads, carved bones, painted textiles, and cast gold and silver objects. A developmental sequence of the increasingly abstract Chavín style has been formulated by John Rowe. The *Lanzón* sculpture represents the earliest phase designated Phase AB, coeval with the functioning of Chavín de Huantar's Old Temple. Phase C is typified by the Tello Obelisk, but has no architectural associations. Phase D sculpture, represented by the stylized male and female avians carved on the New Temple's Black and White Portal, along with the Raimondi Stone of Phase EF, is contemporary with the Chavín cult's spread throughout the north-central Andes.

Suggested Readings

Bennett, W. C. (1944). *The North Highlands of Peru: Excavations in the Callejón de Huaylas and at Chavín de Huántar.* New York: Anthropological Papers of the American Museum of Natural History, 39, part 1.

Benson, E. P., ed. (1971). *Dumbarton Oaks Conference on Chavín.* Washington, D.C.: Dumbarton Oaks Research Library and Collection, Trustees of Harvard University.

Burger, R. L. (1984). *The Prehistoric Occupation of Chavín de Huantar, Peru.* Berkeley and Los Angeles: University of California Press.

Burger, R. L. (1988). "Unity and Heterogeneity within the Chavín Horizon." In *Peruvian Prehistory*, ed. R. Keating. Cambridge: Cambridge University Press, 99–144.

Burger, R. L. (1992). *Chavín and the Development of Andean Civilization.* London: Thames and Hudson.

Burger, R. L. (1993). "The Chavín Horizon: Stylistic Chimera or Socioeconomic Metamorphosis." In *Latin American Horizons*, ed. D. Rice. Washington, D.C.: Dumbarton Oaks Research Library and Collection, Trustees of Harvard University, 41–82.

Burger, R. L., and N. J. van der Merwe (1990). "Maize and the Origin of Highland Chavín Civilization: An Isotopic Persective." *American Anthropologist* 92: 85–95.

Lathrap, D. W. (1973). "Gifts of the Cayman: Some Thoughts on the Subsistence Basis of Chavín." In *Variation in Anthropology: Essays in Honor of John C. McGregor*, ed. D. W. Lathrap and J. Douglas. Urbana: Illinois Archaeological Survey, 91–103.

Lumbreras, L. G. (1977). "Excavaciones en el Templo Antiguo de Chavín (Sector R): Informe de la Sexta Campaña." *Ñawpa Pacha* 15: 1–38.

Lumbreras, L. G. (1989). *Chavín de Huántar en el Nacimiento de la Civilización Andina.* Lima: Instituto de Estudios Andinos (INDEA).

Lumbreras, L. G. (1993). *Chavín de Huantar: Excavaciones en la Galería de las Ofrendas.* Mainz am Rhein: Materialen zur Allgemeinen und Vergleichenden Archäologie, Band 51.

Miller, G., and R. L. Burger (1995). "Our Father the Cayman, Our Dinner the Llama: Animal Utilization at Chavín de Huántar." *American Antiquity* 60: 421–458.

Rowe, J. H. (1967). "Form and Meaning in Chavín Art." In *Peruvian Archaeology: Selected Readings*, ed. J. H. Rowe and D. Menzel. Palo Alto: Peek Publications, 72–103.

Tello, J. C. (1943). "Discovery of the Chavín Culture in Peru." *American Antiquity* 9: 135–160.

Tello, J. C. (1960). *Chavín: Cultura Matríz de la Civilización Andina.* Lima: Publicación Antropológica del Archivo "Julio C. Tello" de la Universidad Nacional Mayor de San Marcos, Volumen 2.

Willey, G. (1951). "The Chavín Problem: A Review and Critique." *Southwestern Journal of Anthropology* 7: 103–144.

SUBTRADITIONS

Highland Chavín

ABSOLUTE TIME PERIOD: 2500–2250 B.P.

RELATIVE TIME PERIOD: The Chavín tradition appears in the Andean highlands during the mid-Early horizon in the Central Andean chronological sequence and immediately precedes the Early Intermediate period. The 2-century span corresponding to the Chavín tradition is referred to as the "Chavín horizon" (Burger 1988, 1993).

LOCATION: The Chavín religious cult was embraced at particular sites in the high *cordilleras* and intermontane valleys of modern Peru's north and north-central highlands, as well as on the adjacent western slopes above the Pacific coast. From Cajamarca region around 6° S. latitude the Chavín tradition extended southward to 10° S. latitude in Huánuco region, yet attenuated influence of the cult has been documented as far south as 13° S latitude in the Ayacucho highlands.

DIAGNOSTIC MATERIAL ATTRIBUTES: The incorporation of design attributes typical of contemporary Janabarriu phase pottery at the Chavín de Huantar center is the most widespread, although unevenly distributed, indicator of inclusion within the Chavín cult's sphere of influence. These attributes include thickened and beveled bottle spouts, dentate rocker-stamp decoration, conventionalized symbols like incised concentric circles and Ss, and modeled representations of Chavín deities and religious themes. The style of artistic representation characteristic of Chavín de Huantar's New Temple appears less commonly throughout the highlands in stone carving, carved and incised bones, cast gold and silver jewelry, painted adobe friezes, and rare petroglyphs. Some sites show sudden growth and the simultaneous intrusion of foreign architectural elements during the mid-Early horizon.

CULTURAL SUMMARY

Environment

The northern portion of the central Andes incorporated within the Chavín tradition is high *cordillera* with seasonally watered intermontane valleys. This highland landscape was more extensively forested prior to the Early horizon than at present (Young 1998). The Cordillera Blanca above Chavín de Huantar reaches well above 6000 m with permanent ice, while farther north in Cajamarca altitudes rarely exceed 4000 m. Today, highland valleys are covered with high grasses, woody shrubs, and isolated forest remnants. Days are warm, and nighttime temperatures dip below freezing only rarely during the coldest months of July and August. South of Huánuco, the Andean plateau is broader, higher, and cooler with greater diurnal temperature variation. Paleoenvironmental data from the southern Andes suggest that the Chavín horizon may coincide with a period of drought (Abbott et al. 1997; Moseley 1997). A drier and cooler mid-Early horizon climate would have depressed the upper altitudinal limits of agriculture (Cardich 1985), perhaps favoring settlement and cultivation on sheltered intermontane valley bottoms. Earthquakes, prolonged droughts, and landslides have always presented environmental hazards.

Settlements

In contrast to coastal centers that were abandoned by the Early horizon, those in the highlands show continuity of occupation and settlement pattern through the Initial period and Early horizon. These sites are typically situated on valley floors and low promontories. Historically, interpretations of the Chavín tradition's distribution have changed with Tello's (1943, 1960), Willey's (1951), and finally Burger's (1988, 1992, 1993) reconsideration of the diagnostic material attributes utilized as identifying criteria. According to Burger's "functional" interpretation, the spotty, archipelago-like distribution of the Chavín religious cult across the central Andes reflects the peaceful establishment of "branch" oracles that functioned alongside local ceremonial traditions (Burger 1992, 1993; Burger and Salazar-Burger 1980). The sudden appearance of the cult during the mid-Early horizon is most evident in the intrusion of Chavín-style elements in local pottery at highland sites like Kotosh, Huaricoto, Pacopampa, Kuntur Wasi, and Ataura (Burger 1984, 1988, 1992; Matos 1973; Tello 1943). It is also conspicuous in the Chavín-style stone sculpture at Yauya, Pacopampa and Kuntur Wasi (Carrion Cachot 1948; Larco 1946; Lyon 1978; Roe 1974; Rosas and Shady 1975; Rowe 1967; Tello 1923). Coinciding with the adoption of the Chavín cult is the adoption of foreign architectural elements like the sunken circular courts at Kuntur Wasi (Kato 1993) and Huaricoto (Burger and Salazar-Burger 1985), and a large U-shaped mound at La Pampa (Burger 1992: 191). The grafting of Chavín features onto local construction traditions reflects a move toward panregional architectural homogenization and the unprecedented expression of common cosmological principles across the central Andes (Burger 1992). Current data indicate that the spread of the Chavín tradition apparently had little impact on highland settlement patterns. Because archaeological work has centered on the public monuments rather than on surrounding settlements and households, few generalizations can be offered regarding the resident populations that presumably supported the centers. Virtually nothing is known of community organization, housing, and population demography. Limited data suggest that early highland habitations were typically constructed of stone and adobe blocks and housed nuclear families.

Economy

According to Burger (1992), the subsistence diversity that characterized the central Andes during the Initial period and Early horizon remained unaltered by the spread of the Chavín cult. Whereas maize, beans, and deer meat were dietary staples in the lower elevation intermontane valleys of the far north, populations at higher elevations south of Chavín de Huantar relied more on high-altitude tubers and camelid meat. In the highest, southernmost reaches of the Chavín tradition, populations subsisted on wild and seasonally cultivated plant foods and camelid meat. Unlike the coastal situation, the Chavín cult spread into highland areas with an ancient tradition of intensive regional and interregional exchange (Burger 1984, 1993; Shady and Rosas 1980). The Chavín horizon establishment of local subsidiary cult oracles brought qualitative rather than quantitative changes in regional interaction. However, external trade with regions like the Ecuadorian Andes and Amazonia became attenuated (Burger 1984, 1992). Chavín tradition interaction spread innovations in transport technology through the north highlands as domesticated llamas and alpacas assumed a new role as pack animals (Miller and Burger 1995). Fine pottery and textiles, semiprecious stones, worked beads, rare marine shells, rare pigments, precious metal artifacts, and obsidian were exchanged widely between emergent elite. Intensified cultural interaction during the Chavín horizon also stimulated innovation in textile weaving and gold and silver casting techniques (Conklin 1978; Lechtmann 1980). Fine, painted textiles, and cast gold and silver objects were likely made by full-time specialists for controlled distribution and exclusive consumption by a priviledged class that had emerged by the end of the Initial period (Burger 1992, 1993). Evidence for socioeconomic stratification in the highlands comes from looted tombs at Chavín de Huantar (Burger 1992) and from chamber tombs at Kuntur Wasi where rich sumptuary goods decorated in the Chavín style were interred with elite personages (Kato 1993; Onuki 1995).

Sociopolitical Organization

As on the coast, direct evidence for sociopolitical organization is scant. However, available information from mortuary contexts does supply evidence for sociopolitical hierarchies in the highlands. The presence of gold and silver adornments, especially gold crowns and jewelry discovered at Kuntur Wasi (Kato 1993; Onuki 1995), and ritual paraphernalia rendered in the Chavín style accompanying interred individuals, suggests that local theocratic hierarchies mimicked the theocratic status ranking at Chavín de Huantar (Burger 1992, 1993). Little additional information is available regarding social organization and political authority. Nor is there evidence from highland settlement patterns or other sources to indicate widespread conflicts or warfare during the Chavín horizon.

Religion and Expressive Culture

The close mortuary association of wealthy, elite individuals with sumptuous grave goods, including jewelry and ritual paraphernalia replete with symbolism, themes, and designs characteristic of Chavín de Huantar's New Temple, suggests that local priestly authority was sanctioned by ties to the highland cult center. These priestly leaders controlled sacred knowledge essential to the functioning of the Chavín cult. Celestial and calendric observation, ritual propitiation to augment agricultural production (Lumbreras 1981, 1989), curing, and divination were likely among the responsibilities of the theocratic elite. An analogy has been drawn between the rituals observed by early Spanish chroniclers at the coastal oracle of Pachacamac and probable cult activities at Chavín de Huantar (Burger 1988, 1992, 1993). In this scenario, branch oracles established in the highlands and elsewhere would have housed the brothers, sisters, sons, and daughters of the principal deity at Chavín de Huantar. This hypothesis, and other interpretations of cult beliefs and ritual practices, is based in large measure on studies of Chavín art and iconography (e.g., Burger 1992; Cordy-Collins 1977, 1980; Rowe 1967). A female deity depicted on a sculpted stone stela at Pacopampa (Lyon 1978) can be interpreted as a wife or daughter of the Staff God at Chavín de Huantar (Burger 1992, 1993). Other portable artifacts decorated with Chavín iconography include carved bones and mortars and pestles, perhaps to grind hallucinogenic plants for ingestion by religious specialists (Burger 1992; Larco 1941). Depictions of individuals holding the hallucinogenic San Pedro cactus and composite representations of human-feline alter egos attest to the ritual ingestion of psychotropic "drugs" by Chavín cult leaders. Many decorated bottles portray felines and human-feline composites in the Chavín style, as well as the same supernaturals depicted at Chavín de Huantar.

References

Abbott, M. B., M. W. Binford, M. Brenner, and K. R. Kelts (1997). "A 3500 C14 Yr. High-Resolution Record of Water Level Changes in Lake Titicaca, Bolivia/Peru." *Quaternary Research* 47: 169–180.

Burger, R. L. (1984). "Archaeological Areas and Prehistoric Frontiers: The Case of Formative Peru and Ecuador." In *Social and Economic Organization in the Prehispanic Andes*, ed. D. L. Browman, R. L. Burger, and M. A. Rivera. Manchester: BAR International Series 194, 33–71.

Burger, R. L. (1988). "Unity and Heterogeneity within the Chavín Horizon." In *Peruvian Prehistory*, ed. R. Keatinge. Cambridge: Cambridge University Press, 99–144.

Burger, R. L. (1992). *Chavín and the Development of Andean Civilization.* London: Thames and Hudson.

Burger, R. L. (1993). "The Chavín Horizon: Stylistic Chimera or Socioeconomic Metamorphosis." In *Latin American Horizons,* ed. D. Rice. Washington, D.C.: Dumbarton Oaks Research Library and Collection, 41–82.

Burger, R. L., and L. Salazar-Burger (1980). "Ritual and Religion at Huaricoto." *Archaeology* 33: 26–32.

Burger, R. L., and L. Salazar-Burger (1985). "The Early Ceremonial Center of Huaricoto." In *Early Ceremonial Architecture in the Andes,* ed. C. B. Donnan. Washington, D.C.: Dumbarton Oaks Research Library and Collection, 111–138.

Cardich, A. (1985). "The Fluctuating Upper Limits of Cultivation in the Central Andes and Their Impact on Peruvian Prehistory." *Advances in World Archaeology* 4: 293–333.

Carrion Cachot, R. (1948). "La Cultura Chavín, Dos Nuevas Colonias: Kuntur Wasi y Ancón." *Revista del Museo Nacional de Antropología y Arqueología* 2: 1.

Conklin, W. J. (1978). "The Revolutionary Weaving Inventions of the Early Horizon." *Ñawpa Pacha* 16: 1–12.

Cordy-Collins, A. (1977). "Chavín Art: Its Shamanic Hallucinogenic Origins." In *Pre-Columbian Art History,* ed. A. Cordy-Collins and J. Stern. Palo Alto: Peek Publications, 353–362.

Cordy-Collins, A. (1980). "An Artistic Record of the Chavín Hallucinatory Experience." *Masterkey* 54, 3: 84–93.

Kato, Y. (1993). "Resultados de las excavaciones en Kuntur Wasi, Cajamarca." In *El Mundo Ceremonial Andino,* ed. L. Millones and Y. Onuki. Osaka: Senri Ethnological Studies 37, National Museum of Ethnology, 203–228.

Larco Hoyle, R. (1941). *Los Cupisniques.* Casa Editora "La Cronica" y "Variedades" Lima: S.A.

Larco Hoyle, R. (1946). "A Culture Sequence for the North Coast of Peru." In *Handbook of South American Indians,* vol. 2, ed. J. Steward, Washington, D.C.: Bureau of American Ethnology Bulletin, no. 143, 149–175.

Lechtman, H. (1980). "The Central Andes: Metallurgy without Iron." In *The Coming of Age of Iron,* ed. T. Wertime and J. Muhly. New Haven: Yale University Press, 267–334.

Lumbreras, L. G. (1981). *Arqueología de la América Andina.* Lima: Editorial Milla Batres.

Lumbreras, L. G. (1989). *Chavín de Huantar en el Nacimiento de la Civilización Andina.* Lima: INDEA.

Lyon, P. J. (1978). "Female Supernaturals in Ancient Peru." *Ñawpa Pacha* 16: 95–140.

Matos Mendieta, R. (1973). "Ataura: Un Centro Chavín en el Valle Mantaro." *Revista del Museo Nacional de Antropología y Arqueología* 38: 93–108.

Miller, G. R., and R. L. Burger (1995). "Our Father the Cayman, Our Dinner the Llama: Animal Utilization at Chavín de Huántar." *American Antiquity* 60: 421–458.

Moseley, M. E. (1997). "Climate, Culture, and Punctuated Change: New Data, New Challenges." *Review of Archaeology* 17, 6: 19–27.

Onuki, Y., ed. (1995). *Kuntur Wasi y Cerro Blanco: Dos Sitios del Formativo en el Norte del Peru.* Japan: Hokusen-sha.

Roe, P. (1974). *A Further Exploration of the Rowe Chavín Seriation and Its Implications for North Central Coast Chronology.* Studies in Pre-Columbian Art and Archaeology, no. 13. Washington, D.C.: Dumbarton Oaks Research Library and Collections.

Rosas, H., and R. Shady (1975). "Sobre el Periodo Formativo en la Sierra del Extremo Norte del Peru." *Arqueológicas* 15: 6–35.

Rowe, J. H. (1967). "Form and Meaning in Chavín Art." In *Peruvian Archaeology: Selected Readings,* ed. J. H. Rowe and D. Menzel. Palo Alto: Peek Publications, 72–103.

Shady R., and H. Rosas (1980). "El Complejo Bagua y el Sistema de Establecimientos durante el Formativo en la Sierra Norte del Peru." *Ñawpa Pacha* 17: 109–142.

Tello, J. C. (1923). "Wira Kocha." *Organo del Museo de Arqueología de la Universidad Mayor de San Marcos, Lima, Inca* 1, 1: 93–320; 1, 3: 583–606.

Tello, J. C. (1943). "Discovery of the Chavín Culture in Peru." *American Antiquity* 9: 135–160.

Tello, J. C. (1960). *Chavín: Cultura Matríz de la Civilización Andina.* Lima: Publicación Antropológica del Archivo "Julio C. Tello" de la Universidad Nacional de San Marcos, II.

Willey, G. R. (1951). "The Chavín Problem: A Review and Critique." *Southwestern Journal of Anthropology* 7, 2: 103–144.

Young, K. R. (1998). "Deforestation in Landscapes with Humid Forests in the Central Andes: Patterns and Processes." In *Nature's Geography: New Lessons for Conservation in Developing Countries,* ed. K. S. Zimmer and K. R. Young. Madison: University of Wisconsin Press, 75–99.

Coastal Chavín

ABSOLUTE TIME PERIOD: 2450–2250 B.P.

RELATIVE TIME PERIOD: The Chavín tradition on the coast appears during the mid-Early horizon in the central Andean chronological sequence, immediately preceding the Early Intermediate period. The 2-century span corresponding to the Chavín tradition is referred to as the "Chavín horizon" (Burger 1988, 1993).

LOCATION: The Coastal Chavín subtradition encompassed the beaches, coastal plains, and river valleys below 500 m in elevation between modern Peru's central Andean *cordillera* and Pacific ocean shoreline. At its maximum extent, the subtradition stretched from the far northern Piura valley at 5° S latitude southward to the Ica valley at 14° S latitude.

DIAGNOSTIC MATERIAL ATTRIBUTES: The incorporation of design attributes typical of contemporary pottery of the Janabarriu phase at the Chavín de Huantar center is the most widespread, although unevenly distributed, indicator of inclusion within the Chavín cult's sphere of influence. These features include thickened and beveled bottle spouts, dentate rocker-stamp decoration, conventionalized symbols like incised concentric circles and Ss, and representations of Chavín deities and religious themes. Nonceramic material evidence from the coast includes elaborate painted textiles, pyro-engraved gourds, carved shells and bones, cast gold and silver jewelry, painted adobe friezes, and rare petroglyphs rendered in the style of stone sculpture at Chavín de Huantar's New Temple.

CULTURAL SUMMARY

Environment

The coast of the central Andes is a long, narrow strip of tropical desert 20–100 km wide, and trending northwest to southeast between the Andean *cordillera* and the Pacific shoreline. Along the coastal plain, desert sand and rocky Andean foothills are separated at intervals by fertile river valleys fed by seasonal mountain runoff. Humans have clustered within these valley oases for millennia. Coastal temperatures are governed by the cold offshore Humboldt current, which generates a cool, humid climate and constant, low cloud cover for much of the year. The cold water and broad continental shelf support an extraordinary abundance of fish, shellfish, birds, and sea mammals, which have always been exploited by coastal peoples. The cyclical intrusion of warm water currents every 8–12 years, called El Niño, generates heavy rains on the Andean slopes, resulting in widespread, often disastrous, coastal flooding. On the central portion of the coast, seasonal fog banks on the lower Andean slopes supply sufficient water to support lush patches of shrubby vegetation called *lomas*. South of 12° S latitude the climate becomes exceedingly arid. The beginning of the Early Horizon c. 2900 B.P. coincides with a series of natural catastrophes in the greater Andean region, including a major drought (Abbott et al. 1997; Moseley 1997) and severe coastal flooding, probably caused by El Niño (Moseley et al. 1981; Nials et al. 1979). The later Chavín Horizon too, may coincide with a cooler, drier period in the Andes (Abbott et al. 1997; Cardich 1985; Moseley 1997). Such climatic perturbations may have precipitated widespread abandonment documented at many coastal centers (Burger 1988, 1992; Onuki 1992).

Settlements

The limited and uneven archaeological reconnaisance conducted on the coast to date shows that settlement patterns changed markedly along the northern and central areas at the beginning of the Early Horizon, with widespread abandonment of the many Lower valley Initial Period settlements and associated U-shaped pyramids (Burger 1992). The timing of these changes suggests that local shrines attached to the flourishing cult centered at highland Chavín de Huantar's New Temple were established at some coastal sites, perhaps as a response to crisis caused by changed environmental and cultural conditions (Burger 1988, 1992). Historically, interpretations of the Chavín tradition's distribution have changed with Tello's (1943, 1960), Willey's (1951), and finally Burger's (1988, 1992, 1993) reconsideration of the diagnostic material attributes utilized as identifying criteria. According to Burger's "functional" interpretation, the spotty, archipelago-like distribution of the Chavín religious cult across the central Andes reflects the peaceful establishment of "branch" oracles that functioned alongside local ceremonial traditions. The sites of Cerro Blanco and Karwa may have housed such oracles.

The presence of the Chavín cult apparently had little direct impact on mid-Early Horizon coastal subsistence practices and settlement patterns. Coastal populations adopting the Chavín cult had resettled in the middle and upper river valleys, although fishing villages like Ancón and Curayacu persisted along the southern shoreline. Some of the the more extensive studies on the north-central coast by the Pozorskis (Pozorski and Pozorski 1987) show that populations remained in the lower Casma valley during the Chavín Horizon. The Casma residents erected crude hamlets atop abandoned Initial Period pyramids at Las Haldas and Sechín Alto and built sprawling settlement compounds with little conspicuous public architecture at San Diego and Pampa Rosario. A single settlement with ceremonial platforms, plazas, and Janabarriu-related pottery flourished at the mid-Casma valley site of Pallka (Tello 1956). In the middle Nepeña valley, a shrine with elaborate adobe decorative friezes in the Chavín style was erected at Cerro Blanco (Daggett 1987a; Larco 1941), but most Nepeña and Santa valley residents lived in small defensible settlements and hilltop fortifications in the mid and upper valleys (Daggett 1987b; Wilson 1988), reflecting heightened insecurity and intravalley conflict. In the middle Moche valley, Huaca Los Chinos is a rare example of coastal Initial Period architectural and ceremonial traditions persisting during the Chavín Horizon (Burger 1992). On the south coast, the Chavín Horizon seems to have been narrowly focused in the Ica valley (Silverman 1996), where ceramics and some rare textiles have been unearthed at Ocucaje, Cerrillos, and Karwa. Chavín Horizon Ica pottery represents a blend of classic Chavín design elements with local elements observed on Initial Period pottery recovered from Disco Verde. Pottery from the Paracas cemeteries served Tello (1943) in his initial formulations of the Chavín culture.

In general, Chavín tradition occupations are poorly understood on the far north and far south coasts where the tradition is most clearly represented by Chavín-style artifacts from looted tombs. The lack of systematic excavations at Chavín tradition habitation sites along the coast leaves us without adaquate information to address problems of community organization, housing, and population demography. Limited data suggest that early coastal habitations were constructed of wattle and daub and/or adobe blocks and housed nuclear families.

Economy

The coastal subsistence economy during the Chavín Horizon was based on intensive agriculture on the valley floors, probably with irrigation, although canals dating from this period have not been preserved. Well-preserved food remains from archaeological contexts attest that maize, beans, sweet potatoes, manioc, squash, peanuts, avacado, and numerous fruits made up staple produce (Pearsall 1992; Pozorski 1983). Maize consumption on the coast becomes widespread at this time (Burger and van der Merwe 1990; Pearsall 1992). On the shoreline, sea mammals and fish were taken for local consumption using watercraft and nets, while mollusks and fish were traded inland. Camelids (llamas) that had been rare on the coast now arrived in the upper valleys and became a significant source of meat protein. The Chavín cult's most obvious economic impact on the coast was its role in stimulating unprecedented regional and interregional economic integration between distant central Andean societies (Miller and Burger 1995). Llamas were increasingly utilized as pack animals, and the earliest dated roads likely used by trade caravans belong to the Early Horizon (Beck 1991). Fine pottery and textiles, semiprecious stones and worked beads, rare marine shells, rare pigments, precious metal artifacts, and obsidian were exchanged widely along such routes. The intensified cultural interaction during the Chavín Horizon stimulated innovation in techniques of textile weaving and gold and silver casting (Conklin 1978; Lechtmann 1980). Fine, painted textiles and cast gold and silver objects were likely made by full-time specialists for controlled distribution and exclusive consumption by a newly emerging, privileged class (Burger 1992, 1993).

Sociopolitical Organization

Direct evidence for sociopolitical organization is scant, but available information from looted mortuary contexts supplies the clearest evidence for the presence of sociopolitical hierarchies. The earliest unequivocal evidence for socioeconomic stratification on the coast comes from looted cemeteries like Chongoyape (Lothrop 1941) in the far north, and Karwa (Cordy-Collins 1979) in the far south, where rich sumptuary goods decorated in the Chavín style were interred with elite personages. Mortuary offerings of fine textiles, gold and silver adornments, and ritual paraphernalia rendered in the Chavín style suggest that a local theocratic hierarchy mimiced the theocratic status ranking at Chavín de Huantar (Burger 1992, 1993). However, the extent to which local leaders dedicated to the Chavín cult acted as political authorities or limited their activities exclusively to cult maintenance remains unclear. Nor is it clear whether cult leaders or other local authorities exercised coercive power to maintain systems of water distribution, construct public architecture, distribute food and trade goods, or coordinate community defense. The construction of defensible settlements, battlements, and fortifications in the upper Casma, Nepeña, Santa, and Virú valleys (Burger 1992; Daggett 1987b; Pozorski and Pozorski 1987; Wilson 1988) does coincide with the Chavín-horizon emergence of economically, socially, and politically stratified societies.

Religion and Expressive Culture

The close mortuary association of wealthy, elite individuals with grave goods that included textiles, jewelry, and ritual periphernalia, replete with symbolism, themes, and designs characteristic of Chavín de Huantar's New Temple, suggests that priestly authority was sanctioned by ties to the highland cult center. These priestly leaders controlled sacred knowledge essential to the functioning of the Chavín cult. Celestial and calendric observation, ritual propitiation of agricultural production (Lumbreras 1981), curing, and divination were likely among the responsibilities of the local theocratic elite that have been described as "shamans" (Cordy-Collins 1977, 1980). An analogy has been drawn between the rituals observed by early Spanish chroniclers at the oracle of Pachacamac and probable cult activities at Chavín de Huantar (Burger 1988, 1992, 1993). In this scenario, branch oracles on the coast and elsewhere would have focused on the brothers, sisters, sons, and daughters of the principal deity at Chavín de Huantar. This hypothesis, and other interpretations of cult beliefs and ritual practices, is based on iconographic studies of Chavín art. A female deity depicted holding staffs on a painted tapestry from the Karwa site (Lyon 1978) can be interpreted as a wife or daughter of the Staff God at Chavín de Huantar (Burger 1992, 1993).

Portable artifacts decorated with Chavín iconography include spatulas and tubes and plant-grinding implements like mortars and pestles (Burger 1992; Carrion 1948). Although local pottery incorporates conventionalized symbols diagnostic of Chavín de Huantar's Janabarriu-style ceramics, decorated bottles often portray felines and human–feline composites in the Chavín style, as well as the same supernaturals depicted at Chavín de Huantar (Larco 1941).

References

Abbott, M. B., M. W. Binford, M. Brenner and K. R. Kelts (1997). "A 3500 C14 Yr. High-Resolution Record of Water Level Changes in Lake Titicaca, Bolivia/Peru." *Quaternary Research* 47: 169–180.

Beck, C. M. (1991). "Cross-cutting Relationships: The Relative Dating of Ancient Roads on the North Coast of Peru." In *Ancient Road Networks and Settlement Hierarchies in the New World*, ed. C. D. Trimbold. Cambridge: Cambridge University Press, 66–79.

Burger, R. L. (1988). "Unity and Heterogeneity within the Chavín Horizon." In *Peruvian Prehistory*, ed. R. Keatinge. Cambridge: Cambridge University Press, 99–144.

Burger, R. L. (1992). *Chavín and the Development of Andean Civilization.* London: Thames and Hudson.

Burger, R. L. (1993). "The Chavín Horizon: Stylistic Chimera or Socioeconomic Metamorphosis." In *Latin American Horizons*, ed. D. Rice. Washington, D.C.: Dumbarton Oaks Research Library and Collection, 41–82.

Burger, R. L., and N. J. van der Merwe (1990). "Maize and the Origin of Highland Chavín Civilization: An Isotopic Perspective." *American Anthropologist* 92: 85–95.

Cardich, A. (1985). "The Fluctuating Upper Limits of Cultivation in the Central Andes and Their Impact on Peruvian Prehistory." *Advances in World Archaeology* 4: 293–333.

Carrion Cachot, R. (1948). "La Cultura Chavín, Dos Nuevas Colonias: Kuntur Wasi y Ancón." *Revista del Museo Nacional de Antropología y Arqueología* 2: 1.

Conklin, W. J. (1978). "The Revolutionary Weaving Inventions of the Early Horizon." *Ñawpa Pacha* 16: 1–12.

Cordy-Collins, A. (1977). "Chavín Art: Its Shamanic Hallucinogenic Origins." In *Pre-Columbian Art History*, ed. A. Cordy-Collins and J. Stern. Palo Alto: Peek Publications, 353–362.

Cordy-Collins, A. (1979). "Cotton and the Staff God: Analysis of an Ancient Chavín Textile." In *The Junius B. Bird Pre-Columbian Textile Conference*, ed. A. Rowe, E. Benson, and A. Schaffer. Washington, D.C.: Textile Museum and Dumbarton Oaks Research Library and Collection, 51–60.

Cordy-Collins, A. (1980). "An Artistic Record of the Chavín Hallucinatory Experience." *Masterkey* 54, 3: 84–93.

Daggett, R. E. (1987a). "Reconstructing the Evidence for Cerro Blanco and Punkurí." *Andean Past* 1: 111–132.

Daggett, R. E. (1987b). "Toward the Development of the State on the North Central Coast of Peru." In *The Origins and Development of the Andean State*, ed. J. Haas, S. Pozorski, and T. Pozorski. Cambridge: Cambridge University Press, 70–82.

Larco Hoyle, R. (1941). *Los Cupisniques.* Lima: Casa Editora "La Cronica" y "Variedades" S.A.

Lechtman, H. (1980). "The Central Andes: Metallurgy without Iron." In *The Coming of Age of Iron*, ed. T. Wertime and J. Muhly. New Haven: Yale University Press, 267–334.

Lothrop, S. K. (1941). "Gold Ornaments of Chavín Style from Chongoyape, Peru." *American Antiquity* 6: 250–261.

Lumbreras, L. G. (1981). *Arqueología de la América Andina.* Lima: Editorial Milla Batres.

Lyon, P. J. (1978). "Female Supernaturals in Ancient Peru." *Ñawpa Pacha* 16: 95–140.

Miller, G. R., and R. L. Burger (1995). "Our Father the Cayman, Our Dinner the Llama: Animal Utilization at Chavín de Huántar." *American Antiquity* 60: 421–458.

Moseley, M. E. (1997). "Climate, Culture, and Punctuated Change: New Data, New Challenges." *Review of Archaeology* 17, 6: 19–27.

Moseley, M. E., R. Feldman, and C. Ortloff (1981). "Living with Crisis: Human Perception of Process and Time." In *Biotic Crises in Ecological and Evolutionary Time*, ed. M. Nitecki. New York: Academic Press, 231–267.

Nials F. L., E. E. Deeds, M. E. Moseley, S. Pozorski, T. Pozorski, and R. Feldman (1979). "El Niño: The Catastrophic Flooding of Coastal Peru." *Field Museum of Natural History Bulletin* 50, 7: 4–14; 50, 8: 4–10.

Onuki, Y. (1992). "Actividades Ceremoniales en la Cuenca del Alto Huallaga." In *El Mundo Ceremonial Andino*, ed. L. Millones and Y. Onuki. Senri Ethnological Studies 37, Osaka: National Museum of Ethnology, 69–96.

Pearsall, D. (1992). "The Origins of Plant Cultivation in South America." In *The Origins of Agriculture: An International Perspective*, ed. C. W. Cowan and P. J. Watson. Washington, D.C.: Smithsonian Institution Press, 173–205.

Pozorski, S. (1983). "Changing Subsistence Priorities and Early Settlement Patterns on the North Coast of Peru." *Journal of Ethnobiology* 3: 15–38.

Pozorski, S., and T. Pozorski (1987). *Early Settlement and Subsistence in the Casma Valley, Peru.* Iowa City: University of Iowa Press.

Silverman, H. (1996). "The Formative Period on the South Coast of Peru: A Critical Review." *Journal of World Prehistory* 10, 2: 95–146.

Tello, J. C. (1943). "Discovery of the Chavín Culture in Peru." *American Antiquity* 9: 135–160.

Tello, J. C. (1956). *Arqueología del Valle de Casma: Cultura Chavín, Santa o Huaylas, Yunga y Sub-Chimu.* Lima: Publicación Antropológica del Archivo "Julio C. Tello" de la Universidad Nacional de San Marcos, I.

Tello, J. C. (1960). *Chavín: Cultura Matríz de la Civilización Andina.* Lima: Publicación Antropológica del Archivo "Julio C. Tello" de la Universidad Nacional de San Marcos, II.

Willey, G. R. (1951). "The Chavín Problem: A Review and Critique." *Southwestern Journal of Anthropology* 7, 2: 103–144.

Wilson, D. (1988). *Prehistoric Settlement Patterns in the Lower Santa Valley, Peru.* Washington, D.C.: Smithsonian Institution Press.

SITES

Ataura

TIME PERIOD: 2900–2200 B.P.

LOCATION: At the confluence of the Mantaro river and its Yacus river tributary, at 3400 m elevation between the modern towns of Jauja and Huancayo.

DESCRIPTIVE SUMMARY

Local Environment

The middle Mantaro is a broad, treeless intermontane valley with rolling alpine grassland terrain and a rainy season between November and May. Days are warm, but nighttime temperatures dip below freezing. High-altitude grains and tubers (e.g., quinoa and potatoes) are most easily cultivated on the slopes and hilltops, although maize can be grown on irrigated river terraces and in moist residual lake beds on the warmer valley bottom. Ataura was well-situated to control movement within or in and out of the Mantaro valley.

Physical Features

The site of Ataura extends nearly 3 ha, and has been divided into three sectors with cultural remains labeled A, B, and C (Matos 1973). Sector A contains three occupational phases, the bottommost pertaining to the late Initial period (Burger 1992; Matos 1978). The upper strata yielded remains of houses and trash middens left by occupations prior to and during the Chavín horizon. Sector B is primarily a cemetery on the slopes above the river terrace. Sector C at the river confluence contains more settlement remnants and the poorly understood remains of a temple structure. Excavations by Matos (1973, 1978) in the settlement areas revealed loosely arranged quadrangular houses with high wall foundations of dressed or carefully selected stone.

Cultural Aspects

Matos (1973) originally observed, and Burger (1992) concurs, that the ceramics in particular reflect the site's participation in the Chavín sphere of interaction. The Ataura ceramics and assemblages at even more southerly sites like Atalla in Huancavelica and Chupas and Jargam Pata de Huamanga in Ayacucho show close stylistic correspondences to the Janabarriu-phase pottery at Chavín de Huantar (Burger 1988, 1992, 1993; Casafranca 1960; Flores 1960; Lumbreras 1974; Matos 1972, 1973, 1978; Ochatoma 1992). Considered together, the assemblages demonstrate a clear Chavín horizon association, despite the lack of stone sculpture and evidence of the Chavín art style often utilized to identify the horizon's distribution (Burger 1993). Botanical remains excavated by Matos from the upper strata midden include locally cultivated maize, beans, squash, and possibly *tarwi*, as well as cotton, chili peppers, and *lucuma* that must have arrived from distant lower elevations. Several kinds of marine shell arrived from the coast, attesting to Ataura's participation in spheres of interregional exchange that expanded during the Chavín horizon. Unfortunately, the limited excavations did not yield direct evidence of social, political, or religious organization. The temple in Sector C probably provided the focus for social, political, and religious activities.

References

Burger, R. L. (1988). "Unity and Heterogeneity within the Chavín Horizon." In *Peruvian Prehistory*, ed. R. Keatinge. Cambridge, MA: Cambridge University Press, 99–144.

Burger, R. L. (1992). *Chavín and the Development of Andean Civilization*. London: Thames and Hudson.

Burger, R. L. (1993). "The Chavín Horizon: Stylistic Chimera or Socioeconomic Metamorphosis." In *Latin American Horizons*, ed. D. Rice. Washington, D.C.: Dumbarton Oaks Research Library and Collection, 41–82.

Casafranca, J. (1960). "Los Nuevos Sitios Arqueológicos Chavinoides en el Departamento de Ayacucho." In *Antiguo Perú: Espacio y Tiempo*, ed. R. Matos Mendieta. Lima: Librería-Editorial Juan Mejía Baca, 325–334.

Flores, Isabel (1960). "Wichqana, Sitio Temprano en Ayacucho." In *Antiguo Perú: Espacio y Tiempo*, ed. R. Matos Mendieta. Lima: Librería-Editorial Juan Mejía Baca, 335–344.

Lumbreras, L. G. (1974). *Peoples and Cultures of Ancient Peru*. Washington, D.C.: Smithsonian Institutution Press.

Matos Mendieta, R. (1972). "Alfareros y Agricultores." In *Pueblos y Culturas de la Sierra Central del Perú*, ed. D. Bonavia and R. Ravines. Lima: Cerro de Pasco Corporation, 34–43.

Matos Mendieta, R. (1973). "Ataura: Un Centro Chavín en el Valle Mantaro." *Revista del Museo Nacional de Antropología y Arqueología* 38: 93–108.

Matos Mendieta, R. (1978). "The Cultural and Ecological Context of the Mantaro Valley during the Formative Period." In *Advances in Andean Archaeology*, ed. D. Browman. The Hague: Mouton, 307–325.

Ochatoma P., J. A. (1992). "Acerca del Formativo en Ayacucho." In *Estudios de Arqueología Peruana*, ed. D. Bonavia. Lima: Fomciencias, 193–213.

Cerro Blanco

TIME PERIOD: 2500–2250 B.P.

LOCATION: In the middle Nepeña river valley, north-central coast of Peru.

DESCRIPTIVE SUMMARY

Local Environment

Cerro Blanco lies at 150 m altitude on Peru's desert coastal plain, approximately 16 km from the shoreline

(Daggett 1987). Like most of Peru's north-central coast, the locality is highly arid, although the valley bottomland surrounding the site can be irrigated for agriculture.

Physical Features

The site of Cerro Blanco consists of two low ceremonial mounds built of stones and adobe 4 and 15 m high, approximately 60 m apart from each other (Daggett 1987). The largest mound covers 14,000 m^2, but only the smaller was excavated by Tello (1942, 1943; Carrión 1948). There is no published field report of the Cerro Blanco excavations, but new details and illustrations have been published by Bischof (1997). The available information affirms that under deep overburden lie at least three constructions, the lowest and most elaborate made up of low stone and adobe walls and platforms. Walls of the earliest building were decorated with low-relief adobe friezes painted in red, yellow, white, and black, and depicting feline and avian motifs in repetition. No detailed plan map of the site has been published, although data at hand have led several scholars to hypothesize a zoomorphic architectural plan. Burger suggests that the layout of the excavated mound resembles "a giant sculpted Chavín supernatural with feline, avian and ophidian attributes" (Burger 1992: 199).

Cultural Aspects

Unfortunately, the Cerro Blanco site report remains unpublished. Burger (1992) suggests that Cerro Blanco may represent the earliest appearance of the Chavín style on the coast, perhaps basing his judgement on the admixture of Chavín and Cupisnique design elements and pottery features that lead Larco (1938) and Daggett (1987) to designate the site as a pre-Chavín, Cupisnique shrine. The site is unique for its era, not only for its zoomorphic plan, but in utilizing painted friezes with repeated motifs in a purely decorative manner (Kroeber 1944). Eccentric eyes and fanged mouth bands are among Cerro Blanco's decorative elements that are characteristic of Chavín de Huantar sculpture (Roe 1974; Rowe 1967; Willey 1951). Whether or not Chavín or Cupisnique predominates stylistically, Cerro Blanco apparently did function within the Chavín religious cult as a local shrine.

References

Bischof, H. (1997). "Cerro Blanco, Valle de Nepeña, Perú- Un Sitio del Horizonte Medio en Emergencia." In *Archaeologica Peruana 2*, ed. E. Bonnier and H. Bischof. Mannheim: Sociedad Arqueológica Peruano-Alemana, Reiss-Museum, 203–234.

Burger, R. L. (1992). *Chavín and the Development of Andean Civilization*. London: Thames and Hudson.

Carrion Cachot, R. (1948). "La Cultura Chavín, Dos Nuevas Colonias: Kuntur Wasi y Ancón." *Revista del Museo Nacional de Antropología y Arqueología* 2: 1.

Daggett, R. E. (1987). "Reconstructing the Evidence for Cerro Blanco and Punkurí." *Andean Past* 1: 111–163.

Kroeber, A. L. (1944). *Peruvian Archaeology in 1942*. New York: Viking Fund Publications in Anthropology, no. 4.

Larco H., R. (1938). *Los Mochicas*, Lima: Tomo I. Casa Editora "La Cronica" y "Variedades."

Roe, P. G. (1974). *A Further Exploration of the Rowe Chavín Seriation and Its Implications for North Central Coast Chronology*. Studies in Pre-Columbian Art and Archaeology, no. 13. Washington, D.C.: Dumbarton Oaks Research Library and Collections.

Rowe, J. H. (1967). "Form and Meaning in Chavín Art." In *Peruvian Archaeology: Selected Readings*, ed. J. H. Rowe and D. Menzel. Palo Alto: Peek Publications, 72–103.

Tello, J. C. (1942). "Origen y Desarrollo de las Civilizaciones Prehistóricas Andinas." In *Actas y Trabajos Científicos del XVII Congreso Internacional de Americanistas, Lima 1939*, Lima: Tomo I, 589–720.

Tello, J. C. (1943). "Discovery of the Chavín Culture in Peru." *American Antiquity* 9: 135–160.

Willey, G. R. (1951). "The Chavín Problem: A Review and Critique." *Southwestern Journal of Anthropology* 7, 2: 103–144.

Chongoyape

TIME PERIOD: Estimated between 2400–2200 B.P.

LOCATION: In the coastal Lambayeque river valley, 50 km from the shore, and 450 linear km from highland Chavín de Huantar.

DESCRIPTIVE SUMMARY

Local Environment

Detailed reports are lacking for the precise localities of two Chavín tradition burial sites looted near the modern town of Chongoyape. Both localities are located on the upper Lambayeque river floodplain where the river exits the Andean foothills and crosses the broad, arid coastal plain of far northern Peru. Details of Chavín-horizon settlement and subsistence in the greater Lambayeque valley remain unknown, but the location would have been appropriate for irrigation agriculture.

Physical Features

The circumstances of discovery of the two Chongoyape burials were reported by Tello (1929), and the mortuary assemblages were analyzed by Lothrop (1941). One burial that was exposed in an irrigation ditch and removed by children in the 1920s apparently contained an adult male interred with personal adornments. Some of the gold objects were recovered by the property owner, and 16 pieces are now housed at the National Museum of the American Indian. Not far away, a second burial was exposed 3 m below the surface by workers enlarging a reservoir. The tomb contained badly preserved skeletons and showed signs of burning. A large assemblage of gold, stone, and ceramic objects that probably belonged to one or more females was acquired by the National Museum of the American Indian apparently intact.

Cultural Aspects

Tello (1929), Lothrop (1941), Willey (1951), Lumbreras (1974), and others agree that the two Chongoyape burial assemblages are of Chavín cultural affiliation. Burger (1988, 1992, 1993) regards the rich assemblages as strong evidence for the emergence of socioeconomic stratification on the coast during the Chavín horizon. The male-associated assemblage consists of three gold crowns and a gold headband; 11 gold ear spools, seven of which were decorated; and a pair of tweezers, all made from a beaten sheet of gold that was shaped and subsequently embossed with feline and serpent imagery typical of the Chavín style (Lothrop 1941). Because the ear spools show a gradient from smaller to larger, Lothrop suggests that they all belonged to the same male who required larger ear spools as he grew and his earlobes became distended. Burger argues further that the possession of such personal adornments by a youth and their eventual interment with the deceased, attests to both the ascribed status conferred by birth and the accumulation of personal wealth by privileged individuals. The burial assemblage believed to have belonged to one or more females contained 129 objects, including many gold beads, finger rings, gorgets, a gold headband, gold and silver pins, an anthracite mirror fragment, and several stone and pottery containers.

References

Burger, R. L. (1988). "Unity and Heterogeneity within the Chavín Horizon." In *Peruvian Prehistory*, ed. R. Keatinge. Cambridge: Cambridge University Press, 99–144.

Burger, R. L. (1992). *Chavín and the Development of Andean Civilization*. London: Thames and Hudson.

Burger, R. L. (1993). "The Chavín Horizon: Stylistic Chimera or Socioeconomic Metamorphosis." In *Latin American Horizons*, ed. D. Rice. Washington, D.C.: Dumbarton Oaks Research Library and Collection, 41–82.

Lothrop, S. K. (1941). "Gold Ornaments of Chavín Style from Chongoyape, Peru." *American Antiquity* 6: 250–261.

Lumbreras, L. G. (1974). *Peoples and Cultures of Ancient Peru*. Washington, D.C.: Smithsonian Institution Press.

Tello, J. C. (1929). *Antigüo Perú: Primera Época*. Lima: Comisión Organizadora del Segundo Congreso Sudamericanos de Turismo.

Willey, G. R. (1951). "The Chavín Problem: A Review and Critique." *Southwestern Journal of Anthropology* 7, 2: 103–144.

Karwa (also Carhua)

TIME PERIOD: 2500–2250 B.P.

LOCATION: On the shoreline of the Bahía de Independencia, southwest of the modern city of Ica, south coast of Peru.

DESCRIPTIVE SUMMARY

Local Environment

The archaeological site at Karwa (also Carhua) has not been fully described, but the surrounding environment is rainless south-coastal desert plain. The site locality is a sandy terrace above the shoreline. Like the Paracas penninsula to the north, the area is famed for its strong afternoon winds. Inhabitants likely obtained water from beneath the ground surface.

Physical Features

Surface evidence at the site of Karwa pertains to at least two post-Chavín occupations (Engel 1981; Tello and Mejta 1979). Surface features include large elongated mounds, an extensive midden deposit, and an associated cemetery. The Chavín horizon finds at Karwa consist of approximately 200 cotton textiles and textile fragments decorated in the Chavín style (Burger 1988, 1992; Cordy-Collins 1976; Roe 1974; Wallace 1991). These were looted during the 1970s from a large rectangular tomb that reportedly contained several individuals, burial offerings including early Ocucaje style pottery, and the cache of textiles (Burger 1988). Burger reports associated sherds resembling Janabarriu-phase pottery dating to approximately 2400 to 2200 B.P. at Chavín de Huantar.

Cultural Aspects

More than 150 of the Karwa textiles have been analyzed for iconographic content (Cordy-Collins 1976, 1979; Roe 1974) and technological attributes (Wallace 1991). The textiles were loosely woven of cotton, and painted with orange, tan, brown, green, and blue vegetable dyes. Chavín-style motifs duplicate design features of stone sculpture structurally incorporated within Chavín de Huantar's New Temple approximately 530 km distant. These date to Phase D in Rowe's (1967) Chavín style seriation (Burger 1988; Cordy-Collins 1976; Roe 1974). Most remarkable is the faithful replication of the Chavín de Huantar pantheon with representations of the Chavín "Staff God," feline and raptorial birds in profile, and the cayman deity. Lyon (1978) observes that the "Staff God" protrayed on Karwa textiles is actually a female or "goddess" (Fig. G), and Burger (1988, 1992, 1993) argues that the "Staff Goddess" was likely a wife or daughter of the Staff God portrayed in Chavín de Huantar stone sculpture and represented a local, branch oracle of the Chavín cult. Pacopampa, Kuntur Wasi, and Chongoyape are among Chavín-horizon sites with iconographic evidence, likewise suggesting that they functioned as branch oracles. The large size of some textiles (up to 4.2 by 2.7 m in one case) leads Conklin (1978), Stone-Miller (1983), and Burger (1988) to propose that they decorated the walls of temples or shrines.

References

Burger, R. L. (1988). "Unity and Heterogeneity within the Chavín Horizon." In *Peruvian Prehistory*, ed. R. Keatinge. Cambridge: Cambridge University Press, 99–144.

Burger, R. L. (1992). *Chavín and the Development of Andean Civilization*. London: Thames and Hudson.

Burger, R. L. (1993). "The Chavín Horizon: Stylistic Chimera or Socioeconomic Metamorphosis." In *Latin American Horizons*, ed. D. Rice. Washington, D.C.: Dumbarton Oaks Research Library and Collection, 41–82.

Conklin, W. J. (1978). "The Revolutionary Weaving Inventions of the Early Horizon." *Ñawpa Pacha* 16: 1–12.

Cordy-Collins, A. (1976). "An Iconographic Study of Chavín Textiles from the South Coast of Peru: The Discovery of a Pre-Columbian Catechism." Ph.D. diss., University of California at Los Angeles.

Cordy-Collins, A. (1979). "Cotton and the Staff God: Analysis of an Ancient Chavín Textile." In *The Julius B. Bird Pre-Columbian Textile Conference*. ed. A. P. Rowe, E. P. Benson, and A. Schaffer. Washington, D.C.: Textile Museum and Dumbarton Oaks Research Library and Collections, 51–60.

Engel, F. (1981). *Andean Ecology: Man, Settlement and Environment in the Andes*. New York: Papers of the Department of Anthropology, Hunter College of the City University of New York.

Lyon, P. J. (1978). "Female Supernaturals in Ancient Peru." *Ñawpa Pacha* 16: 95–140.

Roe, P. G. (1974). *A Further Exploration of the Rowe Chavín Seriation and Its Implications for North Central Coast Chronology*. Studies in Pre-Columbian Art and Archaeology, no. 13, Washington, D.C.: Dumbarton Oaks Research Library and Collections.

Rowe, J. H. (1967). "Form and Meaning in Chavín Art." In *Peruvian Archaeology: Selected Readings*, ed. J. H. Rowe and D. Menzel. Palo Alto: Peek Publications, 72–103.

Stone-Miller, R. (1983). "Possible Uses, Roles and Meanings of Chavin-related Painted Textiles from the South Coast of Peru." In *Investigations of the Andean Past: Proceedings of the First Annual Northeast Conference on Andean Archaeology and Ethnohistory*, ed. D. Sandweiss. Ithaca: Cornell University, 51–74.

Tello, J. C., and T. Mejía X. (1979). *Paracas, Segunda Parte: Cavernas y Necropolis*. Lima: Universidad Nacional Mayor de San Marcos.

Wallace, D. T. (1991). "A Technical and Iconographic Analysis of Carhua Painted Textiles." In *Paracas Art and Architecture*, ed. A. Paul. Iowa City: University of Iowa Press, 61–109.

Kotosh

TIME PERIOD: 4000–1500 B.P.

LOCATION: Kotosh is located at the confluence of the Higüeras and upper Huallaga rivers, and 5 km west of the modern city of Huánuco in Peru's north-central highlands.

DESCRIPTIVE SUMMARY

Local Environment

The site of Kotosh sits at 1950 m on a low river terrace within an unusually arid portion of the otherwise humid eastern slopes of the central Andes (Izumi 1971; Izumi and Sono 1963; Izumi and Terada 1972). Surrounding tropical thorn forests are composed of *algarroba*, *huarango*, cactus, and other xerophytic vegetation. The tropical montane forests of the upper Amazon basin begin approximately 35 km downriver. Modern cultivation in the surrounding valley is done with irrigation. Kotosh's pre-Hispanic populations witnessed two particularly dry periods between 2900 and 2800 B.P. and 2400 and 2200 B.P. (Cardich 1985; Moseley 1997).

Physical Features

The principal site at Kotosh consists of two artificial mounds, the larger designated KT and the smaller KM (Izumi 1971; Izumi and Sono 1963; Izumi and Terada 1972; Onuki 1992). Mound KT measures nearly 14 m high, and, although badly damaged by looters, it contains a sequence of architecture and artifacts spanning the late Preceramic through the Early Intermediate periods. Both mounds contain the preceramic remains of enclosed chambers with ventilated central hearths that Burger and Salazar-Burger (1980) characterize as the architectural signature of an early, widespread "Kotosh Religious Tradition." Later constructions within the mound deposits were only partially excavated, and those dating to the Chavín horizon were partially destroyed by the looters' trench.

Cultural Aspects

Tello (1942, 1943), Lathrap (1971), and Kano (1979) are among archaeologists who have viewed Kotosh as a frontier Andean colony established by migrating Arawak-speaking populations from the Amazon basin, which ultimately provided the constituent elements of Chavín civilization. This migration hypothesis has been undermined by recent research at Chavín de Huantar (Burger 1992). Kotosh is now regarded as an in situ eastern-slope development (Church 1996), and the "Kotosh Chavín Period" is viewed as evidence of the Chavín horizon's intrusive presence in the upper Huallaga basin (Burger 1998, 1992; Izumi 1971). Izumi (1971), who excavated Kotosh, describes the Chavín-horizon constructions as the largest and best-planned at the site and notes the simultaneous introduction of metal artifacts (including gold) and polished stone points. However, the clearest evidence for Chavín-horizon interaction consists of incised bones and especially pottery decorated with Chavín-style iconography (Izumi and Terada 1972; Roe 1974) and design attributes typical of Chavín de Huantar's Janabarriu-phase assemblage (Burger 1988, 1992). Although the existence of moiety-like dual social segments have been hypothesized for Kotosh's Initial-period populace (Burger and Salazar-Burger 1986; Onuki 1992), virtually nothing is known of societal organization at Kotosh during the Chavín horizon.

References

Burger, R. L. (1988). "Unity and Heterogeneity within the Chavin Horizon." In *Peruvian Prehistory*, ed. R. Keatinge. Cambridge: Cambridge University Press, 99–144.

Burger, R. L. (1992). *Chavín and the Development of Andean Civilization*. London: Thames and Hudson.

Burger, R. L., and L. Salazar-Burger (1980). "Ritual and Religion at Huaricoto." *Archaeology* 33: 26–32.

Burger, R. L., and L. Salazar-Burger (1986). "Early Organizational Diversity in the Peruvian Highlands: Huaricoto and Kotosh. In

Andean Archaeology: Papers in Memory of Clifford Evans, ed. R. Matos, S. A. Turpin and H. H. Eling Jr. Monograph XXVII, Institute of Archaeology, Los Angeles: University of California at Los Angeles, 65–82.

Burger, R. L., and L. Salazar-Burger (1992). "The Place of Dual Organization in Early Andean Ceremonialism: A Comparative Review." In *El Mundo Ceremonial Andino*, ed. L. Millones and Y. Onuki. Senri Ethnological Studies 37, Osaka: National Museum of Ethnology, 97–116.

Cardich A. (1985). "The Fluctuating Upper Limits of Cultivation in the Central Andes and their Impact on Peruvian Prehistory." *Advances in World Archaeology* 4: 293–333.

Church, W. (1996). "Prehistoric Cultural Development and Interregional Interaction in the Tropical Montane Forests of Peru." Ph.D. diss., Yale University, New Haven.

Izumi, S., (1971). "The Development of the Formative Culture in the Ceja de Montaña: A Viewpoint Based on the Materials from the Kotosh Sites." In *Dumbarton Oaks Conference on Chavín*, ed. E. P. Benson. Washington, D.C.: Dumbarton Oaks Research Library and Collection, 49–72.

Izumi, S., and T. Sono (1963). *Andes 2: Excavations at Kotosh, Peru, 1960*. Tokyo: Kadokawa.

Izumi, S., and K. Terada (1972). *Andes 4: Excavations at Kotosh, Peru, 1963 and 1966*. Tokyo: University of Tokyo Press.

Kano, C. (1979). *The Origins of the Chavin Culture*. Studies in Pre-Columbian Art and Archaeology, no. 22. Washington, D.C.: Dumbarton Oaks Research Library and Collections.

Lathrap, D. W. (1971). "The Tropical Forest and the Cultural Context of Chavín." In *Dumbarton Oaks Conference on Chavín*, ed. E. P. Benson. Washington, D.C.: Dumbarton Oaks Research Library and Collection, 73–100.

Moseley, M. E. (1997). "Climate, Culture, and Punctuated Change: New Data, New Challenges." *Review of Archaeology* 17, 6: 19–27.

Onuki, Y. (1992). "Actividades Ceremoniales en la Cuenca del Alto Huallaga." In *El Mundo Ceremonial Andino*, ed. L. Millones and Y. Onuki. Osaka: Senri Ethnological Studies 37, National Museum of Ethnology, 69–96.

Roe, P. (1974). *A Further Exploration of the Rowe Chavín Seriation and Its Implications for North Central Coast Chronology*. Studies in Pre-Columbian Art and Archaeology, no. 13. Washington, D.C.: Dumbarton Oaks Research Library and Collections.

Tello, J. C. (1942). "Origen y Desarrollo de las Civilizaciones Prehistóricas Andinas." In *Actas y Trabajos Científicos del XVII Congreso Internacional de Americanistas, Lima 1939, Tomo I*. Lima: 589–720.

Tello, J. C. (1943). "Discovery of the Chavín Culture in Peru." *American Antiquity* 9: 135–160.

Kuntur Wasi

TIME PERIOD: 2900–2000 B.P.

LOCATION: Kuntur Wasi sits atop Cerro La Copa at 2300 m elevation within the upper Jequetepeque river valley, Cajamarca department, north highland Peru.

54 Chavín

DESCRIPTIVE SUMMARY

Local Environment

On the western slope of the northern Peruvian Andes, Kuntur Wasi occupies a promontory overlooking the San Pablo river tributary of the upper Jequetepeque river (Carrion 1948; Onuki 1995). The site locality was probably forested when first settled around 3500 B.P., but only isolated patches of dry montane forest remain on a semiarid steppe environment (Valencia 1992). Irrigation supplements the seasonal rainfall from November to May, allowing modern populations to cultivate a wide variety of mid-elevation crops including maize, beans, and squash. Pre-Hispanic populations witnessed two particularly dry periods between 2900 and 2800 B.P. and 2400 and 2200 B.P. (Cardich 1985; Moseley 1997).

Physical Features

Detailed descriptions of Kuntur Wasi are provided by Carrion (1948) and especially Kato (1993) and Onuki (1995). The ceremonial center of Kuntur Wasi is a temple pyramid covering nearly 1 ha. No associated settlement has yet been documented. The salient design of the temple complex dates to the Kuntur Wasi phase, but architectural elaboration occurred during the following Copa phase. The temple is made up of four succesive terrace platforms. A large terrace with a sunken court and central staircase serves as the base for a three-tiered pyramid nearly 8 m high. Atop the pyramid is a U-shaped array of platforms, columns, and sunken courts around a large rectangular sunken court. A principal platform mound facing the court was clearly the focus of site activities. The builders erected a series of carved stone stela along the axis between the staircases and central platform.

Cultural Aspects

Virtually nothing is known of settlement and subsistence around Kuntur Wasi, although long-distance exchange associated with the temple's functions was an important component of the local economy. Scholars have pointed out that Kuntur Wasi is strategically situated on a natural travel route between early population centers in the coastal Jequetepeque and highland Cajamarca valleys. Art and architectural styles at Kuntur Wasi are typical of the coast-centered Cupisnique culture (Burger 1992; Inokuchi 1998; Onuki 1995). However, the intrusion of the Chavín style by 2400 B.P. indicates that the site assumed the role of regional center

for the Chavín cult (Burger 1992; Carrión 1948). The temple's sculptures are rendered in both the local Cupisnique-variant style, and the intrusive, classic Chavín style. According to Kato (1993: 206–207), Kuntur Wasi phase pottery resembles Janabarriu phase pottery at Chavín de Huantar. However, an alternative interpretation diminishing the Chavín tradition's importance at the site has been presented by Inokuchi (1998). As Kuntur Wasi phase construction began, four high-status individuals were interred under the principal platform mound with elaborate burial offerings. Gold crowns and breastplates are embossed with Cupisnique and classic Chavín-style motifs, while other grave goods include marine shells, gold and chalcedony ear spools, beads, and other personal adornments fashioned from jasper, chalcedony, and *chrisocola* obtained through long-distance exchange. The mortuary evidence suggests that these priviledged individuals interred in the center of the temple had wielded political authority and amassed personal wealth based on their association with the Chavín religious cult (Burger 1992, 1993).

References

Burger, R. L. (1992). *Chavín and the Development of Andean Civilization.* London: Thames and Hudson.
Burger, R. L. (1993). "The Chavín Horizon: Stylistic Chimera or Socioeconomic Metamorphosis." In *Latin American Horizons,* ed. D. Rice. Washington, D.C.: Dumbarton Oaks Research Library and Collection, 41–82.
Carrion Cachot, R. (1948). "La Cultura Chavín, Dos Nuevas Colonias: Kuntur Wasi y Ancón." *Revista del Museo Nacional de Antropología y Arqueología* 2: 1.
Inokuchi, K. (1998). "La Cerámica de Kuntur Wasi y el Problema Chavín." In *Boletín de Arqueología PUCP 2.* Lima: Pontificia Universidad Católica del Perú, 161–180.
Kato, Y. (1993). "Resultados de las excavaciones en Kuntur Wasi, Cajamarca." In *El Mundo Ceremonial Andino,* ed. L. Millones and Y. Onuki. Senri Ethnological Studies 37, Osaka: National Museum of Ethnology, 203–228.
Onuki, Y. ed. (1995). *Kuntur Wasi y Cerro Blanco: Dos Sitios del Formativo en el Norte del Peru.* Tokyo: Hokusen-sha.
Valencia, N. (1992). "Los Bosques Nublados Secos de la Vertiente Occidental de los Andes del Perú." In *Memorias del Museo de Historia Natural 21.* Lima: Universidad Nacional Mayor de San Marcos, 155–170.

Pacopampa

TIME PERIOD: 2900–2200 B.P.

LOCATION: Located at 2140 m elevation in the Chotano river drainage, tributary of the Marañon river in Cajamarca region, north-highland Peru.

DESCRIPTIVE SUMMARY

Local Environment

The ceremonial center of Pacopampa is situated in remnant tropical montane forests of the northeastern Peruvian Andes (Young and León 1993). These humid woodlands have been much deforested since approximately 3000 B.P. Rain is abundant and especially plentiful between November and May. Mid-elevation tubers, maize, and beans can be grown on the surrounding steep slopes. Pre-Hispanic populations witnessed two relatively dry periods between 2900 and 2800 B.P. and 2400 and 2200 B.P. (Cardich 1985; Moseley 1997).

Physical Features

The principal ceremonial complex at Pacopampa is a three-tiered, stepped pyramid constructed by leveling and terracing the upper slopes of a natural hilltop with stone retaining walls (Burger 1992; Fung 1975; Morales 1980, 1993; Rosas and Shady 1970, 1975). The public architecture extended over 9 ha, and most of the structure was built prior to the Chavín horizon. Rows of stone columns and stone sculpture arrayed on the pyramid reflect local traditions and cultural affiliation with Cupisnique societies on the coast. Several stone carvings rendered in the Chavín style, and perhaps the large rectangular sunken court reached by the stone stairway, are Chavín-horizon additions (Burger 1992; Larco 1945; Rosas and Shady 1975). A large resident population presumably supported the ceremonial center at Pacopampa, but only a single, probably special-function, residence has been excavated.

Cultural Aspects

Few details are available regarding Pacopampa's residents. Much of the ceremonial center's attendant population may have resided at nearby smaller sites such as La Capilla and El Mirador. Organic remains from Pacopampa show that a diet including deer meat and perhaps mid-elevation tubers shifted during the Chavín horizon to include maize, beans, and camelid meat (Burger 1992; Miller and Burger 1995; Rosas and Shady 1975). Abundant marine shell and foreign pottery at the site indicate that Pacopampa assumed an important role in inter-regional exchange between the coast and the lowland Amazon tropical forests since its Initial-period establishment. Design elements on mid-Early horizon pottery, and late Chavín-style stone sculpture provide evidence of the site's participation in the Chavín

cult (Burger 1988, 1992; Carrión 1948; Morales 1998; Roe 1974; Rosas and Shady 1970, 1975; Willey 1951). The most important sculpture, a Chavín-style stone stela with a frontal female deity (Fig. H), apparently portrays a staff goddess like that depicted on textiles at the south coast site of Karwa (Larco 1945; Lyon 1978). Like Karwa, Pacopampa may have housed a wife or daughter of the Chavín de Huantar Staff God as a branch oracle (Burger 1988). Residents at Pacopampa's ceremonial complex probably included a priesthood associated with the cult (Burger 1992; Kaulicke 1976; Morales 1993), and an excavated dwelling that produced abundant ritual paraphernalia at El Mirador may have belonged to such a religious specialist.

References

Burger, R. L. (1984a). "Archaeological Areas and Prehistoric Frontiers: the Case of Formative Peru and Ecuador." In *Social and Economic Organization in the Prehispanic Andes*, ed. D. L. Browman, R. L. Burger, and M. A. Rivera. Manchester: BAR International Series, no. 194, 33–71.

Burger, R. L. (1988). "Unity and Heterogeneity within the Chavín Horizon." In *Peruvian Prehistory*, ed. R. Keatinge. Cambridge: Cambridge University Press, 99–144.

Burger, R. L. (1992). *Chavín and the Development of Andean Civilization*. London: Thames and Hudson.

Burger, R. L. (1993). "The Chavín Horizon: Stylistic Chimera or Socioeconomic Metamorphosis." In *Latin American Horizons*, ed. D. Rice. Washington, D.C.: Dumbarton Oaks Research Library and Collection, 41–82.

Cardich, A. (1985). "The Fluctuating Upper Limits of Cultivation in the Central Andes and Their Impact on Peruvian Prehistory." *Advances in World Archaeology* 4: 293–333.

Carrión Cachot, R. (1948). "La Cultura Chavín, Dos Nuevas Colonias: Kuntur Wasi y Ancón." *Revista del Museo Nacional de Antropología y Arqueología* 2: 1.

Fung, R. (1975). "Excavaciones in Pacopampa, Cajamarca." *Revista del Museo Nacional* 41: 129–207.

Kaulicke, P. (1976). *El Formativo de Pacopampa*. Seminario de Historia Rural Andina. Lima: Universidad Nacional Mayor de San Marcos.

Larco Hoyle, R. (1945). *Los Cupisniques*. Buenos Aires: Sociedad Geográfica Americana.

Lumbreras, L. G. (1981). *Arqueología de la América Andina*. Lima: Editorial Milla Batres.

Lyon, P. J. (1978). "Female Supernaturals in Ancient Peru." *Ñawpa Pacha* 16: 95–140.

Miller, G., and R. L. Burger (1995). "Our Father the Cayman, Our Dinner the Llama: Animal Utilization at Chavín de Huántar." *American Antiquity* 60, 3: 421–458.

Morales Ch., D. (1980). *El Dios Felino en Pacopampa*. Seminario de Historia Rural Andina. Lima: Universidad Nacional Mayor de San Marcos.

Morales Ch., D. (1993). Lima: *Compendio Histórico del Perú Tomo I: Historia Arqueológica del Perú. Editorial Milla Batres*.

Morales Ch., D. (1998). "Investigaciones Arqueológicas en Pacopampa, Departamento de Cajamarca." In *Boletín de Arqueología*

PUCP 2. Lima: Pontificia Universidad Católica del Perú, 113–126.

Moseley, M. E. (1997). "Climate, Culture, and Punctuated Change: New Data, New Challenges." *Review of Archaeology* 17, 6: 19–27.

Roe, P. (1974). *A Further Exploration of the Rowe Chavín Seriation and Its Implications for North Central Coast Chronology*. Studies in Pre-Columbian Art and Archaeology, no. 13. Washington, D.C.: Dumbarton Oaks Research Library and Collections.

Rosas, H., and R. Shady (1970). "Pacopampa: Un Complejo Temprano del Período Formativo Peruano." In *Arqueologia y Sociedad* 3: Lima: Museo de Arqueología y Etnología de la Universidad Nacional Mayor de San Marcos, 3–16.

Rosas, H., and R. Shady (1975). "Sobre el Periodo Formativo en la Sierra del Extremo Norte del Peru." In *Arqueológicas* 15: Lima: Instituto Nacional de Cultura, 6–35.

Rowe, J. H. (1967). "Form and Meaning in Chavín Art." In *Peruvian Archaeology: Selected Readings*, ed. J. H. Rowe and D. Menzel. Palo Alto: Peek Publications, 72–103.

Shady, R., and H. Rosas (1980). "El Complejo Bagua y el Sistema de Establecimientos durante el Formativo en la Sierra Norte del Peru." *Ñawpa Pacha* 17: 109–142.

Tello, J. C. (1943). "Discovery of the Chavín Culture in Peru." American Antiquity 9: 135–160.

Tello, J. C. (1960). *Chavín: Cultura Matríz de la Civilización Andina*. Lima: Publicación Antropológica del Archivo "Julio C. Tello" de la Universidad Nacional de San Marcos, II.

Willey, G. R. (1951). "The Chavín Problem: A Review and Critique." *Southwestern Journal of Anthropology* 7, 2: 103–144.

Young, K., and B. León (1993). "Distribution and Conservation of Peru's Montane Forests: Interactions between the Biota and Human Society." In *Tropical Montane Cloud Forests*, comp. and ed. L. Hamilton, J. Juvik, and F. Scatena. Honolulu: East-West Center.

Pallka

TIME PERIOD: 2500–2200 B.P.

LOCATION: Above the Matwa river in the middle Casma valley, north-central coast of Peru.

DESCRIPTIVE SUMMARY

Local Environment

The site of Pallka lies at 900 m altitude on Peru's desert coastal plain, approximately 35 km from the shoreline (Pozorski and Pozorski 1987). Like most of Peru's north-central coast, the locality is highly arid, although the valley bottomland adjacent to the site can be irrigated for agriculture. The site complex sits on an artificially modified river terrace at the base of the valley slope and offers a commanding view of the valley floor. Cactus and xerophytic vegetation typify the area.

Physical Features

Pallka is made up of a main ceremonial mound built of uncut stone with mud mortar and an associated cluster of residential structures (Pozorski and Pozorski 1987; Tello 1956). The better-known ceremonial complex extends 110 m by 220 m, and the mound itself covers 80 m by 50 m and reaches 15 m high. It features rectangular plazas and platforms and one sunken, circular court. Of two associated Early-horizon roads, one approaches the northeast corner of the mound by ascending a broad, ramplike entry. The residential area lies 150 m southwest of the mound. It consists of rectilinear agglutinated rooms with walls of uncut stone, and a nearby trash midden yielded pottery and food remains (Pozorski and Pozorski 1987). An associated cemetary was already heavily looted during Tello's visit to the site in the 1930s.

Cultural Aspects

The site of Pallka remains virtually unexcavated by archaeologists, but Tello assigned the mound complex to the Chavín culture based on the site's polished and decorated ceramic remains (Tello 1943, 1956). Based on more recent work at other early Casma valley sites, the Pozorskis suggest that occupation at Pallka predates the Chavín horizon. Radiocarbon dates are still lacking, yet pottery-design features combine locally derived elements with attributes diagnostic of Chavín de Huantar's Janabarriu-phase assemblage. Pallka was one of the mid-Early horizon centers that prospered while other coastal centers in Casma and elsewhere had long since declined (Burger 1988, 1992, 1993). Its ceremonial architecture and hilltop location apparently reflect influence from the neighboring highlands. Pallka's orientation and internal configuration differ markedly from those of other early Casma valley complexes. The best-known Chavín feature at the site is a bone tube with an incised cayman design rendered in the classic Chavín style (Tello 1956: Fig. 22, 1943: Plate XXIVa; Roe 1974: Fig. 7e; Willey 1951). The economic basis and the social, political, and religious aspects of Pallka's organization remain unstudied to date, but the site clearly functioned within the Chavín cult's sphere of interaction.

References

Burger, R. L. (1988). "Unity and Heterogeneity within the Chavín Horizon." In *Peruvian Prehistory*, ed. R. Keatinge. Cambridge: Cambridge University Press, 99–144.

Burger, R. L. (1992). *Chavín and the Development of Andean Civilization*. London: Thames and Hudson.

Burger, R. L. (1993). "The Chavín Horizon: Stylistic Chimera or Socioeconomic Metamorphosis." In *Latin American Horizons*, ed. D. Rice. Washington, D.C.: Dumbarton Oaks Research Library and Collection, 41–82.

Pozorski, S. and T. Pozorski (1987). *Early Settlement and Subsistence in the Casma Valley, Peru*. Iowa City: University of Iowa Press.

Roe, P. G. (1974). *A Further Exploration of the Rowe Chavín Seriation and Its Implications for North Central Coast Chronology*. Studies in Pre-Columbian Art and Archaeology, no. 13. Washington, D.C.: Dumbarton Oaks Research Library and Collections.

Tello, J. C. (1943). "Discovery of the Chavín Culture in Peru." American Antiquity 9: 135–160.

Tello, J. C. (1956). *Arqueologia del Valle de Casma: Cultura Chavín, Santa o Huaylas, Yunga y Sub-Chimu*. Lima: Publicación Antropológica del Archivo "Julio C. Tello" de la Universidad Nacional de San Marcos, I.

Willey, G. R. (1951). "The Chavín Problem: A Review and Critique." *Southwestern Journal of Anthropology* 7, 2: 103–144.

WARREN B. CHURCH
Department of Environmental Sciences
Columbus State University
Columbus, Georgia
United States

Chimú

ABSOLUTE TIME PERIOD: 1050–480 B.P.

RELATIVE TIME PERIOD: Follows the Moche tradition and precedes the Inka tradition.

LOCATION: The spatial core of the Chimú tradition was the Moche valley of the north coast of Peru. Its maximal extent was along the Pacific coast approximately from the Huarmey valley north to the Piura valley and possibly the Tumbes valley of far northern Peru, a distance of some 1000 km.

MATERIAL ATTRIBUTES: Finely burnished black-ware ceramics including stirrup-spout vessels with surface treatments such as panels of raised stippling or repeated waves, appliquéd animal, human, and mythic figures. Moldmade adobes used to construct rectilinear compounds enclosing architectural features such as baffled entries, ramps and benches, and niches; interior walls decorated with sculpted reliefs depicting waves, fish, pelicans, and other maritime motifs. Settlement patterns vary, but may range from large urban centers to small rural hamlets.

SITES: Cerro de la Virgen, Chan Chan, El Milagro de San Jose, Fárfan, Manchan, Quebrada Santa Cristina.

CULTURAL SUMMARY

Environment

Climate. The Peruvian coast normally receives only 15–40 mm of precipitation because the cold waters of the northward-flowing Humboldt or Peruvian current inhibit near-shore evaporation, creating a coastal desert. Seasonal rainfall east in the Andes flows westward down arable river valleys with runoff reaching the coastal plain in late January, peaking between February and April, and tapering off in May. Periodically, El Niño/Southern Oscillation (ENSO) events disrupt this pattern, creating torrential rainfall, disruption of marine habitats, and general destruction. Extrapolating from ice core data collected in southern Peru, the Chimú experienced a century of drier than normal climate (1050–950 B.P.) followed by 4 centuries of wetter than average climate. Against the backdrop of those general trends, major climatic disruptions associated with ENSO events may have occurred at 1050 B.P. and 650–600 B.P.

Topography. The north coast of Peru is an area of dramatic topographic variety. The western slopes of the Andes rise from sea level to over 6000 m in less than 150 km, creating a complex environmental mosaic along the gradient. The western slope of the Andean Cordillera is incised by numerous river valleys, most of which

58

run west into the Pacific ocean. The deserts between the valleys are expanses of bare rock and dunes without vegetation. In contrast, the coastal valleys are fertile bands of farmland, which can support two or three harvests a year with sufficient water. Chimú tradition developed in the lower river valleys of the north coast of Peru where arable land and rich marine habitats coincide. For millenia, the coastal valleys were the loci of settled life and agriculture, and this was particularly true for the Chimú.

Geology. The steep Andean foothills consist of a Cretaceous batholith of granodiorite to granite, much of it uplifted during the Miocene and early Pliocene. At various points along the Pacific, formations of andesitic volcanic rocks create coastal headlands. Surface geology is shaped by fluvial, alluvial, marine, and aeolian deposits. It has been suggested that tectonic uplift was an important factor in the recent past. Some scholars hypothesize that tectonic uplift disrupted Chimú irrigation systems, while others contend that there is no evidence of Holocene uplift within the Chimú heartland.

Biota. The desert coast generally lacks vegetation except in the irrigated floodplains and river valleys. The only exception are stands of fog-fed plants like the epiphyte *Tillandsia*, which grows on high coastal hills forming so-called *lomas* vegetation. *Lomas* vegetation may have provided pasturage for llamas.

The coastal deserts support few wild animals: fox, burrowing owls, a variety of reptiles, and whitetailed deer. In contrast, coastal waters contain one of the richest fisheries on earth, with normally dense yields of anchovies, sardines, other fish, and shellfish.

Settlements

Settlement System. Settlements ranged from large urban centers, like the Chimú capital of Chan Chan with estimated populations of 40,000–60,000, down to small rural hamlets. A four-tiered settlement hierarchy consisted of (1) the primary center, Chan Chan; (2) secondary centers in many valleys that served as provincial capitals; (3) tertiary settlements often established for specific imperial purposes; and (4) quaternary settlements that were villages and hamlets. The settlement hierarchy is thought to reflect the administrative network of the Chimú state. Chan Chan was the capital and seat of the Chimú kings, while secondary centers like Farfán and Manchan were the loci of political authority in the provinces. Tertiary settlements like Cerro de la Virgen, El Milagro de San Jose, and Quebrada Santa Cristina were smaller communities subject to Chimú authority, whereas most of the rural population lived in small settlements in the shadows of Chimú rule.

Some settlements apparently were established to serve specific political goals. For example, sites associated with the Chimú irrigation canal between the Chicama and Moche valleys seem to be state-sponsored work camps, and Quebrada Santa Cristina in the Casma valley is interpreted as a similar encampment for agricultural workers.

Community Organization. There is no "typical Chimú" community. Even the capital of Chan Chan lacked an overall plan. Royal palaces, noble compounds, and commoners' houses were crammed together in a motley warren of architecture. A common architectural theme was that residential space was surrounded by a perimeter wall enclosing rooms, storage areas, workshops, and patios. This architectural pattern was true of royal compounds and commoners' residences. Although separated by an enormous social divide, commoners' houses physically touched the exterior walls of the Chimú king's palace. There was no overall segregation based on class or occupational differences at Chan Chan. There are no public plazas or open boulevards at Chan Chan. It was a city of life behind walls.

Communities at different tiers in the settlement hierarchy had different architectural elements; in fact, architectural differences are important for defining the hierarchy. For example, the enormous royal *ciudadelas* were unique to Chan Chan because it was the home of the Chimú kings. In contrast, smaller compounds associated with nonroyal elites are found at Chan Chan and provincial centers like Manchan and Farfán.

Housing. Chimú housing reflected adaptation to a natural environment without trees and a social environment based on class. The royal *ciudadelas* were enclosed by adobe brick walls up to 9 m tall; the largest *ciudadela* encloses more than 21 ha with 900 rooms and 7000 sq m of storage. The *ciudadelas* were major public works built by corvée labor. In contrast, commoners' houses made from cane could be built by a few men in a matter of days.

The simple difference between adobe brick and cane wattle was a material indication of class distinctions. Adobe bricks were moldmade, sun dried, and set in mud mortar. Adobe walls were constructed on cobblestone foundations, and the largest walls tapered slightly from base to top. The *ciudadela* walls at Chan Chan were constructed in segments, possibly by different corvée labor groups. Some bricks have makers' marks—lines, dots, and other figures pressed into the brick before it dried—which indicate a group's, rather than an individual's, brick production. Within the *ciudadelas* were plazas, storerooms, complex passageways, kitchens, residential areas, and the royal burial platform.

Cane-walled constructions were much simpler. Canes, 1–2 cm in diameter and 3–4 m long, were collected along the river and trimmed into long, straight poles. Narrow trenches were excavated for the walls; the butts of the canes were set vertically in the trenches, and the trenches filled and tamped down. Then, three bands of horizontal canes were woven through the vertical canes to form a wickerwork. The lower walls were sometimes reinforced with cobbles. Bundles of canes were used as upright supports for doorways and corners. Roofed with mats, the structures were usually not daubed with mud.

The composition of a household similarly varied with class. The household of the legendary founder of the Chimú dynasty, Tacaynamo, contained principal and secondary wives, their offspring, and some forty courtiers including cooks, brewers, artisans, and others whose job was to "honor and adorn his person and his house." Commoner households at the provincial center of Manchan, in contrast, probably consisted of extended families of five to eight people.

Economy

Subsistence. Subsistence was based on agriculture and fishing. There is little evidence for the consumption of wild food resources other than fish and shellfish. Agriculture relied on canal irrigation supplemented in small part by other agrosystems like raised fields and sunken gardens. Principal crops were maize, various common and broad beans, and large pumpkin-like squashes, staples supplemented by important fruits like guanabana, avocado, and other native tree crops. Fishing focused on collecting shellfish like mussels, limpets, chitons, bean clams, and other varieties, and on fishing for near-shore and pelagic fishes like anchovy, sardine, mackereal, tuna, shark, and ray. It is unclear how important llama herding was to coastal subsistence. Llama meat was consumed, llama wool was spun, and llamas were often sacrificed at Chimú sites. Some scholars suggest that *lomas* vegetation supported large llama herds; other archaeologists contend that coastal herds were small and access to llamas relied on highland pastoralists seasonally migrating to the coast.

The pace of agriculture on the coast is set by rainfall in the Andean *cordillera*. With sufficient irrigation water, two crops of maize can be raised annually. Fishing proceeds throughout the year because of the normal stability of the Humboldt current. This pattern, however, is dramatically disrupted during ENSO events. Flooding destroys crops, erodes irrigation systems, and caps fertile fields with hard deposits of silt. Much warmer sea temperatures kill the normal species of phytoplankton and the marine food pyramid they support.

Ethnohistoric sources suggest that fishing folk and farmers may have been specialized with specific lineages or communities focused on a given economic pursuit. Other commoner households have clear archaeological evidence for combining farming and fishing in their subsistence activities.

Industrial Arts. The Chimú farmed with a variety of hand tools. Digging sticks and foot plows were used to turn the soil, and hafted "donut-stones" (*argollas*) were used like hammers to break the clods. Baskets, nets, and pieces of cloth were used to carry earth, crops, and other items. With such tools, the Chimú constructed extensive irrigation systems, including the Moche-Chicama intervalley canal. Analysis of irrigation systems suggests the Chimú had a sophisticated understanding of canal engineering and flow dynamics. Using this knowledge, the Chimú cultivated more land than is currently farmed on the Peruvian coast.

Fishing was with nets and hook and line. Nets were made from spun cotton line and knotted into different mesh sizes to capture different fish species. The Chimú used casting nets and seine nets with bottle gourd floats and stone net weights. Copper fishhooks were used with cotton hand lines. Fishing was either from shore or from small watercraft called *caballitos*. *Caballitos* are buoyant conical bundles of reeds that a sole fisherman straddles like a horse and paddles with a split bamboo oar.

Cloth was woven from cotton thread and llama wool. Thread was spun using a spindle and whorl. Dyed threads were combined in multicolor plies. Using a backstrap loom, a wide variety of cloth was produced, from durable, rough plain weaves to delicately patterned gauzes. Cloth was also decorated by painting, embroidery, and featherwork. Copper needles and wooden pins were used in sewing. Clothing was not tailored, but instead finished panels of cloth were formed into shawls, skirts, ponchos, and loincloths.

Ceramics varied from basic coilmade utilitarian wares to elegant moldmade stirrup-spout jars. Utilitarian wares ranged from cooking pots with volumes of a few liters to large open-mouthed pots for boiling 70–80 l of water and maize to brew *chicha*. The Chimú excelled at moldmade pottery whose sculptural forms depicted humans, anthropomorphized dieties, animals, domesticated plants, and even architecture. Highly burnished black ware was mass-produced, with multiple pots made from a single mold. Pots were fired in open firings, not enclosed kilns.

The Chimú were masterful metallurgists, although few examples of their finest works in silver and gold survive. The Chimú used a copper-arsenic alloy for a variety of items: fishhooks, needles, bracelets, labelets, nose ornaments, bracelets, and other jewelry. The Chimú drew on a long Andean metallurgical tradition that included smelting, molding, soldering, chemical etching, and other techniques. Much of Chimú metalwork was lost to conquest, first by the Inka and later by the Spanish. An indication of the richness of Chimú metallurgy is a 16th century list of gold and silver gold mined by Spaniards from a Chimú tomb at Chan Chan, a treasure equivalent to 80,000 pesos of gold.

Trade. There is debate about the mechanisms of exchange in Chimú economy. It has been suggested that the Chimú public economy was based on a system of state-administered redistribution. The idea is that the Chimú state was the principle economic institution, acquiring human and natural resources and finished products through a labor-based taxation system and then redistributing these revenues in pursuit of state goals. There is some archaeological support for this interpretation; the banks of storerooms at Chan Chan, the clear evidence for state-maintained workers on public constructions, and evidence for corvée labor in monumental constructions all potentially support the redistributive model. It is not clear, however, if this system affected the average citizen of the Chimú empire. Other scholars, drawing on ethnohistoric sources, have argued that occupational specialization (e.g., between farmers and fishing folk) led to exchange between producers and consumers of different items, a "natural" economy. The Andes, in general, have ambiguous evidence for pre-Hispanic markets, and no definite archaeological evidence has been found for Chimú "private" exchange systems.

Division of Labor. In Chimú society, the organization of craft production ranged from part-time to full-time specialists, some of whom were independent and others attached to royal or noble households. To some extent, the level of craft specialization paralleled the administrative hierarchy with more full-time, attached craft specialists at Chan Chan than at other sites. There is little direct archaeological evidence regarding gender-based specializations or status differences associated with crafts. Weavers were probably women, metallurgists were probably men, but evidence is ambiguous or absent for other crafts.

Sociopolitical Organization

Social Organization. Reconstructions of Chimú social organization are tentative and incomplete. Chimú society was almost certainly class based. North coast myths describe the creations of nobles and commoners from separate stars or cosmic eggs. Distinctions in housing and burial techniques and access to luxury items all suggest marked social differences. It is unclear how class and kinship overlapped. Ethnohistoric accounts suggest that class and descent were partly linked; there are references to noble and courtiers whose descendants perpetuated those class distinctions. A handful of kin terms in the Muchik language suggests a distinction between lineal and affinal kin and a pattern in which lineal kin terms are the same for men and women but terms for collaterals vary based on the gender of the speaker. Based on Colonial documents, it has been hypothesized that North-coast kinship was based on exogamous moieties, which, in turn, were subdivided into sections and subsections. Some scholars suggest that a kin-based nested hierarchy of social groups—the community, the moiety, moiety sections, and moiety subsections—were each led by a local lord in a system of dualistic political organization. Ethnohistoric data suggest these leadership positions often passed from father to son, although exceptions, including women leaders, are known. Some scholars suggest this pattern characterized the sociopolitical structure of the entire Chimú state, while others believe it reflects local level polities but not the structure of the Chimú state as a whole.

Political Organization. Some of the different political positions are hinted at by Muchik words: *çie quic,* great lord; *alæc, cacique* or local leader; *fixllca,* gentleman; *paræng,* vassal or subject; *yaná,* servant. The Chimú king occupied the apex of political authority, attended by various courtiers who maintained his person and household. At Chan Chan, nonroyal elites presumably served in various administrative roles, for example, coordinating labor levies, public constructions, and storage of key resources. In the provinces, the Chimú both imposed political authority and coopted local leaders. Chimú governors and generals were posted to the provinces, and local elites were incorporated into the Chimú hierarchy. Perhaps between three and five levels of political authority separated commoner subject and Chimú king.

Responsibility and power varied with political position. The Chimú king was probably a divine king, largely separated from his subjects by *ciudadela* walls. North-coast legends repeatedly state that the death of a king was hidden so the people would consider him immortal. At the same time, kings were responsible for maintaining proper ritual. For example, one myth about a north-coast ruler describes how a destructive El Niño occurred when he attempted to desecrate a sacred idol; in punishment, nobles captured the ruler, bound him, and cast him into the ocean to placate the goddess of the sea. Rulers also had to use their wealth for the common good, most publically in feasts and dances. Leaders were expected to provide large quantities of food and maize beer (*chicha*) at feasts and to corvée labor groups. Such obligatory generosity was expected of leaders at various levels in the political system.

Social Control. Presumably Chimú society, like any complex society, had various institutions and agents of social control, but archaeological and ethnohistoric evidence of them is very poor. There are no references to a judiciary, police force, or other special group designed to keep order, but ethnohistoric sources state theft and adultery were punished by death. Presumably, lords exercised judicial authority, although they probably were catalysts and shapers of common opinion rather than upholders of legal codes. The one obvious mechanism of social control was architecture, particularly the complex patterns of the *ciudadelas*. The tall *ciudadela* walls were, in effect, a mechanism of social control, dividing social groups and restricting access between ruler and king.

Conflict. As the Chimú conquered territories outside the Moche-Chicama heartland, undoubtedly conflicts occurred with polities in other valleys. At present, however, there is scant evidence for warfare at Chimú sites. Most Chimú settlements are located in open valley bottoms rather than on steep, defensible hilltops (unlike earlier north-coast sites), and only a few Chimú fortresses have been documented. Fortified Chimú sites have been discovered in the middle and upper Moche valley; they are structures of walls with concentric parapets located in defensible positions. A small Chimú fort overlooks the provincial center of Farfán, and there is evidence for a battle at the site of Talambo, both in the Jequetepeque valley. But in general, the evidence for Chimú militarism is relatively slim. In contrast to earlier north-coast societies like the Moche, there are few iconographic representations of warfare, taking of prisoners, or human sacrifice in Chimú art. The only documentary reference to Chimú warfare refers to their unsuccessful resistance against the expanding Inka empire.

Religion and Expressive Culture

Religious Beliefs. There is little direct evidence of Chimú religion, but ethnohistoric accounts suggest some of the main outlines of north-coast religious beliefs, ideas that survived Inka domination and, at least for a few centuries, Spanish Catholicism.

The north-coast pantheon was dominated by the Moon (*Si*) and the Sea (*Ni*). Si controlled the elements of nature, protected crops, and caused sea storms, lightning, and thunder. The Moon was considered mightier than the Sun because the Moon was powerful enough to be seen during the day while the Sun was never visible at night. The House of the Moon was in Pacasmayo, and devotees sacrificed their children to the Moon along with offerings of cotton cloth, *chicha*, and fruits.

The Sea was a generous source of food and a major figure in north-coast myths. Comparative analysis of Moche V and Chimú vessels indicates the increasing importance of the sea in iconography, including an anthropomorphized Wave Deity. Offerings of white maize flour, red ocher, and other items were made to the Sea. Another deity, the Moon Animal, first appears in Moche pottery but is also depicted in Chimú ceramics. A crested, fanged imaginary quadruped, the Moon Animal is always associated with lunar and stellar motifs. The moon is depicted as a crescent in which the animal sits or stands as if it were a boat. Although the meanings of the symbol and deity are lost, the Moon Animal was an important north-coast symbol for at least 1000 years.

Two north-coast creation myths describe the creation of humanity. One myth states that humans were born from stars, the other states humans were spawned from cosmic eggs, but both myths recount the separate origins of nobles and commoners. Nobles were the descendants of a golden star or egg, commoners from a copper star or egg. A cosmogonic justification of social differences, the Chimú believed the differences between noble and commoner were spawned in the heavens.

Religious Practitioners. Presumably Chimú religion involved full-time religious specialists—priests, diviners, and curers—but the nature of such specialists is unknown. Chimú pottery lacks the graphic detail that allows scholars to identify priests, unlike Moche fine-line drawings. Ethnohistoric sources refer only to a few local religious specialists. For example, a sorcerer, Mollep or The Lousy, contended that the people would proliferate like his body lice. Male and female sorcerers cast curses, changed themselves into animals, spoke for oracles, and went into trances.

Ceremonies. Ethnohistoric documents about the 17th-century extirpation of native religions give some idea of north-coast religious practices, some of which were probably also practiced by the Chimú. Natives were repeatedly asked if they worshiped idols, if they believed in the omens represented by dreams and certain birds, and if they worshiped *alæc pong* or "cacique stones." These stones apparently were worshiped by specific kin groups.

Offerings were important elements in Chimú ceremonies. The shell of the thorny oyster, *Spondylus* sp., was highly prized and a common offering. *Spondylus* lives only in the warm waters of the Ecuadorian coast, but the importation of *Spondylus* increased dramatically under the Chimú. The lustrous pink shell was used for beads and ornaments, but its most significant role was in ritual. Apparently, *Spondylus* was associated with the sea and rainfall. Caches of ritually buried *Spondylus* have been found at Chimú sites. Other offerings include llamas, coca leaves, quartz crystals, *chicha*, and human sacrifices.

Death and the Afterlife. Based on grave goods buried with the dead, the Chimú almost certainly believed in an afterlife. The Chimú kings were accompanied to their graves by sacrificed young women, perhaps wives and concubines. A recently discovered Chimú architectural model depicts a ceremony within a *ciudadela* plaza, in which the mummies of two females are being feted in a ceremony involving drummers, musicians, a *chicha* brewer, and a ritual specialist directing the event. Commoners had less elaborate burials, but the funerary treatments nonetheless indicate a belief that some form of existence continued beyond the grave. Individuals are frequently buried with food, cooking pots, weaving tools, ornaments, and small pieces of copper often placed in the dead person's mouth.

Suggested Readings

Bruhns, Karen (1976). "The Moon Animal in Northern Peruvian Art and Culture." *Ñawpa Pacha* 14: 21–40.

Keatinge, Richard (1973). "Chimu Ceramics from the Moche Valley, Peru: A Computer Application to Seriation." Ph.D. diss., Department of Anthropology, Harvard University.

Keatinge, Richard, and Geoffrey Conrad (1983). "Imperialist Expansion in Peruvian Prehistory: Chimu Administration of a Conquered Territory." *Journal of Field Archaeology* 10: 255–283.

Klymyshyn, Alexandra (1976). "Intermediate Architecture in Chan Chan, Peru." Ph.D. diss., Department of Anthropology, Harvard University.

Klymyshyn, Alexandra (1987). "The Development of Chimu Administration in Chan Chan." In *The Origins and Development of the Andean State*, ed. J. Haas, S. Pozorski, and T. Pozorski. Cambridge: Cambridge University Press, 97–110.

Kolata, Alan (1978). "Chan Chan: The Form of the City in Time." Ph.D. diss., Department of Anthropology, Harvard University.

Mackey, Carol (1987). "Chimu Administration in the Provinces." In *The Origins and Development of the Andean State*, ed. J. Haas, S. Pozorski, and T. Pozorski. Cambridge: Cambridge University Press, 121–129.

Mackey, Carol, and Alexandra Klymyshn (1981). "Construction and Labor Organization in the Chimu Empire." *Ñawpa Pacha* 19: 99–114.

Moore, Jerry (1981). "Chimu Socio-economic Organization: Preliminary Data from Manchan, Casma Valley, Peru." *Ñawpa Pacha* 19: 115–128.

Moore, Jerry (1985). "Household Economics and Political Integration: The Lower Class of the Chimu Empire." Ph.D. diss. Ann Arbor: University Microfilms.

Moore, Jerry (1992). "Pattern and Meaning in Prehistoric Peruvian Architecture: the Architecture of Social Control in the Chimu State." *Latin American Antiquity* 3: 95–113.

Moore, Jerry (1996). *Architecture and Power in the Prehispanic Andes: The Archaeology of Public Buildings*. Cambridge: Cambridge University Press.

Moseley, Michael (1975). "Chan Chan: Andean Alternative of the Preindustrial City?" *Science* 187: 219–225.

Moseley, Michael, and Alana Cordy-Collins, eds. (1990). *The Northern Dynasties: Kingship and Statecraft in Chimor*. Washington, D.C.: Dumbarton Oaks Research Library and Collection.

Moseley, Michael, and Kent Day, eds. (1982). *Chan Chan: Andean Desert City*. Albuquerque: University of New Mexico Press.

Moseley, Michael, and Carol Mackey (1974). *Twenty-four Architectural Plans of Chan Chan, Peru*. Cambridge, MA: Peabody Museum Press.

Pillsbury, Joanne (1993). "Sculptural Friezes of Chimor." Ph.D. diss., Department of Art History, Columbia University.

Pillsbury, Joanne (1996). "The Thorny Oyster and the Origins of Empire: Implications of Recently Uncovered Spondylus Imagery from Chan Chan, Peru." *Latin American Antiquity* 7: 313–340.

Ramirez, Susan (1996). *The World Upside Down: Cross-Cultural Contact and Conflict in Sixteenth-Century Peru*. Stanford: Stanford University Press.

Rowe, John (1948). "The Kingdom of Chimor." *Acta Americana* 6: 26–59.

Topic, John (1977). "The Lower Class at Chan Chan: A Qualitative Approach." Ph.D. diss., Department of Anthropology, Harvard University.

Topic, J., and M. Moseley (1983). "Chan Chan: A Case Study of Urban Change in Peru." *Ñawpa Pacha* 21: 153–182.

Uceda, Santiago (1997). "Esculturas en miniatura y una maqueta en madera." In *Investigaciones en la Huaca de la Luna, 1995*, ed. S. Uceda, E. Mujica, and R. Morales. Trujillo, Peru: Facultad de Ciencias Sociales, Universidad Nacional de La Libertad, 151–175.

Cerro de la Virgen

TIME PERIOD: 650–550 B.P.

LOCATION: Between the Moche and Chicama valleys of the north-coast of Peru. The site is located 5 km north of the Chimú capital, Chan Chan (see Chan Chan entry) and 2.5 km inland from the modern seaside community of Huanchaco.

DESCRIPTIVE SUMMARY

Local Environment

Cerro de la Virgen is located in the coastal desert of Peru. The site is on a dry rocky quebrada, but Cerro de la Virgen is near prehistoric agricultural fields once irrigated by water from the ancient Moro canal.

Physical Features

Cerro de la Virgen consists of more than 400 agglutinated rooms and associated agricultural fields, cemetery, canal, and road. The residential structures cover an area of 14 ha (Keatinge 1975: 217). Walls had low cobble-faced foundations that supported a perishable (probably cane and matting) upper wall. Rooms varied from 1 m sq to 10 × 10 m. Residential units varied from single rooms to small multiroom clusters (Keatinge 1975: 217–218). A prehistoric road flanked by low retaining walls bisects Cerro del Virgen and continues directly to Chan Chan, but there are administrative structures at the Cerro de la Virgen (Keatinge 1975: 218–220, 1982: 198). It is estimated that at least 1000 people lived at the site (Keatinge 1975: 217).

Although Cerro de la Virgen was heavily looted, excavations in seven relatively intact rooms uncovered numerous features, including hearths, storage vessels, and storage pits. Storage vessels were set in holes in the floor, the mouths surrounded by cobbles, and then capped with half a gourd or cloth. Storage pits were lined with cobbles and plastered with a thick layer of adobe. One type of small room was exclusively for storage, most of its floor taken up by a single storage pit. An estimated 15 percent of the rooms at Cerro de la Virgen were small storage rooms of this type (Keatinge 1975: 223).

Artifacts from Cerro de la Virgen included evidence for fishing, spinning, weaving, and farming. Copper fishhooks, fragments of cotton gill and seine nets, net weights, and abundant deposits of fish scales and bones all indicate the importance of fishing. Spindle whorls, raw cotton, and balls of spun thread and yarn demonstrate that both cotton fiber and llama wool were spun at Cerro de la Virgen. Weaving is indicated by wooden elements of back-strap looms including weaving swords. Finally, copper needles and finished cloth suggest that all steps of textile production—from cleaning raw cotton to sewing finished cloth—took place at Cerro de la Virgen (Keatinge 1975: 223–225).

Stone "donut-stones" were probably used as digging stick weights in the surrounding agricultural fields. Approximately 1600 ha of fields were watered by a feeder ditch from the Moro canal. Much of this area supported cotton rather than food crops (Pozorski 1982: 193). Although a wide variety of plant foods were consumed at Cerro de la Virgen (e.g., maize, common bean, squash, avocado, chilies, and fruits), the site's residents were not growing foodstuffs for export to Chan Chan.

Cultural Aspects

Cerro de la Virgen is one of the few rural Chimú communities to receive intensive archaeological study. This may reflect the overwhelmingly urban nature of Chimú settlement in the Moche valley and the corresponding scarcity of rural villages (Keatinge 1974: 217) and may also reflect incomplete survey data.

Cerro de la Virgen is viewed as a part of a "state-controlled agricultural enterprise" (Keatinge 1975: 276), in which the settlement was established by the Chimú state and its residents required to work the nearby fields. Viewed within a model of the Chimú state emphasizing its administrative character (see Chimú Tradition entry), excavations at Cerro de la Virgen are seen as illuminating "one more aspect of the tightly controlled Chimú socioeconomic system" (Keatinge 1975: 227).

References

Keatinge, Richard (1975). "Urban Settlement Systems and Rural Sustaining Comunities: An Example from Chan Chan's Hinterland." *Journal of Field Archaeology* 2: 215–227.

Keatinge, Richard (1982). "The Chimu Empire in a Regional Perspective: Cultural Antecedents and Continuities." In *Chan Chan: Andean Desert City*, ed. M. Moseley and K. Day. Albuquerque: University of New Mexico Press, 197–224.

Pozorski, Shelia (1982). "Subsistence Systems in the Chimú State." In *Chan Chan: Andean Desert City*, ed. M. Moseley and K. Day. Albuquerque: University of New Mexico Press, 177–196.

Chan Chan

TIME PERIOD: c. 1050–480 B.P.

LOCATION: Approximately 5 km west of the city of Trujillo, department of La Libertad, Peru.

DESCRIPTIVE SUMMARY

Local Environment

Chan Chan is located on the desert coast of northern Peru. Located several kilometers away from the irrigated floodplain of the Moche river, Chan Chan sits on a barren uplifted marine terrace overlooking the Pacific ocean.

Physical Features

Chan Chan is a sprawling city covering some 20 km² with an urban core of 6 km². Lacking a unifying urban plan (Conklin 1990: 64), Chan Chan's urban core contains four principal classes of architecture: (1) 10 large walled compounds, called *ciudadelas*, thought to be the palaces of the Chimú kings; (2) intermediate architecture associated with Chan Chan's nonroyal elites; (3) nonelite commoner dwellings and workshops that housed an estimated 20,000–40,000 people spread throughout the city; and (4) four artificial mounds (*huacas*) located in the eastern half of the city (Conrad 1974, 1982; Day 1973, 1982; Klymyshyn 1976, 1982, 1987; Kolata 1978, 1982, 1990; Moseley 1975, 1990; Topic 1977, 1982, 1990; Topic and Moseley 1983; West 1967, 1970).

The *ciudadelas* are enormous constructions ranging from 6.73–21.2 ha and containing from 113–907 rooms. Enclosed by adobe walls up to 9 m tall, the *ciudadelas* contain plazas, royal burial platforms, walk-in wells, possible storerooms, and distinctive three-sided constructions called U-shaped rooms or *audiencias*. There are 10 *ciudadelas* and although there is debate about the relative sequence of their construction (Cavallaro 1991; Conrad 1982; Day 1973; Kolata 1990; Topic and Moseley 1983; Williams Len 1987), a thin consensus suggests three chronological groups of *ciudadelas*: Early (Chayhuac, Uhle, Tello, Laberinto), Middle (Gran Chimu), and Late (Rivero, Tschudi, Bandelier, Velarde), with the relative position of Ciudadela Squier uncertain. The *ciudadelas* are a unique class of architecture at Chan Chan and within north coast architectural traditions. Individual *ciudadelas* may have been associated with the reign of each of the 10 Chimú kings mentioned in ethnohistoric sources (Conrad 1982; Rowe 1948; cf. Cavallaro 1991; Netherly 1990; Zuidema 1990). The size, complexity, and restricted access of *ciudadelas* suggest their royal association. Many *ciudadelas* have a single entrance, and all have labrynthine access patterns (Moore 1992, 1996). Enclosed plazas fronted by benches and ramps were tightly regulated points of encounter between lord and subject (Moore 1996: 217, 219). Banks of small rooms with stepover thresholds are interpreted as storerooms associated with the Chimú public economy (Klymyshyn 1987).

Except for Ciudadala Tello, the royal compounds contain burial platforms. These now-looted mounds were built from a "concrete" of gravel and mud (*tapia*). Located deep in the recesses of the *ciudadelas*, the burial platforms had a central shaft chamber for the principal burial and auxiliary chambers for subsequent burials and/or sacrifices (Conrad 1974). Ethnohistoric sources (Ramirez 1996) and a recently discovered Chimú architectural model (Uceda 1997) indicate that after a king's death *ciudadelas* were transformed from palaces to royal sepulchers where kin and servants of the deceased ruler attended his mummy.

Intermediate compounds are much smaller than the *ciudadelas*, but contain selected architectural features in common with the royal compounds such as ramps, benches, and occasionally storerooms and *audiencias* (Klymyshyn 1976, 1982). These structures are interpreted as the residences of nonroyal elites, although some intermediate compounds enclose small plazas, possible workshops, and other areas with more public functions (Klymyshyn 1982: 142).

About 1 km² of Chan Chan contains relatively small constructions with cobblestone foundations and cane walls known in the literature as SIAR for small, irregular agglutinated rooms (Topic 1977, 1982, 1990). SIAR are the residences and workshops of Chan Chan's lower classes, many of whom were involved in craft production (Topic 1990: 145–146). The SIAR barrios are generally found in the western and southern margins of Chan Chan's urban core, wedged into spaces occupied by *ciudadalas* and intermediate units. Individual SIAR units are relatively small spaces forming congeries of rooms without replicated plans. Built by the inhabitants and modified as needed, the SIAR contain kitchens, storage bins, multipurpose areas, and workshops for crafts like copper metallurgy, textile production, woodworking, and other minor crafts (Topic 1982: 162–165).

Chan Chan also contains four large mounds or *huacas*; they have received little archaeological attention. The Chan Chan huacas are briefly discussed by Day (1982: 62–63) who describes their locations and general states of destruction. Huaca Obispo is located on the far northern margin of Chan Chan, away from the urban core of the city. The remnants of the heavily looted mound suggest the structure was 100 m by 100 m and perhaps 20 m tall. The mound's core was constructed from cobblestone chamber and fill and covered in adobe bricks and mud plaster forming (Day 1982: 62). No stairways or summit-top structures were observed. Huaca Obispo is located in a large enclosed plaza entered via a single door. Conklin (1990: 61) suggests that Huaca Obispo was a central focus at Chan Chan, oriented toward the mountains and irrigation canals and sharing those orientations with earlier Moche *huacas*. Beyond that, Huaca Obispo seems to sit at the northern boundary of Chan Chan, possibly associated with walls that marked the edge of the city (Conklin 1990: 61). Huaca Toledo is located on the east side of Chan Chan near Ciudadela Bandelier, and like Huaca Obispo it was built in a large enclosed plaza. Extensively looted, Day (1982: 62) estimated that the *huaca* was perhaps 75 m by 75 m at its base and 15 m tall. Little remains but a heap of cobbles, perhaps indicating Huaca Toledo—like Huaca Obispo—was built from cobblestone chamber and fill.

Two other *huacas* are all but destroyed, scarcely indicated by scant remains. Huaca las Conchas is located southeast of Huaca Obispo and northeast of Huaca Toledo; it was built from adobes and was 70 m by 70 m at its base (Day 1982: 62). According to Day (1982: 63), looters discovered walls decorated with appliquéd mud plaster shells and thus the mound's name. Huaca El Higo is east of Ciudadela Chayhuac and may have been the largest *huaca* at Chan Chan. Although the mound "presently consists of mounds of melted adobe and traces of walls" (Day 1982: 63), maps of Chan Chan suggest the mound may have covered some 120 m by 100 m with a height of more than 8 m (Moseley and Mackey 1974: Sheet 1). Like Obispo and Toledo, Huaca El Higo apparently was surrounded by a walled enclosure; however, the extensive destruction in the area makes it impossible to reconstruct.

Kolata (1990) has correlated the construction of the *huacas* with relative sequences for the Chan Chan *ciudadelas*. Based on his seriation of adobe bricks from the *huacas* and *ciudadelas* (Kolata 1978: 82–94), Kolata (1990) suggests that Huaca El Higo was built early in the development of Chan Chan (i.e., in his phase Early

Chimú 1A, c. A.D. 900–1100); Topic and Moseley (1983: 159) suggest absolute dates of A.D. 850–1000. With the expansion of constructions to the north of Chan Chan during Middle Chimu (c. A.D. 1200–1300), both Huaca Obispo and Huaca las Conchas appear in the urban landscape, followed by the construction of Huaca Toledo, along with Ciudadela Bandelier, during Late Chimú 1 (c. A.D. 1300–1400).

Other artificial features of Chan Chan's urban landscape are walk-in wells, sunken gardens and cemeteries. Walk-in wells and sunken gardens (the latter are also called *wachaques* and *mahamaes*) are both excavations down to the water table. Some excavations are large enough to support limited garden crops; others were simply wells with ramps leading from the ground surface down to water level. These features are found within *ciudadelas* and intermediate compounds, in some SIAR barrios, and along the southern flank of Chan Chan.

Cultural Aspects

Chan Chan is pivotal for understanding the development and organization of the Chimú state. It was the Chimú capital and thus the apex of an administrative hierarchy varyingly applied in the core and heartland of the Chimu state. Chan Chan was the most important site in the Moche and Chicama valley during the Late Intermediate period, and satellite communities in this region—like Cerro de la Virgen and El Milagro de San Jose, among others—are clearly articulated to the Chimú economy centered at Chan Chan (Keatinge 1973). Provincial centers, like the sites of Farfan and Manchan, seem to have been variously linked to the capital.

Current understanding of Chan Chan is largely due to research directed by Michael Moseley and Carol Mackey from 1969–1975 and involving more than a dozen scholars. During that research, a model of Chan Chan emerged that emphasized its position within a hierarchical administrative state (Moseley 1975), and this model shaped the interpretation of archaeological data in Chan Chan. In this model, the Chimú state was seen as the major institution within a redistributive public economy, like those envisioned by Service (1975) and others. From this perspective, for example, the SIAR occupations were interpreted as the residences and workshops of an "urban proletariat" (Topic 1982: 173–175) maintained by the agricultural production of rural satelitte communities (Keatinge 1973) whose production was administered by the bureucratic elites of the intermediate compounds (Klymyshyn 1982: 143) and stored within the banks of storerooms in the *ciudadelas* (Day 1982: 338–339).

This model proposed for Chan Chan has had enormous influence on subsequent research into the nature of Chimú society. In essence, the debate forms two sets of questions: (1) Does the model accurately describe the pattern at Chan Chan? and (2) Does the model reflect a basic pattern of Chimú sociopolitical organization throughout the Chimú empire?

When the Inka conquered the Chimú in c. A.D. 1470, Chan Chan became a subject city. According to ethnohistoric sources (Cabello Balboa 1951 [1586]; Rowe 1948), the Chimú, led by King Minchançaman, resisted the Inka forces but were decisively defeated. The Inka took Minchançaman to Cuzco as a royal hostage and placed one of his lesser sons on the throne as a pliant ruler. There is little archaeological evidence for the Inka presence at Chan Chan. The *ciudadelas* were abandoned and many burned, perhaps during the period of Inka rule (Moseley 1990: 15). The Chimú elites left the city and the site's population declined (Donnan and Mackey 1978: 357). The major Inka installation in the region became Chiquitoy Viejo in the Chicama Valley, not Chan Chan (Conrad 1977). Chan Chan's significance diminished further after Francisco Pizarro founded the Spanish city of Trujillo in 1535. Yet the riches of the once-great city were not forgotten. Spaniards organized mining ventures to loot the treasures of Chan Chan, and although the Indians of Trujillo protested, the final sack of the capital of the Chimú empire began (Ramirez 1996: 121–151).

References

Cabello Balboa, Miguel (1951 [1586]). *Miscelanea Antartica*. Lima: Universidad Nacional Mayor de San Marcos.

Cavallaro, Rafael (1991). *Large-site Methodology: Architectural Analysis and Dual Organization in the Andes*. Occasional Papers, no. 5. Calgary: Department of Anthropology, University of Calgary.

Conklin, William (1990). "Architecture of the Chimu: Memory, Function, and Image." In *The Northern Dynasties: Kingship and Statecraft in Chimor*, ed. M. Moseley and A. Cordy-Collins. Washington, D.C.: Dumbarton Oaks Research Library and Collection, 43–74.

Conrad, Geoffrey (1974). "Burial Platforms and Related Structures on the North Coast of Peru: Some Social and Political Implications." Ph.D. diss., Department of Anthropology, Harvard University.

Conrad, Geoffrey (1977). "Chiquitoy Viejo: An Inca Administrative Center in the Chicama Valley, Peru." *Journal of Field Archaeology* 4: 1–17.

Conrad, Geoffrey (1982). "The Burial Platforms of Chan Chan: Some Social and Political Implications." In *Chan Chan: Andean Desert City*, ed. M. Moseley and K. Day. Albuquerque: University of New Mexico Press, 87–117.

Conrad, Geoffrey (1990). "Farfan, General Pacatnamu, and the Dynastic History of Chimor." In *The Northern Dynasties: Kingship and Statecraft in Chimor*, ed. M. Moseley and A. Cordy-Collins. Washington, D.C.: Dumbarton Oaks Research Library and Collection, 227–242.

Day, Kent (1973). "The Architecture of Ciudadela Rivero, Chan Chan, Peru." Ph.D. diss., Department of Anthropology, Harvard University.

Day, Kent (1982). "Ciudadelas: Their Form and Function." In *Chan Chan: Andean Desert City*, ed. M. Moseley and K. Day. Albuquerque: University of New Mexico Press, 55–66.

Keatinge, Richard (1973). "Chimu Ceramics from the Moche Valley, Peru: A Computer Application to Seriation." Ph.D. diss., Department of Anthropology, Harvard University.

Keatinge, Richard (1982). "The Chimu Empire in a Regional Perspective: Cultural Antecedents and Continuities." In *Chan Chan: Andean Desert City*, ed. M. Moseley and K. Day. Albuquerque: University of New Mexico Press, 197–224.

Keatinge, Richard, and Geoffrey Conrad (1983). "Imperialist Expansion in Peruvian Prehistory: Chimu Administration of a Conquered Territory." *Journal of Field Archaeology* 10: 255–283.

Klymyshyn, Alexandra (1976). "Intermediate Architecture in Chan Chan, Peru." Ph.D. diss., Department of Anthropology, Harvard University.

Klymyshyn, Alexandra (1982). "The Elite Compounds in Chan Chan." In *Chan Chan: Andean Desert City*, ed. M. Moseley and K. Day. Albuquerque: University of New Mexico Press, 119–143.

Klymyshyn, Alexandra (1987). "The Development of Chimu Administration in Chan Chan." In *The Origins and Development of the Andean State*, ed. J. Haas, S. Pozorski, and T. Pozorski. Cambridge: Cambridge University Press, 97–110.

Kolata, Alan (1978). "Chan Chan: The Form of the City in Time." Ph.D. diss., Department of Anthropology, Harvard University.

Kolata, Alan (1982). "Chronology and Settlement Growth at Chan Chan." In *Chan Chan: Andean Desert City*, ed. M. Moseley and K. Day. Albuquerque: University of New Mexico Press, 67–85.

Kolata, Alan (1990). "The Urban Concept of Chan Chan." In *The Northern Dynasties: Kingship and Statecraft in Chimor*, ed. M. Moseley and A. Cordy-Collins. Washington, D.C.: Dumbarton Oaks Research Library and Collection, 107–144.

Mackey, Carol (1982). "The Middle Horizon as Viewed from the Moche Valley." In *Chan Chan: Andean Desert City*, ed. M. Moseley and K. Day. Albuquerque: University of New Mexico Press, 321–331.

Mackey, Carol (1987). "Chimu Administration in the Provinces." In *The Origins and Development of the Andean State*, ed. J. Haas, S. Pozorski, and T. Pozorski. Cambridge: Cambridge University Press, 121–129.

Mackey, Carol, and Alexandra Klymyshn (1981). "Construction and Labor Organization in the Chimu Empire" *Ñawpa Pacha* 19: 99–114.

Mackey, Carol, and Alexandra Klymyshn (1990). "The Southern Frontier of the Chimu Empire." In *The Northern Dynasties: Kingship and Statecraft in Chimor*, ed. M. Moseley and A. Cordy-Collins. Washington, D.C.: Dumbarton Oaks Research Library and Collection, 195–226.

Moore, Jerry (1981). "Chimu Socio-economic Organization: Preliminary Data from Manchan, Casma Valley, Peru." *Ñawpa Pacha* 19: 115–128.

Moore, Jerry (1985). "Household Economics and Political Integration: The Lower Class of the Chimu Empire." Ph.D. diss., Ann Arbor: University Microfilms.

Moore, Jerry (1992). "Pattern and Meaning in Prehistoric Peruvian Architecture: The Architecture of Social Control in the Chimu State." *Latin American Antiquity* 3: 95–113.

Moore, Jerry (1996). *Architecture and Power in the Prehispanic Andes: The Archaeology of Public Buildings.* Cambridge: Cambridge University Press.

Moseley, Michael (1975). "Chan Chan: Andean Alternative of the Preindustrial City?" *Science* 187: 219–225.

Moseley, Michael, and Carl Mackey (1974). *Twenty-Four Architectural Plans of Chan Chan, Peru.* Cambridge, MA: Peabody Museum Press.

Pillsbury, Joanne (1993). "Sculptural Friezes of Chimor." Ph.D. diss., Department of Art History, Columbia University.

Pillsbury, Joanne (1996). "The Thorny Oyster and the Origins of Empire: Implications of Recently Uncovered Spondylus Imagery from Chan Chan, Peru." *Latin American Antiquity* 7: 313–340.

Ramirez, Susan (1996). *The World Upside Down: Cross-Cultural Contact and Conflict in Sixteenth-Century Peru.* Stanford: Stanford University Press.

Rowe, John (1948). "The Kingdom of Chimor." *Acta Americana* 6: 26–59.

Service, Elman (1975). *The Origins of the State and Civilization: The Process of Cultural Evolution.* New York: W.W. Norton.

Topic, John (1977). "The Lower Class at Chan Chan: A Qualitative Approach." Ph.D. diss., Department of Anthropology, Harvard University.

Topic, John (1982). "Lower-Class Social and Economic Organization at Chan Chan." In *Chan Chan: Andean Desert City,* ed. M. Moseley and K. Day. Albuquerque: University of New Mexico Press, 145–175.

Topic, John (1990). "Craft Production in the Kingdom of Chimor." In *The Northern Dynasties: Kingship and Statecraft in Chimor,* ed. M. Moseley and A. Cordy-Collins. Washington, D.C.: Dumbarton Oaks Research Library and Collection, 145–176.

Topic, J., and M. Moseley (1983). "Chan Chan: A Case Study of Urban Change in Peru." *Ñawpa Pacha* 21: 153–182.

Uceda, Santiago (1997). "Esculturas en Miniatura y Una Maqueta en Madera." In *Investigaciones en la Huaca de la Luna, 1995,* ed. S. Uceda, E. Mujica, and R. Morales. Trujillo, Peru: Facultad de Ciencias Sociales, Universidad Nacional de La Libertad, 151–175.

West, Michael (1967). "Chan Chan, Peru: An Ancient Urban Metropolis: Results of a Settlement Pattern Study." Ph.D. diss., Department of Anthropology, University of California, Los Angeles.

West, Michael (1970). "Community Settlement Patterns at Chan Chan, Peru." *American Antiquity* 35: 74–86.

El Milagro de San Jose

TIME PERIOD: 650–550 B.P.

LOCATION: In the Quebrada Rio Seco between the Moche and Chicama valleys of the north coast of Peru. The site is located 9.5 km north of the Chimú capital, Chan Chan.

DESCRIPTIVE SUMMARY

Local Environment

El Milagro de San Jose is located in the coastal desert of Peru. The site is on a dry intervalley desert lacking vegetation, but El Milagro de San Jose is surrounded by prehistoric agricultural fields once irrigated by water from the ancient Moro canal.

Physical Features

El Milagro de San Jose consists of a stone-walled building, three much smaller buildings associated with feeder canals, irrigation canals, and prehistoric fields (Keatinge 1974). The largest "Main Structure" is 55 by 45 m and contains courtyards, a kitchen, five three-sided rooms with niches called *audiencias*, and rooms with niches. The architectural features and access patterns of El Milagro de San Jose strongly resemble elite buildings at Chan Chan. Of the three smaller buildings, the largest building has some of the features of the Main Structure (e.g., an *audiencia*), while the smallest structures may be the houses of workers who maintained the canals and tilled the fields.

Two uncorrected, uncalibrated radiocarbon dates from the Main Structure date to 625 B.P. and 645 B.P., however, the excavator believes that C13/C12 correction indicates a construction date in the late 12th century A.D. (Keatinge 1982: 201). Similarities between the *audiencias* at El Milagro de San Jose and *audiencias* in the relatively early Uhle compound at Chan Chan are also thought to indicate an earlier construction date (Moseley and Deeds 1982: 45).

Cultural Aspects

El Milagro de San Jose is interpreted as a rural administrative center, part of the Chimú state's effort to consolidate its rule. Located near a vital irrigation canal and prehistoric field system, the site played an important role in agricultural, production that supported the massive urban center of Chan Chan. El Milagro de San Jose's date suggests that state control of rural agriculture was an early and continuous element of Chimú imperialism.

References

Keatinge, Richard (1974). "Chimu Rural Administrative Centers in the Moche Valley, Peru." 6: 66–82.

Keatinge, Richard (1982). "The Chimu Empire in a Regional Perspective: Cultural Antecedents and Continuities." In *Chan Chan:*

Andean Desert City, ed. M. Moseley and K. Day. Albuquerque: University of New Mexico Press, 197–224.

Moseley, Michael, and Eric Deeds (1982). "The Land in Front of Chan Chan: Agrarian Expansion, Reform and Collapse in the Moche Valley." In *Chan Chan: Andean Desert City*, ed. M. Moseley and K. Day. Albuquerque: University of New Mexico Press, 25–53.

Farfán

TIME PERIOD: c. 750–480 B.P.

LOCATION: Jequetepeque valley, department of Lambayeque, Peru.

DESCRIPTIVE SUMMARY

Local Environment

Farfán is located 12.5 km inland from the Pacific ocean and 3.8 km north of the main channel of the Rio Jequetepeque.

Physical Features

Farfán was the Chimu provincial center in the Jequetepeque valley (Conrad 1990; Keatinge 1982; Keatinge and Conrad 1983). Farfán covers about 1 sq km. The site consists of six adobe brick-walled compounds, various platforms and smaller constructions, cemeteries and canals. Much of the site has been damaged by looting, agriculture, and the construction of the Panamerican highway (Keatinge and Conrad 1983: 265).

Farfán's antiquity—and by extension the date for the Chimú presence in Jequetepeque—is a matter of some debate. Radiocarbon samples from excavations in 1978 produced mixed results with uncalibrated midpoints ranging from 795–405 B.P., all with relatively large standard errors. The excavators believe that relative dates and selected radiocarbon samples suggest a Chimú occupation at Farfán at c. A.D. 1200 (Keatinge and Conrad 1983: 274–276), some 170 years earlier than Chimú deposits at the nearby site of Pacatnamú.

The Farfán compounds are arranged in a rough north-south line. The only compound with a burial platform, Compound II, is the most complicated structure, and it was the focus of excavations in 1978. Compound II is a rectangular walled compound 374 m long and 130 m wide. A pilastered door on the north side of the compound opens onto a large foreplaza. From there, access to the main compound is via a pilastered doorway flanked by two sets of three carved figures; four preserved figures depict a feline crouching behind a smaller human (Keatinge and Conrad 1983: 271–272). Passing through this door, additional interior walls have the effect of baffling passage until a third pilastered entry opens onto an entry court. The open entry court has two low platforms that stand away from the walls and a two-tiered raised platform with niches along the southern wall. A ramp connects the entry court to the raised platform, and from there one moves into a complex of storerooms, an *audiencia* with bins, and snaking corridors. This portion of Compound II is interpreted as administrative in function.

The burial platform in the southern portion of Compound II is approached via a 190-m-long corridor that terminates in the burial platform complex. The burial platform has been looted, but there are traces of associated bins and storerooms. These features were empty as were two rooms adjacent to the burial platform in Compound II.

Cultural Aspects

Farfán's significance stems from its potential role in the Chimú conquest and incorporation of the Jequetepeque valley (Topic 1990: 186–187). Farfán is interpreted as an intrusive administrative center, sharing architectural stylistic traits with some of the much larger walled compounds of the Chimú capital, Chan Chan (Keatinge and Conrad 1983: 280). Ethnohistoric sources suggest Jequetepeque was conquered by the third king of the Chimú dynasty, relatively early in the development of the Chimú empire. Thus, the identification of Farfán as a Chimu provincial center and dating its establishment directly illuminate questions about Chimú imperial expansion (Keatinge and Conrad 1983).

References

Conrad, Geoffrey (1990). "Farfán, General Pacatnamu, and the Dynastic History of Chimor." In *The Northern Dynasties: Kingship and Statecraft in Chimor*. M. Moseley and A. Cordy-Collins. Washington, D.C.: Dumbarton Oaks Research Library and Collection, 227–242.

Keatinge, Richard (1982). "The Chimu Empire in a Regional Perspective: Cultural Antecedents and Continuities." In *Chan Chan: Andean Desert City*, ed. M. Moseley and K. Day. Albuquerque: University of New Mexico Press, 197–224.

Keatinge, Richard, and Geoffrey Conrad (1983). "Imperialist Expansion in Peruvian Prehistory: Chimu Administration of a Conquered Territory." *Journal of Field Archaeology* 10: 255–283.

Topic, Teresa (1990). "Territorial Expansion and the Kingdom of Chimor." In *The Northern Dynasties: Kingship and Statecraft in Chimor*, ed. M. Moseley and A. Cordy-Collins. Washington, D.C.: Dumbarton Oaks Research Library and Collection, 177–194.

Manchan

TIME PERIOD: 650–480 B.P.

LOCATION: In the lower Casma valley on the north coast of Peru.

DESCRIPTIVE SUMMARY

Local Environment

Manchan is located on the coastal desert of Peru. The site is on the southern margin of the Casma valley approximately 9.5 km inland from the Pacific ocean. Manchan sits on a barren terrace lacking vegetation but overlooking the fertile, irrigated agricultural land of the Casma valley.

Physical Features

Manchan covers approximately 63 ha and contains several major classes of archaeological remains (Mackey and Klymyshyn 1981, 1990). A series of agglutinated adobe-walled compounds runs across the northern edge of the site. These agglutinated compounds were built from east to west without interconnecting doorways (Mackey and Klymyshyn 1990: 205). The easternmost compound is the largest and most architecturally complex, and it has a very large plaza, roughly 160 by 85 m in area. The west end of the plaza has a wide bench and an elaborate doorway, and the bases of 65 rounded adobe columns—some painted with ocher and red paint—line the plaza (Mackey and Klymyshyn 1990: 205; Moore n.d.). The rest of the agglutinated compounds contain large plazas, small rooms interpreted as storerooms, and elite residential areas (Mackey 1987).

The northwestern portion of the Manchan contains five isolated adobe compounds exhibiting architectural features—baffled entryways, ramps, and benchs—seen at other Chimú sites (see entries for Chan Chan, Farfán). The most elaborate isolated compound (Isolated Compound 12) has baffled entries, a roughly tripartite plan, ramps that lead from patios, a couple of storerooms, and an *audiencia* variant considered similar

to the U-shaped *audiencias* in Chan Chan (Mackey and Klymyshyn 1990: 206). The other isolated compounds generally share these features, although varying in scale, access, and internal complexity. The discovery of elite burials in these compounds with Chimú hats and loincloths and wooden statues and staffs similar to those found in Chan Chan (Mackey and Klymyshyn 1990: 200) reemphasizes the connection between the isolated compounds at Manchan and Imperial Chimú traditions.

The bulk of Manchan's residences were commoners who lived in simple houses made from riparian cane. There are five barrios of cane-walled residential compounds. Excavations in the largest barrio uncovered a warren of approximately 30 cane-walled enclosures averaging 245 sq m and are linked by sinuous alleys. Each enclosure contained a set of rooms and an open patio. Excavation in the patio areas indicated both domestic and craft economic activities took place including spinning of cotton and llama wool, brewing maize beer (*chicha*), woodworking, and simple copper metallurgy (Moore 1981, 1985, 1989).

Other physical features at Manchan include a large cemetery in the southwestern portion of the site, a cobble enclosure thought to be a llama corral, a large mound of uncertain function built adobe rubble and organic fill, and a *tapia*-walled enclosure on a hillside on the northeastern corner of the site.

Cultural Aspects

Manchan is the largest known Chimú provincial center south of the Virú valley, and research in the 1980s documented Manchan's importance for understanding patterns of political integration in the Chimú empire (Mackey 1987; Mackey and Klymyshyn 1981, 1990; Moore 1981, 1985, 1988, 1989). Manchan appears to be a site-intrusive settlement constructed during the Later Intermediate period (Mackey and Klymyshyn 1990: 198), not a Middle-horizon settlement as Thompson (1961) suggested. Yet, both architectural and ceramic styles suggest a complex intertwining of Imperial Chimú and local Casma valley traditions. Mackey and Klymyshyn (1990) suggest that Manchan represents the center of a local political system coopted by the Chimú empire rather than a Chimú colony or garrison.

Manchan's population was integrated into the Chimú state in various ways. On one hand, local populations employed Chimú iconography and elite goods (press-molded Chimú black ware ceramics, *Spondylus* shell, etc.), and commoners produced items like *chicha* and cloth for elite use. Yet, commoners apparently were economically self-sufficient, unattached craft producers. The lack of storage areas at Manchan suggests the site did not play a major role in the administration and transshipment of bulk items (e.g., agricultural staples.) In rough terms, the Manchan elite were probably more tightly integrated into the Chimú state than were Manchan's commoners. Local political leadership probably drew on indigenous kin-based systems of authority, but gained prestige through incorporation into the Chimú state. The data from Manchan suggest some of the varying strategies of political integration employed by the Chimú Empire.

References

Mackey, Carol (1987). "Chimu Administration in the Provinces." In *The Origins and Development of the Andean State*, ed. J. Haas, S. Pozorski, and T. Pozorski. Cambridge: Cambridge University Press, 121–129.

Mackey, Carol, and Alexandra Klymyshn (1981). "Construction and Labor Organization in the Chimu Empire." *Ñawpa Pacha* 19: 99–114.

Mackey, Carol, and Alexandra Klymyshn (1990). "The Southern Frontier of the Chimu Empire." In *The Northern Dynasties: Kingship and Statecraft in Chimor*, ed. M. Moseley and A. Cordy-Collins. Washington, D.C.: Dumbarton Oaks Research Library and Collection, 195–226.

Moore, Jerry (1981). "Chimu Socio-economic Organization: Preliminary Data from Manchan, Casma Valley, Peru." *Ñawpa Pacha* 19: 115–128.

Moore, Jerry (1985). "Household Economics and Political Integration: The Lower Class of the Chimu Empire." Ph.D. diss. Ann Arbor: University Microfilms.

Moore, Jerry (1988). "Prehistoric Raised Field Agriculture in the Casma Valley, Peru." *Journal of Field Archaeology* 15: 265–276.

Moore, Jerry (1988). "Prehispanic Beer in Coastal Peru: Technology and Social Context of Prehistoric Production." *American Anthropologist* 91: 682–695.

Quebrada Santa Cristina

TIME PERIOD: c. 600–480 B.P.

LOCATION: Approximately 10 km west of the town of Casma, department of Ancash, Peru.

DESCRIPTIVE SUMMARY

Local Environment

Quebrada Santa Cristina is located on the desert coast of northern Peru. Situated on the southern margin of the lower Casma valley, Quebrada Santa Cristina is 1.2 km inland from the Pacific ocean. The site overlooks a large complex of raised agricultural fields.

Physical Features

Quebrada Santa Cristina is a large planned community almost exclusively of cane-walled architecture. The residential area covers 3.11 ha and contains 284 rooms ranging from 8 sq m to 290 sq m in area. The site represents a single occupation thought to have lasted less than 5–10 years (Moore 1991). Ceramics consist of Chimú moldmade black-ware ceramics and vessel forms similar to those discovered at the Chimú capital, Chan Chan. Other artifacts include numerous stone agricultural implements, some evidence for pottery making (ceramic molds, misfired pots, and burnishing stones), but do not include expected numbers of common domestic items like spindle whorls, fishhooks, and fishnets.

The site was constructed by first clearing the rocky slope of stones and then enclosing a roughly rectangular area with a perimeter wall made from canes. This space was in turn subdivided to form room blocks, the largest containing 42 rooms. Concentrations of food debris (shell, macrobotanical remains) and large grinding stones in a few sectors of the site suggest the locations of communal kitchens. Interestingly, plant remains indicate the near-exclusive reliance on storeable maize and beans rather than fresh fruits or vegetables (Moore 1988: 272).

Spatially and chronologically associated with the residential zone is a large complex of raised agricultural fields (Moore 1988, 1991). There are two areas of raised fields, a smaller set (80 ha) on the northern margin of the valley and a larger set (439 ha) on the southern margin directly in front of Quebrada Santa Cristina. The raised fields were built to reclaim waterlogged farmland, the possible result of an El Niño/Southern Oscillation event that triggered torrential flooding in the first half of the 14th century A.D. (Moore 1991: 40).

Cultural Aspects

Quebrada Santa Cristina represents a planned settlement housing agricultural workers, laborers who built the raised fields with the direct support and involvement of the Chimú state. The planned architecture, "nondomestic" residential structures, narrow range of economic activities, and association with the raised fields suggest that Quebrada Santa Cristina was a specialized encampment rather than simply a rural community of commoners. As such, Quebrada Santa Cristina illuminates Chimu agricultural policies (Pozorski 1987), part of a diverse strategy to develop a multivalley empire.

References

Moore, Jerry (1988). "Prehistoric Raised Field Agriculture in the Casma Valley, Peru." *Journal of Field Archaeology* 15: 265–276.

Moore, Jerry (1991). "Cultural Responses to Environmental Catastrophes: Post-El Niño Subsistence on the Prehistoric North Coast of Peru." *Latin American Antiquity* 2: 27–47.

Pozorski, Thomas (1987). "Changing Priorities within the Chimu State: The Role of Irrigation Agriculture." In *The Origins and Development of the Andean State*, ed. J. Haas, S. Pozorski, and T. Pozorski. Cambridge: Cambridge University Press, 111–120.

JERRY MOORE
Department of Anthropology
California State University
Dominguez Hills
Carson, California
United States

Coastal Andean Archaic

Late Preceramic

ABSOLUTE TIME PERIOD: c. 7000–4100 B.P.

RELATIVE TIME PERIOD: Follows the Late Andean Hunting-Collecting tradition and precedes the Early Coastal Andean Formative tradition.

LOCATION: Pacific coast of South America from Ecuador to northern Chile, primarily the narrow coastal desert strip in Peru and northern Chile.

DIAGNOSTIC MATERIAL ATTRIBUTES: Agricultural coastal villages define the Coastal Andean Archaic. The absence of ceramics is also a key diagnostic feature.

CULTURAL SUMMARY

Environment

The Pacific coastline of the Andes is a cool desert environment that has changed little since humans first inhabited the area. Rivers descend from the Andes and deposit rich alluvial fans where they meet the coastline. This alluvium is fertile and relatively lush with grasses, scrub bushes, and small trees, while surrounding areas are hyperarid and almost completely lacking in vegetation. Although deer, birds, and small mammals were present, fish, shellfish, and marine mammals were vital to the Coastal Andean Archaic economy.

Settlements

Coastal Andean Archaic settlements were located along the coastline with access to freshwater from springs. Most settlements were relatively compact agglomerations of dwellings built up without any obvious community plan or layout. Dwellings were both circular and rectangular, and both semisubterranean and surface. The typical dwelling appears to have been circular and semisubterranean with a roof composed of saplings covered with woven mats. However, a wide diversity of dwelling was used by the Coastal Andean Archaic peoples, ranging from circular to rectangular and built from materials as diverse as stone, reed mats, and packed clay. Regardless of their form, most dwellings were relatively small and only large enough to house a single family. Late in the tradition, what appear to be larger dwellings and compounds are present, as are the first large public structures such as pyramids and temples, which come to prominence among the Early Coastal Andean Formative peoples.

Economy

The Coastal Andean Archaic peoples subsisted on a combination of domesticated and wild foods. Domesticated plants raised by the Coastal Andean Archaic peoples included squash, gourds, beans, maize, potatoes, and cotton, among others. Some scholars have suggested that domesticated llamas, guinea pigs, and ducks were also kept, but their context is uncertain. Wild foods came almost exclusively from the sea and included fish, shellfish, and sea mammals. Some inland mammals, such as deer, were also hunted, as were birds, reptiles, and land mollusks.

Technology was relatively simple and was available to everyone. Basic tools included chipped-stone knives, scrapers, and projectile points; stone grinding slabs, mortars, and pestles; bone tools of various kinds; shell hoes and scrapers; wooden digging sticks; and a range of twined textiles such as bags, fishing lines, and nets. Ceramics were not manufactured by the Coastal Andean Archaic peoples. Ornaments used by the Coastal Andean Archaic peoples included textiles and beads made from shell, bone, and stone. Trade between neighboring communities took place, but most items appear to have been manufactured from locally available materials.

Sociopolitical Organization

The large communities inhabited by the Coastal Andean Archaic peoples suggest some degree of political centralization was likely present, if only to maintain peaceful relationships in these communities. Large public works such as pyramids and temples would have required some degree of labor organization. However, evidence for social stratification is not present until late in the tradition and is modest even then. It seems likely that leaders were present, but that they were not strongly differentiated from other members of society.

Leaders' roles would have been as coordinators and facilitators rather than as strong figures of authority.

Religion and Expressive Culture

Burials with grave goods of various kinds, including utilitarian objects, suggest a belief in the afterlife. The development of temples late in the tradition suggests that the Coastal Andean Archaic peoples held religious beliefs similar to those that became elaborated during the Early Coastal Andean Formative Tradition.

Suggested Readings

Burger, Richard (1992). *Chavin and the Origins of Andean Civilization.* London: Thames and Hudson.

Lumbreras, Luis G. (1972). *The Peoples and Cultures of Ancient Peru.* Washington, D.C.: Smithsonian Institution Press.

Moseley, Michael E. (1975). *The Maritime Foundations of Andean Civilization.* Menlo Park: Cummings.

Moseley, Michael E. (1992). *The Incas and Their Ancestors: The Archaeology of Peru.* New York: Thames and Hudson.

Pineda, Rosa Fung (1988). "The Late Preceramic and Initial Period." In *Peruvian Prehistory,* ed. R. W. Keatinge. Cambridge: Cambridge University Press, 67–96.

Peter N. Peregrine
Department of Anthropology
Lawrence University
Appleton, Wisconsin
United States

Early Amazonian

ABSOLUTE TIME PERIOD: 7000–2000 B.P. Radiocarbon dates on charcoal, shells, and carbon on and in the pottery and thermoluminescence dates on the same pottery yielded an age range of 7500–5000 B.P. (8000–5000 cal B.P.) for Taperinha and Pedra Pintada, the two earliest sites of the tradition. This age range is commonly known as the Pottery Archaic. A total of about 34 dates from nine other early sites in the Lower Amazon extend the age a little earlier and later. Roughly similar cultural and food remains were found at all the dated sites. The age range 4000–2000 B.P. is commonly known as the Formative period. The Aroxi culture at Pedra Pintada, for example, yielded dates between 3300–3000 on a human cranium, turtleshell piece, and palm seed. The Ananatuba culture on Marajo island yielded a date of c. 3000 B.P. The earliest radiocarbon dates from the Upper Amazon in Peru and Bolivia, in comparison, were c. 3000 B.P. The earliest dates for pottery from peripheries south of the Amazon mainstream at Carajas were about 1500 B.P.

RELATIVE TIME PERIOD: Follows the Old Amazonian Collecting-Hunting tradition, precedes the Late Amazonian tradition.

LOCATION: The Pottery Archaic subtradition has been excavated and dated in the Brazilian Amazon mainstream, estuary, and coastal plain of the Guianas. Potential sites have also been found along the main rivers and river lakes in Bolivia, Peru, Ecuador, Colombia, and Brazil. The Formative subtradition is found in the same areas and also in the Orinoco.

DIAGNOSTIC MATERIAL ATTRIBUTES: At least partly sedentary villagers relying mainly on fishing and shellfishing supplemented with plant collection, hunting, and probably plant cultivation by the end of the tradition. The pottery tradition begins with simple pottery bowls and ends with more varied pottery. Deposits of the Pottery Archaic subtradition was first identified in excavations in large shell midden sites along the mainstream Amazon and its estuary in the lower Amazon of Brazil and the coastal plain of the Guianas. Most of the pottery sherds found in the earliest sites are from plain sand-tempered bowls. Only a few sherds at each site were decorated, with red paint, incision, or corrugation, depending on the site. Some pottery at some of the later sites of the tradition is shell tempered, but grit or sand temper continues to be more common. About 1000 sherds have been recovered from the early Holocene levels of Taperinha, of which about 3 percent are decorated with repeated geometric grooved designs. Later, Formative subtradition sites have more elaborate pottery with broadline incision, zoned incised hatched, red and white paint, modeling, *adorno* bowls, and animal effigy vessels. Some of these Formative subtradition sites have griddles; others have decorative stamps and tobacco effigy pipes. The most common figurative images are zoomorphic, but there are rare anthropomorphic animals, too. Grit temper is common, but sherd temper was characteristic of the sites on Marajo island at the south of the Amazon. Bone and shell were made into tools, such as scrapers and simple figurative carvings. Some sites have crude flaked lithics, others not.

CULTURAL SUMMARY

Environment

The environment of this culture tends to be the floodplains of the Amazon and its tributaries. The numerous identified numerous subfossil plant and animal remains and the plant stable isotopes from early sites such as Taperinha and Pedra Pintada in Para indicate that vegetation was similar to today but somewhat moister and denser during the early part of the period. Forest signatures dominate the isotope record. Climate records from pollen cores in the Guianas, Monte Alegre, and the Ecuadorian Amazon suggest that river levels are high in the early and middle Holocene. Pollen from near Monte Alegre reveals tropical forest vegetation and human disturbance species of the types encouraged by cutting and burning, but because there is no evidence of agricultural pollen in the early part of the tradition, the earliest clearings may have been for settlement and hunting purposes. The fauna are familiar taxa known in the area today. Freshwater taxa, especially fish and shellfish, make up the most numerous fauna, as in earlier and later periods. Manatee and crocodile bones are present but very rare. Among land fauna, small creatures, such as frogs, turtles, tortoises, lizards, and rodents, are the most common, but always less common than fish and shellfish.

Settlements

An Early Amazonian site has been excavated at Taperinha, near Santarem on the lower Amazon in Para, Brazil. This mound still stands about 6 m high and appears to have been about 5 ha in area originally. The mound is composed primarily of shells of freshwater pearly mussels. It is encircled by a nonmound zone containing faunal remains and artifacts. The nonmound areas contain scattered, flexed human skeletons.

At Pedra Pintada site, pottery and food remains of the Paituna culture have yielded dates in the early range of the tradition. The deposit consists of shellfish, fish, and carbonized fruits mixed with thick grit-tempered pottery. A later deposit of the later Aroxi culture also has been excavated at Pedra Pintada cave. Its pottery is an oxidized ware with coarse sand tempering. The Aroxi deposit contains numerous human burials that are very poorly preserved, except for their teeth.

Economy

The subsistence remains found in the Taperinha mound consist of large quantities of shells of freshwater pearly mussels, fishbones, and turtle and tortoise shells. Remains of plant foods and larger fauna are very rare, although lizards and frogs were identified among the land fauna. Deposits of the tradition at Pedra Pintada also had numerous fragments of mussel shells, fishbones, and turtle carapaces, and there were carbonized palm fruits, as well. At both sites, shells are the most common food remain, but allometric considerations suggest that fish and shellfish were equally important in the diet. Later deposits, such as the Aroxi culture deposit at Pedra Pintada, lack the superabundance of shells found earlier and include thick griddle sherds. Because no maize has been found at eastern sites of the tradition, manioc may have been a Formative staple food cooked on griddles. At Pedra Pintada, Aroxi bone chemistry has essentially a forest signature, which does not admit important consumption of maize. The fauna seem to have furnished the protein component of the subsistence in this particular area. In the far west, in the Ecuadorian Amazon, pollen profiles suggest quite intensive maize cultivation by about 3000 years ago, but human bone chemistries suggest consumption was low until the end of the prehistoric period. Disturbances in the laminae of cores suggest that rare traces of maize phytoliths as early as 6000 years ago in pollen cores from lake Ayauchi, Ecuador, may be related to intrusions in the cores, rather than to early maize cultivation. Health was probably generally good among people of the populations, because their teeth show very few pathologies.

Sociopolitical Organization

The settlements of this tradition appear to have been small villages or temporary, recurrently occupied campsites. Although postholes have been uncovered at Taperinha, broad-area excavation will be necessary to determine the size and shape of structures. Community composition and organization, therefore, are difficult to reconstruct. In the Antilles, sites of related Formative cultures are large, communal houses of poles, thatch, and earth floors. The archaeological remains are similar to common indigenous house forms in the Amazon in the 20th century. If one can speculate about social organization based on the parallels, then it may be that the Formative communities were made up of one or more communally housed residence groups of nuclear families related through either the husband or the wife. As for gender relations and division of labor, the most important foods of the tradition, whether fish and shellfish early in the tradition or fish and root crops late in the tradition, are those produced by women and children. In terms of crafts, traditionally indigenous Amazonian women are the pottery makers and the painters, so given the importance of the craft and its highly elaborate, ritualized decoration in the later part of the tradition, we can perhaps guess that women as well as men gained status and influence as shaman and artists.

Religion and Expressive Culture

So little figurative art has been found in the earliest sites that it is not possible to speculate about its content, although few designs known are similar to those found in later cultures. The art of the later cultures is dominated by images of animals and geometric motifs suggesting parts of animals, such as ears and eyebrows. The only humanlike images bear both animal features and human hands, feet, posture, and ornaments. These mixed images tend to be larger and more central than the purely animal images. Interpreted from the point of view of current Amazonian cosmology, the art suggests beliefs in shamanic ancestor worship, in which part animal, part human ancestral spirits act as intermediaries between people and the other world. So far, no urn burials of this tradition have been noted. Burials are either flexed, as at Pedra Pintada and Taperinha, or extended, as at Yarinacocha in Peru. If the later urn burial is an adjunct of ranking based on ancestry, then one might conclude that ranking was not a feature of the Early Amazonian Tradition cultures.

Suggested Readings

Evans, C., and B. J. Meggers (1960). "Archaeological Investigations in British Guiana." *Bulletin of the Bureau of American Ethnology* 177.

Lathrap, D. (1970). *The Upper Amazon.* New York: Praeger.

Piperno, D. R. (1995). "Plant Microfossils and Their Application in the New World Tropics." In *Archaeology in the Lowland American Tropics: Current Analytical Methods and Recent Applications*, ed. P. Stahl. Cambridge: Cambridge University Press, 130–153.

Piperno, D. R., and D. M. Pearsall (1998). *The Origins of Agriculture in the Lowland Tropics.* San Diego: Academic Press.

Roosevelt, A. C. (1980). *Parmana: Prehistoric Maize and Manioc Subsistence along the Amazon and Orinoco.* New York: Academic Press.

Roosevelt, A. C. (1989). "Resource Management in Amazonia before the Conquest: Beyond Ethnographic Projection." In *Resource Management in Amazonia: Indigenous and Folk Strategies*, eds. W. Balee and D. Posey. Advances in Economic Botany, vol. 7. New York: New York Botanical Garden, 30–62.

Roosevelt, A. C. (1995). "Early Pottery in the Amazon: Twenty Years of Scholarly Obscurity." In *The Emergence of Pottery: Technology and Innovation in Ancient Societies*, eds. W. Barnett and J. Hoopes. Washington, D.C.: Smithsonian Institution, 115–131.

Roosevelt, A. C. (1997). "The Excavations at Corozal, Venezuela: Stratigraphy and Ceramic Seriation." *Yale University Publications in Anthropology* 83.

Roosevelt, A. C. (1998). "Paleoindian and Archaic Occupations in the Lower Amazon: A Summary and Comparison." In *Explorations in American Archaeology: Essays in Honor of Wesley R. Hurt*, ed. M. G. Plew. Lanham, MD: University Press of America, 165–191.

Roosevelt, A. C. (1999). "The Maritime-Highland-Forest Dynamic and the Origins of Complex Society." In *History of the Native Peoples of the Americas. South America*, eds. F. Salomon and S. Schwartz. Cambridge: Cambridge University Press, 264–349.

Roosevelt, A. C., Rupert Housley, Maura Imazio da Silveira, Silvia Maranca, and Richard Johnson (1991). "Eighth Millennium Pottery from a Prehistoric Shell Midden in the Brazilian Amazon." *Science* 254: 1621–1624.

ANNA ROOSEVELT
Department of Anthropology
The Field Museum
and
Department of Anthropology
University of Illinois
Chicago, Illinois
United States

Early Coastal Andean Formative

Initial Period

ABSOLUTE TIME PERIOD: 4100–3000 B.P.

LOCATION: A narrow coastal desert strip 20–50 km wide running along the Pacific coast within the modern borders of Peru between the La Leche valley in the north and the Lurin valley in the south.

RELATIVE TIME PERIOD: Follows the Late Coastal Andean Archaic tradition and precedes the Late Coastal Andean Formative tradition.

DIAGNOSTIC MATERIAL ATTRIBUTES: Pottery is relatively thin and unevenly fired, with principal forms being neckless ollas, short-necked jars, and open bowls. Some thin-walled stirrup-spout vessels occur in sites along the north coast. Twined and woven cotton textiles are present. Sites are dominated by very large bilaterally symmetrical flat-topped mounds associated with rectangular and circular plazas. Medium-sized stone mounds are often present and laid out in precisely aligned rows.

REGIONAL SUBTRADITIONS: Central Coast Early Coastal Andean Formative, North Coast Early Coastal Andean Formative, North-Central Coast Early Coastal Andean Formative.

IMPORTANT SITES: Cardal, Cerro Blanco, Cerro Sechin, Garagay, Huaca de los Reyes, Huaca Lucia, La Florida, Las Haldas, Monte Grande, Pampa de las Llamas-Moxeke, Punkuri, Purulen, Sechin Alto, Taukachi-Konkan.

CULTURAL SUMMARY

Environment

Climate. The Early Coastal Formative tradition evolved in a hyperarid desert environment that has changed little since the Pleistocene. The coast is a cool desert with relatively high humidity that ranges in temperature from about 60° F in the winter to about 80° F in the summer.

Topography. The Early Coastal Formative tradition is present within the confines of most major coastal river valleys as well as along the coastline adjacent to favorable places for fish and shellfish exploitation. Significant topographic changes include the aggradation of river valleys and the progradation of alluvial deposits at river mouths, which eventually filled in most estuaries that once supplied ready sources of aquatic food.

Geology. The Early Coastal Formative region is characterized by numerous river valleys that descend the western slopes of the Andes mountains, opening up to wider alluvial fan deposits within 30 km of the Pacific coastline. Feeding laterally into the main river channels are various colluvial channels that contain water and sediment only during rare El Niño rain events. Outside the river valleys, conditions are hyperarid, characterized by bedrock overlain by eolian deposits of various ages. Granodiorite, andesite, and basalt are readily available in most areas for use in construction.

Biota. The Early Coastal Formative region is characterized by river valleys substantially altered by human intervention. Natural floodplains with associated vegetation are fairly narrow in most coastal valleys. At the beginning of the Early Coastal Formative, irrigation agriculture was introduced, and cultivation zones quickly expanded out onto desert areas previously completely lacking in plant growth. This rapid expansion drastically reduced the area of natural vegetation, which included "*algarrobo*" trees and scrub bushes while also eliminating most of the edible land fauna such as whitetailed deer. Animal protein was obtained throughout the time period, primarily from the Pacific ocean in the form of fish and shellfish.

Settlements

Settlement System. Early Coastal Formative settlements seem to consist of four primary kinds of sites: (1) large centers with multiple symmetrical platform mounds of various sizes laid out according to a precise plan and often associated with a substantial residential population; (2) centers with one large symmetrical platform mound that may or may not be associated with a substantial residential population; (3) farming villages, located along the edges of river valleys, which contain abundant refuse and evidence of habitation structures; and (4) fishing villages, located along the coastline between river valleys, which contain ample evidence of refuse and habitation structures. There seems to have been a settlement hierarchy in which the largest settlements served as the centers of valleywide polities while smaller sites served various economic support roles. Most significant were the inland villages and centers, which exchanged agricultural products for marine products gathered by inhabitants of the coastal villages. Exchange of products was controlled by the large centers through smaller centers characterized by a single mound, which served as the bureaucratic node for the exchange network.

Community Organization. The two larger types of sites are generally well planned with a central axis that bisects and is defined by the main mounds and central plazas of the site. Smaller mounds and structures line the sides of the main plazas. Smaller villages show little evidence of planning save for an occasional small mound that has

a bilaterally symmetrical layout. Inhabitants of fishing villages provided marine products for themselves as well as for inhabitants of all types of sites situated within the river valleys. Villages and larger centers had farming populations that grew and supplied food for themselves as well as for people in coastal fishing villages. Production of ceramics and important artifacts such as groundstone bowls and mortars appears to have taken place at the major centers.

Housing. Early Coastal Formative houses tend to be small (2–4 m on a side) and rectangular or quadrangular in shape, presumably for nuclear families. Double-faced stone walls form the base of each structure, with the original superstructure constructed of either cane or wood covered with mud plaster. At a few sites, the houses seem to be clustered into groups surrounded by a low wall, perhaps delineating some sort of community or kinship unit. Higher status houses tend to be slightly larger (4–6 m on a side), with quarried stone making up more of the height of the structures' walls. A few sites contain small circular stone structures (about 3 m in diameter), containing central hearths with subfloor flues, which rest on low rectangular platforms. The superstructures of these buildings was cane covered with mud plaster. It is likely that these were ritual buildings used by small groups, similar to sweat houses used by certain North American Indian groups.

Population, Health, and Disease. Larger sites probably housed about 1000–3000 people. Smaller sites held only a few hundred individuals.

Economy

Subsistence. The Early Coastal Formative subsistence was based on permanent agriculture practiced within the irrigated coastal river valleys. Wild food resources came almost exclusively from the Pacific ocean.

Wild Foods. Almost no wild plant food sources were utilized or even available to the people of the Early Coastal Formative tradition. Very early within the tradition, whitetailed deer were hunted within the vegetation zones of the river floodplains, but these animals were quickly eliminated and their habitats destroyed by the expansion of irrigation agriculture. Fish and shellfish were gathered by inhabitants of coastal fishing villages who exchanged these products for inland agricultural products. The marine products offered a stable year-round source of protein.

Domestic Foods. The vast majority of the food eaten by the people of this time period came from irrigation agriculture. The primary domesticates were peanuts, common beans, lima beans, squash, potatoes, sweet potatoes, avocadoes, *lucuma*, guava, and *cansaboca*. Cotton and gourd were also grown for industrial purposes. Depending on the river valley, from one to three crops per year could be grown.

Industrial Arts. Early Coastal Formative technology was simple and available to everyone. Most items were probably manufactured by individuals within households.

Utensils. Primary utensils were (1) thin-walled pottery, which was unevenly fired and made from local soils; (2) scrapers and hoes made from large, locally available marine shells; (3) ceramic spindle whorls; (4) flaked stemmed projectile points; (5) pointed wooden digging sticks; and (6) ground-stone vessels, mortars, and pestles made of locally available stone. Pottery forms include neckless ollas, short-necked jars, and open bowls decorated with punctations, incising, and appliqué bumps. Some solid ceramic figurines are also present.

Ornaments. Both woven and twined textiles are present. Beads made of marine shell, bird bones, turquoise, biotite, and *chrysocolla* are the most common types of ornaments. Red pigment is commonly found, some of which may have been used as body paint.

Trade. Very little physical evidence has been found of possible trade items. Most artifacts appear to have been made of locally available materials. A few small pieces of *Spondylus* shell have been recovered, suggesting at least some minor long-distance trade with people along the southern coast of Ecuador. Such trade probably involved several parties in a down-the-line type of exchange system.

Division of Labor. Specialists may have been present during this time period to produce ceramics and stone vessels/mortars, but no definite workshops have yet been reported.

Differential Access or Control of Resources. Elites appear to have controlled the production and distribution of food and some manufactured items as well as the distribution of irrigation water.

Sociopolitical Organization

Political Organization. Settlement patterns and artifact distributions suggest that polities were organized around a single individual or small group of individuals. Site-size hierarchy suggests that two, possibly three, levels of authority existed in some places, representing a chiefdom or incipient state level organization. Enormous mound constructions, used for various purposes, were associated with the highest level of authority, which exercised a certain degree of coercive power to ensure the construction and maintenance of these buildings.

Conflict. There is little direct evidence for conflict reflected in architecture. However, one site displays iconography suggesting possible conflict between two groups involving human body dismemberment.

Religion and Expressive Culture

Religious Beliefs. Iconography suggests that religious beliefs included supernatural beings in the form of animals such as felines, caimans, crustaceans, and spiders. Human forms are also quite common, possibly representing major deities, cultural heroes, and participants in ritual human sacrifice.

Ceremonies. Public ceremonies most likely took place in large rectangular and circular plazas associated with large flat-topped mounds, many of which were once decorated with impressive polychrome mud sculptures. Private rituals may have occurred within small rooms on mound summits and within small roofed circular structures that contained central ventilated hearths.

Arts. Inhabitants of this time period used a variety of media for art. Monumental art included mud sculptures or friezes on the walls of large mounds, rendered in both naturalistic and geometric forms. A limited amount of stone sculpture was also incorporated into the walls of substantial structures. Portable art, both geometric and naturalistic, was depicted on ceramics; ground-stone vessels; and both woven and twined textiles. Part-time or full-time specialists may have been needed to effect some of the more elaborate artistic accomplishments.

Death and Afterlife. Few burials have been recovered from the period. Most contain few if any grave goods, reflecting the relative scarcity of exotic materials and goods available during the Early Coastal Formative. Status differences do not seem to have been expressed through grave goods at this time.

Suggested Readings

Burger, Richard L. (1992). *Chavin and the Origins of Andean Civilization*. London: Thames and Hudson.

Donnan, Christopher, ed. (1985). *Early Ceremonial Architecture in the Andes*. Washington, D.C.: Dumbarton Oaks Research Library and Collection.

Haas, Jonathan, Shelia, Pozorski, and Thomas Pozorski, eds. (1987). *The Origins and Development of the Andean State*. Cambridge: Cambridge University Press.

Keatinge, Richard (1988). *Peruvian Prehistory*. Cambridge: Cambridge University Press.

Moseley, Michael (1983). "Central Andean Civilization." In *Ancient South Americans*, ed. J. Jennings. San Francisco: W. H. Freeman, 179–239.

Moseley, Michael (1992). *The Incas and Their Ancestors*. London: Thames and Hudson.

Pozorski, Shelia, and Thomas Pozorski (1987). *Early Settlement and Subsistence in the Casma Valley, Peru*. Iowa City: University of Iowa Press.

Pozorski, Shelia, and Thomas Pozorski (1992). "Early Civilization in the Casma Valley, Peru." *Antiquity* 66: 845–870.

Richardson, James (1994). *People of the Andes*. Washington, D.C.: Smithsonian Books.

Tello, Julio C. (1956). *Arqueologia del valle de Casma: Culturas Chavin, Santa o Huaylas Yunga y Sub-Chimu*. Lima: Universidad Nacional Mayor de San Marcos.

SUBTRADITIONS

Central Coast Early Coastal Formative

TIME PERIOD: 4100–3000 B.P.

LOCATION: A narrow coastal strip 20–50 km wide along the Pacific coast from the Fortaleza valley in the north to the Lurin valley in the south.

DIAGNOSTIC MATERIAL ATTRIBUTES: Pottery is relatively thin and unevenly fired, with principal forms being neckless ollas, short-necked jars, and open bowls. Twined and woven cotton textiles are present. Sites are dominated by enormous, U-shaped bilaterally symmetrical flat-topped mounds associated with rectangular and circular plazas.

CULTURAL SUMMARY

Environment

The climate experienced by the people of this subtradition was cool and hyperarid, much like the modern climate. The topography of the area is characterized by a long, narrow coastal desert strip periodically cut by numerous river channels that descend the western slopes of the Andes mountains (Burger 1992; Richardson 1994). Vegetation, mostly confined to the narrow coastal river valleys, is present well beyond the confines of natural floodplains because of irrigation agriculture, which has supported coastal life for at least the last 4000 years (Moseley 1983, 1992). Most food eaten by people consisted of domesticated plants grown in the river valleys. Fish and shellfish from the Pacific ocean provided most of the animal protein consumed by people of this subtradition (Fung 1988).

Settlements

Central Coast Early Coastal Formative settlements seem to consist of three primary kinds of sites: (1) centers with one or more large symmetrical platform mounds that may or may not be associated with a substantial residential population (Burger 1992; Patterson 1985); (2) farming villages, located along the edges of river valleys, which contain abundant refuse and evidence of habitation structures; and (3) fishing villages, located along the coastline between river valleys, which contain ample evidence of refuse and habitation structures. The major platform mounds are often U-shaped in plan and were built over a relatively long period of time in numerous construction phases (Burger 1987, 1992; Burger and Salazar-Burger 1991; Williams 1985). A partial settlement hierarchy apparently existed, in which the larger settlements served as centers of local polities with smaller sites serving various support roles (Burger 1992). Inhabitants of inland coastal sites grew agricultural products that were exchanged for marine fish and shellfish gathered by people living in coastal fishing villages (Fung 1988). Ceramics and ground-stone artifacts were apparently produced at the major centers. House size ranges from 2–4 m on a side for lower status dwellings to 4–6 m on a side for higher status dwellings. Double-faced stone walls form the base of each structure with the original superstructure constructed of either cane or wood covered with mud plaster (Burger 1992; Burger and Salazar-Burger 1991). Some of the larger sites may have housed several hundred people, whereas smaller sites contained only several dozen to a few hundred individuals (Burger 1992).

Economy

The people of the Central Coast Early Coastal Formative relied almost exclusively on irrigation agriculture to grow a wide variety of plant foods, including peanuts, common beans, lima beans, squash, potatoes, sweet potatoes, avocadoes, *lucuma*, guava, *cansaboca*, gourd, and cotton (Burger 1992; Fung 1988). Marine fish and shellfish provided most of the animal protein during this time period; deer were occasionally hunted (Burger 1992; Fung 1988). Primary utensils were thin-walled pottery, unevenly fired, made from local soils. Characteristic pottery forms include neckless ollas, short-necked jars, open bowls, and bottles decorated with punctations, incisions, appliqué bumps, and occasional figurative designs (Burger 1992; Fung 1988; Patterson 1985; Ravines et al. 1982). Both woven and twined textiles are present (Burger 1992; Ravines et al. 1982). Beads made of marine shell, bird bone, turquoise, and *chrysocolla* are the most common types of ornaments. There is little evidence of trade, with most artifacts being made out of locally available materials. A few pieces of *Spondylus* shell recovered from secure context suggest minor long-distance trade with the people of the southern coast of Ecuador (Burger 1992). Such trade was probably down-the-line type of exchange involving several parties. Specialists may have produced some of the finer artifacts, although no workshops have yet been found. Elites probably had some control over the production and distribution of food and some manufactured items as well as the distribution of irrigation water (Burger 1992).

Sociopolitical Organization

Settlement patterns and artifact distributions suggest that polities were organized around a single individual or small group of individuals. Site-size hierarchy suggests that two levels of authority existed in some places, representing a chiefdom level organization (Burger 1992; Patterson 1985; Ravines 1982, 1984). Large mounds, constructed in multiple phases over a period of centuries and used for various purposes, were associated with community leaders who were able to persuade their followers to build and maintain these buildings (Burger 1992). There is little direct evidence for conflict reflected in architecture.

Religion and Expressive Culture

Iconography suggests that religious beliefs included supernatural beings in the form of animals such as felines, crustaceans, and spiders (Bischof 1994; Burger 1992; Patterson 1985). Human forms are common, possibly representing major deities or cultural heroes (Bischof; Burger 1992; Ravines and Isbell 1975). Public ceremonies most likely took place in large rectangular and circular plazas associated with large flat-topped mounds (Burger 1992; Ravines 1982, 1984; Ravines and Isbell 1975). Private rituals possibly occurred within small rooms on mound summits (Burger 1992). Inhabitants of this time period used a variety of media for art. Monumental art included mud sculptures or friezes on the facades of large mounds, rendered in both naturalistic and geometric forms (Bischof 1994; Burger 1992; Burger and Salazar-Burger 1991). Portable art, both geometric and naturalistic, was depicted on ceramics; and both woven and twined textiles (Ravines et al. 1982). Part-time or full-time specialists may have been needed to effect some of the more elaborate artistic accomplishments. Relatively few burials have been recovered from the period. A few contain exotic grave goods, reflecting the limited access to such materials at this time period (Burger 1992; Moseley 1992).

Suggested Readings

Bischof, Henning (1994). "Toward the Definition of Pre- and Early Chavin Art Styles in Peru." *Andean Past* 4: 169–228.

Burger, Richard (1987). "The U-shaped Pyramid Complex, Cardal, Peru." *National Geographic Research* 3, 3: 363–375.

Burger, Richard L. (1992). *Chavin and the Origins of Andean Civilization*. London: Thames and Hudson.

Burger, Richard, and Lucy Salazar-Burger (1991). "Recent Investigations at the Initial Period Center of Cardal, Lurin Valley." *Journal of Field Archaeology* 18: 275–296.

Fung, Rosa (1988). "The Late Preceramic and Initial Period." In *Peruvian Prehistory*, ed. R. Keatinge. Cambridge: Cambridge University Press, 67–96.

Moseley, Michael (1983). "Central Andean Civilization." In *Ancient South Americans*, ed. J. Jennings. San Francisco: W. H. Freeman, 179–239.

Moseley, Michael (1992). *The Incas and Their Ancestors*. London: Thames and Hudson.

Patterson, Thomas (1985). "The Huaca La Florida, Rimac Valley, Peru." In *Early Ceremonial Architecture in the Andes*, ed. C. B. Donnan. Washington, D.C.: Dumbarton Oaks Research Library and Collection, 59–69.

Ravines, Rogger (1982). *Panorama de la arqueologia Andina*. Lima: Instituto de Estudios Peruanos.

Ravines, Rogger (1984). "Sobre la formacion de Chavin: Imagenes y simbolos." *Boletin de Lima* 35: 27–45.

Ravines, Rogger, and William Isbell (1975). "Garagay: Sitio ceremonial temprano en el valle de Lima." *Revista del Museo Nacional* 41: 253–275.

Ravines, Rogger, Helen Engelstad, Victoria Palomino, and Daniel Sandweiss (1982). "Materiales arqueologicos de Garagay." *Revista del Museo Nacional* 46: 135–233.

Richardson, James (1994). *People of the Andes*. Washington, D.C.: Smithsonian Books.

Williams, Carlos (1985). "A Scheme for the Early Monumental Architecture of the Central Coast of Peru." In *Early Ceremonial Architecture in the Andes*, ed. C. B. Donnan. Washington, D.C.: Dumbarton Oaks Research Library and Collection, 227–240.

North Coast Early Coastal Formative

TIME PERIOD: 4100–3000 B.P.

LOCATION: A narrow coastal strip 20–50 km wide along the Pacific coast from the La Leche valley in the north to the Viru valley in the south.

DIAGNOSTIC MATERIAL ATTRIBUTES: Pottery is relatively thin and unevenly fired with principal forms being neckless ollas, short-necked jars, open bowls, and stirrup-spout vessels. Twined and woven cotton textiles are present. Sites are dominated by large, U-shaped bilaterally symmetrical flat-topped mounds associated with colonnades and rectangular plazas.

CULTURAL SUMMARY

Environment

The climate experienced by the people of this subtradition was cool and hyperarid, much like the modern climate. The topography of the area is characterized by a long, narrow coastal desert strip periodically cut by numerous river channels that descend the western slopes of the Andes mountains (Burger 1992; Richardson 1994). Vegetation, mostly confined to the narrow coastal river valleys, is present well beyond the confines of natural floodplains because of irrigation agriculture, which has supported coastal life for at least the last 4000 years (Moseley 1983, 1992). Most food eaten by people of this subtradition consisted of domesticated plants grown in the river valleys. Fish and shellfish from the Pacific ocean provided most of the animal protein consumed (Fung 1988).

Settlements

North Coast Early Coastal Formative settlements seem to consist of three primary kinds of sites: (1) centers with one or more large symmetrical platform mounds that may or may not be associated with a substantial residential population (Alva 1987, 1988; T. Pozorski 1982; Ravines 1985); (2) farming villages, located along the edges of river valleys, which contain abundant refuse and evidence of habitation structures; and (3) fishing villages, located along the coastline between river valleys, which contain ample evidence of refuse and habitation structures. The major platform mounds are often U-shaped in plan, contain colonnades, and were constructed in only one or two relatively large construction phases (T. Pozorski 1995; Shimada 1981, 1982; Shimada et al. 1982). There seems to have been a settlement hierarchy in which the largest settlements served as the centers of valleywide polities with smaller sites serving various economic support roles. Inhabitants of inland coastal sites grew agricultural products that were exchanged for marine fish and shellfish gathered by people living in coastal fishing villages (Pozorski and Pozorski 1979). Ceramics and ground-stone artifacts were apparently produced at the major centers (T. Pozorski 1976; Ulbert 1994). House sizes range from 2–4 m on a side for lower status dwellings to 4–6 m on a side for higher status dwellings. Double-faced stone walls form the base of each structure with the original superstructure constructed of either cane or wood covered with mud plaster (Tellenbach 1986). The larger sites probably housed between 1000–3000 people, whereas smaller sites contained only a few hundred individuals.

Economy

The people of the North Coast Early Coastal Formative relied almost exclusively on irrigation agriculture to grow a wide variety of plant foods including peanuts, common beans, lima beans, squash, potatoes, sweet potatoes, avocadoes, *lucuma*, guava, *cansaboca*, gourd, and cotton (S. Pozorski 1976; Pozorski and Pozorski 1979). Although whitetailed deer were consumed early in the subtradition, these animals quickly disappeared because of overexploitation and the destruction of their habitat by the expansion of irrigation agriculture in coastal river valleys. Marine fish and shellfish provided most of the animal protein during this time period (Pozorski and Pozorski 1979). Primary utensils were (1) thin-walled pottery, which was unevenly fired and made from local soils; (2) shell scrapers and hoes; (3) pointed wooden digging sticks; and (4) ground-stone vessels, mortars, and pestles. Characteristic pottery forms include neckless ollas, short-necked jars, open bowls, and stirrup-spout vessels decorated with punctations, incisions, and appliqué bumps (T. Pozorski 1976; Tellenbach 1986; Ulbert 1994). Both woven and twined textiles are commonly present (Burger 1992; Moseley 1992; Richardson 1994). Beads made of marine shell, bird bone, turquoise, and *chrysocolla* are the most common types of ornaments. There is little evidence of trade; most artifacts are made of locally available materials. A few pieces of *Spondylus* shell recovered from secure context suggest minor long-distance trade with the people of the southern coast of Ecuador (Burger 1992). Such trade was probably down-the-line type of exchange involving several parties. Specialists may have produced some of the finer artifacts as suggested by the discovery of numerous pottery kilns in the La Leche valley (Burger 1992). Elites probably controlled the production and distribution of food and some manufactured items as well as the distribution of irrigation water (T. Pozorski 1976).

Sociopolitical Organization

Settlement patterns and artifact distributions suggest that polities were organized around a single individual or small group of individuals. Site size hierarchy suggests that two, possibly three, levels of authority existed in some places, representing a chiefdom or possibly incipient state level organization (T. Pozorski 1980, 1982). Large mounds, constructed in relatively few phases and used for various purposes, were associated with the highest level of authority, which exercised a certain degree of coercive power to ensure the construction and maintenance of these buildings (T. Pozorski 1995). There is little direct evidence for conflict reflected in architecture.

Religion and Expressive Culture

Iconography suggests that religious beliefs included supernatural beings in the form of animals such as felines. Human forms are common, possibly representing major deities or cultural heroes. Public ceremonies most likely took place in large rectangular plazas associated with large flat-topped mounds (Burger 1992; T. Pozorski 1982; Pozorski and Pozorski 1993). Private rituals possibly occurred within small rooms on mound summits and within small roofed circular structures that contained central ventilated hearths (Pozorski and Pozorski 1996). Inhabitants of this time period used a variety of media for art. Monumental art included mud sculptures or friezes on the walls of large mounds, rendered in both naturalistic and geometric forms (Moseley and Watanabe 1974; T. Pozorski 1975, 1980). Portable art, both geometric and naturalistic, took the form of ceramics, ground-stone vessels, and both woven and twined textiles. Part-time or full-time specialists may have been needed to effect some of the more elaborate artistic accomplishments. Relatively few burials have been recovered. Most contain few if any grave goods, reflecting the relative scarcity of exotic materials and goods available during the Early Coastal Formative (Burger 1992; Moseley 1992). Status differences do not seem to have been expressed through grave goods at this time.

References

Alva, Walter (1987). "Resultados de las excavaciones en el valle de Zaña, norte del Peru." In *Archaologie in Peru—Archaometrie: 1985*, ed. W. Bauer. Stuttgart: Konrad Theiss Verlag, 61–78.

Alva, Walter (1988). "Investigaciones en el complejo Formativo con arquitectura monumental de Purulen, costa norte del Peru (informe preliminar)." *Beiträge zur Allgemeinen und Vergleichenden Archäologie* 8: 283–300.

Burger, Richard L. (1992). *Chavin and the Origins of Andean Civilization*. London: Thames and Hudson.

Fung, Rosa (1988). "The Late Preceramic and Initial Period." In *Peruvian Prehistory*, ed. R. Keatinge. Cambridge: Cambridge University Press, 67–96.

Moseley, Michael (1983). "Central Andean Civilization." In *Ancient South Americans*, ed. J. Jennings. San Francisco: W. H. Freeman, 179–239.

Moseley, Michael (1992). *The Incas and Their Ancestors*. London: Thames and Hudson.

Moseley, Michael, and Luis Watanabe (1974). "The Adobe Sculpture of Huaca de los Reyes: Imposing Artwork from Coastal Peru." *Archaeology* 27: 154–161.

Pozorski, Shelia (1976). "Prehistoric Subsistence Patterns and Site Economics in the Moche Valley, Peru." Ph.D. diss., Department of Anthropology, University of Texas, Austin.

Pozorski, Shelia, and Thomas Pozorski (1979). "An Early Subsistence Exchange System in the Moche Valley, Peru." *Journal of Field Archaeology* 6: 413–432.

Pozorski, Thomas (1975). "El complejo Caballo Muerto: Los frisos de barro de la Huaca de los Reyes." *Revista del Museo Nacional* 41: 211–251.

Pozorski, Thomas (1976). "Caballo Muerto, a Complex of Early Ceramic Sites in the Moche Valley, Peru." Ph.D. diss., Department of Anthropology, University of Texas, Austin.

Pozorski, Thomas (1980). "The Early Horizon Site of Huaca de los Reyes: Societal Implications." *American Antiquity* 45: 100–110.

Pozorski, Thomas (1982). "Early Social Stratification and Subsistence Systems: The Caballo Muerto Complex." In *Chan Chan: Andean Desert City*, ed. M. E. Moseley and K. C. Day. Albuquerque: University of New Mexico Press, 225–253.

Pozorski, Thomas (1995). "Huaca de los Reyes Revisited: Clarification of the Archaeological Evidence." *Latin American Antiquity* 6: 335–339.

Pozorski, Thomas, and Shelia Pozorski (1993). "Early Complex Society and Ceremonialism on the Peruvian North Coast." In *El Mundo Ceremonial Andino*, ed. L. Millones and Y. Onuki. Osaka: National Museum of Ethnology, 45–68.

Thomas Pozorski, and Shelia Pozorski (1996). "Ventilated Hearth Structures in the Casma Valley, Peru." *Latin American Antiquity* 7: 341–353.

Ravines, Rogger (1985). "Early Monumental Architecture in the Jequetepeque Valley, Peru." In *Early Ceremonial Architecture in the Andes*, ed. C. Donnan. Washington, D.C.: Dumbarton Oaks Research Library and Collection, 209–226.

Richardson, James (1994). *People of the Andes.* Washington, D.C.: Smithsonian Books.

Shimada, Izumi (1981). "The Batan Grande-La Leche Archaeological Project: The First Two Seasons." *Journal of Field Archaeology* 8: 405–446.

Shimada, Izumi (1982). "Horizontal Archipelago and Coast-Highland Interaction in North Peru: Archaeological Models." In *El hombre y su ambiente en los Andes Centrales,* ed. L. Millones and H. Tomoeda. Osaka: National Museum of Ethnology, 137–210.

Shimada, Izumi, Carlos Elera, and Melody Shimada (1982). "Excavaciones efectuadas en el centro ceremonial de Huaca Lucia-Cholope, del Horizonte Temprano, Batan Grande, costa norte del Peru: 1979–1981." *Arqueologicas* 19: 109–210.

Tellenbach, Michael (1986). *Las excavaciones en el asentamiento formativo de Montegrande, valle de Jequetepeque en el norte del Peru.* Munich: Verlag C. H. Beck.

Ulbert, Cornelius (1994). *Die Keramik der formativzeitlichen Siedlung Montegrande, Jequetepequetal, Nord-Peru.* Mainz: Verlag Philipp von Zabern.

North-Central Coast Early Coastal Formative

TIME PERIOD: 4100–3000 B.P.

LOCATION: A narrow coastal strip 20–50 km wide along the Pacific coast from the Chao valley in the north to the Huarmey valley in the south.

DIAGNOSTIC MATERIAL ATTRIBUTES: Pottery is relatively thin and unevenly fired, with principal forms being neckless ollas, short-necked jars, and open bowls. Twined and woven cotton textiles are present. Sites are dominated by enormous, U-shaped bilaterally symmetrical flat-topped mounds associated with colonnades and rectangular and circular plazas.

CULTURAL SUMMARY

Environment

The climate experienced by the people of this subtradition was cool and hyperarid, much like the modern climate. The topography of the area was characterized by a long, narrow coastal desert strip periodically cut by numerous river channels that descend the western slopes of the Andes mountains (Burger 1992; Richardson 1994). Vegetation, mostly confined to the narrow coastal river valleys, is present well beyond the confines of natural floodplains because of irrigation agriculture, which has supported coastal

life for at least the last 4000 years (Moseley 1983, 1992). Most food consisted of domesticated plants grown in the river valleys. Fish and shellfish from the Pacific ocean provided most of the animal protein (Fung 1988).

Settlements

North-Central Coast Early Coastal Formative settlements seem to consist of four primary kinds of sites: (1) large centers with multiple symmetrical platform mounds of various sizes carefully laid out according to a precise plan and often associated with a substantial residential population (S. Pozorski 1987; S. Pozorski and T. Pozorski 1991, 1992, 1994a, 1994b); (2) centers with one or more large symmetrical platform mounds that may or may not be associated with a substantial residential population (Larco Hoyle 1941; Maldonado 1992; S. Pozorski and T. Pozorski 1987; Tello 1943); (3) farming villages, located along the edges of river valleys, which contain abundant refuse and evidence of habitation structures; and (4) fishing villages, located along the coastline between river valleys, which contain ample evidence of refuse and habitation structures. The major platform mounds are often U-shaped in plan, contain colonnades, and were constructed in only one or two relatively large construction phases (Grieder 1975; Matsuzawa 1978; S. Pozorski and T. Pozorski 1992). There seems to have been a settlement hierarchy in which the largest settlements served as the centers of valleywide polities while the smaller sites served various economic support roles (S. Pozorski and T. Pozorski 1986, 1991, 1992, 1994b). Inhabitants of inland coastal sites grew agricultural products that were exchanged for marine fish and shellfish gathered by people living in coastal fishing villages (Fung 1969; S. Pozorski and T. Pozorski 1992). Ceramics and ground-stone artifacts were apparently produced at the major centers (T. Pozorski and S. Pozorski 1992). House size ranges from 2–4 m on a side for lower status dwellings to 4–6 m on a side for higher status dwellings. Double-faced stone walls form the base of each structure, with the original superstructure constructed of either cane or wood covered with mud plaster (S. Pozorski and T. Pozorski 1986, 1987). The larger sites probably housed between 1000–3000 people, whereas smaller sites contained only a few hundred individuals (S. Pozorski and T. Pozorski 1994a).

Economy

The people of the North-Central Coast Early Coastal Formative relied almost exclusively on irrigation agriculture to grow a wide variety of plant foods, including peanuts, common beans, lima beans, squash, potatoes, sweet potatoes, avocadoes, *lucuma*, guava, *cansaboca*, gourd, and cotton (Fung 1969; S. Pozorski 1987; S. Pozorski and T. Pozorski 1987). Although whitetailed deer were consumed early in the subtradition, these animals quickly disappeared because of overexploitation and the destruction of their habitat by the expansion of irrigation agriculture in coastal river valleys. Marine fish and shellfish provided most of the animal protein during this time period (S. Pozorski and T. Pozorski 1987). Primary utensils were (1) thin-walled pottery, which was unevenly fired and made from local soils; (2) shell scrapers and hoes; (3) pointed wooden digging sticks; and (4) ground-stone vessels, mortars, and pestles. Characteristic pottery forms include neckless ollas, short-necked jars, open bowls, and bottles decorated with punctations, incisions, appliqué bumps, and graphite paint (Fung 1969; Grieder 1975; S. Pozorski and T. Pozorski 1987). Both woven and twined textiles are commonly present (Burger 1992; S. Pozorski and T. Pozorski 1987). Beads made of marine shell, bird bone, turquoise, biotite, and *chrysocolla* are the most common types of ornaments. There is little evidence of trade, with most artifacts being made out of locally available materials. A few pieces of *Spondylus* shell recovered from secure context suggest minor long-distance trade with the people of the southern coast of Ecuador (Burger 1992). Such trade was probably down-the-line type of exchange involving several parties. Specialists may have produced some of the finer artifacts, although no workshops have yet been found. Elites probably controlled the production and distribution of food and some manufactured items as well as the distribution of irrigation water (S. Pozorski 1987; S. Pozorski and T. Pozorski 1986, 1987).

Sociopolitical Organization

Settlement patterns and artifact distributions suggest that polities were organized around a single individual or small group of individuals. Site-size hierarchy suggests that two, possibly three, levels of authority existed in some places, representing a chiefdom or possibly incipient state level organization (S. Pozorski and T. Pozorski 1987, 1992). Large mounds, constructed in relatively few phases and used for various purposes, were associated with the highest level of authority who exercised a certain degree of coercive power to ensure the construction and maintenance of these buildings (S. Pozorski and T. Pozorski 1986, 1987, 1992). There is little direct evidence for conflict reflected in architecture.

Religion and Expressive Culture

Iconography suggests that religious beliefs included supernatural beings in the form of animals such as felines and fish (Bischof 1994; Larco Hoyle 1941; Maldonado 1992; Tello 1943). Human forms are common, possibly representing major deities or cultural heroes (Bischof 1997; Samaniego et al. 1995; Tello 1956). Public ceremonies most likely took place in large rectangular and circular plazas associated with large flat-topped mounds (Burger 1992; S. Pozorski and T. Pozorski 1986, 1987; T. Pozorski and S. Pozorski 1993). Private rituals possibly occurred within small rooms on mound summits and within small, roofed, circular structures that contained central ventilated hearths (T. Pozorski and S. Pozorski 1996). Inhabitants of this time period used a variety of media for art. Monumental art included mud sculptures or friezes and stone carvings on the facades of large mounds, rendered in both naturalistic and geometric forms (Bischof 1994, 1997; Maldonado 1992; S. Pozorski and T. Pozorski 1986; Samaniego et al. 1995; Tello 1956). Portable art, both geometric and naturalistic, took the form of ceramics; ground-stone vessels; and both woven and twined textiles (S. Pozorski and T. Pozorski 1987). Part-time or full-time specialists may have been needed to produce some of the more elaborate artistic accomplishments. Relatively few burials have been recovered from the period. Most contain few if any grave goods, reflecting the relative scarcity of exotic materials and goods available during the Early Coastal Formative (Burger 1992; Moseley 1992). Status differences do not seem to have been expressed through grave goods at this time.

References

Bischof, Henning (1994). "Toward the Definition of Pre- and Early Chavin Art Styles in Peru." *Andean Past* 4: 169–228.

Bischof, Henning (1997). "Cerro Blanco, valle de Nepeña, Peru—Un sitio del Horizonte Temprano en emergencia." In *Archaeologica Peruana 2: Arquitectura y Civilization en los Andes Prehispanicos*, ed. E. Bonnier and H. Bischof. Mannheim: Sociedad Arqueologica Peruano-Alemana and Reiss-Museum, 202–234.

Burger, Richard L (1992). *Chavin and the Origins of Andean Civilization*. London: Thames and Hudson.

Fung, Rosa (1969). "Las Aldas: Su ubicacion dentro del proceso historico del Peru antiguo." *Dedalo* 5, 9–10: 1–208.

Fung, Rosa (1988). "The Late Preceramic and Initial Period." In *Peruvian Prehistory*, ed. R. Keatinge. Cambridge: Cambridge University Press, 67–96.

Grieder, Terence (1975). "A Dated Sequence of Building and Pottery at Las Haldas." *Ñawpa Pacha* 13: 99–112.

Larco Hoyle, Rafael (1941). *Los Cupisniques*. Lima: Casa Editora La Cronica y Variedades S.A. Ltda.

Maldonado, Elena (1992). *Arqueologia de Cerro Sechin, Tomo I: Arquitectura*. Lima: Pontificia Universidad Catolica del Peru.

Matsuzawa, Tsugio (1978). "The Formative Site of Las Haldas, Peru: Architecture, Chronology, and Economy." *American Antiquity* 43: 652–673.

Moseley, Michael (1983). "Central Andean Civilization." In *Ancient South Americans*, ed. J. Jennings. San Francisco: W. H. Freeman, 179–239.

Moseley, Michael (1992). *The Incas and Their Ancestors*. London: Thames and Hudson.

Pozorski, Shelia (1987). "Theocracy vs. Militarism: The Significance of the Casma Valley in Understanding Early State Formation." In *The Origins and Development of the Andean State*, ed. J. Haas, S. Pozorski, and T. Pozorski. Cambridge: Cambridge University Press, 15–30.

Pozorski, Shelia, and Thomas Pozorski (1986). "Recent Excavations at Pampa de las Llamas-Moxeke, a Complex Initial Period Site in Peru." *Journal of Field Archaeology* 13: 381–401.

Pozorski, Shelia, and Thomas Pozorski (1987). *Early Settlement and Subsistence in the Casma Valley, Peru*. Iowa City: University of Iowa Press.

Pozorski, Shelia, and Thomas Pozorski (1991). "Storage, Access Control, and Bureaucratic Proliferation: Understanding the Initial Period (1800–900 B.C.) Economy at Pampa de las Llamas-Moxeke, Casma Valley, Peru." *Research in Economic Anthropology* 13: 341–371.

Pozorski, Shelia, and Thomas Pozorski (1992). "Early Civilization in the Casma Valley, Peru." *Antiquity* 66: 845–870.

Pozorski, Shelia, and Thomas Pozorski (1994a). "Early Andean Cities." *Scientific American* 270: 66–72.

Pozorski, Shelia, and Thomas Pozorski (1994b). "Multi-Dimensional Planning at Pampa de las Llamas-Moxeke on the North Central Coast of Peru." In *Meaningful Architecture: Social Interpretations of Buildings*, ed. M. Locock. Avebury: Worldwide Archaeology Series, 45–65.

Pozorski, Thomas, and Shelia Pozorski (1992). "Early Stone Bowls and Mortars from Northern Peru." *Andean Past* 3: 165–186.

Pozorski, Thomas, and Shelia Pozorski (1993). "Early Complex Society and Ceremonialism on the Peruvian North Coast." In *El Mundo Ceremonial Andino*, ed. L. Millones and Y. Onuki. Osaka: National Museum of Ethnology, 45–68.

Pozorski, Thomas, and Shelia Pozorski (1996). "Ventilated Hearth Structures in the Casma Valley, Peru." *Latin American Antiquity* 7: 341–353.

Richardson, James (1994). *People of the Andes*. Washington, D.C.: Smithsonian Books.

Samaniego, Lorenzo, Mercedes Cardenas, Henning Bischof, Peter Kaulicke, Erman Guzman, and Wilder Leon (1995). *Arqueologia de Cerro Sechin, Tomo II: Escultura*. Lima: Pontificia Universidad Catolica del Peru.

Tello, Julio C (1943). "Discovery of the Chavin Culture in Peru." *American Antiquity* 9: 135–160.

Tello, Julio C (1956). *Arqueologia del valle de Casma: Culturas Chavin, Santa o Huaylas Yunga y Sub-Chimu*. Lima: Universidad Nacional Mayor de San Marcos.

SITES

Cardal

TIME PERIOD: 3300–2900 B.P.

LOCATION: On the south side of the lower Lurin valley, Peru.

DESCRIPTIVE SUMMARY

Local Environment

Cardal is located along the cultivated south margin of the Lurin valley within a hyperarid desert environment (Burger 1992). Adjacent to the site are foothills of the Andes mountains.

Physical Features

The site is a large U-shaped mound, oriented slightly east of due north, which borders a large central plaza on three sides. The tallest part of the mound is at the base of the U and is ascended by a wide, steep staircase from the central plaza. On the mound summit is a central atrium bordered by a frieze depicting a massive mouth band with interlocking teeth and fangs. The main mound shows evidence of at least five separate construction phases, indicating that the mound and site grew slowly over a long period of time. The site also has 10 sunken circular plazas, two of which are located within the central plaza and eight of which are situated along one side and the base of the U-shaped mound. Just south of the main mound are the remains of a small number of houses for a resident population (Burger 1987, 1992; Burger and Salazar-Burger 1991).

Cultural Aspects

Cardal is one of a number of large U-shaped centers located in the interconnected central coast valleys of Chillon, Rimac, and Lurin. Cardal was one of a number of competing centers concerned with public gathering for ritual and nonritual purposes, and perhaps it served as the main center for a polity centered in the lower Lurin valley. Because the resident population was small, public gatherings consisted mainly of people normally living in smaller outlying settlements, who would gather at the site periodically for special events. The numerous sunken circular courts at the site may represent private ritual areas for certain lineage groups, somewhat like Hopi kivas of the U.S. Southwest (Burger 1987, 1992; Burger and Salazar-Burger 1991).

References

Burger, Richard (1987). "The U-Shaped Pyramid Complex, Cardal, Peru." *National Geographic Research* 3, 3: 363–375.

Burger, Richard L (1992). *Chavin and the Origins of Andean Civilization*. London: Thames and Hudson.

Burger, Richard, and Lucy Salazar-Burger (1991). "Recent Investigations at the Initial Period Center of Cardal, Lurin Valley." *Journal of Field Archaeology* 18: 275–296.

Cerro Blanco

TIME PERIOD: 3500–3000 B.P.

LOCATION: On the north side of the Nepeña valley, Peru.

DESCRIPTIVE SUMMARY

Local Environment

Cerro Blanco is located within modern irrigated land near the middle of the Nepeña valley and north of the Nepeña river. Bordering the modern irrigated land is a hyperarid desert environment with sand dunes and the foothills of the Andes mountains.

Physical Features

The site, covering about 3 ha, consists of a U-shaped mound made of stone and conical adobes, which opens to the northeast. The southeast wing has been partially truncated and separated from the remainder of the site by a modern road. Various excavation campaigns within the southeast wing have exposed several low walls and a platform decorated with polychrome clay friezes with anthropomorphic, feline, and avian characteristics—all rendered in a rectilinear style (Bischof 1997; Burger 1992; Tello 1943).

Cultural Aspects

Scholars usually interpret Cerro Blanco as a religious edifice (Bischof 1997; Burger 1992). Its dating is in dispute. Based on the iconography of the friezes, some scholars feel that this site dates to the Late Coastal Formative, c. 2500 B.P., and is a coastal manifestation of the highland Chavin culture (Bischof 1997; Burger 1992; Tello 1943). Others (T. Pozorski and S. Pozorski 1987) believe that this site is another example of a decorated coastal mound dating to the latter half of the Early Coastal Formative based on its layout and the use of conical adobes in its construction. Lack of radiocarbon dates and information concerning associated ceramics has hampered its proper chronological placement.

References

Bischof, Henning (1997). "Cerro Blanco, valle de Nepeña, Peru—Un sitio del Horizonte Temprano en emergencia." In *Archaeologica Peruana 2: Arquitectura y Civilizacion en los Andes Prehispanicos*, ed. E. Bonnier and H. Bischof. Mannheim: Sociedad Arqueologica Peruano-Alemana and Reiss-Museum, 202–234.

Burger, Richard L (1992). *Chavin and the Origins of Andean Civilization*. London: Thames and Hudson.

Pozorski, Shelia, and Thomas Pozorski (1987). *Early Settlement and Subsistence in the Casma Valley, Peru*. Iowa City: University of Iowa Press.

Tello, Julio C (1943). "Discovery of the Chavin Culture in Peru." *American Antiquity* 9: 135–160.

Cerro Sechin

TIME PERIOD: 4000–3300 B.P.

LOCATION: On the south side of the Sechin branch of the Casma valley, Peru.

DESCRIPTIVE SUMMARY

Local Environment

Cerro Sechin is located in a small sandy colluvial plain at the base of a granitic hill within a hyperarid desert environment. To the north and east of the site lies modern cultivated land of the Sechin branch of the Casma valley (Burger 1992; S. Pozorski and T. Pozorski 1987; Tello 1943, 1956).

Physical Features

Cerro Sechin consists of a low mound, made of quarried hill stone, measuring 53 m on a side and flanked by at least two other smaller stone constructions. The outstanding feature of the main mound is its outer facade that contains some 400 carved sculptures depicting warrior figures holding weapons alternating with mutilated victims, severed human heads, and other body parts. The outer facade is the last of four building phases of the main mound. The earlier construction phases, made of conical adobes, include (1) an inner chamber decorated with two painted jaguars; (2) a second facade decorated with at least one clay frieze of a severed human head; and (3) a third facade decorated with a clay frieze of two large fish (Burger 1992; Maldonado 1992; S. Pozorski and T. Pozorski 1987; Samaniego et al. 1995).

Cultural Aspects

Cerro Sechin is the smallest but best-known of the four sites that make up the 10.5-km-sq Sechin Alto

Complex. Given the large size and location of the Sechin Alto Complex within a hyperarid environment, it is quite likely that its inhabitants practiced large-scale irrigation agriculture to meet their subsistence needs. Although clearly not the major site within the complex, Cerro Sechin nevertheless served a special purpose because of the unique nature of its stone sculptured facade. The exact nature of its purpose or function is highly debated. Some scholars believe the site served as a center for ritual human sacrifice, whereas others believe that it served as a memorial to commemorate a military victory, either an actual battle or a mythical one (Burger 1992; S. Pozorski and T. Pozorski 1987; Samaniego et al. 1995). Other than the iconography itself, no additional evidence has come to light to support any particular functional interpretation. The site was substantially reoccupied by various later cultures until c. 700 B.P.

References

Burger, Richard L (1992). *Chavin and the Origins of Andean Civilization*. London: Thames and Hudson.

Maldonado, Elena (1992). *Arqueologia de Cerro Sechin, Tomo I: Arquitectura*. Lima: Pontificia Universidad Catolica del Peru.

Pozorski, Shelia, and Thomas Pozorski (1987). *Early Settlement and Subsistence in the Casma Valley, Peru*. Iowa City: University of Iowa Press.

Samaniego, Lorenzo, Mercedes Cardenas, Henning Bischof, Peter Kaulicke, Erman Guzman, and Wilder Leon (1995). *Arqueologia de Cerro Sechin, Tomo II: Escultura*. Lima: Pontificia Universidad Catolica del Peru.

Tello, Julio C (1943). "Discovery of the Chavin Culture in Peru." *American Antiquity* 9: 135–160.

Tello, Julio C (1956). *Arqueologia del valle de Casma: Culturas Chavin, Santa o Huaylas Yunga y Sub-Chimu*. Lima: Universidad Nacional Mayor de San Marcos.

Garagay

TIME PERIOD: 3600–2900 B.P.

LOCATION: On the north side of the lower Rimac valley, Peru.

DESCRIPTIVE SUMMERY

Local Environment

Garagay is located on a flat colluvial plain on the north side of the Rimac valley, situated within a hyper-arid desert environment (Burger 1992). Since the mid-1980s, the site has been surrounded by a suburb of Lima.

Physical Environment

Modern urban development that surrounds Garagay has disturbed or destroyed any smaller constructions or midden that may have been associated with the site. The remaining civic-ceremonial constructions consist of a large U-shaped mound, opening toward the northeast, which borders a huge rectangular plaza. A small circular plaza is located in front of the southeast wing of the U. The most dominant part of the U configuration is its base, which consists of a mound 385 by 155 by 23 m tall. Smaller atria are present on the summits of the mounds forming the U. On the walls of these atria are remnants of polychrome friezes representing spiders with feline attributes and human warrior figures. The friezes are associated with small votive figurines and paraphernalia such as hallucinogenic San Pedro cactus spines. The size and placement of the friezes and the associated artifacts suggest that the most important rituals were performed and witnessed only by small groups of people rather than by large crowds that could have gathered in the plazas. Both the base and southeast wing of the U were built in several construction stages (Burger 1992; Ravines 1982, 1984; Ravines and Isbell 1975; Ravines et al. 1984).

Cultural Aspects

Garagay is one of several centers dating to the latter half of the Early Coastal Formative within the interconnected central coast Chillon-Rimac-Lurin valley complex. Presumably it was the main center for large public and small private gatherings pertaining to a small polity situated in the lower Rimac valley (Ravines 1982, 1984; Ravines and Isbell 1975). The society responsible for the construction and use of this center was possibly not as complex as those farther north on the Peruvian coast, where large mounds were built in fewer construction phases which required substantially more labor in order to be completed within a reasonable amount of time.

References

Burger, Richard L (1992). *Chavin and the Origins of Andean Civilization*. London: Thames and Hudson.

Ravines, Rogger (1982). *Panorama de la arqueologia Andina*. Lima: Instituto de Estudios Peruanos.

Ravines, Rogger (1984). "Sobre la formacion de Chavin: Imagenes y simbolos." *Boletin de Lima* 35: 27–45.

Ravines, Rogger, and William Isbell (1975). "Garagay: Sitio ceremonial temprano en el valle de Lima." *Revista del Museo Nacional* 41: 253–275.

Ravines, Rogger, Helen Engelstad, Victoria Palomino, and Daniel Sandweiss (1984). "Materiales arqueologicos de Garagay." *Revista del Museo Nacional* 46: 135–233.

Huaca de los Reyes

TIME PERIOD: 3800–3400 B.P.

LOCATION: On the north side of the Moche valley, Peru.

DESCRIPTIVE SUMMARY

Local Environment

Huaca de los Reyes is located along the margin of modern cultivation at the mouth of a colluvial fan within a hyperarid desert environment. Adjacent to the site are foothills of the Andes mountains (Pozorski 1980, 1982).

Physical Features

The site is located in the center of the Caballo Muerto Complex, a group of eight mound sites that range in date from the Early Coastal Formative to the Late Coastal Formative (Pozorski 1980, 1982). It is one of the best-preserved early monumental sites on the coast of Peru. The site consists of two main contiguous mounds that face eastward, each associated with a pair of wing structures that form two overlapping U configurations. Several ancillary mounds, colonnades of square pillars, and room blocks also form numerous U configurations, all bordering various plazas and courts. The site reflects a high degree of bilateral symmetry and formal planning. The three largest plazas decrease in size along the central axis of the site from east to west. Access to plazas, courts, and rooms becomes increasingly restrictive as one passes from east to west. Most notable is the presence of dozens of clay friezes set in niches and on the faces of pillars and pilasters that border the sides of two of the main plazas as well as two ancillary plazas. The content of the friezes includes large anthropomorphic feline heads, standing bipedal human figures, subsidiary fanged profile heads, and profile felines (Moseley and Watanabe 1974; Pozorski 1975, 1980, 1982, 1995).

Cultural Aspects

Huaca de los Reyes represents the pinnacle of achievement in monumental art and architecture produced by the Cupisnique culture, an early coastal culture that contributed certain iconographic themes to later Chavin art. The U-shaped mounds bordering large plazas plus the use of colonnades are typical features of early north coast architecture. Most of what is visible on the surface belongs to a single construction phase (Pozorski 1980, 1982, 1995). The site most likely served as the main center of an early polity in the Moche valley. The planning of the site, which includes the correlation among plaza size, frieze size and content, and accessibility, reflects the guidance of a strong central authority that directed its construction as well as the ranked or stratified nature of the society itself. It appears that only select people or groups were allowed into certain sectors of the site (Pozorski 1980, 1982). The larger, repetitive friezes border the second largest plaza of the site and were undoubtedly meant to impress hundreds of visitors at one time when gathered in the plaza. Other, smaller friezes displaying a more varied content are associated with smaller plazas that can only be reached by way of narrow corridors and staircases (Pozorski 1975, 1980, 1982, 1995). The friezes strongly suggest that religious worship played a major role at the site, but with several dozen undecorated rooms also present, it is also possible that other administrative or storage functions were also carried out here as well (Pozorski and Pozorski 1993).

References

Moseley, Michael, and Luis Watanabe (1974). "The Adobe Sculpture of Huaca de los Reyes: Imposing Artwork from Coastal Peru." *Archaeology* 27: 154–161.

Pozorski, Thomas (1975). "El complejo Caballo Muerto: Los frisos de barro de la Huaca de los Reyes." *Revista del Museo Nacional* 41: 211–251.

Pozorski, Thomas (1980). "The Early Horizon Site of Huaca de los Reyes: Societal Implications." *American Antiquity* 45: 100–110.

Pozorski, Thomas (1982). "Early Social Stratification and Subsistence Systems: The Caballo Muerto Complex." In *Chan Chan: Andean Desert City*, ed. M. E. Moseley and K. C. Day. Albuquerque: University of New Mexico Press, 225–253.

Pozorski, Thomas (1995). "Huaca de los Reyes revisited: Clarification of the Archaeological Evidence." *Latin American Antiquity* 6: 335–339.

Pozorski, Thomas, and Shelia Pozorski (1993). "Early Complex Society and Ceremonialism on the Peruvian North Coast." In *El Mundo Ceremonial Andino*, ed. L. Millones and Y. Onuki. Osaka: National Museum of Ethnology, 45–68.

Huaca Lucia

TIME PERIOD: 3500–2600 B.P.

LOCATION: On the north side of the La Leche valley, Peru.

DESCRIPTIVE SUMMARY

Local Environment

Huaca Lucia is located in a scrub forest zone bordered by modern cultivated land within an arid desert environment. Scattered foothills of the Andes mountains are also present (Shimada 1981).

Physical Features

Huaca Lucia is part of the huge Batan Grande complex that covers over 50 sq km and contains sites ranging in date from the Early Coastal Formative to c. A.D. 1200. Found in a heavily looted state, excavators were able to reveal that the mound, made of conical adobes, is two-tiered and measures about 50 m on a side. Along its north facade is a wide staircase that leads up to the lower tier of the mound containing a colonnade of 24 round columns. These columns are made of conical adobes and once held a roof some 3.5–4 m above the floor of the colonnade. Traces of mural paintings were also found during excavations (Burger 1992; Shimada 1981, 1982; Shimada et al. 1982).

Cultural Aspects

Huaca Lucia probably served as the main religious edifice for a small polity situated in the La Leche valley. Although not large by early coastal standards, the unusual width of its central staircase (16 m), its mural paintings, and the impressive colonnade overlooking a plaza area strongly suggest its primary use as a gathering area for ritual purposes (Burger 1992; Shimada 1981, 1982; Shimada et al. 1982).

References

Burger, Richard L (1992). *Chavin and the Origins of Andean Civilization*. London: Thames and Hudson.
Shimada, Izumi (1981). "The Batan Grande-La Leche Archaeological Project: The First Two Seasons." *Journal of Field Archaeology* 8: 405–446.
Shimada, Izumi (1982). "Horizontal Archipelago and Coast-Highland Interaction in North Peru: Archaeological Models." In *El hombre y su ambiente en los Andes Centrales*, ed. L. Millones and H. Tomoeda. Osaka: National Museum of Ethnology, 137–210.
Shimada, Izumi, Carlos Elera, and Melody Shimada (1982). "Excavaciones efectuadas en el centro ceremonial de Huaca Lucia-Cholope, del Horizonte Temprano, Batan Grande, costa norte del Peru: 1979–1981." *Arqueologicas* 19: 109–210.

La Florida

TIME PERIOD: 4100–3700 B.P.

LOCATION: On the north side of the lower Rimac valley, Peru.

DESCRIPTIVE SUMMARY

Local Environment

La Florida is located on a flat alluvial plain north of the Rimac river within a hyperarid desert environment. Since the 1950s, the site has been surrounded by the urban development of Lima (Patterson 1985).

Physical Features

The site is considered one of the oldest and largest U-shaped mound complexes on the central coast (Burger 1992; Moseley 1992; Patterson 1985; Williams 1985). The main mound forms the base of the U shape and is considerably taller than both of the low wing mounds forming the arms of the U. Together, the three mounds border a large rectangular plaza. Immediately in front of the main mound is a small rectangular vestibule formed by low stone walls. A central staircase leads to a central atrium on the summit of the main mound (Patterson 1985). Limited excavations revealed that the main mound was constructed in at least three separate stages. Aerial photographs show that many smaller structures once surrounded the U-shaped complex before being destroyed by urban expansion (Patterson 1985).

Cultural Aspects

La Florida appears to have been an early version of a civic-ceremonial center that probably served as the main gathering area for people living within a small polity in the lower Rimac valley. The architectural configuration is somewhat similar to slightly later U-shaped complexes such as Garagay and Cardal on the central coast. Presumably, La Florida functioned in much the same way as these later sites, as a gathering area for large and small groups of people who came together for religious and nonreligious purposes. The site is also similar in that it was the product of multiple construction stages built over a few hundred years (Burger 1992; Patterson 1985).

References

Burger, Richard L (1992). *Chavin and the Origins of Andean Civilization*. London: Thames and Hudson.

Moseley, Michael (1992). *The Incas and Their Ancestors*. London: Thames and Hudson.

Patterson, Thomas (1985). "The Huaca La Florida, Rimac Valley, Peru." In *Early Ceremonial Architecture in the Andes*, ed. C. B. Donnan. Washington, D.C.: Dumbarton Oaks Research Library and Collection, 59–69.

Williams, Carlos (1985). "A Scheme for the Early Monumental Architecture of the Central Coast of Peru." *Early Ceremonial Architecture in the Andes*, ed. C. B. Donnan. Washington, D.C.: Dumbarton Oaks Research Library and Collection, 227–240.

Las Haldas

TIME PERIOD: 4000–3300 B.P.

LOCATION: On the Pacific coast some 20 km south of the Casma valley, Peru.

DESCRIPTIVE SUMMARY

Local Environment

Las Haldas is located on a low hill that rests on a rocky cliff overlooking the Pacific ocean within a hyperarid desert environment. A rolling sandy pampa borders the site on the north, south, and east. To the west is the Pacific ocean bordered by sandy beaches and rocky outcrops.

Physical Features

Las Haldas, covering 40 ha, consists of dozens of mounds, rooms, plazas, and courts that, for the most part, rest on midden deposits some 4–5 m deep. The main structure is a mound with several tiers built on a natural hill to enhance its apparent height. This mound overlooks four rectangular plazas that extend 300 m to the northeast. Within the second rectangular plaza is a deep sunken circular plaza. Along the west side of the main mound is a series of smaller mounds that overlook a small sunken circular plaza (Fung 1969; Grieder 1975; Matsuzawa 1978; S. Pozorski and T. Pozorski 1987).

Cultural Aspects

It is generally assumed that the main mound and associated plazas functioned as a temple or religious edifice. However, there is also evidence suggesting that this structure was unfinished or at least utilized very little (Grieder 1975). Virtually all of the surface architecture as well as the top 2–3 m of midden at Las Haldas date to the Early Coastal Formative. The architectural layout of the main mound and the associated ceramics point to a connection with the inland site of Sechin Alto that lies within the Sechin branch of the Casma valley (Fung 1969; S. Pozorski and T. Pozorski 1987). This connection likely took the form of a subsistence exchange system whereby marine fish and shellfish were exchanged for inland agricultural products. Underlying the Early Coastal Formative occupation at Las Haldas is a midden deposit, dating to the Late Coastal Archaic, which is substantially smaller in area than the Early Coastal Formative occupation. Overlying the main mound is a later occupation, very limited in area, dating to the Late Coastal Formative.

References

Fung, Rosa (1969). "Las Aldas: Su ubicacion dentro del proceso historico del Peru antiguo." *Dedalo* 5, 9–10: 1–208.

Grieder, Terence (1975). "A Dated Sequence of Building and Pottery at Las Haldas." *Ñawpa Pacha* 13: 99–112.

Matsuzawa, Tsugio (1978). "The Formative Site of Las Haldas, Peru: Architecture, Chronology, and Economy." *American Antiquity* 43: 652–673.

Pozorski, Shelia, and Thomas Pozorski (1987). *Early Settlement and Subsistence in the Casma Valley, Peru*. Iowa City: University of Iowa Press.

Monte Grande

TIME PERIOD: 3500–3000 B.P.

LOCATION: On the north side of the middle Jequetepeque valley, Peru.

DESCRIPTIVE SUMMARY

Local Environment

Monte Grande is located at 430 m above sea level on a series of low ridges at the mouth of a colluvial fan bordered by low-lying peaks of the Andes mountains (Tellenbach 1986). Formerly, cultivated land was located just south of the site, but since the mid-1980s, the area is now occupied by the reservoir associated with the Gallito Ciego dam.

Physical Features

The site, covering more than 13 ha, contains 14 small stone mounds associated with several dozen smaller structures made of small stones and cane (Burger 1992; Pozorski 1976; Tellenbach 1986). Two of the largest mounds were excavated in the early 1980s. Each of these mounds has a wide staircase that leads up from a rectangular plaza situated in front of each mound. The stone architecture was covered by clay plaster with some evidence of modeled sculptures on their front facades. Other unexcavated mounds, together with low wing structures, form U-shaped configurations that border rectangular plazas. Most of the smaller structures served as dwelling units for the site's inhabitants (Burger 1992; Tellenbach 1986).

Cultural Aspects

Monte Grande was presumably the civic and religious center of a small polity situated in the middle Jequetepeque valley. Its ceramic assemblage contains elements of the coastal Cupisnique culture, but also has elements that are similar to ceramics found at such highland sites as Huacaloma near Cajamarca (Ulbert 1994). Given its midvalley position, it is likely that Monte Grande was actively involved in coastal-highland interchange during the Early Coastal Formative.

References

Burger, Richard L (1992). *Chavin and the Origins of Andean Civilization.* London: Thames and Hudson.

Pozorski, Thomas (1976). "Caballo Muerto, a Complex of Early Ceramic Sites in the Moche Valley, Peru." Ph.D. diss., Department of Anthropology, University of Texas, Austin.

Tellenbach, Michael (1986). *Las excavaciones en el asentamiento formativo de Montegrande, valle de Jequetepeque en el norte del Peru.* Munich: Verlag C. H. Beck.

Ulbert, Cornelius (1994). *Die Keramik der formativzeitlichen Siedlung Montegrande, Jequetepequetal, Nord-Peru.* Mainz: Verlag Philipp von Zabern.

Pampa de las Llamas-Moxeke

TIME PERIOD: 4000–3400 B.P.

LOCATION: On the north side of the Casma branch of the Casma river valley, Peru.

DESCRIPTIVE SUMMARY

Local Environment

Pampa de las Llamas-Moxeke is located on a rocky colluvial fan within a hyperarid desert environment. The site is bordered on three sides by granitic foothills of the Andes mountains. The southern third of the site is partially obscured by modern cultivation associated with the Casma river (S. Pozorski and T. Pozorski 1986, 1987).

Physical Features

The site, covering approximately 220 ha, contains hundreds of mounds and structures made of stone set in mud mortar. The main axis of the site is formed by two large mounds, Moxeke and Huaca A, which are separated from each other by a series of large rectangular and square plazas. The northeast face of Moxeke once was decorated with a series of very large anthropomorphic clay friezes set in niches. Huaca A is decorated with very large clay friezes along the back walls of two recessed atria. One of these friezes consists of a pair of felines each measuring 10 m across. Lining the main plazas of the site are over 110 medium-sized mounds and compounds. Hundreds of other smaller low-walled structures located on the west and east sides of the site housed the site's inhabitants. Other structures present at the site include a large circular plaza; two small buildings with central ventilated hearths, somewhat reminiscent of North American Indian sweat houses; and a unique I-shaped court similar in form to I-shaped ball courts found in Mesoamerica (S. Pozorski and T. Pozorski 1991, 1994; T. Pozorski and S. Pozorski 1995, 1996).

Cultural Aspects

Pampa de las Llamas-Moxeke served as a major center within a valleywide polity for most of its existence. Given the large size of the site and its location within a hyperarid environment, it is quite likely that inhabitants practiced large-scale irrigation agriculture to meet their subsistence needs. The large size and sheer number of the mounds at the site plus their precise layout and modular construction suggest the presence of a stratified society headed by a strong central authority (S. Pozorski and T. Pozorski 1986). Moxeke was probably a temple (Tello 1956), whereas Huaca A was a large communal warehouse (S. Pozorski and T. Pozorski 1986, 1991, 1994). The medium-sized mounds probably served as bureaucratic edifices to control the production and distribution of food and commodities in and out of the site (S. Pozorski and T. Pozorski 1991). Plazas likely served as public gathering areas. The ventilated hearth structures probably served as small ritual chambers. Artifactual and subsistence remains point to a trade relationship with coastal fishing villages, which served as satellites supplying marine products (shellfish, fish) in exchange for inland coastal agricultural products (S. Pozorski and T. Pozorski 1987). There is little evidence of trade with areas outside the Casma valley. To date, it is unclear if the Casma valley polity had dominance over any of the neighboring valleys to the north or south.

References

Pozorski, Shelia, and Thomas Pozorski (1986). "Recent Excavations at Pampa de las Llamas-Moxeke, A Complex Initial Period Site in Peru." *Journal of Field Archaeology* 13: 381–401.

Pozorski, Shelia, and Thomas Pozorski (1987). *Early Settlement and Subsistence in the Casma Valley, Peru.* Iowa City: University of Iowa Press.

Pozorski, Shelia, and Thomas Pozorski (1991). "Storage, Access Control, and Bureaucratic Proliferation: Understanding the Initial Period (1800–900 B.C.) Economy at Pampa de las Llamas-Moxeke, Casma Valley, Peru." *Research in Economic Anthropology* 13: 341–371.

Pozorski, Shelia, and Thomas Pozorski (1994). "Multi-Dimensional Planning at Pampa de las Llamas-Moxeke on the North Central Coast of Peru." In *Meaningful Architecture: Social Interpretations of Buildings*, ed. M. Locock. Avebury: Worldwide Archaeology Series, 45–65.

Pozorski, Thomas, and Shelia Pozorski (1995). "An I-Shaped Ball-Court Form at Pampa de las Llamas-Moxeke, Peru." *Latin American Antiquity* 6: 274–280.

Pozorski, Thomas, and Shelia Pozorski (1996). "Ventilated Hearth Structures in the Casma Valley, Peru." *Latin American Antiquity* 7: 341–353.

Tello, Julio C (1956). *Arqueologia del valle de Casma: Culturas Chavin, Santa o Huaylas Yunga y Sub-Chimu.* Lima: Universidad Nacional Mayor de San Marcos.

Punkuri

TIME PERIOD: 3500–3000 B.P.

LOCATION: On the north side of the Nepeña valley, Peru.

DESCRIPTIVE SUMMARY

Local Environment

Punkuri is located within modern irrigated land near the middle of the Nepeña valley and north of the Nepeña river. Outside of modern irrigated land is a hyperarid desert environment with sand dunes and the foothills of the Andes mountains.

Physical Features

The site consists of a small mound measuring 45 m on a side, made of stone and conical adobes. The most prominent feature of this site was a large sculpted clay figure of a feline once located at the base of a central staircase within the center of the mound (Bischof 1994; Burger 1992; Larco Hoyle 1941; Tello 1943). Associated with this frieze was the burial of a human female, which contained imported *Spondylus* shell and *Strombus* shell, turquoise beads, and an elaborate incised stone bowl. An earlier construction phase contains the remains of clay friezes containing abstract geometric and avian motifs (Bischof 1994; Burger 1992).

Cultural Aspects

Although this site was excavated in 1933, there is general agreement that it dates to the Early Coastal Formative (Bischof 1994; Burger 1992; T. Pozorski and S. Pozorski 1987). Scholars usually interpret Punkuri as a probable religious edifice (Bischof 1994; Burger 1992). It is likely to have been contemporary with another Nepeña valley site, Cerro Blanco, which was also decorated with clay friezes.

References

Bischof, Henning (1994). "Toward the Definition of Pre- and Early Chavin Art Styles in Peru." *Andean Past* 4: 169–228.

Burger, Richard L (1992). *Chavin and the Origins of Andean Civilization.* London: Thames and Hudson.

Larco Hoyle, Rafael (1941). *Los Cupisniques.* Lima: Casa Editora La Cronica y Variedades S.A. Ltda.

Pozorski, Shelia, and Thomas Pozorski (1987). *Early Settlement and Subsistence in the Casma Valley, Peru.* Iowa City: University of Iowa Press.

Tello, Julio C (1943). "Discovery of the Chavin Culture in Peru." *American Antiquity* 9: 135–160.

Purulen

TIME PERIOD: 3400–3000 B.P.

LOCATION: On the south side of the lower Zaña valley, Peru.

DESCRIPTIVE SUMMARY

Local Environment

Purulen is located on a series of gently rolling hills made of eroding granitic bedrock and compact sand, set within a hyperarid desert environment. The site lies south of modern cultivation and is adjacent to at least two old channels of the Zaña river drainage (Alva 1988).

Physical Features

The site, extending over an area of some 3 sq km, consists of 15 small and medium-sized stone mounds oriented slightly east of north. Most of these mounds are made up of two to three superposed platforms containing a sunken atrium at the summit. Each mound has a wide central staircase leading up from a rectangular forecourt. Excavations of the largest mound revealed the presence of thick cylindrical cane columns that supported small roofs. Remains of perishable cane and clay buildings were found on portions of the summit. Habitation refuse and the remains of small houses situated among the various mounds indicate that a substantial population once inhabited the site (Alva 1987, 1988; Burger 1992).

Cultural Aspects

Although the individual mounds are not huge by early coastal standards, the presence of 15 mounds distributed over an area of 3 sq km makes Purulen one of the most extensive early mound complexes on the north coast. Presumably, it was the center for civic and ceremonial activities of a small polity within the Zaña valley, similar to other early centers in coastal valleys to the north and south. The associated incised Cupisnique pottery and radiocarbon dating place the complex within the last few centuries of the Early Coastal Formative. Much work remains to be done at this complex that shows little sign of later occupation or modern looting.

References

Alva, Walter (1987). "Resultados de las excavaciones en el valle de Zaña, norte del Peru." In *Archaologie in Peru—Archaometrie: 1985*, ed. W. Bauer. Stuttgart: Konrad Theiss Verlag, 61–78

Alva, Walter (1988). "Investigaciones en el complejo Formativo con arquitectura monumental de Purulen, costa norte del Peru (informe preliminar)." *Beiträge zur Allgemeinen und Vergleichenden Archäologie* 8: 283–300.

Burger, Richard L (1992). *Chavin and the Origins of Andean Civilization*. London: Thames and Hudson.

Sechin Alto

TIME PERIOD: 4000–3300 B.P.

LOCATION: Within the Sechin branch of the Casma valley, Peru.

DESCRIPTIVE SUMMARY

Local Environment

Sechin Alto is located in the north branch of the Casma valley within a larger hyperarid desert setting. The actual site is immediately south of the Sechin river and is surrounded by modern irrigation agriculture. The valley is, in turn, bordered by the foothills of the Andes mountains (S. Pozorski 1987; S. Pozorski and T. Pozorski 1987, 1992, 1994).

Physical Features

The site, covering over 200 ha, consists of several large mounds and walled structures made of quarried hill stones set in mud mortar. The largest of these mounds measures 300 m by 250 m by 35 m tall and is the largest mound construction for its time period in the New World. Within the central part of the mound summit is a central core, measuring 90 m by 30 m and made of conical adobes, which is physically distinct from the mainly stone construction that surrounds it. This huge mound faces a series of four rectangular plazas that stretch some 1.5 km to the east. Two of these rectangular plazas contain large circular plazas. Large- and medium-sized stone mounds are situated to the south, east, and west of the main mound and also line the north and south sides of the four rectangular plazas (S. Pozorski 1987; S. Pozorski and T. Pozorski 1987, 1992, 1994).

Cultural Aspects

The site of Sechin Alto is the largest of four sites that comprise the 10.5-sq-km Sechin Alto Complex. Given the large size of the site and its location within a hyperarid environment, it is quite likely that the inhabitants practiced large-scale irrigation agriculture to meet their subsistence needs. The site as well as the complex as a whole served as the main center for a valleywide polity. Architectural, artifactual, and subsistence evidence indicates the existence of an exchange system with the coastal sites such as Tortugas and Huaynuna and, near the end of its period of dominance, the site of Las Haldas. Inland agricultural products were exchanged for coastal marine fish and shellfish. The main mound of Sechin Alto probably served as the locus for various functions including administrative activity, storage, and ritual activity. This mound was reoccupied around 500 B.C. by people who leveled much of the summit and placed houses, platforms, and plazas on top of the much earlier construction (S. Pozorski 1987; S. Pozorski and T. Pozorski 1987, 1992, 1994).

References

Pozorski, Shelia (1987). "Theocracy vs. Militarism: The Significance of the Casma Valley in Understanding Early State Formation." In *The Origins and Development of the Andean State*, ed. J. Haas, S. Pozorski, and T. Pozorski. Cambridge: Cambridge University Press, 15–30.

Pozorski, Shelia, and Thomas Pozorski (1987). *Early Settlement and Subsistence in the Casma Valley, Peru.* Iowa City: University of Iowa Press.

Pozorski, Shelia, and Thomas Pozorski (1992). "Early Civilization in the Casma Valley, Peru." *Antiquity* 66: 845–870.

Pozorski, Shelia, and Thomas Pozorski (1994). "Early Andean Cities." *Scientific American* 270: 66–72.

Taukachi-Konkan

TIME PERIOD: 4000–3300 B.P.

LOCATION: On the north side of the Sechin branch of the Casma river valley, Peru.

DESCRIPTIVE SUMMARY

Local Environment

Taukachi-Konkan is located on a sandy colluvial fan within a hyperarid desert environment. Foothills of the Andes mountains border the site on the west, north, and east. Along the south side is the modern cultivated north branch of the Casma valley (S. Pozorski and T. Pozorski 1987, 1992, 1994).

Physical Features

The site, covering some 60 ha, contains several large mounds and dozens of smaller mounds and structures made of stones set in mud mortar. These structures border a series of large rectangular plazas as well as three circular plazas. The most notable large mound, the Mound of the Columns, located at the west end of the site, contains a colonnaded area that once supported a roof covering the eastern half of the mound summit (S. Pozorski and T. Pozorski 1992, 1994). At least two other large mounds seem to be unfinished and were never utilized. Modular room construction and precise planning are evident in most of the mounds. Other notable structures included three ventilated hearth structures, similar in form to North American Indian sweat houses (T. Pozorski and S. Pozorski 1996). Later reoccupation severely altered many of the surface features within the eastern half of the site.

Cultural Aspects

Taukachi-Konkan is one of four large sites that form the immense Sechin Alto Complex, a 10.5-sq-km complex that served as the major center of a valleywide polity between 4000–3300 B.P. (S. Pozorski and T. Pozorski 1987, 1992). Given the large size of the site and its location within a hyperarid environment, it is quite likely that the inhabitants practiced large-scale irrigation agriculture to meet their subsistence needs. The Mound of the Columns appears to have served as an elite residence or palace for an important person, perhaps the ruler of the Sechin Alto Complex. The medium-sized mounds lining the plazas probably served as bureaucratic edifices for controlling the production and distribution of food and commodities entering and leaving the site. The three ventilated hearth structures probably served as small ritual chambers (T. Pozorski and S. Pozorski 1996). Taukachi-Konkan participated in a subsistence exchange system with the coast, possibly with the site of Las Haldas, 20 km south of the Casma valley. Within this system, coastal shellfish and fish were exchanged for inland agricultural products. Taukachi-Konkan was intensively reoccupied after 1000 B.P. by the Chimu culture and the local culture characterized by Casma Incised pottery.

References

Pozorski, Shelia (1987). "Theocracy vs. Militarism: The Significance of the Casma Valley in Understanding Early State Formation." In *The Origins and Development of the Andean State*, ed. J. Haas, S. Pozorski, and T. Pozorski. Cambridge: Cambridge University Press, 15–30.

Pozorski, Shelia, and Thomas Pozorski (1987). *Early Settlement and Subsistence in the Casma Valley, Peru.* Iowa City: University of Iowa Press.

Pozorski, Shelia, and Thomas Pozorski (1992). "Early Civilization in the Casma Valley, Peru." *Antiquity* 66: 845–870.

Pozorski, Shelia, and Thomas Pozorski (1994). "Early Andean Cities." *Scientific American* 270: 66–72.

Pozorski, Thomas, and Shelia Pozorski (1996). "Ventilated Hearth Structures in the Casma Valley, Peru." *Latin American Antiquity* 7: 341–353.

SHELIÀ AND THOMAS POZORSKI
Department of Psychology and Anthropology
University of Texas–Pan American
Edinburg, Texas
United States

Early East Brazilian Uplands

ABSOLUTE TIME PERIOD: 11,000–5000 B.P.

RELATIVE TIME PERIOD: Follows the Late Paleoindian tradition, precedes the Late East Brazilian Uplands tradition.

LOCATION: The Brazilian highlands. Bounded on the north by the Amazon valley, on the west by the lowlands of the Matto Grosso, on the south by the Pampas on the southern part of the state of Rio Grande do Sul, and on the east by the coastal plain.

DIAGNOSTIC MATERIAL ATTRIBUTES: Most Early Brazilian Uplands sites occur in rock shelters, although open sites exist. Projectile points are made from bone and stone. Stone points tend to have contracting stems and square or slightly hooked shoulders. Not all sites, however, have projectile points. Long and narrow stone scrapers are more common, and some sites have large hooked stone knives. A few Early East Brazilian Upland sites have bola stones, a trait in common with the prehistoric cultures in the Pampas region to the south. Polished and grooved axes are also present. Although most sites have the remains of modern fauna, several of the sites in the states of Minas Gerais and Bahia contain bones of extinct Pleistocene megafauna as well as modern fauna.

REGIONAL SUBTRADITIONS: Flake and Core Tool, Itaparica, Serranópolis, Southern Brazilian Core Tool.

IMPORTANT SITES: Abrigo 6, Abrigo do Pilao, Jose Vieria, GO-JA-01, GO-JA-03, Gruta do Padre.

CULTURAL SUMMARY

Environment

Climate. There were major climatic changes during the Early East Brazilian Uplands tradition. In the early part of the period, a dry climate existed, but this changed to a more moist one by the mid-Holocene. The end of the tradition saw a late Holocene return to drier conditions. From region to region of this vast area, there were undoubtedly variations from this general pattern. Average temperatures and average rainfall have not been determined, but this figure would be meaningless over a long time period in this vast area.

Topography. The Brazilian uplands are characterized by many changes in altitude from the river valleys to the coastal range. For example, in the state of Paraná, the uplands are bordered on the west by the large river, the Rio Paraná. On the east, the uplands are bordered by the coastal range that is higher than any mountains in the uplands. On the uplands in the state of Bahia are mountain ranges of quartzite and limestone. In the limestone areas, which have a karst topography, there are sinkholes, underground rivers, and vertical cliffs.

Rock shelters formed by solution and wind and water erosion are present. A large section of highlands have a limestone bedrock of Solutrean age. Available for the making of artifacts, although varying from one region to the next, are quartzite, quartz crystal, and chert. The uplands have very few impediments to movement. There are passes through the coastal range, and the rivers could be crossed by dugout canoes.

Biota. The earliest sites are associated with extinct Pleistocene megafauna such as the glyptodon, short-nosed cave bear, saber-toothed tiger, horse, and camel. In Holocene times, the region contained peccaries, monkeys, armadillos, agoutis, pacas, tapirs, capybaras, anteaters, three-toothed sloth, marmosets, rheas, parrots, giant land snails, freshwater mussels, turtles, snakes, iguanas, and lizards. Flora varied from the *caatinga* in the north with giant cacti and trees with edible fruits, to the *cerrado*, which had more deciduous trees, to the coniferous forests in the south. On the Atlantic side of the coast range are tropical rain forests.

Settlement

Most Early East Brazilian Uplands settlements were in rock shelters. The size of these communities was limited by the size of the shelter itself, and most could have housed only an extended family. Open sites are less common, although they tend to be found more frequently in the southern part of the tradition. These open sites are little more than lithic scatters along streams. There are few published descriptions of open-air sites and no descriptions of housing or community forms.

Economy

The Early East Brazilian Uplands peoples were hunters and gatherers. Early in the tradition, there was apparently some hunting of Pleistocene megafauna, but for most of the tradition contemporary species (and their direct ancestors) were primary game animals. Few floral remains have been recovered, but one can assume a wide range of plants was collected and used.

Tools were made from both bone and stone. Both flake and core tools were used at different times and, presumably, for different functions. Ceramics were not manufactured.

Sociopolitical Organization

Although there is no direct evidence, scholars assume that the extended family group formed the basis of both social and political organization for the Early East Brazilian Uplands peoples.

Suggested Readings

Bruhns, Karen (1994). *Ancient South America.* Cambridge: Cambridge University Press.

Bryan, Alan, and Ruth Gruhn (1993). *Brazilian Studies.* Corvallis, OR: Center for the Study of the First Americans, Oregon State University.

Hurt, Wesley (1998). *Explorations in American Archaeology: Essays in Honor of Wesley R. Hurt.* Lanham, Md.: University Press of America.

Willey, Gordon R (1971). *An Introduction to American Archaeology,* vol. 2: *South America.* Engelwood Cliffs, NJ: Prentice-Hall.

SUBTRADITIONS

Flake and Core Tool

TIME PERIOD: 11,000–8500 B.P.

LOCATION: From the extreme western edge of the highlands of Minas Gerias (that is, from the Araguarí river) southward to the valley of the Parapanema river, which forms the boundary of the states of Paraná and São Paulo.

DIAGNOSTIC MATERIAL ATTRIBUTES: The major characteristic of the Flake and Core Tool subtradition is that sites contain both flake and core artifacts. Flake tools include plano-convex and thick flake knives. The raw materials for most stone artifacts are chert, quartzite, and indurated and friable sandstone obtained in form of cobbles. Flakes with cortex occur in the form of wedges. Other flakes are used for knives, side scrapers, end scrapers, denticulated scrapers, and ovoid scrapers. There are also willowleaf-shaped knives. Blades were used for knives, side scrapers, choppers. Core tools include choppers, perforators, and denticulated scrapers. Lithics were made by direct percussion; rare pieces show bipolar flaking. The flakes for tools are generally thick. Knives varied from 5–15 cm in length and 1–4 cm thick.

CULTURAL SUMMARY

Environment

There is considerable variation in the environment depending on the location. For example, along the Parapanema river, there are many rapids and waterfalls. Fish are abundant and easy to catch because of the barriers to their movement. Game animals include capybaras, pacas, deer, and cotias. In the same general area, the second and third highlands of Paraná are divided by a basalt escarpment. During the months of summer, October to March, the mean precipitation is 1348 mm, and in the months of winter, April to September, 594 mm, with a mean annual precipitation of 1942 mm in the vicinity of the town of Cambará. At the other extreme of the same area, that is Londrina, maximum precipitation in summer is 945 mm, and in winter is 444 mm, with a mean annual of 1389 mm. In contrast, the area of Minas Gerais is a dry savannah in the winter, while in the rainy season (from October to March) it has precipitation from 1300–1900 mm. In short, the environment varies tremendously.

Settlements

Settlements of the Flake and Core Tool subtradition are situated on elevated areas, 50–150 m above levels of rivers and c. 2 km from the edge of the principal rivers. Sites are usually scattered over an area of 200 m or more in diameter and are very shallow. Sites are often associated with elongated mounds, 5.50 m or so in length and 2.50 m in width and with a maximum height of some 1.10 m. Over these mounds were usually 10 cm of grass and the remains of bushes and small trees. Excavation of these mounds revealed that they were constructed using soil from the immediate vicinity. Mixed with the strata of the mounds were flakes and cores typical of this subtradition.

References

Anonymous (1995). *Projeto Executivo, Programa de Salvamento Arqueológico — Atividades do Centro de Estudos e Pesquisas Arqueológicas da Universidade Federal da Universidade Federal do Paraná, Cemig*. Minas Gerais: Companhia Energética de Minas Gerais, Belo Hizonte.

Bigarella, Joao J., and Maria R. Mousinho (1965). *Significaco Paleográfico e Paleoclimático dos depósitos Rudáceos, Boetim Paranense de Geografia*. Paraná: Curitiba.

Chymz, Igor (1967). "Dados parcias sôbre a arquelogia do vale do Rio Paranapanema." In *Programa Nacional de Pesquisas Archaeológicas: Resultados Preliminares do Primero Ano, 1965–1966*. Publicaçoes Avulsas N. 06. Pará: Museu Paraense Emílio Goeldi, Belêm, 59–78.

Itaparica

ABSOLUTE TIME PERIOD: 11,000–2000 B.P.

LOCATION: Goiás westward through Minas Gerais, Bahia, and Pernambuco.

DIAGNOSTIC MATERIAL ATTRIBUTES: Tools are primarily unifacial, but bifacial examples occur in small quantities. Tools are primarily made of flakes, but there are small numbers fabricated from cores. Unifacial projectile points are common but not universally present, and only a few sites in Goaias have bone projectile points. Unifacial scrapers, flaked entirely over the dorsal surface with a keel-shaped or carinated cross-section, are common but not present in all sites. *Lesmas*, when present, indicate that a site belongs to the Itaparica subtradition. These are large willowleaf-shaped knives that may be symmetrical or have a diagonal cutting edge at one end. Schmitz (1980: 186–225) states that the sites of this subtradition in Goiás have lithic artifacts that are unifacial and made of large flakes accompanied by pecked or ground tools to grind or crush. There seems to have been two artifact groups represented in this subtradition (Martin et al. 1986; 118–119). The oldest group, 8000–7000 B.P., has plano-convex and biconvex tools that are usually fragmented transversely; the second group, 7000–3000 B.P., has flaked artifacts made of discoidal pebbles, flakes with dorsal ridges. The second group abandoned the technique of pressure retouching. The core tools were bifacial (Hurt 1969). According to LaRoche (1981: 45), the oldest site, the Lago de Casa, Muncipio de Bom Jardin, Pernambuco, contains bones of extinct animals such as the mastodon. This site produced unifacial choppers, burins, fan-shaped scrapers, ovoid unifacial scrapers with pressure flaked retouched edges, *lesmas*, unifacial drills, square-stemmed unifacial projectile points, pentagonal-shaped projectile points, and triangular-shaped projectile points that resemble Mousterian and Levallois types. Economic activity is generalized hunting and secondarily fishing and gathering.

CULTURAL SUMMARY

Environment

There are many varieties of local environment because this subtradition is spread over a wide area. The area of this subtradition in the state of Goías has three to four dry months, a mean annual precipitation of 1500 mm, with the rainy season from December to February, and the coldest months being June to August. The mean annual temperature varies from 18–20° C. The hottest months are December to March. In the coldest months frost can occur. According to Schmitz (1980), the area of this subtradition in Goías during the period from 10,500–7000 B.P. was relatively dry, mixed with warmer and more humid, the period from 7000–5000 B.P. was very humid; and 4500–3000 B.P. was hot and dry. In the area of Minas Gerais, where the sites were located, 11,000–8000 B.P. was hot and dry.

In the area of the Itaparica subtraditon, there are four basic types of vegetation. The *campo limpo* on the highest elevations contains grasslands without trees. The *cerrado* has small trees and bushes mixed with some grasslands. The *floresta mesófila* has tropical, *latifoliadas*, *subcaducifólias* forests, on the most fertile soils in floodplains of rivers. In some areas in the states of Bahia and Pernambuco are the *caatinga*, vegetation of arid and semiarid regions, xerophystic vegetation such as low thorny bushes and trees and cacti. Trees include the *caju* and *umbu*, which produce edible fruits. Fauna includes two types of deer, armadillos, anteaters, rheas, seriema, paca, agouti, capybara, peccary, coati, cayman, turtles, and mollusks. There are also large terrestrial gastropods. During the rainy season, the trees produce a large variety of fruits and nuts.

Settlements

The majority of the sites occur in rock shelters, although a few open sites are present in Pernambuco.

Economy

Judging by the tools, such as the projectile points, scrapers, and knives, the main economic activity was hunting of modern fauna, although the content of a few very old open sites in Pernambuco, such as Cha do Caboclo, dated 11,000 B.P., indicates the possibility that the mammoth and other extinct megafauna were also hunted (La Roche 1975).

References

Calderón, Valentin (1969). *Nota prévia sobre arqueologia das regios central e sudeste da Bahia*. Programa Nacional de Pesquisas Arqueológicas, 2, Resultados Preliminares do Segundo Ano, 1966–1967. Pará: Publicaçoes Avulsas No. 10, Museu Paraense Emílio Goeldi, Belém.

Hurt, Wesley (1969). "Tradition Itaparica." In *Clio, Série Arqueolóica, Numero 5*. Recife: University of Pernambuco, 55–58.

LaRoche, A. F. (1975). Contribuçoes para a pré-historia pernambucana. Ginásio Pernambucano. Recife. Martin, Gabriela, Jacionira Silva, Rocha, Marcos Galindo Lima, 1986, 99–135. Industrias Líticas, no Vale do Medio Sao Francisco (Pernambuco, Brasil). Clio, Série Arqueológico, Numero 8, Universidade Federal de Pernambuco.

LaRoche, A. F. (1981). Martin, Gabriela Jacionira, Silva Rocha, Marcos Galindo Lima. (1986). Industrias líticas em no vale do Médio Sao Francisco (Pernambuco, Brasil). Cliom Série Arqueológico – 3, Numero 9. Universidade Federal Pernambuco, Recife: 99–136

Schmitz, Ignacio (1980). "A Evoluçao ds Cultura no Sudoeste de Goiás." In *Estudos de Arquelogia e Préhistória Brasiieira em Memória de Alfredo Teodoro Rusins, Pesquisas, Antrpológia no 211*. Instituto Anchietano de Pesquisas, Rio Grande ddo Sul: Sao Leopoldo, 114–225.

Serranópolis

ABSOLUTE TIME PERIOD: 9510–6690 B.P.

LOCATION: In southeast area of the state of Goiás, on the right side of the Rio Paranaiba. It is in the center of the Brazilian highlands at the continental divide with the Rio Araguaia.

DIAGNOSTIC MATERIAL ATTRIBUTES: The sites of this subtradition are all located in rock shelters. Open sites, if any exist, have not been described in publications. Bone projectile points and fishooks are common, as are scrapers are made of mollusk shells. Human burials are flexed.

CULTURAL SUMMARY

Environment

Climate is tropical and hot with an attenuated dry season. The dry season lasts 3–4 months in June to August. July is the coldest month, and September is warmest month. Annual precipitation varies from 1250–1500 mm. During the time of the subtradition, the climate was becoming warmer with an oscilating amount of precipitation. The fauna did not vary much from that of present day, except it was much more numerous. Included were tapir, anteater, peccary, agouti, capybara, and paca, capybara, turtle, cayman, deer, terrestrial gastrops, and fish. Vegetation included palm trees, *xixá*, *guaroba*, and *jatobá*, *araça*. and *caju*, all of which produced fruits, nuts, or both.

Settlements

Settlements were confined to rock shelters and were probably not any larger than an extended family.

Economy

The economic base of the Serranopolis subtradition was hunting, fishing, and gathering of large terrestrial gastropods, which are edible. The tools are better made than those of the earlier Itaparica subtradition in the area. Stone artifacts included small scrapers, projectile points, drills, pitted hammer stones, and smoothing stones; bone artifacts included projectile points, fish-hooks, and scrapers made of mollusk shells.

Reference

Schmitz, Pedro Ifnacio (n.d.). *A Evoluçao da Cultura no Sudoeste Sudoeste de Goías.* Rio Grfande do Sul: Instituto Anchietano de Pesquisas. UNISINOS.

Southern Brazilian Core Tool

ABSOLUTE TIME PERIOD: 6680–6000 B.P.

LOCATION:: From the area of the Rio Ivai, northwestern Paraná, south to the northern highlands of Rio Grande do Sul.

DIAGNOSTIC MATERIAL ATTRIBUTES: The major diagnostic trait is the preponderance of tools made of cores in relation to those made of flakes. The majority of sites are located between 200–300 m from the margins of the main rivers. Sites are generally found on low hills. Friable sandstone, indurated sandstone, chalcedony, and volcanic rocks, such as red basalt were the main raw materials for artifacts. Core tools included choppers, pestles, knifes, picks, and a great variety of scrapers: square, rectangular, circular, plano-convex, and side-notched (Chynz 1969: 111). In the northeast highlands of Rio Grande do Sul, the Core subtradition has some hook-shaped or "boomerang-shaped" lithic tools (Miller 1969: 48), which indicate a relation with the Altoparanaense Tradition to the south of the Rio Grande Highlands and in Uruguay. The Altoparanaense Tradition is dated c. 6000 B.P. (Menghin and Wachnitz 1958). According to Brochado (1969: 26), the tools in the highlands of northwest Rio Grande do Sul are both unifaced and bifaced. Here also are large tools with a point on opposite ends.

CULTURAL SUMMARY

Environment

The type of environment varies according to the location. The area of the valley of the Rio Ivaí in northwest Paraná, where some of the sites of the Core Tool subtradition occur, is on the second and third highlands. The division of these two highlands is marked by a basalt escarpment, and the valley of this river cuts through Permian sandstone. Above this sandstone are the upper Triassic sandy clays and calcarous sandstone. These formations are crossed by veins and dikes of diabase that causes falls and rapids in the Rio Ivaí. The valley of this river has forests primarily composed of palm trees mixed with Aruacanian pines. Where the Rio Ivaí parallels the basalt escarpment, there is a subtropical rainforest with lianas, epiphytes, and palms. The mean temperature of the second highlands is 17.8° C with a miniumum of −4.6° C. The annual precipitation is 1736 mm, being most accentuated in the summer months from October to March. In times past, large animals, such as capybaras and anteaters, were present. Fish are plentiful in the rivers. In summer, many trees produce nuts and fruits such as the *palmito*, *jerivá*, *macaúba*. On the other hand, in the highlands of northern Rio Grande do Sul, the area is characterized by great lakes. There are also navigable rivers, with small rapids that have their sources in the basalt highlands in the Serra Geral (mountains with an altitude of 3000 m). The highlands have a maximum temperature of 40° C in January and minimum of −9° C in July. Rainfall is evenly distributed in the winter, and the mean annual precipitation is 2000 mm. Before the time of conquest, the highlands were covered with tropical latifolida trees, while the river valley had gallery forests of mainly aruacarias. The highlands of Rio Grande do Sul were rich in game animals, fish, fruits, nuts, and raw material for artifacts.

Settlements

All sites of this subtradition are open and are located near the falls and rapids of small tributaries of larger rivers and lie on elevated areas above periodic flooded lowlands. The majority of sites lie 200–300 m from the river's edges. Sites are small, roughly 10 by 20 m, although one site had material scattered over an area of 200 sq m. Archaeological material generally occurs between depths of 20–40 cm, although one site had artifacts between levels 40–80 cm. The greater the depth generally, the better made the artifacts.

References

Brochado, José, Proenza Th. (1969). "Pesquisas arqueológicas efetu-adas no noroeste do Rio Grande do Dul, Programa Nacional de Pesquisas Archaeológicas, 2, Resultatdos Preliminares do Segundo

Ano, 1666–1667." In *Publicações Avulsas No. 10.* Pará: Bêlem, 11–28.

Chymz, Igor (1969). "Dados Parcais Sôbre a Arqueologia do Vale do Rio Ivaí in Programa Nacional de Pesquisas Arqueológicas: Resultados Preliminaraes do Sequndo Ano-1966–1967." *Publicações Avulsas no. 10.*, Museu Paraense Emílio Goeldi. Pará: Belém, 95–118.

Menghin, Osvaldo F. A., and Herman Waschitnitz (1958). *Forschungen über die Chronologie de Altoparanákultur.* Buenos Aires: Acta Prehistorica.

Miller, Eurico Th. (1969). "Pesquisas Arqueológicas Efetuadas no Noreste do Sul (Alto Uruguai). Programa Nacional de Pesquisas Archaeológicas, 2." *Resultados Preliminares de Segundo Ano,* 1966–1967. Publicações Svulsas No. 10. Pará: Museu Paraense Emílio Goeldi, Bêlem, 33–54.

SITES

Abrigo 6, Cerca Grande

ABSOLUTE TIME PERIOD: 9028–100 B.P.

LOCATION: The site is situated in a rock shelter at the south end of the cliffs in the area of Cerca Grande, to the north of Belo Horizonte, Minas Gerais, Brazil.

DESCRIPTIVE SUMMARY

Local Environment

Cerca Grande is a limestone cliff fronting on a ephemeral lake. There were five other rock shelters with evidence of human habitation in the base of the same cliff. The climatic changes of the past are reflected in the height of various caves and rock shelters in the cliff formed by various past oscillations of this lake. Abrigo 6 is a solution cave at the south end of the cliff and was formed by the highest lake level, 25 m above the present-day base of the lake. The cultural deposits rest on top a layer of calcite crystals. The vegetation of the general area is the type known as a *cerrado* forest of medium-size trees, such as palms, *gameleiras*, and *Ipês*. On top of the limestone plateau in which the rock shelter is located, not only do these trees occur but also cacti, orchids, and xerophitic shrubs. The present-day fauna include marmosets, pacas, and armadillos, but they are no longer common. Parakeets occur in large numbers. The bones of extinct Pleistocene megafauna were excavated by Peter Wilhelm Lund in the local area 1825–1880 (Couto 1950). Lund found the remains of *Platyonix, Clymodotherium, Heplophorus, Megatherium,* and *Smilodon.*

Physical Features

At one time, a large rock fell from the ceiling, and a part of the base intruded in the ash of the uppermost level of the cultural deposits. Under the base of the diagonally inclined boulder and a portion of upper cultural deposits, an empty space was formed. This space was soon filled with refuse. This refuse in time had been cemented by mineral water dripping through fissures in the ceiling. In the refuse stratum were found completely flexed human burials. This mineralized stratum was designated as Level 1, which was 1 m thick. Level 2, a highly consolidated level, was composed of ash with other refuse of human occupation, while Level 3 had the same content but was less consolidated. On the other hand, Level 4, while composed of the same material, was much harder. Levels 5–7 were composed of red-colored and gray alternating layers. Level 8 had the same content as Level 4 and contained evidence of human occupation. The lowermost level of refuse (Level 8) produced radiocarbon dates of 7700 B.P. and 7076 B.P.

Cultural Aspects

The 12 human burials encountered in the rock shelter lay in a completely flexed position. The grave of one of the burials was outlined with rock slabs, and some of the other burials were covered with rocks. The artifacts and the content of the refuse areas indicate that the inhabitants of this rock shelter had an economy based on hunting and gathering. A major diagnostic trait of the toolkit was the many artifacts made of quartz crystals. Tools consisted of contracted-stemmed and barbed projectile points. There were also choppers and pitted hammer stones. An unexplained anomaly at this early date were grooved and polished stone axes and adzes.

References

Couto, Carlos de Paula (1950). *Memórias Sôbre a Paleontologia Brasileira, Peter Wilhelm Lund,* transl. Couto. Rio de Janeiro: Instituto Livro.

Hurt, Wesley, and Oldemar Blasi (1969). "O Projecto Arqueológico Lagoa Santa, Minas Gerais, Brasil (Nota Final)." *Arquivos do Museu Paranaense, Nova Série, Arqueologia* no. 4, Curitiba.

Abrigo do Pilao (BA-CE-17)

TIME PERIOD: 9600–900 B.P.

LOCATION: Situated in a rock shelter, on the south side of Serra da Pedra Blanca, a limestone ridge, facing south, north of the town of Central, Bahia.

DESCRIPTIVE SUMMARY

Local Environment

The site is within a dry belt of Northeast Brazil. Dry season averages about 7 months in duration from April through October and occasionally may be longer than a year. At the time of the excavation project, May 1984, it had not rained for 5 years. Average rainfall is 489 mm. Daytime temperatures may climb above 40° C and in winter drop below 13° C. In the southwest part of the Municipio, where the Abrigo de Pilao is located, is a northwest-trending mountain range composed mainly of quartzite, called the Serra Azul. The mountains were the source of raw materials for making tools by the prehistoric inhabitants of the Municipio de Central. The Rio Verde, a permanent river, which has its origin in the Serra Azul, lies on the west side of the Municipio. This was the source for the freshwater mussels, a major food supply for the prehistoric peoples and material for making tools. The rock shelter of Pilao is located in a karst plateau with numerous sinkholes and cliffs containing solution caves and rock shelters. The area is covered with a *caatinga* type of forest, which includes thorny bushes and trees. There are also giant and smaller types of cacti and the *Umbu* trees that produce edible fruits. Contemporary fauna includes peccaries, deer, jaguars, smaller mammals such as the pacas, agouti, armadillos, marmosets, lizards, and snakes. These animals are rare today because they have been overhunted, but were plentiful in ancient times. Birds are present but not very common.

Physical Features

The site has an east and west chamber and is encompassed in a rock shelter that extends along a cliff about 17 m. The small flaked tools in the main early Holocene level, dated between 9600–8000 years ago, were never intentionally edge-trimmed. Instead, the raw material quartzite and quartz crystals had a natural sharp cutting edge. Other tools and rejected material in the manufacturing process consisted of flakes and chunks of quartz, quartzite, chert, and limestone, plus limestone pounders, choppers, and hammer stones. Scrapers made of mussels from the Verde river and a few bone artifacts, such as two projectile points, complete the assemblage of the early occupations. Tools were heavy and made of large limestone flakes in the upper part of a red zone within in the eastern chamber. In addition, Bryan and Gruhn conclude that, because there is a stratigraphic separation and a distinctive pebble and flake-tool industry, which did not persist into the overlying ash and silt zone, the limestone pebble tools from the lower red silt zone were used earlier than the main early Holocene occupation. Thus at least two very early occupations are present.

Cultural Aspects

Intentionally edge-trimmed flaked tools are rare. The 0–10 cm stratum contained 50 percent of the artifacts. This stratum also contained fragments of mussel shells, utilized quartz flakes, utilized chert flakes, quartzite hammer stones, large limestone flakes, two bifacial flakes, an engraved ax blade, two grooved and polished stone axes, red ocher, and ceramics. The ceramics were thick, incompletely fired, giving a dark core in their cross-section. The temper is a fine quartz grit. Some sherds had a grooved surface made by the potter's fingers. Others had a red slip and a brushed surface. These traits indicate that the last occupation should be assigned to the Simple Brazilian Ceramic subtradition. In summary, Bryan and Gruhn (1993: 109) conclude that there were at least four discrete occupations in the Abrigo de Piloa. The most intensive occupation, between 9600–8800 B.P. was probably by hunters and gatherers, as were the two earlier occupations. The final occupation, about 900 years ago, was probably by horticulturists who made ceramics.

Reference

Bryan, Alan C., and Ruth Gruhn. (1993). *Archaeological Research at Six Cave or Rockshelter Sites in Interior Bahia, Brazil*. Brazilian Studies Center for the Study of First Americans, Corvallis: Oregon State University.

José Vieira

ABSOLUTE TIME PERIOD: c. 8635 B.P. (preceramic level) undated (ceramic level).

LOCATION: The site is situated on the left bank of the Rio Ivaí, about 20 km north of the city of Gaúcha, state of Paraná.

DESCRIPTIVE SUMMARY

Local Environment

According to Laming and Emperaire (1959: 129), the cliff on which the site is situated is about 15 m above the mean level of the river. The cliff where the river has cut its bed has at its base conglomerate and probably is of the Quaternary age. On top of this conglomerate, 2–4 m thick, is a blue argillous sand. Above this is a sandy clay compound; finally, near the surface, are stratified light-colored and black sands. Apparently the lower strata (Levels 3 and 4) are the result of flooding of the river, while the upper strata (Levels 1 and 2) seem to be of aeolian origin because they are above the floodline. Archaeologically and geologically, there is a hiatus between the lower and upper levels. The final formation of the area corresponds to a period of droughts and wind that appears to be general of the Paraná river valley.

Physical Features

The geological and archaeological history of the José Viera begins with a period of alluvial formation. Near the end of the alluvial period, humans occupy the cliff. By the end of the alluvial period, pottery-making humans occupy the cliff. This alluvial period is followed by a period of aeolian deposits. Climate is dry and with strong winds predominant. Ceramic-making humans continue to occupy the cliff. The area is finally abandoned, and aeolian sands cover it.

Cultural Aspects

Only one polished stone, a small chisel, was found in the aeolian deposits. All other tools are of flaked stone and are crudely made. These flake tools occur in all levels and are made from split water-rounded stones. In spite of Laming and Emperaire's conclusion that all but one tool was made of flakes, their illustrations indicate some of the other tools (such as choppers) are made

from cores (1959: Figs. 19, 20, 21, and 22). Tools were both unifacial and bifacial. Judging by use marks, unmodified flakes were used as scrapers. Flake tools include end scrapers, pointed scrapers, and knives. The proportion and quality of bifacial tools increase with age, while the presence of both flake and core tools indicates that the preceramic strata belong to the Flake and Core Tool subtradition. The type of ceramics found in the upper layers is typical of Tupigurani types, such as sherds decorated with geometric patterns of red, rarely brown, on a white slip and examples with plastic decorations such as fingertip or punctated. In the aeolian layers were found the burials of two women and one child, but they were in very poor condition

Reference

Laming, Annette, and José Emperaire (1959). "A Jazida José Vieira, Un Sito Guarani e Precerâmico." In *Arqueologico* no. 0, Secçao. Paraná: Universidade do Paraná, Curitiba.

GO-JA-O1

TIME PERIOD: 10,750–9000 B.P.

LOCATION: The rock shelter is located in the state of Goiás on the right side of the Rio Paranaíba.

DESCRIPTIVE SUMMARY

Local Environment

The region is in the center of the Brazilian uplands, varying in altitude from the 300 m in the bottom of the river valleys to 1000 m in the highest elevation on the divide of the Rio Araguaia. The present climate is hot with an attenuated dry season. The dry season is from 3–4 months of June to August. The month of June is the coldest and September the hottest month. It rains from 70 to 130 days a year, with 1250–1400 mm annual precipitation. According to Ab'Saber (1977), the climate at the end of the Pleistocene when the site was first occupied, was colder and drier than at present. Open grasslands were probably larger than at present. On the basis of evidence in the strata in the rock shelter it can be deduced, according to Schmitz (1984), that at the beginning of the Holocene, 11,000–8500 B.P., the region was colder and drier, but around 8500 B.P. the temperature became warmer and more humid. Anteater, peccary, capybara, paca, agouti, coatis, and small rodents inhabit the region. In the river and swamps are cayman, turtles, and mollusks. There are also large terrestrial gastropods in the area. During the rainy season, the trees produce a great variety of nuts and fruits, fibers, and medicinal leaves.

Physical Features

Site GO-JA-01 is in a rock shelter in a cliff of sandstone and quartzitc. Thc shelter is 65 m at the mouth and at a depth of 20 m and has 170 cm of kitchen refuse. Inside the shelter, it is dry, but in the rainy season drops of water fall from the ceiling. On the walls are many pictographs and petroglyphs.

Cultural Aspects

Judging by the site, it was probably inhabited by an extended family. The surrounding savannas were probably inhabited by many game animals, and hunting was the main economic activity, followed by fishing and the gathering of the large terrestrial gastropods. Wild fruits and nuts were also collected. The site was occupied from 10,750–9000 B.P., and the artifacts included a unifacial industry made of large flakes. A diagnostic tool was the lesma, a leaf-shaped point that had at one end a diagonal cutting edge. This tool is characteristic of the Itaparica subtradition in which site GO-JA-01 belongs. These tools are accompanied by pointed tools and smoothing instruments for crushing fruits. There were also bone points or spatulas.

References

Ab'Saber A.N. (1977). Domínios Mortoclimáticos na América do Sul. São Paulo: Universidade de São Paulo, Instituto de Geografia.

Schmitz, Pedro Ignacio. (n.d.). A Evoluçao da Cultura no Sudoeste de Goiás. Instituto Anchietano de Pesquisas. Rio Grande do Sul: USINOS.

Schmitz, P. J. (1984). Caçadores e Coletores do Pré-história do Brasil. Instito Anchietano de Pesquisas. Rio Grande do Sul: UNISINOS, Sao Leopoldo.

GO-JA-03

TIME PERIOD: 9765–5729 B.P.

LOCATION: Southwest of the state of Goias, in the municipio of the same name, valley of the Verdinho river, a tributary on the right side of the Paranaiba river.

DESCRIPTIVE SUMMARY

Local Environment

The site, in the area of the Verdinho river, has 3–4 dry months, with an mean annual precipitation of 1500 mm, largely falling during the rainy season from December through February. The coldest months are June through August, while the mean annual temperature varies from 18° to 20° C. The mean annual temperatures of the coldest months vary from 15°–10° C, and frost may occur. The site is at the contact of two different vegetation series, the cerrado, a regime of low trees and shrubs, and a semideciduous forest. There are also grasslands and gallery forests by the rivers. The open grasslands have a great variety of fruit-bearing trees, such as caju, murici, and guariroba. Mammals in prehistoric times included the peccary, armadillo, deer, paca, agouti, tapir, capybara, turtles, and cayman. The rock shelters that were inhabited had their mouths to the north or east.

Physical Features

The site is situated in a rock shelter at the base of a cliff 64 m high. The opening is 80 m wide but has a depth of only 6–14 m. The cliff is formed of sandstone beds, with some silicified, which was excellent material for making artifacts. The roof of the rock shelter is tilted toward the interior, forming the continuation of the face of the cliff. Great irregularities in the ceiling form compartments in the shelter without closing the space. There are also large rocks that have fallen from the ceiling. A large rock in the center of the rock shelter is covered with petroglyphs as are the sides of the site. Stratum 7 has a charcoal lens with a date of 5720 radiocarbon years, while the lowermost stratum (10) composed of sand with sandstone fragments, has a date of 9765 radiocarbon years. The uppermost strata (35 cm deep) of the ceramic-making Jatai focus produced two skeletons, an adult and an infant. They lay on their backs with their legs open. Accompanying them was a large quantity of perforated beads. Between the two burials was a rock and the base of a stake that possibly marked the sepulcher.

References

Schmitz, Pedro Ignacio. (n.d.). A Evoluçao da Cultura no Sudoeste de Goiás. Instituto Anchietano de Pesquisas. Rio Grande do Sul: USINOS.

Altair Sales Barbosa, Andre Luis Jazcobus, and Maria Barberi Ribeiro (1989). "Arqueologia nos Cerrados do Brazil Central, Serranópolis

I, Pesquisas." In *Antropologia* no. 44. Rio Frande do Sul: Instituto Anchietano de Pesquisas, Sao Leopoldo.

Gruta do Padre (PE.SF.16)

TIME PERIOD: 5630–c. 2000 B.P.

LOCATION: In the valley of the Médio Sao Francisco river, near the Itaparica waterfalls, município de Petrolândia.

DESCRIPTIVE SUMMARY

Local Environment

Although there is abundant rain in the headwaters of the Sao Francisco river, in its middle course it enters a semiarid region with high evaporation. At present, the mean annual precipitation is less than 500 mm, with many months without any rain. This dry season extends over 9–10 months, with precipitation concentrated in the months of January to March. The vegetation is the dry *caatinga* type, small trees and bushes averaging 2.50–3 m. These grow in small groups of forests with interving areas without any vegetation. Thorny bushes and palms are common. The land has smooth undulations with an average altitude of 300 m. The area during the period between 6000–5000 B.P. had an extremely hot and dry climate. Beginning at 10,000 B.P., the perennial flow of the Sao Francisco river attracted hunters to the region.

Physical Features

The Gruta do Padre faces the Sao Francisco river, and the mouth of the rock shelter is 8 m wide and 2–70 m high. It extends into the cliff 9.74 m. Because of the large numbers of human bones found in the rock shelter, early researchers, such as Carlos Estevao, suggested that the site was a cemetery and that a fire had been ignited over the burials and their accompanying artifacts. Over this, flagstones were placed. These fires destroyed bones but helped preserve textiles, seeds, and nuts. On the basis of the finds he made in this site, Calderón named it the Itaparica Tradition. Theoretically, the people of the Itaparaica Tradition grew maize, cremated their dead, and wove various textiles. The growing of maize in a relatively recent site such as the Gruta do Padre, dated 2000 B.P., is entirely possible, but

for sites in the Itaparica Tradition such as G0-JA-01, dated 11,000 B.P., is out of the question. The stratigraphy of the Gruta de Padre and its content, as excavated by Calderón, was as follows: Level 0–20 cm contained many rock fragments and goat manure. There were also burned shell, human teeth, and remains of fiber. There were also cremated bones of four individuals. Level 20–60 cm contained large amounts of ash and bone fragments. The piles of bones and ash were covered with flagstones. Level 60–65 cm was gray-colored when dry and coffee-colored when wet. Also had carbonate concretions. Level 75–90 cm deposits were yellow-colored and hardened with silicate. It contained a large number of stone artifacts and charcoal.

Cultural Aspects

According to Calderón, the rock shelter had three human occupations: the oldest, which had 1 m of deposits, had a date of 5630 B.P. and corresponds with Strata IV–III, and two later occupations, separated by a period of no occupation, the last being a cemetery. The oldest occupation had plano-convex stone tools, with edges trimmed by percussion and pressure. Types included circular or semicircular scapers, side scrapers, ovoid scrapers, choppers, *lesmas*, flake knives, drills, and worked flakes. They were made of quartz and fine sandstone, quartzite and chalcedony and hematite. The most recent tools were plano-convex, polished tools, choppers, pestles, and blades. There were also keeled scrapers characteristic of the Itaparica subtradition.

References

Calderón, Valentin (1969). "Nota prévia sobre arqueologica das regiLes e sudeste da Bahia." In *Pronapa* 2. Pará: Museu Paraense Emílio Goeldi, Bélem, 37–58.

Estévao. Carlos (1943). "O ossuário da Gruta do Padre, em Itaparica e algumas notícisd sobre remanescentes indigines do Nordeste, Rio de Janeiro." *Impressa Naciomsl Separata do Boletim do Museu Nacional* 14–15 (1938–1942): 150–210.

Martin, Gabriela Jacionira, Silva Rocha, and Marcos Galindo Lima (1986). "Industrias líticas em no vale do Médio Sao Francisco (Pernambuco, Brasil)." In *Cliom Série Arqueológico* 3, Numero 9. Recife: Universidade Federal Pernambuco, 99–136.

WESLEY HURT (deceased)
compiled by
PETER N. PEREGRINE
Department of Anthropology
Lawrence University
Appleton, Wisconsin
United States

Early Highland Andean Archaic

ABSOLUTE TIME PERIOD: 7000–4500 B.P.

RELATIVE TIME PERIOD: Follows the Late Andean Hunting-Collecting tradition and is followed by the Late highland Andean Archaic tradition.

LOCATION: The Andes mountains and mountain valleys from Ecuador to northern Chile, to the west of lowland tropical forest regions.

DIAGNOSTIC MATERIAL ATTRIBUTES: Chipped-stone industry including relatively small, leaf-shaped, diamond-shaped, or shouldered projectile points and unifacial tools. Industries include bone tools, rare ground stone, and ornaments of mineral, shell, or bone. Cave occupation sites, with some open-air camps. Pictographs in a variety of pigment colors.

REGIONAL SUBTRADITIONS: Central Andean Archaic, North Andean Archaic, Southern Andean Archaic.

IMPORTANT SITES: Asana, Guitarrero Cave, Pachamachay Cave, Puente.

CULTURAL SUMMARY

Environment

Climate. The general climate of the Archaic traditions appears reasonably similar to that of the present; glacial retreats from the last stadial of the Pleistocene are fairly complete prior to human occupation. Temperature ranges vary across altitude more than with seasons, with frequent subfreezing nightly temperatures at higher altitudes, and warmer and less fluctuating temperatures in valley settings. Rainfall concentrated in period of November through April.

Topography. Archaic occupations are found throughout the rugged highlands, excepting only extremely high regions above about 4600 m. Major topographic physiotypes include the high plains and hilly topography above 3700 m, and the highland valleys, with altitudes ranging from as low as 1300–3700 m.

Geology. Much of the Andean highlands consists of rock exposures and relatively thin soils, although substantial Pleistocene and Holocene sediments occur in valley bottoms. The Andes mountains have varied formation origin, but frequently sedimentary limestones and similar rocks are found above intrusive igneous and surrounding metamorphosed formations. Extrusive rocks are present in northern and southern ends of the central Andes, making obsidian common in Ecuador and southern Peru; other flakeable stone resources include a variety of cherts and fine-grain crystalline igneous rocks. Hydrothermal alteration leads to metal-producing mineral deposits.

Biota. At higher humanly occupied altitudes, the common formation is the *puna*, or open grasslands, inhabited by grazing animals such as wild camelids, especially the vicuña, and deer. Highland valley settings typically featured a sparse scrub vegetation limited by local rain shadows; camelids, especially the guanaco, and deer were present, if sparse. Rainfall seasonality leads to a more seasonal biota in the highland valley setting compared with the *puna*.

Settlements

Settlement System. Sites include apparent base camps as well as quarry and other task-specific locations; ceremonial facilities are relatively rare, with the possible exception of shelters with rock art. At higher altitudes, occupation was primarily in caves, which offered cold protection; sites at lower elevations often include open-air camps. In highland valleys and the southern *puna* there was significant residential mobility, leading to a highly seasonal use of sites according to local resource availability. The less seasonal *puna* environment of the central Andes allowed relatively low degrees of mobility, with corresponding high intensity occupations.

Community Organization. Some base-camp sites show differentiation between residential, refuse, and task-oriented areas, but these are highly variable between cave and open-air contexts.

Housing. Fragmentary structures, but few complete examples of houses are known. Most seem to have been light pole-and-thatch constructions of very modest size, often with one or more hearths, capable of sheltering no more than nuclear families, and even then only for sleeping. Some examples of modest stone foundations are known, and corrals for animals make their appearance toward the end of the archaic. Special-function structures for ceremonial purposes have been argued for certain sites, but are not widely known.

Population, Health, and Disease. Modest site size of most highland Archaic sites indicates that band-sized groups of around 15–50 people were the common residential units. Some population clusters with density relatively high for hunter gatherers may have existed, but in general a dispersed, fairly sparse population is the rule, with residential bases spaced between 15–100 km apart. Overall site density ranges between 0.01–0.2 sites per km^2, including nonresidential sites; population densities may have fallen in the range of 0.001–0.05 persons per km^2. It appears probable that relatively separate populations existed in highland valley and *puna*

settings. The general impression from the relatively few known human remains of this period is that of a healthy and robust population with good dental condition. Child mortality does not appear to have been particularly high for a hunter-gatherer population.

Economy

Subsistence. At the outset of the Archaic, hunting and gathering was the sole source of food, but some use of domesticated species occurs by the end of the period. Populations in highland valleys maintained a pattern of seasonal mobility in order to position themselves near the seasonally available resources of this zone. *Puna* populations of the central Andes were less mobile because of reduced resource seasonality. A sexual division of labor in subsistence tasks is likely, but little direct evidence is available to confirm it.

Wild Foods. Archaic peoples were broad-spectrum foragers, using a broad and variable range of natural resources, depending on their location. Seed-, fruit-, and tuber-bearing plants were important, especially in sub-*puna* settings. Hunting was increasingly important at higher altitudes where edible plants become scarce. Camelids (vicuña, guanaco) and deer were primary large-bodied game, while *viscacha* (a rabbit-like animal), wild guinea pig, and a variety of terrestrial and lake-based birds contributed to a small game component of the diet.

Domestic Foods. In the later Archaic, there appears to be a regional and quite variable use of domesticate species, perhaps mostly focused in highland valley areas. Early use of a domesticated *Chenopodium* has been argued for fairly early *puna* sites, but undoubtedly contributed a minor food component. Both grain and tuber crops, including maize, beans, and perhaps potatoes, were probably cultivated in some highland valleys before the end of the period, but evidence is sparse. Use of apparently domesticated alpacas may have occurred prior to 6000 B.P. in *puna*-edge sites, while more centrally located *puna* sites seem to maintain a primary reliance on hunting throughout the period.

Industrial Arts. Primary technologies include fracturing, grinding, and polishing of stone; shaping and polishing of bone; preparation of hides for clothing and shelter; preparation of pigments for ornamentation of rock surfaces and probably the human body. Technologies involving perishable materials are less well known, because highland preservation conditions are not ideal as on the desert coast to the west of the Andes. There is evidence for basket and mat weaving, and at least by the end of the period textile production had begun.

Utensils. Chipped-stone tools are the best known artifacts of the highland Archaic. This industry used percussion and pressure flakers of antler and bone to fashion struck flakes into a variety of tool forms. Most tools are small (<3 cm), including bifacially flaked projectile points that vary significantly in form over time and also space. The remainder of the chipped tools are unifacially retouched flakes with a variety of edge forms and utilized but largely unmodified flakes. Stone raw materials vary by locality, but cherts, quartzites, and basalts predominate, with obsidian used near the relatively rare sources of this material. Heat alteration of chert is frequently seen for improving technical and functional qualities of the stone. This industry predominantly consists of tools useful in hunting and processing animals and also for maintenance and production of tools in wood or bone. Grinding stones for milling foodstuffs are relatively rare compared with chipped-stone tools. They are somewhat more frequent in highland valley sites, but are generally rather unformed pieces of stone with surfaces ground and polished from use. Bone tools are present, largely in the form of pointed and polished tools including awls and needles, but given the abundance of available bone, these tools are not strikingly common. Pottery is completely absent.

Ornaments. Nonutilitarian worked artifacts are relatively rare and consist mostly of local materials. Beads of stone or bone are perhaps most common, with marine and eastern jungle shell present, but rare. Minerals including crystals, fossils, and colorants were collected, and there appears to have been consistent use of hematite and limonite, probably as a paint for artistic decoration on the human body and elsewhere. Baked clay was used, but rarely, as a modeling medium for rudimentary figurines. The striking rarity of ornaments and the suggestive fragmentary remains of basketry and netting under unusually good preservation conditions suggest that decoration may have been focused on perishable items.

Trade. There is little evidence for organized or concerted trade over significant distances in the highland Andes. Very minor amounts of exotic obsidian and shell are found in Archaic sites, but most people living at this time probably never touched or saw these materials. They probably reflect sequential passing of materials through local, unorganized exchange that may have occurred during sporadic contacts by individuals or temporary meetings of multiple residential groups. The relative lack of exchanged items within a very diverse region such as the Andes may speak to relative isolation of groups within environmental zones and to a small amount of travel beyond group boundaries.

Division of Labor. There is very little evidence for occupational specialization in the form of craft production. Artifacts from the Archaic could easily have been produced by any competent individual within the society with a relatively short learning time. Patterns of projectile point style may indicate that some stone tool production was sex-specific, probably by males, but other evidence for a sexual division of labor is based mostly on inference from known hunter gatherers, and not direct evidence.

Differential Access or Control of Resources. Evidence from burials suggests that individuals were not distinguished by accumulated possessions that would argue for preferential resource control during life. The use of immediately available raw materials that were mostly available over large areas would have made difficult any control of essential materials. There are some suggestions that adjacent residential groups may have had access to a different range of ornamental resources, either through rare trade contacts or territorial control.

Sociopolitical Organization

Social Organization. The size of residential sites suggests most people lived in band-sized groups of around 25, as documented ethnographically for many hunter gatherers. The small size of the few and fragmentary living structures indicates that smaller units existed within the local residential group, perhaps nuclear families. No known evidence points to strong kinship or descent ties between families or individuals. Patterns of projectile point style over time and space suggest considerable local group continuity in projectile point makers, probably men, for some *puna* areas. Strong stylistic differentiation between adjacent residential sites argues for long-term continuity and stability in group composition over significant lengths of time. This suggests that the pronounced fluidity of social composition seen in such ethnographic hunter gatherers such as the Kalahari San of Africa may not apply in some regions of the Andean Archaic. Skeletal evidence from one *puna* area shows strong uniformity in genetic characteristics within a residential group that might hint at some level of local group endogamy.

Political Organization. Neither the artifact nor burial record shows patterns in the slightest suggestive of a distinction between individuals in terms of authority.

Simply put, there are no consistently available, distinguishing materials that could have been used to signify authority, and no evidence of craft investment or material accumulation that might have served in a similar fashion. All evidence points towards a highly egalitarian condition among these foragers.

Social Control. Although there is no evidence for authority capable of imposing social control on an autocratic basis, some patterns in rock art depictions suggest that there may have been social observances, perhaps in the form of rituals, designed to achieve certain behavior patterns. The consistent portrayal of camelids expulsing young from their social groups and the repetitive and palimpsested depiction of pregnant animals may hint at beliefs related to exogamy and reproduction in humans.

Conflict. To date, there is no evidence for individual or organized violence in he form of harmed individuals, defensive features to sites, or human-specific weaponry. Paired young–old simultaneously interred burials at one *puna* site could hint at coercive behavior, but this remains unclear. Given the limited skeletal evidence from this period, however, there is no reason to argue that interpersonal conflict was any different from that observed in small group, nonauthoritarian groups in other times and places.

Religion and Expressive Culture

Religious Beliefs. There is little basis for knowing the religious beliefs of this temporally remote and nondepictive society. It may be telling that camelids are the overwhelmingly predominant depiction in rock art and are not usually shown in a hunting context. It seems possible that spirits related to these animals were important in Archaic beliefs, in a relationship similar to that of South African rock art and corresponding hunter-gatherer belief systems.

Ceremonies. Ceremonial contexts have been argued for the Archaic residential site of Asana, involving cleared public space with small altarlike features and perhaps miniature representations of architecture and animals.

Arts. Rock art is the primary expressive art surviving to the present from the highland Archaic. The predominant depictions are of camelids, usually in groups, perhaps with some portrayal of social behavior. Images are painted in a variety of colors, with red predominating, but also with the use of black, white, and yellow pigments.

Death and Afterlife. Burials suggest a careful disposal of the dead, probably in most cases away from primary occupation sites. Artifacts accompanying the dead suggest some belief in an afterlife, but they are neither abundant nor informative. A few tools of either stone or bone and ornaments or clothing decorations of bone, teeth, or shell are all that are known in the way of funerary offerings. Burial position and orientation of the dead are not consistent, even within sites, suggesting that funerary ritual was not highly institutionalized or related to highly specific beliefs.

Suggested Readings

Aldenderfer, M. (1998). *Montane Foragers: Asana and the South-Central Andean Archaic.* Iowa City: University of Iowa Press.

Cardich, A. (1958). "Los Yacimientos de Lauricocha y la Nueva Interpretación de la Prehistoria Peruana." *Studia Praehistórica* 1.

Cardich, A. (1964). *Lauricocha: Fundamentos para una Prehistória de los Andes Centrales. Studia Praehistórica* 3.

Lavallée, D., M. Julien, J. Wheeler, and C. Karlin (1985). *Telarmachay: Chasseurs et Pasteurs Préhistoriques des Andes*, I. Paris: Institut Francais D'Études Andines.

Lynch, T. F. (1967). "The Nature of the Andean Preceramic." *Occasional Papers of the Idaho State Museum* 21.

Lynch, T. F. (1980). *Guitarrero Cave: Early Man in the Andes.* New York: Academic Press.

MacNeish, R. S., A. Garcia Cook, L. G. Lumbreras, R. K. Vierra, and A. Nelken-Turner (1981). *Prehistory of the Ayacucho Basin, Peru: vol. II: Excavations and Chronology.* Ann Arbor: University of Michigan Press.

MacNeish, R. S., R. K. Vierra, A. Nelken-Turner, and C. J. Phagan. (1980). *Prehistory of the Ayacucho Basin, Peru: vol. III: Nonceramic Artifacts.* Ann Arbor: University of Michigan Press.

Nuñez A., L. (1983). "Paleoindian and Archaic Cultural Periods in the Arid and Semiarid Regions of Northern Chile." *Advances in World Archaeology*, 2: 161–203.

Rick, J. W. (1980). *Prehistoric Hunters of the High Andes.* New York: Academic Press.

Rick, J. W. (1983). *Cronología, Clima, y Subsistencia en el Precerámico Peruano.* Lima: Instituto Andino de Estudios Arqueológicos.

Rick, J. W. (1988). "The Character and Context of Highland Preceramic Society." In *Peruvian Prehistory*, ed. by R. W. Keatinge. New York: Cambridge University Press, 3–40.

Salazar, E. (1979). *El Hombre Temprano en la Región del Ilaló, Sierra del Ecuador.* Cuenca, Ecuador: La Universidad de Cuenca.

SUBTRADITIONS

Central Andean

TIME PERIOD: 10,000–1700 B.P.

LOCATION: High Andean valleys, and high *puna* grasslands of western South America from about 8° S latitude to about 15° S latitude. This area makes up the central highlands of present-day Peru. It is a somewhat geographically broader definition than the Central Andean Preceramic Tradition of Lynch (1980).

DIAGNOSTIC MATERIAL ATTRIBUTES:: Small-sized chipped-stone tools with bifacial projectile points made to distinctive outline shapes, including leaf- and lanceolate-shape, shouldered and denticulate, and occasionally flat-based or triangular shapes. Subsistence emphasis is on broad-spectrum exploitation of a variable species list, but with at least some emphasis on hunting of deer or wild camelids.

CULTURAL SUMMARY

Environment

The central Peruvian Andes have two relatively distinct zones of archaic occupation: the highland valleys and the *puna* zone (Rick 1983; Tosi 1960). The highland valleys are varied environments, but tend to be steeply sloping valley walls and small areas of alluvial bottomland with a natural vegetation of scrub or spiny forest located in altitude ranging from about 2000–3700 m. Food resources for humans include a wide range of plant foods, many highly seasonal, and large- and small-bodied game. Most resources were dispersed and low density in most places over most of the year. Rainfall ranges from sparse to moderate, and thus moisture highly controls these environments. Temperatures are also moderate because of heat-sheltering effects of the valleys. Altitude, rain shadows, rain seasonality, and other effects on rainfall determine the productivity of these environments for hunter-gatherer cultures. The wet season of November to April brings rapid plant growth and probably a concentration of deer and wild camelids (particularly the guanaco) into lower reaches of valley systems; the dry season of May to October sees progressive drying from lower toward higher altitudes, with game dispersing in search of remaining vegetation and scattered higher water sources. Overall, the highland valleys are sudivided into broad altitude bands or subzones of resource availability. The *puna* zone consists of high grasslands generally ranging from about 3700–4700 m in altitude, with greater overall rainfall than the highland valleys, and a relatively cold average temperature. It has less geographic rainfall variability and seasonality within the central Andes than the highland valley zone, but does have the same wet and dry season timings. Plant food resources for humans consist primarily of the vicuña, guanaco, and deer, with a minor availability of wild grains, tubers, berries, cactus fruit, greens, and small game. Resources are generally distributed in a fine-grain mosaic of resource microzones.

Settlements

Although Lynch (1967, 1971) originally postulated a broad pattern of transhumance between sierra and coast for this period in the central Andes, it seems more likely that there was little annual movement between far-flung zones, and in some areas even the *puna* and highland valley human populations may have been distinct. In situations where small valley and *puna* areas are highly interlaced, landscape utilization may have been more broad-ranging. In the central *puna* zone surrounding Lake Junín, extensive investigations have documented a number of sites, although the investigators vary in their views concerning settlement patterns (Kaulicke 1980; Lavallée et al. 1985; Rick 1980). The density of sites per km^2 and the density of material remains in these sites deposits all suggest that the *puna* was intensively occupied, in places by hunter gatherers of low residential mobility. *Puna*-edge settlements may have been part of broader movement patterns. Sites are generally in caves and rock shelters, probably reflecting a desire for heat protection. Deposits in *puna* sites can range up to 5 m thick, with exceptionally high densities of stone tools and faunal materials. Highland valley archaic sites are known from many parts of Peru, but the largest scale investigations have been in the Callejón de Huaylas (Lynch 1970, 1980) and the Ayacucho valley (MacNeish et al. 1980, 1981). In this setting, sites appear to be more scattered and much lower in density per km^2 and with lower quantities of remains per site (Rick 1988). This suggests a pattern of shifting residential bases, probably responding to seasonal resource availability and quite possibly implying altitudinal shifts within a yearly cycle. Cave and rock-shelter occupations are also present in the valleys, but open-air sites are considerably more common in this warmer setting. In both regions, evidence of houses is relatively rare, but post molds have been noted in cave and open sites, representing partially preserved structures.

Economy

In the highland valley environments, archaic people apparently utilized significant amounts of plant foods, from the relatively few reports on prehistoric plant remains from sites (Smith 1980). Nevertheless, the majority of reported subsistence remains are those of animals, which include guanaco, deer, guinea pig, and a variety of small animals (Vierra 1975; Wing 1972). There is no clear evidence of use of domesticated animals from the valley context during this time period, but the abundance of guinea pig remains in certain sites may suggest a coexistence with humans. In the *puna*, especially as documented in the Junín area, the use of plants is limited, but well documented and methodologically explored for certain sites (Pearsall 1980, 1988, 1989). There may be some experimentation with seed crops such as *Chenopodium* at a relatively early date, but this was likely to have been of minor economic importance. Intense use of camelids, particularly the vicuña, is found in the later part of this period, while the beginning shows somewhat greater, although minority use of deer (Wheeler et al. 1976). Intensive use of the vicuña is now well documented (Moore 1988, 1998) and clearly indicates an increasingly year-round, strategized use of this animal by hunters dietarily specialized in meat (Rick and Moore 2001). The presence of domesticated camelids has been argued for the Junín site of Telarmachay, based on tooth form and a high percentage of newborn animals (Wheeler 1984, 1985), but other *puna* sites have rather different records, suggesting variability in the timing and degree of dependence on domestic animals at this time. Stone tools from the valley and *puna* settings are quite similar in technology, form, and function, including a variety of time-sensitive, but locally variable projectile point forms. In the *puna*, at least, these have been shown to document important social variability (Rick 1996). The chipped-stone toolkit is primarily oriented toward hunting and processing of animals, including abundant evidence for hide processing (Lavallée et al. 1985). Over time within the Archaic, projectile points come to dominate the tool assemblage in all documented *puna* sites, while highland valley sites seem to show the opposite trend. The meaning is unclear, but suggests that over time subsistence systems of the two zones diverged functionally, with hunting remaining a strong emphasis of the *puna* populations well beyond the end of the Archaic period. Raw materials vary between most highland valley and *puna* sites, arguing that toolmakers primarily procured lithic resources within their local environs. Other tools include rare grinding stones and pointed bone tools that probably served as needles and awls.

Sociopolitical Organization

To date there is no evidence to suggest any organization other than a relatively egalitarian condition within band-sized local residential groups. Sites are modest in size and produce very few artifacts that can even be considered ornamental, much less connoting status differentials of any type. The relatively few burials known have few preserved objects accompanying them, and these again do not suggest any significant variability in material possessions between individuals (Beynon and Siegel 1981; Cardich 1964). Distribution of projectile point styles over space and time in the Junín *puna* has been argued to indicate decreased mobility over the course of the Archaic, along with increasing localization of style within specific sites. For this area, at least, a certain amount of social stability is likely, with long-lasting local residential groups occupying specific, modest-sized territories for many generations (Rick 1986). Interaction and exchange seem quite limited both between the highlands and other zones such as the coast and between the two highland zones themselves. Shell, available in abundance on the Pacific coast of the Andean region, and obsidian, available in scattered point sources within the highlands, do not travel very great distances, compared to known hunter gatherers such as those of western North America. It appears there was little incentive to personal distinction through material possessions, further arguing for an egalitarian condition at this time.

Religion and Expressive Culture

In terms of durable material culture, this is one of the less expressive post-Pleistocene cultures, with a very sparse presence of extrafunctional artifacts. A small handful of stone and shell beads and other worked stone and bone items, together with minor collections of local minerals and fossils, mostly unworked, are the only evidence of attention to pursuits beyond subsistence. It is likely that the art of making clothing, probably from wild camelid hides, may have been quite advanced. The only arena with a substantial expressive component is rock art, usually painted in red iron-based pigments, but also known to use black, yellow, and white colorants. It is likely that a substantial portion of the known pictographs of the central Andes dates from hunting-gathering periods, given the predominant camelid subject matter, and the relative rarity of clear herding depictions (Cardich 1964). This art is usually associated with archaic sites, although often with secondary camps as opposed to primary residential sites (Rick 1980). Human forms and geometric pictographs are relatively quite rare, and thus camelids may be portrayed more as elements of archaic belief systems than as hunting fuarry.

References

Beynon, D. E., and M. I. Siegel (1981). "Ancient Human Remains from Central Peru." *American Antiquity* 46: 167–178.

Cardich, A. (1958). "Los Yacimientos de Lauricocha y la Nueva Interpretación de la Prehistoria Peruana." *Studia Praehistórica* 1.

Cardich, A. (1964). "Lauricocha: Fundamentos para una Prehistória de los Andes Centrales." *Studia Praehistórica* 3.

Kaulicke, P. (1980). *Beiträge zur Kenntnis der Lithischen Perioden in der Puna Junins, Peru.* Bonn: University of Bonn.

Lavallée, D., M. Julien, J. Wheeler, and C. Karlin (1985). *Telarmachay: Chasseurs et Pasteurs Préhistoriques des Andes*, I. Paris: Institut Francais D'Études Andines.

Lynch, T. F. (1967). "The Nature of the Andean Preceramic." *Occasional Papers of the Idaho State Museum* 21.

Lynch, T. F. (1970). "Excavations at Quishqui Puncu in the Callejón de Huaylas, Peru." *Occasional papers of the Idaho State University Museum* 26.

Lynch, T. F. (1971). "Preceramic Transhumance in the Callejón de Huaylas, Peru." *American Antiquity* 36: 139–148.

Lynch, T. F. (1980). *Guitarrero Cave: Early Man in the Andes.* New York: Academic Press.

MacNeish, R. S., A. Garcia Cook, L. G. Lumbreras, R. K. Vierra, and A. Nelken-Turner (1981). *Prehistory of the Ayacucho Basin, Peru: vol. II: Excavations and Chronology.* Ann Arbor: University of Michigan Press.

MacNeish, R. S., R. K. Vierra, A. Nelken-Turner, and C. J. Phagan. (1980). *Prehistory of the Ayacucho Basin, Peru: vol. III: Nonceramic Artifacts.* Ann Arbor: University of Michigan Press.

Moore, K. M. (1988). "Hunting and Herding Economies on the Junin Puna." In *Economic Prehistory of the Central Andes*, ed. E. S. Wing and J. C. Wheeler. London: BAR International Series 427, 154–166.

Moore, K. M. (1998). "Measures of Mobility and Occupational Intensity in Highland Peru." In *Identifying Seasonality and Sedentism in Archaeological Sites: Old and New World Perspectives*, ed. T. R. Rocek and O. Bar-Yosef. Cambridge, MA: Peabody Museum Bulletin 6, 181–196.

Nuñez A., L. (1983). "Paleoindian and Archaic Cultural Periods in the Arid and Semiarid Regions of Northern Chile." *Advances in World Archaeology*, 2: 161–203.

Pearsall, D. M. (1980). "Pachamachay Ethnobotanical Report: Plant Utilization at a Hunting Base Camp." In *Prehistoric Hunters of the High Andes*, by J. W. Rick, New York: Academic Press, 191–232.

Pearsall, D. M. (1988). "Interpreting the Meaning of Macroremain Abundance: The Impact of Source and Context." In *Current Paleobotany*, ed. C. A. Hastorf and V. S. Popper. Chicago: University of Chicago Press, 97–118.

Pearsall, D. M. (1989). "Adaptation of Prehistoric Hunter-Gatherers to the High Andes: The Changing Role of Plant Resources." In *Foraging and Farming: The Evolution of Plant Exploitation*, ed. D. R. Harris and G. C. Hillman. London: Unwin Hyman, 318–332.

Rick, J. W. (1980). *Prehistoric Hunters of the High Andes.* New York: Academic Press.

Rick, J. W. (1983). *Cronología, Clima, y Subsistencia en el Precerámico Peruano.* Lima: Instituto Andino de Estudios Arqueológicos.

Rick, J. W. (1988). "The Character and Context of Highland Preceramic Society." In *Peruvian Prehistory*, ed. R. W. Keatinge. New York: Cambridge University Press, 3–40.

Rick, J. W. (1996). "Projectile Points, Style, and Social Process in the Preceramic of Central Peru." In *Stone Tools: Theoretical Insights into Human Prehistory*, ed. G. Odell. New York: Plenum Press, 245–278.

Smith C. E. Jr., (1980). "Plant Remains from Guitarrero Cave." In *Guitarrero Cave: Early Man in the Andes*, ed. T. F. Lynch. New York: Academic Press, 87–120.

Tosi, J. A. (1960). *Zonas de Vida Natural en el Perú.* Boletin Técnico, no. 5. Lima: Instituto Interamericano de Ciencias Agricolas, Zona Andina.

Vierra, R. K. (1975). "Structure versus Function in the Archaeological Record." Ph.D. diss., University of New Mexico. Ann Arbor: University Microfilms.

Wing, E. S. (1972). "Utilization of Animal Resources in the Peruvian Andes." In *Andes 4: Excavations at Kotosh, Peru, 1963 and 1966*, ed. S. Izumi and K. Terada. Tokyo: University of Tokyo Press, 327–351.

Wheeler, J. C. (1984). "On the Origin and Early Development of Camelid Pastoralism in the Andes." In *Animals and Archaeology 3: Early Herders and Their Flocks*, ed. J. Clutton Brock and C. Grigson. London: BAR International Series 202, 395–410.

Wheeler, J. C. (1985). "De la Chasse a L'Elevage." In *Telarmachay: Chasseurs et Pasteurs Préhistoriques des Andes*, I, ed. D. Lavallée, M. Julien, J. Wheeler, and C. Karlin. Paris: Institut Francais D'Études Andines, 61–80.

Wheeler, J. C., E. Pires-Ferreira, and P. Kaulicke (1976). "Preceramic Animal Utilization in the Central Peruvian Andes." *Science* 194: 483–490.

North Andean

TIME PERIOD: 7000–4500 B.P.

LOCATION: Highlands of Ecuador and far northern Peru.

DIAGNOSTIC MATERIAL ATTRIBUTES: Stone tools of various types, including stemmed forms.

CULTURAL SUMMARY

Environment

The Andes of Ecuador have a rather different topography and geology than the central Andes of Peru, with much more apparent volcanic activity. Long slopes of major volcanic cones constitute a fair portion of the landscape, and many of these volcanoes have laid major amounts of volcanic ash over the land's surface. This may in part be responsible for the scarcity of sites that might be called Archaic in the Ecuadorian highlands. The same is less true for the relatively dissected and somewhat lower sierra of northern Peru, which suffers more from a lack of concerted investigations (but see Church 1994). This northern area of the Andes is somewhat more humid than the central Andes, and most of the occupied area today tends to be at the altitude of the highland valleys of the central Andes, but with a more open setting and moderate temperatures. Given the paucity of known Archaic sites, there is little room for speculation on the human utilization of this landscape in these remote times.

Settlements

There are no reasonable data on the basis of which to infer the distribution of sites or people on the Archaic landscape. Given the size of the few known sites, principally Chobshi Cave (Lynch and Pollock 1980) and sites such as El Inga (Bell 1965) and others in the Ilaló region (Salazar 1979, 1980), there is little likelihood that social units larger than typical hunter-gatherer bands are present.

Economy

The major data available on Archaic subsistence come from Chobshi Cave in the sierra of southern Ecuador. Here, excavation in a generalized and mixed deposit of mostly Archaic age produced a fairly substantial faunal sample, which suggests that whitetail and *pudu* deer, along with rabbit and agouti or *paca* were likely dietary constituents (Lynch and Pollock 1980). We know nothing of plant resource exploitation from this period. Stone tool industries are the primary data of these limited sites, but lack of reliable dating for a series of diverse tool collections allows only the most general of statements. First is that tool forms, including heavily stemmed and shouldered points and possibly burins, seem to differ in part from the tools of the better-known central Andean Archaic. There are broad similarities, including generalized unifacial tool forms, but these may be poor evidence for any cultural continuity. Second is that fairly high-quality raw materials, which include abundant obsidian for parts of the Ecuadorian highlands, may have led to an emphasis on blade-based tools and perhaps on some of the elaborate projectile point forms. As in the central Andean Archaic, however, these raw materials do not seem to be exchanged over major distances. Chobshi Cave, for instance, has very few obsidian tools, and yet it is only around 230 km from the obsidian-rich El Inga area.

Religion and Expressive Culture

The only evidence for this type of cultural behavior may be rock art, but its dating is uncertain (Porras 1980).

References

Bell, R. E. (1965). *Archaeological Investigations at the Site of El Inga, Ecuador*. Quito: Editorial Casa de la Cultura Ecuatoriana.

Church, W. (1994). "Early Occupations at Gran Pajatén." Peru. *Andean Past* 4:281–318.

Lynch, T. F., and S. Pollock. (1980). "Chobshi Cave and Its Place in Andean and Ecuadorean Archaeology." In *Anthropological Papers in Memory of Earl H. Swanson, Jr*. Pocatello: Idaho Museum of Natural History.

Porras G., P. I. (1980). *Arqueología del Ecuador*. Otavalo, Editorial Gallocaption. Ecuador.

Rick, J. W., and K. M. Moore. (2001). "Specialized Meat-Eating in the Holocene: An Archaeological Case from the Frigid Tropics of High-Altitude Peru." In *Meat-Eating and Human Evolution*, edited by C. B. Stanford and H. T. Bunn. Oxford: Oxford University Press, 237–260.

Salazar, E. (1979). *El Hombre Temprano en la Región del Ilaló, Sierra del Ecuador*. Cuenca, Ecuador: La Universidad de Cuenca.

Salazar, E. (1980). *Talleres Prehistóricos en los Altos Andes del Ecuador*. Cuenca, Ecuador: La Universidad de Cuenca.

Southern Andean

TIME PERIOD: 7000–4500 B.P.

LOCATION: High Andean valleys and high *puna* grasslands and deserts of western South America from about 15° S latitude to about 25° S latitude. Today this is the far southern sierra of Peru and the arid northern sierra of Chile.

DIAGNOSTIC MATERIAL ATTRIBUTES: Chipped-stone tools with lanceolate bifacial projectile points. Subsistence relied on deer, camelids, rodents, birds, and a broad range of plants.

CULTURAL SUMMARY

Environment

The Andes highlands of southern Peru and northern Chile are a dry, and relatively resource-sparse environment. They consist of a number of altitude-layered environments partly centered around small rivers running toward the Pacific, and partly consisting of higher altitude expanses of sparse grassland and virtually vegetation-free desert. Rainfall seasonality and unpredictability become increasingly strong as one proceeds south from Peru, and oasis-like settings occur wherever water is present, whether lake or spring in origin. The wet season occurs December–April, and overall rainfall generally is in the range of 20–40 cm per year, except for small areas of wet *puna* in the north, which can have as much as 80 cm per year. The spotty distribution of water leads to corresponding scattered minor concentrations of water-dependent resource species. Important species include deer, guanaco, and vicuña, along with various rodents and birds in the animal kingdom; plants include a range of dryland seed, berry, and tuber-producing species. Some disagreements exist about the paleoclimatic conditions that may have existed in the Archaic (Aldenderfer 1989; Lynch 1986; Nuñez 1983), much of which may represent real variability between local environments. During the Archaic, however, it does not appear that climates were sufficiently different from the present to have had major impact on our reconstructions of cultures of the time.

Settlements

This same variety of local conditions, combined with a fairly spotty archaeological record, has led to a variety of reconstructions of landscape utilization in the south Andean Archaic. A major problem is whether Archaic highland cultures subsisted entirely within the sierra, or whether they also occupied coastal or near-coastal areas within a seasonal round (Nuñez and Dillehay 1979). There is no question that there is greater rainfall and perhaps temperature seasonality in this southern region than in the central Andes, which might have promoted a long-distance residential mobility that might have spanned coast and sierra. Yet it appears that the majority of evidence from both southern Peru (Aldenderfer 1989) and northern Chile (Nuñez 1986) would argue that coast and sierra mostly harbored separate forager populations. Most models for local settlement patterns in the Archaic include significant levels of mobility within and between adjacent sierra zones, but the degrees of mobility and their changes through time are contested. For Chile, Nuñez (1983) has argued that the most of the Archaic shows decreasing residential mobility, until the end when a shift from hunting to herding actually dictates greater movement. Aldenderfer (1989) suggests that the trend to increased sedentism continues throughout the Archaic, as population filled in, restricting group movement by social circumscription. Although these may represent adaptations to regionally diverse environments, the actual knowledge of site distributions and characteristics remains too limited to fully validate any of the models.

Economy

The basic subsistence mode of the southern Andean Archaic is hunting gathering, primarily based on a mix of large game (camelids, deer), small animals (guinea pig, *viscacha*, and various birds including lake fowl) and plants, although documentation of plant exploitation is primarily inferred through the ubiquity of fairly informal grinding stones. Occasional finds of plant remains under exceptional preservation conditions include tubers and cactus fragments. Domestication of camelids has been inferred for the very end of this period or shortly thereafter, using a number of methods (Aldenderfer 1989; Hesse 1982; Pollard and Drew 1975), but results are not conclusive, and it appears that if herding was occurring during these times, it was probably late and of small scale. Some seasonal movements are inferred that would have allowed repositioning of hunter-gatherer groups for efficient exploitation of seasonal resources; this frequently suggests residence in the higher, dry *puna* areas during the wet season of November–April. Aldenderfer (1989) argues that the foundations of Andean ecological complementarity, the use of resources from a variety of altitude-stratified environmental zones, have their origins in the Archaic period. Subsistence technology largely consists of chipped-stone tools, including a variety of shapes of projectile points with lanceolate forms predominating and various unifacial knife and scraper-like tools. Use of caves for habitation is frequent, increasing with greater altitude, but depends on bedrock outcrop availability, which can be rare in some high basin situations. Residential structures tend to be ephemeral, judging from the scattered and small postholes documented in most sites, and only relatively late is there evidence of more substantial structures (Aldenderfer 1998; Nuñez 1983). Structures at the end of the Archaic in northern Chile include semisubterranean, slab-lined pit houses with storage pits in their floors, suggesting a fair degree of permanence in these sites (Le Paige 1970).

Sociopolitical Organization

The small size of sites and the relatively similar range of grave goods found with burials argue that the southern Archaic, like its northerly Andean neighboring cultures, was of a small group, relatively egalitarian structure. Unless there is some erosional process that dispersed deposits, sites are usually in the range of 50–500 m^2, a reasonable range for groups averaging 25 persons. Organization within local residential groups is rarely evident in the archaeological record, but the lack of artifacts that could signal major status differences argues that there was little social differentiation. On a larger scale, Aldenderfer (1989) has argued for ethnic differences between coastal and highland Archaic populations in the southern Andean area, mostly based on distinct subsistence systems. There is evidence for exchange of materials between coast and sierra, with marine shell usually occurring in highland sites (Nuñez 1983). Aldenderfer has argued that the presence of artifacts made of raw materials from outside local areas may indicate the exchange of tokens, defined as material culture items designed to signify and reinforce sharing relationships. The environmental unpredictability of this region would have made any form of resource sharing beneficial, be it local or long-distance. Other models for explaining these distributions include various forms of group mobility and casual exchange without underlying political-economic motives.

Religion and Expressive Culture

For the latest Archaic times Aldenderfer (1998) has interpreted prepared floors and rock arrangements at the site of Asana in the Moquegua region of Peru as evidence of organized ceremonialism. Although the evidence is open to multiple interpretations, there is evidence of an increasingly elaborate community organization over time at this site, which may well reflect group ritual activities. As with the Archaic in the central Andes, there is generally a scarcity of artifacts that involve artistic expression or religious belief. Like other Andean regions, rock art is widely distributed (for example, see Muelle 1970; Neira 1968; Nuñez 1983). It tends to depict animals, sometimes in apparent hunting scenes, although human figures are also present. In the case of the North Chilean site of Puripica 1, petroglyphs of camelids were carved into rocks forming the walls of habitation structures (Nuñez 1983). Human burials are surprisingly rare from the southern Archaic, suggesting that inhumations were rarely made in the primary habitation sites that have been the focus of archaeological excavations.

References

Aldenderfer, M. S. (1989). "The Archaic Period in the South-Central Andes." *Journal of World Archaeology* 3 2.

Aldenderfer, M. S. (1998). *Montane Foragers: Asana and the South-Central Andean Archaic.* Iowa City: University of Iowa Press.

Hesse, B. (1982). "Animal Domestication and Oscilating Climates." *Journal of Ethnobiology* 2: 1–15.

Le Paige, G. (1970). *Industrias Líticas de San Pedro de Atacama.* Santiago: Editorial Orbe.

Lynch, T. F. (1986). "Climate Change and Human Settlement around the Late-Glacial Laguna de Punta Negra, Northern Chile: The Preliminary Results." *Geoarchaeology* 1: 145–162.

Muelle, Jorge (1970). "Las Pinturas de Toquepala." In *100 Años de Arqueología en el Perú*, ed. R. Ravines. Lima: Edición Petróleos del Perú/Instituto de Estudios Peruanos, 151–154.

Neira, M. (1968). "Un Nuevo Complejo Litico y Pinturas Rupestres en la Gruta SU-3 de Sumbay." *Revista de la Facultad de Letras (Arequipa)*, 5: 43–75.

Nuñez A., L. (1983). "Paleoindian and Archaic Cultural Periods in the Arid and Semiarid Regions of Northern Chile." *Advances in World Archaeology* 2: 161–203.

Nuñez A., L. (1986). "Evidencias Arcaicas de Maices y Cuyes en Tiliviche: Hacía el Semisedentarismo en el Litoral Fertil y Quebradas del Norte de Chile." *Chungará* 16/17: 25–47.

Nuñez A., L., and T. Dillehay (1979). *Movilidad Giratoria, Armonia Social, y Desarrollo en los Andes Meridionales: Patrones de Tráfico e Interacción Económica.* Antofagasta: Universidad de Chile.

Pollard, G., and I. Drew (1975). "Llama Herding and Settlement in Prehispanic Northern Chile: Application of Analysis for Determining Domestication." *American Antiquity* 40: 296–305.

SITES

Asana

TIME PERIOD: 10,500–3500 B.P.

LOCATION: Along the banks of the Rio Asana in the southern Peruvian highlands at an altitude of 3435 m.

DESCRIPTIVE SUMMARY

Local Environment

The Asana site lies in a small basin along the banks of a tributary of the Rio Osmore. The site sits on and intergrades with alluvial and colluvial sediments transported by the adjacent stream and sliding from the relatively unstable hillslope above. As such, the site's surroundings include the stream and its bed, boulder-laden slopes, and a vegetation best described as a dryland bushy scrub with cactus, scattered in and around the rocky landscape. Average rainfall is about 25 cm per yr., while average temperature may be in the range of 10° C.

Physical Features

The site consists of flat, thinly stratified cultural deposits interlayered with natural soil layers over a maximum 3 m depth. The site originally covered more than the 300 m² excavated by Aldenderfer (1998), but parts were either cut by stream erosion or scoured away by landslides. Six depositional complexes are described for Asana (Aldenderfer 1998), almost continuously covering the time period mentioned for the site. Within the many layers of each complex are numerous features including hearths, postholes, and clay floors. A rather low-density assemblage of chipped-stone tools typical of the highland Archaic was excavated at Asana, including small bifacial projectile points, unifacial tools, and cores and flakes, some utilized (Aldenderfer 1998). Animal bones are present from large and small game, but usually in quite small fragments.

Cultural Aspects

Asana is important as the most completely excavated and documented site of the southern Highland Archaic. It represents a residential base, probably occupied seasonally, by small hunter-gatherer groups with gradual transitions toward animal domestication. Over time, the site changes considerably in function and occupation intensity with various adaptational responses of pioneering and evolving local groups. At the end of the Archaic period, organizational complexity of the group living at Asana seems to increase, with the preparation of extensive, post-delimited floor surfaces and possible ceremonial facilities. Aldenderfer (1998) has argued for certain parallels in ceremonial activity with ethnographically known Aymara from the southern Andes.

References

Aldenderfer, M. (1998). *Montane Foragers: Asana and the South-Central Andean Archaic*. Iowa City: University of Iowa Press.

Guitarrero Cave

TIME PERIOD: 11,000–c. 2200 B.P.

LOCATION: On the west side of the highland valley of the Santa river, the Callejón de Huaylas, at an altitude of 2580 m.

DESCRIPTIVE SUMMARY

Local Environment

Guitarrero Cave is located in an outcrop of ortho-quartzite, about 150 m directly above the Santa river. It is on a very steep slope of bedrock and scree, with a dry, low vegetation of spiny bushes, low cacti, and bromeliads.

Physical Features

The cave has a chamber of about 100 m^2, tapering rapidly from an approximately 18-m-wide mouth. Ceiling height decreases from about 5–6 m at the mouth to about 2 m in the interior chamber. The floor of the cave was originally fairly flat, prior to extensive disturbance by later cultures and looters, but outside the cave mouth the talus rapidly falls away toward the river below. Lynch (1980) recognized four major stratigraphic complexes (I, the deepest, to IV, the most superficial), the uppermost having a number of subdivisions. Although the deposits were mostly less than 1 m in depth, an uneven underlying bedrock and the extensive disturbance of the deposits left a stratigraphic headache for the excavators. In this dry and rain-sheltered situation, the cave's deposits remained dry in large part, allowing exceptional preservation of perishable materials.

Cultural Aspects

Guitarrero is particularly important for producing plant remains of beans and corn, but their stratigraphic context and dating has been complex. Similarly, the early dating of the lowest level remains unclear, but it seems likely that the site witnessed a major occupation interval around 10,000–7500 B.P., with probable later use. The excavations produced 580 stone tools and associated debitage, most of which are typical of the Andean Archaic: a range of projectile point forms, along with a knife or scraper-like unifacial component. Most tools had extensive retouch designed to produce edges of a given configuration; in this sense, this is a reasonably formal industry.

The relatively modest number of animal bones from the site includes a wide range of small animals, including birds and rodents, and deer outnumber the camelids by a considerable margin, as expected in a highland valley setting. Artifacts unusually preserved in this site include textiles, basketry, cordage, leather, wood, and other plant remains. Fire-making tools of wood and basketry of twining, interlinking, and looped technologies are documented. Overall, Guitarrero gains its importance from the broad range of cultural materials documented there, including early domesticates. The site probably represents a camp of rather short duration, perhaps occupied for special purposes that its shelter would promote. Given the relatively mild climate and the known open-air sites in the near vicinity (Lynch 1970), it is likely that residential bases were placed in open and less inclined topography. Guitarrero probably was part of a highland valley settlement pattern involving fairly extensive mobility because of the relatively low productivity of this quite dry environment (Lynch 1971).

References

Lynch, T. F. (1970). "Excavations at Quishqui Puncu in the Callejón de Huaylas, Peru." *Occasional Papers of the Idaho State University Museum* 26.

Lynch, T. F. (1971). "Preceramic Transhumance in the Callejón de Huaylas, Peru." *American Antiquity* 36: 139–148.

Lynch, T. F. (1980). *Guitarrero Cave: Early Man in the Andes.* New York: Academic Press.

Pachamachay Cave

TIME PERIOD: In the range of 12,000–10,000 B.P. to 1800 B.P.

LOCATION: In the *puna* to the west of lake Junin, central Peru, at an altitude of 4300 m.

DESCRIPTIVE SUMMARY

Local Environment

Pachamachay Cave is located in a limestone outcrop typical of the puna bedrock of central Peru—highly distorted sea bottom sediments uplifted by the formation of the Andes. The site is located in a major expanse of *puna* grasslands—the vegetation formation of this major altitudinal zone, which includes a variety of bunch grasses, minor stunted shrubs and trees in rocky outcrops, and polster plants in water-saturated settings. Local climate is cold, with an average temperature of about 5° C, an annual rainfall of 80 cm, and wet and dry seasons running from November through April and May through October, respectively.

Physical Features

This is a small cave, measuring up to 4 m wide and 7 m deep, whose height has been greatly diminished by the 3-m-deep plug of occupation debris that fills the cave mouth and extends down the talus slope in front of the cave. The cave floor is relatively flat, and a small level space extends in front of the cave, from which the talus slope falls away at a considerable angle for about a 10-m drop. Archaeological deposits, in addition to filling the cave, extend over most of the talus for a total area of about 300 m². Site stratigraphy was found to include about 33 superimposed layers in the cave mouth area (Rick 1980), of which the uppermost 11 layers are of ceramic age, and the lower 22 are preceramic. There is little evidence of recent disturbance except in superficial layers inside the cave, and inhabitants of the site dug few intrusive features. The preceramic layers in the cave mouth have exceptionally high concentrations of chipped-stone tools and debris, and their extension on the talus slope below also contain a massive amount of animal bone, mostly of camelids such as the vicuña. Fragments of living structures are evident in the cave mouth terrace area, in the form of postholes and small remnants of rock walls.

Cultural Aspects

This site is a great example of an Archaic *puna* residential camp; a similar example is Panaulauca Cave nearby (Bocek and Rick 1984; Rick 1980). Analysis of this and similar sites indicates an occupation of low-mobility inhabitants who intensively exploited the closely surrounding *puna* environment for hunted prey, primarily the vicuña. At least by the later Archaic, residence was year-round, resource use is overwhelmingly local, and a network of similar residential sites surrounds Pachamachay. The amount and character of cultural materials present in the deposit at this time can account for a full-time and constant residence by a band-sized group practicing intensive hunting as the basis of their lifeway. Herding may be known by the late Archaic, but not until the end of the Archaic does settlement pattern change and presumably with it the mode of subsistence.

References

Bocek, B., and J. W. Rick (1984). "La Época Precerámica en la Puna de Junín: Investigaciones en la Zona de Panaulauca." *Chungará* 13: 109–127.

Rick, J. W. (1980). *Prehistoric Hunters of the High Andes.* New York: Academic Press.

Puente

TIME PERIOD: 10,000–4000 B.P.

LOCATION: On the slope of a small stream canyon in the Ayacucho valley, south-central highlands of Peru, at an altitude of 2582 m.

DESCRIPTIVE SUMMARY

Local Environment

The site is set at the foot of a major outcrop above a strongly sloping talus that reaches down to the Wichqana creek below. Vegetation surrounding the site is a dry, low thorn scrub—an intermixture of low grasses and ground plants, with scattered cactus and spiny tree shrubs. Current grazing land use has left much of the area without ground cover, leading to extensive erosion and gullying in the area. Local bedrock is consolidated volcanic ash. The climate of the site area is that of the lower highland valleys, with an average temperature around 15° C.

Physical Features

The Puente site is a shallow rock shelter set in a canyon wall, whose roof collapsed over time. The site is estimated at about 20 m by 10 m in size, prior to the erosional distribution of materials down the talus (MacNeish et al. 1981a, 1981b). The site's 3-m-deep cultural deposits were finely stratified, containing 16 major occupational layers that include 38 total stratigraphic zones, all dating to the preceramic period. Erosion has clearly truncated many site layers, which end abruptly at the outer end of the deposit. The site produced abundant chipped-stone tools from the relatively complete excavation of its deposits (MacNeish et al. 1981a, 1981b; Vierra 1975). The majority of these tools are made in basalt, a local material. In general, the tools conform to the standard of the highland Archaic: small bifacial projectile points of varied form, together with standardized unifacially flaked tools and utilized flakes. Abundant animal remains were produced from the site, the large animals including predominantly deer as opposed to camelids, but smaller animals were also

quite abundant, such as guinea pig (Vierra 1975). Features in the site include hearths, structural fragments such as postholes, and human burials.

Cultural Aspects

The Puente site is important for leaving a detailed record of hunter-gatherer occupation in the lower altitude areas of the highland valleys of the central Andes. The finely stratified and well-dated site deposits (MacNeish et al. 1981a, 1981b) give exceptional detail on the adaptations of small, band-sized organizational units that probably used Puente as one stopping point on their annual subsistence rounds.

References

MacNeish, R. S., A. Garcia Cook, L. G. Lumbreras, R. K. Vierra, and A. Nelken-Turner (1981). *Prehistory of the Ayacucho Basin, Peru, vol. II: Excavations and Chronology.* Ann Arbor: University of Michigan Press.

MacNeish, R. S., R. K. Vierra, A. Nelken-Turner, and C. J. Phagan (1981b). *Prehistory of the Ayacucho Basin, Peru, vol. III: Nonceramic Artifacts.* Ann Arbor: University of Michigan Press.

Vierra, R. K. (1975). "Structure versus Function in the Archaeological Record." Ph.D. diss., University of New Mexico. Ann Arbor: University Microfilms.

JOHN RICK
Department of Anthropological Sciences
Stanford University
Stanford, California
United States

Early Parana-Pampean

ABSOLUTE TIME PERIOD: C. 7000–1500 B.P.

RELATIVE TIME PERIOD: Follows the Late Andean Hunting-Collecting tradition and includes the initial colonization of some parts of the Parana-Pampas region. Precedes the Late Parana-Pampean tradition.

LOCATION: Parana-Pampas region.

DIAGNOSTIC MATERIAL ATTRIBUTES: Distinctive triangular stemmed projectile points.

CULTURAL SUMMARY

Environment

Three major environments are included within the Parana-Pampas region. These include the northern river lowlands and alluvial plains, the flat grasslands of the Pampas proper, and the southern arid flatlands of northern and eastern Patagonia. Thus flat grassland topography dominates the region. Large rivers flow west-to-east across these flatlands at rather wide intervals. Game animals such as the guanaco and rhea were plentiful on these grasslands, as were fish in the rivers.

Settlements

Early Parana-Pampean settlements are small and ephemeral, often consisting of little more than a scattering of kitchen and stone-tool production refuse. In some areas caves were inhabited, and these have provided a better picture of the material culture of the Early Parana-Pampean peoples, but not much more information about their settlements or dwellings.

Economy

The Early Parana-Pampean peoples were hunter gatherers. Guanaco, rhea, and deer were hunted on the grasslands, fish were taken in the rivers, and a diversity of plant foods was collected from both areas. Hunting was done with distinctive triangular stemmed projectile points, often with concave bases. These are often small and may indicate the use of the bow and arrow. Bolas were also used for hunting on open grasslands. Scrapers, knives, and flat grinding stones were used to work hide by the Early Parana-Pampean peoples.

Sociopolitical Organization

The Early Parana-Pampean peoples were apparently nomadic or seminomadic hunter gatherers with a simple technology. As such, based on comparisons to similar hunter gatherers living today, it seems likely, that they were both egalitarian and acephalous. The nuclear or extended family probably formed the basis of both social and political organization.

Suggested Readings

Bird, Junius (1988). *Travels and Archaeology in South Chile*, ed. J. Hyslop. Iowa City: University of Iowa Press.

Borrero, Luis A., and Nora V. Franco (1997). "Early Patagonian Hunter-Gatherers: Subsistence and Technology." *Journal of Archaeological Research* 53: 219 239.

Willey, Gordon R. (1971). *An Introduction to American Archaeology, vol. Two: South America.* Engelwood Cliffs, NJ: Prentice-Hall.

PETER N. PEREGRINE
Department of Anthropology
Lawrence University
Appleton, Wisconsin
United States

Highland Andean Formative

ABSOLUTE TIME PERIOD: 3500–2200 B.P.

RELATIVE TIME PERIOD: Usually defined by the first occurrence of ceramics, this period includes the phases commonly known as the Initial Period and the Early Horizon. In the northern half of the area, the Chavin state emerges midway through this phase, and there the period ends with the collapse of Chavin; in the southern half of the area, the period ends with the beginning of the Andean Regional Development phase.

LOCATION: High Andes from Ecuador to northern Chile.

DIAGNOSTIC MATERIAL ATTRIBUTES: Sedentary agriculturalists with a reliance on maize and domesticated animals, living in large villages and ceremonial centers. Ranking or stratification is present, as is pottery manufacture and metallurgy.

REGIONAL SUBTRADITIONS: Chiripa, Huamachuco, Pucara, Wichqana, Cajamarca; see the Chavin entry for discussion of other northern areas.

CULTURAL SUMMARY

Environment

Topography. The highland area includes occupation areas between roughly 2500–4500 m. For the most part, this is characterized by a treeless high altitude grassland, including roughly 25 percent of the area of Peru and Bolivia. Some areas, in the vicinity of Lake Titicaca, are characterized by large expanses of tablelands, bounded on the east and west by two parallel sierra ranges. Farther north in Peru, the two ranges are closer, resulting in fractured expanses, with grasslands along long meandering ridges and mesas separated by deep valleys. Valley slopes may have growths of the native Andean trees in small copses; valley areas are also characterized by various shrubby vegetation. Grassland environment, however, dominates the zone, changing from the dry *puna* in the south, to the wet *puna* in midcountry, to the much more temperate *paramo* in the north.

Climate. Climatic details are very sketchy, but it appears that this was a period of slightly warmer temperatures than the preceding phase. Upper limits of cultivation were 100–300 m higher than today. On one hand, the high elevation means significantly less atmospheric insulation, so that temperatures warm up and cool down rapidly diurnally. But on the other hand, the proximity to the equator means that the permanent snowline is often over 4800–5000 m.

Geology. The uplifted strata of the Andes provided access to a variety of mineral resources: metal ores (gold, silver, copper, lead, tin, platinum); good-quality cryptocrystallines (obsidian and various cherts); gemstone

123

minerals (turquoise, sodalite, lapis lazuli, fossil amber), which were exploited locally and traded long distance.

Biota. The *puna* grasslands were ideal environment for deer and wild camelids (vicuña and guanaco) and also at this time supported significant herds of domestic camelids, alpaca and llama. This zone was the home for a large number of root varieties, many of which were domesticated by this time (multiple varieties of potatoes, *oca*, *papa lisa*, *olluco*, and *arracacha*) as well as several varieties of chenopods and other seeds.

Settlements

Settlement System. Unity of ceramic substyles indicates that there are discrete polities. Settlement-pattern surveys are incomplete for most of this time period. In the Titicaca basin, where substantial survey has been completed, the early part of this period seems characterized by larger villages controlling areas within a day's journey; only at the end of this period does a settlement hierarchy of larger scale begin to emerge.

Community Organization. Community location at this period usually was situated so as to secure access both to good pasture lands (often at slightly higher elevations) for llama and alpaca herds, and also to agricultural lands where various root and seed crops could be grown. Villages at higher elevations, above the climatic limits allowing agriculture, were situated near springs, lakes, or marshy areas, which provided both water for the herds and rich fodder. In the southern highlands, various raised field systems were initiated, to help extend the upper limits of secure cultivation.

Housing. Principal housing construction materials were adobe and fieldstone. Although there is a tendency to have roundhouses in areas that employ fieldstone and rectangular houses where adobes were employed, the reverse occurs. There are microregional patterns, but no clear overarching preferred style. Houses tend to be small, usually with a maximum dimension of no more than 4–5 m, thus providing primarily dormitory/sleeping space and storage space from rafters, with many daily activities taking place outside the structure. Storage structures are common in villages in agriculture zones, usually internal to or attached to the house, rather than separate. It is widely assumed that the village leader had a larger structure, but insufficient study is available to prove this assumption.

Population, Health, and Disease. Most villages are small, with population estimates no more than 100 to perhaps 200–300. There are many smaller hamlet-sized settlements as well. The emerging political or religious centers have larger populations, but estimates of their population sizes vary by a factor of 10 or more. The first good evidence of geophagy (earth-eating) occurs in this period. Very specific clays were sought and consumed (up until the present), earths, that on one hand bind with the residual phytotoxins, completing the detoxification process for many of the tubers, and on the other hand, provide bioavailable trace elements (such as the typical trace elements amounts of manganese, copper, zinc, and iron, which we get in our vitamins today). The agropastoral regime characteristic of the next two millennia is firmly in place, with thus more secure diets. Nevertheless, living at such high elevations, minor climatic variations produce much greater impacts on the productive systems, and we begin to see population cycles that are intimately integrated into regional climatic cycles.

Economy

Subsistence. The basic format is an agropastoral based economy. Herding of llamas and alpacas now is widely established throughout the region. Herders generally followed an annual cycle: moving the herds up to higher elevations in the austral winter/dry season and down to the village area or lower agricultural fields in the austral summer/wet season. Because of the high elevations involved, extensive cloud cover can drop the temperature enough that snow can fall in the austral summer in the southern highland area. The late austral summer is the time of birth of young llamas and alpacas; they need to be kept lower to avoid thermal stress from such unseasonable weather, as well as to take advantage of the rich grasses that grown in the rainy season. The agropastoral herders also have major labor demands in the local fields, harvesting the various grain and tuber crops at the end of the rainy season. By the time of the austral winter/dry season, agricultural labor demands are mainly over, the young camelids are strong enough to handle major diurnal temperature variations, and the thus previously less exploited grasslands at higher elevations now provide ideal grazing. As agropastoral communities, villagers were required to integrate the labor demands of both plant agriculture and herding. The agriculture labor demands are those rather typical world wide, with sowing with the first rains, weeding the young plants, protecting the ripening fields from predators, and the short but intense period of harvesting mature crops.

Wild Foods. Herders particularly had opportunities to take guanaco, vicuña, and deer, as well as small rodents (vizcacha, wild guinea pigs), land birds (a partridge-size bird as well as smaller species), and waterbirds (sierra flamingoes, geese, ducks, grebes, and coots). Communities near larger streams and lakes also engaged in fishing. A wide variety of wild plants from the grasslands and marshy areas was also collected.

Domestic Foods. Llamas, alpacas, and guinea pigs provided the major domestic meat resources. Maize became ubiquitous in northern highland villages during this time and is thought to provide part of the surplus that allowed the Chavin development. Maize is important in the next chronological phase in the southern highlands and seems only to make pioneering entrees at this period. Primary agriculture in the highland remained focused on the various native seed plants (the chenopod quinoa, *caniwa*, and amaranth grains) and tubers (a wide range of white potato varieties, as well as other tubers such as *oca*, *ulluco*, *papa lisas*, *arracacha*, and the like). Root crops typically have short "shelf life." By this period, in the southern highlands where climatic conditions were appropriate, various "freeze-drying" techniques were now in place. These procedures had double rewards: not only did they modify the tubers into products that could be stored and retained reconstituted edibility for up to a decade or longer, but the freeze-drying process also destroyed most of the phytotoxins in the tubers. Most of the agricultural plants in this zone have significant levels of phytotoxins (which prevent or inhibit predation as well as human consumption). Thus until a technique was developed to detoxify grains and roots, plant agriculture in the highlands was not a reasonable mechanism for production of food surpluses.

Industrial Arts. The assemblage of industrial arts present in the Inca empire was in place, although some of these industries were in their early developmental stages. Most important for status validation as well as wealth production are textile production and metallurgy. Woven textiles replaced simpler looped and twined textiles; cotton and camelid wool fiber textiles are widespread; incipient sophistication in design production can be seen particularly in the southern highlands. Base metal production of gold, silver, and copper items is common, but the only alloy present is the first stages of arsenical bronze production, at the end of the period.

Utensils. The stone and bone kitchen utensils from the previous period continue to be utilized, but now are supplemented by a new technology, that of ceramics. Early wares are rather simple shapes, with plastic surface decoration (rocker stamping, zone-punctate, incision, etc.) often preceding the first use of painted designs.

Ornaments. Stone (turquoise, sodalite, lapis lazuli, various copper-based ores), bone, shell, and textile are the principal manufactured items of ornamentation, with access to these items usually limited to individuals of high status. Certain styles of textiles appear limited to the elites.

Trade. The first regular llama trade caravans begin. In some sites associated with the Chavin tradition, the first developed roads may be identified. From evidence such as differential patterns of body parts as well as from items preserved in arid coastal areas, it appears that these early caravans were involved in trading staples (dried llama meat, wool, potatoes, and other highland tubers and grains) as well as lighter status-validating goods (various mineral ores, gemstones jewelry, metal goods) with lowland coastal and jungle areas for foodstuffs and raw materials, as well as lowland manufactured items.

Division of Labor. Most crafts are presumed to be fabricated as cottage industries or at the household industry. Textile production, in terms of collecting wool, spinning the wool, and yarn production involved all members of the household; actual weaving of cloth and clothing items appears to be primarily controlled by women. Some activities, such as long-distance caravan trade, major seasonal movements of herds, and hunting, appear to be limited to men. Lapidary arts and metallurgy seem somewhat more specialized; the assumption has been made that these artisans were attached in some way to the religious and/or political elites, rather than being independent craftsmen.

Differential Access or Control of Resources. Religious and political elites appear to have maintained control over certain classes of goods, particularly metals, and certain stone items (turquoise, obsidian, sodalite, and the like). On the coast and in the highland in later periods, this included control of access to more perishable items, such as colorful Amazonian parrot features, and certain types of woolen textiles; this no doubt also transpired in the highland in this period as well, although we do not yet have the evidence to demonstrate it.

Sociopolitical Organization

Social Organization. Most scholars believe that the modern clan-like *ayllu* organization was in place by this time period and have seen the villages as residence locations of single *ayllus*. These are generally viewed as groups emphasizing resource control (whether it be herding or agricultural lands), through real or fictive descent linkages.

Political Organization. The period is characterized by the coalescing and aggrandizing of local political groups into larger and larger units, such that by the end of the temporal period, this long linear tract of high Andean lands is subdivided into perhaps half a dozen larger polities. Except for payment of tribute to the larger centers, a good deal of local autonomy appears to have prevailed.

Social Control. Political and religious elites exist, but the precise mechanisms by which they secured and maintain political control are much debated.

Conflict. The preferred method of warfare was apparently based on man-to-man direct contact, using clubs. Other potential weapons include slings and spears, but these do not seem to have been employed often. The few centuries prior to the end of this period exhibit increasing blunt trauma injuries in males between the ages of 15 and 35, including shattered forearms (the shield arm) and cranial depressions (from club blows). In the southern highlands, the last few centuries see the first occurrence of isolated human crania, interpreted as "trophy heads," the presence of which is expanded in the next period.

Religion and Expressive Culture

Religious Beliefs. Religious deities and concepts in the northern area are antecedent to the later Chavin culture. Among the northern highland components is a manifestation usually called the Kotosh tradition. This involves the use of possible clan-based or *ayllu*-based religious structures. The typical model is a subterranean structure of relatively small size, able to hold no more than a score of individuals, with a central fire pit for burnt offerings and low benches around the side of the structure, which may be either ovoid or rectangular. There is some suggestion of the type of dualism that is much more evident in the southern highlands. In the south, the earliest recovered manifestations belong to the Pajano tradition. This appears to incorporate two themes: one of metamorphosis and a second of dualism. Around the southern half of lake Titicaca, there are now scores of sites known, which have one or more stone monoliths raised in a central location, with the most frequent images

being of frogs/toads, lizards, otters-like animals, and fish. Late in the Formative, these monoliths become regularly associated with rectangular subterranean structures, with a new emphasis on dualism, often with apparent male/female representations on the opposite side of the same stela, incorporating on the side panels images of snakes, fish, felines, and the like. This latter substyle becomes known as the "Yaya-Mama" tradition, after the Inca-language terms for "father-mother." The manifestations at this time begin to be incorporated in ceramics as well. At the site of Pucara, at the north end of lake Titicaca, the two principal representations on ceremonial ware are "Camelid Woman" and "Feline Man," possibly antecedents to the later religious dualism of Pachamama (an earth mother goddess) and Viracocha (a sky-based male creator god) of the Inca period.

Ceremonies. In the southern sector, public religious ceremonies were held in the open-air subterranean temples, no doubt somewhat like the "theater state" public religious ceremonies of the Tiwanaku state, which evolves out of the Pajano tradition. In the northern area, the Kotosh-tradition religious structures seem to have been limited to only participants from a smaller kin-based group, perhaps the *ayllu*. There is no evidence yet of full-time religious specialists; we presume that the kin-or polity-based elites fulfilled the duties of the principal religious practitioners.

Arts. A wide variety of media was employed, including stone, metal, textiles, pottery, and adobes. Important deities were carved on large stone stela, while a variety of religious and secular images were inscribed on more portable items of stone jewelry and ceremonial use. Metal objects were still rare and mainly limited to elite usages; because of the linkages between religion and political power, most of the images on metal items were of religious themes. Textiles and ceramics display a wide variety of both religious images and secular decorations, depending on their intended use for everyday life or for more ceremonial occasions. The adobe walls of elite residences as well as adobe walls of public buildings were decorated with painted murals of both religious themes and geometric designs. Remnants of pigment suggest that some of the stone buildings may have been similarly decorated.

Religious Practitioners. The small size of the northern highland structures suggests the principal religious specialists were the *ayllu* or clan head. The larger Pajano temples in the southern highland suggest a separation of religious and secular authority, but evidence is yet unclear. The enclosed nature of the Kotosh-tradition structures suggests private ceremonies; the open central location of the Pajano structures suggests more public religious manifestations.

Death and Afterlife. The care taken with burial of the dead and the various artifacts included with the burial indicate a belief in some sort of afterlife, apparently available to all levels of society. The metamorphic theme popular in the southern highland formative suggests a transition for the ethical or religious Andean to transcend this world to the next.

Suggested Readings

Albarracin-Jordan J. (1996). *Tiwanaku: Arqueologia regional y dinamica segmentaria.* La Paz: Plural Editores.

Bonnier, E., and C. Rozenberg (1988). "Du sanctuaire au hameau: À propos de la neolithisation dans la cordillere des Andes centrales." *L'Anthropologie* 92, 3: 983–996.

Browman, D. L. (1981). "New Light on Andean Tiwanaku." *American Scientist* 69, 4: 408–419.

Chavez, S. J. (1992). "The Conventionalized Rules in Pucara Pottery Technology and Iconography: Implications for Socio-political Development in the Northern Lake Titicaca Basin." Ph.D. diss., Michigan State University, East Lansing.

Kidder, A., II (1943). *Some Early Sites in the Northern Lake Titicaca Basin.* Papers of the Peabody Museum of American Archaeology and Ethnology, vol. 27, no. 1. Cambridge, MA: Harvard University Press.

Mohr-Chavez, K. L. (1977). "Marcavalle: The Ceramics from an Early Horizon Site in the Valley of Cusco, Peru, and Implications for South Highland Socio-Economic Interaction." Ph.D. diss., University of Pennsylvania, Philadelphia.

Moseley, M. E. (2001). *The Incas and Their Ancestors: The Archaeology of Peru.*, 2nd ed. London: Thames and Hudson.

Stanish, C., E de la Vega, L. Steadman, C. Chavez Justo, K. L. Frye, L Onofre Mamani, M. T. Seddon, and P Calisaya Chuquimia (1997). *Archaeological Survey of the Juli-Desaguadero Region of Lake Titicaca.* Fieldiana, Anthropology (n.s.) no. 29. Chicago: Field Museum of Natural History.

Steadman, L. H. (1995). "Excavations at Camata: An Early Ceramic Chronology for the Western Titicaca Basin, Peru." Ph.D. diss., University of California, Berkeley.

Terada, K. (1985). "Early Ceremonial Architecture in the Cajamarca Valley." In *Early Ceremonial Architecture in the Andes,* ed. C. B. Donnan. Washington, D.C.: Dumbarton Oaks Research Library and Collection, 191–208.

Terada, K., and Y. Onuki, ed. (1982). *Excavations at Huacaloma in the Cajamarca Valley, Peru, 1979.* Report 2 of the Japanese Scientific Expedition to Nuclear America. Tokyo: University of Tokyo Press.

Terada, K., and Y. Onuki, ed. (1985). *The Formative Period in the Cajamarca Basin, Peru: Excavations at Huacaloma and Layzon, 1982.* Report 3 of the Japanese Scientific Expedition to Nuclear America. Tokyo: University of Tokyo Press.

SUBTRADITIONS

Chiripa

TIME PERIOD: 3500–1800 B.P.

LOCATION: Chiripa sites are clustered around the "Little Lake" of lake Titicaca in the altiplano of Bolivia and Peru, at elevations between c. 3800–4100 m.

DIAGNOSTIC MATERIAL ATTRIBUTES: Chiripa-phase sites are defined by ceramics and religious architecture. The ceramics usually exhibit a dominance of fiber-tempering and are decorated with geometric painted designs executed in red on a whitish cream slip; in later phases, flat-bottomed bowls are very typical. Sites either include or are within nearby access to subterranean temples with sculpture of the Pajano style early on, and later of the Yaya-Mama substyle. Small concave dart points are the diagnostic hunting component; housing is of either fieldstone or adobe construction and may include both round and rectangular forms.

CULTURAL SUMMARY

Environment

The lake Titicaca basin is characterized by essentially a dry *puna* ecotype environment, mainly high grasslands with little associated stunted native shrubs or trees in protected enclaves. Thus the Chiripa communities are basically agropastoral economies, but are also much influenced by the presence of lake Titicaca. Herding of llamas and alpacas and planting of various tubers and seed plants dominate the economy along both the sites closer to the lake shore and those farther inland. Sites appear to be preferentially located near to the lake shore, however, for two reasons. On one hand, the lake provided additional resources, in terms of fisheries and a wide variety of waterbirds. But more important, the lake as a large heat sink provided ameliorating conditions for agricultural production, and the shores beginning in this period are dense with raised field complexes, which capitalized on the environmental conditions. Of lesser importance until later periods are the locations of a variety of lithic and mineral (especially copper ores) resources in the area. Beginning around 3500 B.P., climatic changes in the Titicaca basin changed to the extent that the lake levels rose rapidly to near-modern shorelines. Prior to this time, the lake had been as much as 85–100 m lower than today, which meant that lake levels were too low to feed the Rio Desaguadero, the modern outflow of the lake. Thus until roughly 3500 years ago, the lake would have exhibited a salt concentration not appropriate for any agricultural purpose. In addition, pollen samples suggest that the modern *totora* (a cattail plant), which are so critically important for the fisheries and a number of technical constructions, were also in low abundance, until the rainfall shift, which raised the level of the lake and shifted the salinity to a more freshwater aspect. Although the millennium-long pattern was a shift from a hotter, drier environment of 4000–6000 years ago to a moister environment, pollen evidence, lake cores, glacial ice cores, and other evidence suggest century-long periods of climatic variations. There is thus, for example, some evidence that the Roman Warm period of Europe was also identifiable in similar impacts in the Titicaca basin.

Settlements

The "type site" of this subtradition is Chiripa, Bolivia, located on the north shore of the Taraco peninsula, on the Little lake of lake Titicaca. Originally any ceramic ware that exhibited fiber temper was assigned to this subtradition. The problem began becoming clear, however, when a number of the sites that produced fiber-tempered ceramics did not also include the typical red-on-cream geometric designs that were diagnostic of the type site. In the Titicaca basin, there are now at least half a dozen small polities posited: Qaluyu and Camata at the north end of the basin, Sillumocco and Ckackachipata on the southwest side, Titimani on the southeast side, Chiripa on the south side, and still yet unnamed clusters in the little explored northeast sector. These settlement clusters, at least during the first millennium, around larger lakeside villages that have a subterranean temple, associated Pajano and Yaya-Mama style monoliths, also may include artificially constructed mounds. Housing stock may include both oval and rectangular structures, although rectangular houses seem more frequent. Habitation terraces are often constructed on hill slopes; houses have prepared clay floors. Structures with adobe wall constructions frequently have plastered or "stuccoed" walls, which may retain evidence of red, yellow, green, or white pigments.

Economy

The economic focus reflects changing environmental conditions. Populations immediately prior to the Chiripa phases appear to have focused on herding and dryland agriculture, whereas the changing conditions at the lake now opened up the possibility for fishing, as well as utilizing low-lying shoreside areas by constructing raised fields for plant agriculture. The increased productivity permitted larger sedentary communities and supported the construction of public architecture. This period marks the first evidence for the development of new technologies such as copper smelting. Llama trade caravans seem to have gone regularly to lower elevation areas to trade. What was being traded? Evidence from contemporary coastal sites indicates that highland tubers and grains were among the pack goods, in addition to a variety of animal products, ranging from whole animals to cured and dried llama meat, to wool, leather, and so on. The large numbers of bone tools associated with textiles recovered from work at Chiripa itself have been interpreted as evidence of production of textiles for wealth goods. There is a dramatic increase in the number of andesite hoes during this period, suggesting clear agricultural intensification. Although the sample is small, sites of this period appear to show the beginnings of specialization: artifacts related to textile production dominate one site; waste material from production of obsidian artifacts is significant at a second; productions features associated with the production of *charqui* (dried camelid meat) at a third, and so on.

Sociopolitical Organization

Present incomplete survey of the Titicaca basin area has suggested the presence of half a dozen or more political units at this time. Although ceramic patterns make it possible to define a northern basin influence, defined from the type sites of Qaluyu/Pucara, and a southern basin influence from the type site of Chiripa, which is what archaeologists initially did in trying to understand the complexities of the basin, it is now clear that archaeologists were not so smart or so lucky as to identify the only two major cultural centers in their work at these two centers. Rather there is a cluster of traits that is more typical of the northern basin, as contrasted to one that may be more typical of the southern basin, but it is not a simple matter of continuum. Rather there existed a series of small political entities, controlling larger or smaller geographic zones, in the basin. To date, these all seem to display some kind of religious architecture, in terms of a semisubterranean temple or a platform mound (or both), associated with regional variants of the Pajano and later the Yaya-Mama sculpture traditions. The ranked society of the early part of the Formative appears to have changed into a more hereditary social and political ranking by the upper Formative.

Religion and Expressive Culture

The religious themes are related earlier to the Pajano stela tradition and later include the Yaya-Mama sub-style. Early examples are difficult to neatly encapsulate; some include lacustrine quadrupeds, otter-like animals, some tadpole or minnow representations, others frogs/toads, salamander/lizard, and a few include the small mountain cat (*titi*) and camelids. Where there is any clustering, it appears to relate to a lacustrine theme suggesting metamorphosis of spirit. Later examples of stone sculpture seem to parallel themes in some of the ceramic styles; thus the "camelid-woman" and "feline-man" of the northern basin ceramics seem to have their counterpart in the Yaya-Mama substyle, which often displayed humanlike male and female representations on the opposite side of the same stela. This standardization of religious themes emerges as the first evidence of supralocal regional centers becomes clear. This feature appears to be the beginning of the "religious theater" that is seen for Tiwanaku, where principal public buildings were situated so that large public religious presentations could be conducted on behalf of the citizenry.

References

Albarracin-Jordan, J. (1996). *Tiwanaku: Arqueologia regional y dinamica segmentaria*. La Paz: Plural Editores.

Bennett, W. C. (1936). Excavations in Bolivia. *Anthropological Papers of the American Museum of Natural History* 35, 4: 329–507.

Bermann, M. (1994). *Lukurmata: Household Archaeology in prehispanic Bolivia*. Princeton: Princeton University Press.

Browman, D. L. (1978a). "Toward the Development of the Tiahuanaco (Tiwanaku) State." In *Advances in Andean Archaeology*, ed. D. L. Browman. The Hague: Mouton, 327–349.

Browman, D. L. (1978b). "The Temple of Chiripa." In *Actas y Trabajos del III Congreso Peruano del Hombre y la Cultura Andina*, 2, ed. R. Matos Mendieta. Lima: Editorial Lacontay, 807–813.

Browman, D. L. (1981). "New Light on Andean Tiwanaku." *American Scientist* 69, 4: 408–419.

Browman, D. L. (1989). "Chenopodium Cultivation, Lacustrine Resources and Fuel Usage at Chiripa, Bolivia." In *New World Paleoethnobotany*, ed. E. Voight and D. Pearsall. *Missouri Archaeologist* 47: 137–172.

Browman, D. L. (1993). "Altiplano Comestible Earth: Prehistoric and Historic Geophagy of Highland Peru and Bolivia." *Geoarchaeology* 8, 5: 413–425.

Chavez, S. J. (1992). "The Conventionalized Rules in Pucara Pottery Technology and Iconography: Implications for Socio-political Development in the Northern Lake Titicaca Basin." Ph.D. diss., Michigan State University, East Lansing.

Chavez, S. J., and K. L. Mohr-Chavez (1970). "Newly Discovered Monoliths from the Highlands of Puno, Peru." *Expedition* 12, 4: 25–39.

Chavez, S. J., and K. L. Mohr-Chavez (1976). A Carved Stela from Taraco, Puno, Peru, and the Definition of an Early Style of Stone Sculpture from the Altiplano of Peru and Bolivia. *Ñawpa Pacha* 13: 45–8.

Cordero Miranda, G. (1977). "Descubrimiento de una estela litica en Chiripa." In *Arqueologia en Bolivia y Peru (Jornadas Peruano-Bolivianas de Estudio Cientifico del Altiplano Boliviano y del Sure del Peru)*, vol. 2. La Paz: Editorial Casa Municipal de La Cultura Franz Tamayo, 229–232.

Erickson, C. L. (1988). "An Archaeological Investigation of Raised Field Agriculture in the Lake Titicaca Basin of Peru." Ph.D. diss., University of Illinois, Urbana.

Faldin Arancibia, J. D. (1991). "La ceramica de Chiripa en los valles de Larecaja y Munecas." *Pumapunku* (n.s.) 2: 119–132.

Graffam, G. C. (1990). "Raised Fields without Bureaucracy: An Archaeological Examination of Intensive Wetland Cultivation in the Pampa Koani Zone, Lake Titicaca Bolivia." Ph.D. diss., University of Toronto, Toronto.

Kent, J. (1982). "The Domestication and Exploitation of South American Camelids: A Method of Analysis and Their Application to Circum-lacustrine Archaeological Sites in Bolivia and Peru." Ph.D. diss., Washington University, St. Louis.

Kidder, A., II (1943). "Some Early Sites in the Northern Lake Titicaca Basin." Papers of the Peabody Museum of American Archaeology and Ethnology, vol. 27, no. 1. Cambridge, MA: Harvard University Press.

Kidder, A., II (1956). "Digging in the Titicaca Basin." *University Museum Bulletin* (University of Pennsylvania) 20, 3: 16–29.

Lanning, E. P. (1967). *Peru before the Incas*. Englewood Cliffs, NJ: Prentice Hall.

Mohr, K. L. (1966). "An Analysis of Pottery of Chiripa, Bolivia." M.A. thesis, University of Pennsylvania, Philadelphia.

Mohr-Chavez, K. L. (1977). "Marcavalle: The Ceramics from an Early Horizon Site in the Valley of Cusco, Peru, and Implications for South Highland Socio-economic Interaction." Ph.D. diss., University of Pennsylvania, Philadelphia.

Mohr-Chavez, K. L. (1989). "The Significance of Chiripa in Lake Titicaca Developments." *Expedition* 30, 3: 17–26.

Morris, C., and A. Von Hagen (1993). *The Inka Empire and Its Andean Origins*. New York: Abbeville Press.

Moseley, M. E. (2001). *The Incas and Their Ancestors: The Archaeology of Peru*, 2nd ed. London: Thames and Hudson.

Mujica Barreda, E. (1978). "Nueva hipotesis sobre el desarrollo temprano del altiplano, del Titicaca y de sus areas de interaccion." *Arte y Arqueologia* 5/6: 285–308.

Mujica Barreda, E. (1987). "Cusipata: Una fase Pre-Pukara en la cuenca norte del Titicaca." *Gaceta Arqueologia Andina* 4, 13: 22–28.

Ponce Sangines, C. (1970). *Las culturas Wankarani y Chiripa y sus relacion con Tiwanaku*. La Paz: Academia Nacional de Ciencias de Bolivia, no. 25.

Portugal Ortiz, M. (1981). "Expansion del estilo escultorico Pa-ajanu." *Arte y Arqueologia* 7: 149–159.

Portugal Ortiz, M. (1985). "Excavaciones arqueologicos en Titimani, Parte I." *Arqueologia Boliviana* 2: 41–64.

Portugal Ortiz, M. (1988). "Excavaciones arqueologicos en Titimani, Parte II." *Arqueologia Boliviana* 3: 51–81.

Portugal Ortiz, M. (1989). "Estilo escultorico Chiripa en la peninsula de Santiago de Huata." *Textos Antropologicos* 1: 45–78.

Portugal Ortiz, M. (1991). "La prospeccion efectuada en zonas de la provincia Camacho, Dpto. de La Paz." *Textos Antropologicos* 2: 9–42.

Portugal Ortiz, M. (1992). "Aspects de la cultura Chiripa." *Textos Antropologicos* 3: 9–26.

Posnansky, A. (1945). *Tihuanacu: The Cradle of American Man*, vols. 1 and 2. New York: J. J. Augustin.

Smith, C. T., W. M. Denevan, and P. Hamilton (1968). "Ancient Ridged Fields in the Region of Lake Titicaca." *Geographical Journal* 134: 353–367.

Stanish, C., and L. Steadman (1994). *Archaeological Research at Tumatumani, Juli, Peru*. Fieldiana, Anthropology (n.s.), no. 23. Chicago: Field Museum of Natural History.

Stanish, C., E de la Vega, L. Steadman, C. Chavez Justo, K. L. Frye, L Onofre Mamani, M. T. Seddon, and P Calisaya Chuquimia (1996). "Archaeological Survey in the Southwestern Lake Titicaca Basin." *Dialogo Andino* 14/15: 97–143.

Stanish, C., E de la Vega, L. Steadman, C. Chavez Justo, K. L. Frye, L Onofre Mamani, M. T. Seddon, and P Calisaya Chuquimia (1997). *Archaeological Survey of the Juli-Desaguadero Region of Lake Titicaca*. Fieldiana, Anthropology (n.s.), no. 29. Chicago: Field Museum of Natural History.

Steadman, L. H. (1995). "Excavations at Camata: An Early Ceramic Chronology for the Western Titicaca Basin, Peru." Ph.D. diss., University of California, Berkeley.

Huamachuco

TIME PERIOD: 3000–1500 B.P. (and later).

LOCATION: Condebamba river basin, the southern part of the Cajamarca-Condebamba macrobasin, situated between the eastern and western cordillera, which merges to form the Crisnejas river, a major tributary to the Rio Maranon of the Amazonian drainage basin. Huamachuco is 100 km south of Cajamarca.

DIAGNOSTIC MATERIAL ATTRIBUTES: Major diagnostic is the megalithic architecture that evolves during the Andean Regional Development period, which becomes a feature of the subsequent state installations of the Wari. Diagnostic ceramics include specific forms of tripod bowls and pedestal vases, as well as an inventory of specific bichrome and polychrome painted motifs.

CULTURAL SUMMARY

Environment

The highland area includes occupation areas between roughly 2500–4500 m. For the most part, this is characterized by a treeless high-altitude grassland, mainly wet *puna* in nature, bounded on the east and west by two parallel sierra ranges. The two ranges vary in distance, resulting in fractured expanses, with grasslands along long meandering ridges and mesas separated by deep valleys. Valley slopes may have growths of the native Andean trees in small copses; valley areas are also characterized by various shrubby vegetation. Climatic details are very sketchy, but it appears that this was a period of slightly warmer temperatures than the preceding phase, allowing agriculture at elevations 100–300 m higher than today. The *puna* grasslands were ideal environment for the deer and wild camelids (vicuña and guanaco) and also at this time supported significant herds of domestic camelids, alpaca and llama. This zone was the home for a large number of domesticated tubers, including multiple varieties of potatoes, *oca*, *isanu*, *ullucu*, *maca*, *arracacha*, and the like, as well as several varieties of chenopods, lupines, and other seed-producing plants. Maize, which was introduced into the highland in the previous period, is grown at the lower elevation sites, but while of increasing importance, does not yet seem to have attained the importance that characterizes it later during the Inca occupation.

Settlements

During the Andean Formative and Developmental period, settlements are generally composed of round or oval fieldstone single-room dwellings with prepared clay floors (mainly for storage and sleeping purposes) in the rural agropastoral communities. There are some larger centers, which appear to have political dominion over specific areas, which in addition to larger size, also include rectangular structures of more than one room, presumed to be residences of elites. Some of the communities are at such a high elevation that agriculture is not possible and seem to be likely specialized herding hamlets; some of the settlements are in lower (2500–3000 m) elevations, contain large numbers of agricultural tools, and may have been primarily agriculturally based hamlets. Most of the settlements, however, include evidence of both herding and agriculture. Sites at the upper end of the settlement range, above 3900–4000 m, tend to be limited to herding activities. Hamlet sizes seem to run from an estimated six to eight households (perhaps a population of 50–75) up to somewhat larger concentrations, perhaps 200–300 persons in size. During much of this period, settlements seem to be particularly situated with an eye toward defensibility, and there is an evident trend or shift also from the much larger settlements of the Highland Andean Formative.

Cerro Campana East is typical of one of the larger hierarchical centers for the early half of this period. It is composed of a series of residential terraces with circular and rectangular fieldstone houses, with prepared yellow plaster or clay floors. A major road accesses the site; in the center is a single story (in contrast to the multistory later examples) circular gallery, associated with a water source (as are the later examples as well), the principal public architecture of the site. At the outer edge of the settlement is a set of llama corrals. Cerro Amaru at Marcahuamachuco is believed to have been constructed during the later part of this time period and continued in use during the subsequent Wari epoch. It is viewed as a major pilgrimage center, with appropriate galleries and halls, also associated with water sources, making it the principal ritual and feasting center for lineage affiliation and group identity for the nearby region.

Exotic goods at this period are often perceived as items derived from offerings from long-distance pilgrimages rather than sumptuary goods of elites or trade. The presence of so many large roofed halls with rows of niches, as places for honoring lineage or *ayllu* ancestors, implies the site was intended to serve as a central place where a number of lineages could hold their feasts together, but in separate facilities. The megalithic architecture that first is identified at places like Cerro Campana East, and that is so characteristic of Marcahuamachuco, predates architecture of the same stylistic canons of the later Wari state and is currently thus believed to have been adopted by the Wari from Huamachuco.

Economy

The economy was mixed agropastoral, with herding particularly important at higher elevations and plant agriculture at lower elevations. Agriculture was primarily predicated on native tubers (such as potatoes, *oca*, *ulluco*, *isanu*, *maca*, and the like) and other plants such as chenopods, amaranths, legumes, cucurbits, and beans. Meat sources were from both domestic animals (llama, alpaca, and guinea pig) and hunted wild game (such as deer, various rodents, and birds). During this period, an elaborate network of irrigated terraces was first constructed, indicating that maize (which was first introduced into this region during the Formative tradition, and which requires more moisture than the local annual rainfall produces predictably) was becoming or had become a major component of the economy. Metal artifacts, which were relatively rare in the previous period, are increasingly common and important and include not only gold, silver, and copper, but also gilded copper and some arsenic bronze alloys. Typical metal items include club heads, maceheads, projectile points, chisels, adzes, plates, pins, *tupus*, needles, tweezers, as well as ingots and scraps of pure metal.

Huamachuco pottery never attains the prestige value of the kaolin-based Cajamarca wares to the south and is relatively limited in its distribution outside the core area. Textile manufacture is an important economic activity in this region, as deduced from the number of weaving tools (although little in the way of textile materials has been preserved in the wet climate). During the early portion of the Regional Development tradition (2200–1800 B.P.), locally known as the Purpucala phase, there is little evidence of interaction of the Huamachuco region with surrounding areas. Because, however, there is evidence of significantly more interaction between Cajamarca, only a short distance south, and several of the coastal areas to the direct west of Huamachuco, such as the Recuay and Moche culture zones, one suggestion is that the major road over which trade caravans traversed somehow bypassed the valley. However, by the end of the Regional Development period, that is by 1800–1500 B.P., the trade pattern has changed. Significant interaction between the Recuay sites such as Pashash and Tablachaca in the Callejon de Huaylas and Huamachuco now is in evidence, and major ceramic linkages are seen between the Huamachuco and Cajamarca areas. High-prestige Cajamarca floral cursive and Cajamarca floral wares begin to appear, as well as various Recuay influences. Huamachuco is believed to have secured major control of trade to the Pacific coast, dominating trade through (a) Cajamarca to the coast and (b) Recuay and the Callejon de Huaylas to the coast. By the end of the Andean Regional period, Marcahuamachuco was associated with a major north-south highway and network of connecting roads, which linked the Cajamarca and Huamachuco areas and led to the expansion into the cis-Andean area on the western slopes. Huamachuco became the principal regional prestige center with its political center at Marcahuamachuco redirecting adjoining regional trade during the Andean Regional tradition period.

Sociopolitical Organization

There is a relatively dramatic change during this period from the Purpucala phase, with its hilltop small communities and thus presumed rather localized political organization, to the new monumental architecture of Marcahuamachuco, with its apparent hierarchical control over the entire Huamachuco region. Although there is an ancient tradition of long, narrow buildings with rectangular and curvilinear galleries and niched walls beginning in the Formative, this pattern expands robustly during the later part of the Regional Andean Development tradition, with a massive series of rectangular galleries (or niched halls), circular galleries, and curvilinear galleries, with large roofed areas, situated around patios or courtyards, of three stories or more, now characterizing the central settlement. The rectangular buildings, with regular patterns of niches on one or more interior walls, with evidence of burials, are interpreted as being evidence of a major pilgrimage center, a ritual and feasting center, where activities took place reaffirming lineage (*ayllu*) affiliation and group identity. The presence of so many niched halls for honoring lineage ancestors at Marcahuamachuco implies the site was intended to serve as a central place where a number of lineages could hold their feasts together, but in separate facilities. This was a ceremonial center for a multilineage confederation where manipulation of water, fertility, and lineage were correlated at these sites. Ideology emphasized cooperation between lineages that were autonomous and relatively equal in rank.

The reconstruction is thus one of a kind of federation of segmentary lineages, a series of hierarchically nested minor-*ayllu*, *ayllu*, major-*ayllu* organization, rather than a centralized potentate. However, traits and features such as road construction, clear agglutination of populations, processes of centralization, development of administrative hierarchy, and increase in warfare all correlate with the formations of elites. The interactions as evidenced by warfare, trade, communication along the road network, resulted in a major transformation with unification of Huamachuco area into single large territory. The improved inter-regional trade mechanisms (new roads) and agricultural intensification (new irrigated terraces) are seen as providing new surpluses to be mobilized by the elite. At the end of the period, new contacts with the militant Wari empire to the south is seen in evidence of extensive unrest and new fortifications being built at Huamachuco, as well as in neighboring areas like the Recuay subtradition area.

Religion and Expressive Culture

Significant religious shifts are defined for the latter part of the Early Intermediate period (c. 1600–1300 B.P.), which would include McCown's Middle Huamachuco, Julien's Middle Cajamarca, and Topic's Early Huamachuco. As noted, there was an ancient tradition of long, narrow gallery-style buildings with niches in the Huamachuco area, beginning with one-

story examples from Cerro Campana in Formative to the multistory rectangular, circular, and curvilinear galleries, niched halls, and wall tombs at Marcahuamachuco. Specific association of the religious architecture with water sources, by means of canals and wells, continues to be observed. Open sepulcher, or *chullpa*-like, above ground multistoried burial structures or mausoleums became a significant feature of the religious architecture, not only in Huamachuco, but in places to the north like the Chota-Cutervo basin, and to the east, as at Wilkawain and other earlier sites in the Recuay zone of the upper Callejon de Huaylas. Marcahuamachuco is the principal regional pilgrimage center, where ritual feasting was a major component of honoring; reconfirming local group affiliation, with real or theoretical founding ancestors, is hypothesized to have been the primary raison d'être of Marcahuamachuco. This was a ceremonial center for a multilineage confederation where manipulation of water, fertility, and lineage was realized. Ideology emphasized cooperation between lineages that were autonomous and relatively equal in rank.

References

Bonnier, E., and C. Rozenberg (1988). "Du sanctuaire au hameau: À propos de la neolithisation dans la cordillere des Andes centrales." *L'Anthropologie* 92, 3: 983–996.

Isbell, W. H. (1997). *Mummies and Mortuary Monuments: A Postprocessual Prehistory of Central Andean Social Organization*. Austin: University of Texas Press.

Loten, H. S. (1987). *Burial Tower 2 and Fort A, Marcahuamachuco*. Peterborough, ON: Trent University Occasional Papers in Anthropology, no. 3.

Lumbreras, L. G. (1974). *The Peoples and Culture of Ancient Peru*, trans. B. J. Meggers. Washington, D.C.: Smithsonian Institution.

McCown, T. D. (1945). *Pre-Incaic Huamachuco: Survey and Excavations in the Region of Huamachuco and Cajabamba*. University of California Publications in American Archaeology and Ethnology 29, 3: 223–399. Berkeley and Los Angeles: University of California Press.

Moseley, M. E. (2001). *The Incas and Their Ancestors: The Archaeology of Peru*, 2nd ed. London: Thames and Hudson.

Terada, K. (1985). "Early Ceremonial Architecture in the Cajamarca Valley." In *Early Ceremonial Architecture in the Andes*, ed. C. B. Donnan. Washington, D.C.: Dumbarton Oaks Research Library and Collection, 191–208.

Thatcher, J. P. (1972). "Continuity and Change in the Ceramics of Huamachuco, North Highlands, Peru." Ph.D. diss., University of Pennsylvania, Philadelphia.

Topic, J. R., (1986). "A Sequence of Monumental Architecture from Huamachuco." In *Perspectives on Andean Prehistory and Protohistory*, ed. D. H. Sandweiss and D. P. Kvietok. Ithaca: Cornell University Latin American Studies Program, 63–83.

Topic, J. R., and T. L. Topic (1982). *Huamachuco Archaeological Project: Preliminary Report on the First Season, July–August 1981*. Peterborough, ON: Trent University Department of Anthropology.

Topic, J. R., and T. L. Topic (1983). *Huamachuco Archaeological Project: Preliminary Report on the Second Season, June–August 1982*. Peterborough, ON: Trent University Department of Anthropology.

Topic, T. L., and J. R. Topic (1984). *Huamachuco Archaeological Project: Preliminary Report on the Third Season, June–August 1983*. Peterborough, ON: Trent University Occasional Papers in Anthropology, no. 1.

Topic, T. L., and J. R. Topic (1987). *Huamachuco Archaeological Project: Preliminary Report of the 1986 Field Season*. Peterborough, ON: Trent University Occasional Papers in Anthropology, no. 4.

Topic, J. R., and T. L. Topic (1992). "The Rise and Decline of Cerro Amaru: An Andean Shrine during the Early Intermediate Period and Middle Horizon." In *Ancient Images, Ancient Thoughts: The Archaeology of Ideology*, ed. A. S. Goldsmith, S. Garvie, D. Selin, and T. Smith. Calgary: Proceedings of the 23rd Chacmool Conference, University of Calgary, 167–180.

Pucara

TIME PERIOD: 3200–1700 B.P.

LOCATION: Pucara and Qaluyu sites are clustered around the north end of lake Titicaca in the altiplano of Peru, at elevations between c. 3800–4100 m.

DIAGNOSTIC MATERIAL ATTRIBUTES: Pucara-phase (and its initial development, usually known as the Qaluyu-phase) sites are defined by ceramics and religious architecture. Housing is of either fieldstone or adobe construction and may include both round and rectangular forms.

CULTURAL SUMMARY

Environment

The lake Titicaca basin is characterized by essentially a dry *puna* ecotypeenvironment, mainly high grasslands with little associated stunted native shrubs or trees in protected enclaves. Thus the Pucara and Qaluyu communities are basically agropastoral economies, but are also much influenced by the presence of lake Titicaca. Herding of llamas and alpacas and planting of various tubers and seed plants dominate the economy along both habitation sites closer to the lake shore and those further inland. Sites appear to preferentially be located near to the lake shore, however, for two reasons. On one hand, the lake provided additional resources, in terms of fisheries and waterbirds. But more important, the lake as a large heat sink provided ameliorating conditions for agricultural production, and the shores beginning in this period are dense with raised field complexes, which capitalized on the environmental conditions. Of lesser importance at the beginning, but of significant utility at the end of the time period, is the variety of lithic and mineral (especially copper ores) resources in the area. Beginning around 3500 B.P., climatic changes in the Titicaca basin changed to the extent that lake levels rose rapidly to near-modern shorelines. Prior to this time, the lake had been as much as 85–100 m lower than today, which meant that lake levels were too low to feed the Rio Desaguadero, the modern outflow of the lake. Thus until roughly 3500 years ago, the lake would have exhibited a salt concentration not appropriate for any agricultural purpose. In addition, pollen samples suggest that the modern *totora* (a cattail plant), which is so critically important for the fisheries and a number of technical constructions (such as fishing boats and roofing thatch), also was in low abundance, until the rainfall shift, which raised the level of the lake and shifted the salinity to a more freshwater aspect. Although the millennium-long pattern was a shift from a hotter, drier environment of 4000–6000 years ago to a moister environment, pollen evidence, lake cores, glacial ice cores, and other evidence suggest century-long periods of climatic variations. There is thus, for example, some evidence that the Roman Warm period of Europe was also identifiable in similar impacts in the Titicaca basin. This is believed to be reflected in the enhanced agricultural production, with evidence by the end of the period of growing some minor amounts of maize, a crop that previously had to be imported from lower elevations.

Settlements

The "type site" of this subtradition is Pucara, Peru, and Qaluyu, just 4 km distance from Pucara, located on the north end of the lake Titicaca basin. Housing stock was predominantly of rectangular structures, with round or oval varieties less common, constructed of fieldstone or adobe. Houses often had prepared clay floors; structures of adobe frequently had clay washes or "stucco," which display remnants of red, yellow, green, and/or white paint. Habitation terraces were constructed where necessary to provide flat residential use areas. During the early portion of this cultural period, at least half a dozen small polities are posited: Qaluyu and Camata at the north end of the basin, Sillumocco and Ckackachipata on the southwest side, Titimani on the southeast side, Chiripa on the south side, and still yet unnamed clusters in the little explored northeast sector.

Increasingly during this phase, there are trends toward coalescing into two supralocal regional centers, one centered at Pucara at the north end of the Titicaca basin, and one represented by the Qeya phase of the site of Tiwanaku at the south end of the basin. There appears to be a hierarchical nested organization in place; secondary centers include examples of artificial mounds, stone enclosures, and sunken temples or courts, which link to the larger complexes at Pucara and Tiwanaku. Early in the area, there is a good deal of variation in both style and content of religious themes; but by the end of the period, there is a substantial level of standardization of theme and style. Such standardization is often viewed in archaeology as indicative of more intense centralization of sociopolitical control.

Economy

The economic focus reflects changing environmental conditions. Populations immediately prior to the Qaluyu and Pucara phases appear to have focused on herding and dryland agriculture, whereas the changing conditions at the lake now opened up the possibility for fishing as well as utilizing low-lying shore-side areas by constructing raised fields for plant agriculture. The increased productivity permitted larger sedentary communities and supported the construction of public architecture. This period marks the development of new technologies such as copper smelting. There is evidence of some specialization among communities: specialization not only in terms of focus on a specific subsistence resource, such as herding, fishing, or farming, but specialization in terms of production of metal goods, lithic items, textiles, ceramics, and other manufactured goods. Llama trade caravans traversed regular routes: north and south between communities in the *puna* and altiplano, trading different specialties; and east and west to the Amazonian jungle and Pacific coastal lowlands, to secure products not available in the highlands.

Sociopolitical Organization

The current interpretation of sociopolitical organization in the Titicaca basin links it tightly with the emerging religious traditions. At the early part of this period, there exists a series of small political entities, controlling larger or smaller geographic zones in the basin, as defined by both patterns of display of images on stone stela and on ceramic assemblages. By the middle part of the period (if not earlier), most of the larger presumed centers of these polities have some kind of religious architecture, in terms of a semisubterranean

temple or a platform mound (or both), associated with regional variants of the Pajano and later the Yaya-Mama sculpture traditions. There appears to be a tendency toward increasing nested hierarchical organization. Thus by the later part of this subtradition, two centers of regional influence have emerged: Pucara at the north end of the basin, and Tiwanaku (Qeya subtradition) at the southern end of the basin. The organizing principles, as intuited from the available evidence, seems to be around a kind of religious theater, of religious and political elites controlling the performance of required religious ceremony at large open mound and temple locations, where it is assumed that large numbers of the regional population gathered for annual ritual occasions.

Religion and Expressive Culture

The religious themes are related earlier to the Pajano stela tradition and later include the Yaya-Mama substyle. Early examples are difficult to neatly encapsulate; some include lacustrine quadrupeds, otter-like animals, some tadpole or minnow representations, others frogs/toads, salamander/lizard, and a few include the small mountain cat (*titi*) and camelids. Where there is any clustering, it appears to relate to a lacustrine theme suggesting metamorphosis of spirit. Later examples of stone sculpture seems to parallel themes in some of the ceramic styles; thus the "camelid-woman" and "feline-man" of the northern basin ceramics seem to have their counterpart in the Yaya-Mama substyle, which often displayed humanlike male and female representations on the opposite side of the same stela. This appears to be the beginning of the "religious theater" that is seen for Tiwanaku, where principal public buildings were situated so that large public religious presentations could be conducted on behalf of the citizenry. What we define as Pucara-style religious deities now widely appear on stone stelae at secondary hierarchical centers at the north end of the basin; the Early Tiwanaku (or Derived Pajano) series of religious representations characterize the religious artwork on stone monuments in the southern end of the basin.

References

Browman, D. L. (1978a). "Toward the Development of the Tiahuanaco (Tiwanaku) State." In *Advances in Andean Archaeology*, ed. D. L. Browman. The Hague: Mouton, 327–349.

Browman, D. L. (1981). "New Light on Andean Tiwanaku." *American Scientist* 69, 4: 408–419.

Browman, D. L. (1989). "Chenopodium Cultivation, Lacustrine Resources and Fuel Usage at Chiripa, Bolivia." In *New World*

Paleoethnobotany, ed. E. Voight and D. Pearsall. *Missouri Archaeologist* 47: 137–172.

Carlevato, D. C. (1989). "Late Ceramics from Pucara, Peru: An Indicator of Changing Site Function." *Expedition* 30, 3: 39–45.

Chavez, S. J. (1976). "The Arapa and Thunderbolt Stelae: A Case of Stylistic Identity with Implications for Pucara Influences in the Area of Tiahuanaco." *Ñawpa Pacha* 13: 3–24.

Chavez, S. J. (1982). "Notes on Some Stone Sculpture from the Northern Lake Titicaca Basin." *Ñawpa Pacha* 19: 79–91.

Chavez, S. J. (1989). "Archaeological Reconnaissance in the Province of Chumbivilcas, South Highland Peru." *Expedition* 30, 3: 27–38.

Chavez, S. J. (1992). "The Conventionalized Rules in Pucara Pottery Technology and Iconography: Implications for Socio-political Development in the Northern Lake Titicaca Basin." Ph.D. diss., Michigan State University, East Lansing.

Chavez, S. J., and K. L. Mohr-Chavez (1970). "Newly Discovered Monoliths from the Highlands of Puno, Peru." *Expedition* 12, 4: 25–39.

Chavez, S. J., and K. L. Mohr-Chavez (1976). "A Carved Stela from Taraco, Puno, Peru, and the Definition of an Early Style of Stone Sculpture from the Altiplano of Peru and Bolivia." *Ñawpa Pacha* 13: 45–8.

Conklin, W. J. (1985). "Pucara and Tiahuanaco Tapestry: Time and Style in a Sierra Weaving Tradition." *Ñawpa Pacha* 21: 1–44.

Erickson, C. L. (1988). "An Archaeological Investigation of Raised Field Agriculture in the Lake Titicaca Basin of Peru." Ph.D. diss., University of Illinois, Urbana.

Flores Ochoa, J. A. (1987). "Cultivation in the Qocha of the South Andean Puna." In *Arid Land Use Strategies and Risk Management in the Andes: A Regional Anthropological Perspective*, ed. D. L. Browman. Boulder: Westview Press, 271–296.

Franco Inojosa, J. M. (1940a). "Informe sobre los trabajos arqueologicos de la Mision Kidder en Pukara, Puno." *Revista del Museo Nacional* 9, 1: 128–136.

Franco Inojosa, J. M. (1940b). "Investario de los especimenes existentes en el Museo Arqueologico de la Municipalidad de Pucara (Provincia de Lampa)." *Revista del Museo Nacional* 9, 1: 137–142.

Franquemont, E. M. (1986). "The Ancient Pottery from Pucara, Peru." *Ñawpa Pacha* 24: 1–30.

Kidder, A., II (1943). *Some Early Sites in the northern Lake Titicaca Basin*. Papers of the Peabody Museum of American Archaeology and Ethnology, vol. 27, no. 1. Cambridge, MA: Harvard University Press.

Kidder, A., II (1964). "South American High Cultures." In *Prehistoric Man in the New World*, ed. J. D. Jennings and E. Norbeck. Chicago: University of Chicago Press, 451–486.

Lumbreras, L. G., and H. Amat (1968). "Secuencia arqueologica del altiplano occidental del Titicaca." In *Proceedings of the 37th International Congress of Americanists, Buenos Aires 1966* 2: 75–106.

Mohr-Chavez, K. L. (1977). "Marcavalle: The Ceramics from an Early Horizon Site in the Valley of Cusco, Peru, and Implications for South Highland Socio-economic Interaction." Ph.D. diss., University of Pennsylvania, Philadelphia.

Mohr-Chavez, K. L. (1985). "Early Tiahuanaco-Related Ceremonial Burners from Cuzco, Peru." *Dialogo Andino* 4: 137–178.

Moseley, M. E. (2001). *The Incas and Their Ancestors: The Archaeology of Peru*, 2nd ed. London: Thames and Hudson.

Mujica Barreda, E. (1978). "Nueva hipotesis sobre el desarrollo temprano del altiplano, del Titicaca y de sus areas de interaccion." *Arte y Arqueologia* 5/6: 285–308.

Mujica Barreda, E. (1979). "Excavaciones en Pucara, Puno." In *Arqueologia Peruano*, ed. R. Matos Mendieta. Lima: Universidad Nacional Mayor de San Marcos, 183–197.

Mujica Barreda, E. (1987). "Cusipata: Una fase Pre-Pukara en la cuenca norte del Titicaca." *Gaceta Arqueologia Andina* 4, 13: 22–28.

Rowe, J. H. (1942). "Sitios arqueologicos en la region de Pucara." *Revista del Instituto Arqueologico, Cuzco* 10/11: 66–75.

Rowe, J. H., and K. T. Brandel (1971). "Pucara Style Pottery Designs." *Ñawpa Pacha* 7/8: 1–16.

Schaedel, R. P. (1948). "Monolithic Sculpture of the Southern Andes." *Archaeology* 1, 2: 66–73.

Schaedel, R. P. (1952). "An Analysis of Central Andean Stone Sculpture." Ph.D. diss., Yale University.

Smith, C. T., W. M. Denevan, and P. Hamilton (1968). "Ancient Ridged Fields in the Region of Lake Titicaca." *Geographical Journal* 134: 353–367.

Steadman, L. H. (1995). "Excavations at Camata: An Early Ceramic Chronology for the Western Titicaca Basin," Peru. Ph.D. diss., University of California, Berkeley.

Valcarcel, L. E. (1925). "Informe sobre las exploraciones arqueologicas en Pukara." *Revista Universitaria del Cuzco* 48: 14–21.

Valcarcel, L. E. (1932a). "El personaje mitico de Pukara." *Revista del Museo Nacional* 1, 1: 18–30, 122–123.

Valcarcel, L. E. (1932b). "El Gato de Agua." *Revista del Museo Nacional* 1, 2: 3–27.

Valcarcel, L. E. (0000). "Litoesculturas y ceramica de Pukara (Puno)." *Revista del Museo Nacional* 4, 1: 25–28.

Wichqana

TIME PERIOD: 3000–1900 B.P.

LOCATION: Middle Mantaro valley region, from 2300 up to 3900 m, Ayacucho and Huancavelica departments, Peru.

DIAGNOSTIC MATERIAL ATTRIBUTES: The Wichqana subtradition is defined almost exclusively on its inventory of ceramic attributes. This inventory can be subdivided into three components: first, the general assemblage of vessel shapes typical throughout the Peruvian sierra formative period; second, the specific decorative techniques and iconographic themes that relate to Chavin influence on the region; and third, the assemblage of ceramic traits borrowed from the adjacent Paracas Pacific coastal area during the latter half of the Wichqana subtradition.

CULTURAL SUMMARY

Environment

The Middle Mantaro sector from 2300 m up to 3900 m includes the subtropical ecological zones of the riverine thorny forest and the scrub thorny forest in the lower elevations, grading into the dry mountain parkland and *puna* grasslands at upper elevations.

Below about 3400 m, lands are almost exclusively employed for farming purposes, based on irrigation agriculture, as rainfall is seasonal and is 600 mm a year or less. Crops include maize, beans, cucurbits, and a variety of local fruits. Above 3400 m, the crops shift to chenopod grains and the various tubers, with llama and alpaca pastoralism. Animals hunted included deer, guanaco, vicuña, a number of rodents, and birds.

Settlements

The Wichqana Regional Highland Formative or Early Horizon settlements in the Central/South Central Peruvian highlands are generally composed of round or oval fieldstone single-room dwellings (mainly for storage and sleeping purposes) in the rural agropastoral communities. There are some larger centers, which appear to have political dominion over specific areas, which in addition to larger size, also include rectangular structures of more than one room, presumed to be residences of elites. Some of the communities are at such a high elevation that agriculture is not possible and seem to be likely specialized herding hamlets; some of the settlements are in lower (2500–3000 m) elevations contain large numbers of agricultural tools, and may have been primarily plant agriculturally based hamlets. Most of the settlements, however, include evidence of both herding and agriculture. Hamlet sizes seem to run from an estimated six to eight households (perhaps a population of 50–75) up to somewhat larger concentrations, perhaps 200–300 persons in size.

Economy

The subsistence base for the Wichqana subtradition was primarily agropastoral, a mix of camelid pastoralism (llama and alpaca herding) and indigenous plant agriculture, including an emphasis on tubers such as potato, *oca*, *ullucu*, *arracacha*, *maca*, and the like, and on indigenous seeds and grains such as *tarwi*, *quinoa*, and *caniwa*. Hunting is still a significant component of the economy in the *puna* and high-elevation sites, with wild camelids (guanaco and vicuña) and deer as larger game, and various rodents (such as viscacha) and birds (such as a partridge-like bird) being well represented. Both wild and domestic guinea pigs are also frequently a significant part of the subsistence inventory. Interregional exchange is most often evident in various high-quality stones employed for hunting, butchering, and hide-processing activities. Obsidian is often imported from sites several hundred kilometers' distance. Occasional ceramic trade vessels from Andean centers both to the north and south of the Middle Mantaro, as well

as from the Paracas area on the Pacific coast to the west, occur in larger sites of the Wichqana area. Based on ceramic influences, it appears that there was more interchange with areas to the north of Wichqana during the early part of the period, and more interactions with the coastal areas during the latter part of the Wichqana period. Textiles of cotton and wool are important trade goods during this time period, and a number of new fabrication techniques are first identified for central highland communities. Metal fabrication appears to be limited to use of artifacts from copper, silver, and gold, mainly used as high-status decorative gear.

Sociopolitical Organization

The available settlement surveys suggest some nature of hierarchical political organization in place, with smaller agropastoral villages apparently linked to slightly larger centers with public religious architecture. Individuals from high-status tomb burials often have "tabular erecta" cranial deformation, a feature not present in presumed peasant burials. In addition, some of the elite burials also have supernumerary or trophy heads included, a feature characteristic of the elites in the adjacent coastal Paracas area at this period. These features taken together are the basis for presuming that there is a developing political bureaucracy, one based on hereditary access to position. The political organization in its evolutionary phases here gives rise to the subsequent Huarpa subtradition during the Andean Regional Development tradition and Wari tradition in this same region and thus is of particular interest as part of the roots of the second set of major Andean empires.

Religion and Expressive Culture

The U-shape configuration of the platform temple at the site of Wichqana, in conjunction with ceramics with Chavinoid iconography, indicates that the Wichqana-phase people were participating in an at least attenuated form of the Chavin culture. The U-shaped platform mound, semicircular temple structures on artificial terraced platform mounds found at Wichqana-phase sites like Wichqana and Chupas indicate the same kind of priestly importance as that defined for the Chavin.

Note: The Cajamarca subtradition is included in the Andean Regional Development tradition, 1–17.

References

Bonavia, D. (1970). "Investigaciones arqueologicaas en el Mantaro Medio." *Revista del Museo Nacional* 35: 211–294.

Casafranca, J. (1960). "Los nuevos sitios arqueologicos Chavinoides en el Departamento de Ayacucho." In *Antiguo Peru—Espacio y Tiempo*, ed. R. Matos Mendieta. Lima: Libreria Mejia Baca, 325–334.

Flores Espinoza, I. (1960). "Wichqana, sitio temprano en Ayacucho." In *Antiguo Peru—Espacio y Tiempo*, ed. R. Matos Mendieta. Lima: Libreria Mejia Baca, 335–344.

Gonzalez Carre, J. E. (1982). *Historia Prehispanica de Ayacucho*. Ayacucho: Universidad Nacional de San Cristobal de Huamanga.

Lumbreras, L. G. (1960a). "Algunos problemas de arqueologia Peruana." In *Antiguo Peru—Espacio y Tiempo*, ed. R. Matos Mendieta. Lima: Libreria Mejia Baca, 129–148.

Lumbreras, L. G. (1960b). "Esquema arqueologico de la sierra central del Peru." *Revista del Museo Nacional* 28: 64–117.

Lumbreras, L. G. (1974a). *The Peoples and Culture of Ancient Peru*, trans. B. J. Meggers. Washington, D.C.: Smithsonian Institution.

Lumbreras, L. G. (1974b). *Las Fundacion de Huamanga*. Lima: Editorial Nueva Edicion.

Lumbreras, L. G. (1981). "The Stratigraphy of the Open Sites." In *Prehistory of the Ayacucho Basin*, 2, ed. R. S. MacNeish, A. Garcia Cook, L. G. Lumbreras, R. K. Vierra, and A. Nelken-Terner. Ann Arbor: University of Michigan Press, 167–198.

MacNeish, R. S. (1981). "Synthesis and Conclusions." In *Prehistory of the Ayacucho Basin*, 1, ed. R. S. MacNeish, A. Garcia Cook, L. G. Lumbreras, R. K. Vierra, and A. Nelken-Terner. Ann Arbor: University of Michigan Press, 199–252.

MacNeish, R. S., T. C. Patterson, and D. L. Browman (1975). *The Central Peruvian Prehistoric Interaction Sphere*. Andover, MA: Papers of the R. S. Peabody Foundation for Archaeology, no. 7.

Moseley, M. E. (1992). *The Incas and Their Ancestors: The Archaeology of Peru*. London: Thames and Hudson.

Ochatoma Paravicino, J. A. (1992). "Acerca de Formativa en Ayacucho." In *Estudios de Arqueologia Peruana*, ed. D. Bonavia. Lima: Fomciencias, 193–214.

Ochatoma Paravicino, J. A., A. Pariahuaman, and U. Larrea (1984). "Cupisnique en Ayacucho?" *Gaceta Arqueologia Andina* 3, 9: 10–11.

DAVID BROWMAN

Department of Anthropology
Washington University
St. Louis, Missouri
United States

Huari

ABSOLUTE TIME PERIOD: 1200–950 B.P.

RELATIVE TIME PERIOD: Follows the Andean Regional Development tradition, precedes the Andean Regional States tradition.

LOCATION: Nucleus of state located in the central highlands of the Ayacucho and Huanta basins with extension of polity to Cajamarca in the north highlands to Moquegua in the far south coast; from the western central and south coasts to the eastern south highlands near Cuzco.

DIAGNOSTIC MATERIAL ATTRIBUTES: Pottery, architecture, textiles, carved stone, carved wood, carved bone, feather work, sculpted stone statuary, and metal ornaments. Planned orthogonal architectural buildings with corbeled floor supports, niches, corridors, galleries, open courtyards, drainage canals, and open plazas, as well as specialized irregular buildings such as D-shaped ceremonial structures.

REGIONAL SUBTRADITIONS: Huarpa, Nasca (Nasca Phase 8, Loro, and Atarco).

IMPORTANT SITES: Azangaro, Conchopata, Huari, Jincamocco, Pachacamac, Pikillacta, Cerro Baul, Honcopampa, Jargampata, Viracochapampa.

CULTURAL SUMMARY

Environment

Climate. Based on ice-core analysis, the climactic condition prior to the Middle horizon was a dramatically dry period of time from A.D. 570–610, followed by a intensively wet period and another dry period A.D. 650–730.

Topography. The Huari heartland is located in two broad basin areas, the southern Huamanga basin surrounding Huari and Conchopata and the northern Huanta basin surrounding Azangaro. These basins sweep down from the 4400+ m high *puna* areas to the lower, 2200–2600 m *chawpi-yunga* valley bottoms. Between these two extremes are the camelid herding and grazing area of the *puna* at 4100–4400 m, the tuber-growing area of the 3400–4100-m *suni*, and the maize-growing area of the 2600–3400-m *kechwa*. These basin areas are heavily eroded into numerous ridges and small mesa extensions delineated by deep ravines. At the bases of some of these mesas are small caches of alluvial plains suitable for farming. Highland runoff produces shallow torrential rivers such as the Pongora, Chachi, and Huarpa, which flow north into the Mantaro river.

Geology. Geologically complex, the Huari site was built on a surface of exposed volcanic rock overlying sedimentary deposits that in many sections eroded away, creating underground caves and a number of sinkholes. The rock deposits were an important source of building material. Important clay deposits exist throughout this area.

Biota. The Huari region is characterized as a lower montane savanah or dry forest of cacti, *molle* trees, and little arable land and few natural springs. Felines, cameloids, and deer are among the larger mammals and condors, eagles, and falcons are among the larger birds.

Settlements

Settlement System. Known Huari sites are generally distinguished by planned, rectangular enclosures, known as orthogonal architecture. Within the perimeters of these enclosures were multiroomed habitation units or patios of narrow rooms, corridors, and open courtyards. The larger sites included walled streets and large walled plazas. Valley-wide surveys indicate four "site size modes" with administrative architecture recognized in the three larger sizes.

Community Organization. The Huari site is on a unique 3 × 4-km oval-shaped mesa accessed by a narrow 0.5-km-wide land bridge to the basin's eastern slope. Current farming is possible through irrigation from a narrow canal following this ridge into the mesa and from seasonal rains. Subfloor excavations indicate that city planning included drainage ditches for water and sewage management.

Housing. Urban housing was arranged into open courtyards surrounded by narrow galleries known as patio groups. Low benches are usually found against the walls of the courtyard. Because preservation of wood is impossible in the highlands, the roofs are assumed to be beamed and thatched. The walls contained a few doorways, recessed niches, and no windows.

Population, Health, and Disease. Preservation does not allow for many burial remains. The size of the Huari site suggests a concentrated population of approximately 50,000.

Economy

Subsistence. Terraced agriculture and open fields are in proximity to most Huari sites, although dating is problematic. Iconography documents the following cultivated plants: quinoa, *tarwi*, ullucu, oca, potato, corn, and anu.

Industrial Arts. Microtool production at the Huari site indicates that primary lithic workshops were located elsewhere. Stone maceheads, hoes, ground-stone metates, and manos suggest defensive warfare and agriculture processing. Huarpa culture contributed the tradition of ceramic spoons and ladles.

Ornaments. Numerous stone beads and partially worked turquoise fragments, as well as iconographic depictions of broad collared necklaces and ears pools, indicate individual adornment. Modeled human faces on pottery vessels also depict a Huari practice of painting or possibly tattooing the face as ethnic or social markers.

Trade. Exotic materials such as *Spondylus princeps* from Ecuador and lapis lazuli from Chile indicate far-reaching trade relations. Obsidian for microtool production was brought to the Huari site.

Division of Labor. Craft specialization is implied by the quality and abundance of certain artifacts, especially when found in concentrated ritual locations. Ceramic workshops are implied by the abundance of vessel scrapers made from discarded sherds and bead workshops by the concentrated areas of turquoise debitage.

Differential Access or control of resources. Huari regional sites suggest planned control over resources and habitation. The population's means of access to these resources is unknown.

Sociopolitical Organization

Social Organization. Iconography depicts many elite dressed males whose roles may be those of priestly leaders or warriors. Some ceramic vessels depict men with burdened llamas who might be traveling traders. Only a few ceramic vessels depict females who are carrying children and burdens tied on their backs.

Political Organization. The exquisitely crafted textiles and pottery document the identity of several Huari individuals or ethnic groups in roles of dualistic confrontation and hierarchical religious leadership.

Social Control. Planned architecture at Middle Horizon sites indicates Huari's political policy to control resources and populations in distant regional centers. By A.D. 900, during the height of Huari empire domination, these individuals wore four-cornered hats and tunics with religious iconography. The Huari site and empire began to dissipate by A.D. 1000, perhaps simply because of weakening leadership or incipient increases in regional autonomy. In any case, later Moche and Chimu cultures appear to have borrowed many Huari styles of art and architectural planning, indicating that the Huari phenomenon had far-reaching temporal influence.

Conflict. The Huari site appears to be defensively situated on a mesa with steep ravines on three sides. However, Huari architecture is also found built into the sides of the ravine below the main architectural core on the mesa above. A small pinnacle within 1 km due west was covered with stone macehead fragments. Iconography indicates confrontational stances between no more than two individuals. Thus inter-regional conflicts or wars are not yet known from archaeological data.

Religion and Expressive Culture

Religious Beliefs. The dominant Huari religious theme is represented by the image of a frontal, standing deity holding a staff on each side with smaller attendant beings on each side in profile positions facing the deity. This theme is depicted on pottery and textiles. Huari culture was believed to have originated at the Bolivian site of Tiwanaku where this theme was carved across the top of a megalithic stone slab doorway. However, similar themes are found in early Chavin and Pucara cultural art. Other mythical features are depicted on human depictions, such as protruding felinelike canines and half-moon eyes that are either in a cross-eyed or wall-eyed position. Circled dot eyes are more traditionally indicated on human depictions; thus the half-moon eyes may indicate altered states of intoxication or hallucination. Deity depictions include examples of male and female, suggesting abundance and fertility.

Ceremonies. Burials of ritually broken oversized urns and face-neck jars occurred at the highland sites of Conchopata, Huari, and Ayapata and at coastal sites of Pacheco, Maymi, and Ocoña and are believed to represent "offerings" to Huari deities. Human sacrifice is associated with one of the Conchopata offerings.

Arts. Huari art consists of abstract designs that evolved from coastal Nasca culture and elaborate anthropomorphic icons that evolved from pan-Andean beliefs in central deities and attendant angels or spirits. The most common medium for Huari art is pottery and textiles.

Death and Afterlife. Few intact burials are known from the Huari heartland. Five females were buried with ritual pottery at the Conchopata site. From Huari coastal locations, multiwrapped mummy bundles indicate that earlier traditions of body preservation continued through Huari culture into historic times.

Suggested Readings

Anders, M. B. (1986). "Wari Experiments in Statecraft: A View from Azangaro." In *Andean Archaeology: Papers in Memory of Clifford Evans*, cd. R. Matos, S. Turpin, and H. Eling. Los Angeles: Institute of Archaeology, University of California, Monograph 27, 201–224.

Arnold, D. E. (1975). "Ceramic Ecology of the Ayacucho Basin, Peru: Implications for Prehistory." *Current Anthropology* 16: 183–205.

Benavides Galle, M. C. (1984). *Caracter del Estado Wari.* Ayacucho, Peru: Universidad Nacional de San Cristóbal de Huamanga.

Bennett, W. C. (1953). *Excavations at Wari, Ayacucho, Peru.* New Haven: Yale University Publication, no. 49.

Brewster-Wray, C. C. (1983). "Spatial Patterning and the Function of a Huari Architectural Compound." In *Investigations of the Andean Past, First Annual Northeast Conference on Andean Archaeology and Ethnohistory*, ed. D. H. Sandweiss. Ithaca: Cornell Latin American Studies Program, Cornell University, 125–135.

Browman, D. L. (1976). "Demographic Correlations of the Wari Conquest of Junin." *American Antiquity* 41: 465–477.

Conklin, W. J. (1970). "Peruvian Textile Fragments from the Beginnings of the Middle Horizon." *Textile Museum Journal* 3: 15–24.

Donnan, C. B. (1972). "Moche-Huari Murals from Northern Peru." *Archaeology* 25: 85–95.

González Carré, E., and J. G. Pérez (1976). *Wari: El Primer Imperio Andino.* Ayacucho, Peru: Concejo Provincial de Huamanga.

Harcourt, R. d' (1922). "La Céramique de Cajamarquilla-Nieveria." *Journal de la Société des Américanistes* 14: 107–118.

Isbell, W. H. (1977). *The Rural Foundation for Urbanism: Economic and Stylistic Interaction between Rural and Stylistic Communities in Eight-Century Peru.* Urbana: University of Illinois Press.

Isbell, W. H. (1997). *Mummies and Mortuary Monuments: A Postprocessual Prehistory of Central Andean Social Organization.* Austin: University of Texas Press.

Isbell, W. H., and A. Gwynn Cook (1987). "Ideological Origins of an Andean Conquest State." *Archaeology* 40: 26–33.

Isbell, W. H., and G. F. McEwan, eds. (1991). *Huari Political Organization: Prehistoric Monumental Architecture and State Government. A Round Table held at Dumbarton Oaks, May 17–19, 1985.* Washington, D.C.: Dumbarton Oaks.

Isbell, W. H., and K. J. Schreiber (1978). "Was Wari a State?" *American Antiquity* 43: 372–389.

Katterman, G. (1986). "Stylistic Analysis of Type 1B and 1C Tapestry Tunics from the Middle Horizon Wari Culture of Ancient Peru." M.A. thesis, University of Arizona, Tucson.

Knobloch, P. J. (1983). "A Study of the Andean Huari Ceramics from the Early Intermediate Period to the Middle Horizon Epoch 1." Ph.D. diss., Department of Anthropology, State University of New York, Binghamton.

Knobloch, P. J. (1989). "Artisans of the Realm: Art of the Wari Empire and Its Contemporaries." In *Ancient Art of the Andean World*, ed. S. Masuda and I. Shimada. Tokyo: Iwanami Shoten, Publishers.

Kroeber, A. L. (1944). *Peruvian Archeology in 1942.* New York: Viking Fund Publications in Anthropology, no. 4.

Kroeber, A. L., and D. Collier, Carmichael P. H., ed. (1998). *The Archaeology and Pottery of Nazca, Peru: Alfred Kroeber's 1926 Expedition.* Walnut Creek: AltaMira Press.

Lapiner, A. (1975). *Pre-Columbian Art of South America.* New York: Harry N. Abrams.

Larco Hoyle, R. (1996). *Perú: Archaeología Mundi.* Cleveland: World.

Lumbreras, L. G. (1974). *The Peoples and Cultures of Ancient Peru.* Washington, D.C.: Smithsonian Institution Press.

Lumbreras, L. G. (1977). *Las Fundaciones de Huamanga.* Lima: Editorial Nueva Educación.

MacNeish, R. S., A. García Cook, L. G. Lumbreras, R. K. Vierra, and A. Nelken-Terner (1981). *Prehistory of the Ayacucho Basin, Peru, vol. 2: Excavations and Chronology.* Ann Arbor: University of Michigan Press.

Menzel, D. (1964). "Style and Time in the Middle Horizon." *Ñawpa Pacha* 2: 1–106.

Menzel, D. (1968). "New Data on the Huari Empire in Middle Horizon Epoch 2A." *Ñawpa Pacha* 6: 47–114.

Menzel, D. (1977). *The Archaeology of Ancient Peru and the Work of Max Uhle.* Berkeley: Robert H. Lowie Museum of Anthropology, University of California.

O'Neale, L. M. (1976). "Notes on Pottery Making in Highland Peru." *Ñawpa Pacha* 14: 41–59.

Ravines Sánchez, R. H. (1968). "Un Depósito de Ofrendas del Horizonte Medio en la Sierra Central del Perú." *Ñawpa Pacha* 6: 19–46.

Raymond, J. S. (1979). "A Huari Ceramic Tapir Foot?" *Ñawpa Pacha* 17: 81–86.

Rowe, J. H. (1961). "Stratigraphy and Seriation." *American Antiquity* 26: 324–330.

Rowe, J. H. (1962). "Stages and Periods in Archaeological Interpretation." *Southwestern Journal of Anthropology* 18: 40–54.

Rowe, J. H., D. Collier, and G. Willey (1950). "Reconnaissance Notes on the Site of Huari near Ayacucho, Peru." *American Antiquity* 16: 120–137.

Sawyer, A. R. (1975). *Ancient Andean Art in the Collections of the Krannert Art Museum.* Urbana-Champaign: University of Illinois.

Schmidt, M. (1929). *Kunst und Kultur von Peru.* Berlin: Propyläen-Verlag.

Shady, R. (1982). "La Cultura Nievería y la Interacción Social en el Mundo Andino en la Época Huari." *Arqueológicas* 19: 5–108.

Spielvogel, R. B. (1955). "Wari: A Study of Tiahuanaco Style." Ph.D. diss., Department of Anthropology, Yale University.

Stone, B. J. (1984). "The Socio-economic Implications of Lithic Evidence from Huari, Peru." Ph.D. diss., Department of Anthropology, State University of New York, Binghamton.

Tello, J. C. (1942). *Origen y Desarrollo de las Civilizaciones Prehistóricas Andinas, Actas del XXVII Congreso de Americanistas de 1939.* Lima: Librería e Imprenta Gil.

Thompson, L. G., E. Mosley-Thompson, J. F. Bolzan, and B. R. Koci (1983). "A 1500-Year Record of Tropical Precipitation in Ice Cores from the Quelccaya Ice Cap, Peru." *Science* 229: 971–973.

Ubbelohde-Doering, H. (1965). *On the Royal Highways of the Inca: Archaeological Treasures of Ancient Peru.* New York: Frederick A. Praeger.

Wagner, L. J. (1981). "Information Exchange as Seen in Middle Horizon Two Ceramics from the Site of Huari, Peru." Ph.D. diss., Department of Anthropology, University of Wisconsin, Madison.

Yacovleff, E., and F. L. Herrera (1934). "El Mundo Vegetal de los Antiguos Peruanos." *Revista del Museo Nacional* 3: 243–322.

Yacovleff, E., and F. L. Herrera (1935). "El Mundo Vegetal de los Antiguos Peruanos (conclusión)." *Revista del Museo Nacional* 4: 31–102.

SUBTRADITIONS

Huarpa

TIME PERIOD: 1650–1150 B.P.

LOCATION: Ayacucho-Huanta basins.

DIAGNOSTIC MATERIAL ATTRIBUTES: Pottery displaying black-on-white geometric designs.

CULTURAL SUMMARY

Environment

Located in a tropical highland valley area from 2200 m to over 4000 m, the environment varies dramatically through closely neighboring ecological zones from tropical thorn forest, through dry forest and moist pasture, into alpine conditions for herding.

Settlements

Scattered small habitations are found throughout the Ayacucho-Huanta valley with one large site, Ñawimpukyu, located 2 km southeast of modern Ayacucho (González Carré 1967; Lumbreras 1974, 1977).

Economy

Pottery manufacture is well documented (Benavides 1971; Bennett 1953; Knobloch 1976, 1983; Lumbreras 1960) with the possibility of craft specialization because of the high proportion of standardized bowl sizes and exterior design patterns (Knobloch 1976).

Sociopolitical Organization

Ñawimpukyu is suggested as a possible capital of a Huarpa statelike polity (Lumbreras 1974, 1977). The distribution of ceramic substyles indicates that the "Kumun Senqa" style of large, red storage jars originated in the northern Huanta area and may have been distributed through the Huari areas through exchange (González Carré 1967; Knobloch 1976). Initial contact with south-coast Nasca culture indicates that Huarpa society was amenable to foreign interaction, and pottery displays the artistic influence of such contact. The typical Huarpa black-on-white style (Rowe et al. 1950) was gradually replaced by increased curvilinear designs in various colors (Menzel 1964), developing into the local substyles of "Cruz Pata" and "Chakipampa" (Knobloch 1991; Lumbreras 1977). The Huarpa occupation of the

Huari site area indicates that this culture and its foreign interaction may have contributed significantly to the later development of the Huari culture in both processes of urbanization and state formation (Paulsen 1983).

Religion and Expressive Culture

The Huarpa-style pottery documents little if any religious behavior. The art is basically geometric, with some human imagery in modeled faces, face-neck jars, and figurines. The faces display tear lines drawn as vertical black lines beneath the eyes. These designs may represent the Huarpa practice of facial painting or tattooing, which appears to continue into Middle horizon Huari culture (Knobloch 1983).

References

Benavides Calle, M. (1971). "Análisis de la Cerámica Huarpa." *Revista del Museo Nacional* 37: 63–88.

Bennett, W. C. (1953). *Excavations at Wari, Ayacucho, Peru.* New Haven: Yale University Publication, no. 49.

González Carré, J. E. (1967). "Periodo Intermedio Temprano, Arqueología de Ayacucho Wamani." *Wamani* 2: 96–107.

Knobloch, P. J. (1976). "A Study of the Huarpa Ceramic Style of the Andean Early Intermediate Period." M.A. thesis, Department of Anthropology, State University of New York, Binghamton.

Knobloch, P. J. (1983). "A Study of the Andean Huari Ceramics from the Early Intermediate Period to the Middle Horizon Epoch 1." Ph.D. diss., Department of Anthropology, State University of New York, Binghamton.

Knobloch, P.J. (1991). "Stylistic Date of Ceramics from the Huari Centers". In *Huari Political Organization: Prehistoric Monumental Architecture and State Government: A Round Table Held at Dumbarton Oaks, May 17–19, 1985,* ed. W.H. Isbell and G.F. McEwan. Washington, D.C.: Dumbarton Oaks, 247–258.

Lumbreras, L. G. (1960). "Espacio y Cultura en los Andes." *Revista del Museo Nacional* 21: 177–200.

Lumbreras, L. G. (1974). *The Peoples and Cultures of Ancient Peru.* Washington, D.C.: Smithsonian Institution Press.

Lumbreras, L. G. (1977). *Las Fundaciones de Huamanga.* Lima: Editorial Nueva Educación.

Menzel, D. (1964). "Style and Time in the Middle Horizon." *Ñawpa Pacha* 2: 1–106.

Paulsen, A. C. (1983). *Huaca del Loro Revisited: the Nasca-Huarpa Connection.* Ithaca: Investigations of the Andean Past, First Annual Northeast Conference on Andean Archaeology and Ethnohistory.

Rowe, J. H., D. Collier, and G.R. Willey (1950). "Reconnaissance Notes on the Site of Huari, Near Ayacucho, Peru." *American Antiquity* 16: 120–137.

Nasca (Loro, Atarco)

TIME PERIOD: 1350–1950 B.P.

LOCATION: The south coast of Pisco, Ica, Nasca, and Acari river drainage basins.

DIAGNOSTIC MATERIAL ATTRIBUTES: Nasca Phase 8, Loro and Atarco style pottery; scattered communities with key sites of Huaca del Loro and Pacheco.

CULTURAL SUMMARY

Environment

Characterized as a coastal desert (Carmichael 1988) with limited access to water; thus a vast development of wells and interconnecting underground water tunnels known as *puquios* was engineered (Schreiber and Lanchos Rojas 1988).

Settlements

Occupation is located close to rivers although above the areas that were utilized for agriculture, both from river overflow and controlled irrigation. Several surveys and site excavations help document the distribution of Nasca habitation (Kroeber and Collier 1998; Robinson 1957; Silverman 1993; Strong 1957; Tello 1942). The stylistic analysis and chronological dating of pottery (Gayton and Kroeber 1927; Menzel 1964) indicate that toward the end of the Early Intermediate Period populations decreased or moved into the highlands during the Middle Horizon, which may be due to significant drought conditions recorded by ice-core analysis (Thompson et al. 1983).

Economy

Extensive analysis of flora iconography suggests that the Nasca culture harvested guava, pears, lucuma, aji, pacai, peanuts, beans, corn, manioc, jicama, and *yacon* (O'Neale and Whitaker 1947; Sawyer 1979).

Sociopolitical Organization

Burials provide little evidence of a social elite, but rather suggest a warrior elite with burials associated with trophy heads. Early Nasca art depicts farmers, warriors, fishermen, musicians, and everyday activities that possibly continued into the Middle horizon (Knobloch 1983). The Pacheco offering of elaborate religious pottery may indicate a priestly sociopolitical group within the Nasca population (Menzel 1964). Based on mortuary data, Carmichael (1988) proposed a Nasca tradition of small, independent political units or, minimally, chiefdoms, as opposed to other suggestions of "urbanized state" (Lanning 1967) or "regional state" (Silverman 1987).

Religion and Expressive Culture

A long tradition of elaborate anthropomorphic deities found on pottery (Eisleb 1976; Gayton and Kroeber 1927; Kroeber and Strong 1924; Putnam 1914; Schleiser 1959; Seler 1961; Silverman 1993; Uhle 1914; Zuidema 1971); textiles (Harcourt 1962; Reid 1986; Sawyer 1979), and the world-famous ground drawings on the Pampa de Ingenio between the Ingenio and Nasca river valleys (Isbell 1978; Reiche 1976) document a religious concern for fertility, warfare, and ritual sacrifice. From analysis of the occupation at Cahuachi, Nasca valley known as the "Room of the Posts," Silverman (1993) suggested that panpipes, *Spondylus* shell, *huarango* pods, and trophy heads support the rituals of ancestor worship as symbolized by the carved *huarango* posts.

References

Carmichael, P.H. (1988). "Nasca Mortuary Customs: Death and Ancient Society on the South Coast of Peru." Ph.D. diss., Department of Archaeology, University of Calgary, Canada.

Eisleb, D. (1976). *Altperuanische Kulturen: Nazca II*. Berlin: Musuem für Völkerkunde.

Gayton, A. H., and A. L. Kroeber (1927). "The Uhle Pottery Collections from Nazca." *University of California Publications in American Archaeology and Ethnology* 24: 1–46.

Harcourt, R. d' (1962). *Textiles of Ancient Peru and Their Techniques*. Seattle: University of Washington Press.

Isbell, W. H. (1978). "The Prehistoric Ground Drawings of Peru." *Scientific American* 239: 140–153.

Knobloch, P.J. (1983). "A Study of the Andean Huari Ceramics from the Early Intermediate Period to the Middle Horizon Epoch 1." Ph.D. diss., Department of Anthropology, State University of New York, Binghamton.

Kroeber, A. L., and D. Collier, Carmichael, P. H., ed. (1998). *The Archaeology and Pottery of Nazca, Peru: Alfred Kroeber's 1926 Expedition*. Walnut Creek: AltaMira Press.

Kroeber, A. L., and W. D. Strong (1924). "The Uhle Pottery Collections from Ica." *University of California Publications in American Archaeology and Ethnology* 21: 95–120.

Lanning, E. P. (1967). *Peru Before the Incas*. Englewood Cliffs, NJ: Prentice-Hall.

Menzel, D. (1964). "Style and Time in the Middle Horizon." *Ñawpa Pacha* 2:1–106.

O'Neale, L. M., and T. W. Whitaker (1947). "Embroideries of the Early Nazca Period and the Crop Plants Depicted on Them." *Southwestern Journal of Anthropology* 3: 294–321.

Putnam, E. K. (1914). "The Davenport Collection of Nazca and other Peruvian Pottery." *Proceedings of the Davenport Academy of Ancient Peru* 13: 17–46.

Reiche, M. (1976). *Mystery on the Desert*, 2 ed. Stuttgart: Heinrich Fink GmbH.

Reid, J. W. (1986). *Textile Masterpieces of Ancient Peru*. New York: Dover.

Robinson, D.A. (1957). "An Archaeological Survey of the Nasca Valley, Peru." MA thesis, Department of Sociology and Anthropology, Stanford University, California.

Sawyer, A. R. (1979). "Painted Nasca Textiles." In *The Junius B. Bird Pre-Columbian Textile Conference, May 19th and 20th, 1973*, ed. A. P. Rowe, E. P. Benson, and A. Schaffer. Washington, D.C.: Textile Museum and Dumbarton Oaks, 129–150.

Schlesier, K. H. (1959). "Stilgeschichtliche Einordnung der Nazca-Vasenmalereien: Beiträg zur Geschichte der Hochkulturen des Vorkolumbischen Peru." *Annali Lateranansi* 23: 9–236.

Schreiber, K. J., and J. Lancho Rojas (1988). "Los Puquios de Nasca: Un Sistema de Galerías Filtrantes." *Boletín de Lima* 59: 51–62.

Seler, E. (1961). *Die buntbemalten Gefässe von Nasca im südlichen Peru und die Hauptelemente ihrer Verzierung*. Graz: Akademische Druck-U., Gesammelte Abhandlungen zur Amerikanischen Sprach- und Altertumskunde 4.

Silverman, H. (1987). "A Nasca 8 Occupation at an Early Nasca Site: The Room of the Posts at Cahuachi." *Andean Past* 1: 5–55.

Silverman, H. (1993). *Cahuachi in the Ancient Nasca World*. Iowa City: University of Iowa Press.

Strong, W. D. (1957). "Paracas, Nazca, and Tiahuanacoid Cultural Relationships in South Coast Peru." *Memoirs of the Society for American Archaeology* 13: 1–48.

Tello, J.C. (1942). *Origen y Desarrollo de las Civilizaciones Prehistóricas Andinas, Actas del XXVII Congreso de Americanistas de 1939*. Lima: Librería Imprenta Gil.

Thompson, L. G., E. Mosley-Thompson, J. F. Bolzan, and B. R. Koci (1983). "A 1500-Year Record of Tropical Precipitation in Ice Cores from the Quelccaya Ice Cap, Peru." *Science* 229: 971–973.

Uhle, M. (1914). "The Nazca Pottery of Ancient Peru." *Proceedings of the Davenport Academy of Sciences* 13: 1–16.

Zuidema, R. T. (1971). *Meaning in Nazca Art*. Götesburg: Götesburg Etnografiska Museum, Arstryck, 35–54.

SITES

Azangaro

TIME PERIOD: 1200–1000 B.P.

LOCATION: Huanta valley, north of Ayacucho.

DESCRIPTIVE SUMMARY

Local Environment

A productive agricultural zone between 2200–2600 m with a water source from nearby springs and within a tropical highland ecology of variable climatic conditions (Anders 1986a, 1986b).

Physical Features

The site documents the Huari diagnostic architecture of orthogonal construction from a preconceived plan. From extensive excavations, Martha Anders (1986a, 1986b, 1991) divided the site into three sectors. The North Sector measures 175 × 144 m and contains large rectangular subdivisions, some having the diagnostic Huari features of open courts surrounded by narrow galleries. The Central Sector measures 175 × 169.5 m and contains 40 rows of conjoined rooms in a rigid, gridlike pattern, arranged on either side of a central corridor and bordered by corridors. The South Sector measures 175 × 133.5 m and contains a few planned courtyards and gallery but is somewhat irregular. The gateway entrance is double walled and appears to provide strictly controlled access to the enclosure. Canals brought water to the site.

Cultural Aspects

Pottery dates most of the occupation of Azangaro to Middle Horizon Epoch 2 with a predominance of Huamanga-style designs (Knobloch 1991). From detailed analysis of irregularity in the site's construction, Anders proposed that various work crews probably imposed group variation. Anders also proposed that Azangaro was built as a calendrical/ceremonial center, a possible capital of a Huari province, and that the division of the Central Sector into two parts might indicate a duality of authority (Anders 1986a, 1986b, 1991).

References

Anders, M. B. (1986a). "Wari Experiments in Statecraft: A View from Azangaro." In *Andean Archaeology: Papers in Memory of Clifford Evans*, ed. R. Matos, S. Turpin, and H. Eling. Los Angeles: Institute of Archaeology, University of California, Monograph 27, 201–224.

Anders, M. B. (1986b). "Dual Organization and Calendars Inferred from the Planned Site of Azangaro: Wari Administrative Strategies." Ph.D. diss., Department of Anthropology, Cornell University.

Anders, M. B. (1991). "Structure and Function at the Planned Site of Azangaro: Cautionary Notes for the Model of Huari as a Centralized Secular State." In *Huari Political Organization: Prehistoric Monumental Architecture and State Government: A Round Table held at Dumbarton Oaks, May 17–19, 1985*, ed. W. H. Isbell and G. F. McEwan. Washington, D.C.: Dumbarton Oaks, 165–197.

Knobloch, P. J. (1991). "Stylistic Date of Ceramics from the Huari Centers." In *Huari Political Organization: Prehistoric Monumental Architecture and State Government: A Round Table Held at Dumbarton Oaks, May 17–19, 1985*, ed. W. H. Isbell and G. F. McEwan. Washington, D.C.: Dumbarton Oaks, 247–258.

Conchopata

TIME PERIOD: 1200–1000 B.P.

LOCATION: The eastern suburbs of Ayacucho, along the western edge of a mesa and airport runway.

DESCRIPTIVE SUMMARY

Local Environment

Tropical highland ecology at approximately 2700 m in an extremely arid environmental zone with little modern evidence of agricultural production. Average temperatures vary between 12–18° C, with rainfall averaging 500–1000 mm (Pozzi-Escot B. 1991).

Physical Features

The site contains numerous agglutinated walled rooms, D-shaped ceremonial centers, and pits of ceramic offerings and human sacrifice (Isbell and Cook 1987; Pozzi-Escot B. 1991).

Cultural Aspects

In 1942, Julio Tello first discovered oversized ceremonial urns that appeared to be ritually smashed and buried. Subsequent excavations and analyses of the site defined the pottery as the Conchopata style of the Middle Horizon, with iconographic associations with the Gateway of the Sun in Bolivia (Bustamente 1950; Casafranca 1951; Lumbreras 1960, 1974; Medina 1952). Menzel (1964) suggested that these urns documented an introduction of Tiwanaku-based religion to Huari during Middle Horizon Epoch 1A. From salvage operations in 1977, Cook (1984–1985) analyzed additional Huari iconography from large, elaborate face-neck jars that again depicted the 'Central Deity Theme' of Tiwanaku's Gateway of the Sun, but in rather abstract renditions. Based on iconographic analysis, Knobloch (1983, 1991) suggested that the Conchopata rituals occurred at the end of Middle Horizon Epoch 1, documenting the development of the elaborate Huari religion that was probably contemparary with the Tiwanaku Classic phase. Recent excavations by Ochatomay Cabrera (1999) add further examples of the Conchopata style, with additional information of flora, flauna, and Huari elites.

References

Benavides Calle, M. (1965). "Estudio de la Cerámica Decorada de Conchopata." B.S. thesis, Universidad Nacional de San Cristóbal de Huamanga, Ayacucho, Peru.

Bustamante, M. (1950). *Apuntes Tomados en Wari Waka Urara: Basurales de Cerámica: Épocas y Períodos de Civilización Anteriores al Incanato*. Ayacucho: Annuario del Museo Histórico Regional de Ayacucho 1.

Casafranca, J. (1951). *Una Entrevista al Inspector de la Zona Arqueológic de la Sierra Central del Perú*. Ayacucho: Annuario del Museo Histórico Regional de Ayacucho 2.

Cook, A. Gwynn (1984–1985). "The Middle Horizon Ceramic Offerings from Conchopata." *Ñawpa Pacha* 22–23: 49–90.

Isbell, W. H., and A. G. Cook (1987). "Ideological Origins of an Andean Conquest State." *Archaeology* 40: 26–33.

Knobloch, P. J. (1983). "A Study of the Andean Huari Ceramics from the Early Intermediate Period to the Middle Horizon Epoch 1." Ph.D. diss., Department of Anthropology, State University of New York, Binghamton.

Knobloch, P. J. (1991). "Stylistic Date of Ceramics from the Huari Centers." In *Huari Political Organization: Prehistoric Monumental Architecture and State Government: A Round Table Held at Dumbarton Oaks, May 17–19, 1985*, ed. W. H. Isbell and G. F. McEwan. Washington, D.C.: Dumbarton Oaks, 247–258.

Lumbreras, L. G. (1960). "La Cultura de Wari, Ayacucho." *Etnología y Arqueología* 1: 130–226.

Lumbreras, L. G. (1974). *Las Fundaciones de Huamanga*. Lima: Editorial Nueva Educación.

Medina, P. M. (1952). *Estudio de los Pocras*. Ayacucho: Annuarío del Museo Histórico Regional de Ayacucho 3.

Menzel, D. (1964). "Style and Time in the Middle Horizon." *Ñawpa Pacha* 2: 1–106.

Ochatoma Paravicino, J. and M. Cabrera Romero (1999). *Recientes Descubrimentos en el Sitio Huari de Conchopata–Ayacucho. Texto de la presentación al 64th Annual Meeting of the Society for American Archaeology, Chicago, Illinois*. Facultad de Ciencias Sociales: Universidad Nacional de San Cristóbal de Huamanga.

Pozzi-Escot B., D. (1991). "Conchopata: A Community of Potters." In *Huari Political Organization: Prehistoric Monumental Architecture and State Government: A Round Table Held at Dumbarton Oaks, May 17–19, 1985*, ed. W. H. Isbell and G. F. McEwan. Washington, D.C.: Dumbarton Oaks, 81–92.

Huari

TIME PERIOD: 1200–1000 B.P.

LOCATION: 11 km north of Ayacucho, the Huari capital is located on a mesa at approximately 13° 14′ S latitude, 74° 10′ W longitude.

DESCRIPTIVE SUMMARY

Local Environment

Tropical highland ecology with variable climactic conditions. The site is located in an arid forest zone known as *kechwa*, which allows cultivation of tubers, grains, beans, squash, peppers, and corn.

Physical Features

The site of Huari has been systematically mapped (Bennett 1953; Isbell et al. 1991), and several sectors and buildings have been excavated (Benavides 1979, 1984, 1991; Bragayrac 1991; Brewster-Wray 1983, 1990; Knobloch 1976, 1983; Wagner 1981). The excavations often produce 3–4 m of deep cultural refuse that indicates the lengthy and intensive prehistoric occupation of the site. Many forms of architecture occur at the site, including the Huari diagnostic orthogonal "patio group." Other structures include ceremonial complexes of D-shaped buildings associated with walled niches for possible burial crypts. Curious subterranean corridors and rooms as well as multistoried megalithic slab structures built like a small house of cards also suggest ritual practices. A semisubterranean temple of cut-stone walls and floors was filled in, and a patio group was built over it (Isbell et al. 1991). The site is situated somewhat defensively on a mesa with steep ravines, but Huari architecture is also found along the side of these ravines.

Cultural Aspects

William Isbell has been the leading scholar in proposing the political dominance of Huari urbanism and state formation (Isbell 1971, 1977, 1978, 1985, 1986, 1987a, 1987b, 1991, 1997). His research argues for the pristine development of such social institutions that were perhaps antecedent to later Chimu and Inca cultural models. Huari culture is defined mainly by its unique and well-documented architectural features and pottery styles such as the Early Intermediate Period Huarpa and Middle Horizon Chakipampa, Ocros, Black Decorated, Robles Moqo, Vinaque, Huamanga—just to name a few. At Huari, coastal Nievería, and Moche, imports (Lumbreras 1960) and north highland Cajamarca pottery (Knobloch 1991) have also been identified. Pottery and similar architectural features found at Huari sites such as Azangaro, Jincamocco, Pikillaqta, Marca Huamachuco (Topic 1991), and Moquegua (Feldman 1989; Moseley et al. 1991) help to document the outward movement of Huari's political agenda of controlling many environmental areas and regional polities. Human images on Huari artifacts and their occurrence at Huari sites indicate that elites or priests wore ethnic and religious symbols while visiting their domain in order to validate their social and political power (Knobloch 1989). The decline of the Huari polity appears to have been the gradual abandonment of the site and adaptation of Huari social models into Chimu and Inca culture of the Late Intermediate Period and Late Horizon.

References

Benavides Catte, M. (1979). *Notas sobre excavaciones en Cheqo Wasi*. Investigaciones: Revista de ciencias historico sociales, l. Ayacucho: Universidad de San Cristóbal de Huamanga.

Benavides Calle, M. (1984). *Caracter del Estado, Wari*. Ayacucho, Peru: Universidad Nacional de San Cristóbal de Huamanga.

Benavides Calle, M. (1991). "Cheqo Wasi, Huari." In *Huari Political Organization: Prehistoric Monumental Architecture and State Government: A Round Table Held at Dumbarton Oaks, May 17–19, 1985*, ed. W. H. Isbell and G. F. McEwan. Washington, D.C.: Dumbarton Oaks, 55–69.

Bennett, W. C. (1953). *Excavations at Wari, Ayacucho, Peru*. New Haven: Yale University Publication, no. 49.

Bragayrac D., E. (1991). "Archaeological Excavations in the Vegachayoq Moqo Sector of Huari." In *Huari Political Organization: Prehistoric Monumental Architecture and State Government: A Round Table Held at Dumbarton Oaks, May 17–19, 1985*, ed. W. H. Isbell and G. F. McEwan. Washington, D.C.: Dumbarton Oaks, 71–80.

Brewster-Wray, C. C. (1983). "Spatial Patterning and the Function of a Huari Architectural Compound." In *Investigations of the Andean Past, First Annual Northeast Conference on Andean Archaeology and Ethnohistory*, ed. D. H. Sandweiss. Ithaca: Cornell Latin American Studies Program, Cornell University, 125–135.

Brewster-Wray, C. C. (1990). "Moraduchayuq: An Administrative Compound at the Site of Huari, Peru." Ph.D. diss., Department of Anthropology, State University of New York, Binghamton.

Feldman, R. A. (1989). "A Speculative Hypothesis of Wari Southern Expansion." In *The Nature of Wari: A Reappraisal of the Middle Horizon Period in Peru*. ed. M. Czwarno, F. M. Meddens, and A. Morgan. Oxford: BAR International Series 525, 72–97.

Isbell, W. H. (1971). "Un pueblo rural ayacuchano durante el imperio Huari." *Actas y Memorias del 39 Congreso Internacional de Americanstas* 3: 89–105.

Isbell, W. H. (1977). *The Rural Foundation for Urbanism: Economic and Stylistic Interaction between Rural and Stylistic Communities in Eighth-Century Peru*. Urbana: University of Illinois Press.

Isbell, W. H. (1978). "El imperio Huari: Estado o ciudad?" *Revista del Museo Nacional* 43: 227–241.

Isbell, W. H. (1985). "El Origen del Estado en el Valle de Ayacucho." *Revista Andina* 3: 57–106.

Isbell, W. H. (1986). "Emergence of City and State at Wari, Ayacucho, Peru, during the Middle Horizon." In *Andean Archaeology: Papers in Memory of Clifford Evans, Monograph 27*, ed. M. R. Matos, S. A. Turpin, and H. H. Eling. Los Angeles: Institute of Archaeology, University of California, 189–200.

Isbell, W. H. (1987a). "State Origins in the Ayacucho Valley, Central Highlands, Peru." In *The Origins and Development of the Andean State*, ed. J. Haas, S. Pozorski, and T. Pozorski. Cambridge: Cambridge University Press, 83–90.

Isbell, W. H. (1987b). "City and State in Middle Horizon Huari." In *Peruvian Prehistory*, ed. R. W. Keatinge. Cambridge: Cambridge University Press, 164–189.

Isbell, W. H. (1991). "Huari Administration and the Orthogonal Cellular Architecture Horizon." In *Huari Political Organization: Prehistoric Monumental Architecture and State Government: A Round Table Held at Dumbarton Oaks, May 17–19, 1985*, ed. W. H. Isbell and G. F. McEwan. Washington, D.C.: Dumbarton Oaks, 293–315.

Isbell, W. H. (1997). *Mummies and Mortuary Monuments: A Postprocessual Prehistory of Central Andean Social Organization*. Austin: University of Texas Press.

Isbell, W. H., and G.F. McEwan, eds. (1991). *Huari Political Organization: Prehistoric Monumental Architecture and State Government: A Round Table Held at Dumbarton Oaks, May 17–19, 1985*, Washington, D.C.: Dumbarton Oaks.

Isbell, W. H., C. Brewster-Wray, and L. E. Spickard (1991). "Architecture and Spatial Organization at Huari." In *Huari Political Organization: Prehistoric Monumental Architecture and State Government: A Round Table Held at Dumbarton Oaks, May 17–19, 1985*, ed. W. H. Isbell and G. F. McEwan. Washington, D.C.: Dumbarton Oaks, 19–53.

Knobloch, P. J. (1976). "A Study of the Huarpa Ceramic Style of the Andean Early Intermediate Period." M.A. thesis, Department of Anthropology, State University of New York, Binghamton.

Knobloch, P. J. (1983). "A Study of the Andean Huari Ceramics from the Early Intermediate Period to the Middle Horizon Epoch 1." Ph.D. diss., Department of Anthropology, State University of New York, Binghamton.

Knobloch, P. J. (1989). "Artisans of the Realm: Art of the Wari Empire and Its Contemporaries." In *Ancient Art of the Andean World*, ed. S. Masuda and I. Shimada. Tokyo: Iwanami Shoten, Publishers.

Knobloch, P. J. (1991). "Stylistic Date of Ceramics from the Huari Centers" In *Huari Political Organization: Prehistoric Monumental Architecture and State Government: A Round Table Held at Dumbarton Oaks, May 17–19, 1985*, ed. W.H. Isbell and G. F. McEwan. Washington, D. C.: Dumbarton Oaks, 247–258.

Lumberas, L. G. (1960). "Espacio y cultura en los Andes." *Revista del Museo Nacional*, 21: 177–200. Lima.

Moseley, M. M., R. A. Feldman, P. S. Goldstein, and L. Watanabe (1991). "Colonies and Conquest: Tiahuanaco and Huari in Moquegua." In *Huari Political Organization: Prehistoric Monumental Architecture and State Government: A Round Table Held at Dumbarton Oaks, May 17–19, 1985*, ed. W. H. Isbell and G. F. McEwan. Washington, D.C.: Dumbarton Oaks, 121–140.

Topic, J. (1991). "Huari and Huamachuco." In *Huari Political Organization: Prehistoric Monumental Architecture and State Government: A Round Table Held at Dumbarton Oaks, May 17–19, 1985*, ed. W. H. Isbell and G. F. McEwan. Washington, D.C.: Dumbarton Oaks, 141–164.

Wagner, L. J. (1981). "Information Exchange as Seen in Middle Horizon Two Ceramics from the Site of Huari, Peru." Ph.D. diss., Department of Anthropology, University of Wisconsin, Madison.

Jincamocco

TIME PERIOD: 1200–1000 B.P.

LOCATION: Carahuarazo valley, province of Lucanas, southern department of Ayacucho, just west of Cabana Sur at approximately 14° 17′ S latitude and 73° 58′ W longitude.

DESCRIPTIVE SUMMARY

Local Environment

Located at approximately 3350 m altitude, the Carhuarazo Valley is comparatively dry compared with other highland valleys, because of rain-shadow effect.

There are three biotic zones: *janca* or permanent snow; dry *puna* or bunch grass and shrubs; dry sierra scrub or thorny, cacti and trees. The lower area is intensively terraced and provides habitation areas (Pulgar Vidal 1987; Schreiber 1992; Tosi 1960; Troll 1968).

Physical Features

The site was first described in a 1586 Spanish *visita* by Luís de Monzón (1881). John Rowe (1963) pointed out this citation as possible indications of a Huari site. In 1974, William Isbell and his graduate students, Katharina Schreiber and Patricia Knobloch, were the first archaeologists to investigate and map the site and to discover from its pottery and architectural features that Rowe's suggestion was correct (Schreiber 1992). Schreiber returned to the site, naming it Jincamocco, and worked with Christina Brewster-Wray on its initial excavation. Diagnostic Huari architectural features such as "patio groups" of open courtyards with narrow galleries and low benches and interconnecting walled corridors were encountered. The rectangular enclosure measures 130 by 260 m and occupies a low, flat promontory (Schreiber 1991).

Cultural Aspects

Schreiber conducted an extensive survey of the valley to determine Huari's intrusive presence and extensive disruption of regional settlements prior to Middle Horizon, during, and after, as well as determining the first evidence of a Middle Horizon road system (Schreiber 1984). The pottery showed some early Epoch 1B designs but was predominately of the Epoch 2 Viñaque style (Knobloch 1991, Schreiber 1991, 1992). Obsidian lithics and debitage and animal bones from deer, llama, and guinea pig indicate extensive occupation of this Huari outpost.

References

Knobloch, P. J. (1991). "Stylistic Date of Ceramics from the Huari Centers." In *Huari Political Organization: Prehistoric Monumental Architecture and State Government: A Round Table Held at Dumbarton Oaks, May 17–19, 1985*, ed. W.H. Isbell and G. F. McEwan. Washington, D. C.: Dumbarton Oaks, 247–258.

Monzón, Luís de (1881). "Descripción de la tierra del repartimiento de los Rucanas Antamarcas de la corona real, jurisdición de la ciudad de Guamanga. Año de 1586." *Relaciones Geográficas de Indias – Perú*, Tomo I, pp. 197–215. Congreso Intenacional de Americanistas, Madrid.

Pulgar Vidal, J. (1987). *Geografía del Perú: Las Ocho Regiones Naturales, la Regionalización Transversal, la Microregionalización*. Lima: Promoción Editorial Inca.

Rowe, J. H. (1963). "Urban Settlements in Ancient Peru." *Ñawpa Pacha* 1: 1–28.

Schreiber, K. J. (1984). "Prehistoric Roads in the Carahuarazo Valley." In *Current Archaeological Projects in the Central Andes: Some Approaches and Results*, ed. A. Kendall. Oxford: BAR International Series 210, 75–94.

Schreiber, K. J. (1991). "Jincamocco: A Huari Administrative Center in the South Central Highlands of Peru." In *Huari Political Organization: Prehistoric Monumental Architecture and State Government: A Round Table Held at Dumbarton Oaks, May 17–19, 1985*, ed. W. H. Isbell and G. F. McEwan. Washington, D.C.: Dumbarton Oaks, 199–213.

Schreiber, K. J. (1992). *Wari Imperialism in Middle Horizon Peru*. Anthropological Papers, no. 87, Museum of Anthropology. Ann Arbor: University of Michigan.

Tosi, J. (1960). *Zonas de Vida Natural en el Perú*. Boletín Técnica, no. 5. Lima: Instituto Inter-Americano de Ciencias Agrícolas de la OEA: Zona Andina.

Troll, C. (1968). *Geo-Ecology of the Mountainous Regions of the Tropical Americas: Proceedings of the UNESCO Mexico Symposium 1966*. Bonn: Dummlers Verlag.

Pachacamac

TIME PERIOD: 1200–950 B.P.

LOCATION: Central coast, south of Lima.

DESCRIPTIVE SUMMARY

Local Environment

Coastal desert within view of the Pacific ocean and close to the irrigated farmland of the Lurín river valley.

Physical Features

An enclosed compound of artificially created pyramidal temples built of sedimentary rock and adobe brick, atop high natural features with various urban features of high-walled enclosed living and minor ceremonial centers. Julio Tello directed numerous investigations of this site during the 1940s but left no technical report (Shimada 1991). Middle Horizon pyramids were formed by terraced steps with remnants of colorful frescoes (Bonavia 1985; Muelle and Wells 1939) as depicted on the "Pachacamac Temple" or "Red Temple" (Paredes 1985), whereas post-Huari enclosures or "castle houses" have a diagnostic ramp feature (Shimada 1991). Walled streets and enclosures imply a very constricted and controlled authority over the habitation of this site.

Cultural Aspects

Uhle's (1903; Shimada 1991) initial analysis of Pachacamac-style pottery established a long tradition of cultural association with the Tiwanaku culture of Bolivia. Later archaeological research confirmed that the Pachacamac culture was more directly related to the Huari expansionist state of the Middle Horizon Epoch 2, although Pachacamac appears to have maintained a unique autonomy (Menzel 1964, 1977). The distribution of Pachacamac-style pottery and its antecedent, Middle Horizon Epoch 1 Nievería-style pottery, indicate a broad central coast influence from Ancón in the north to Ica in the south with major occupations at Pachacamac and Cajamarquilla in the Rimac valley (Bueno 1974–1975, 1982; Gayton 1927; Harcourt 1922; Jiménez Borja 1985; Schmidt 1929; Sestieri 1964; Strong 1925; Stumer 1954; Van Stan 1967).

From iconographic analysis of pottery in the extensive Pachacamac collection at the Museum für Völkerkunde, Berlin, and from Huari, Knobloch (1989) proposed that individuals traveled between these cultures and the Nievería culture in Middle Horizon Epoch 1B and contributed to the development of the Huari religion in Middle Horizon Epoch 2. This far-reaching interaction may have established the long tradition of Pachacamac as an "oracle" site (Patterson 1985). The most diagnostic feature of Pachacamac art is the anthropomorphic bird icon known as the "Pachacamac Griffin" (Menzel 1964).

References

Bonavia, D. (1985). *Mural Paintings in Ancient Peru*, transl. P. J. Lyon. Bloomington: Indiana University Press.

Bueno, A. (1974–1975). "Cajamarquilla y Pachacamac: Dos Ciudades de la Costa Central del Perú." *Boletín Bibliográfico de Antropología Americana* 36: 171–201.

Bueno, A. (1982). *El Antiguo Valle de Pachacamac: Espacio, Tiempo y Cultura*. Lima: Editorial Los Pinos.

Gayton, A. H. (1927). "The Uhle Collections from Nievería." *University of California Publications in American Archaeology and Ethnology* 21: 305–329.

Harcourt, R. d' (1922). "La Céramique de Cajamarquilla-Nievería." *Journal de la Société des Américanistes* 14: 107–118.

Jiménez Borja, A. (1985). "Pachacamac." *Boletín de Lima* 38, 7: 40–54

Knobloch, P. J. (1989). "Artisans of the Realm: Art of the Wari Empire and Its Contemporaries." In *Ancient Art of the Andean World*, ed. S. Masuda and I. Shimada. Tokyo: Iwanami Shoten, Publishers.

Menzel, D. (1964). "Style and Time in the Middle Horizon." *Ñawpa Pacha* 2: 1–106.

Menzel, D. (1977). *The Archaeology of Ancient Peru and the Work of Max Uhle*. Berkeley: Robert H. Lowie Museum of Anthropology, University of California.

Muelle, J. C., and R. Wells (1939). "Las Pinturas del Templo de Pachacamac." *Revista del Museo Nacional* 8: 275–282.

Paredes B., P. (1985). "La Huaca Pintada o El Templo de Pachacamac." *Boletín de Lima* 7: 70–77.

Patterson, T. C. (1985). "Pachacamac: An Andean Oracle under Inca Rule." In *Recent Studies in Andean Prehistory, Papers from the Second Annual Northeast Conference on Andean Archaeology and Ethnohistory*, ed. D. P. Kvietok and D. H. Sandweiss. Ithaca: Cornell University Latin American Studies Program, 159–175.

Schmidt, M. (1929). *Kunst und Kultur von Peru*. Berlin: Propyläen-Verlag.

Sestieri, P. C. (1964). "Excavations of Cajamarquilla, Peru." *Archaeology* 17: 12–17.

Shimada, I. (1991). *Pachacamac: A reprint of the 1903 edition by Max Uhle and Pachacamac Archaeology: Retrospect and Prospect*, Monograph 62. Philadelphia: University Museum of Archaeology and Anthropology, University of Philadelphia.

Strong, W. D. (1925). *The Uhle Pottery Collections from Ancon*. Berkeley: University of California Publications in American Archaeology and Ethnology 21.

Stumer, L. M. (1954). "Population Centers of the Rimac Valley of Peru." *American Antiquity* 20: 130–148.

Uhle, M. (1903). *Pachacamac: Report of the William Pepper, M.D., LL.D., Peruvian Expedition of 1896*. Philadelphia: University of Pennsylvania Press.

Van Stan, I. (1967). *Textiles from Beneath the Temple of Pachacamac, Peru: A Part of the Uhle Collection of the University Museum, University of Pennsylvania*. Museum Monograph 7. Philadelphia: University of Pennsylvania Press.

Pikillacta

TIME PERIOD: 1200–1000 B.P.

LOCATION: Lucre basin of the Cuzco valley.

DESCRIPTIVE SUMMARY

Local Environment

Located at 3200 m altitude along a low ridge and measures approximately 1680 by 1120 m in the very fertile Cuzco valley, drained by the Huatanay river. The climate is mild, although rains can cause heavy flooding. The site is located near a lagoon and marshland area (McEwan 1984).

Physical Features

The rigid gridlike layout follows the diagnostic orthogonal attributes of Huari-style architecture. The site's enormous size of abutting, walled enclosures matches the size of Inca Cuzco, but because of its proximity to the Inca capital, this site has been the subject of only a few investigations (Harth-Terre 1959; Sanders 1973; Valcárcel 1933). In 1982, Gordon McEwan (1989) conducted the first extensive mapping and excavation research. He divided the site into several sectors: two central sectors of "patio groups" with open courtyards surrounded by narrow galleries are interpreted as the center of civil administration (McEwan 1991). Another sector of 501 small rectangular buildings was suspected as storage rooms, but McEwan's excavations (which followed the unreported excavations of Dr. Luis Barreda in 1978) found only domestic-type occupation. The remainder of the site consists of large, enclosed plazas or *canchones*, which may have been in preparation for further building or llama corrals. The walls are massively high, suggesting second-story buildings with corbeled projecting stones that may have supported beamed floors and roofs. The roofs were probably thatched (McEwan 1991). Valley-wide survey indicates that the site was situated in a basin where defensive sites were positioned near any of the access points into this area.

Cultural Aspects

Excavations produced Huari-style pottery in the Chakipampa and Ocros styles dating the site to Epoch 1B or early 2A (Menzel 1968), although most of the pottery dates to Epoch 1B (Knobloch 1991). There was one example of a face-neck jar with cheek decoration of a banded rectangle, which is very typical of a Huari individual and may indicate Huari ethnic identity (Knobloch 1991). McEwan proposes that the two main functions of the site were residential and ceremonial. Variation in construction may indicate social status differentiation. Rather than storage rooms or *colccas*, the small rectangular rooms may have housed a military garrison or some large group of service personnel reporting to administrative officials housed in the larger "patio groups" or to religious leaders who may have carried out ceremonial obligations in the two large plaza areas (McEwan 1991). Recently, McEwan's (1998) study of niched halls suggests ritual use in ceremonies of ancestral worship. From a study of two caches of small turquoise or soladite human figurines (Engl and Engl 1969; Valcárcel 1933), Cook (1992) also suggested that Huari occupants practiced ancestor worship to ensure rights of inheritance and fulfill administrative goals.

References

Cook, A. Gwynn (1992). "The Stone Ancestors: Idioms of Imperial Attire and Rank among Huari Figurines." *Latin American Antiquity* 3: 341–364.

Engl, L., and T. Engl (1969). *Twilight of Ancient Peru: The Glory and Decline of the Inca Empire*. New York: McGraw-Hill.

Harth-Terre, E. (1959). *Pikillacta—Ciudad de Positos y Bastimientos del Imperio Incaico*. Cuzco: Revista de Museo e Instituto Arqueológico 3–19.

Knobloch, P. J. (1991). "Stylistic Date of Ceramics from the Huari Centers." In *Huari Political Organization: Prehistroic Monumental Architecture and State Government: A Round Table Held at Dumbarton Oaks, May 17–19, 1985*, ed. W. H. Isbell and G. F. McEwan. Washington, D. C.: Dumbarton Oaks, 247–258.

McEwan, Gordon (1984). "The Middle Horizon in the Valley of Cuzco, Peru: The Impact of Wari Occupation of Pikillacta in the Lucre Basin." Ph.D. diss., Department of Anthropology, University of Texas, Austin. Texas.

McEwan, G. F. (1989). "The Wari Empire in the Southern Peruvian Highlands: A View from the Provinces." In *The Nature of Wari: A Reappraisal of the Middle Horizon Period in Peru*, ed. R. M. Czwarno, R. M. Meddens and A. Morgan. Oxford, England: BAR International Series 525, 53–71.

McEwan, G. F. (1991). "Investigations at the Pikillacta Site: A Provincial Huari Center in the Valley of Cuzco." In *Huari Political Organization: Prehistoric Monumental Architecture and State Government: A Round Table Held at Dumbarton Oaks, May 17–19, 1985*, ed. W. H. Isbell and G. F. McEwan. Washington, D.C.: Dumbarton Oaks, 93–119.

McEwan, G. F. (1998). "The Function of Niched Halls in Wari Architecture." *Latin American Antiquity* 9: 68–96.

Sanders, W. T. (1973). "The Significance of Pikillacta in Andean Culture History." *Occasional Papers in Anthropology, Pennsylvania State University* 8: 38–428.

Valcárcel, L. E. (1933). "Esculturas de Pikillacta." *Revista del Museo Nacional* 2: 19–48.

Patricia J Knobloch
La Mesa, California
United States

Inca

ABSOLUTE TIME PERIOD: c. 800–468 B.P.

RELATIVE TIME PERIOD: Follows the Andean Regional States tradition and precedes the historic period ushered in by the Spanish Conquest in 468 B.P.

LOCATION: The Andean highlands. The original Inca homeland was the Cuzco valley of south-central Peru, but the Inca empire eventually encompassed the Andean highlands and much of the Pacific coastal zone from northern Ecuador at the Colombian border, to north-central Chile and northwestern Argentina, in the vicinity of Santiago and Mendoza.

DIAGNOSTIC MATERIAL ATTRIBUTES: Megalithic architecture and fine cut-stone masonry. Rectangular structures, often with gabled roofs and trapezoidal doors and niches. Limited repertoire of highly standardized polychrome pottery vessels typically decorated with geometric design, the tall-necked jar known as the *aríbalo* being the quintessential Inca vessel form. Planned provincial administrative centers with standard architectural features, including a central ceremonial platform (*ushnu*), storage facilities (*qollka*), a house for "chosen women" (*aqllawasi*), and large rectangular halls (*kallanka*). Carved or otherwise modified natural rock outcrops. Large-scale agricultural terracing, hydraulic systems, and road networks. Miniature human and camellid forms cast in metal. *Tocapu* (geometric design blocks).

REGIONAL SUBTRADITIONS: Imperial Heartland (Cuzco basin and Urubamba valley), Antisuyu (eastern flanks and foothills of Andes), Chinchaysuyu (northern highlands), Collasuyu (southern highlands), Cuntisuyu (south coast).

IMPORTANT SITES: Cuzco, Hatux Xauxa, Huánaco Pampa, Incallacta, Ingapirca, Island of the Sun, Machu Picchu, Ollantaytambo, Pachaeamac, Rumicucho, Samaipata, Tomebamba.

CULTURAL SUMMARY

Environment

Climate. The Inca empire encompassed the area from the equator to approximately 34° south latitude along the spine of the Andes. In this mountainous environment, climate varies more with elevation than with distance from the equator. Consequently, hot low-lying valleys are found relatively close to the cold plateaus of the highlands. The higher elevations are characterized by coldness and aridity with perpetual snows beginning at approximately 4500 m. Rainfall is light in the highlands and usually confined to a 3-month season annually. The coastal zone dominated by the Inca includes one of the driest deserts on earth. Arid conditions prevail nearly the entire length of the Pacific coast, except for parts of Ecuador where the tropical forest reaches the sea.

Coastal temperatures are moderated by winds off the cold Humboldt current, a phenomenon that also contributes to the low-lying clouds that hang perpetually over much of the Pacific coast. The eastern flanks of the Andes, or the *montaña* zone, is tropical in character. The upper portion of this zone, called the *ceja de montaña*, is a permanent cloud forest where relative humidity typically exceeds 90 percent.

Topography. The Inca empire, which extended some 3500 km along the mountainous backbone of South America, encompassed some of the world's most rugged terrain. The Andean range, which runs the full length of the continent, is characterized by tall peaks, many of which are between 5000 and 7000 m tall, and deep valleys. At its widest, the Andean massif spans 900 km from east to west. From its central girth, the Andes divide into a series of parallel ranges. To the south, the eastern and western *cordilleras* diverge to frame the altiplano, an immense high-altitude plateau some 800 km in length, the central feature of which is Lake Titicaca. The Andes also bifurcate to the north and eventually splinter into a series of narrow parallel ranges in Colombia. The intermontane valleys and high plateaus of the Andes were the homeland of the Inca proper.

In addition to the highlands, the Inca also succeeded in dominating two other distinct physiographic provinces: the Pacific coast and the eastern Andean slopes. In Peru, the relatively narrow coastal strip is dissected at intervals by westward-flowing rivers that descend from the highlands to create a series of narrow green oases perpendicular to the shore. To the east, the Andes drop off sharply, the terrain of the *montaña* zone being deeply dissected by the fast-moving streams that ultimately drain into the Amazon river.

Geology. The Andean range extends 7500 km along the Pacific boundary of South America. As part of the circumpacific mountain system, the Andes are a region of great seismic and volcanic activity. The orogenic history of the western edge of the continent extends back to the Precambrian period. Subsequent tectonics of the Paleozoic era were characterized by intense folding; activity during the later Mesozoic and Cainozoic periods involved violent fracture faulting. Large sections of the Andean range are intersected by deep fractures that can be regarded as tectonic grabens. The great plutonic batholith that underlies the Andean range is made up of granodiorites, tonalites, gabbros and diorites. It is because of this plutonic formation that the Andes are referred to as a magmatic mountain range. The igneous rock is intercalated with various metamorphic and sedimentary formations. The Andes contain some of the richest ore deposits in the world, from which enormous quantities of copper, tin, silver, lead, zinc, and gold are extracted.

Biota. The flora and fauna of the highlands follow the pattern of vertical stratification created by the abrupt changes in elevation. A series of three vertically arrayed ecozones is generally recognized in the highlands: *yunga*, *quechua*, and *puna*. The *yunga* zone lies below 1500 m, is warm and dry, and has a natural xerophytic vegetation. The *quechua*, an intermediate zone dissected by valleys and *quebradas*, ranges from approximately 1500–3500 m above sea level. This was the principal zone of human settlement in the Andes. Prior to the advent of agriculture, this zone likely supported dense forests, although little evidence of these stands remain today. The *puna* zone above extends from approximately 3500 m to the snow fields, which begin between 4500 and 4800 m. The *puna* is characterized by a cold, dry climate and rolling grassy plains that serve as pasturage for the flocks of llamas, alpacas, and vicuñas native to this zone. In the northern Andes, where elevations are somewhat lower, rainfall more abundant, and the grasses thicker and coarser, this upper zone is known as the *páramo*.

On the dry Pacific coast, terrestrial fauna is limited, but the marine resources of this zone are exceptionally rich, the cold coastal waters supporting huge numbers of fish, shellfish, sea mammals, and seabirds. The only plant life native to the coastal desert is the unique "fog vegetation" of the *lomas*, or low-lying hills, which are shrouded in fog banks several months per year. The semitropical *montaña* zone of the eastern Andean flanks is home to numerous animal species, including monkeys, jaguars, snakes, bears, and colorful birds whose feathers were highly prized. Plants of particular economic importance from the *montaña* include the hardwood *chonta*, medicinal herbs, chili peppers (*ají*), and hallucinogenic plants. Coca, a plant of considerable ritual importance for the Inca, is also native to this zone.

Settlements

Settlement System. The Inca empire, known in Quechua as Tawantinsuyu or the Kingdom of the Four Quarters, was centrally administered from the capital city of Cuzco. Inca Cuzco had two principal sectors: a sacred inner core inhabited by the Inca nobility, priests, and government officials, which functioned as the center of religious and political activity, and the outlying residential districts, inhabited by lower nobility, ethnic lords, craft specialists, and other *mitmaqkuna* populations.

Other types of settlements in the Inca heartland included rural villages, of from 5 to 20 households, and the royal estates of the Inca elite. The rural agricultural villages undoubtedly existed much as they had prior to the Inca's meteoric rise to power. From these communities, residents would leave daily to farm surrounding agricultural fields or depart for lengthier periods to exploit the resources of more distant ecozones. The royal estates of the Inca elite were lavishly constructed sites that served as country retreats for the ruling elite. Examples include the sites of Ollantaytambo, Machu Picchu, Chinchero, and Pisac, all of which are located in the fertile Urubamba valley below Cuzco. Such palatial estates typically encompassed the best agricultural lands and displayed the finest Inca masonry.

During their short period of imperial rule, the Inca also constructed numerous planned settlements. These provincial administrative centers served as the nodes that connected the hinterlands to the capital of Cuzco. Common features of these Inca administrative centers included buildings of fine stone masonry, quantities of Inca polychrome pottery, and a central plaza typically flanked by large rectangular structures, or *kallanka*. In addition to housing military personnel and state corvée laborers, the *kallanka* also served as the foci of civic-ceremonial and public feasting events. Other buildings, known as *aqllawasi*, functioned as warehouses for the state's "chosen women." The central plazas of the provincial sites often contained an *ushnu*, or royal dais, as well. Other common elements of the Inca administrative centers were rows of round, towerlike structures known as *qollka*, which served as state storage facilities.

Special religious sanctuaries or oracle sites, such as Tambo Machay near Cuzco or the coastal *huaca* (shrine) of Pachacamac, were a kind of special-purpose site in the Inca settlement system. Hilltop fortresses, or *pucaras*, were another type of special-purpose site. As the Inca empire expanded into frontier zones, *pucaras* were often constructed to garrison the military, control the movements of the local population, and/or for surveillance purposes.

Community Organization.

Most native villages in the Andes grew organically with little evidence of planning. There were no regular streets or public plazas, and houses were widely spaced rather than concentrated. Towns and administrative centers constructed by the state, however, displayed a considerable degree of planning, although no two sites were identical. Each settlement was adapted to the particular topographical, social, astronomical, and economic conditions of its location. There were no universal rules that dictated the precise form of a settlement, but Inca builders drew on a common set of elements and principles. State settlements were typically laid out following either an orthogonal (uneven grid) or a radial pattern. The large architectural blocks that resulted each contained a number of enclosed rectangular compounds (*kanchas*). A division of the site into two parts, representing the idea of upper (*hanan*) and lower (*hurin*) halves, is also often visible in the layout. Large public plazas are another common element of state sites and could be either centrally or laterally located. These plazas were often astronomically aligned and contained an *ushnu*. The *kallanka*, or great halls, typically lined the perimeter of the main plaza.

Housing.

The basic architectural unit of the Inca was the rectangular room with no internal divisions. Humble peasant homes and kingly palaces alike were based on this fundamental building block. The simplest structures, including domestic residences, had unworked fieldstone or adobe walls and a hip roof made of wooden poles covered with thatch. Although single-story structures were the norm, two-story buildings were not uncommon. Both doors and wall niches were typically trapezoidal in shape. Double or triple jamb doors were indicative of elite residences or sacred structures.

If the rectangular room was the basic architectural unit of the Inca, the basic composite form was the *kancha*, a group of three or more rectangular structures arranged symmetrically around a central patio. These complexes were probably inhabited by the extended family.

Beyond the Inca heartland, house forms varied as the conquerors did not require subjects to adopt a uniform state style. Consequently, houses of Inca subjects followed regional traditions and were as likely to be round as rectangular or constructed of sod blocks as of stone.

Population, Health, and Disease.

Most Andean villages contained fewer than 100 families. The number of residents at the planned Inca settlements probably did not normally exceed that of other Andean villages, although the size may have fluctuated periodically with the arrival of state officials or military forces. The population of the capital city of Cuzco is estimated to have been between 15,000 and 20,000 and climbs to 100,000 if residents of the surrounding "suburban" areas are included. Ethnohistoric information suggests that the entire population of the Inca state may have numbered between 6,000,000–10,000,000 prior to the

Spanish invasion in 468 B.P. Epidemics of smallpox and measles which swept the Andes following the Spanish invasion, decimated the region, reducing highland populations by as much as 75 percent and eradicating many of the coastal communities.

Economy

Subsistence. The subsistence base of Tawantinsuyu was agricultural, and production was tightly controlled by the state. Land improvements, which included the construction of terraces, irrigation canals, and dams, were undertaken by the state on a massive scale and intended to increase agricultural yields. Once a region was conquered by the Inca, all lands were declared to be the property of the state. A portion of these agricultural lands was "returned" to the community for its own support; another portion was set aside for the Inca state; and another dedicated to the state religion. Inca subjects were required to work the confiscated lands and forward the produce to state coffers. Labor was the only form of tribute demanded by the state of its citizens. Both men and women engaged in agricultural activities. Land was not owned by individuals but rather by the *ayllu*, the traditional Andean corporate group.

Wild Foods. The collection of wild plants, particularly greens and fruits, and the occasional hunting of deer and guanaco supplemented the Andean diet but was generally of minor importance. All game was declared the property of the state by the Inca and hunting was allegedly strictly controlled. Fishing was important on the coast and on the shores of Lake Titicaca.

Domestic Foods. The two most important crops in the Andes were maize, which can be grown up to 2300 m above sea level, and potatoes, which can be cultivated to almost 4000 m. Maize held considerably more ceremonial and symbolic significance for the Inca, than did potatoes. Other important high-altitude crops included quinoa, *tarwi*, *oca*, *ulluco*, and legumes. Camelid herding also figured prominently in the state economy. Although llamas and alpacas were of principal importance for their wool, they also served as pack animals and occasionally as sources of meat. Large herds were claimed as the exclusive property of Inca rulers. Other Andean domesticates included guinea pigs (*cuyes*), Muscovy duck, and dogs.

Industrial Arts. Inca built on the technological achievements and knowledge of the Andean civilizations that preceded them. Cloth, being of both ceremonial and practical significance in Inca society, was one of the most important manufactures. Textiles were woven primarily of wool, although cotton from the coast was also utilized. Weaving was undertaken by both men and women, using backstrap and upright looms. Metal artifacts included knives, axes, and chisels of bronze; items of personal adornment, such as *tupu* pins, made of copper; and luxury and ceremonial objects such as cups, plates, ear plugs, and figurines made of gold and silver. Production techniques included smelting, alloying, casting, cold hammering, and repoussé. Inca state pottery was highly standardized in terms of both form and decoration and was likely produced by specialists. Stoneworking was highly advanced, employing techniques of hammering and abrasion. Monumental architecture was the enduring achievement of the Inca. The great public structures were built by professional architects and master masons with the aid of a massive labor force supplied by the state. Using only simple tools to shape the huge stone blocks and rollers and ramps to haul and place them, the Inca created structures of lasting beauty.

Utensils. Cooking, eating, and serving utensils were typically made of clay, gourds, or wood. The state ceramic assemblage was confined to a few basic vessel shapes that included the tall-necked jar (*aríbalo*), the smaller pedestal-based cooking pot, and the bird-handled plate. Special-purpose or high-status vessels were sometimes manufactured in stone or precious metal. A unique type of grinding implement consisting of a heavy lunate-shaped rocker stone paired with a flat stone slab was common to most Andean households. The fundamental agricultural implement was the wooden foot plow (*chaquitaclla*). The main hunting implements were the sling and the bola. In warfare, the Inca military utilized clubs with star-shaped stone heads, battle axes, spears, slings, and bolas.

Ornaments. Both men and women wore jewelry. Males of the elite class wore large cylindrical ear plugs of metal or wood, bracelets of gold and silver, and metal pectorals that denoted military prowess. Women used large metal pins (*tupu*) to fasten their shawls and wore necklaces of bone or shell beads. Small squares filled with repeating geometric designs (*tocapu*) were the fundamental decorative device of Inca clothing. Cranial reshaping was practiced by a number of ethnic groups in the Inca empire, and face paint was used in battle and in mourning. Ornamentation of buildings beyond the structural beauty of their design and construction was rare. Bas-relief carvings are occasionally observed on building exteriors, and double and triple jambed doorways were used to mark the importance of certain structures.

Trade. Neither trade nor markets figured in the Inca economy. Nonlocal goods were normally acquired through direct access to or control over the zones of production. Following an ancient Andean pattern involving the permanent deployment of community members to vertically stratified ecozones (the vertical archipelago model), colonies of state subjects known as *mitmaqkuna* could be relocated to special resource zones to extract desired goods. Such products were funneled to the imperial capital or local administrative centers, from which they were subsequently redistributed by the state.

In the Inca empire, taxes were paid in the form of labor rather than in kind. Each community was required to cultivate the lands appropriated by the state in its district. The produce from these lands went to state storage facilities and was used to support state activities. In addition, each community contributed a designated number of individuals to perform specific tasks for the state on an annual basis (*mit'a*). Such tasks could include military duty, construction of state facilities, and service to nobles.

Division of Labor. Specific goods associated with the Inca state, including pottery, cloth, and metal artifacts, were produced by full-time craft specialists who were retained by the state. Within the family, clearcut differences existed in the types of work performed depending on age and sex. Most family members typically shared in the agricultural labor, although men and women were responsible for different aspects of this work, as for instance, in the case of sowing, where men broke the ground and women planted the seed. Children helped their parents, guarded fields before harvest, tended flocks, and collected firewood. Adult males were responsible for fulfilling the family's labor tribute obligations and also made the family footwear. Women were responsible for the maintenance of the household, child rearing, food preparation, and domestic cloth production.

Differential Access to Resources. The Inca controlled production of state polychrome pottery, fine cloth (*cumbi*), and precious metals. Such items were distributed as gifts by the Inca ruler to the nobility or to those who had distinguished themselves through service to the state. The Inca claimed exclusive access to hunting territories and game such as deer and waterfowl. The state also exerted control over its female subjects and, thus, to some extent, over the reproduction of society. Young women chosen for their physical perfection were periodically removed from their families and sent to live in state-run convents. These chosen women (*aqllakuna*) were distributed as gifts by the Inca to deserving warriors, select nobility, and political allies.

Sociopolitical Organization

Social Organization. The traditional Andean system of social organization rested on the notion of *ayllu*, a corporate group whose members exchanged labor and were often related through kinship. An Andean community was typically made up of several distinct *ayllus*, each of which constituted an endogamous entity. Inheritance was reckoned bilaterally, with daughters inheriting from their mothers, and sons from their fathers.

The Inca recognized a series of age groups for purposes of census taking and taxation. Marriage marked the transition to full adulthood. Polygyny was practiced by the Inca elite. The wives and offspring of the emperor formed a royal *ayllu* known as a *panaqa*, which lived off the wealth produced by the ruler during his reign and which maintained his mummy, after death. The principal wife of the Inca ruler, the *Coya*, was his sister. There was no standard of succession to the throne although customarily the emperor selected his heir from among his most competent sons.

Inca society was highly stratified with the "Incas-by-blood" of the Cuzco lineages making up the uppermost echelons of the status hierarchy. Below them were the "Incas-by-privilege," a class made up mainly of the original, non-Inca inhabitants of the Cuzco valley, individuals who had distinguished themselves through outstanding service to the state, and all those whose native language was Quechua. Males of the Inca elite distinguished themselves physically through the use of large ear ornaments. It was this practice that gave rise to the Spanish term *orejones* ("big ears") to refer to the Inca aristocracy.

The provincial nobility made up the next tier in the sociopolitical hierarchy of the state. Members of this class were typically the local ethnic elite who had ruled their provinces prior to the Inca conquest. Below the ethnic elite were the commoners, the backbone of the Inca state, who made their living through agricultural labor.

Political Organization. The Inca empire was centrally administered from the capital city of Cuzco. Conceptually the empire was divided into four great quarters, hence the Quechua name Tawantinsuyu, or "Kingdom of the Four Quarters." Each of these was subdivided into provinces, many of which corresponded to the territories of the indigenous tribes and states subsumed by the empire. These provinces were further subdivided into an upper (*hatun*) and a lower (*hurin*) half, with the upper division taking precedence over the lower in public ceremonies. Each moiety had a varying number of *ayllus*.

The Inca governed their empire through a highly formalized hierarchical system. At the apex stood the Inca sovereign, who ruled by divine right and claimed lineal descent from the sun. Below him were the lords of the four sectors (*suyu*) of the empire, who oversaw the imperial governors of each of the provinces within their sector. The provincial governors purportedly each had responsibility for 10,000 families. Following a decimal system of organization, there were two tiers of Inca officials below the governor, the higher of which supervised two subordinates responsible for the management of 500 families each. Local ethnic leaders, known as *curacas*, served as intermediaries between the imperial hierarchy and the local populace. Theoretically, each *curaca* had under his control 100 families.

Social Control. Although the Inca state managed its subjects with a firm hand, it was not generally abusive. Typical punishments included public rebuke, exile, and loss of office. Seemingly minor crimes could draw harsh penalties. Adultery, for instance, was punishable by torture or death. Crimes, in general, seem to have been relatively rare. Imperial laws were upheld and enforced by regular state officials; there was no special class of state police.

Conflict. One of the key factors in the rapid rise of the Inca state was the military. The Inca army consisted of men drawn from around the empire, who served in fulfillment of their rotational labor obligations (*mit'a*) to the state. Soldiers on active duty were fully supported by the state. Like other elements of the state apparatus, the army was hierarchically organized according to a decimal system. Most military operations involved either hand-to-hand combat or assaults on hilltop fortresses to which the local combatants often retreated. Military prowess was the chief way for commoners to improve their social status within the state, and individuals sought distinction in warfare. Weapons used by Inca forces included the sling, the bola, the star-headed mace, spears, and clubs. Protective gear, including helmets and quilted body armor, was worn in battle.

Religion and Expressive Culture

Religious Beliefs. Inca state religion has been characterized as more pragmatic than mystical, concerned more with food production and the curing of disease than spiritual salvation. The Inca recognized the existence of a supreme deity known as Wiraqocha, who was understood to be the creator of the world. The second most important deity in the Inca pantheon was Inti, the sun and father of the Inca sovereign. Other deities included Illapa (lightening), Killa (moon), Choque Chinchay (the constellation of Orion), and Chasqa Koyllur (Venus). The earth (Pachamama), water (Mamacocha), and mountains (Apus) were also understood to possess supernatural qualities.

The Inca portrayed himself as the direct descendant of the sun. The first Inca, Manco Capac, was said to have emerged from a cave together with his three brothers and four sisters. The eight siblings set out in search of an appropriate site to settle. They eventually arrived in the valley of Cuzco, defeated the local population, and founded what would become the capital of the last indigenous empire in the Andes.

Inca religion was fundamentally animistic insofar as inanimate objects were understood to have a spiritual content. The sun and moon, certain stars, the sea, the earth, rivers and springs, hills, snow-capped peaks, caves, and outcrops all had special significance for the Inca. Rocks were particularly laden with symbolic meaning; numerous Inca myths reference the transformation of men into stones or vice versa. Special boulders or outcrops of particular importance were often integrated into Inca architecture. Small unmodified stones were carried as personal charms; other stone objects carved in the shape of camellids were objects of domestic ritual. The mummified remains of ancestors were also venerated by the Inca. Viewed as the sacred progenitors of the lineage, the mummies of ancestors were consulted on important matters and served as the focal points of both state and family ritual.

Religious Practitioners. All religious shrines (*huacas*) had at least one resident attendant, and the larger had sizeable staffs. Such individuals, including both men and women, were full-time ritual specialists. The women were selected from the larger corps of chosen women (*aqllakuna*) maintained by the state. They formed their own order presided over by a priestess of the highest nobility. Besides tending the shrine, making appropriate sacrifices, and praying, the priests and priestesses also engaged in interpreting oracles, hearing confessions, and diagnosing illnesses. Because consultation with the supernatural was considered an imperative prior to the undertaking of any important action, divination was also a central activity of ritual specialists, who employed coca, guinea pig and llama entrails, dreams, and direct questioning of the oracles to this end.

Ceremonies. Within Andean society, ritual was an essential aspect of daily life. People engaged in private acts, such as the sharing of coca or praying to the snow-capped peaks (*apu*), which expressed deeply held religious beliefs everyday. Public ceremonies of the Inca were elaborate, highly formal affairs. The state ceremonial calendar corresponded closely to the agricultural cycle of the highlands, with many rituals explicitly linked to crop productivity. Public ceremonies were also performed during times of crisis and to mark important historic events such as the coronation or death of the emperor. Most such ceremonies involved the exhibition of sacred idols and images, dancing, feasting, oratory, and the heavy consumption of corn beer (*chicha*). Sacrifices accompanied nearly every religious rite and typically involved guinea pigs, llamas, coca, or *chicha*, although children were sometimes immolated as well. Public ceremonies were typically conducted outdoors in one of the central plazas.

Arts. Song and dance were important elements of most public ceremonies. Dance costumes could be elaborate and often involved masks and animal skins. Instruments were simple and included small flutes of cane and bone, ceramic panpipes, skin drums, gourd and shell trumpets, and metal bells. The affluence and pageantry associated with the Inca court led to the production of large quantities of beautiful objects. The most common design elements in Inca art involved simple geometric patterns. Other common motifs included plants, flowers, insects, humans, llamas, and pumas. The possession of luxury items or goods produced in the state style signified the status and rank of the individual.

Death and Afterlife. The dead were generally considered a source of protection for the family. They were guardians (*mallki*) to whom descendants could appeal for special favors or requests. Inca rulers were typically mummified on death and retained as valued state advisers and lineage patriarchs in the sacred temple of the Sun (*Coricancha*) in Cuzco. Common people were normally buried in caves or rock shelters with offerings of food, pottery, and clothing. Beyond the Inca heartland, burial practices followed traditional norms and varied considerably, although the interments of ethnic elite not infrequently contained Inca-style items.

Suggested Readings

Bauer, Brian (1992). *The Development of the Inca State*. Austin: University of Texas Press.

Bray, Tamara (2000). "Imperial IWCA Iconography: The Art of Empire in the Andes." *RES Journal of Anthropology and Aesthetics* 38: 168–178.

Cieza de León, Pedro de (1962). *La Crónica del Perú* [1553]. Madrid: Espasa Calpe.

Cobo, Bernabé (1964). *Historia del Nuevo Mundo* [1653]. Madrid: Biblioteca de Autores Españoles, Ediciones Atlas.

Collier, George A., Renato I. Rosaldo, and John D. Wirth, eds. (1982). *The Inca and Aztec States, 1400–1800: Anthropology and History.* New York: Academic Press.

D'Altroy, Terence N. (1992). *Provincial Power in the Inka Empire*. Washington, D.C.: Smithsonian Institution Press.

Garcilaso de la Vega, el Inca (1966). *Royal Commentaries of the Incas and the General History of Peru* [1609], trans. H. Livermore. Austin: University of Texas Press.

Gasparini, Graziano, and Luise Margolies (1980). *Inca Architecture*, trans. P. J. Lyon. Bloomington: Indiana University Press.

Guaman Poma de Ayala, Felipe (1936). *Nueva Corónica y Buen Gobierno* [1614]. Paris: Institut d'Ethnologie, Université de Paris.

Hemming, John, and Edward Ranney (1982). *Monuments of the Inca*. Albuquerque: University of New Mexico Press.

Hyslop, John (1990). *Inka Settlement Planning*. Austin: University of Texas.

Malpass, Michael (1996). *Daily Life in the Inca Empire*. Westport: Greenwood Press.

McIntyre, Loren (1975). *The Incredible Incas and Their Timeless Land.* Washington, D.C.: National Geographic Society.

Metraux, Alfred (1969). *The History of the Incas*. New York: Schocken Books.

Morris, Craig (1988). "Progress and Prospect in the Archaeology of the Inca." In *Peruvian Prehistory*, ed. R. Keatinge. Cambridge: Cambridge University Press, 233–256.

Moseley, Michael (1992). *The Inca and Their Ancestors*. London: Thames and Hudson.

Murra, John V. (1980). *Economic Organization of the Inka State*. Greenwich: JAI Press.

Rostworowski de Diez Canseco, María (1988). *Historia del Tahuantinsuyu*. Lima: Instituto de Estudios Peruanos.

Rowe, John H. (1946). "Inca Culture at the Time of the Spanish Conquest." In *Handbook of South American Indians*, vol. 2: *The Andean Civilizations*, ed. J. Steward. Washington, D.C.: Bureau of American Ethnology Bulletin, Smithsonian Institution, 183–330.

Silverblatt, Irene (1987). *Moon, Sun, and Witches*. Princeton: Princeton University Press.

Zuidema, R. Tom (1964). *The Ceque System: The Social Organization of the Capital of the Inca*. Leiden: E. J. Brill.

SUBTRADITIONS

Imperial Heartland

TIME PERIOD: 800–468 B.P.

LOCATION: Cuzco basin and Urubamba valley, south-central highlands of Peru.

DIAGNOSTIC MATERIAL ATTRIBUTES: Fine (Cuzco-style) masonry consisting of well-fitted coursed or polygonal stone blocks; high density of monumental structures exhibiting fine cut-stone masonry; elaborate agricultural terracing; specialized mortuary architecture typically involving underground passages, tunnels, and modified caverns to house ancestral mummies of royal families;

high density of carved rock outcrops and other *huacas* (shrines) making up nodes on lines of the *ceque* system; lack of *ushnu* at sites outside of Cuzco proper; lack of *qollka* storage facilities; orthogonal site plans; use of perforated stones such as eye bonders and ring stones in architecture; triple-jambed niches and windows; asymmetrical, steeply sloped gabled roofs; formal water reservoirs; high density of Inca polychrome pottery.

CULTURAL SUMMARY

Environment

The imperial heartland of the Inca empire, encompassing the Cuzco basin and the nearby Urubamba river valley, is found in the south-central highlands of Peru. It is a rugged region of high mountain valleys and snow-capped peaks. The climate, tempered by the proximity of the eastern jungles, is relatively mild, with the lower Urubamba valley being a few degrees warmer than the Cuzco basin. Rainfall is limited and confined to a 4-month period between December and April. The vegetation consists primarily of grasses, low bushes, and cactuses.

Settlements

The city of Cuzco was as much the hub of the imperial heartland as it was the sacred center of Tawantinsuyu, or the Kingdom of the Four Quarters. Various Inca policies and practices gave the capital city a cosmopolitan character, effectively creating a microcosm of the empire (Cieza de León 1962: 243; Hyslop 1990: 63–65; Rowe 1967; Zuidema 1983). Inca Cuzco had two principal sectors: the sacred inner core inhabited by the Inca nobility, priests, and government officials, and the outlying residential districts inhabited by lower nobility, ethnic lords, craft specialists and other *mitayoq* populations. Cuzco was further divided into quarters and halves by four main roads that intersected in the central plaza and led to the four great sectors of the empire (Hyslop 1990: 57–59). Each quarter of Cuzco was associated with one of the four imperial quarters of the empire, Chinchaysuyu and Antisuyu being associated with the upper (*hanan*) half of Cuzco, and Collasuyu and Cuntisuyu being associated with lower (*hurin*) Cuzco. The population of the metropolitan area at the time of the Spanish conquest is estimated at approximately 100,000 (Rowe 1967; Ruiz de Arce 1933; Sancho 1917).

The land surrounding Cuzco, including the immediately adjacent Vilcanota-Urubamba valley, was intensively developed by the Inca. This region, which constitutes the imperial heartland, contains almost continuous tracts of finely built agricultural terraces, paved roads, hydraulic works, and Inca residences (MacLean 1986; Niles 1982, 1993). Nearly every Inca ruler maintained an estate in the sacred Urubamba valley (Niles 1987; Rowe 1985). These properties were lavishly constructed and served as country retreats for the ruling elite. Examples include the sites of Ollantaytambo, Machu Picchu, Chinchero, Calca, Huayllabamba, Yucay, Quispiguanca, and Pisac (Betanzos 1968; Farrington 1995; Kendall 1974, 1976; Niles 1988, 1993; Niles and Batson 1999; Protzen 1993; Zuidema 1990). Such palatial estates typically encompassed the best agricultural lands and displayed the finest Inca masonry. Like Cuzco, many display an orthogonal site layout (Hyslop 1990: 191–222). They also often contained beautifully wrought tombs in associated rock outcrops (Niles 1987: 121–124). Interestingly, they do not appear to have contained *ushnu* (Hyslop 1990: 101).

Other types of settlements in the imperial heartland include planned residential communities, which typically contained from 15–70 single-room rectangular structures with fieldstone foundations arranged in rows (Bouchard 1983; Gasparini and Margolies 1980; Heffernan 1996; Kendall 1974, 1985; Niles 1984, 1987). Such towns are normally found on hillsides between 200–500 m above the valley floor, affording easy access to the valuable agricultural lands below (Niles 1987: 44–46). Niles (1987: 24–58) suggests that the standardized structures at these sites were built to house nuclear families and that they were probably utilized by agricultural workers fulfilling their labor tribute obligations to the state.

Architectural elements that appear to be exclusive to the imperial heartland include the use of perforated stones such as eye bonders and ring stones in construction (Kendall 1985: 262); triple-jambed niches and windows (Kendall 1985: 264); and asymmetrical, steeply sloped gabled roofs (Kendall 1985: 272). The widespread use of fine-cut stone masonry in constructions and higher densities of Inca polychrome pottery (Lunt 1984, 1987) are other characteristics of the heartland. Interestingly, the region contains few examples of *qollka* or *kallanka* (Gasparini and Margolies 1980: 67–68).

Economy

The subsistence base of the Inca was agricultural, and production was tightly controlled by the state (Morris 1982, 1985; Murra 1980; Rowe 1946). Land improvements, which included the construction of terraces, irrigation canals, and dams, were undertaken by the state on a massive scale and intended to increase agricultural yields (Malpass 1987; Morris 1982; Niles 1982; Sherbondy 1982). Such works are especially evident in the imperial heartland. The two most important crops in the Andes were maize, which can be grown up to 3500 m above sea level, and potatoes, which can be cultivated to almost 4000 m. Of the two, maize held considerably more ceremonial and symbolic significance (Murra 1960). The fertile soils and warmer temperatures of the sheltered Urubamba valley made it particularly well suited to the production of maize and other valued items such as *ají* (hot pepper) (Niles 1993; Rostworowski 1962). Hunting and fishing also figured in the local economy (Villanueva 1970). The produce from the royal estates supported the ruler and his court during his lifetime and was used to maintain the ruler's descendants and his mummy cult after his death (Cobo 1964, bk. 12, ch. 4, 3:155; Conrad and Demarest 1984; Niles 1987, 1993).

The Inca state economy was a redistributive one that exploited ancient principles of reciprocity to its own benefit (D'Altroy and Earle 1985; Morris 1982, 1985; Murra 1980; Wachtel 1977). Morris describes this system as "institutionalized reciprocity." Taxes were paid in the form of labor rather than in kind, and each community was required to cultivate the lands appropriated by the Inca state in its district (Murra 1980; Rowe 1946). The produce from these lands went to state storage facilities and was used to support imperial activities (D'Altroy and Earle 1985; LaLone 1982; Morris 1967). Specific goods associated with the Inca state, including pottery, cloth, and metal artifacts, were produced by full-time craft specialists who were retained by the state and often lodged in the vicinity of Cuzco (Julien 1993; Morris 1974). Neither trade nor markets figured prominently in the Inca economy (Murra 1980, 1995). Nonlocal goods were normally acquired through direct access to or control over vertically differentiated zones of production (Murra 1975, 1985). Such products were funneled to the imperial capital and subsequently redistributed by the state (D'Altroy and Earle 1985; Murra 1980).

Sociopolitical Organization

The imperial heartland constituted the core of the Inca empire. As such, it served as a model of social, political, cosmological, and spatial organization. The Inca built upon the traditional Andean system of social organization, which rested on the notion of *ayllu*. The *ayllu* was a corporate group whose members exchanged labor and were often related through kinship. An Andean community was typically made up of several

distinct *ayllus*, each of which constituted an endogamous entity. Polygyny was practiced by the Inca elite, and the wives and offspring of the emperor formed a royal *ayllu* known as a *panaqa* (Rowe 1946; Zuidema 1990). The principal wife of the Inca ruler, the Coya, was his sister. Inheritance was reckoned bilaterally, with daughters inheriting from their mothers, and sons from their fathers (Silverblatt 1987).

Inca society was highly stratified with the "Incas-by-blood" of the Cuzco lineages making up the uppermost echelons of the status hierarchy. These were the occupants of the sacred central precinct of Cuzco. Each Inca ruler, whether living or mummified, maintained a palatial residence within the imperial center for his wives, children, and retainers. Below the royal lineages were the "Incas-by-privilege," a class consisting mainly of the original, non-Inca inhabitants of the Cuzco valley, individuals who had distinguished themselves through outstanding service to the state, and all those whose native language was Quechua (Rowe 1946; Zuidema 1990). Members of this class, together with the provincial nobility, who were the next tier in the sociopolitical hierarchy of the state, maintained residences in the perimeter districts surrounding the capital (Agurto 1980; Chávez Ballón 1970; Hyslop 1990: 35). The latter were typically ethnic elite who had ruled their provinces prior to the Inca conquest. Below this stratum were the commoners, the backbone of the Inca state, who made their living through agricultural labor (Bauer 1992a; Murra 1980; Rowe 1946; Zuidema 1989, 1990). In the imperial heartland, members of this class occupied the planned residential communities that lay beyond the suburban perimeter of Cuzco (Hyslop 1990: 49–50; Niles 1984).

Religion and Expressive Culture

As the sacred center of the Inca empire, Cuzco served as the focal point of state ceremonial and religious activity. Most Inca ceremonies and ritual were conducted in the open air, the great plaza of Huacaypata serving as one of the principal sites of state religious activity (Rowe 1946). Inca state ceremonials typically involved elaborate sacrifices, dances, drinking, and recitations. State rituals were attended by the emperor and the entire royal court as well as the mummies of former rulers, which were brought out from their temples together with the images of religious deities (Conrad and Demarest 1984; Pizarro 1921 [1571]; Rowe 1946; Zuidema 1973).

The Coricancha, a temple dedicated to the cult of the sun god Inti located in *hurin* Cuzco, was the most sacred shrine in the empire. Inti was the most powerful deity in the imperial pantheon next to the creator god Wiracocha. The Inca emperor, who fashioned himself as the son of the sun, claimed lineal descent from the solar deity to legitimize his power. The cult of the sun was the official religion of the Inca state, and it was imposed throughout the empire. Although the deities of the subject populations were not eradicated, the images of these gods were taken to Cuzco where they were essentially held hostage (Conrad 1981; Rowe 1946).

The Coricancha was the origin point of the 41 vectors making up the Inca *ceque* system (Zuidema 1964, 1977, 1983). The *ceque* system represented a unique form of spatiotemporal organization that integrated the agricultural cycle, astronomy, calendrics, religious ritual, kinship, and social divisions with the physical landscape of the surrounding area through a series of conceptual lines defined by specific landmarks (Zuidema 1964, 1983, 1990). The imperial heartland contains a high density of these landmarks, which were considered to be *huacas* or holy places. Over 350 *huacas* are located within a 20-mile radius of Cuzco (Bauer 1992b; Cobo 1964, bks. 13, 14; Rowe 1979; Zuidema 1964). These include temples and other buildings, cult objects, tombs, battlefields, hills, caves, springs, forts, lookout points, and rock outcrops (Rowe 1946: 296, 1979; Zuidema 1964).

References

Agurto, Santiago (1980). *Cuzco-traza urbana de la ciudad Inca.* UNESCO, Proyecto Per 39, Instituto Nacional de Cultural de Perú. Cuzco: Imprenta Offset Color, S.R.L.

Bauer, Brian (1992a). *The Development of the Inca State.* Austin: University of Texas Press.

Bauer, Brian (1992b). "Ritual Pathways of the Inca: An Analysis of the Collasuyu Ceques in Cuzco." *Latin American Antiquity* 3, 3: 183–205.

Betanzos, Juan de (1968). *Suma y Narración de los Incas* [1551]. Biblioteca de Autores Españoles. Madrid: Atlas.

Bouchard, Jean (1983). *Contribución à l'Étude de l'Architecture Inca: Établissements de la Vallée du Rio Vilcanota-Urubamba.* Paris: Éditions de la Maison des Sciences de l'Homme.

Chávez Ballón, Manuel (1970). "Ciudades Incas: Cuzco, capital del imperio." *Wayka* 3: 1–15.

Cieza de León, Pedro de (1962). *La Crónica del Perú* [1553]. Madrid: Espasa Calpe.

Cobo, Bernabé (1964). *Historia del Nuevo Mundo* [1653]. Madrid: Biblioteca de Autores Españoles, Ediciones Atlas.

Conrad, Geoffrey (1981). "Cultural Materialism, Split Inheritance, and the Expansion of Ancient Peruvian Empires." *American Antiquity* 46: 3–26.

Conrad, Geoffrey, and Arthur Demarest (1984). *Religion and Empire: The Dynamics of Aztec and Inca Expansionism.* Cambridge: Cambridge University Press.

D'Altroy, Terence, and Timothy Earle (1985). "Staple Finance, Wealth Finance, and Storage in the Inka Political Economy." *Current Anthropology* 26, 2: 187–206.

Farrington, Ian (1995). "The Mummy, Palace and Estate of Inka Huayna Capac at Quispiguanca." *Tawantinsuyu* 1: 55–64.

Gasparini, Graziano, and Luise Margolies (1980). *Inca Architecture,* trans. P.J. Lyon. Bloomington: Indiana University Press.

Heffernan, Ken (1996). *Limatambo: Archaeology, History, and the Regional Societies of Inca Cusco.* London: British Archaeological Reports, International Series 664.

Hyslop, John (1990). *Inka Settlement Planning.* Austin: University of Texas.

Julien, Catherine (1993). "Finding a Fit: Archaeology and Ethnohistory of the Incas." In *Provincial Inca: Archaeological and Ethnohistorical Assessment of the Impact of the Inca State,* ed. M. Malpass. Iowa City: University of Iowa Press, 177–233.

Kendall, Ann (1974). "Architecture and Planning at the Inca Sites in the Cusichaca Area." *Baessler Archiv* 22: 73–137.

Kendall, Ann (1976). "Preliminary Report on Ceramic Data and the Pre-Inca Architectural Remains of the (Lower) Urubamba Valley." *Baessler Archiv* 24: 41–159.

Kendall, Ann (1985). *Aspects of Inca Architecture: Description, Function, and Chronology.* Oxford: British Archaeological Reports, International Series 242.

LaLone, Darrell (1982). "The Inca as a Nonmarket Economy: Supply on Command vs. Supply and Demand." In *Contexts for Prehistoric Exchange,* ed. J. Ericson, and T. Earle. New York: Academic Press, 291–316.

Lunt, Sarah (1984). "An Introduction to the Pottery from the Excavations at Cusichaca, Department of Cuzco." In *Current Archaeological Projects in the Central Andes, Forty-ninth International Congress of Americanists.* ed. A. Kendall London: BAR International Series, 307–319.

Lunt, Sarah (1987). "Inca and Pre-Inca Pottery from Cusichaca, Department of Cuzco, Peru." Ph.D. diss., London University Institute of Archaeology, University College, London.

MacLean, Margaret (1986). "Sacred Land, Sacred Water: Inca Landscape Planning in the Cuzco Area." Ph.D. diss., Department of anthropology, University of California, Berkeley.

Malpass, Michael (1987). "Prehistoric Agricultural Terracing at Chijra in the Colca Valley, Peru." In *Pre-Hispanic Agricultural Fields in the Andean Region,* ed. W. Denevan, K. Mathewson, and G. Knapp. Oxford: British Archaeological Report, International Series, no. 359, 45–66.

Morris, Craig (1967). "Storage in Tawantinsuyu." Ph.D. diss., Department of Anthropology, University of Chicago.

Morris, Craig (1974). "Reconstructing Patterns of Non-Agricultural Production in the Inca Economy: Archaeology and documents in Instituted Analysis." In *Reconstructing Complex Societies,* ed. C. Moore. Cambridge, MA. Supplement to Bulletin of the American Schools of Oriental Research, no. 20, 49–68.

Morris, Craig (1978). "The Archaeological Analysis of Andean Exchange Systems." In *Social Archaeology: Beyond Subsistence and Dating,* ed. C. Redman et al. New York: Academic Press, 303–327.

Morris, Craig (1982). "Infrastructure of Inka Control in the Peruvian Central Highlands." In *The Inca and Aztec States, 1400–1800,* ed. G. Collier, R. Rosaldo, and J. Wirth. New York: Academic Press, 153–171.

Morris, Craig (1985). "From Principles of Ecological Complementarity to the Organization and Administration of Tawantinsuyu." In *Andean Ecology and Civilization,* ed. S. Masuda, I. Shimada, and C. Morris. Tokyo: University of Tokyo Press, 477–490.

Murra, John (1960). "Rite and Crop in the Inca State." In *Culture and History,* ed. S. Diamond. New York: Columbia University Press, 393–407.

Murra, John (1975). "El control vertical de un máximo de pisos ecológicos en la economía de las sociedades andinas." In *Formaciones Económicas y Políticas del Mundo Andino*, ed. J. Murra. Lima: Instituto de Estudios Peruanos, 59–115.

Murra, John (1980). *Economic Organization of the Inka State*. Greenwich: JAI Press.

Murra, John (1985). "The Archipiélago Vertical' Revisited." In *Andean Ecology and Civilization*, ed. S. Mazuda, I. Shimada, and C. Morris. Tokyo: University if Tokyo Press, 3–14.

Murra, John (1995). "Did Tribute and Markets Prevail in the Andes before the European Invasion?" In *Ethnicity, Markets, and Migration in the Andes: At the Crossroads of History and Anthropology*, ed. B. Larson, O. Harris, and E. Tandeter. Durham: Duke University Press, 57–72.

Niles, Susan (1982). "Style and Function in Inca Agricultural Works near Cuzco." *Ñawpa Pacha* 20: 163–182.

Niles, Susan (1984). "Architectural Form and Social Function in Inca Towns near Cuzco." In *Current Archaeological Projects in the Central Andes: Some Approaches and Results*, ed. A. Kendall. Oxford: British Archaeological Reports, International Series 210, 205–223.

Niles, Susan (1987). *Callachaca: Style and Status in an Inca Community*. Iowa City: University of Iowa Press.

Niles, Susan (1988). "Looking for "Lost" Inca Palaces." *Expedition* 30: 56–64.

Niles, Susan (1993). "The Provinces in the Heartland: Stylistic Variation and Architectural Innovation near Inca Cuzco." In *Provincial Inca: Archaeological and Ethnohistorical Assessment of the Impact of the Inca State*, ed. M. Malpass. Iowa City: University of Iowa Press, 146–176.

Niles, Susan, and Robert Batson (in press). "Sculpting the Yucay Valley: Style and Technique in Late Inka Architecture." In *Variations in the Expressions of Inka Power*, ed. M. M. Ramiro Matos, R. Burger, and C. Morris. Washington, D.C.: Dumbarton Oaks Press.

Pizarro, Pedro (1921). *Relation of the Discovery and Conquest of the Kingdoms of Peru* [1571]. New York: Cortes Society.

Protzen, Jean Pierre (1993). *Inca Architecture and Construction at Ollantaytambo*. Oxford: Oxford University Press.

Rostworowski de Diez Canseco, María (1962). "Nuevos datos sobre tenencia de tierras reales." *Revista del Museo Nacional* (Lima) 21: 130–194.

Rowe, John H. (1946). "Inca Culture at the Time of the Spanish Conquest." In *Handbook of South American Indians*, vol. 2, *The Andean Civilizations*, ed. J. Steward. Washington, D.C.: Bureau of American Ethnology Bulletin, Smithsonian Institution 143, 183–330.

Rowe, John H. (1967). "What Kind of a Settlement was Inca Cuzco?" *Ñawpa Pacha* 5: 59–76.

Rowe, John H. (1979). "An Account of the Shrines of Ancient Cuzco." *Ñawpa Pacha* 5: 59–76.

Rowe, John H. (1985). "Probanza de los Incas nietos de conquistadores." *Histórica* 9, 2: 193–245.

Ruiz de Arce, Juan (1933). "Relación de los servicios en Indias de don Juan Ruiz de Arce, conquistador del Perú [1543]." *Boletín de la Academia de la Historia* (Madrid) 102, 2: 327–384.

Sancho de la Hoz, Pedro (1917). "Relación para S. M. de lo sucedido en la conquista [1534]." In "*Colección de Libros y Documentos Referentes a la Historia del Perú*, 5, ed. H. Urteaga. Lima: San Martí, 122–202.

Sherbondy, Jeannette (1982). "Canal Systems of Hanan Cuzco." Ph.D. diss., Department of Anthropology, University of Illinois, Urbana.

Silverblatt, Irene (1987). *Moon, Sun, and Witches*. Princeton: Princeton University Press.

Villanueva, Horacio (1970). "Documentos sobre Yucay, siglo XVI." *Revista del Archivo Histórico del Cuzco* 13: 1–148.

Wachtel, Nathan (1977). *Vision of the Vanquished*. New York: Harper and Row.

Zuidema, R. Tom (1964). *The Ceque System: The Social Organization of the Capital of the Inca*. Leiden: E. J. Brill.

Zuidema, R. Tom (1973). "Kinship and Ancestor Cult in Three Peruvian Communities: Hernández Príncipe's Account in 1622." *Bulletin de l'Institut Francés de Études Andines* 2, 10: 16–33.

Zuidema, R. Tom (1977). "The Inca Calendar." In *Native American Astronomy*, ed. A. Aveni. Austin: University of Texas Press, 219–259.

Zuidema, R. Tom (1983). "Hierarchy and Space in Incaic Social Organization." *Ethnohistory* 30, 2: 49–75.

Zuidema, R. Tom (1989). "The Moieties of Cuzco." In *Attraction of Opposites: Thought and Society in the Dualistic Mode*, ed. D. Maybury-Lewis and U. Amagor. Ann Arbor: University of Michigan Press, 255–275.

Zuidema, R. Tom (1990). *Inca Civilization in Cuzco*. Austin: University of Texas Press.

Antisuyu

TIME PERIOD: C. 530–468 B.P.

LOCATION: Eastern slopes and foothills of the Andes, encompassing the tropical montane forest zone known as the *ceja de montaña* ("eyebrow of the jungle"), stretching an indeterminate distance to the northwest and southeast from Cuzco into Ecuador and Bolivia.

DIAGNOSTIC MATERIAL ATTRIBUTES: Lack of formal Inca road; use of local fieldstone for constructions; lack of fine cut-stone masonry; agricultural terraces associated with sites.

CULTURAL SUMMARY

Environment

The eastern quarter of the empire, known as Antisuyu, incorporates the montane forest zone of the eastern slopes of the Andean cordillera. The swift rivers and deep canyons characteristic of this zone region create an extremely broken topography. It is a region of high rainfall and dense vegetation with temperatures ranging between 0–15° C. The upper portion of this zone, known as the *ceja de montaña*, is a permanent cloud forest where relative humidity typically exceeds 90 percent. The eastern montane forest is home to numerous animal species including monkeys, jaguars, snakes, bears, and colorful birds whose feathers were highly prized. It is a zone of unparalleled ecological diversity. Plants of particular economic importance from the *montaña* include the hardwood *chonta*, medicinal herbs, chili peppers (*aji*), and hallucinogenic plants. Coca, a plant of considerable ritual importance for the Inca, is also native to this zone. The eastern tropical montane forest has traditionally been considered a cultural and ecological transition zone between the highlands and the Amazonian lowlands. The imperial boundaries of this rugged sector have never been clearly defined. It was generally viewed as an inhospitable environment by highland dwellers, was difficult to access, and is sparsely populated even today.

Settlements

Hyslop (1984: 265) notes that Antisuyu was never furnished with a primary Inca road. Hence there was no direct linkage to the imperial capital or internal connections between the different provinces of this quarter. Most entries into this region were made via side roads that branched north or east off the main imperial highway. Hyslop suggests that road construction in this sector was particularly difficult because of the dense vegetation and steep slopes. What roads are found in the Antisuyu quarter are necessarily narrow and required considerable effort to engineer.

Few Inca sites have been identified in the Antisuyu district. Those present appear to be small scale and primarily residential in nature, generally conforming to local settlement patterns and utilizing similar construction techniques. The primary distinguishing feature at sites believed to have an Inca component is the presence of rectangular structures; these contrast sharply with the circular forms favored by the local population (Bonavía and Ravines 1968; Isbell 1968; Schjellerup 1992: 359–360; Thompson 1971, 1973). In the case of Abiseo (also known as Gran Pajatén), for instance, both structural types exhibit the same construction technique and utilize the same locally available schist slabs for construction material (Bonavía 1968a; Bonavía and Ravines 1968: 156; Rojas Ponce 1967). Most of the late prehistoric period sites in the Antisuyu district typically have large tracts of agricultural terracing associated (Bonavía 1967–1968: 276–278, 1968b; Bonavía and Ravines 1968: 157; Isbell 1968; von Hassel 1905: 301, 305).

Cochabamba, in the Chachapoyas province of northeastern Peru, is one of the only reported sites with obvious Inca architecture and pottery within the Antisuyu quarter (Bandelier 1907, 1940; Schjellerup 1979–1980, 1984, 1998). Several compounds at Cochabamba are outfitted with doors and baths exhibiting fine cut-stone masonry, although the main construction technique involves low *pirca*-style wall foundations supporting *tapia* or adobe upper walls (Schjellerup 1984: 164–169). Imperial Inca polychrome pottery has also been recovered at the site (Schjellerup 1984: 169). In addition, numerous rectangular storage structures (*qollka*) have been documented in the vicinity of Cochabamba (Schjellerup 1984: 172–176).

There are no major Inca administrative centers in Antisuyu (Bonavía 1978, 1981). Lyon (1981: 4) suggests that much of the intent of Inca settlement in Antisuyu was defensive, although cultivation of specialty crops such as coca, cotton, and chili pepper, and access to valued resources were also likely to have been important considerations. Gade (1979) conjectures that the minimal Inca presence in Antisuyu was related to the threat of tropical disease. He points out that the few Inca sites found in this region are all situated above 2700 m, well beyond the range of the flies that carried the dreaded leishmania pathogen endemic to the region below 2400 m. Lyon (1981) believes that the limits of imperial expansion in Antisuyu may have been tied to transportation considerations, noting that Inca sites seem to terminate at the point along any given river system where canoe transport becomes imperative (see also Renard-Casevitz and Saignes 1988: 52, who make a similar point with respect to the range of llamas).

Based on historical information, it has generally been assumed that numerous military installations existed along the eastern border of the empire for defense against marauding hordes of tropical forest dwellers. The Ortíz inspection of 1567 (1972: 25–50), for example, mentions that there were three or four Inca fortresses positioned east of Huánaco to guard the frontier; Saignes (1985: 18–28) notes early reports of such fortifications in the upper Beni river region of northeastern Bolivia (see also Denevan 1966: 23). The archaeological evidence amassed to date, however, does not substantiate the ethnohistoric reports (Hyslop 1990: 157–160). A high concentration of military sites has been documented in eastern Bolivia near the boundary of the Andean-Amazonian macroregions (Byrne de Caballero 1978; Nordenskiold 1917, 1942, 1956–1957), but the evidence for Inca fortifications diminishes as one proceeds northwest along the edge of the eastern frontier into Peru and Ecuador (Hyslop 1990: 157–160). For all the historical speculation, there is remarkably little archaeological evidence of Inca fortifications along the eastern frontier.

The eastern montane forests were traditionally viewed as a zone of refuge by highland peoples

(Renard-Casevitz et al. 1988) and served as a base of guerilla operations for the rebel leader, Manco Inca, following the Spanish invasion (Pizarro 1921). The site of Vilcabamba, established deep within the jungles of Antisuyu, functioned as the capital for the remnants of the Inca state for several decades after the fall of Cuzco (Hemming and Ranney 1982: 160–163; Lyon 1981; Savoy 1970).

Economy

The subsistence base of the Inca was agricultural, and production was tightly controlled by the state (Morris 1982, 1985; Murra 1980; Rowe 1946). Land improvements, which included the construction of terraces, irrigation canals, and dams, were undertaken by the state on a massive scale and intended to increase agricultural yields (Malpass 1987; Morris 1982; Niles 1982; Sherbondy 1982). The two most important crops in the Andes were maize, which can be grown up to 3500 m above sea level, and potatoes, which were cultivated to almost 4000 m. Of the two, maize held considerably more ceremonial and symbolic significance (Murra 1960). Coca, another highly valued crop, is native to the *montaña* zone of Antisuyu, where it grows between 500 and 1800 m elevation (Plowman 1981). The terracing found at Inca sites in Antisuyu was likely dedicated to coca and/or maize production (Bonavia and Ravines 1968; Donkin 1984: 122–125; Isbell 1974; Raymond 1988: 296–297).

The Inca state economy was a redistributive one that exploited ancient principles of reciprocity to its own benefit (D'Altroy and Earle 1985; Morris 1982, 1985; Murra 1980; Wachtel 1977). Morris describes this system as "institutionalized reciprocity." Taxes were paid in the form of labor rather than in kind, and each community was required to cultivate the lands appropriated by the Inca state in its district (Murra 1980; Rowe 1946). The produce from these lands went to state storage facilities, such as those reported at Cochabamba in the Chachapoyas district, and was used to support imperial activities (D'Altroy and Earle 1985; LaLone 1982; Morris 1967). Specific goods associated with the Inca state, including pottery, cloth, and metal artifacts, were produced by full-time craft specialists who were retained by the state and often lodged in the vicinity of Cuzco (Julien 1993; Morris 1974).

Although in general markets and trade did not figure prominently in the Inca economy (Murra 1980, 1995), there may have been somewhat more emphasis on trade and exchange on the eastern frontier (Gade 1972; Lyon 1981; Myers 1981; Renard-Casevitz and Saignes 1988:

70–73; Uhle 1909). The tropical forests east of the Andes were the source of a number of important products, including hardwoods, coca, feathers, wax, honey, medicinal herbs, and hallucinogens, but the Inca never succeeded in completely dominating this important resource zone. Rather, the imperial boundary seems to have remained fairly porous along the this frontier, with the Inca trading back and forth across it.

Sociopolitical Organization

One of Pachacuti's first imperial gestures after defeating the Chanca and securing the Cuzco basin was to annex the lower Urubamba valley, portions of which came to be associated with Antisuyu (Cabello Balboa 1951: 300–301; Sarmiento 1943: 100–110). Additional campaigns were undertaken in this quarter by Pachacuti's heir, Topa Inca, to expand Inca control of the region (Cabello Balboa 1951: 334–335; Cobo 1979: 142; Sarmiento 1943: 128–130). Huayna Capac, who succeeded Topa Inca c. 507 B.P., also fought a number of battles along the eastern frontier, subduing the rebellious Chachapoyas of northeastern Peru and the Chiriguano of northeastern Bolivia during his reign (Cabello Balboa 1951: 361; Cieza 1973: 226–228; Cobo 1979: 154; Sarmiento 1943: 142). In general, the eastern edge of Tawantinsuyu seems to have been a fluid frontier against which the Inca expanded and receded several times in the face of strong resistance from the local population.

The archaeological evidence indicates that the eastern flanks of the Andean cordillera were densely occupied during the Regional States (Late Intermediate) period (Bonavía 1967–1968; Church 1996; Hastings 1985; Onuki 1985; Schjellerup 1992). The inhabitants of this region lived in nucleated settlements located in readily defensible positions on hilltops or ridges. Each village seemingly operated as an independent political entity with a structure based on the Andean model of the *ayllu* (Espinoza 1967; Oberem 1980; Renard-Casevitz et al. 1988; Schjellerup 1998). There is no evidence that the ethnic groups of Antisuyu were ever politically unified. The residents of this region maintained extensive contacts with both Amazonian and Andean groups and were participants in a vast exchange network (Myers 1981; Reeve 1994).

The Inca generally regarded the inhabitants of Antisuyu as unpredictable savages and cannibals, the antithesis of civilized society (Cieza 1962: 439; Renard-Casevitz and Saignes 1988). Yet there was also a certain respect accorded the inhabitants of this region as masters of an environment that highland dwellers perceived as dangerous. The most powerful shamans and sorcerers hailed from this realm. Various scholars have suggested that the eastern slopes were colonized by highlanders as early as the Middle horizon (Bonavía 1964; Bonavía and Ravines 1967: 62, 1968; Hastings 1985; Kauffmann 1987; Lyon 1981: 9; Raymond 1976). The Inca may have relocated some relatively compatible *mitmaq* populations to Antisuyu (Cieza de León 1962: 393; Lyon 1981: 7; Rostworowski 1963), it does not appear that they required highland subjects to live there except on a temporary basis to perform labor service (Gade 1979: 275) or that they themselves ever resided in this region.

Inca society was highly stratified with the "Incas-by-blood" of the Cuzco lineages being the uppermost echelons of the status hierarchy. Below them were the "Incas-by-privilege," a class consisting mainly of the original, non-Inca inhabitants of the Cuzco valley, individuals who had distinguished themselves through outstanding service to the state, and all those whose native language was Quechua. The provincial nobility was the next tier in the sociopolitical hierarchy of the state. Members of this class were typically the ethnic elite who had ruled their provinces prior to the Inca conquest. Below this stratum were the commoners, the backbone of the Inca state, who made their living through agricultural labor (Bauer 1992; Murra 1980; Rowe 1946; Zuidema 1989, 1990).

The Inca governed their empire through a highly formalized hierarchical system. At the apex stood the Inca sovereign, who ruled by divine right and claimed lineal descent from the sun. Below him were the lords of the four sectors (*suyu*) of the empire, who oversaw the imperial governors of each of the provinces within their sector. The provincial governors purportedly each had responsibility for 10,000 families. Following a decimal system of organization, there were two tiers of Inca officials below the governor, the higher of which supervised two subordinates responsible for the management of 500 families each. Local ethnic leaders, known as *curacas*, served as intermediaries between the imperial hierarchy and the local populace. Theoretically, each *curaca* had under his control 100 families (Julien 1982; Rowe 1946).

Religion and Expressive Culture

Inca religion was fundamentally animistic insofar as inanimate objects were understood to have a spiritual content. The sun and moon, certain stars, the sea, the earth, rivers and springs, hills, snow-capped peaks, caves, and outcrops all had special significance for the Inca. Rocks were particularly laden with symbolic meaning; numerous Inca myths reference the transformation of men into stones or vice versa. Special boulders or outcrops of particular importance were often integrated into Inca architecture or became the focal points of imperial sites around the empire (Cobo 1990; Rowe 1946; Zuidema 1990).

Within Andean society, ritual was an essential aspect of daily life. People engaged in private acts, such as the sharing of coca or praying to the snow-capped peaks (*apu*), which expressed deeply held religious beliefs everyday. Public ceremonies of the Inca were elaborate, highly formal affairs. The state ceremonial calendar corresponded closely to the agricultural cycle of the highlands, with many rituals explicitly linked to crop productivity. Public ceremonies were also performed during times of crisis and to mark important historic events such as the coronation or death of the emperor. Most such ceremonies involved the exhibition of sacred idols and images, dancing, feasting, oratory, and the heavy consumption of corn beer (*chicha*). Public ceremonies were typically conducted outdoors (Rowe 1946; Zuidema 1990).

Sacrifices accompanied nearly every religious rite and often involved guinea pigs, llamas, coca, and *chicha*, although children were sometimes immolated as well. Guaman Poma (1936: 268–269) depicts residents of Antisuyu offering a small child and a plate of burning fat to several hilltop *huacas* and an anthropomorphized jaguar. He indicates in the text that the people of Antisuyu worshiped the jaguar (*otorongo*), the great snake (*amaru*), and the coca plant, and that they made sacrifices of children, white guinea pigs (*conejo blanco*), coca, maize, *mullo* (*Spondylus* shell), feathers, and blood to the hilltop dieties.

Ethnic groups in the Andes typically had their own distinctive style of dress. Guaman Poma (1936: 167) depicts the captain from Antisuyu clothed in a feather garment wearing a crownlike headdress, and holding a bow and arrow. A sheaf of arrows is arrayed on his back like a large halo. Rowe (1946: 275) notes that the principal weapon of the Indians of Antisuyu was the bow and arrow and that this was a device used exclusively by the lowland tribes. Guaman Poma (1936: 175) represents a female from this region wearing only a short skirt and a bead necklace. She is depicted barefoot, appears to have a stomach tatoo, and is attended by a bird and a monkey. In his illustrations of people from Antisuyu, Guaman Poma usually represents them half-naked (1936: 291, 322), a convention likely intended to signal their uncivilized character.

The dead were generally considered a source of protection in the late pre-Columbian era. They were guardians (*mallki*) to whom descendants could appeal for special favors or requests. Inca rulers were typically mummified on death and retained as valued state advisers and lineage patriarchs in the sacred temple of the Sun (Coricancha) in Cuzco. Common people were normally buried in caves or rock shelters with offerings of food, pottery, and clothing. In the imperial provinces, burial practices followed traditional norms and varied considerably, although the interments of ethnic elite frequently contained Inca-style items. Guaman Poma (1936: 291–292) suggests that the Indians of the Anti-suyu region typically buried their dead inside hollow tree trunks in the jungle.

References

Bandelier, Adolph (1907). *The Indians and Aboriginal Ruins near Chachapoyas in Northern Peru.* New York: Historical Records and Studies.

Bandelier, Adolph (1940). "Los indios y las ruinas aborigines cerca de Chachapoyas en el norte del Perú." *Chaski* (Lima) 1, 2: 13–59.

Bauer, Brian (1992). *The Development of the Inca State.* Austin: University of Texas Press.

Bonavía, Duccio (1962). *Investigaciones en la Ceja de Selva de Ayacucho.* Arqueológicos: Publicaciones del Instituto de Investigaciones Antropológicas 6. Lima: Museo Nacional de Antropología y Arqueología.

Bonavía, Duccio (1967–1968). "Investigaciones arqueológicas en el Mataro medio." *Revista del Museo Nacional* (Lima) 35: 211–294.

Bonavía, Duccio (1968a). *Las Ruinas de Abiseo.* Lima: Universidad Peruana de Ciencias y Tecnología.

Bonavía, Duccio (1968b). "Nucleos de población en la ceja de selva de Ayacucho." *Actas y Memorias del XXXVIIth Annual Congreso Internacional de Americanistas* 1: 75–83.

Bonavía, Duccio (1978). "Ecological Factors Affecting the Urban Transformation in the Last Centuries of the Pre-Columbian Era." *Advances in Andean Archaeology,* ed. D. Browman. The Hague: Mouton, 393–410.

Bonavía, Duccio (1981). "Tello y la arqueología de la ceja de selva." *Histórica* 5, 2: 149–158.

Bonavía, Duccio, and Rogger Ravines (1967). "Las fronteras ecológicas de la civilización andina." *Amaru* 2: 61–69.

Bonavía, Duccio, and Rogger Ravines (1968). "Villas del horizonte tardío en la ceja de selva del Perú: Algunas consideraciones." *Actas y Memorias del XXXVIIth Annual Congreso Internacional de Americanistas* 1: 153–160.

Byrne de Caballero, Geraldine (1978). "Incarracay: Un centro administrativo incaico." *Arte y Arqueología* (La Paz) 5–6: 309–316.

Cabello Balboa, Miguel (1951). *Miscelánea Antártica* [1586]. Quito: Editorial Ecuatoriana.

Church, Warren (1996). "Prehistoric Cultural Development and Interregional Interaction in the Tropical Montane Forests of Peru." Ph.D. diss., Department of Anthropology, Yale University.

Cieza de León, Pedro de (1962). *La Crónica del Perú* [1553]. Madrid: Espasa Calpe.

Cieza de León, Pedro de (1973). *El Señorio de los Incas.* Lima: Editorial Universo.

Cobo, Bernabé (1964). *Historia del Nuevo Mundo* [1653]. Madrid: Biblioteca de Autores Españoles, Ediciones Atlas.

Cobo, Bernabé (1979). *History of the Inca Empire.* Austin: University of Texas Press.

Cobo, Bernabé (1990). *Inca Religion and Customs,* ed. R. Hamilton. Austin: University of Texas Press.

D'Altroy, Terence, and Timothy Earle (1985). "Staple Finance, Wealth Finance, and Storage in the Inka Political Economy." *Current Anthropology* 26, 2: 187–206.

Denevan, William (1966). *The Aboriginal Cultural Geography of the Llanos de Mojos in Northeastern Bolivia.* Ibero-Americana 48. Berkeley and Los Angeles: University of California Press.

Donkin, R. A. (1984). *Agricultural Terracing in the Aboriginal New World.* Viking Fund Publications in Anthropology 56. Tucson: University of Arizona Press.

Espinoza S., Waldemar (1967). "Los señorios étnicos de Chachapoyas y la alianza Hispano-Chacha." *Revista Histórica* (Lima) 30: 224–332.

Fejos, Paul (1944). *Explorations in the Cordillera Vilcabamba.* Viking Fund Publications in Anthropology, no. 3. New York.

Gade, Daniel (1972). "Comercio y colonización en la zona de contacto entre la sierra y las tierras bajas del valle del Urubamba." *Actas y Memorias del XXXVIIIth Congreso Internacional de Americanistas* 4: 207–221.

Gade, Daniel (1979). "Inca and Colonial Settlement, Coca Cultivation, and Endemic Disease in the Tropical Forest." *Journal of Historical Geography* 5: 263–279.

Guaman Poma de Ayala, Felipe (1936). *Nueva Corónica y Buen Gobierno* [1614]. Paris: Institut d'Ethnologie, Université de Paris.

Hastings, Charles (1985). "The Eastern Frontier: Settlement and Subsistence in the Andean Margins of Central Peru." Ph.D. diss., Department of Anthropology, University of Michigan. University Microfilms.

Hemming, John, and Edward Ranney (1982). *Monuments of the Incas.* Albuquerque: University of New Mexico Press.

Hyslop, John (1984). *Inka Road System.* New York: Academic Press.

Hyslop, John (1990). *Inka Settlement Planning.* Austin: University of Texas.

Isbell, William (1968). "New Discoveries in the Montaña of Southeastern Peru." *Archaeology* 21, 2: 108–114.

Isbell, William (1974). "Ecología de la expansión de los Quechua-hablantes." *Revista del Museo Nacional* (Lima) 40: 139–155.

Julien, Catherine (1982). "Inca Decimal Administration in the Lake Titicaca Region." In *The Inca and Aztec States, 1400–1800: Anthropology and History,* ed. G. Collier, R. Rosaldo, and J. Wirth. New York: Academic Press, 119–151

Julien, Catherine (1993). "Finding a Fit: Archaeology and Ethnohistory of the Incas." In *Provincial Inca: Archaeological and Ethnohistorical Assessment of the Impact of the Inca State,* ed. M. Malpass. Iowa City: University of Iowa Press, 177–233.

Kauffmann Doig, Federico (1987). *Andes Amazónicos: Investigaciones Arqueológicas 1980–1986 (Expedición Antisuyo).* Lima: Banco Continental.

LaLone, Darrell (1982). "The Inca as a Nonmarket Economy: Supply on Command vs. Supply and Demand." In *Contexts for Prehistoric Exchange,* ed. J. Ericson and T. Earle. New York: Academic Press, 291–316.

Lyon, Patricia J. (1981). "An Imaginary Frontier: Prehistoric Highland-Lowland Interchange in the Southern Peruvian Andes." In *Networks of the Past: Regional Interaction in Archaeology,* ed. P. Francis, F. Kense, and P. Duke. Calgary: University of Calgary Press, 3–18.

Malpass, Michael (1987). "Prehistoric Agricultural Terracing at Chijra in the Colca Valley, Peru." In *Pre-Hispanic Agricultural Fields in the Andean Region*, ed. W. Denevan, K. Mathewson, and G. Knapp. Oxford: British Archaeological Report, International Series, no. 359, 45–66.

Morris, Craig (1967). "Storage in Tawantinsuyu." Ph.D. diss., Department of Anthropology, University of Chicago.

Morris, Craig (1974). "Reconstructing Patterns of Non-agricultural Production in the Inca Economy: Archaeology and Documents in Instituted Analysis." In *Reconstructing Complex Societies*, ed. C. Moore. Supplement to Bulletin of the American Schools of Oriental Research, no. 20., Cambridge, MA, 49–68.

Morris, Craig (1978). "The Archaeological Analysis of Andean Exchange Systems." In *Social Archaeology: Beyond Subsistence and Dating*, ed. C. Redman et al. New York: Academic Press, 303–327.

Morris, Craig (1982). "Infrastructure of Inka Control in the Peruvian Central Highlands." In *The Inca and Aztec States, 1400–1800*, ed. G. Collier, R. Rosaldo, and J. Wirth. New York: Academic Press, 153–171.

Morris, Craig (1985). "From Principles of Ecological Complementarity to the Organization and Administration of Tawantinsuyu." In *Andean Ecology and Civilization*, ed. S. Masuda, I. Shimada, and C. Morris. Tokyo: University of Tokyo Press, 477–490.

Murra, John (1960). "Rite and Crop in the Inca State." In *Culture and History*, ed. S. Diamond. New York: Columbia University Press, 393–407.

Murra, John (1975). "El control vertical de un máximo de pisos ecológicos en la economía de las sociedades andinas." In *Formaciones Económicas y Políticas del Mundo Andino*, ed. J. Murra. Lima: Instituto de Estudios Peruanos, 59–115.

Murra, John (1980). *Economic Organization of the Inka State*. Greenwich: JAI Press.

Murra, John (1995). "Did Tribute and Markets Prevail in the Andes before the European Invasion?" In *Ethnicity, Markets, and Migration in the Andes: At the Crossroads of History and Anthropology*, ed. B. Larson, O. Harris, and E. Tandeter. Durham: Duke University Press, 57–72.

Myers, Thomas (1981). "Aboriginal Trade Networks in Amazonia." In *Networks of the Past: Regional Interaction in Archaeology*, ed. P. Francis, F. J. Kense, and P. G. Duke. Calgary: Archaeological Association, University of Calgary, 19–30.

Niles, Susan (1982). "Style and Function in Inca Agricultural Works near Cuzco." *Ñawpa Pacha* 20: 163–182.

Nordenskiold, Erland von (1917). "The Guarani Invasion of the Inca Empire in the Sixteenth Century: An historical Indian Migration." *Geographical Review* 9: 103–121.

Nordenskiold, Erland von (1942). "Fortifications in Ancient Peru and Europe." *Ethnos* 7: 1–9.

Nordenskiold, Erland von (1956–1957). "Incallajta: Ciudad fortificada fundado por el Inca Tupac Yupanqui." *Khana: Revista Municipal de Arte y Letras* (La Paz) 21–24: 6–22.

Oberem, Udo (1980). *Los Quijos*. Colección Pendoneros. Otavalo, Ecuador: Instituto Otavaleño de Antropología.

Onuki, Yoshio (1985). "The Yunga Zone in the Prehistory of the Central Andes: Vertical and Horizontal Dimensions in Andean Ecological and Cultural Processes." In *Andean Ecology and Civilization*, ed. S. Masuda, I. Shimada, and C. Morris. Tokyo: University of Tokyo Press, 339–356.

Ortíz de Zúñiga, Iñigo (1972). *Visita a la Provincial de León de Huánaco en 1562. Torro II*, In *Documentos para la Historia y Etnología de Huánaco y la Selva Central*, 2nd ed. J. Murra. Huánaco, Peru: Universidad Nacional Hermilio Valdizán.

Pizarro, Pedro (1921). *Relation of the Discovery and Conquest of the Kingdoms of Peru* [1571]. New York: Cortes Society.

Plowman, Timothy (1981). "Amazonian Coca." *Journal of Ethnopharmacology* 3: 195–225.

Raymond, Scott (1976). "Late Prehistoric and Historic Settlements in the Upper Montaña of Peru." In *Canadian Archaeology Abroad*, ed. P. Shinnie, J. Robertson, and F. Kense. Calgary: University of Calgary Press, 205–214.

Raymond, Scott (1988). "A View from the Tropical Forest." In *Peruvian Prehistory*, ed. R. Keatinge. Cambridge: Cambridge University Press, 279–300.

Reeve, Mary Elizabeth (1994). "Regional Interaction in the Western Amazon: The Early Colonial Encounter and the Jesuit Years." *Ethnohistory* 41: 106–138.

Renard-Casevitz, F. M., and T. Saignes (1988). "Los piedemonte oriental de los Andes: Realidades geographicas y representaciones incop." In *Al Este de los Andes: Relaciones entre las Sociedades Amazónicas y Andinas entre los siglos XV y XVII*, 2 vol. Quito: Abya-Yala Press, 43–55.

Renard-Casevitz, F. M., T. Saignes, and A. C. Taylor (1988). *Al Este de los Andes: Relaciones entre las Sociedades Amazónicas y Andinas entre los siglos XV y XVII*, 2 vols. Quito: Abya-Yala Press.

Rojas Ponce, P. (1967). "The Ruins of Pajatén." *Archaeology* 20, 1.

Rostworowski de Diez Canseco, Maria (1963). "Dos manuscritos inéditos con datos sobre Manco II, tierras personales de los Incas y mitimaes." *Nueva Corónica* (Universidad Nacional Mayor de San Marcos, Lima) 1: 223–239.

Rowe, John H. (1946). "Inca Culture at the Time of the Spanish Conquest." In *Handbook of South American Indians, vol. 2: The Andean Civilizations*, ed. J. Steward. Washington, D.C.: Bureau of American Ethnology Bulletin, Smithsonian Institution, 183–330.

Saignes, Thierry (1985). *Los Andes Orientales: Historia de un Olvido*. Cochabamba, Bolivia: Instituto Francés de Estudios Andinos and Centro de Estudios de la Realidad Económica y Social.

Sarmiento de Gamboa, Pedro (1943). *Historia de los Incas* [1572]. Buenos Aires: Editores Emece.

Savoy, Gene (1970). *Antisuyo: The Search for the Lost Cities of the Amazon*. New York: Simon and Schuster.

Schjellerup, Inge (1979–1980). "Documents on Paper and in Stone: A Preliminary Report on the Inca Ruins in Cochabamba, Province of Chachapoyas." *Folk* 21–22: 299–311.

Schjellerup, Inge (1984). "Cochabamba: An Incaic Administrative Centre in the Rebellious Province of Chachapoyas." In *Current Archaeological Projects in the Central Andes, Forty-ninth International Congress of Americanists*, ed. A. Kendall. London: BAR International Series 210, 161–187.

Schjellerup, Inge (1992). "Patrones de asentamiento en las faldas de los Andes de la región de Chachapoyas." In *Estudios de Arqueología Peruana*, ed. D. Bonavía. Lima: Fomsciencias.

Schjellerup, Inge (1998). *Incas and Spaniards in the Conquest of the Chachapoyas*. Gottenberg: University of Gottenberg Press.

Sherbondy, Jeannette (1982). "Canal Systems of Hanan Cuzco." Ph.D. diss., Department of Anthropology, University of Illinois, Urbana.

Thompson, Donald (1971). "Late Prehispanic Occupations in the Eastern Peruvian Andes." *Revista del Museo Nacional, Lima* 37: 117–123.

Thompson, Donald (1973). "Archaeological Investigations in the Eastern Andes of Northern Peru." In *Actas y Memorias del XL Congreso Internacional de Americanistas* (Genoa) 1: 363–369.

Uhle, Max (1909). "La esfera de influencias del país de los Incas." *Revista Histórica* (Lima) 4: 5–40.

von Hassel, J. M. (1905). "Ríos altos Madre de Dios y Paucartambo." *Boletín de la Sociedad Geográfica de Lima* 17: 300–311.

Wachtel, Nathan (1977). *Vision of the Vanquished*. New York: Harper and Row.

Zuidema, R. Tom (1989). "The Moieties of Cuzco." In *Attraction of Opposites: Thought and Society in the Dualistic Mode*, ed. D. Maybury-Lewis and U. Amagor. Ann Arbor: University of Michigan Press, 255–275.

Zuidema, R. Tom (1990). *Inca Civilization in Cuzco*. Austin: University of Texas Press.

Chinchaysuyu

TIME PERIOD: 537–468 B.P.

LOCATION: Central and northern Andean highlands from the imperial capital of Cuzco to the Ecuadorian-Colombian border, stretching from the Pacific coast to the eastern montaña.

DIAGNOSTIC MATERIAL ATTRIBUTES: Large administrative centers; stand-alone monumental platforms as seen at Huánaco Pampa and Ingapirca; royal highway more formally elaborated; use of stone superstructure and fiber suspension bridges.

CULTURAL SUMMARY

Environment

Chinchaysuyu, as the northern quarter of the Inca empire was known, was the second largest in size, encompassing all of modern Ecuador and more than two-thirds of Peru. Stretching from the Pacific coast of northern Peru to the tropical slopes of the eastern Andes, it embraced the spectrum of Andean ecozones from desert coastal plains to intermontane valleys and plateaus to the steamy jungles of the eastern slopes. Moving from south to north, the Andes decrease in elevation, and the climate becomes correspondingly moister, with the dry *puna* of the central highlands giving way to the wetter *páramo* grasslands of the Ecuadorian sierra. Given that many of the major drainages in this sector flow north and east, there was greater opportunity for contact between highland Andean and tropical eastern lowland groups. The ecological and ethnic diversity of this sector of the empire engendered a very heterogeneous approach to imperial Inca rule.

Settlements

The capital city of Cuzco was linked to the provinces of Chinchaysuyu through a highland and a coastal road.

The Cuzco-Quito segment of the *capac ñan*, or royal Inca road, was the most elaborate and elegantly constructed in the entire empire (Hyslop 1984: 257). Unlike other stretches of the Inca highway, this 2000-km-long segment evidences formal construction consisting of stone pavement, sidewalls, stairs, and bridges along its entire length. The coastal road was not nearly as elaborate, many of the barren sections between irrigated valleys consisting of little more than a footpath (Hyslop 1984: 260–262). On the north coast, in particular, the Inca appeared to have simply adapted the preexisting road network of the conquered Chimú.

No other sector of the empire had as many large Inca administrative centers situated along the *capac ñan* as the Cuzco-Quito route of Chinchaysuyu (Hyslop 1990: 257, 279). Examples of such centers include Hatun Xauxa (Costin et al. 1989; D'Altroy 1981, 1987, 1992; D'Altroy and Hastorf 1984; Earle et al. 1987; Hastorf 1983, 1990, 1993), Pumpu (Brown 1991; Matos 1994), Huánaco Pampa (Morris and Thompson 1985), and Ingapirca (Fresco 1983, 1984). Common features of these Inca administrative centers include buildings of fine stone masonry, quantities of Inca polychrome pottery, and a central plaza typically flanked by large rectangular structures, or *kallanka* (Gasparini and Margolies 1980; Hemmings and Rainey 1982; Hyslop 1984, 1990). In addition to housing military personnel and state corvée laborers, the *kallanka* also served as the focal point of civic-ceremonial and public feasting events.

Other buildings at these sites known as *aqllawasi* functioned as warehouses for the state's 'chosen women' (Silverblatt 1987). The central plazas of the provincial sites typically contained an *ushnu*, or royal dais, as well. Another common element of the Inca administrative centers in this sector of the empire were rows of round, tower-like structures known as *qollka*, which served as state storage facilities (D'Altroy and Hastorf 1984; Morris 1967). These are particularly prevalent at the sites of Huánaco Pampa and Hatun Xauxa. Inca administrative centers were typically built on unoccupied land. As these were the principal state constructions, Inca occupation of this sector had relatively little impact on existing settlement patterning.

In the far northern highlands of Ecuador, the Inca constructed a variety of different site types including *pucaras*, or hilltop fortresses (Almeida 1984; Bray 1991, 1992; Oberem 1969; Plaza Schuller 1976); *tambos*, or roadside facilities (Meyers 1976; Oberem 1988); administrative centers (Fresco 1983, 1984; Hyslop 1984: 19–34; Salomon 1986); and *huacas*, or shrines (Dorsey 1901; Hyslop 1984: 19–34; McEwan and Silva 1989). Tomebamba, located in the southern highlands of Ecuador, was the most important Inca center in the northern Andes (Alcina Franch 1982; Bamps 1887; Idrovo 1988, 2000; Uhle 1923). Various ethnohistoric sources describe Tomebamba as a second Cuzco, suggesting that the site was deliberately created in the image of the sacred capital of the Inca empire (Cabello 1951; Cieza 1962: 142–147). Coyoctor is a finely carved rock outcrop located in the same Cañari territory. The *tambo* of San Agustin de Callo, approximately 65 km south of Quito, is the northernmost known example of fine Inca masonry (Bedoya 1978: 193–204; Hyslop 1984: 284).

Whereas the Inca presence in the far northern highlands is well attested, there is little to no Inca architecture on the north coast (Hyslop 1990: 40). Sites situated along the royal highway on the north coast show no characteristics of Inca architecture. Archaeological investigation at several of these sites, including Farfan (Keatinge and Conrad 1983), Chiquitoy Viejo (Conrad 1977), and Tambo Real (Helsley 1980), demonstrate, rather, that the architecture was quite varied. As Lumbreras (1974: 221) suggests, where urbanism and its attendant infrastructure were extant, as in the case of Chimú, the Inca apparently preferred to continue using local administrative centers, architecture, and engineering works (also Hyslop 1990: 40–54, 250). As a consequence, settlement patterns changed little on the north coast with the imposition of Inca rule (Ramirez 1990). The chief evidence of Inca influence in this area is the presence of Inca polychrome pottery and Inca local hybrid wares (Bonavía and Ravines 1971; Hayashida 1994, 1999; Hyslop 1990: 40).

The same is true for the northern Peruvian highlands in the vicinity of Cajamarca and Huamachuco (Hyslop 1984: 56–67). Various archaeological investigations have failed to produce any significant evidence of Inca occupation, although it is known that this region was incorporated into the empire early on (Pineda 1980; Reichlen and Reichlen 1970: 498; Thatcher 1972; Topic and Chiswell 1992; Topic and Topic 1993).

Economy

The subsistence base of the Inca was agricultural, and production was tightly controlled by the state (Morris 1982, 1985; Murra 1980; Rowe 1946). Land improvements, which included the construction of terraces, irrigation canals, and dams, were undertaken by the state on a massive scale and intended to increase agricultural yields (Malpass 1987; Morris 1982; Niles 1982; Sherbondy 1982). The two most important crops in the Andes were maize, which can be grown up to 3500 m above sea level, and potatoes, which can be cultivated to almost 4000 m. Of the two, maize held considerably more ceremonial and symbolic significance (Murra 1960). Coca, another highly valued crop in the pre-Columbian world with a limited production range, was known to have been cultivated in the coastal valleys of this sector (Plowman 1984: 133; Rostworowski 1970, 1973, 1988).

The Inca state economy was a redistributive one that exploited ancient principles of reciprocity to its own benefit (D'Altroy and Earle 1985; Morris 1982, 1985; Murra 1980; Wachtel 1977). Morris describes this system as "institutionalized reciprocity." Taxes were paid in the form of labor rather than in kind, and each community was required to cultivate the lands appropriated by the Inca state in its district (Murra 1980; Rowe 1946). The produce from these lands went to state storage facilities such as those found at Hatun Xauxa and Huánaco Pampa and was used to support imperial activities (D'Altroy and Earle 1985; LaLone 1982; Morris 1967). Specific goods associated with the Inca state, including pottery, cloth, and metal artifacts, were produced by full-time craft specialists who were retained by the state and often lodged in the vicinity of Cuzco (Julien 1993; Morris 1974).

Although in general trade and markets did not figure prominently in the Inca economy (Murra 1980, 1995), there appears to have been somewhat more emphasis on commerce and exchange in the Chinchaysuyu district. The importance of long-distance traders (*mindaláes*) comparable to the *pochteca* of the Aztec world is well documented in the far northern highlands (Rappaport 1988; Salomon 1978, 1986). Long-distance exchange was also an important aspect of several coastal economies within the Chinchaysuyu province as well (Morris 1988; Ramirez 1990; Rostworoski 1970, 1975; Sandweiss 1992). It is interesting to note that the zones where commercial activity has been documented are generally located at the outer edges of imperial Inca control (Patterson 1987).

Sociopolitical Organization

The annexation of Chinchaysuyu was initiated during the northern campaigns of Pachacuti and Topa Inca, which began c. 537 B.P. The far northern reaches of this sector were consolidated by Huayna Capac during the last decade of that century (Rowe 1945, 1946). Many different ethnic groups occupied this region prior to the Inca expansion. These ranged in level of political development from the statelike organization of the Chimú on the north coast of Peru, to the smaller chiefdoms of northern Ecuador, to the bellicose tribes of the Cañari region. The polities of the northern and central highlands offered varying amounts of resistance prior to capitulating to the Inca invaders. The Wanka groups of the upper Mantaro valley of the central highlands fell rather rapidly to Inca forces (D'Altroy 1992: 77–79); the Caranqui of northern Ecuador were said to have defended their territory against the Inca for 17 years (Bray 1991, 1992; Jijón y Caamaño 1914; Oberem 1969, 1981). The northernmost reach of Tawantinsuyu was extended almost to the Colombian border during the reign of Huayna Capac.

The Kingdom of Chimú, which encompassed the entire coast of Peru north of the Chincha valley, rivaled that of the Inca in the mid-15th century in terms of size and wealth. But the Chimú were defeated by Inca forces under the command of Topa Inca (Rowe 1946). The Chimú king was subsequently exiled to Cuzco and a puppet ruler installed in his place (Cieza 1973: 206; Davies 1995: 132–136). The Inca admired the accomplishments of the Chimú and the skill of their artisans. Large contingencies of Chimú potters and metal workers were deported to Cuzco and pressed into service for the state (Cieza 1973: 206; Netherly 1988).

Inca society was highly stratified with the "Incas-by-blood" of the Cuzco lineages, the uppermost echelons of the status hierarchy. Below them were the "Incas-by-privilege," a class consisting mainly of the original, non-Inca inhabitants of the Cuzco valley, individuals who had distinguished themselves through outstanding service to the state, and all those whose native language was Quechua. The provincial nobility was the next tier in the sociopolitical hierarchy of the state. Members of this class were typically the ethnic elite who had ruled their provinces prior to the Inca conquest. Below this stratum were the commoners, the backbone of the Inca state, who made their living through agricultural labor (Bauer 1992; Murra 1980; Rowe 1946; Zuidema 1989, 1990).

The Inca governed their empire through a highly formalized hierarchical system. At the apex stood the Inca sovereign, who ruled by divine right and claimed lineal descent from the sun. Below him were the lords of the four sectors (suyu) of the empire, who oversaw the imperial governors of each of the provinces within their sector. The provincial governors purportedly each had responsibility for 10,000 families. Following a decimal system of organization, there were two tiers of Inca officials below the governor, the higher of which supervised two subordinates responsible for the management of 500 families each. Local ethnic leaders, known as curacas, served as intermediaries between the imperial hierarchy and the local populace. Theoretically, each curaca had under his control 100 families (Julien 1982; Rowe 1946).

Religion and Expressive Culture

Inca religion was fundamentally animistic insofar as inanimate objects were understood to have a spiritual content. The sun and moon, certain stars, the sea, the earth, rivers and springs, hills, snow-capped peaks, caves, and outcrops all had special significance for the Inca. Rocks were particularly laden with symbolic meaning; numerous Inca myths reference the transformation of men into stones or vice versa. Special boulders or outcrops of particular importance were often integrated into Inca architecture or became the focal points of imperial sites around the empire (Cobo 1990; Rowe 1946; Zuidema 1990). The Inca typically sought to arrogate the sacred power of local huacas and holy places to themselves by installing state constructions at these sites, as seen, for example, in the case of Pachacamac, Ingapirca, and La Plata island in Chinchaysuyu.

Within Andean society, ritual was an essential aspect of daily life. People engaged in private acts, such as the sharing of coca or praying to the snow-capped peaks (apu), which expressed deeply held religious beliefs everyday. Public ceremonies of the Inca were elaborate, highly formal affairs. The state ceremonial calendar corresponded closely to the agricultural cycle of the highlands, with many rituals explicitly linked to crop productivity. Public ceremonies were also performed during times of crisis and to mark important historic events such as the coronation or death of the emperor. Most such ceremonies involved the exhibition of sacred idols and images, dancing, feasting, oratory, and the heavy consumption of corn beer (chicha). Public ceremonies were typically conducted outdoors in one of the central plazas (Rowe 1946; Zuidema 1990).

Sacrifices accompanied nearly every religious rite and typically involved guinea pigs, llamas, coca, and chicha, although children were sometimes immolated as well. Guaman Poma (1936: 266) depicts residents of Chinchaysuyu offering the lord of Pachacamac a child and a plate of food. He indicates in the text that different ethnic groups within Chinchaysuyu made different types of offerings, the Wanka, for instance, sacrificing dogs, conejo (guinea pig), food, coca, and mullu (Spondylus shell), while the Yauyos presented chicha, mullu, food, and conejos (Guaman Poma 1936: 267).

Ethnic groups in the Andes typically had their own distinctive style of dress, with affiliation most often signaled through headgear. Guaman Poma (1936: 165) depicts the war captain from Chinchaysuyu wearing a traditional uncu, or knee-length shirt, with fringed leggings and sandals. A large, double-ringed headdress envelopes his face, and he holds a club and a spear.

Guaman Poma represents a woman from this district wearing a typical floor-length dress with a waistband composed of individual design squares and a long shawl fastened in front by a *tupu* pin (1936: 173). The Chinchaysuyu damsel wears a skullcap for headgear and holds a small coca purse in one hand and a possible weaving implement in the other.

The dead were generally considered a source of protection in the late pre-Columbian era. They were guardians (*mallki*) to whom descendants could appeal for special favors or requests. Inca rulers were typically mummified upon death and retained as valued state advisers and lineage patriarchs in the sacred temple of the Sun (Coricancha) in Cuzco. Common people were normally buried in caves or rock shelters with offerings of food, pottery, and clothing. In the imperial provinces, burial practices followed traditional norms and varied considerably, although the interments of ethnic elite frequently contained Inca-style items. Guaman Poma (1936: 289–290) indicates that the norm for residents of the Chinchaysuyu district was to bury the dead in smaller-sized domed towers that may have served as family crypts.

References

Alcina Franch, José (1982). "Tomebamba y el problema de los indios Cañaris da la sierra sur del Ecuador." *Anuario de Estudios Americanos* 37: 403–433.

Almeida, Eduardo (1984). "El Pucara de Rumichucho." In *Miscelánea Antropológica Ecuatoriana*. Serie Monografía 1. Quito: Museo del Banco Central del Ecuador.

Bamps, Anatole. (1887). *Tomebomba antigue cite del' des Iwkas*. Louvain: Impe. Lefeve.

Bauer, Brian (1992). *The Development of the Inca State*. Austin: University of Texas Press.

Bedoya, Marur, Angel. (1978). "Incaico de Ingapirca en Cañal." *Revista Geographica* (Quito) 7: 133–149.

Bonavía, Duccio, and Rogger Ravines (1971). "Influence Inca sur la cote nord du Perou." *Boletín de la Societé Suisge des Americanistes* 35: 3–18.

Bray, Tamara (1991). "The Effects of Inca Imperialism on the Northern Frontier: An Archaeological Investigation." Ph.D. diss., Department of Anthropology, State University of New York, Binghamton. University Microfilms.

Bray, Tamara (1992). "Archaeological Survey in Northern Highland Ecuador: Inca Imperialism and the País Caranqui." *World Archaeology* 24, 2: 218–233.

Brown, David (1991). "Administration and Settlement Planning in the Provinces of the Inka Empire: A Perspective from the Inka Capital of Pumpu on the Junín Plain in the Central Highlands of Peru." Ph.D. diss., Department of Anthropology, University of Texas, Austin. University Microfilms.

Cabello Balboa, Miguel (1951). *Miscelánea Antártica: Una historia del Perú Antiguo* [1586]. Lima: Universidad Nacional Mayor de San Marcos.

Cieza de León, Pedro de (1962). *La Crónica del Perú* [1553]. Madrid: Espasa Calpe.

Cieza de León, Pedro de (1973). *El Señorío de los Incas*. Lima: Editorial Universo.

Cobo, Bernabé (1990). *Inca Religion and Customs*. Austin: University of Texas Press.

Cohen, Mark (1973). "Two Methods for Estimating the Late Horizon Population of the Rimac Province, Peru." *Journal of the Steward Anthropological Society* 5, 1: 1–23.

Conrad, Geoffrey (1977). "Chiquitoy Viejo: An Inca Administrative Center in the Chicama Valley, Peru." *Journal of Field Archaeology* 4: 1–18.

Costin, Cathy, T. Earle, B. Bowen, and G. Russell. (1989). "Impact of Inka Conquest on Local Technology in the Upper Mantaro Valley, Peru." In *What's New? A Closer Look at the Process of Innovation*, ed. S. van der Leeuw and R. Torrance. London: Unwin and Hyman, 107–139.

D'Altroy, Terence (1981). "Empire Growth and Consolidation: The Xauxa Region of Peru under the Incas." Ph.D. diss., Department of Anthropology, University of California, Los Angeles. University Microfilms.

D'Altroy, Terence (1987). "Transitions in Power: Centralization of Wanka Political Organization under Inca Rule." *Ethnohistory* 34, 1: 78–102.

D'Altroy, Terence (1992). *Provincial Power in the Inka Empire*. Washington, D.C.: Smithsonian Institution Press.

D'Altroy, Terence, and Timothy Earle (1985). "Staple Finance, Wealth Finance, and Storage in the Inka Political Economy." *Current Anthropology* 26, 2: 187–206.

D'Altroy, Terence, and Christine Hastorf (1984). "Distribution and Contents of Inca State Storehouses in the Xauxa Region of Peru." *American Antiquity* 49: 334–349.

Davies, Nigel (1995). *The Incas*. Niwot: University Press of Colorado.

Dillehay, Tom (1977). "Tawantinsuyu Integration of the Chillon Valley, Peru: A Case of Inca Geo-political Mastery." *Journal of Field Archaeology* 4: 397–405.

Dorsey, George (1901). *Archaeological Investigations on the Island of La Plata, Ecuador*. Field Columbian Museum Publication, no. 56, Anthropological Series 2, 5.

Earle, Timothy, T. D. Altroy, C. Hastorf, C. Scott, C. Cootin, G. Russell, and E. Sandeful. (1987). *Archaeological Field Research in the Upper Mantaro, Peru, 1982–1983: Investigations of Inka Expansion and Exchange*. Los Angeles: Institute of Archaeology, UCLA, Monograph Series, no. 28.

Fresco, Antonio (1983). "Arquitectura de Ingapirca (Cañar-Ecuador)." *Boletín de los Museos del Banco Central del Ecuador* 3: 195–212.

Fresco, Antonio (1984). *La Arqueología de Ingapirca (Ecuador): Costumbres funerarias, cerámica y otros materiales*. Quito: Gráficas Mediavilla Hnos.

Gasparini, Graziano, and Luise Margolies (1980). *Inca Architecture*, trans. P. J. Lyon. Bloomington: Indiana University Press.

Guaman Poma de Ayala, Felipe (1936). *Nueva Corónica y Buen Gobierno* [1614]. Paris: Institut d'Ethnologie, Université de Paris.

Hastorf, Christine (1983). "Prehistoric Agricultural Intensification and the Political Development in the Jauja Region of Central Peru." Ph.D. diss., Department of Anthropology, University of California, Los Angeles. University Microfilms.

Hastorf, Christine (1990). "The Effect of the Inka State on Sausa Agricultural Production and Crop Consumption." *American Antiquity* 55: 262–290.

Hastorf, Christine (1993). *Agriculture and the Onset of Inequality before the Inca*. Cambridge: Cambridge University Press.

Hayashida, Francis (1994). "Producción cerámica en el imperio inca: Una visión global y nuevos datos." In *Tecnología y Organización de la Producción de cerámica en los Andes*, ed. I. Shimada. Lima: Fondo Editorial, P.U.C.P., 443–476.

Hayashida, Francis (1999). "Style, Technology, and State Production: Wka Poltery Manufacture in the Leche Valley." *Latin American Antiquity* 10: 337–352

Helsley, Anne (1980). "Excavations at Cerro Tambo Real, Lambayeque, Peru." M.A. thesis, Department of Anthropology, Princeton University.

Hemmings, John, and Edward Rainey (1982). *Monuments of the Incas*. Albuquerque: University of New Mexico Press.

Hyslop, John (1984). *Inka Road System*. New York: Academic Press.

Hyslop, John (1990). *Inka Settlement Planning*. Austin: University of Texas.

Idrovo, Jaime (1988). "Tomebamba: Primera fase de conquista incasica en los Andes septentrionales." In *La Frontera del Estado Inca*, ed. T. Dillehay and P. Netherly. Oxford: British Archaeological Reports, International Series 442, 87–104.

Jijón y Caamaño, Jacinto (1914). *Contribución al Conocimiento de los Aborígenes de la Provincial de Imbabura*. Madrid: Blas y Cia. Impresores.

Keatinge, Richard, and Geoffrey Conrad (1983). "Imperialist Expansion in Peruvian Prehistory." *Journal of Field Archaeology* 10: 255–283.

LaLone, Darrell (1982). "The Inca as a Nonmarket Economy: Supply on Command vs. Supply and Demand." In *Contexts for Prehistoric Exchange*, ed. J. Ericson and T. Earle. New York: Academic Press, 291–316.

Lumbreras, Luis (1974). *Peoples and Cultures of Ancient Peru*. Washington, D.C.: Smithsonian Institution Press.

Malpass, Michael (1987). "Prehistoric Agricultural Terracing at Chijra in the Colca Valley, Peru." In *Pre-Hispanic Agricultural Fields in the Andean Region*, ed. W. Denevan, K. Mathewson, and G. Knapp. Oxford: British Archaeological Report, International Series, no. 359, 45–66.

Matos M., Ramiro (1994). *Pumpu: Centro Administrativo Inka de la Puna de Junín*. Lima: Editorial Horizonte.

McCown, Theodore (1945). *Pre-incaic Huamachuco: Survey and Excavations in the Region of Huamachuco and Cajabamba*. Los Angeles: University of California Publications in American Archaeology and Ethnology 39, 4.

McEwan, Colin, and María Isabel Silva (1989). "Qué fueron a hacer los Incas en la costa central del Ecuador?" In *Relaciones Interculturales en el área Ecuatorial del Pácifico durante la Época Precolombina*, ed. J. F. Bouchard and M. Guinea. Oxford: Proceedings of the 46th International Congress of Americanists, British Archaeological Reports, International Series, 163–185.

Menzel, Dorothy (1966). "The Pottery of Chincha." *Ñawpa Pacha* 4: 77–153.

Menzel, Dorothy, and John H. Rowe (1966). "The Role of Chincha in Late Pre-Spanish Peru." *Ñawpa Pacha* 4: 63–76.

Meyers, Albert (1976). *Die Inka en Ekuador*. Bonn: Bonner Amerikanistiche Studien, no. 8.

Morris, Craig (1967). "Storage in Tawantinsuyu." Ph.D. diss., Department of Anthropology, University of Chicago.

Morris, Craig (1974). "Reconstructing Patterns of Non-agricultural Production in the Inca Economy: Archaeology and Documents in Instituted Analysis." In *Reconstructing Complex Societies*, ed. C. Moore. Supplement to Bulletin of the American Schools of Oriental Research, no. 20, 49–68.

Morris, Craig (1978). "The Archaeological Analysis of Andean Exchange Systems." In *Social Archaeology: Beyond Subsistence and Dating*, ed. C. Redman et al. New York: Academic Press, 303–327.

Morris, Craig (1982). "Infrastructure of Inka Control in the Peruvian Central Highlands." In *The Inca and Aztec States, 1400–1800*, ed. G. Collier, R. Rosaldo, and J. Wirth. New York: Academic Press, 153–171.

Morris, Craig (1985). "From Principles of Ecological Complementarity to the Organization and Administration of Tawantinsuyu." In *Andean Ecology and Civilization*, ed. S. Masuda, I. Shimada, and C. Morris. Tokyo: University of Tokyo Press, 477–490.

Morris, Craig (1988). "Más alla de las fronteras de Chincha." In *La Frontera del Estado Inca*, ed. T. Dillehay and P. Netherly. Oxford: British Archaeological Reports, International Series 442, 131–140.

Morris, Craig, and Donald Thompson (1985). *Huánaco Pampa: An Inca City and Its Hinterland*. London: Thames and Hudson.

Murra, John (1960). "Rite and Crop in the Inca State." In *Culture and History*, ed. S. Diamond. New York: Columbia University Press, 393–407.

Murra, John (1975). "El control vertical de un máximo de pisos ecológicos en la economía de las sociedades andinas." *Formaciones Económicas y Políticas del Mundo Andino*, ed. J. Murra. Lima: Instituto de Estudios Peruanos, 59–115.

Murra, John (1980). *Economic Organization of the Inka State*. Greenwich: JAI Press.

Murra, John (1985). "The 'Archipiélago Vertical' Revisited." In *Andean Ecology and Civilization*, ed. S. Mazuda, I. Shimada, and C. Morris. Tokyo: University of Tokyo Press, 3–14.

Murra, John (1995). "Did Tribute and Markets Prevail in the Andes before the European Invasion?" In *Ethnicity, Markets, and Migration in the Andes: At the Crossroads of History and Anthropology*, ed. B. Larson, O. Harris, and E. Tandeter. Durham: Duke University Press, 57–72.

Netherly, Patricia (1978). "Local Level Lords on the North Coast of Peru." Ph.D. diss., Cornell University.

Netherly, Patricia (1988). "El reino Chimor y el Tawantinsuyu." In *La Frontera del Estado Inca*, ed. T. Dillehay and P. Netherly. Oxford: British Archaeological Reports, International Series 442, 105–129.

Niles, Susan (1982). "Style and Function in Inca Agricultural Works near Cuzco." *Ñawpa Pacha* 20: 163–182.

Oberem, Udo (1969). "La fortaleza de montaña de Quitoloma en la sierra septentrional del Ecuador." *Boletín de la Academia Nacional de Historia* 52, 114: 196–205.

Oberem, Udo (1981). "Los Caranquis de la sierra norte del Ecuador y su incorporación al Tahuantinsuyu." In *Contribución a la Etnohistória Ecuatoriana*, ed. S. Moreno. Otavalo, Ecuador: Instituto Otavaleño de Antropología, Pendoneros, no. 20, 73–102.

Oberem, Udo (1988). "El período incaico en el Ecuador." In *Nueva Historia del Ecuador*, vol. II, ed. E. Ayala Mora. Quito, Ecuador: Corporación Editora Nacional, 135–165.

Patterson, Thomas (1987). "Merchant Capital and the Formation of the Inca State." *Dialectical Anthropology* 12: 217–227.

Pineda Quevado, José (1980). "Patrones de Asentamientos Prehispánicos en el valle de Condebamba." M.A. thesis, Programa Académico de Arquitectura, Urbanismo, y Artes, Universidad Nacional de Ingeniería, Lima.

Plaza Schuller, Fernando (1976). *La incursión Inca en el Septentrión Andino Ecuatoriano*. Otavalo, Ecuador: Instituto Otavaleño de Antropología, Serie Arqueología.

Plowman, Timothy (1984). "The Origin, Evolution, and Diffusion of Coca, Erythroxylum spp., in South and Central America." In *Pre-Columbian Plant Migration*, ed. D. Stone. Cambridge, MA: Papers of the Peabody Museum of Archaeology and Ethnology 76, 129–163.

Ramirez, Susan (1990). "The Inca Conquest of the North Coast: A Historian's View." In *The Northern Dynasties: Kingship and State-*

craft in Chimor, ed. M. Moseley and A. Cordy-Collins. Washington, D.C.: Dumbarton Oaks, 507–537.

Rappaport, Joanne (1988). La organización socio-territorial de los Pastos: Una hipótesis de trabajo. *Revista de Antropología* 4(2):73–103.

Reichlen, Henry, and Paule Reichlen (1970). "Reconocimientos arqueológicos en los Andes de Cajamarca." In *Cien Años de la Arqueología en el Peru*, ed. R. Ravines. Lima: Instituto de Estudios Peruanos y Petróleos de Peru, 461–501.

Rostworowski de Diez Canseco, Maria (1970). "Mercaderes del valle de Chincha en la época prehispánica." *Revista Española de Antropología Americana* 5: 135–177.

Rostworowski de Diez Canseco, Maria (1973). "Plantaciones prehispánicas de coca en la vertiente del Pacífico." *Revista del Museo Nacional, Lima* 39: 193–224.

Rostworowski de Diez Canseco, Maria (1975). "Pescadores, artesanos y mercaderes costeños en el Perú prehispánico." *Revista del Museo Nacional, Lima* 38: 250–314.

Rostworowski de Diez Canseco, Maria (1988). *Conflicts over Coca Fields in XVIth Century Peru.* Ann Arbor: Memoirs of the Museum of Anthropology, University of Michigan, 21, 4.

Rowe, John (1945). "Absolute Chronology in the Andean Area." *American Antiquity* 10: 265–284.

Rowe, John H. (1946). "Inca Culture at the Time of the Spanish conquest." In *Handbook of South American Indians, vol. 2: The Andean Civilizations*, ed. J. Steward. Washington, D.C.: Bureau of American Ethnology Bulletin, Smithsonian Institution 143, 183–330.

Rowe, John H. (1948). "The Kingdom of Chimor." *Acta Americana* 6: 26–59.

Salomon, Frank (1978). Pochteca and mindalá: a comparison of long-distance traders in Ecuador and Mesoamérica. *Journal of Steward Anthropology* 9(1–2): 231–247.

Salomon, Frank (1986). *Native Lords of Quito in the Age of the Incas.* New York: Cambridge University Press.

Salomon, Frank (1987). "A North Andean Status Trader Complex under Inka Rule." *Ethnohistory* 34: 63–77.

Sandweiss, Dan (1992). *The Archaeology of Chincha Fishermen: Specialization And Status in Inka Peru.* Pittsburgh: Bulletin of the Carnegie Museum of Natural History, no. 29.

Sherbondy, Jeannette (1982). "Canal Systems of Hanan Cuzco." Ph.D. diss., Department of Anthropology, University of Illinois, Urbana.

Silverblatt, Irene (1987). *Moon, Sun, and Witches.* Princeton: Princeton University Press.

Thatcher, John (1972). "Continuity and Change in the Ceramics of Huamachuco, North Highlands, Peru." Ph.D. diss., Department of Anthropology, University of Pennsylvania. University Microfilms.

Topic, John, and Coreen Chiswell (1992). "Inka Storage in Huamachuco." In *Inka Storage Systems*, ed. T. Levine. Norman: University of Oklahoma Press, 206–233.

Topic, John, and Theresa Topic (1993). "A Summary of the Inca Occupation of Huamachuco." In *Provincial Inca: Archaeological and Ethnohistorical Assessment of the Impact of the Inca State*, ed. M. Malpass. Iowa City: University of Iowa Press, 17–43.

Uhle, Max (1923). *Las Ruinas de Tomebamba.* Quito: Imprenta Julio Sáenz Rebolledo.

Wachtel, Nathan (1977). *Vision of the Vanquished.* New York: Harper and Row.

Zuidema, R. Tom (1989). "The Moieties of Cuzco." In *Attraction of Opposites: Thought and Society in the Dualistic Mode*, ed. D. Maybury-Lewis and U. Amagor. Ann Arbor: University of Michigan Press, 255–275.

Zuidema, R. Tom (1990). *Inca Civilization in Cuzco.* Austin: University of Texas Press.

Collasuyu

TIME PERIOD: 570–468 B.P.

LOCATION: Southern Andean highlands, encompassing the Titicaca basin and most of Bolivia, northwestern Argentina, and northern Chile.

DIAGNOSTIC MATERIAL ATTRIBUTES: Lack of large administrative centers; large burial towers of fine cut stone; use of the corbeled arch; decorative stepped motif associated with earlier Tiwanaku culture incorporated into Inca niches, doors, and lintels; lack of cut-stone masonry south of the Titicaca basin; rectangular rather than trapezoidal wall apertures south of the Titicaca basin.

CULTURAL SUMMARY

Environment

Collasuyu was the largest quarter of the Inca empire. Lying to the south of Cuzco, it stretched from the desert shores of the Chilean coast to the edge of the tropical eastern lowlands in Bolivia and south into the highlands of northwestern Argentina. The most salient aspect of the Collasuyu environment was the *altiplano*, an immense high-altitude plateau some 800 km in length, the central feature of which is lake Titicaca. This enormous body of water mitigates the severity of the alpine environment, permitting the cultivation of potatoes and quinoa around its perimeter from 3500–3900 m above sea level. Above these limits, the dry *puna* grasslands support immense herds of llamas and alpacas. The lands around lake Titicaca were densely settled by Aymara-speaking peoples and was highly productive, making them an early target of Inca expansionism.

Settlements

The Collasuyu road was less elegant than that of the northern quarter, but this does not imply that it was any less utilized or important (Hyslop 1984; Stehberg and Carvajal 1988). As Hyslop (1984: 264) suggests, it may well have been a function of the more level terrain in this sector, which only would have required less engineering effort. There is a curious lack of large-scale Inca administrative centers in the Collasuyu district (D'Altroy et al. 1999; Davies 1995: 139; Fock 1961; Gasparini and Margolies 1980: 118; Hyslop 1990: 279; Ryden 1947; Tschopik 1946). Probable imperial centers in Collasuyu rarely exceed 5 ha in size, which is considerably smaller than similar sites in the northern quarter (Hyslop 1990: 279). There is, however, a high density of *ushnus* in Collasuyu, according to Hyslop (1990: 95), though they are typically smaller in size than those found elsewhere.

On the *altiplano*, the Inca appeared to have modified preexisting settlement patterns by forcing people to relocate from fortified hilltop sites to new towns situated around the lakeshore (Cieza 1973: 83; Hyslop 1990: 119; Julien 1983). Hyslop's (1976, 1977, 1979) survey work in this region offers some confirmation of this imperial strategy. Late prehistoric-period habitation units in the Collasuyu district were usually round (Hyslop 1984: 306; Ryden 1947; Tschopik 1946). The use of the corbeled arch, an ancient architectural tradition in the *altiplano*, was incorporated into Inca structures in the Collasuyu province, as seen in the *chulpas* at Sillustani and the Pilco Kayma palace on the Island of the Sun (Gasparini and Margolies 1980: 153–156). The Inca also used the stepped motif derived from the antecedent Tiwanaku culture as a decorative device in some of their constructions in this region (Kendall 1985: 39).

No certain Inca storage facilities have been identified in the entire area around lake Titicaca (Hyslop 1984: 291), although there are large numbers of *qollka* in the Cochabamba district of Bolivia (Wachtel 1982). Numerous rectangular enclosures have been found in association with Inca *tambos* in Collasuyu, however, particularly in Northwest Argentina (Hyslop 1990: 292). These features have been interpreted as corrals for camelids, one of the principal resources of this region. If they served as state holding pens, these structures might be viewed as the functional equivalent of *qollkas* for animals (Hyslop 1990: 180–185).

There is little evidence of fine Inca masonry south of the central part of Bolivia (Dillehay and Gordon 1988; Hyslop 1990: 4; Iribarren 1978; Niemeyer 1986; Niemeyer and Schiappacasse 1988; Santoro and Muñoz 1981). Rather, the Inca seem to have adapted existing settlements to suit their own residential and administrative needs. This is especially true in Argentina and Chile, where, despite obvious evidence of Inca occupation (Calderari and Williams 1991; Williams 1991), there are no good examples of planned settlements or fine stone masonry constructions (González 1983). A construction technique involving the use of either double rows of fieldstones or partially worked stones bonded with mud mortar was an important attribute of Inca construction

in this region (Lynch 1993: 132; Raffino 1981: 77). Square or rectangular wall apertures are found almost to the exclusion of the trapezoidal form south of lake Titicaca (González 1983: 341; Hyslop 1990: 10, 285). There is also a notable lack of carved boulders and outcrops south of central Bolivia (Hyslop 1990: 125). Hyslop (1990: 285) suggests the possibility that the southernmost portion of Collasuyu was ruled indirectly by the Inca via the indigenous polities of the Titicaca basin.

The southern border of the Inca empire is not entirely clear but likely reached to the Maipo river just south of Santiago, Chile (Hyslop 1984: 212, 1990: 156; Silva 1977–1978, 1983). Unlike the northern frontier, which was heavily fortified, there is little evidence of military installations or defensive features along the southern border (Hyslop 1990: 155–163).

Economy

The subsistence base of the Inca was agricultural, and production was tightly controlled by the state (Morris 1982, 1985; Murra 1980; Rowe 1946). Land improvements, which included the construction of terraces, irrigation canals, and dams, were undertaken by the state on a massive scale and intended to increase agricultural yields (Malpass 1987; Morris 1982; Niles 1982; Sherbondy 1982). The two most important crops in the Andes were maize, which can be grown up to 3500 m above sea level, and potatoes, which can be cultivated to almost 4000 m. Of the two, maize held considerably more ceremonial and symbolic significance (Murra 1960).

The chief resource of Altiplano region was the extensive camelid herds that grazed in the higher *puna* zone west of lake Titicaca (Murra 1965). Fishing also figured prominently in the economies of the ethnic groups that inhabited the shores of lake Titicaca (Julien 1983; Ramos Gavilán 1976). Several scholars have suggested that the principal reason for the Inca occupation of the far southern reaches of Collasuyu (Northwest Argentina and Chile) was the exploitation of mineral wealth (González 1983; Llagostera 1976).

The Inca state economy was a redistributive one that exploited ancient principles of reciprocity to its own benefit (D'Altroy and Earle 1985; Morris 1982, 1985; Murra 1980; Wachtel 1977). Morris describes this system as "institutionalized reciprocity." Taxes were paid in the form of labor rather than in kind, and each community was required to cultivate the lands appropriated by the Inca state in its district (Murra 1980; Rowe 1946). The produce from these lands went to state storage facilities such as those found at Cochabamba in Bolivia and was used to support imperial activities (D'Altroy and Earle 1985; LaLone 1982; Morris 1967; Wachtel 1982).

Specific goods associated with the Inca state, including pottery, cloth, and metal artifacts, were produced by full-time craft specialists who were retained by the state (Julien 1993; Morris 1974). In the Collasuyu district, for instance, the Inca established a large community of specialized weavers, feather workers, and potters dedicated to full-time production for the state near Huancane at the north end of lake Titicaca (Murra 1978; see also LaLone and LaLone 1987; Lorandi 1984). Neither trade nor markets figured prominently in the Inca economy (Murra 1980, 1995). Nonlocal goods were normally acquired through direct access to or control over vertically differentiated zones of production (Murra 1975, 1995). Such products were funneled to the imperial capital and subsequently redistributed by the state (D'Altroy and Earle 1985; Murra 1980).

Sociopolitical Organization

The Collasuyu region, birthplace of the much admired Tiwanaku civilization, held special significance for the Inca. The sanctuaries of the Copacabana peninsula and the islands of the Sun and Moon in lake Titicaca were among the holiest shrines in the Andean world. The conquest of the lord of this region, the Colla Capac Zapana, and the annexation of his kingdom was purportedly one of the first objectives of Inca expansionism under Pachacuti (Cieza 1962, ch. 41–43; Cobo 1979: 141; Sarmiento 1943: 109). According to historical sources, Bolivia, Northwest Argentina (Tucumán), and Chile were subjugated during the independent reign of Topa Inca (529–507 B.P.) (Rowe 1946), although there is some evidence of contact prior to imperial consolidation (Muñoz and Chacama 1990; Pärssinen and Siiriäinen 1997).

The *altiplano* was originally the home of the Aymara, a large Andean population sharing a common language distinct from Quechua (Cieza de León 1962: 260–263; Diez de San Miguel 1964 [1567]; LaBarre 1948). Important ethnic divisions included the Qolla, Lupaqa, and Pacajes (Julien 1983: 42). Murra (1968, 1970) provides an analysis of an Aymara kingdom as it existed in the mid-16th century. The Inca classified the people of the Titicaca basin into two groups: the Aymara and the Uru. The Aymara were the wealthier, higher-status group that had a herding and farming economy; the Uru, who were poorer and considered lower-status, lived on reed islands in or at the edges of lake Titicaca and made their living through fishing and weaving (Julien 1982, 1983).

In the *altiplano* region, the Inca built on the indigenous political organization, which was based on hereditary dynasties (Julien 1983). Hyslop (1977, 1979) suggests that the strength of some of the local leaders was enhanced and underwritten by the Inca, as in the case of the Lupaqa leader Cari. In Northwest Argentina and Chile, pre-Incaic social organization was more on the order of tribes than chiefdoms, which may, in part, account for the Inca's more minimal investment in these areas (González 1983).

Inca society was highly stratified with the "Incas-by-blood" of the Cuzco lineages making up the uppermost echelons of the status hierarchy. Below them were the "Incas-by-privilege," a class consisting mainly of the original, non-Inca inhabitants of the Cuzco valley, individuals who had distinguished themselves through outstanding service to the state, and all those whose native language was Quechua. The provincial nobility was the next tier in the sociopolitical hierarchy of the state. Members of this class were typically the ethnic elite who had ruled their provinces prior to the Inca conquest. Below this stratum were the commoners, the backbone of the Inca state, who made their living through agricultural labor (Bauer 1992; Murra 1980; Rowe 1946; Zuidema 1989, 1990).

The Inca governed their empire through a highly formalized hierarchical system. At the apex stood the Inca sovereign, who ruled by divine right and claimed lineal descent from the sun. Below him were the lords of the four sectors (*suyu*) of the empire, who oversaw the imperial governors of each of the provinces within their sector. The provincial governors purportedly each had responsibility for 10,000 families. Following a decimal system of organization, there were two tiers of Inca officials below the governor, the higher of which supervised two subordinates responsible for the management of 500 families each. Local ethnic leaders, known as *curacas*, served as intermediaries between the imperial hierarchy and the local populace. Theoretically, each *curaca* had under his control 100 families (Julien 1982; Rowe 1946).

Religion and Expressive Culture

Inca religion was fundamentally animistic insofar as inanimate objects were understood to have a spiritual content. The sun and moon, certain stars, the sea, the earth, rivers and springs, hills, snow-capped peaks, caves, and outcrops all had special significance for the

Inca. Rocks were particularly laden with symbolic meaning; numerous Inca myths reference the transformation of men into stones or vice versa. Special boulders or outcrops of particular importance were often integrated into Inca architecture or became the focal points of imperial sites around the empire. The Inca typically sought to arrogate the sacred power of local *huacas* and holy places to themselves by installing state constructions at these sites, as seen, for example, in the case of the Islands of the Sun and Moon in lake Titicaca (Cobo 1990; Rowe 1946; Zuidema 1990).

Within Andean society, ritual was an essential aspect of daily life. People engaged in private acts, such as the sharing of coca or praying to the snow-capped peaks (*apu*), which expressed deeply held religious beliefs everyday. Public ceremonies of the Inca were elaborate, highly formal affairs. The state ceremonial calendar corresponded closely to the agricultural cycle of the highlands, with many rituals explicitly linked to crop productivity. Public ceremonies were also performed during times of crisis and to mark important historic events such as the coronation or death of the emperor. Most such ceremonies involved the exhibition of sacred idols and images, dancing, feasting, oratory, and the heavy consumption of corn beer (*chicha*). Public ceremonies were typically conducted outdoors in one of the central plazas (Rowe 1946; Zuidema 1990).

Sacrifices accompanied nearly every religious rite and typically involved guinea pigs, llamas, coca, and *chicha*, although children were sometimes immolated as well. Guaman Poma (1936: 270) depicts residents of Collasuyu offering the lord of the mountain a black llama and bundles of coca. He indicates in the text that different ethnic groups within Collasuyu made different types of offerings, the Puquinacolla, for instance, sacrificing white llamas, *chicha*, *mullu* (*Spondylus* shell), and fish, while the Pomacanches presented gold and silver and children of 12 years of age (Guaman Poma 1936: 271).

There seem to have been a disproportionately large number of mountaintop offertory shrines in Collasuyu. Of 35 such high-altitude sites identified by Beorchia, 32 were found in Chile, Argentina, and Bolivia (see also McEwan and Silva 1989: 177–181; Reinhard 1996; Schobinger 1966). Most of these contain buildings or enclosures of low stone walls and small platforms (González 1983: 351). Beyond these mountaintop immolations, no important Inca religious sites have been identified south of Samaipata in southwestern Bolivia (Meyers 1993; Meyers and Ulbert 1998).

Ethnic groups in the Andes typically had their own distinctive style of dress, with affiliation most often signaled through headgear. Julien (1983: 43) reports that the diagnostic element of dress among the Qolla proper was the man's headdress, which consisted of a tall brimless hat that narrowed at the top. Guaman Poma (1936: 169) depicts the war leader from Collasuyu sporting a truncated conical headdress bearing a lunate emblem on the front and a distinctive neckpiece that may relate to the hat. The captain holds a spear in one hand and a bolalike object in the other. Rowe (1946: 275) states that the Collasuyu were experts in the use of the multistranded bolas as a weapon. Guaman Poma represents an elite female from this region wearing a floor-length skirt, a long shawl fastened in front by a *tupu* pin, and a distinctive cowl-like head cover (1936: 177). With her one exposed hand, she points to a small dog standing near her feet. The Aymara of the Collasuyu district practiced cranial deformation through the application of pressure to the infant's skull (Rowe 1946: 236–237). The hat shapes represented by Guaman Poma (1936: 169, 177, 324) may correspond to the distinctive modified head shapes of the Collasuyu.

The dead were generally considered a source of protection in the late pre-Columbian era. They were guardians (*mallki*) to whom descendants could appeal for special favors or requests. Inca rulers were typically mummified on death and retained as valued state advisers and lineage patriarchs in the sacred temple of the Sun (Coricancha) in Cuzco. Common people were normally buried in caves or rock shelters with offerings of food, pottery, and clothing. In the imperial provinces, burial practices followed traditional norms and varied considerably, although the interments of ethnic elite frequently contained Inca-style items. Guaman Poma (1936: 293–294) suggests that the Collasuyu typically buried their dead in stone towers known as *chulpas*. Under Inca influence, some local elite constructed *chulpas* with Cuzco-style fine masonry (Hyslop 1990: 119).

References

Bauer, Brian (1992). *The Development of the Inca State*. Austin: University of Texas Press.

Beorchia, Antonio (1978). "Análisis comparativo, descripción de los santuarios de altura y conclusiones provisorias en base a los antecedentes conocidos hasta junio de 1978." *Revista del Centro de Investigaciones Arqueológicas de Alta Montaña, San Juan, Argentina* 3: 11–24.

Calderari, Milena, and Veronica Williams (1991). "Re-evaluación de los estilos cerámicos incaicos en el noroeste Argentino." *Revista Comechingonia* (Cordoba, Argentina) 9: 75–95.

Cieza de León, Pedro de (1962). *La Crónica del Perú* [1553]. Madrid: Espasa Calpe.

Cieza de León, Pedro de (1973). *El Señorio de los Incas*. Lima: Editorial Universo.

Cobo, Bernabé (1979). *History of the Inca Empire*. Austin: University of Texas Press.

Cobo, Bernabé (1990). *Inca Religion and Customs*. Austin: University of Texas Press.

D'Altroy, Terence, and Timothy Earle (1985). "Staple Finance, Wealth Finance, and Storage in the Inka Political Economy." *Current Anthropology* 26, 2: 187–206.

D'Altroy, Terence, Ana María Lorandi, and Verónica Williams (in press). "The Inka Occupation of the South Andes." In *Variations in the Expressions of Inka Power*, ed. M. Ramiro Matos, R. Burger, and C. Morris. Washington, D.C.: Dumbarton Oaks Press.

Davies, Nigel (1995). *The Incas*. Niwot: University Press of Colorado.

Diez de San Miguel, Garci (1964). *Visita hecha a la provincial de Chucuito* [1567]. Lima: Casa de la Cultura del Perú.

Dillehay, Thomas, and Américo Gordon (1988). "La actividad prehispánica de los Incas y su influencia en la Araucania." In *La Frontera del Estado Inca*, ed. T. Dillehay and P. Netherly. Oxford: British Archaeological Reports, International Series 442, 215–234.

Fock, Nils (1961). "Inka Imperialism in Northwest Argentina and Chaco Burial Forms." *Folk* 3: 67–90.

Gasparini, Graziano, and Luise Margolies (1980). *Inca Architecture*, trans P. J. Lyon. Bloomington: Indiana University Press.

González, Alberto Rex (1981). "La ciudad de Chicoana: su importancia histórica y arqueológica." *Síntomas* (Buenos Aires) 3: 15–21.

González, Alberto Rex (1983). "Inca Settlement Patterns in a Marginal Province of the Empire: Sociocultural Implications." In *Prehistoric Settlement Patterns: Essays in Honor of Gordon R. Willey*, ed. E. Vogt. Cambridge, MA: Harvard University Press, 337–360.

Guaman Poma de Ayala, Felipe (1936). *Nueva Corónica y Buen Gobierno* [1614]. Paris: Institut d'Ethnologie, Université de Paris.

Hyslop, John (1976). "An Archaeological Investigation of the Lupaca Kingdom and Its Origins." Ph.D. diss., Department of Anthropology, Columbia University.

Hyslop, John (1977). "Chulpas of the Lupaca Zone of the Peruvian High Plateau." *Journal of Field Archaeology* 4: 149–170.

Hyslop, John (1979). "El área Lupaqa bajo el dominio incaico: Un reconocimiento arqueológico." *Histórica* (Lima) 3, 1: 53–79.

Hyslop, John (1984). *Inka Road System*. New York: Academic Press.

Hyslop, John (1990). *Inka Settlement Planning*. Austin: University of Texas.

Iribarren, Jorge (1978). "Manifestations of Inca Culture in Two Provinces of Chile." In *Advances in Andean Archaeology*, ed. D. Browman. The Hague: Mouton, 443–448.

Julien, Catherine (1982). "Inca Decimal Administration in the Lake Titicaca Region." In *The Inca and Aztec States, 1400–1800: Anthropology and History*, ed. G. Collier, R. Rosaldo, and J. Wirth. New York: Academic Press, 119–151.

Julien, Catherine (1983). *Hatunqolla: A View of Inca Rule from the Lake Titicaca Region*. University of California Publications in Anthropology 15. Berkeley and Los Angeles: University of California Press.

Julien, Catherine (1993). "Finding a Fit: Archaeology and Ethnohistory of the Incas." In *Provincial Inca: Archaeological and Ethnohistorical Assessment of the Impact of the Inca State*, ed. M. Malpass. Iowa City: University of Iowa Press, 177–233.

Kendall, Ann (1985). *Aspects of Inca Architecture: Description, Function, and Chronology*. Oxford: British Archaeological Reports, International Series 242.

LaBarre, Weston (1948). *The Aymara Indians of the Lake Titicaca Plateau, Bolivia*. Arlington: Memoirs of the American Anthropological Association, no. 68.

LaLone, Darrell (1982). "The Inca as a Nonmarket Economy: Supply on Command vs. Supply and Demand." In *Contexts for Prehistoric Exchange*, ed. J. Ericson and T. Earle. New York: Academic Press, 291–316.

LaLone, Mary, and Darrell LaLone (1987). "The Inka State in the Southern Highlands: State Administration and Production Enclaves." *Ethnohistory* 34, 1: 47–62.

Llagostera, Agustín (1976). "Hipótesis sobre la expansión incaica en la vertiente occidental de los Andes meridionales." *Anale Universidad del Norte* 10: 203–218.

Lorandi, Ana María (1983). "Mitayos y Mitmaqkuna en el Tawantinsuyu meridional." *Histórica* (Lima) 7, 1: 3–50.

Lorandi, Ana María (1984). "Soñocamayoc: Los olleros del Inka en los centros de manufactureros de Tucumán." *Revista del Museo de La Plata* 8: 303–327.

Lynch, Thomas (1993). "The Identification of Inca Posts and Roads from Catarpe to Río Frío, Chile." In *Provincial Inca: Archaeological and Ethnohistorical Assessment of the Impact of the Inca State*, ed. M. Malpass. Iowa City: University of Iowa Press, 117–144.

Malpass, Michael (1987). "Prehistoric Agricultural Terracing at Chijra in the Colca Valley, Peru." In *Pre-Hispanic Agricultural Fields in the Andean Region*, ed. W. Denevan, K. Mathewson, and G. Knapp. Oxford: British Archaeological Report, International Series, no. 359, 45–66.

McEwan, Colin, and María Isabel Silva (1989). "Que fueron a hacer los Incas en la costa central del Ecuador?" In *Relaciones Interculturales en el área Ecuatorial del Pácifico durante la Época Precolombina*, ed. J. F. Bouchard and M. Guinea. Oxford: Proceedings of the 46th International Congress of Americanists, British Archaeological Reports, International Series 503, 163–185.

Meyers, Albert (1993). "Trabajos arqueológicos en Samaipata, Departamento de Santa Cruz, Bolivia." *Boletín de la Sociedad de Investigaciones en el Arte Rupestre Boliviano* 7: 48–58.

Meyers, Albert, and C. Ulbert (1998). "Archaeological Investigations in Eastern Bolivia: The Samaipata Project." *Tawantinsuyu* 3: 79–85.

Morris, Craig (1967). "Storage in Tawantinsuyu." Ph.D. diss., Department of Anthropology, University of Chicago.

Morris, Craig (1974). "Reconstructing Patterns of Non-Agricultural Production in the Inca Economy: Archaeology and Documents in Instituted Analysis." In *Reconstructing Complex Societies*, ed. C. Moore. Cambridge, MA. Supplement to Bulletin of the American Schools of Oriental Research, no. 20, 49–68.

Morris, Craig (1978). "The Archaeological Analysis of Andean Exchange Systems." In *Social Archaeology: Beyond Subsistence and Dating*, ed. C. Redman et al. New York: Academic Press, 303–327.

Morris, Craig (1982). "Infrastructure of Inka Control in the Peruvian Central Highlands." In *The Inca and Aztec States, 1400–1800*, ed. G. Collier, R. Rosaldo, and J. Wirth. New York: Academic Press, 153–171.

Morris, Craig (1985). "From Principles of Ecological Complementarity to the Organization and Administration of Tawantinsuyu." In *Andean Ecology and Civilization*, ed. S. Masuda, I. Shimada, and C. Morris. Tokyo: University of Tokyo Press, 477–490.

Muñoz Ovalle, I., and J. Chacama Rodriguez (1990). "Cronología por termoluminiscencia para los períodos Intermedio Tardío y Tardío en la sierra de Arica." *Revista Chungará* 20: 19–45.

Murra, John (1960). "Rite and Crop in the Inca State." In *Culture and History*, ed. S. Diamond. New York: Columbia University Press, 393–407.

Murra, John (1965). "Herds and Herders in the Inca State." In *Man, Culture, and Animals*. Washington, D.C.: American Association for the Advancement of Science, 185–216.

Murra, John (1968). "An Aymara Kingdom in 1567." *Ethnohistory* 15, 2: 115–151.

Murra, John (1970). "Información etnológica e histórica adicional sobre el reino Lupaqa." *Historia y Cultura* 4: 49–62.

Murra, John (1975). "El control vertical de un máximo de pisos ecológicos en la economía de las sociedades andinas." In *Formaciones Económicas y Políticas del Mundo Andino*, ed. J. Murra. Lima: Instituto de Estudios Peruanos, 59–115.

Murra, John (1978). "Los olleros del Inka: Hacia una historia y arqueología del Qollasuyu." In *Historia, Problema, y Promesa: Homenaje a Jorge Basadre*, ed. F. Miró, F. Pease, and D. Sobrevilla. Lima: Fondo Editorial, 415–423.

Murra, John (1980). *Economic Organization of the Inka State*. Greenwich: JAI Press.

Murra, John (1995). "Did Tribute and Markets Prevail in the Andes before the European Invasion?" In *Ethnicity, Markets, and Migration in the Andes: At the Crossroads of History and Anthropology*, ed. B. Larson, O. Harris, and E. Tandeter. Durham: Duke University Press, 57–72.

Niemeyer, Hans (1986). "La ocupación incaica de la cuenca alta del Río Copiapó." *Comechingonia, Revista de Antropología e Historia* 4: 165–294.

Niemeyer, Hans, and Virgilio Schiappacasse (1988). "Patrones de asentamiento incaicos en el Norte Grande de Chile." In *La Frontera del Estado Inca*, ed. T. Dillehay and P. Netherly. Oxford: British Archaeological Reports, International Series 442, 141–179.

Niles, Susan (1982). "Style and Function in Inca Agricultural Works near Cuzco." *Ñawpa Pacha* 20: 163–182.

Pärssinen, Marti, and Ari Siiriäinen (1997). "Inka-style Ceramics and Their Chronological Relationship to the Inka Expansion in the Southern Lake Titicaca Area (Bolivia)." *Latin American Antiquity* 8, 3: 255–272.

Raffino, Rudolfo (1981). *Los Inkas del Kollasuyu*. La Plata, Argentina: Editorial Ramos Americana.

Ramos Gavilán, Alonso (1976). *Historia de Nuestra Señora de Copacabana* [1621]. La Paz: Cámara Nacional de Comercio y Industria.

Reinhard, Johan (1996). "Peru's Ice Maiden." *National Geographic* 189, 6: 62–81.

Rowe, John H. (1946). "Inca Culture at the Time of the Spanish Conquest." In *Handbook of South American Indians*, vol. 2: *The Andean Civilizations*, ed. J. Steward. Washington, D.C.: Bureau of American Ethnology Bulletin, Smithsonian Institution 143, 183–330.

Ryden, Stig (1947). *Archaeological Researches in the Highlands of Bolivia*. Göteborg, Sweden: Elanders Boktryckeri Aktiebolag.

Santoro Vargas, Calogero, and I. Muñoz Ovalle (1981). "Patrón habitacional incaico en el área de Pampa Alto Ramírez (Arica, Chile)." *Revista Chungará* 7: 144–171.

Sarmiento de Gamboa, Pedro (1943). *Historia de los Incas* [1572]. Buenos Aires: Editores Emece.

Schobinger, Juan (1966). "Investigaciones arqueológicas en la sierra de Famatina." *Anales de Arqueología y Etnología, Universidad Nacional de Cuya, Mendoza, Argentina* 2: 139–193.

Sherbondy, Jeannette (1982). "Canal Systems of Hanan Cuzco." Ph.D. diss., Department of Anthropology, University of Illinois, Urbana.

Silva Galdames, Osvaldo (1977–1978). "Consideraciones acerca del período Inca en la cuenca de Santiago (central Chile)." *Boletín del Museo Arqueológico de La Serena, Chile* 16: 211–243.

Silva Galdames, Osvaldo (1983). "Detuvo la batalla del Maule la expansión Inca hacia el sur de Chile?" *Cuadernos de Historia, Universidad de Chile, Santiago* 3: 7–25.

Stehberg, Rubén, and Nazareno Carvajal (1988). "Red vial incaica en los términos meridionales del imperio: Tramo valle del Limari-Valle del Maipo." In *La Frontera del Estado Inca*, ed. T. Dillehay and P. Netherly. Oxford: British Archaeological Reports, International Series 442, 181–214.

Tschopik, Marion (1946). *Some Notes on the Archaeology of the Department of Puno*. Cambridge, MA: Papers of the Peabody Museum of American Archaeology and Ethnology 27, 3.

Wachtel, Nathan (1977). *Vision of the Vanquished*. New York: Harper and Row.

Wachtel, Nathan (1982). "The Mitimas of the Cochabamba Valley: The Colonization Policy of Huayna Capac." In *The Inca and Aztec States, 1400–1800: Anthropology and History*, ed. G. A. Collier, R. I. Rosaldo, and J. D. Wirth. New York: Academic Press, 199–229.

Williams, Veronica (1991). "Control estatal incaico en el noroeste Argentino: Un caso de estudio de Potrero-Chaquiago (Provincial de Catamarca)." *Arqueología: Revista de la Sección Prehistoria, Universidad de Buenos Aires* 1: 75–103.

Zuidema, R. Tom (1989). "The Moieties of Cuzco." In *Attraction of Opposites: Thought and Society in the Dualistic Mode*, ed. D. Maybury-Lewis, and U. Amagor. Ann Arbor: University of Michigan Press.

Zuidema, R. Tom (1990). *Inca Civilization in Cuzco*. Austin: University of Texas Press.

Cuntisuyu

TIME PERIOD: 524–468 B.P.

LOCATION: Southwest quarter of the empire extending from Cuzco to the Pacific coast, the northern boundary intercepting the coast in the vicinity of the Chincha valley, and the southern limit located near the Moquegua valley.

DIAGNOSTIC MATERIAL ATTRIBUTES: A suite of architectural features in the coastal sector, including the use of rectangular adobe bricks in architecture, plastered and sometimes painted wall surfaces, structures with joined rooms, flat rather than gabled roofs, and the occasional use of friezes as a decorative device; lack of formal road construction in much of the quadrant.

CULTURAL SUMMARY

Environment

The small southwestern sector of the Inca empire known as Cuntisuyu includes the region around Arequipa and the near south coast of Peru. This quarter is dominated by the dry western slopes of the cordillera and the desert coastal plain. Normally no rain falls below approximately 1800-m elevation in this region, leaving the western flanks and coastal plain barren of vegetation. The coastal zone of Cuntisuyu is minimally watered by a number of rivers that exit the mountains during the highland rainy season. Because the coastal plain is wider in this region than it is farther north, several of these rivers, including the Ica and the Nazca, expire well before reaching the sea. For this reason, most population centers are found several kilometers inland. The coastal climate is conditioned by the effects of the Humboldt current, a cold flow that sweeps north along the coast, producing moderate air temperatures ranging between 66–73° F.

Settlements

The Inca road system within the Cuntisuyu district is not well documented (Hyslop 1984: 222). From Cuzco, the royal road to Cuntisuyu apparently exited the south side of the central plaza and passed through the ancient parish of Belén on the outskirts of the city (Urton 1990: 24). It continued through the province of Paruro, proceeding south to a point at which it crossed the Apurimac river over a famous suspension bridge spanning a 45-m gorge (Bauer 1990: 54–58; Urton 1990: 24, 92–93). From the Apurimac, the royal road likely proceeded south toward the region of Arequipa, although the exact route has not been documented (but see Stanish and Pritzker 1983). Bauer's (1990: 58) survey of the region south of Cuzco suggests that the Inca relied heavily on preexisting road networks in this area. In the coastal zone of Cuntisuyu, Hyslop (1984: 262) notes that there is a lack of formally constructed Inca roads. This is particularly noteworthy insofar as the Inca ruins in this sector are more pronounced than elsewhere on the Pacific coast.

Relatively few Inca sites have been identified in the highland sector of Cuntisuyu. The largest known is that of Maucallacta, located approximately 20 km south of Cuzco (Bauer 1990: 142–160, 185–200; Kendall 1985: 377–383; Muelle 1945; Pardo 1946). This site features fine cut-stone masonry, a U-shaped plaza, and a series of triple-jambed niches (Bauer 1990: 143–144). Maucallacta is an exceptional site for a number of reasons: it has a unique, fan-shaped layout that ignores common principles of Inca site planning (Hyslop 1990: 219–220); it is located well off the main Inca highway; its central plaza lacks an *ushnu*; and there are no *qollka* associated with it (Bauer 1990: 151–160). Based on the archaeological and ethnohistoric evidence, Bauer (1990: 154) suggests that Maucallacta was an Inca religious center intimately linked to the Inca origin myth (also Urton 1990: 32–37).

One of the few other Inca sites reported from the highland sector of Cuntisuyu is Torata Alta, located in the upper Moquegua valley (Stanish and Pritzker 1983). This site, one of the southernmost in the empire evidencing an orthogonal layout (Hyslop 1990: 197), has been interpreted as a small Inca administrative center.

Although essentially uniform, Inca architecture admitted some local variation to allow for the availability of different building materials and to accommodate local conditions. This is especially apparent in the case of coastal Cuntisuyu, where the Inca adapted their state architecture to the traditions of the local cultures and the hot, dry climate (Gasparini and Margolies 1980: 4; Hyslop 1990; Menzel 1971; Rowe 1946: 229; Wallace 1971). Fine Inca masonry is rare on the coast, having been observed at only a handful of sites, including Paredones in the Nazca valley (Hyslop 1990: 284, 328, n.13) and Huaytará in the upper Pisco valley (Gasparini and Margolies 1980: 255–259). One of the best preserved Inca sites on the south coast is Tambo Colorado in the Pisco valley (Engel 1957; Menzel 1959, 1971; Urteaga 1938–1939). With its great trapezoidal plaza, laterally positioned *ushnu*, tapia walls, and remnant polychrome paint, it constitutes a good example of an Inca installation that integrates Inca principles of organization with coastal technical traditions (Gasparini and Margolies 1980: 178).

Hyslop (1990: 267) suggests that the south coast shared a sufficient number of unique features to merit recognition as a distinct architectural subarea. These included the use of rectangular adobe bricks (Hyslop 1990: 267; Menzel 1959: 130); plastered and sometimes painted wall surfaces that utilized yellow, black, red, and white pigment (Kendall 1985: 52; Menzel 1959: 131); agglutinated rooms, flat roofs, the intermittent use of rectangular rather than trapezoidal niches and doors, and the occasional use of friezes as decorative devices (Hyslop 1990: 267, 285–286; Menzel 1959: 131). Unlike other parts of the empire, there is little evidence that sacred stones or rock outcrops affected the placement or organization of state facilities on the south coast (Hyslop 1990: 125).

Menzel (1959: 232) contends that where centralized authority and its attendant infrastructure were extant, as in the case of the Ica and Chincha valleys, the Inca preferred to utilize local centers, often adding no more than a few imperial-style structures (Hyslop 1990: 266–267; Menzel 1971; Menzel and Rowe 1966). Where the political infrastructure was lacking, as in the case of the Nasca, Acarí, and Yauya valleys, the Inca established administrative centers apart from existing sites, leaving the local villages essentially intact (Menzel 1959: 232). Consequently, local settlement patterns appear to have changed little with the imposition of Inca rule on the south coast (Hyslop 1990; Menzel 1959). The chief evidence of Inca influence in some sectors of the coast is the presence of imperial polychrome pottery and Inca-local hybrid wares (Kroeber and Strong 1924; Menzel 1971, 1976; Uhle 1924b).

Economy

The subsistence base of the Inca was agricultural, and production was tightly controlled by the state (Morris 1982, 1985; Murra 1980; Rowe 1946). Land improvements, which included the construction of terraces, irrigation canals, and dams, were undertaken by the state on a massive scale and intended to increase agricultural yields (Morris 1982; Niles 1982; Sherbondy 1982). Such state efforts are exemplified in the Colca valley, located to the northwest of Arequipa, which was extensively terraced (Malpass 1987; Shea 1987). The two most important crops in the Andes were maize, which can be grown up to 3500 m elevation in some cases, and potatoes, which can be cultivated to almost 4000 m. Of the two, maize held considerably more ceremonial and symbolic significance (Murra 1960). Fishing was an important component of the local economy on the south coast as was the extraction of guano (Cieza 1962: ch. 55; Julien 1985; Rostworowski 1974, 1977; Watanabe et al. 1990).

The Inca state economy was a redistributive one that exploited ancient principles of reciprocity to its own benefit (D'Altroy and Earle 1985; Morris 1982, 1985; Murra 1980; Wachtel 1977). Morris describes this system as "institutionalized reciprocity." Taxes were paid in the form of labor rather than in kind, and each community was required to cultivate the lands appropriated by the Inca state in its district (Murra 1980; Rowe 1946). The produce from these lands went to state storage facilities and was used to support imperial activities (D'Altroy and Earle 1985; LaLone 1982; Morris 1967). Specific goods associated with the Inca state, including pottery, cloth, and metal artifacts, were produced by full-time craft specialists who were retained by the state and often lodged in the vicinity of Cuzco (Julien 1993; Morris 1974).

Although in general trade and markets did not figure prominently in the Inca economy (Murra 1980, 1995), there appears to have been considerable emphasis on commerce and exchange in the coastal sector of Cuntisuyu. The importance of long-distance exchange has been well documented for the Chincha valley of the south coast, and the Ica valley, with its tradition of fine pottery production, is implicated as well (Menzel 1976; Morris 1988; Rostworowski 1970, 1974, 1975; Sandweiss 1992).

Sociopolitical Organization

The highland sector of Cuntisuyu nearest Cuzco was home to several ethnic groups that came into the orbit of the Inca early on (Bauer 1990). Given their proximity to the imperial capital, they were among a number of surrounding groups designated as "Incas-by-privilege" by the state (Rowe 1946: 261). Archaeological and ethnohistoric evidence suggests that the Cuntisuyu quadrant was associated with the ancestral origins of the Inca people and thus held special significance (Bauer 1991; Urton 1990: 57–59). The indigenous people of this district were assigned to the lower status (*hurin*) moiety of the Inca and constituted eligible marriage partners for the Inca nobility (Urton 1990). Archaeological research suggests that this region was annexed rather than conquered by the Inca and that local settlement patterns were little affected by the change (Bauer 1990, 1992). The Arequipa region further to the south was likely brought under imperial control by either Pachacuti or his son Topa Inca by 529 B.P. (Julien 1991; Rowe 1945: 272–273).

The south coast was initially raided by Pachacuti's general, Capac Yupanqui, c. 560 B.P., but not conquered (Menzel 1959; Rowe 1945: 270). A later campaign directed by Topa Inca c. 524 B.P. brought the south coast firmly under imperial control (Menzel 1959; Rowe 1945: 271–272). Although the Ica, Nazca, and Acarí valleys reportedly submitted peacefully to Inca forces, there is some disagreement as to whether the Chincha yielded without a struggle or resisted (Davies 1995: 70–71).

The valley of Chincha, which lay almost due west of Cuzco, was one of the most powerful kingdoms on the coast during the Regional States (Late Intermediate) period. The lord of Chincha reportedly commanded 30,000 tributaries, ruled over a complex society organized according to occupational specialization, and maintained ties with distant lands through a vast network of seafaring merchants (Menzel and Rowe 1966; Rostworowski 1970, 1974, 1977). Rather than dismembering the Chincha polity, the Inca entered into a political alliance with this valley and bestowed on the lords of Chincha many privileges (Menzel and Rowe 1966; Morris 1988; Rostworowski 1970).

Inca society was highly stratified with the "Incas-by-blood" of the Cuzco lineages making up the uppermost echelons of the status hierarchy. Below them were the

"Incas-by-privilege," a class consisting mainly of the original, non-Inca inhabitants of the Cuzco valley, individuals who had distinguished themselves through outstanding service to the state, and all those whose native language was Quechua. The provincial nobility was the next tier in the sociopolitical hierarchy of the state. Members of this class were typically the ethnic elite who had ruled their provinces prior to the Inca conquest. Below this stratum were the commoners, the backbone of the Inca state, who made their living through agricultural labor (Bauer 1992; Murra 1980; Rowe 1946; Zuidema 1989, 1990).

Menzel (1959, 1977) observes that in situations where social stratification was already present, such as in the Ica and Chicha valleys, evidence of Inca influence was concentrated among the elite. This suggests that local elite manipulated their relationship with the state to amplify preexisting social differences. In valleys like Acarí, where the social hierarchy appears to have been less elaborated, Inca influence appears to more evenly distributed among the local population (Menzel 1959; Rowe 1956).

The Inca governed their empire through a highly formalized hierarchical system. At the apex stood the Inca sovereign who ruled by divine right and claimed lineal descent from the sun. Below him were the lords of the four sectors (*suyu*) of the empire who oversaw the imperial governors of each of the provinces within their sector. The provincial governors purportedly each had responsibility for 10,000 families. Following a decimal system of organization, there were two tiers of Inca officials below the governor, the higher of which supervised two subordinates responsible for the management of 500 families each. Local ethnic leaders, known as *curacas*, served as intermediaries between the imperial hierarchy and the local populace. Theoretically, each *curaca* had under his control 100 families (Julien 1982; Rowe 1946).

Religion and Expressive Culture

Inca religion was fundamentally animistic insofar as inanimate objects were understood to have a spiritual content. The sun and moon, certain stars, the sea, the earth, rivers and springs, hills, snow-capped peaks, caves and outcrops all had special significance for the Inca. Rocks were particularly laden with symbolic meaning; numerous Inca myths reference the transformation of men into stones or vice versa. Special boulders or outcrops of particular importance were often integrated into Inca architecture or became the focal points of imperial sites around the empire (Cobo 1990; Rowe

1946; Zuidema 1990). An example of this tendency in the Cuntisuyu quadrant is seen in the case of Puma Orqo, an elaborately modified rock outcrop decorated with twin carved pumas, which is within visual proximity of the large Inca center of Maucallacta (Bauer 1990, 1991; Pardo 1946; Urton 1990: 57–61).

Within Andean society, ritual was an essential aspect of daily life. People engaged in private acts, such as the sharing of coca or praying to the snow-capped peaks (*apu*), which expressed deeply held religious beliefs everyday. Public ceremonies of the Inca were elaborate, highly formal affairs. The state ceremonial calendar corresponded closely to the agricultural cycle of the highlands, with many rituals explicitly linked to crop productivity. Public ceremonies were also performed during times of crisis and to mark important historic events such as the coronation or death of the emperor. Most such ceremonies involved the exhibition of sacred idols and images, dancing, feasting, oratory, and the heavy consumption of corn beer (*chicha*). Public ceremonies were typically conducted outdoors in the large central plazas (Rowe 1946; Zuidema 1990).

Sacrifices accompanied nearly every religious rite and frequently involved guinea pigs, llamas, coca, and *chicha*, although children were sometimes immolated as well. Guaman Poma (1936: 270) depicts residents of Cuntisuyu offering a child and a guinea pig to a small figure on a hilltop. He indicates in the text that the people of Cuntisuyu sacrificed guinea pigs (*conejo*), silver, feathers, coca, *mullu* (*Spondylus* shell), raw meat, blood, and children of 12 years of age to the sea, the hills, and the *yungas* (Guaman Poma 1936: 273).

Ethnic groups in the Andes typically had their own distinctive style of dress, with affiliation most often signaled through headgear. According to Uhle (1903: 39), the inhabitants of Cuntisuyu wore braided cords (*llaut'a*) of different colors coiled around the head. Guaman Poma (1936: 171) depicts a war captain from Cuntisuyu wearing a rolled headband, a probable *llaut'a*, holding a spear in one hand and a bladelike object in the other. The coastal tribes were reportedly experts in the use of spear throwers and darts as weapons (Rowe 1946: 275). Guaman Poma (1936: 179) portrays an elite female from Cuntisuyu, wearing a calf-length dress and a shawl pinned by a *tupu*, holding a small bird on her finger. The woman wears no headdress, calling attention to the broadly flattened shape of her head. Rowe (1946: 236–237) notes that cranial deformation was widely practiced among coastal tribes.

The dead were generally considered a source of protection in the late pre-Columbian era. They were guardians (*mallki*) to whom descendants could appeal for special favors or requests. Inca rulers were typically mummified on death and retained as valued state advisers and lineage patriarchs in the sacred temple of the Sun (Coricancha) in Cuzco. Common people were normally buried in caves or rock shelters with offerings of food, pottery, and clothing. In the imperial provinces, burial practices followed traditional norms and varied considerably, although the interments of ethnic elite frequently contained Inca-style items (Menzel 1959, 1966, 1976, 1977; Uhle 1924a, 1924b). Guaman Poma (1936: 295–296) suggests that the Indians of the Cuntisuyu region had mortuary customs similar to those of the Collasuyu people, although the archaeological evidence indicates that coastal burials usually involved deep tombs (Cieza 1962: ch. 53; Menzel 1971, 1976, 1977: 8–10; Uhle 1924a, 1924b).

References

Bauer, Brian (1990). "State Development in the Cusco Region: Archaeological Research on the Incas in the Province of Paruro." Ph.D. diss., Department of Anthropology, University of Chicago.

Bauer, Brian (1991). "Pacariqtambo and the Mythical Origins of the Inca." *Latin American Antiquity* 2, 1: 7–26.

Bauer, Brian (1992). *The Development of the Inca State*. Austin: University of Texas Press.

Cabello Balboa, Miguel (1951). *Miscelánea Antártica* [1586]. Quito: Editorial Ecuatoriana.

Cieza de León, Pedro de (1962). *La Crónica del Perú* [1553]. Madrid: Espasa Calpe.

Cobo, Bernabé (1990). *Inca Religion and Customs*. Austin: University of Texas Press.

D'Altroy, Terence, and Timothy Earle (1985). "Staple Finance, Wealth Finance, and Storage in the Inka Political Economy." *Current Anthropology* 26, 2: 187–206.

Davies, Nigel (1995). *The Incas*. Niwot: University Press of Colorado.

Engel, Frederic (1957). "Early Sites in the Pisco Valley of Peru: Tambo Colorado." *American Antiquity* 23, 1: 34–45.

Gasparini, Graziano, and Luise Margolies (1980). *Inca Architecture*, trans. P. J. Lyon. Bloomington: Indiana University Press.

Guaman Poma de Ayala, Felipe (1936). *Nueva Corónica y Buen Gobierno* [1614]. Paris: Institut d'Ethnologie, Université de Paris.

Hyslop, John (1984). *Inka Road System*. New York: Academic Press.

Hyslop, John (1985). *Inkawasi: The New Cuzco*. Oxford: British Archaeological Reports, International Series 234.

Hyslop, John (1990). *Inka Settlement Planning*. Austin: University of Texas Press.

Julien, Catherine (1985). "Guano and Resource Control in Sixteenth-Century Arequipa." In *Andean Ecology and Civilization*, ed. S. Masuda, I. Shimada, and C. Morris. Tokyo: University of Tokyo Press, 185–231.

Julien, Catherine (1991). *Condesuyu: The Political Division of Territory under Inca and Spanish Rule*. Bonn: Bonner Amerikanistische Studien 19.

Julien, Catherine (1993). "Finding a Fit: Archaeology and Ethnohistory of the Incas." In *Provincial Inca: Archaeological and Ethnohistorical Assessment of the Impact of the Inca State*, ed. M. Malpass. Iowa City: University of Iowa Press, 177–233.

Kendall, Ann (1985). *Aspects of Inca Architecture: Description, Function, and Chronology*. Oxford: British Archaeological Reports, International Series 242.

Kroeber, Alfred, and William Strong (1924). *The Uhle Pottery Collections from Ica*. University of California Publications in American Archaeology and Ethnology 21, 3.

LaLone, Darrell (1982). "The Inca as a Nonmarket Economy: Supply on Command vs. Supply and Demand." In *Contexts for Prehistoric Exchange*, ed. J. Ericson, and T. Earle. New York: Academic Press, 291–316.

Malpass, Michael (1987). "Prehistoric Agricultural Terracing at Chijra in the Colca Valley, Peru." In *Pre-Hispanic Agricultural Fields in the Andean Region*, ed. W. Denevan, K. Mathewson, and G. Knapp. Oxford: British Archaeological Report, International Series, no. 359, 45–66.

Menzel, Dorothy (1959). "The Inca Occupation of the South Coast of Peru." *Southwestern Journal of Anthropology* 15, 2: 125–142.

Menzel, Dorothy (1966). "The Pottery of Chincha." *Ñawpa Pacha* 4: 77–153.

Menzel, Dorothy (1971). *Estudios Arqueológicos en los Valles de Ica, Pisco, Chincha, y Cañete*. Lima: Arqueología y Sociedad, Museo de Arqueología y Etnología de la Universidad Mayor de San Marcos, 6.

Menzel, Dorothy (1976). *Pottery Style and Society in Ancient Peru: Art as a Mirror of History in the Ica Valley, 1350–1570*. Berkeley and Los Angeles: University of California Press.

Menzel, Dorothy (1977). *The Archaeology of Ancient Peru and the Work of Max Uhle*. Berkeley: R. H. Lowie Museum, University of California.

Menzel, Dorothy, and John H. Rowe (1966). "The Role of Chincha in Late Pre-Spanish Peru." *Ñawpa Pacha* 4: 63–76.

Morris, Craig (1967). "Storage in Tawantinsuyu." Ph.D. diss., Department of Anthropology, University of Chicago.

Morris, Craig (1974). In "Reconstructing Patterns of Non-agricultural Production in the Inca Economy: Archaeology and Documents in Instituted Analysis." In *Reconstructing Complex Societies*, ed. C. Moore. Cambridge, MA. Supplement to Bulletin of the American Schools of Oriental Research, no. 20, 49–68.

Morris, Craig (1978). "The Archaeological Analysis of Andean Exchange Systems." In *Social Archaeology: Beyond Subsistence and Dating*, ed. C. Redman et al. New York: Academic Press, 303–327.

Morris, Craig (1982). "Infrastructure of Inka Control in the Peruvian Central Highlands." In *The Inca and Aztec States, 1400–1800*, ed. G. Collier, R. Rosaldo, and J. Wirth. New York: Academic Press, 153–171.

Morris, Craig (1985). "From Principles of Ecological Complementarity to the Organization and Administration of Tawantinsuyu." In *Andean Ecology and Civilization*, ed. S. Masuda, I. Shimada, and C. Morris. Tokyo: University of Tokyo Press, 477–490.

Morris, Craig (1988). "Más alla de las fronteras de Chincha." In *La Frontera del Estado Inca*, ed. T. Dillehay and P. Netherly. Oxford: British Archaeological Reports, International Series 442, 131–140.

Muelle, J. (1945). "Pacarectambo: Apuntes de viaje." *Revista del Museo Nacional* (Lima) 14: 153–160.

Murra, John (1960). "Rite and Crop in the Inca State." In *Culture and History*, ed. S. Diamond. New York: Columbia University Press, 393–407.

Murra, John (1975). "El control vertical de un máximo de pisos ecológicos en la economía de las sociedades andinas." In *Formaciones Económicas y Políticas del Mundo Andino*, ed. J. Murra. Lima: Instituto de Estudios Peruanos, 59–115.

Murra, John (1980). *Economic Organization of the Inka State*. Greenwich: JAI Press.

Murra, John (1985). "The 'Archipiélago Vertical' Revisited." In *Andean Ecology and Civilization*, ed. S. Mazuda, I. Shimada, and C. Morris. Tokyo: University if Tokyo Press, 3–14.

Murra, John (1995). "Did Tribute and Markets Prevail in the Andes before the European Invasion?" In *Ethnicity, Markets, and Migration in the Andes: At the Crossroads of History and Anthropology*, ed. B. Larson, O. Harris, and E. Tandeter. Durham: Duke University Press, 57–72.

Niles, Susan (1982). "Style and Function in Inca Agricultural Works near Cuzco." *Ñawpa Pacha* 20: 163–182.

Pardo, Luís (1946). "La metropoli de Paccarictambu: El adoratorio de Tamputtocco y el itinerario del camino seguido por los hermanos ayar."*Revista del Instituto Arqueológico del Cusco* 2: 2–46.

Rostworowski de Diez Canseco, María (1970). "Mercaderes del valle de Chincha en la época prehispánica: Un documento y unos comentarios." *Revista Española de Antropología Americana* 5: 135–177.

Rostworowski de Diez Canseco, María (1974). "Coastal Fisherman, Merchants, and Artisans in Pre-hispanic Peru." In *The Sea in the Precolumbian World*, ed. E. Benson. Washington, D.C.: Dumbarton Oaks, 167–187.

Rostworowski de Diez Canseco, Maria (1975). "Pescadores, artesanos y mercaderes costeños en el Perú prehispánico." *Revista del Museo Nacional, Lima* 38: 250–314.

Rostworowski de Diez Canseco, María (1977). *Etnía y Sociedad: Costa Peruána Prehispánica*. Lima: Instituto de Estudios Peruanos.

Rowe, John (1945). "Absolute Chronology in the Andean Area." *American Antiquity* 10: 265–284.

Rowe, John H. (1946). "Inca Culture at the Time of the Spanish Conquest." In *Handbook of South American Indians, vol. 2: The Andean Civilizations*, ed. J. Steward. Washington, D.C.: Bureau of American Ethnology Bulletin, Smithsonian Institution 143, 183–330.

Rowe, John H. (1956). "Archaeological Explorations in Southern Peru, 1954–1955: Preliminary Report of the Fourth University of California Archaeological Expedition." *American Antiquity* 22, 2: 135–151.

Sandweiss, Dan (1992). *The Archaeology of Chincha Fishermen: Specialization and Status in Inka Peru*. Pittsburgh: Bulletin of the Carnegie Museum of Natural History, no. 29.

Sarmiento de Gamboa, Pedro (1943). *Historia de los Incas* [1572]. Buenos Aires: Editores Emece.

Shea, Daniel (1987). "Preliminary Discussion of Prehistoric Settlement and Terracing at Achoma, Colca Valley, Peru." In *Pre-Hispanic Agricultural Fields in the Andean Region*, ed. W. Denevan, K. Mathewson, and G. Knapp. Oxford: British Archaeological Report, International Series, no. 359, 67–77.

Sherbondy, Jeannette (1982). "Canal Systems of Hanan Cuzco." Ph.D. diss., Department of Anthropology, University of Illinois, Urbana.

Stanish, Charles, and Irene Pritzker (1983). "Archaeological Reconnaissance in Southern Peru." *Field Museum of Natural History Bulletin* 54: 6–17.

Uhle, Max (1903). *Pachacamac*. Philadelphia: Department of Archaeology, University of Pennsylvania.

Uhle, Max (1924a). "Explorations at Chincha." *University of California Publications in Archaeology and Ethnology* 21, 2: 55–94.

Uhle, Max (1924b). "Notes on the Ica Valley." *University of California Publications in Archaeology and Ethnology* 21, 3: 121–132.

Urteaga, Horacio (1938–39). "Tambo Colorado." *Boletín de la Sociedad Geográfica de Lima* 40–41: 86–94.

Urton, Gary (1990). *The History of a Myth*. Austin: University of Texas Press.

Wachtel, Nathan (1977). *Vision of the Vanquished*. New York: Harper and Row.

Wallace, Dwight (1971). *Sitios Arqueológicos del Perú (Segunda Entrada): Valles de Chincha y de Pisco*. Arqueológicos: Publicaciones del Instituto de Investigaciones Antropológicas 13. Lima: Museo Nacional de Antropología y Arqueología.

Watanabe, L., M. Moseley, and F. Cabieses eds. (1990). *Trabajos arqueológicos en Moquegua, Perú*, 3 vols. Lima: Editorial Escuela Nueva.

Zuidema, R. Tom (1989). "The Moieties of Cuzco." In *Attraction of Opposites: Thought and Society in the Dualistic Mode*, ed. D. Maybury-Lewis, and U. Amagor. Ann Arbor: University of Michigan Press, 255–275.

Zuidema, R. Tom (1990). *Inca Civilization in Cuzco*. Austin: University of Texas Press.

SITES

Cuzco

TIME PERIOD: 562–468 B.P.

LOCATION: Cuzco is located in the south-central highlands of Peru at approximately 13° S latitude.

DESCRIPTIVE SUMMARY

Local Environment

Cuzco is situated at an elevation of 3400 m above sea level on an alluvial fan at the head of a high mountain valley surrounded by snow-capped peaks. The climate, which is tempered by the proximity of the eastern jungles, is relatively mild with a mean annual temperature of 40° F. Although there is little seasonal variation in temperature, there can be extreme differences between day and night. The region experiences a marked rainy season between December and April. The environment is classified as moist *puna*, and the vegetation consists primarily of grasses, low bushes, and cactus.

Physical Features

The Inca empire was centrally administered from the capital city of Cuzco. The founder of Cuzco was the first Inca king, Manco Capac, who, according to legend, conquered the earlier inhabitants of the valley and settled there with several brothers and sisters (Betanzos 1968; Rowe 1944; Valcárcel 1939; Zuidema 1990). Cuzco was subsequently rebuilt by Pachacuti during the mid-15th century, to mark his miraculous defeat of the Chancas and to signal the imperial aspirations of the Inca (Betanzos 1968; Sarmiento de Gamboa 1943). With Pachacuti, Cuzco was transformed into a monumental representation of the power of the state, becoming both the symbolic and political center of the Inca world. In its dual role as the seat of government and the ceremonial center of Tawantinsuyu, the city encompassed aspects of both the sacred and the secular. Cuzco is recognized today as the oldest continuously inhabited city in the western hemisphere (Rowe 1944: 5). Although the importance of Inca Cuzco is obvious, surprisingly little archaeological work has been conducted there (but see Bauer 1992a; Dwyer 1971; Franco and Llanos 1940; Pardo 1957; Rowe 1944, 1957; Valcárcel 1934, 1935; Valencia 1970).

The political heart of the capital was situated between two canalized rivers, the Tullumay and the Saphy (Farrington 1983; Hyslop 1990: 34–35). The central precinct is said to be laid out in the shape of a puma (Gasparini and Margolies 1980: 45–51; Rowe 1968; see Zuidema (1985) for alternative interpretation), with the head being the great temple-fortress of Saqsaywaman, the underbelly the main public square of Huacaypata, and the tail ending in the confluence of the two rivers. The principal roads out of Cuzco, which led to the four quarters of the empire, intersected in the main plaza. These divided the city into quadrants as well as upper (*hanan*) and lower (*hurin*) halves, reflecting fundamental principles of Inca social and spatial organization (Zuidema 1990).

One of the central features of Cuzco was the large central plaza, the floor of which was said to have been covered with a deep layer of sand imported from the Pacific coast (Hyslop 1990: 37–39; Polo de Ondegardo 1916: 109–110; Sherbondy 1982: 16). In the center of the plaza was a sacred rock sheathed in gold, to which offerings were made (Aveni 1981; Betanzos 1968: 33; Molina 1943: 30–31; Pizarro 1978; Zuidema 1981). The plaza was fronted on three sides by impressive buildings, including the *aqllawasi* (house of the chosen women), several *kallanka* (great halls), and the palace of Huayna Capac (Garcilaso 1966; Hyslop 1990: 40–44; Pizarro 1978; Rowe 1979).

Cuzco contained at least three major temples dedicated to the state deities. The greatest of these was the Coricancha, or the Temple of the Sun (Hyslop 1990: 44–48; Gasparini and Margolies 1980: 220–234; Lehmann-Nitsche 1928; Rowe 1979). Although the Coricancha was purportedly erected by Manco Capac as one of his first acts (Betanzos 1968: 14; Hyslop 1990: 32), it was subsequently rebuilt and greatly enhanced by Pachacuti

(Betanzos 1968; Cieza 1967; Pizarro 1978). According to Spanish witnesses, the temple was awash in gold and housed both religious idols and the mummies of past Inca rulers (Pizarro 1978; Ruiz de Arce 1933; Sancho de la Hoz 1917). In addition, the Coricancha constituted the origin point of the Inca *ceque* system, an abstract organizational schema involving the use of a series of radiating sight lines that integrated time, space, ritual, and social groups within a coherent framework (Bauer 1992b; Zuidema 1964, 1981, 1990).

At the opposite end of the city from the Coricancha was Saqsaywaman, the greatest architectural complex ever built by the Inca. Situated on a natural hill immediately above Cuzco, the temple-fortress of Saqsaywaman is a construction of Cyclopean proportion. Utilizing enormous cut-stone blocks, many weighing 100 tons or more, the Inca built three immense zigzag ramparts using the finest polygonal masonry (Garcilaso de la Vega 1966; Hemming and Ranney 1982). Above these walls, they constructed at least two great towers that served as storehouses for state property (Hemming and Ranney 1982; Pizarro 1978; Valcárcel 1934, 1935).

Cultural Aspects

Imperial Cuzco was a planned settlement deliberately constructed to showcase the power and wealth of the Inca rulers. The city stood both as a symbol of imperial might and a model of social and cosmological order (Hyslop 1990; Gasparini and Margolies 1980; Rowe 1968). In developing their own imperial style, the Inca likely drew on their knowledge of the architectural history of different Andean cultures gained through conquest: the monumentality of ancient Huari, the fine stonework of Tiwanaku, and the royal compounds of Chanchan (Gasparini and Margolies 1980: 44).

Only the royal Inca lineages (*panaqas*), priests, and government officials were permitted to live within the central precinct of the city, which served as the seat of religious-political activity. Each Inca ruler, whether living or mummified, maintained a palatial residence within the imperial center for his wives, children, and retainers. All others, including the "Incas-by-privilege," provincial elite, craft specialists, and general laborers, lived in residential districts outside the limits of the sacred center (Agurto 1980; Chávez Ballón 1970; Hyslop 1990: 35–51). Various rules for entering and exiting the sacred city as well as for how to comport oneself within were strictly followed. The population of the entire metropolitan area at the time of the Spanish conquest has been estimated at 100,000 (Agurto 1980; Azevedo 1982; Ruiz de Arce 1933; Sancho 1917). As the sacred and symbolic center of the Inca universe, Cuzco was the focal point of political, ritual, and ceremonial activity within the empire (Zuidema 1990).

References

Agurto, Santiago (1980). *Cuzco-traza urbana de la ciudad Inca.* UNESCO, Proyecto Per 39, Instituto Nacional de Cultural de Perú. Cuzco: Imprenta Offset Color, S.R.L.

Aveni, Anthony (1981). "Horizon Astronomy in Incaic Cuzco." In *Archaeoastronomy in the Americas*, ed. R. Williamson. Santa Barbara: Ballena Press, 305–316.

Azevedo, Paulo de (1982). *Cusco-ciudad histórica: Continuidad y cambio.* Proyecto Regional de Patrimonio Cultural, PNUD/UNESCO. Lima: Ediciones PEISA.

Bauer, Brian (1992a). *The Development of the Inca State.* Austin: University of Texas Press.

Bauer, Brian (1992b). "Ritual Pathways of the Inca: An Analysis of the Collasuyu Ceques in Cuzco." *Latin American Antiquity* 3, 3: 183–205.

Betanzos, Juan de (1968). *Suma y Narración de los Incas* [1551]. Biblioteca de Autores Españoles. Madrid: Atlas.

Chávez Ballón, Manuel (1970). "Ciudades Incas: Cuzco, capital del imperio." *Wayka* 3: 1–15.

Dwyer, Edward (1971). "Early Inca Occupation of the Valley of Cuzco, Peru." Ph.D. diss., Department of Anthropology, University of California, Berkeley.

Farrington, Ian (1983). "Prehistoric Intensive Agriculture: Preliminary Notes on River Canalization in the Sacred Valley of the Incas." In *Drained Field Agriculture in Central and South America*, ed. J. Darch. Oxford: British Archaeological Reports, International Series 189, 221–235.

Franco, J., and L. Llanos (1940). "Trabajos arqueológicos en el Departamento del Cuzco: Sajsawaman." *Revista del Museo Nacional, Lima* 9, 1: 22–31.

Garcilaso de la Vega, el Inca (1966). *Royal Commentaries of the Incas and the General History of Peru* [1609], trans. H. Livermore. Austin: University of Texas Press.

Gasparini, Graziano, and Luise Margolies (1980). *Inca Architecture*, trans. P. Lyon. Bloomington: Indiana University Press.

Hemming, John, and Edward Ranney (1982). *Monuments of the Inca.* Albuquerque: University of New Mexico Press.

Hyslop, John (1990). *Inka Settlement Planning.* Austin: University of Texas.

Lehmann-Nitsche, Robert (1928). "Arqueología Peruana: Coricancha, el Templo del Sol en el Cuzco y las imágenes de su altar mayor." *Revista del Museo de La Plata* 31: 1–260.

Molina, Cristóbal (1943). "Relación de las fabulas y ritos de los Incas [1575]." In *Los Pequeños Grandes Libros de Historia Americana*, Serie 1. Lima: Librería e Imprenta D. Miranda, 5–84.

Pardo, Luis (1957). *Historia y Arqueología del Cuzco.* Callao: Imprenta Colegio Militar Leonico Pardo.

Pizarro, Pedro (1978). *Relación de l descubrimiento y conquista del Perú* [1571]. Lima: Pontifica Universidad Católica de Perú.

Polo de Ondegardo, Juan (1916). "Relación de los fundamentos acerca del notable daño que resulta de no guardar a los indios sus fueros [1571]." In *Colección de Libros y Documentos Referentes a la Historia del Perú*, ed. H. Urteaga. Lima: San Martí, 45–188.

Rowe, John (1944). *An Introduction to the Archaeology of Cuzco.* Cambridge, MA: Papers of the Peabody Museum of American Archaeology and Ethnology, Harvard University 27, 2.

Rowe, John (1957). "La arqueología del Cuzco como historia cultural." *Revista del Museo e Instituto Arqueológico de la Universidad Nacional del Cuzco* 10, 16–17: 34–48.

Rowe, John H. (1968). "What Kind of A Settlement Was Inca Cuzco?" *Ñawpa Pacha* 5: 59–76.

Rowe, John H. (1979). "An Account of the Shrines of Ancient Cuzco." *Ñawpa Pacha* 17: 2–80.

Rowe, John (1991). "Los monumentos perdidos de la plaza mayor del Cuzco incaico." *Saqsaywaman* (Cuzco) 3: 81–109.

Ruiz de Arce, Juan (1933). "Relación de los servicios en Indias de don Juan Ruiz de Arce, conquistador del Perú [1543]." In *Boletín de la Academia de la Historia* (Madrid) 102, 2: 327–384.

Sancho de la Hoz, Pedro (1917). "Relación para S. M. de lo sucedido en la conquista [1534]." In *Colección de Libros y Documentos Referentes a la Historia del Perú*, 5, ed. H. Urteaga. Lima: San Martí, 122–202.

Sarmiento de Gamboa, Pedro (1943). *Historia de los Incas* [1572]. Buenos Aires: Editores Emece.

Sherbondy, Jeannette (1982). "Canal Systems of Hanan Cuzco." Ph.D. diss., Department of Anthropology, University of Illinois, Urbana.

Valcárcel, Luis (1934). "Sajsawaman redescubierto." *Revista del Museo Nacional* (Lima) 3: 3–36, 211–233.

Valcárcel, Luis (1935). "Sajsawaman redescubierto." *Revista del Museo Nacional* (Lima) 4: 1–24, 161–203.

Valcárcel, Luis (1939). "Sobre el origen del Cuzco." *Revista del Museo Nacional* (Lima) 8: 190–233.

Valencia, Alfredo (1970). "Dos tumbas de Saqsaywaman." *Revista Española de Antropología Americana* 5: 67–75.

Zuidema, R. Tom (1964). *The Ceque System of Cuzco: The Social Organization of the Capital of the Inca.* Leiden: E. J. Brill.

Zuidema, R. Tom (1981). "Inka Observations of the Solar and Lunar passages through Zenith and Anti-Zenith at Cuzco." In *Archaeoastronomy in the Americas*, ed. R. Williamson. Santa Barbara: Ballena Press, 316–342.

Zuidema, R. Tom (1985). "The Lion in the City." In *Animal Myths and Metaphors*, ed. G. Urton. Salt Lake City: University of Utah Press, 185–250.

Zuidema, R. Tom (1990). *Inca Civilization in Cuzco.* Austin: University of Texas Press.

Huánaco Pampa

TIME PERIOD: 520–468 B.P.

LOCATION: Huánaco Pampa is located in the central Andean highlands of Peru near the headwaters of the Marañon river, approximately 700 km northwest of Cuzco on the royal Inca road to Quito.

DESCRIPTIVE SUMMARY

Local Environment

The site of Huánaco Pampa is situated near the edge of a broad upland plain, or *pampa*, at an elevation of nearly 3800 m above sea level. This cold, treeless environment, known as the *puna*, is characterized by expanses of thick, tough *ichu* grass punctuated by numerous small lakes and bogs. The *puna* is typically cold, rainy, and windy, with temperatures ranging from daytime highs of 21° C to near freezing at night. It is the native habitat of the Andean camelids (llamas and alpacas), while potatoes are the primary cultigen of this zone.

Physical Features

Because of its remote location, Huánaco Pampa is one of the best-preserved provincial Inca administrative centers in the empire. Located on the main Inca highway between Cuzco and the northern provinces, Huánaco Pampa contains the remains of nearly 4000 structures and covers an area of 2 sq km (Morris and Thompson 1985: 56). The site is dominated by an immense rectangular plaza over half a kilometer in length. In the center of the plaza sits a massive *ushnu*, 32 × 48 × 4 m tall, constructed of fine-cut masonry (Shea 1966). The rest of the city, which radiates from the central plaza, is divided into four major sections (Harth-terré 1964; Morris 1984; Morris and Thompson 1970). The eastern sector contains the most impressive architecture and is believed to have been the palace compound of the Inca royalty (Morris 1976, 1984). Two magnificent *kallanka* and a series of eight fine cut-stone gateways with carved pumas link the great central plaza with the smaller interior courts of this compound. Residences of the *aqllakuna* (chosen women) and associated workshops, where spinning, weaving, and brewing were undertaken, were identified in the northern sector (Morris 1974; Murra and Morris 1976). The numerous small circular structures found around the site, not a common element of Inca architecture, likely represent the residences of the local, non-Inca workforce (Morris and Thompson 1985: 62). On the hillside adjacent to the south of the city, the Inca erected orderly rows of some 500 storehouses, or *qollka*. Archaeological excavations revealed that these once contained potatoes, maize, and other foodstuffs received by the state as tribute (Morris 1972, 1974, 1976, 1986).

Cultural Aspects

Huánaco Pampa was one of the largest administrative centers in the Inca empire. Founded c. A.D. 1475 during the reign of Topa Inca, the center was constructed on a previously unoccupied site (Morris 1972), although the region immediately surrounding was inhabited by several different ethnic groups (Grosboll 1987; Ortíz de Zúñiga 1967, 1972; Thompson 1968, 1972; Thompson and Murra 1966). There are numerous structures present at the site, but it has been suggested that the permanent population was relatively small (Morris and Thompson 1985). The site contains no features that could be interpreted as defensive or military in nature (Gasparini and Margolies 1980: 103). Based on the archaeological evidence, Morris (1982, 1986) suggests that rather than having had a primarily bureaucratic or military function, Huánaco Pampa served essentially as a center of state hospitality and the ritual fulfillment of state obligations of reciprocity toward its subjects.

References

Gasparini, Graziano, and Luise Margolies (1980). *Inca Architecture*, trans. P. Lyon. Bloomington: Indiana University Press.

Grosboll, Sue (1987). "Ethnic Boundaries within the Inca Empire: Evidence from Huánaco, Peru." In *Ethnicity and Culture*, ed. R. Auger et al. Calgary: University of Calgary Press, 115–124.

Harth-terré, Emilio (1964). "El pueblo de Huánaco Viejo." *Arquitecto Peruano* 1–20: 320–321.

Morris, Craig (1972). "State Settlements in Tawantinsuyu: A Strategy of Compulsory Urbanism." In *Contemporary Archaeology*, ed. M. Leone. Carbondale: University of Southern Illinois Press, 391–401.

Morris, Craig (1974). "Reconstructing Patterns of Non-agricultural Production in the Inca Economy: Archaeology and Documents in Institutional Analysis." In *Reconstructing Complex Societies: An Archaeological Colloquium*, ed. C. Moore. Chicago: American Schools of Oriental Research (Suppl. Bulletin, no. 20), 49–68.

Morris, Craig (1975). "Sampling in the Excavation of Urban Sites: The Case of Huánaco Pampa." In *Sampling in Archaeology*, ed. J. Mueller. Tucson: University of Arizona Press,

Morris, Craig (1976). "Master Design of the Inca." *Natural History* 85, 10: 58–67.

Morris, Craig (1982). "The Infrastructure of Inka Control in the Peruvian Central Highlands." In *The Inca and Aztec States, 1400–1800: Anthropology and History*, ed. G. A. Collier, R. I. Rosaldo, and J. D. Wirth. New York: Academic Press, 153–172.

Morris, Craig (1986). "Storage, Supply, and Redistribution in the Economy of the Inka State." In *Anthropological History of Andean Polities*, ed. J. Murra, N. Wachtel, and J. Revel. New York: Academic Press, 59–68.

Morris, Craig, and Donald Thompson (1970). "Huánaco Viejo: An Inca Administrative Center." *American Antiquity* 35: 344–362.

Morris, Craig, and Donald Thompson (1985). *Huánaco Viejo: An Inca Administrative Center*. London: Thames and Hudson.

Murra, John (1962). "An Archaeological Restudy of an Andean Ethnohistorical Account." *American Antiquity* 28: 1–4.

Murra, John, and Craig Morris (1976). "Dynastic Oral Tradition, Administrative Records, and Archaeology in the Andes." *World Archaeology* 7: 269–282.

Ortíz de Zúñiga, Iñigo (1967). *Visita de la Provincia León de Huánaco en 1562*, Tomo I, ed. J. Murra. Huánaco, Peru: Universidad Nacional Hermilio Valdizán.

Ortíz de Zúñiga, Iñigo (1972). *Visita de la Provincia León de Huánaco en 1562*, Tomo II, ed. J. Murra. Huánaco, Peru: Universidad Nacional Hermilio Valdizán.

Shea, Daniel (1966). "El conjunto arquitectónico central en la plaza de Huánaco Viejo." *Centro de Investigación Antropológica, Huánaco* 1: 108–116.

Thompson, Donald (1968). "Huánaco, Peru: A Survey of a Province of the Inca Empire." *Archaeology* 21, 3: 174–181.

Thompson, Donald (1968). "Incaic Installations at Huánaco and Pumpu." *Actas y Memorias del XXXVII Congreso Internacional de Americanistas* (Buenos Aires) 1: 67–74.

Thompson, Donald (1972). "Peasant Inca Villages in the Huánaco Region." *Verhandlungen des XXXVIII Internationalen Americanisten Kongresses* (Stuttgart-Munchen) 4: 61–66.

Thompson, Donald, and John Murra (1966). "Inca Bridges in the Region of Huánaco Viejo." *American Antiquity* 31: 632–639.

Incallacta

TIME PERIOD: c. 528–468 B.P.

LOCATION: Near the town of Pocona, Cochabamba province, central Bolivia, at the eastern edge of the Inca empire.

DESCRIPTIVE SUMMARY

Local Environment

Located at an altitude of approximately 3000 m above sea level, the site occupies a high river terrace between two streams. Vegetation at the site is dense and xerophytic.

Physical Features

Incallacta is considered a military fortification because of its defensive features and its strategic location (Hyslop 1990: 176). The central portion of the site, as well as the steep hill to the north, is enclosed by stone walls (Hyslop 1990: 176). The massive north wall reaches 5 m in height and is 1.5–2 m thick (Hyslop 1990: 180). Notable features of this wall include its zigzag layout reminiscent of Saqsaywaman, the small oblique windows built into the wall along certain segments, and the low stone bench attached to the interior side of the wall along which troops could have patrolled (Hyslop 1990: 180).

The central portion of the site is a large, irregularly shaped plaza divided into two halves by a large terrace wall (Ellefsen 1973a, 1973b; Gasparini and Margolies 1980: 119; Hyslop 1990: 83). Situated on the northeast side of the plaza is an immense rectangular structure, or *kallanka*, with 12 doors that face onto the plaza (Gasparini and Margolies 1980: 207–212). Numerous other structures including several stone circular foundations interpreted as *qollka* (storage houses), a possible barracks complex behind the large *kallanka*, and various other groupings of rectangular structures arranged around patios (*kancha*) are also present at the site (Gasparini and Margolies 1980: 119; Hyslop 1990: 179). Buildings at Incallacta are typically constructed of a double row of stones set in mortar; many of the walls were subsequently plastered and painted (Hyslop 1990: 179).

A large rock with an artificially flattened surface presumed to be an *ushnu* feature is found at the edge of the plaza rather than in the center, a situation noted at only a few other Inca sites, including Tambo Colorado and Pachacamac on the Peruvian coast (Hyslop 1990: 85, 179). Another interesting feature of the site is a unique towerlike structure with zigzag walls, thought to have calendrical or astronomical significance (Hyslop 1990: 227). Prominently located on a steep slope in the western sector of the site, the structure is approximately 7 m in length and 4.5 m tall (Hyslop 1990: 227).

Cultural Aspects

Incallacta is one of largest Inca military installations in the southern sector of the empire (Nordenskiold 1915). The site formed one of a series of fortifications protecting the Inca frontier against the unconquered tribes of the eastern lowlands (González and Cravotto 1977; Hyslop 1990: 82–85, 176–180). Being more elaborate in construction than most Inca fortress sites, it is thought that Incallacta may have also served as the state administrative center for the region (Hyslop 1990: 182).

Construction of the site is attributed to the ruler Topa Inca Yupanqui. Historic sources, which refer to the site as Cuzcotuiro or Cuzcotuyo (Rowe 1985: 215–217), indicate that it was populated by *mitmaqkuna* and Inca lords (*orejones*) who were tasked with defending the area (Hyslop 1990: 176; Wachtel 1982). The site was reportedly attacked and partially destroyed by the Guaraní, an eastern lowland tribe, in 1525 (Gasparini and Margolies 1980: 210).

References

Ellefsen, Bernardo (1973a). "La división en mitades de la ciudad incaica." *Bulletin de l'Institut Francais d'Études Andines* 2, 4: 23–28.

Ellefsen, Bernardo (1973b). "El patrón urbano incaico según el Professor Zuidema y su relación con Incallacta." *Bulletin de l'Institut Francais d'Études Andines* 2, 4: 29–34.

Gasparini, Graziano, and Luise Margolies (1980). *Inca Architecture*, trans. P. J. Lyon. Bloomington: Indiana University Press.

González, Alberto Rex, and Antonio Cravotto (1977). *Estudio arqueológico e inventario de las ruinas de Inkallajta*. Paris: UNESCO Informe Técnico, PP/1975–76/3.411.6.

Hyslop, John (1990). *Inka Settlement Planning*. Austin: University of Texas Press.

Nordenskiold, Erland von (1915). "Incallacta, eine befestigte und von Inca Tupac Yupanqui angelegte Stadt." *Ymer* 2: 169–185.

Rowe, John H. (1985). "Probanza de los incas nietos de conquistadores." *Histórica* 9, 2: 193–245.

Wachtel, Nathan (1982). "The Mitimas of the Cochabamba Valley: The Colonization Policy of Huayna Capac." In *The Inca and Aztec States, 1400–1800: Anthropology and History*, ed. G. A. Collier, R. I. Rosaldo, and J. D. Wirth. New York: Academic Press, 199–229.

Ingapirca

TIME PERIOD: 520–468 B.P.

LOCATION: Province of Cañar, southern highlands of Ecuador, about 35 km due north of Cuenca.

DESCRIPTIVE SUMMARY

Local Environment

The site is located at the upper, eastern end of the Cañar river basin in the bare, rolling hills of southern Ecuador. At an elevation of 3160 m above sea level, Ingapirca occupies a transitional zone between the fertile sub-Andean valleys and the cold wet grasslands, or *páramos*. The climate of this region is cool, with an average annual temperature of 10–14° C.

Physical Features

Ingapirca, which means "Inca walls" in Quechua, is a name loosely applied to archaeological ruins throughout the former Inca empire. In Ecuador, Ingapirca is the name given to the best-preserved Inca site in the country (Alcina Franch 1978; Bedoya 1978a; Cueva 1971; Fresco 1983). Located in Cañari territory, the site of Ingapirca contains both monumental architecture and high-quality stonework (Bedoya 1978a; Fresco 1984; Humboldt 1878; Juan and Ulloa 1748). The site is best known for a large oval structure of fine Inca masonry called El Castillo. The oval form is rare in Inca architecture (Gasparini and Margolies 1980: 289–299) and may, in this case, have had some astronomical significance (Ziolkowski and Sadowski 1984). Other Inca constructions at the site include rectangular residential structures, storage units, waterworks, and agricultural terraces (Alcina Franch 1978; Bedoya 1978a, 1978b; Fresco 1984).

Archaeological evidence indicates that many of the Inca structures at Ingapirca were erected over preexisting architectural features. Radiocarbon dates and associated Cashaloma pottery indicate that the site was occupied by the local Cañari population prior to the Inca invasion of the region (Hyslop 1990: 262). The sector of the site referred to as Pilaloma is believed to have been the original Cañari precinct. Excavations in this area revealed a walled enclosure containing a series of rectangular rooms organized around a central patio. A monolith in the center of the patio marked the location of a shallow sepulcher containing the remains of 11 individuals and a wealth of funerary offerings, including Cashaloma pottery vessels, copper objects, and *Spondylus* shell (Fresco and Cobo 1978).

Cultural Aspects

The Cañaris were conquered by Topa Inca Yupanqui toward the close of the 15th century after considerable resistance (Engwall 1995; Oberem 1981; Salomon 1987). Ethnohistoric and archaeological data suggest that Ingapirca, known originally as Hatun Cañar, was the principal settlement and sacred origin place of the ancient Cañari nation (Arriaga 1922; Fock and Krener 1978; Idrovo 1979). A well-known strategy of Inca imperial expansion was to symbolically subordinate local deities and sacred places to the state religion. The superimposition of Inca structures over the Cañari capital likely reflects a conscious effort on the part of the Inca lords to dominate and coopt the sacred significance of this site.

References

Alcina Franch, José (1978). "Ingapirca: Arquitectura y áreas de asentamiento." *Revista Española de Antropología Americana* 8: 127–146.

Arriaga, Jesús (1922). *Apuntes de Arqueología Cañar*. Cuenca, Ecuador: Imprenta del Clero.

Bedoya Maruri, Angel (1978a). "Monumento Incaico de Ingapirca en Cañar." *Revista Geográfica* (Quito) 7: 133–149.

Bedoya Maruri, Angel (1978b). *La Arqueología en la región interandina de Ecuador*. Quito: Casa de la Cultura Ecuatoriana.

Cueva, Juan (1971). "Descubrimientos arqueológicos en Ingapirca." *Revista de Antropología* 3: 215–226.

Engwall, Evan (1995). "Turbulent Relations Recast: The Mythohistory of the Cañaris and the Inca Empire." *Journal of the Steward Anthropological Society* 23, 1–2: 345–361.

Fock, Niels, and Eva Krener (1978). "Los Cañaris del Ecuador y sus conceptos etnohistóricos sobre los Incas." In *Amerikanistische Studien: Festschrift für Hermann Trimborn*, ed. R. Hartmann and U. Oberem. St. Agustin: Haus Volker und Kulturen, Anthropos-Institut, 170–181.

Fresco, Antonio (1983). "Arquitectura de Ingapirca (Cañar-Ecuador)." *Boletín de los Museos del Banco Central del Ecuador* 3: 195–212.

Fresco, Antonio (1984). *La Arqueología de Ingapirca (Ecuador): Costumbres funerarias, cerámica y otros materiales*. Quito, Ecuador: Gráficas Mediavilla Hnos.

Fresco, Antonio, and Waina Cobo (1978). "Consideraciones et-nohistóricas acerca de una tumba de poso y cámera de Ingapirca (Ecuador)." *Revista Española de Antropología Americana* 14: 85–101.

Gasparini, Graziano, and Luise Margolies (1980). *Inca Architecture*, trans. P. Lyon. Bloomington: Indiana University Press.

Humboldt, Alejandro von (1878). *Sitios de las Cordilleras y Monumentos de los Pueblos Indígenas de América*. Madrid: Imprenta y Librería de Gaspar.

Hyslop, John (1990). *Inka Settlement Planning*. Austin: University of Texas Press.

Idrovo, Jaime (1979). "*Aspectos funerarios entre los Cañaris de Ingapirca*." Paris: U.E.R. d'Art et Archéologie.

Juan, Jorge, and Antonio de Ulloa (1748). *Relación Histórica del Viaje a la América Meridional*. Madrid: Antonio Marín, Impresor.

Oberem, Udo (1981). "Los Cañaris y la conquista española de la sierra ecuatoriana: otro cápitulo de las relaciones interétnicas en el siglo XVI." In *Contribución a la Etnohistória Ecuatoriana*, ed. S. Moreno. Otavalo, Ecuador: Instituto Otavaleño de Antropología, Pendoneros, no. 20, 129–152.

Salomon, Frank (1987). "Ancestors, Grave Robbers, and the Possible Antecedents of Cañari "Inca-ism." In *Natives and Neighbors in South America*, ed. H. Sklar and F. Salomon. Göteberg: Etnografiska Museum, Etnologiska Studier, vol. 38, 207–232.

Ziolkowski, Marius, and Robert Sadowski (1984). "Informe acerca de las investigaciones arqueoastronómicas en el área central de Ingapirca (Ecuador)." *Revista Española de Antropología Americana* 14: 103–125.

Island of the Sun

TIME PERIOD: 528–468 B.P.

LOCATION: In the southern part of lake Titicaca, just off of the Copacabana peninsula, Bolivia.

DESCRIPTIVE SUMMARY

Local Environment

The mountainous Island of the Sun is located at the south end of lake Titicaca, the highest navigable body of water in the world. The elevation of the island is 3850 m above sea level, and the climate is generally cold and arid. The Island of the Sun, which is oriented northwest-southeast, is approximately 10 km in length. The associated Island of the Moon (Koati) is located approximately 5 km to the east.

Physical Features

The Island of the Sun, together with the nearby Island of the Moon and the Copacabana peninsula, made up one of the most sacred districts in the Inca empire. The most important part of this religious complex was the northern end of the Island of the Sun. The center of ritual activity at the north end was a large plaza associated with a great rock (Bandelier 1910; Hyslop 1990: 76–77; Stanish and Bauer 1999). In Inca times, this rock was said to have been covered with gold plates on one side and fine *cumbi* cloth on the other (Cobo 1964, Bk.13; Hyslop 1990: 77). Inca myths relate that the sun arose from within or behind the great rock (Hyslop 1990: 76–77). The plaza reportedly contained an altar and a large basin and was presumably the site of ritual libation and sacrifice (Cobo 1964, Bk. 13; Hyslop 1990: 77–78).

The approach to the north end of the Island of the Sun was via a well-defined route along which were located a number of Inca structures and features. The most impressive of these is a two-story building at the south end of the island, known as Pilco Kayma. This exceptional structure incorporates corbeled vaults and numerous first floor chambers with double- and triple-jamb wall niches (Gasparini and Margolies 1980: 154). Other Inca buildings on the island included *qollkas*, a possible *aqllawasi*, and residential structures (Hemming and Ranney 1982: 58; Hyslop 1990). Fine Inca terraces also cover much of the Island of the Sun (Hyslop 1990: 286). At the north end, these terraces, together with a stone wall, form part of a barrier that partitions the sacred precinct (Hyslop 1990: 286).

Cultural Aspects

The islands of lake Titicaca were considered sacred by the local populace long before their appropriation by the Inca. It is likely for this reason that the islands figure so prominently in Inca origin myths. The Island of the Sun was variously construed by the Cuzqueños as the birthplace of the sun, of humankind, and of the Inca dynasty (Hemming and Ranney 1982: 54–64). The Inca structures found on the Island of the Sun and the nearby Island of the Moon were likely built during the reign of Topa Inca Yupanqui, following his reconquest of this region c. A.D. 1472 (Cobo 1964, Bk. 13: 190–191). Decorative elements such as the stepped motif and recessed cruciforms observed on some structures are reminiscent of Tiwanaku and suggest the use of local builders in their construction (Gasparini and Margolies 1980: 154).

Both historical and archaeological evidence indicates that the Islands of the Sun and Moon were dedicated exclusively to religious activity and treated as an imperial Mecca by the Inca (Bandelier 1910; Hyslop 1990: 301–303; Mesa and Gisbert 1972; Ramos Gavilán 1976; Reinhard 1992: 101–109; Stanish and Bauer 1999). Pilgrims traveling to the sacred sanctuaries of the islands would undergo purification rituals on the Copacabana peninsula prior to crossing (Ramos Gavilán 1976). Landing at the south end of the Island of the Sun, the pilgrims would follow a processional route punctuated by various Inca buildings and features to the sacred northern promontory (Cobo 1964; Stanish and Bauer 1999). These structures presumably served as stations where specific rituals were performed as part of the sojourn (Hyslop 1990: 301–303). Finds of both Tiwanaku and Inca offertory artifacts off the northern tip of the island reflect the historic continuity of religious tradition in this region (Reinhard 1992: 103). Inca materials recovered from the underwater reef include numerous carved stone boxes and several miniature gold statuettes (Reinhard 1992: 101–109).

References

Bandelier, Adolph (1910). *The Islands of Titicaca and Coati.* New York: Hispanic Society of America.

Cobo, Bernabé (1964). *Historia del Nuevo Mundo* [1653]. Madrid: Biblioteca de Autores Españoles, Ediciones Atlas.

Gasparini, Graziano, and Luise Margolies (1980). *Inca Architecture,* trans. P. J. Lyon. Bloomington: Indiana University Press.

Hemming, John, and Edward Ranney (1982). *Monuments of the Inca.* Albuquerque: University of New Mexico Press.

Hyslop, John (1990). *Inka Settlement Planning.* Austin: University of Texas Press.

Mesa, José de, and Teresa Gisbert (1972). "La arquitectura incaica en Bolivia." *Boletín del Centro de Investigaciones Históricas y Estéticas* (Caracas) 13: 129–168.

Ramos Gavilán, Alonso (1976). *Historia de Nuestra Señora de Copacabana* [1621]. La Paz: Cámara Nacional de Comercio, y Industria.

Reinhard, Johan (1992). "Sacred Peaks of the Andes." *National Geographic* 181, 3: 84–111.

Stanish, Charles, and Brian Bauer (in press). "Pilgrimage and the Geography of Power in the Inka State." In *Variations in the Expressions of Inka Power,* ed. R. Matos, R. Burger, and C. Morris. Washington, D.C.: Dumbarton Oaks Press.

Machu Picchu

TIME PERIOD: c. 550–470 B.P.

LOCATION: 120 km northwest of Cuzco in the Urubamba river valley, Peru.

DESCRIPTIVE SUMMARY

Local Environment

The site of Machu Picchu, at 2560 m above sea level, sits atop a mountain saddle that drops precipitously on three sides to the Urubamba river 600 m below. At the north end of this spur rises the towering pinnacle of Huayna Picchu, while behind it hovers the peak of Machu Picchu, which gives its name to the site. The rugged eastern slopes of the Andes in this zone are dissected by fast-flowing streams and steep valleys of sheer granite cliffs. The climate is humid and rainy, supporting an extreme degree of biodiversity. The vegetation surrounding the site includes a dense tropical rainforest of hardwoods, bromeliads, ferns, and grasses.

Physical Features

The site of Machu Picchu laid virtually undisturbed from the time of its abandonment in the early 16th century until its dramatic rediscovery by Hiram Bingham in 1911. Occupying a strategic position atop a steep ridge in the Urubamba canyon, this most famous of South American sites is recognized for its remarkable preservation and the extreme beauty of its architecture. Much of the hilltop on which the site sits was terraced. These terraces likely served both for agricultural purposes and erosion control (Hemming and Ranney 1982: 126). Machu Picchu lies at the end of a chain of Inca towns and agricultural stations connected by a spur of the royal Inca road (Hyslop 1990; Meisch 1985). The entire Urubamba valley, from Pisac to Machu Picchu, is full of ceremonial sites, small residential clusters, and large expanses of terraced agricultural works, suggesting the esteem in which the valley was held by the Inca (Fejos 1944; Niles 1988).

The site of Machu Picchu has three basic architectural elements: elite residential compounds, religious structures, and terraces. Staircases and sculpted rocks also abound at the site. The carved stones, with their stepped surfaces, carved channels, and molded protrusions, were likely considered *huacas,* or sacred shrines (Hyslop 1990: 108–112; MacLean 1986). Many of the modified outcrops and boulders are incorporated into the architecture and most sectors of the site seem to have a sacred stone around which they were constructed (Bingham 1913: 471). The site is organized according to the Inca principle of upper (*hanan*) and lower (*hurin*) halves. These two halves occupy either side of a central plaza (Gasparini and Margolies 1980; Hemming and Ranney 1982). The western (*hanan*) sector contains the majority of the religious architecture, while the eastern half consists primarily of residential structures (Bingham 1913, 1979).

One of the most important temple groupings in the western sector is the Torreón. The main feature of this structure is a curved wall that surrounds a large carved rock altar (Hemming and Ranney 1982: 133; Hyslop 1990: 229–232). Immediately below the Torreón is a natural cave into which the Inca carved several large niches and a stepped partition. Adjacent to the Torreón is a series of cascading "baths" or fountains. Beyond it lies a cluster of finely crafted residential structures known as the "King's Group." From here, a long stairway leads to the most sacred sector of the site, at the heart of which is an open area known as the Sacred Plaza (Bingham 1979; Hemming and Ranney 1982). The plaza, delineated on the east side by the famous Temple of Three Windows, contains three structures into which are incorporated several phenomenally large building stones. Beyond the Sacred Plaza, a series of staircases leads to the summit of the religious complex, which is crowned by the famous carved stone projection known as the Intihuatana ("hitching post of the sun").

The eastern half of the city includes a dense concentration of residential structures representing a variety of architectural types including one-, two-, and three-story buildings, a double *masma*, and a barracks-like structure, or *kallanka* (Hemming and Ranney 1982). The domestic structures were typically arranged around a central courtyard to form a self-contained compound (*kancha*), although each compound at Machu Picchu was unique in some aspect (Bingham 1979: 79). The majority of these structures display features associated with elite architecture such as fine cut-stone masonry or double-jambed doors, suggesting the high status of their occupants. The site contains approximately 200 residential structures, which would suggest a total population of no more than 1000 (Hemming and Ranney 1982: 133).

Cultural Aspects

The construction of Machu Picchu was carefully planned and executed within a relatively short period, probably with the use of *mit'a* labor. The architecture is uniformly late imperial Inca in style (Hemming and Ranney 1982: 133). The site of Machu Picchu has lent itself to numerous interpretations, including that of frontier citadel (Bingham 1979), military outpost, sanctuary of the Inca's "chosen women" (Bingham 1913, 1979), astronomical observatory (Dearborn and Schreiber 1986; Dearborn and White 1982, 1983; Dearborn et al. 1987), sacred religious center (Reinhard 1991, 1992), and last refuge of the Inca (Bingham 1979; Valcárcel 1935).

However, the small size, fine masonry, and architectural components of the site combine to suggest that Machu Picchu was likely constructed as the royal estate of an Inca emperor (Rowe 1985). Such country estates

would be visited periodically by the ruler and his royal retinue. Here the royal family would relax, hunt, and entertain other elites (Niles 1988). A document written in 1568 suggests that the imperial sector within which Machu Picchu is located pertained to the emperor Inca Pachacuti (Rowe 1985).

Over the course of investigations at the site, Bingham's crew located approximately 143 burials, the majority of which had simply been placed in shallow caves and crevices on the slopes below the urban area (Bingham 1913, 1979). The expedient nature of these burials, the paucity of associated grave goods, and the indicators of stress noted on the remains (Eaton 1916) suggest that these individuals were not of the elite class but more likely the servants and retainers of the Inca. This lends support to the interpretation of the site as a country estate of the Inca nobility.

Defensive features of the site include its strategic location atop a narrow ridge, the presence of a deep dry moat and double wall on the one approachable side, the sentry post atop Huayna Picchu, and the single, securable entry to the site at the southwest corner (Hemming and Ranney 1982). Although Bingham (1913, 1979) was impressed by the military value of these features, Fejos was not, suggesting that they more likely served to enforce sacred partitioning.

References

Bingham, Hiram (1913). "In the Wonderland of Peru." *National Geographic* 24, 4: 387–573.

Bingham, Hiram (1979) [1930]. *Machu Picchu: A Citadel of the Inca.* New York: Hacker Art Books.

Dearborn, David, and Katharina Schreiber (1986). "Here Comes the Sun: The Cuzco-Machu Picchu Connection." *Archaeoastronomy* 9, 1–4: 114–122.

Dearborn, David, and Raymond White (1982). "Archaeoastronomy at Machu Picchu." In *Ethnoastronomy and Archaeoastronomy in the American Tropics,* ed. A. Aveni and G. Urton. New York: Annals of the New York Academy of Sciences 385, 249–259.

Dearborn, David, and Raymond White (1983). "The Torreón of Machu Picchu as an Observatory." *Archaeoastronomy* 5: S37–S45.

Dearborn, David, Katharina Schreiber, and Raymond White (1987). "Intimachay, a December Solstice Observatory." *American Antiquity* 52: 346–352.

Eaton, George (1916). "The Collection of Osteological Materials from Machu Picchu." *Memoirs of the Connecticut Academy of Arts and Sciences* 5: 3–96.

Fejos, Paul (1944). *Archaeological Explorations in the Cordillera Vilcabamba.* Viking Fund Publications in Anthropology 3, New York.

Gasparini, Graziano, and Luise Margolies (1980). *Inca Architecture,* trans. P. J. Lyon. Bloomington: Indiana University Press.

Hemming, John, and Edward Ranney (1982). *Monuments of the Inca.* Albuquerque: University of New Mexico Press.

Hyslop, John (1990). *Inka Settlement Planning.* Austin: University of Texas Press.

MacLean, Margaret (1986). "Sacred Land, Sacred Water: Inca Landscape Planning in the Cuzco Area." Ph.D. diss., University of California, Berkeley.

Meisch, Lynn (1985). "Machu Picchu: Conserving an Inca Treasure." *Archaeology* 6: 18–25.

Niles, Susan (1988). "Looking for "Lost" Inca Palaces." *Expedition* 30, 3: 56–64.

Reinhard, Johan (1991). *Machu Picchu: The Sacred Center.* Lima: Nuevas Imagenes.

Reinhard, Johan (1992). "Sacred Peaks of the Andes." *National Geographic* 181, 3: 84–111.

Rowe, John H. (1985). "Probanza de los incas nietos de conquistadores." *Histórica* 9, 2: 193–245.

Rowe, John H. (1990). "Machu Picchu a luz de documentos de siglo XVI." *Histórica* 14, 1: 139–154.

Valcárcel, Luis (1935). "Los trabajos arqueológicos en el departamento de Cuzco." *Revista del Museo Nacional* 4: 163–208.

Ollantaytambo

TIME PERIOD: c. 560–468 B.P.

LOCATION: Southern highlands of Peru in the Urubamba river valley, approximately 70 km northwest of Cuzco.

DESCRIPTIVE SUMMARY

Local Environment

The site is located at the confluence of Patakancha and Urubamba rivers at an elevation of 2800 m above sea level. The climate is relatively arid, and the average annual temperature is 18° C.

Physical Features

Ollantaytambo is one of the best preserved examples of an Inca town and is particularly interesting for the variety of architectural styles, building types, and masonry techniques it exhibits (Bingham 1916; Pardo 1946; Protzen 1993; Sawyer 1980; Squier 1877). Ollantaytambo is also remarkable for the number of unfinished construction projects found there, the evidence of which remains in situ.

The site is dominated by a hilltop religious precinct known as the Fortress. On the alluvial floodplain below, the town of Ollantaytambo is divided into east and west sectors by the Patakancha river. The larger, eastern half is laid out on a grid that accommodates numerous walled residential compounds or *kancha*. These highly standardized compounds consisted of a central patio surrounded by four structures arranged so as to leave a small open courtyard in each corner (Bingham 1916; Gasparini and Margolies 1980; Protzen 1993). Each block in the grid system was a double compound that shared a central wall, although they were not otherwise linked. The western sector of Ollantaytambo, situated at the foot of the religious precinct, was not gridded but rather was organized around a central plaza (Protzen 1993: 66–70). The structures facing this main plaza are monumental in scale and exhibit unusually large doorways (Protzen 1993: 68). The area appears less residential and was more likely utilized for ceremonial or military purposes (Hyslop 1990: 194). Many of the structures in Ollantaytambo exhibit trapezoidal niches on the interior walls and prestigious double-jambed doors.

The religious or ceremonial sector of the site occupies a rocky spur overlooking the Urubamba river. An imposing flight of terraces with associated staircases leads to the main temple sector at the top. This component of the site was never fully finished. It is capped, however, by a spectacular megalithic wall of six elegantly carved monoliths, possibly intended to have been part of a temple or platform structure (Protzen 1993). Several aspects of the masonry found in the temple district, such as the subtly "tailed" joints in the "wall of the unfinished gate" (Harth-terré 1965: 158) and the stone fillet between the six great monoliths, are unique to Ollantaytambo (Protzen 1993: 82). The stone for the structures in the temple district was quarried from an area 5 km away on the opposite side of the river (Hemming and Ranney 1982; Protzen 1986). The blocks were dragged to the construction site via an impressive ramp that was integrated into the southwestern flank of the temple hill. In addition to the temple sector, there are two other architectural units on the hilltop. These areas contain simpler rectangular structures of fieldstone and mortar construction (Llanos 1936; Protzen 1993). Above and below the main temple area are numerous carved rocks, fountains, and shrines (Hemming and Ranney 1982; Protzen 1993).

Much of the Urubamba valley in the Ollantaytambo region is elaborately terraced. Although these features were used for agricultural purposes, they also symbolized the ability of the Inca to dominate the landscape and their subject population. Finely engineered irrigation canals around Ollantaytambo brought water to terraces from sources as far as 10 miles away (Protzen 1993). Produce from the Ollantaytambo area was housed in narrow rectangular storage structures that cling to the steep slopes above and behind the main site (Nuñez del Prado 1966–67; Protzen 1993). The town was connected to the royal Inca road (*capac ñan*) by a suspension bridge over the Urubamba river, the pier and abutments of which are still in use today (Protzen 1993: 20).

Cultural Aspects

The people of the pre-Incaic settlement of Ollantaytambo and the lower Urubamba valley were reportedly conquered by the Inca Pachacuti (Cobo 1964; Sarmiento de Gamboa 1943, ch. 35). Pachacuti subsequently absorbed Ollantaytambo into his personal estate and ordered the construction of elaborate buildings (Sarmiento de Gamboa 1943, ch. 40). The location of the site, its architectural features, the fine stone masonry, and the documentary evidence suggest that it functioned as a royal country estate of the Inca ruler Pachacuti (Niles 1988; Protzen 1993).

At least two Inca construction phases are recognized at the site (Gibaja 1984; Kendall 1985; Protzen 1993). The first pertains to the initial building period, which probably began around A.D. 1440. Both documentary evidence and the presence of specific masonry techniques at the site suggest that stonemasons from the Qollasuyu sector of the empire were brought to oversee construction (Hemming and Ranney 1982: 110; Sarmiento de Gamboa 1943, ch. 40: 12; Protzen 1993: 269). Several generations later, Ollantaytambo was used as the temporary headquarters of the rebel leader Manco Inca in his campaign against the Spanish. From this stronghold, Manco repelled Pizarro's forces in 1536 (Hemming and Ranney 1982: 99–117; Pizarro 1978; Protzen 1993). The second episode of construction activity at the site, which involved both remodeling and new building, is attributed to Manco Inca's postconquest occupation. A series of defensive features was probably added during this phase, including a chain of fortified guard stations, a strategic rechannelization of the Urubamba river, a flight of steep outer terraces, and a formidable walled and gated entry at the eastern end (Protzen 1993).

References

Bingham, Hiram (1916). "Further Explorations in the Land of the Incas: The Peruvian Expedition of 1915 of the National Geographic Society and Yale University." *National Geographic* 29, 5: 413–473.

Cobo, Bernabé (1964). *Historia del Nuevo Mundo* [1653]. Madrid: Biblioteca de Autores Españoles, Ediciones Atlas.

Gasparini, Graziano, and Luise Margolies (1980). *Inca Architecture*, trans. P. J. Lyon. Bloomington: Indiana University Press.

Gibaja, Arminda (1984). "Sequencia cronológica de Ollantaytambo." In *Current Archaeological Projects in the Central Andes: Some Approaches and Results; Proceedings of the 44th International Congress of Americanists*, ed. A. Kendall. Oxford: British Archaeological Reports, International Series, no. 210, 225–243.

Harth-Terré, Emilio (1965). "Técnica y arte de la cantería incaica." *Revista Universitaria* (*Cuzco*) 51–52: 152–168.

Hemming, John, and Edward Ranney (1982). *Monuments of the Inca.* Albuquerque: University of New Mexico Press.

Hyslop, John (1990). *Inka Settlement Planning.* Austin: University of Texas Press.

Kendall, Ann (1985). *Aspects of Inca Architecture: Description, Function, and Chronology.* Oxford: British Archaeological Reports, International Series, no. 242.

Llanos, Luis (1936). "Trabajos arqueológicos en el Departamento de Cuzco." *Revista del Museo Nacional* (Lima) 5, 2: 123–156.

Niles, Susan (1988). "Looking for "Lost" Inca Palaces." *Expedition* 30: 56–64.

Nuñez del Prado, Oscar (1966–1967). "La vivienda Inca actual." *Revista Universitaria* (*Cuzco*) 130–133: 320–324.

Pardo, Luis (1946). "Ollantaitampu (una ciudad megalítica)." *Revista de la Sección Arqueológica de la Universidad Nacional del Cuzco* 2: 47–73.

Pizarro, Pedro (1978) [1571]. *Relación del Descubrimiento y Conquista de los reinos del Perú.* Lima: Pontífica Universidad Católica del Perú.

Protzen, Jean Pierre (1986). "Inca Stonemasonry." *Scientific American* 254, 2: 94–105.

Protzen, Jean Pierre (1993). *Inca Architecture and Construction at Ollantaytambo.* Oxford: Oxford University Press.

Sarmiento de Gamboa, Pedro (1943). *Historia de los Incas* [1572]. Buenos Aires: Editores Emece.

Sawyer, Alan (1980). "Squier's Palace at Ollanta." *Ñawpa Pacha* 18: 63–73.

Squier, George (1877). *Peru: Incidents of Travel and Exploration in the Land of the Incas.* London: Macmillan.

Rumicucho

TIME PERIOD: 530–468 B.P.

LOCATION: On the equator, approximately 30 km north of Quito, Pichincha province, Ecuador.

DESCRIPTIVE SUMMARY

Local Environment

The site sits atop a low hill almost directly on the equator. The elevation of Rumicucho is 2405 m above sea level. The hilltop site is located at the edge of a semidesertic esplanade that drops off steeply into the canyon of the Guayllabamba river immediately to the east. The area receives very little rain (3–4 cm per year), is subject to frequent high winds, and has sandy soils and xerophytic vegetation.

Physical Features

The site of Rumicucho is traditionally described as a *pucara* or hilltop fortress, on the basis of its strategic location and presumed defensive terracing (Almeida 1984; Plaza 1976). But the archaeological materials recovered through excavation, together with other features of the site, suggest additional or alternative functions as well (Almeida 1984). Unlike other Inca fortresses, Rumicucho was not impregnable; there are no defensive ditches or moats, and the construction technique is finer than at most other pucaras.

The hill on which the site is located rises only 24 m above the plain, although it does afford a panoramic view of the surrounding region. Rumicucho occupies a portion of this hilltop, which measures 525 m long by 150 m wide and is oriented north-south. The top of the hill is ringed by a series of three concentric stone-faced terraces that give it the stepped appearance of a wedding cake. The terrace walls vary in height from 1–1.5 m. The hilltop is partitioned into five sectors or levels, each of which exhibits different types of features (Almeida 1984). The northernmost sector has a large open area enclosed by a stone wall and containing a small circular structure and a large rock (Almeida 1984: 27–29). The central sector, which is the highest, consists of a large rectangular platform that may have once held an *ushnu* (Hyslop 1990: 98–99). A set of stairs at either end of this platform provides access to the adjacent levels. The southernmost sector, which contains the most complex architecture on the site, may have been the residential zone (Almeida 1984: 30). Access to this sector is limited to two baffled entryways in the surrounding enclosure wall. All of the walls at the site are of typical *pirca* construction, which involves the use of minimally finished and fitted stones for the exterior wall surfaces and the filling of the interior core of the wall with rubble (Almeida 1984).

Cultural Aspects

Topa Inca Yupanqui likely ordered construction of Rumicucho during or shortly after the first Inca incursion into northern Ecuador toward the end of the 15th century (Oberem 1981; Salvador Lara 1972, 1980). Its strategic hilltop location and its basic architecture suggest that Rumicucho may have served as a frontier garrison for Inca troops (Almeida 1984; Plaza 1976). The lack of armaments and other defensive features at the site, however, tends to undercut this interpretation. Other aspects of the site, such as the circular structures and its location on the equator, suggest that Rumicucho may have held some ceremonial or religious significance linked to astronomical phenomena (Almeida 1984: 116). The presence of considerable domestic debris, including both local Caranqui and imperial Inca pottery, stone and bone

utensils, and quantities of faunal remains, suggests that the site had a significant residential component (Almeida 1984). The vast majority of the faunal remains recovered pertains to llama (Almeida 1984: 97–102). Excavations also produced a substantial number of bone artifacts related to textile manufacture, including needles, spindle whorls, and combs, suggesting specialized on-site production possibly related to tribute requirements (Almeida 1984: 77–84).

References

Almeida, Eduardo (1984). "Investigaciones arqueológicas en el Pucará de Rumicucho." In *El Pucará de Rumichucho*, ed. E. Almeida, and H. Jara. Quito: Miscelánea Antropológica Ecuatoriana, Serie Monografía 1, Museo del Banco Central del Ecuador.

Hyslop, John (1990). Inka *Settlement Planning* Austin: University of Texas Press.

Oberem, Udo (1988). "El período incaico en el Ecuador." In *Nueva Historia del Ecuador*, vol. II, ed. E. Ayala Mora. Quito: Corporación Editora Nacional, 135–165.

Plaza Schuller, Fernando (1976). *La Incursión Inca en el Septentrión Andino del Ecuador*. Otavalo, Ecuador: Instituto Otavaleño de Antropología.

Salvador Lara, Jorge (1972). "Quito en la prehistória." *Revista de la Universidad Católica del Ecuador* 1: 231–275.

Salvador Lara, Jorge (1980). "La resistencia del Reino de Quito contra la expansión incaica." *Historia del Ecuador*, Tomo II. Quito: Salvat Editores Ecuatoriana. 129–150.

Samaipata

TIME PERIOD: 528–468 B.P.

LOCATION: Santa Cruz province, southwestern Bolivia.

DESCRIPTIVE SUMMARY

Local Environment

The site is located at an elevation of 1650 m above sea level on the eastern slopes of the Andes. The climate is pleasant and the vegetation lush.

Physical Features

Samaipata is the largest of all known carved rock outcrops in the Inca empire, its sculpted surface covering approximately 10,000 sq m (Hyslop 1990: 122; Trimborn 1959, 1967). The general orientation of this massive outcrop of variegated sandstone is east-west, as are the principal channels and troughs carved into its relatively flat upper surface. Hundreds of shelves and steps have been sculpted into the gently sloping south face of the outcrop, while a series of elaborate rectangular niches adorns the north side (Hyslop 1990: 123). Spectacular relief carvings of felines, a bird, and a snake are found on the eastern side of the monument (D'Orbigny 1835–1847; Hyslop 1990: 123; Pucher 1945). Double zigzag channels forming three long, parallel rows of rhomboids are carved into the top of the outcrop. An unusual set of alternating rectangular and triangular shelves arranged in a ring is found on the highest elevation of the rock.

The Samaipata monument is associated with an Inca settlement that has not yet been fully mapped or tested (Meyers 1998). The estimated size of this settlement is approximately 30 ha (Rivera 1984: 46; Tapia 1984). Recent excavations have unearthed the remains of an Inca *kallanka*, or barracks, a residential compound (*kancha*), and storage facilities (*qollka*) (Meyers 1993).

Cultural Aspects

The site was purportedly the seat of the local Inca governor who controlled the easternmost extension of the Inca state (Boera and Rivera 1979; Hyslop 1990: 122). Historical sources suggest that Samaipata functioned as a fortress, but the lack of defensive features and the location of the site some distance from the actual eastern frontier argue against this interpretation (Hyslop 1990: 122; Trimborn 1967). The orderly arrangement of carved motifs and elements on the outcrop gives the overall impression of careful planning. Like other carved stones around the empire, however, the actual function is not entirely clear. Sacred rocks were regularly integrated into Inca architectural planning and obviously exerted some influence on site selection. In some cases, they may have functioned as offertory sites; in others, they may have constituted stations for the performance of ritual activity or the observance of astronomical phenomena (Hyslop 1990: 102–128).

References

Boera Rojo, Hugo, and Oswaldo Rivera Sundt (1979). *El Fuerte preincaico de Samaipata*. La Paz-Cochabamba: Editorial Los Amigos del Libro.

D'Orbigny, Alcide (1834–1847). *Voyage dans l'Amérique méridionale* Paris: F. G. Lemault .

Hyslop, John (1990). *Inka Settlement Planning*. Austin: University of Texas Press.

Meyers, Albert (1993). "Trabajos arqueológicos en Samaipata, Departamento de Santa Cruz, Bolivia." *SIARB, Boletín de la Sociedad de Investigaciones en el Arte Rupestre Boliviano* 7: 48–58.

Meyers, Albert, and C. Ulbert (1998). "Archaeological Investigations in Eastern Bolivia: The Samaipata Project." *Tawantinsuyu* 3: 79–85.

Pucher, Leo (1945). *Ensayo sobre el arte pre-histórico de Samaypata*. Sucre, Bolivia: Museo Arqueológico de la Universidad de San Francisco.

Rivera Sundt, Oswaldo (1984). "La horca del Inka." *Arqueología Boliviana, Instituto Nacional de Arqueología, La Paz* 1: 91–101.

Tapia Pineda, Félix (1984). "Excavaciones arqueológicas en el sector habitacional de el Fuerte de Samaipata, Santa Cruz." *Arqueología Boliviana, Instituto Nacional de Arqueología, La Paz* 1: 49–62.

Trimborn, Hermann (1959). *Archäologische Studien in den Kordilleren Boliviens*. Berlin: Baessler Archiv, Beiträge zur Volkerkunde Beiheft 2.

Trimborn, Hermann (1967). *Archäologische Studien in den Kordilleren Boliviens*. Berlin: Baessler Archiv, Beiträge zur Volkerkunde Beiheft 5.

Tomebamba

TIME PERIOD: 520–470 B.P.

LOCATION: Province of Azuay, southern highlands of Ecuador, beneath the modern town of Cuenca.

DESCRIPTIVE SUMMARY

Local Environment

The site is located in a large river basin in the bare, rolling hills of the southern Ecuadorian highlands at an elevation of 2530 m above sea level. The climate is semiarid, averaging under 1 m of rainfall per year, and relatively mild, with a mean annual temperature of 15° C.

Physical Features

The site of Tomebamba was first excavated by Max Uhle in the early 1920s (Uhle 1923). Many of the ruins he described now lie beneath the modern city of Cuenca (see also Bamps 1887). The architectural remains Uhle encountered were vast in scale and included what he interpreted as religious structures, a central plaza, a palatial residence, guard's quarters, and a nunnery (*aqllawasi*). Elaborate waterworks, including pools, baths, and canals, as well as terraces and roads, were also recorded (Cordero and Aguirre 1994; Hyslop 1990: 140–142). The palatial sector, known as Puma Pungo, is believed to have been the royal residence of Huayna Capac (Idrovo 2000; Uhle 1923). Substantial quantities of Inca pottery have been recovered from this portion of the site (Idrovo 1984, 1988). Tomebamba was devastated by Atahualpa during the Inca civil war that ensued following the death of Huayna Capac in A.D. 1527 (Alcina Franch 1986; Engwall 1995; Rostworowski

1988: 148–178). Although the site lay in ruins by the time the Spanish chronicler Cieza de León passed through some 20 years later, it was nonetheless impressive enough for him to describe it as one of the most magnificent Inca sites in all the empire.

Cultural Aspects

Tomebamba was the principal Inca administrative center for the northern sector of the empire. The site was founded by Topa Inca Yupanqui during the military campaigns he led against the indigenous Cañari population A.D. 1460–1470 (Larrea 1971). Huayna Capac, successor to Topa Inca and penultimate ruler of the empire, was born in Tomebamba and resided there for much of his life; it was he who commissioned much of the monumental construction (Alcina Franch 1982; Bamps 1887). Various ethnohistoric sources describe Tomebamba as a second Cuzco, suggesting that the site was deliberately created in the image of the sacred capital of the Inca empire (Cabello Balboa 1951; Cieza 1962 [1553]: 142–147). Indeed, certain features of the local landscape are reminiscent of the Cuzco valley (Idrovo 1984, 2000). This resemblance was not lost on the Inca, who sought to magnify the similarities through the imposition of Cuzqueño place names upon the local topography. Many of these toponyms are still in place today (Arriaga 1922).

References

Alcina Franch, José (1982). "Tomebamba y el problema de los indios Cañaris de la sierra sur del Ecuador." *Anuario de Estudios Americanos* 37: 403–433.

Alcina Franch, José (1986). "Los indios Cañaris de la sierra sur del Ecuador." *Miscelánea Antropológica Ecuatoriana* 6: 141–188.

Arriaga, Jesús (1922). *Apuntes de Arqueología Cañar* Cuenca, Ecuador: Imprenta del Clero.

Bamps, Anatole (1887). *Tomebamba: Antique Cité de l'Empire des Incas.* Louvain: Imprimèrie Lefever.

Cabello Balboa, Miguel (1951). *Miscelánea Antártica* [1586]. Lima: Instituto de Etnología, Facultad de Letras, Universidad Nacional Mayor de San Marcos.

Cieza de León, Pedro de (1962). *La Crónica del Perú* (1st part) [1553]. Madrid: Espasa Calpe.

Cordero, Juan, and Leonardo Aguirre (1994). *La Ciudad de Tomebamba, Museo de Sitio.* Cuenca: Banco Central del Ecuador.

Engwall, Evan (1995). "Turbulent Relations Recast: The Mythohistory of the Cañaris and the Inca Empire." *Journal of the Steward Anthropological Society* 23, 1–2: 345–361.

Hyslop, John (1990). *Inka Settlement Planning.* Austin: University of Texas Press.

Idrovo, Jaime (1984). "Prospection archéologique de la vallée de Cuenca, Ecuador (Secteur Sud, ou l'emplacement de la villa Inca de Tomebamba)." Ph.D. diss., Université de Paris, Panteon Sorbonne.

Idrovo, Jaime (1988). "Tomebamba: Primera fase de conquista Incasica en los Andes septentrionales." In *La Frontera del Estado Inca*, ed. T. Dillehay and P. Netherly. Oxford: British Archaeological Reports, International Series, 87–104.

Idrovo, Jaime (2000). *Tomebamba: Arqueologia e Historia de una Ciudad Imperial.* Cuenca: Ediciones del Museo del Banco Central del Ecuador.

Larrea, Carlos Manuel (1971). *La Cultura Incásica del Ecuador.* Mexico City: Instituto Panamericano de Geografía e Historia.

Rostworowski de Diez Canseco, María (1988). *Historia del Tahuantinsuyu.* Lima: Instituto de Estudios Peruanos.

Uhle, Max (1923). *Las Ruinas de Tomebamba.* Quito: Imprenta Julio Sáenz Rebolledo.

TAMARA L. BRAY
Department of Anthropology
Wayne State University
Detroit, Michigan
United States

Late Amazonian

ABSOLUTE TIME PERIOD: 2000–50 B.P. Several hundred radiocarbon dates have been run for the culture in the eastern, western, and southern Amazon. The 25 dates for the polychrome subtradition from Marajo island in the east range from about A.D. 400 to 1100. Polychrome culture sites in Ecuador, Peru, and Colombia in the western Amazon tend to have later dates: from about A.D. 1100 to 1400, but a culture in the Ecuadorian Amazon has dates as early as about 2000 years ago. The latest subtradition is the Incised and Punctate culture horizon. Radiocarbon dates from sites in many regions show that the main florescence of this culture dated between A.D. 1000 and 1500. However, both the Parmana and Santarem areas have also produced numerous radiocarbon dates between A.D. 500 and 1000 for early stages of the tradition. The earlier dates in these areas may mean that the tradition began in the east and spread west, but perhaps there are too few dated areas of the horizon tone to establish statistically significant regional differences.

RELATIVE TIME PERIOD: Follows the Early Amazonian tradition and continues into the historic period.

LOCATION: The Polychrome Horizon is known from the mainstream Amazon, its tributaries, and the Guianas coastal plain. Sites of the Incised and Punctate tradition have been noted in a wide area in lowland South America both east and north of the Andes. It is found along the entire mainstream of the Amazon, the Guianas, the Columbian and Venezuelan Orinoco, and northern Colombia. It also extends into the well-drained upland tropical forests of the Andean foothills in Ecuador.

DIAGNOSTIC MATERIAL ATTRIBUTES: Sedentary and possibly socially ranked mixed horticulturalists and intensive agriculturalists living in large villages often placed on large mounds. Some cultures also have representative mounds. Subsistence ranges from possible manioc cultivation to intensive maize cultivation late in the period. Fishing is the most important source of faunal food, but late prehistoric period people have stable isotope ratios that suggest a dominance of maize in their protein supply. People made elaborately decorated pottery and sculptures and often buried their dead in urns in large cemeteries used for long periods. The characteristic polychrome subtradition pottery bears elaborate polychrome and/or incised and modeled decoration. The forms include *adorno* bowls, effigies of many kinds, anthropomorphic zoomorphic burial urns, female rattle figurines, and pendant pigment pots, stools, etc. The Incised and Punctate subtradition pottery corpus also includes *adorno* bowls, diverse effigies, burial bowls, female figurine rattles, but in addition has large statues or effigy vessels representing realistic human images.

CULTURAL SUMMARY

Environment

The lower Amazon late prehistoric complex societies tended to be focused on the land in and alongside the main river floodplain, which extends east to the mouth of the Amazon and north along the Guiana's coasts. In this zone, annually renewed, cultivable alluvial soils are abundant in lower land. The uplands bear extensive areas of heavily weathered soils, including oxisols, ultisols, and alfisols. All the upland soils are appropriate at least for slash-and-burn cultivation. Although often the weathered soils are often classed as poor soils for permanent agriculture, their agricultural utility depends on the original bedrock. Thus, soils developed on quartz-rich sandstone require long fallowing, but those developed on limestone, shale, or limey sandstone can be more intensively cropped. Late prehistoric sites in all the different areas of the lower Amazon have produced some evidence of plant cultivation, ranging from specimens of crop plants to pollen of cultivated field weeds. The backwaters, side channels, and lakes of the rivers are full of fish, easiest to catch in the dry season, but available year-round. Game is less abundant by far, but easy to catch, either in the rainy season when isolated on levee islands or in the dry season when gathered about water sources. Wild plant food is abundant, especially in river forests and swamps, but also in upland forests. Today, disturbance-adapted fruit trees abound in the forests, relics of the many centuries of indigenous human occupation. Swampy or seasonally flooded land may bear edible, grain-bearing grasses and other herbs, all of which were used for food by the indigenous people, according to the early historical sources.

The sites of some upper Amazon complex societies, such as the Polychrome Caimito in Peru and Napo in Ecuador, occur along river floodplains. In the seasonally swampy lowlands of the Bolivian Amazon, which are similar to those of Marajo at the mouth of the Amazon, there are artificial habitation mounds and cemeteries, causeways, and large areas of raised cultivation fields. There are also, however, substantial occupations in the hinterland volcanic terra firmer away from floodplains. Faldas de Sangay is an example of one of these occupations. Such densely forested upland localities did furnish land suitable for intensive agriculture, contrary to general expectation based on assumptions about low humid tropical soil fertility. The evidence of agriculture consists of pollen profiles from upland lakes, which show abundant maize pollen and phytoliths.

Settlements

In the eastern Amazon in Brazil and the Guianas and the southwestern Amazon in Bolivia, the most conspicuous sites are large earth habitation mounds built in lowland, swampy river floodplains. In the Ecuadorian Amazon, there are both habitation mounds and mounds in the shape of animals and humans. On Marajo island in the eastern Brazilian Amazon, the mounds are platforms between 1–20 ha in area and from 1–20 m in height. The platforms occur either singly or in groups, in a few cases as many as 20–40 together. The platforms upheld large villages containing 5–20 large, oblong communal houses with earth floors and thatch roofs. Domestic structures, garbage, and ceremonial features were geophysically surveyed and excavated at two Marajo sites: Teso dos Bichos and Guajara. The structures contain central groups of adobe hearths of oblong trough form. Between the houses and cemeteries, the inhabitants placed black soil garbage fill, made plantations, and carried out ceremonial activities. Near each house is one or more discrete, multilevel cemeteries that were protected with shedlike structures and prepared earth floors. The sites show a separation of domestic and ceremonial activities, with the former occurring in the houses and the latter in the open. However, so far, no evidence has come out to suggest that there were significant differences in status between houses and between mounds. But perhaps future research to compare mound and nonmound sites and cemeteries and houses within mounds may expose such differences.

Survey and excavations at Incised and Punctate subtradition sites at Santarem and Caverna da Pedra Pintada have produced post and floor evidence for large, communal residences with bell-shaped pits. The bell-shaped pits at Santarem were filled with large amounts of broken finely decorated pottery and/or large human effigies and shells of large turtles.

Burials of the tradition were usually placed in pottery vessels of varying size and decoration. Most burials are secondary, sometimes painted and wrapped in fiber coverings. There are some rare flexed inhumations and very rare, late cremations in bowls, at Santarem sites. Sometimes placed with the urns were fancy whole vessels and musical instruments, such as rattles and ocarinas. On Marajo, the burials were grouped densely into cemeteries that were apparently used for many years, because they hold several superimposed layers of urns. Although broad area excavation of a cemetery has yet to be carried out, the stratigraphy of the cemeteries exposed in test pits suggests that the cemeteries might have been roofed sheds where the urns were set on the ground in a display. When the shed was filled, it may be that the urns were buried and a new level of urns begun above them.

In addition to the mounds, on Marajo there were also small nonmound sites, which may have been seasonal campsites or alternatively dwellings of a group of commoners. Among Santarem sites, some are very large, like Santarem, at c. 4 sq km, and some are small, like that at Pedra Pintada, only about 100 sq m. But all have the incised and punctate pottery and some painted pottery. The main distinction that might be made among Incised and Punctate sites is the size and presence of special objects, such as the large pottery statues, found at Santarem. Such differences could possibly be interpreted as differences between chiefly centers and supporting villages, but this would be quite speculative. In the southern Amazon, several large sites with multiple rings of larger houses have been mapped.

Economy

The subsistence remains from the excavations on Marajo had a forest/riverine focus. People cultivated and collected tree fruits, especially palms, and possibly grew root crops. There is also rare hard-kernel maize and seeds of native herbs. Faunal food consisted mainly of numerous small fishes. Very large fish as much as 2 m long occur only in ceremonial deposits. The burials reveal that populations included some tall sturdy people with characteristically Amazonian, not Andean, cranial morphology. There are also a few delicately built, small-statured people. Skeletons have minor anemic pathologies, probably from parasite infections, and have heavy tooth wear and gum problems. Stable carbon isotope ratios of human skeletons indicate a mixed subsistence. Individuals varied appreciably in their ratios, suggesting some socioeconomic differentiation.

Carbon isotope ratios and species of plants and animals from the sites suggest a mosaic habitat of forest and river floodplain at the time.

Investigation of subsistence at Santarem, Taperinha, and Caverna de Pedra Pintada in the lower Amazon and sites near Parmana in the middle Orinoco suggests that communities of the tradition focused on resources from both floodplains and interfluves. Many sites have produced evidence of intensive agriculture with maize as the staple, but manioc was important in some areas, to judge from remains of griddles and grater chips. Small fishes seem to have been the protein supplement, but rare bones of large animals such as tapir and shells of large turtles have also been found at Santarem-area sites. The few human skeletons analyzed are of tall

people with dental problems. Stable carbon isotope ratios on human skeletons from Yarinacocha in the upper Amazon of Peru and from Parmana in Venezuela fit a diet heavily reliant on maize and fish. Subsistence remains from the Bolivian Amazon have not yet been analyzed, but that region has extensive raised field systems, causeways, and residential mounds related to the horizon. In the Andean foothills in the Ecuadorian Amazon, there are extensive mound groups, as large as 12 sq km in one case, which appear to be associated with incised and punctate and geometric polychrome pottery of the horizon. No subsistence remains have been described, but pollen cores from nearby lake Ayauchi include abundant maize and manioc pollen by this time if not before. In the Bolivian Amazon, large areas of raised fields are known, in some cases extending over as much as 10,000 sq km. As yet, however, the particular crops cultivated on such fields are not identified.

In general, the pottery of different Polychrome or Incised and Punctate sites seems to have been made locally. Polychrome subtradition pottery is known for its polychrome painting, executed most often in red and brown or black on white. Occasionally purplish red and yellow colors also appear. The red, brown, and black seem to be watercolors. The white seems to be fired. Most vessels also have modeled and incised ornaments, and there are large numbers of vessels decorated primarily in incision, excision, and modeling. Shapes are incredibly diverse, including plates, pedestal plates, bowls, jars, pigment pots with handles for suspension, urns, spindle whorls, round stools, funnels, disks, public covers, rattle figurines, human effigy vessels. Of the human images, those identifiable by sex are mostly women. Only one clear male representation is known, modeled and incised on a pigment pot. Among the animals, the most common identifiable ones are creatures of the ground or water, such as turtles or ducks. Typical stone artifacts in the Polychrome sites include simple ground lithics in imported rocks of volcanic origin.

Sites at or near Santarem at the mouth of the Tapajos river on the Amazon mainstream in Para, Brazil, produce elaborate appliqué, incised, and punctate pottery decorated with geometric, human, and animal plastic motifs and sometimes with rectilinear polychrome painted motifs or a red wash. The forms include ceremonial display vessels, such as pedestal vessels, numerous female and rare male rattle figurines, bird ocarinas, animal effigy vessels, and large statues or effigy vessels depicting men or women. The large images are either of women standing or sitting, sometimes holding bowls or a baby, or of men, often sitting, holding rattles. The women and men both have long slit ear lobes. The women wear headbands with carvings attached and elaborate braided hairdos, and the men wear radial headdresses and decorated shoulder bags.

Some sites have also produced elaborate and diverse ground-stone and lapidary objects for cutting, chopping, carving, staff emblems and the like. Many pendants and headband ornaments were made of green jade. Art imagery in both pottery and rock objects includes raptorial birds and carnivorous animals not common in the earlier Polychrome tradition. They include images of animals attacking humans or other animals, animals eating food or human limbs, alter ego figures of men, women, or animals with a large animal on their shoulders, holding their heads and sometimes biting them.

Sociopolitical Organization

The nature of sites and art at Polychrome subtradition sites on Marajo suggests wealthy, perhaps ranked communities that nonetheless were not necessarily organized under central authority figures. If the iconography can be interpreted directly, which may not be the case, women were important in ritual, as they must have been in crafts and subsistence. They are definitely shown in shamanic activity, as is the lone male image. Men may have had important ritual roles as hunters and warriors. Many of the male long bones in museums are very robust in muscular development of the sort that can be built up through active, physical sports and footraces.

In the Incised and Punctate subtradition, on the other hand, differences in size and artifacts between sites suggest the possibility that there might have been regional centers. Conquest records suggest the existence of paramount war chiefs based in centers. They also mention notions of nobles and commoners. Perhaps the large pottery statues could be connected with the nobles. However, all habitation sites, even sites in caves, contain some of the highly decorated incised and punctate and painted pottery, so the fine art was available to everyone, apparently.

The largest sites are found in the realm of the Incised and Punctate culture of Faldas de Sangay in the Ecuadorian Amazon. A cluster of mounds covering as much as 12 sq km is described at that site in particular. Such sites, which are both rare figurative mounds and numerous habitation mounds, might have been chiefly centers, but little mapping and broad-area excavation have been carried out in that region.

Religion and Expressive Culture

Aesthetic and ritual culture was very highly developed in the tradition. Although many of the objects found in archaeological sites are not made today in Amazonia, some researchers have suggested that the imagery of the art of the tradition seems consonant with current Amazonian cosmology. Certainly, one can find resonances. For example, the division of the world into a male half and a female half could perhaps be discerned in the iconography of the art. Marajo art seems female oriented with its emphasis on water animals and animals that crawl on the ground. Santarem art, on the other hand, might be related to concepts of the male half, with its emphasis on raptorial birds and voracious felines. Alternatively, the imagery that appears to be male oriented could also be interpreted as imagery of rulership. Large female effigies often form the foundation of elaborate vessels covered with small animal figures. Perhaps such images represent the shamanic mistresses of the animals known from modern Amazonian cosmology. An additional element in Santarem art is art of the night and death, imaged in bats and vultures. Both cultures emphasized the processing of dead bodies, either by defleshing and bundling or by burning. Conquest-period records for the vague Santarem area mention the practice of ritual endocannibalism, in which the bodies of dead relatives were burned and then made into a drink with beer, for relatives to imbibe. Certain images and some objects could be related to elite culture. The slit earlobes were considered signs of rank at the time of the conquest. Stools, although not limited to chiefs today, were reportedly employed in ceremonies involving elites at the time of the conquest.

Suggested Readings

Acuna, C. de (1891). *Nuevo descubrimiento del gran rio de las Amazonas.* Madrid: Colleccion de Livros que Tratan de America Raros o Curiosos, Tomo 2.

Athens, J. S. (1989). "Pumpuentsa and the Pastasa Phase in Southeastern Lowland Ecuador." *Ñawpa Pacha* 24: 1–29.

Bezerra de Meneses, Ulpiano (1972). *Arqueologia Amazonica (Santarem).* Sao Paulo: Museu de Arqueologia e Etnologia, Universidade de São Paulo.

Bettendorf, J. (1910). "Chronica da Missao dos padres da Companhia de Jesus no estado do Maranhao." *Revista do Instituto Geografico e Historico* (Rio de Janeiro) 72, 1.

Bevan, B. W. (1989). *Geophysical Surveys at Three Sites along the Lower Amazon River.* Pitman, NJ: Geosight.

Brochado, Jose P. (1980). "The Social Ecology of the Marajoara Culture." M.A. thesis, University of Illinois, Urbana.

Correa, C. G. (1965). *Estatuas de ceramica na cultura Santarem.* Publicacoes Avulsas do Museu Paraense Emilio Goeldi, no. 4.

de Heriarte, M. (1964). *Descripcam do Estado do Maranham, Para, Corupa e rios das Amazonas, feito por Mauricio de Heriarte, Ouvidorgeral Provedormor e Auditor, que foi pelo Gobernador D. Pedro de Mello, no anno 1662.* Faksimile—Ausgabe aus den MSS 5880 und 5879 der Österreichischen National-Bibliothek, Vienna and Graz: Academische Druck und Verlagsansstalt.

de la Penha, G., ed. (0000). *O Museu Paraense Emilio Goeldi*. Sao Paulo: Museu Paraense Emilio Goeldi, Banco Safra SA, and CNPq.

Denevan, W. (1966). *An Aboriginal Cultural Geography of the llanos de Mojos de Bolivia*. Ibero-Americana no. 48. Berkeley and Los Angeles: University of California Press.

Derby, O. (1879). "The Artificial Mounds of the Island of Marajo." *American Naturalist* 13: 224–229.

Dougherty, B., and H. Calandra (1981–1982). "Excavaciones arqueologicas en La Loma Alta de Casarabe, Llanos de Moxos, Departemento del Beni, Bolivia." *Relaciones de la Sociedad Argentina de Antropologia* n.s. 14, 2: 9–48.

Erickson, C. (1980). "Sistemas agricolas prehispanicos en los llanos de Mojos." *America Indigena* 404: 731–755.

Evans, C., and B. J. Meggers (1960). "Archaeological Investigations in British Guiana." *Bulletin of the Bureau of American Ethnology* 177.

Evans, C., and B. J. Meggers (1968). *Archaeological Investigations on the Rio Napo, Eastern Ecuador*. Washington D.C.: Smithsonian Contributions to Anthropology, no. 6.

Hartt, C. F. (n. d.). "Contribution to the Ethnology of the River of the Amazons." Unpublished manuscript in the Peabody Museum, Harvard University, Cambridge, MA.

Heckenberger, Michael J. (1996). "War and Peace in the Shadow of Empire: Social Change in the Upper Xingu of Southeastern Amazonia, A.D. 1400–2000." Ph.D. diss., Department of Anthropology, University of Pittsburgh.

Heckenberger, Michael J., James B. Peterson, and Eduardo Goes Neves (1997). "Village Size and Permanence in Amazonia: Two Archaeological Examples from Brazil." *Latin American Antiquity* 10: 353–376.

Hilbert, P. P. (1968). *Archäologische Untersuchungen am Mittleren Amazonas*. Marburger Studien zur Volkerkunde, no. 1. Berlin: Dietrich Reimer Verlag.

Lathrap, D. (1970). *The Upper Amazon*. New York: Praeger.

Medina, E., ed. (1934). *The Discovery of the Amazon according to the Account of Friar Gaspar de Carvajal and Other Documents*. New York: American Geographical Society.

Meggers, B. J. (1952). "The Archaeological Sequence on Marajo Island, Brazil, with Special Reference to the Marajoara Culture." Ph.D. diss., Department of Anthropology, Columbia University.

Meggers, B. J. (1971). *Amazonia: Man and Nature in a Counterfeit Paradise*. Chicago: Aldine.

Meggers, B. J. (1972). *Prehistoric America*. Chicago: Aldine-Atherton.

Meggers, B. J. (1988). "The Prehistory of Amazonia." In *People of the Tropical Forest*, ed. J. S. Denslow and C. Padoch, Berkeley: University of California Press and Smithsonian Traveling Exhibition Service, 54–62.

Meggers, B. J., and C. Evans (1957). *Archaeological Investigations at the Mouth of the Amazon*. Bureau of American Ethnology, Bulletin 167. Washington D.C.: Smithsonian Institution Press.

Nimuendaju, C. U. (1949). "Os Tapajo." *Boletim do Museu Paraense Emilio Goeldi* 10: 93–108.

Nordenskiold, E. (1930). *L'Archéologie du Bassin de L'Amazone*. Ars Americana 1. Paris: Les Editions G. van Oest.

Palmatary, H. (1950). "The Pottery of Marajo Island." *Transactions of the American Philosophical Society* n.s. 39, 3.

Palmatary, H. (1960). "The Archaeology of the Lower Tapajos Valley." *Transactions of the American Philosophical Society* n.s. 50, 3.

Piperno, D. R. (1995). "Plant Microfossils and Their Application in the New World Tropics." In *Archaeology in the Lowland American Tropics: Current Analytical Methods and Recent Applications*, ed. P. Stahl. Cambridge: Cambridge University Press, 130–153.

Piperno, D. R., and D. M. Pearsall (1998). *The Origins of Agriculture in the Lowland Tropics*. San Diego: Academic Press.

Porras, P. A. (1987). *Investigaciones Archaeologicas a Las Faldas de Sangay, Provincia Moroma Santiago*. Quito: Artes Graficas Senal.

Porro, A. (1994). "Social Organization and Political Power in the Amazon Floodplain: The Ethnohistorical Sources." In *Amazonian Indians from Prehistory to the Present*, ed. A. C. Roosevelt. Tucson: University of Arizona Press, 79–94.

Roe, P. (1981). *The Cosmic Zygote: Cosmology in the Amazon Basin*. New Brunswick, NJ: Rutgers University Press.

Roosevelt, A. C. (1980). *Parmana: Prehistoric Maize and Manioc Subsistence along the Amazon and Orinoco*. New York: Academic Press.

Roosevelt, A. C. (1989). "Resource Management in Amazonia before the Conquest: Beyond Ethnographic Projection." In *Resource Management in Amazonia: Indigenous and Folk Strategies*, ed. W. Balee and D. Posey. Advances in Economic Botany, vol. 7. New York: New York Botanical Garden, 30–62.

Roosevelt, A. C. (1991). *Moundbuilders of the Amazon: Geophysical Archaeology on Marajo Island, Brazil*. San Diego: Academic Press.

Roosevelt, A. C. (1993). "The Rise and Fall of the Amazon Chiefdoms." In *Le remontée de l'Amazone: Anthropologie et histoire des societés amazoniennes*, ed. A.-C. Taylor and P. Descola. Paris: L'Homme 33, 126–128, 255–284.

Roosevelt, A. C. (1997). *The Excavations at Corozal, Venezuela: Stratigraphy and Ceramic Seriation*. New Haven: Yale University Publications in Anthropology, no. 83.

Roosevelt, A. C. (1999). "The Maritime-Highland-Forest Dynamic and the Origins of Complex Society." In *History of the Native Peoples of the Americas: South America*, ed. F. Salomon and S. Schwartz. Cambridge: Cambridge University Press, 264–349.

Roosevelt, A. C. (1999). "The Development of Prehistoric Complex Societies: Amazonia, a Tropical Forest." In *Complex Polities in the Ancient Tropical World*, ed. E. A. Bacus and L. J. Lucero. Archaeological Papers of the American Anthropological Association, no. 9, 13–34.

Roosevelt, A. C. (in press). Amazonia, A Dynamic Human Habitat. In *Pre-Columbian New World Ecosystems*, ed. D. Lentz. New York: Columbia University Press.

Roosevelt, A. C., ed. (1994). *Amazonian Indians from Prehistory to the Present: Anthropological Perspectives*. Tucson: University of Arizona Press.

Salazar, Ernesto (1998). "De vuelta al Sangay: Investigaciones arqueologicas en el alto Upano, Amazonia Ecuatoriana." *Bulletin de l'Institut Francais des Études Andines* 27: 213–240.

Schann, Denise Pahl (1997). *A Linguagem Iconografica da Ceramic Marajoara*. Porto Alegre: Pontifica Universidade Catolica do Rio Grande do Sul, Colecao Arqueologicqa 3.

Smith, N. (1980). "Anthrosols and Human Carrying Capacity in Amazonia." *Annals of the Association of American Geographers* 70: 533–566.

Steward, J., and L. Faron (1959). *Native Peoples of South America*. New York: McGraw-Hill.

ANNA ROOSEVELT
Department of Anthropology
The Field Museum
and
Department of Anthropology
University of Illinois
Chicago, Illinois
United States

Late Andean Hunting-Collecting

ABSOLUTE TIME PERIOD: c. 8000–6000 B.P.

RELATIVE TIME PERIOD: Follows the Early Andean Hunting-Collecting and precedes the Early Highland Andean Archaic.

LOCATION: Highlands of the western flanks of the Andes and adjacent altiplano, ranging in elevation from roughly 2000–4500 m, encompassing a region from southern Ecuador to northern Chile.

DIAGNOSTIC MATERIAL ATTRIBUTES: A variety of projectile point styles, including lanceolate, foliate, rhomboidal, and stemmed forms; settlement patterns reflect a number of alternatives, ranging from seasonal transhumance within highland zones through sedentary occupations of high altiplano grasslands.

REGIONAL SUBTRADITIONS: Central Andean, Circum Titicaca, Northern Andean, South-central Andean.

IMPORTANT SITES: Asana, Chobshi Cave, Guitarrero Cave, Lauricocha, Pachamachay, Pikimachay, Quelcatani, Telarmachay, Toquepala, Viscachani, Cubilán, Hakenasa, Panalauca, Patapatane, Puente.

CULTURAL SUMMARY

Environment

Climate. The Late Andean Hunting-Collecting Tradition developed during a period of increasing desiccation along the western flanks of the Andes. The rate and severity of this desiccation, however, were tempered by local factors of high mountain and plateau topography. At 8000 B.P., climate was generally somewhat cooler and wetter than the present, but by 6000 B.P., it was more arid, and temperatures were similar to or slightly warmer than in modern times.

Topography. The tradition is found within the relatively narrow valleys of the major rivers of the western flanks of the Andes and its adjacent plateau (*puna* or altiplano). Sites are found in an elevational range from roughly 2000–4500 m. The valleys are narrow and surrounded by steeply sloping mountains that are cut by smaller stream courses, many of which flow only during the rainy season (November–April). The terrain is rugged. The altiplano, in contrast, is best characterized as a rolling plane dotted with numerous small lakes and crossed by permanent streams.

Geology. The region is dominated by the mass of the Andes, which are generally of volcanic origin. The Andean are composed of two chains, or *cordillera*, between which lie the altiplano, which is best seen as a large, open, high-elevation plateau or basin. The highlands are drained by a series of regularly spaced, parallel river valleys. Many of these valleys, especially at higher elevations, are relatively narrow and surrounded by very steep slopes; they show distinctive traces of glacial outwash formations that followed deglaciation some time after 13,000 B.P. Glacial features, like moraines, can be observed at the highest elevations. High-quality lithic materials are common and are often stratified by elevation. Tool-grade obsidian is found in a number of major flows extending from northern Ecuador to southern Peru.

Biota. Life zones along the western flanks of the Andes are vertically stratified by rapid elevational change. In some valleys, it is possible to go from 0–4000 m in less than 150 km. Thus, life zones with very distinct ecologies are found in close proximity. However, because the western flanks of the Andes are in a rain shadow, primary productivity is somewhat diminished. Life zones are also influenced by latitude—in general, rainfall is more abundant in the northern regions (southern Ecuador, northern Peru), and diminishes as one moves farther south. However, the rugged mass of the Andean chain produces significant microecological variability. The western flanks of the Andes are composed of two major ecological zones: the high sierra and the *puna*. The high sierra is characterized by generally low primary productivity, a patchy distribution of plant resources that is tethered to water sources and small, widely dispersed *bofedales* (high-quality pasture), and very low rainfall that falls during a short rainy season from November through April. The *puna* is characterized by relatively abundant, seasonal (November–March) rainfall, cool to cold temperatures, and high primary productivity of grasses palatable to the native Andean camelids, especially the vicuña. Because much of the *puna* is humid, seasonal variation in plant and animal abundance is less marked than in lower elevation zones.

Settlements

Settlement System. Settlement systems are for the most part composed of a series of site types familiar to students of hunting and gathering peoples: base camps, which are occupied for a significant portion of the year by much of the co-residential group, logistical camps that serve different ends and are created by different segments of the population depending on the scale and frequency of residential moves, and field camps, which are very short-term uses of sites as hunting blinds,

butchery sites, plant-gathering loci, and other places on the landscape used on a sporadic, ad hoc basis primarily for resource procurement. Special-purpose sites include quarries and caches. These site types are articulated into settlement systems that have greater or lesser degrees of residential and logistical mobility, span of occupation, and composition. These systems appear to be in great part determined by local resource constellations within the broader ecological zones of the western flanks of the Andes.

Community Organization. Relatively few sites have been excavated at the scale required to gain significant insight into community organization or are of a small size such that variability in use is tightly constrained. Open-air sites with residential architecture, such as Asana, have layouts consistent with varying lengths of occupation. Longer term residential use of the site shows concern for midden placement at site margins and refuse cleanup, as well as placement of messy activities away from residential areas. Rockshelters generally have structures built within them and use talus slopes as middens, although shelter backwall areas sometimes are used for this purpose.

Housing. Residential structures are small, ranging in covered floor area from 3.5 m^2–6 m^2, circular in form, and defined by combinations of post molds, stone circles, or prepared clay surfaces. Most are presumed to have been covered with hides, brush, or other perishable materials.

Population, Health, and Disease. Very few skeletal remains of this period have been encountered, thus making it difficult to generalize about health status.

Economy

Subsistence. Diet throughout this period is based almost wholly on wild foods. Hunting of mammals of all sizes was important, as was plant collection. However, some environments, such as the altiplano, had limited plant foods available, and thus hunting predominated. The role of domesticates in some areas is hotly debated.

Wild Foods. Hunted species in the lower elevation zones (from roughly 2000–3500 m) include deer, primarily whitetailed, but also *pudu* in Ecuador and *huemul* farther south, rabbit, guinea pig, and other small mammals. Plant species of importance include cactus fruits, tubers of a variety of species, and *Chenopodium* sp. (*quinoa*). At higher elevations, camelids, including the guanaco and vicuña, were dietary staples.

Domestic foods. The abundance and important of domesticated plant species are hotly debated. Potential domesticates include various species of beans (common and lima), peppers, and tubers. The antiquity of these domesticates is under question, but it seems probable that some were part of the diet by 6000 B.P. in the north-central Andes.

Industrial Arts. The technology of this tradition is simple and consists of a variety of stone, wooden, bone, and fiber tools.

Utensils. Utensils consist of stone tools, including projectile points, unfacial scrapers used to process hide, wood, bone, and antler, other unfacial and bifacial cutting, graving, chopping, and general-purpose tools. Ground-stone tools, used to process hides, grind plant foods, ocher, and resins, are also common, as are hammer stones, crude pestles and mortars, and some polished stone. Bone tools include those used in weaving, awls, combs, pressure flakers (also made of antler), and needles. Wooden tools include fragments of fire drills. Fragments of gourd containers have been found, as have been remains of cordage and baskets.

Ornaments. Ornaments are relatively scarce in this tradition and include bone and stone beads as well as bone and tooth pendants.

Trade. Regarding subsistence, it seems clear that these groups were self-sufficient. However, there does appear to have been a low-level circulation of lithic materials, especially obsidian, across fairly large distances. It is probable that this exchange was a form of down-the-line trading, although it is also possible that some direct access to these sources could have been practiced. Some have argued that the appearance of finished projectile points made of exotic, nonlocal materials indicates an exchange system designed to cement social ties between individuals.

Division of Labor. The only division of labor observable in the archaeological record of this tradition is the presence of logistical camps used, presumably by males, as hunting blinds or stations. Although it is probable that other field camps existed, these cannot be seen empirically.

Sociopolitical Organization

Social Organization. There is very little direct evidence of the social organization of these peoples. However, it is clear that group size was relatively small and that

regional scale population density in every major subtradition was also low.

Political Organization. What limited information exists suggests that these groups were egalitarian, and that whatever prestige or status differences existed were based on gender and occupation. Neither is there evidence for the accumulation of wealth.

Religion and Expressive Culture

Religious Beliefs. Although rupestral art exists in this tradition, it is unclear to what extent it can be related to religious belief and ritual. Fantastic figures, including geometric forms, may represent a conception of the supernatural.

Ceremonies. Although there is no direct evidence for ceremonies per se, public architecture is found at a few sites. Generally, these public structures are larger than contemporary domestic residences and have no features within them that indicate residential use. They are ovoid in form and have special-purpose features in them, such as steam baths. These structures are usually found surrounded by domestic structures, not by a plaza or open space. Ethnographic analogy suggests these structures may have served as sweat lodges or community houses. No feasting took place within them or near them.

Arts. Rupestral art is common at many sites of this tradition, and much of it is focused on representations of camelids or deer, the principal hunted species of the region. Human forms are also present, and these are sometimes shown in scenes suggestive of hunting. Other animals, such as the puma, are found at some sites, as are geometric motifs, such as grids of lines, dots, and blotches of color. Depictions of camelids and puma are often very detailed and highly naturalistic, whereas human figures are crude, often thick, stick figures.

Death and Afterlife. The dead are buried as individuals in and around residential sites. Artifacts found with them appear to reflect gender and show no signs of differential wealth accumulation. Burials are infrequently recovered, possibly suggesting an alternative form of disposal than interment.

Suggested Readings

Aldenderfer, M. (1989). "The Archaic Period in the South-Central Andes." *Journal of World Prehistory* 3: 117–158.

Aldenderfer, M. (1998). *Montane Foragers: Asana and the South-Central Andean Archaic.* Iowa City: University of Iowa Press.

Aldenderfer, M. (in press). *Quelcatani: The Evolution of a Pastoral Lifeway.* Washington, D.C.: Smithsonian Institution Press.

Lavallée, D. (1987). *Telarmachay: Chasseurs et Pasteurs Préhistoriques de Andes 1.* Institut Français d Études Andines. Paris: Éditions Récherche sur les Civilisations.

Lynch, T. (1967). *The Nature of the Central Andean Preceramic.* Pocatello: Occasional Papers of the Idaho State Museum 21.

Lynch, T. (1980). *Guitarrero Cave: Early Man in the Andes.* New York: Academic Press.

MacNeish, R., R. Vierra, A. Nelken-Terner, R. Lurie, and A. Cook (1983). *Prehistory of the Ayacucho Basin, Peru. vol. IV: The Preceramic Way of Life.* Ann Arbor: University of Michigan Press.

Ravines, R. (1972). "Secuencia y Cambios en los Artefactos Liticos del Sur del Peru." *Revista del Museo Nacional* 38: 133–184.

Rick, J. (1980). *Prehistoric Hunters of the High Andes.* New York: Academic Press.

Rick, J. (1988). "The Character and Context of Highland Preceramic Society." In *Peruvian Prehistory*, ed. R. Keatinge. Cambridge: Cambridge University Press, 3–40.

Stothert, K., and J. Quilter (1991). "Archaic Adaptations of the Andean Region 9000 to 5000 B.P." *Revista de Arqueología Americana* 4: 25–53.

SUBTRADITIONS

Central Late Andean Hunting-Collecting

TIME PERIOD: 8000–6000 B.P.

LOCATION: On the altiplano and adjacent western flanks of the Andes from the Rio Santa to the southern reaches of the department of Ayacucho, Peru.

DIAGNOSTIC MATERIAL ATTRIBUTES: A variety of projectile point forms, including large, triangular-bladed stemmed points; large foliates with and without ears; smaller bipointed foliates; some lanceolate forms.

CULTURAL SUMMARY

Environment

This tradition is found across a series of different environments on the altiplano or western flanks of the Andes, encompassing an elevational range from roughly 2500–4500 m. Moving from the Santa to the north toward Ayacucho in the south, there is a significant decrease in rainfall in the high sierra valleys. Rainfall on the altiplano across this continuum, in contrast, varies relatively little. Although there is real variability in the types of plant communities observed, most of the valleys fall into the high sierra environmental zone, which is characterized by generally low primary productivity and a patchy distribution of resources that are tethered to water sources. Plant growth, except for xerophytic species such as cacti, is concentrated on the valley bottoms. Animal species include *huemul* and whitetailed deer, small mammals, and rodents. In some valleys, guanaco were also common. In contrast, the altiplano in this region is characterized by intense seasonal (November–March) rainfall, cool to cold temperatures, and high primary productivity of grasses palatable to the native Andean camelids, especially the vicuña. There are few plant species, however, of dietary importance to humans. At 8000 B.P., climate was generally somewhat cooler and wetter than the present, but by 6000 B.P., it was more arid, and temperatures were similar to or slightly warmer than in modern times. However, changes associated with increasing desiccation were strongly affected by local factors of high mountain and plateau topography, slope, and aspect.

Settlements

Three distinct settlement systems have been defined in the central Andes during this period. Although they share some broad similarities, their differences are related to specific local constellations of resources present. One system has been defined for the Callejon de Huaylas and includes sites within an elevational range from roughly 2500 m to just over 4000 m (Lynch 1980). Movement occurs within the river valley itself on a seasonal basis, with people living at lower elevations until the onset of the dry season, when groups of foragers would move toward the high elevations of the valley. Settlement patterns in this instance would show a series of residential bases up and down the valley as well as a number of logistical camps or hunting blinds set up in favorable areas. Although this system is plausible, none of the larger residential bases has been encountered in the valley to date (Rick 1988). In contrast, an essentially sedentary settlement system has been postulated for Pachamachay. Based on the extraordinary quantities of lithics and bone recovered from the site, Rick (1980) has argued that the site was occupied year-round by hunter gatherers who hunted camelids, specifically the vicuña. Settlement data in the vicinity of the site reveal no other candidate for a base camp, and all indicators point the use of the site as a residential base. Smaller logistical camps are found around the site, and these are occupied for varying lengths of time, but never permanently. Sedentary occupations have also been postulated for the Lauricocha sites (Cardich 1976), but here, the data seem less convincing because extensive settlement pattern studies have not been conducted. A variant of the *puna* settlement system seen in this tradition is one associated with Telarmachay, which is located near the rim of the *puna*. The site is said to have been occupied only during the wet season, and dry season sites are located in the valleys below (Lavallée 1987). However, the settlement pattern data that support this assertion have yet to be published in detail, making it difficult to assess this argument. Finally, in the Ayacucho highlands, MacNeish (1983) postulates a settlement system of fission-fusion, in which macrobands occupy favorable niches during the wet season and then break into microbands and disperse into other habitats during the dry season. Other known sites include hunting and other logistical camps. This pattern of fission-fusion dominates the Piki phase (7800–6400 B.P.) and continues until early into the following Chihua phase.

Economy

Economy in this tradition varies with location. In the Callejon de Huaylas system, economy is focused on the exploitation of small mammals and deer, but not camelids, as well as a wide range of plant resources, including tubers, cactus fruits, and other seed-bearing plants. At least at Guitarrero Cave, Lynch (1980), based on the work of Kaplan (1980) and Smith (1980), argues that some cultivated plants are present by 8000 B.P. These include beans (*Phaseolus vulgaris*), certain tubers (*Ullucus tuberosus* and *Oxalis* sp.), peppers (*aji, Capsicum* sp.), and squash (*Curcurbita*). The importance to the diet of these potential cultivars, however, is much debated, and currently, Guitarrero Cave is the only site in the Andean highlands with such floral remains. There are, however, other sites at lower elevations, such as sites from the Nanchoc Tradition, which are said to have the remains of cultivated plants that date to between 8000–6000 B.P. (Dillehay et al. 1989; Rossen et al. 1996). Cordage and basketry have been discovered at Guitarrero Cave. The economy at Pachamachay, Panalauca, and other sites found on the altiplano at elevations beyond 4000 m is very much focused on vicuña hunting, which was found in great density on the wet *puna* grasslands. Although some deer (most likely *huemul*) were also taken, camelids formed the greatest part of the diet. Plant foods were scarce and included seed-bearing plants like *Opuntia* sp. and *Calandrina* (Bocek and Rick 1984; Pearsall 1980). Lithic materials used by these peoples were of local origin. Although the economy at sites like Telarmachay was similar, there are greater proportions of high sierra plant and animal species exploited when compared with sites in the deep interior of the altiplano, such as Pachamachay (Lavallée 1987). In Ayacucho region, diet in the Piki phase used of all major environmental zones within the highlands. Small mammals, deer, camelids, and guinea pig (*Cavia*) were important to the diet as were plants, some of which are said to have been cultivated, including *Chenopodium* sp., squash, and gourd (MacNeish 1983).

Sociopolitical Organization

All archaeological indicators point to an egalitarian society. The limited mortuary evidence available reveals no wealth- or status-related distinctions, and what residential structures have been discovered suggest that any size variation within them was based upon household size, and not rank. Public structures are not known from this subtradition, but this may be in great part because of the very biased sample of sites excavated, the majority of which are rockshelters. The few open-air sites excavated, such as Quishqui Puncu, have been interpreted as hunting or logistical camps (Lynch 1970).

Religion and Expressive Culture

As in other areas of the Andes at this time, rupestral art is an important aspect of culture. Art that probably dates to this period has been found at a number of cave and rockshelter sites on the altiplano, including the Lauricocha sites (Cardich 1959, 1964), sites on the Junin *puna* such as Pachamachay, and some logistical sites near it (Rick 1980, 1988), Telarmachay (Lavallée 1987), and others. Most of the motifs depict animals, including camelids, puma, fox or dog, deer, and birds, but humans are often present as are geometric forms of a variety of shapes and sizes. Most authors have assumed this art to be related to hunting ritual or simple depiction of important scenes from daily life. Mortuary patterns show show possible ritual activities. At the Puente site in Ayacucho, MacNeish and Vierra (1983) describe a child burial dating to the Piki phase, which consisted of a skull and a few long bones wrapped in a fabric and buried in a shallow pit. Although they offer a number of hypotheses, it appears that this burial most probably reflects a secondary or bundle burial, which will become very common throughout the Andes in later times. Mortuary evidence from other sites suggests that children were buried with greater quantities of grave goods than were adults (Stothert and Quilter 1991: 32).

References

Bocek, B., and J. Rick (1984). "La Epoca Precerámica en la Puna de Junin." *Chungará* 13: 109–127.

Cardich, A. (1958). *Los Yacimientos de Lauricocha*. Buenos Aires: Studia Praehistorica I.

Cardich, A. (1959). "Los Yacimientos de Lauricocha y la Nueva Interpretación de la Prehistoria Peruana." *Actas y Trabajos del II Congreso Nacional de Historia del Peru* 1: 93–106.

Cardich, A. (1976). "Vegetales y Recolecta en Lauricocha: Algunas Inferencias sobre Asentamientos Subsistencias Preagrícolas en los Andes Centrales." *Relaciones de la Sociedad Argentina de Antropología* 10: 27–41.

Dillehay, T., P. Netherly, and J. Rossen (1989). "Middle Preceramic Public and Residential Sites on the Forested Slope of the Western Andes, Northern Peru." *American Antiquity* 54: 733–759.

Kaplan, L. (1980). "Variation in the Cultivated Beans". In *Guitarrero Cave: Early Man in the Andes*, ed. T. Lynch. New York: Academic Press, 145–148.

Lavallée, D. (1987). *Telarmachay: Chasseurs et Pasteurs Préhistoriques de Andes 1*. Institut Français d' Études Andines. Paris: Éditions Recherche sur les Civilisations.

Lynch, T. (1970). *Excavations at Quishqui Puncu in the Callejon de Huaylas, Peru*. Pocatello: Occasional Papers of the Idaho State University Museum, 26.

Lynch, T. (1980). *Guitarrero Cave: Early Man in the Andes*. New York: Academic Press.

MacNeish, R. (1983). "The Ayacucho Preceramic as a Sequence of Cultural Energy-Flow Systems." In *Prehistory of the Ayacucho Basin, Peru. vol. IV: The Preceramic Way of Life*, ed. R. MacNeish, R. Vierra, A. Nelken-Terner, R. Lurie, and A. Cook. Ann Arbor: University of Michigan Press, 236–280.

MacNeish, R., and R. Vierra (1983). "The Preceramic Way of Life in the Thorn Forest Riverine Ecozone." In *Prehistory of the Ayacucho Basin, Peru. vol. IV: The Preceramic Way of Life*, ed. R. MacNeish, R. Vierra, A. Nelken-Terner, R. Lurie, and A. Cook. Ann Arbor: University of Michigan Press, 48–129.

Pearsall, D. (1980). "Pachamachay Ethnobotanical Report: Plant Utilization at a Hunting Base Camp." In *Prehistoric Hunters of the High Andes*, ed. J. Rick. New York: Academic Press, 234–256.

Rick, J. (1980). *Prehistoric Hunters of the High Andes*. New York: Academic Press.

Rick, J. (1988). "The Character and Context of Highland Preceramic Society." In *Peruvian Prehistory*, ed. R. Keatinge. Cambridge: Cambridge University Press, 3–40.

Rossen, J., T. Dillehay, and D. Ugent (1996). "Ancient Cultigens or Modern Intrusions: Evaluating Archaeological Plant Remains in an Andean Case Study." *Journal of Archaeological Science* 23: 391–407.

Smith, C. E. (1980). "Plant Remains from Guitarrero Cave." In *Guitarrero Cave: Early Man in the Andes*, ed. T. Lynch. New York: Academic Press, 87–120.

Stothert, K., and J. Quilter (1991). "Archaic Adaptations of the Andean Region 9000 to 5000 B.P." *Revista de Arqueología Americana* 4: 25–53.

Circum-Titicaca Late Andean Hunting-Collecting

TIME PERIOD: 8000–6000 B.P.

LOCATION: The Titicaca basin of southeastern Peru, eastern Bolivia, and extreme northeasten Chile.

DIAGNOSTIC MATERIAL ATTRIBUTES: A variety of projectile point forms, including large, triangular-bladed stemmed points; large foliates with and without ears; smaller bipointed foliates; some lanceolate forms.

CULTURAL SUMMARY

Environment

The Titicaca basin at this time was relatively cool and dry. Around 7700 B.P., Lake Titicaca reached its lowest stand, which may have been from 50 m to over 180 m below modern lake levels (Abbott et al. 1997a, 1997b; Binford et al. 1997; Cross et al. 1997; Seltzer et al. 1998). This would have made the lake more saline and significantly reduced its potential for human utilization. The lake remained at this low stand until at least 6000 B.P., when it may have experienced a slight rise (Wirrmann and Mourguiart 1995). Prior to 5000 B.P., conditions in the interior basin were characterized by extreme aridity, and sources of permanent, potable water, such as *bofedales*, springs, and the rivers themselves, would have been significant resource pulls. Interior rivers, such as the Ilave and Ramis, would have been deeply channeled, and their superior terraces (T2 and T3) would have formed prior to 8000 B.P. (Aldenderfer and Klink 1996: 15–17). Stream discharge rates would have been low, and seasonal inundation of lower terraces and floodplains would have been limited. Low rainfall, plus little floodplain transformation because of annual floods, would have led to limited, low-density and low-abundance plant growth, especially for the weedy species of economic value to humans. Although animals would have been tethered to stream courses, their territories, especially those for the guanaco, would have been relatively large (as they are the modern sierra on the western flanks of the Andes [Aldenderfer 1998: 45]), and depending on the severity of aridity, may have led to some seasonal movement by this species. Encounter rates for both animals and plants, then, would have been lower than in the modern era. Under conditions of low regional population density, these patchy low-productivity environments would have promoted some degree of residential mobility by the foragers of the region.

Settlements

Systematic survey projects in the circum-Titicaca are relatively few and until recently, have focused their attention on the margins of Lake Titicaca (Frye 1999;

Stanish et al. 1997). These projects have found few sites dating to the period 8000–6000 B.P., suggesting that lake margin and near-lake environments were not of importance to the hunter gatherers of the region. This is consistent with the ecology of the lake at this time. More recent surveys, specifically those of Aldenderfer (1996) in the Rio Ilave drainage and Klink (1999) in the Rio Huenque, both of which drain the deep interior of the basin, have discovered very substantial numbers of sites along their terraces. In the interior, sites are large, dense, and show multiple reoccupations. Although the analyses of the materials recovered by these surveys have not been completed, it is clear that there is a range of site types, including residential bases, short-term camps, and other logistical sites. Excavations at sites of this period are almost nonexistent, and the only site to have received systematic exploration is Quelcatani, a rock shelter found at 4420 m on the extreme southern margin of the basin. Hunters occupied the site as early as 7500 B.P., and it remained a short-term residential base or logistical camp throughout the period (Aldenderfer in press). Small, circular or ovoid structures were built along the back wall of the site. Although much work remains to be done, it is clear from these surveys and excavation projects that population densities were highest in the interior drainages and high plateaus during this period, and that the lake margin and near-lake environments were relatively little used. Very little is known at present of the scale and timing of residential mobility. There is a sense that mobility was practiced up and down stream courses, and that in the deep interior, some sites were occupied during the rainy season by logistical parties of hunters.

Economy

The limited data available show that hunting was important to the peoples of this tradition. Projectile points, including whole forms, those broken in process, and discarded, exhausted tools, are encountered in very large quantities at open-air residential sites as well as rock shelters. Species hunted include deer (both white-tailed and *huemul*) as well as the camelids (guanaco and vicuña). Small mammal species are not commonly observed as a component of the diet. Knowledge of plant foods in the diet is very limited. At Quelcatani, wild forms of chenopods are present, as are small quantities of other *puna* plants. Lithic raw materials are for the most part local, implying that trade for this material was uncommon. Obsidian from sources in Arequipa, located well over 250 air km, however, has been found at a few sites. This probably indicates

down-the-line trading of small quantities of this material over long distances, rather than direct access to the source.

Sociopolitical Organization

No hierarchy can be inferred from the settlement pattern data, and the size and scale of known sites are consistent with the low population sizes and densities typical of band-level societies. Warfare is unknown.

Religion and Expressive Culture

Rupestral art at cave and rock-shelter sites is characteristic of this tradition. Motifs include imagery of camelids, deer, puma, and other species. Some human figures are known, and frequently, these are shown with motions that indicate hunting, such as thrusting spears or sticks into animals. Simple geometric images are also found, including dot patterns, grids, and blots of color. The meaning of this art, however, is unknown.

References

Abbott, M., M. Binford, M. Brenner, and K. Kelts (1997a). "A 3500-year 14C High-Resolution Record of Water-Level Changes in Lake Titicaca, Bolivia/Peru." *Quaternary Research* 47: 169–180.

Abbott, M., G. Seltzer, K. Kelts, and J. Southon (1997b). "Holocene Paleohydrology of the Tropical Andes from Lake Records." *Quaternary Research* 47: 70–80.

Aldenderfer, M. (1996) "Pedestrian and Buried Sites Reconnaissance for Early to Late Preceramic Archaeological Sites in the Rio Ilave Drainage, southern Peru." Report submitted to the National Geographic Society, (Project Number 5245–94).

Aldenderfer, M. (1998). *Montane Foragers: Asana and the South-Central Andean Archaic*. Iowa City: University of Iowa Press.

Aldenderfer, M. (in press). *Quelcatani: The Prehistory of a Pastoral Lifeway on the High Puna*. Washington, D.C.: Smithsonian Institution Press.

Aldenderfer, M., and C. Klink (1996). "Archaic Period Settlement in the Lake Titicaca Basin: Results of a Recent Survey." Paper presented at the 36th annual meeting of the Institute for Andean Studies, Berkeley.

Binford, M., A. Kolata, M. Brenner, J. Janusek, M. Seddon, M. Abbott, and J. Curtis (1997). "Climate Variation and the Rise and Fall of an Andean Civilization." *Quaternary Research* 47: 235–248.

Cross, S., P. Baker, G. Seltzer, S. Fritz, and R. Dunbar (1997). "Holocene Paleohydrology of Lake Titicaca." *Transactions of the American Geophysical Union Annual Meeting* F30.

Frye, K. (1999). "Settlement Pattern Research near Chuquito, Southern Peru." Unpublished manuscript.

Klink, C. (1999). "Informe Preliminar de un Reconocimiento Arqueologico del Rio Huenque, Peru." Unpublished manuscript.

Seltzer, G. P. Baker, P., S. Cross, and R. Dunbar (1998). "High-Resolution Seismic Reflection Profiles from Lake Titicaca, Peru-Bolivia: Evidence for Holocene Aridity in the Tropical Andes." *Geology* 26: 167–170.

Stanish, C., E. de la Vega, L. Steadman, C. Chavez, K. Frye, L. Onofre Mamani, M. Seddon, and P. Calisaya (1997). "Archaeological Survey in the Juli-Desaguadero Region of Lake Titicaca Basin, Southern Peru." *Fieldania Anthropology* n.s. 29.

Wirrmann, D., and P. Mourguiart (1995). "Late Quaternary Spatio-temporal Limnological Variations in the Altiplano of Bolivia and Peru." *Quaternary Research* 43: 344–354.

Northern Andean Late Hunting-Collecting

TIME PERIOD: 8000–6000 B.P.

LOCATION: On the western flanks of the Andes and adjacent altiplano (or *paramo*) in the southern Ecuadorian highlands.

CULTURAL SUMMARY

Environment

The few known sites of this tradition are found on the western flanks of the Andes in the southern Ecuadorian highlands in an elevational range from c. 2000–3100 m. At lower elevations, the modern climate is warm and moist, and primary productivity is high. At higher elevations, sites are found in the *paramo* grasslands, which are used today for farming but would have been highly productive environments for deer and other large mammal species. Most of the sites of this tradition are located within 30–40 km on the other side of the *paramo* of the western boundary of the tropical forest ecological zone. Although firm connections with the Amazon basin are not known of the sites of this period, it is clear they are situated within an environment of considerable ecological diversity.

Settlements

Very little is known of the range of site types in this tradition. Chobshi Cave, at 2400 m, probably served as a short-term residential site for a small band of foragers (Lynch 1989). Other smaller, open-air sites, like the slightly earlier Cubilán, which are found on the *paramo* grasslands, likely served as a hunting camp or a logistical camp devoted to the exploitation of game (Temme 1982).

Economy

Again, although data are scarce, faunal evidence recovered from Chobshi Cave shows that deer, both whitetailed and *pudu*, were of considerable importance to the diet as were small mammals. Direct evidence of plant remains, however, has yet to be systematically recovered from any site of this tradition, but given the significant plant productivity of this region in the past, plants were likely important to diet. Exchange (or more probably down-the-line trading) of obsidian from northern Ecuadorian sites occurred during this time as well.

Sociopolitical Organization

All archaeological indicators point to an egalitarian society. Site sizes are small, population density insofar as it is known is low, and the artifacts present at the few known sites of this tradition appear to be utilitarian in nature with no evidence of wealth accumulation.

References

Lynch, T. (1989). "Chobshi Cave in Retrospect". *Andean Past* 2: 1–32.

Temme, M. (1982). "Excavaciones en el Sitio Precerámico de Cubilán (Ecuador)." *Miscelánea Antropológica Ecuatoriana* 2: 135–164.

South-Central Late Andean Hunting-Collecting

TIME PERIOD: 8000–6000 B.P.

LOCATION: On the western flanks of the south-central Andes from the southern half of the department of Arequipa, Peru, to extreme northern Chile.

DIAGNOSTIC MATERIAL ATTRIBUTES: A variety of projectile point forms, including large, triangular-bladed stemmed points; large foliates with and without ears; smaller bipointed foliates; some lanceolate forms.

CULTURAL SUMMARY

Environment

This tradition is found in the valleys of the western flanks of the Andes and encompasses a elevational range from roughly 2500–4500 m. Although most of this range lies within the high sierra environmental zone, which is characterized by generally low primary productivity and a patchy distribution of resources that are tethered to water sources, areas beyond 4000 m fall into a zone labeled the *puna* rim, which is composed of puna plant communities that are smaller and more spatially restricted when compared with similar communities on the altiplano or plateau. Many of the major streams that drain the western flanks have their headwaters in the *puna* rim. Distance from high elevation to the Pacific coast is often very short, ranging from 120–150 km. The area is characterized by a rainy season from November through March, with the remainder of the year fairly dry. From 8000–6000 B.P., the western flanks of the Andes underwent increasing desiccation. Higher elevations would have had more rainfall, and consequently, plant and animal densities would have been greatest in the *puna* rim and upper reaches of the high sierra. However, all life would have been tethered to stream courses and the occasional spring. The lower elevation areas of the sierra would have had low densities of plants and animals, but some of these species, like the wild ancestors of *Chenopodium* sp., are found in great natural abundance in this zone in modern times.

Settlements

Patchy, low-density resources would have promoted some degree of residential mobility (Aldenderfer 1998). In great part, mobility would have been influenced by seasonal variation in resource density and abundance, but for some resources, like the vicuña on the *puna* rim, would have been available year-round. Given the generally low densities of resources in the valleys, mobility would have also responded to resource depletion. Settlement patterns of this type have been observed in the Rio Osmore (or Moquegua), one of the major western-flank streams (Aldenderfer 1998; Cardona 1997; Cardona and Oquiche 1994), and are labeled the Muruq'uta phase (7800–6000 B.P.; Aldenderfer 1998, 2000). A similar pattern called the Asana phase (8000–6000 B.P.) has been described in the valleys of extreme northern Chile (Santoro 1989). Mobility ranges from the lower high sierra to the *puna* rim. Residential bases, such as Asana (Aldenderfer 1998), are located near high-density resource patches, which are exploited through the occupation of logistical camps used for short stays, such as Coscori and Tala. Hunting blinds and other locations complement the settlement pattern. Residential bases have small, circular structures with floors made of a locally available, prepared white clay that is pooled and shaped.

Economy

The economy of this tradition is based on hunting and gathering of wild plant and animal resources. To date, no cultivated or domesticated resources have been found. Plant species of importance include the wild ancestors of *Chenopodium* sp., tubers, and other seed-bearing plants. Animal resources include *huemul* and whitetailed deer, guanaco, and vicuña. Tools used include scrapers, projectile points, and other chipped-stone implements as well as ground-stone tools used for hide working, plant processing, and other grinding tasks. Raw materials used are predominantly local, although there is some very low level procurement of obsidian from sources well to the north of these sites as well as far nonlocal materials from the distant *puna* (Aldenderfer 1999).

Sociopolitical Organization

All archaeological indicators point to an egalitarian society. The limited mortuary evidence available reveals no wealth- or status-related distinctions, and what residential structures have been discovered suggest that any size variation within them was based upon household size, not rank. Public architecture, however, has been discovered at Asana. These public structures are larger than contemporary domestic residences and have no features within them that indicate residential use. They are ovoid in form and have special-purpose features in them, such as steam baths. These structures are usually found surrounded by domestic structures, not by a plaza or open space. Ethnographic analogy suggests these structures may have served as sweat lodges or community houses. No feasting took place within them or near them (Aldenderfer 1991).

Religion and Expressive Culture

Rupestral art at cave and rock-shelter sites is characteristic of this tradition. Motifs include imagery of camelids, deer, puma, and other species. Some human figures are known, and frequently, these are shown with motions that indicate hunting, such as thrusting spears or sticks into animals. Simple geometric images are also found, including dot patterns, grids, and blots of color. The meaning of this art, however, is unknown. One of the most outstanding examples of art in this tradition is from Toquepala (Ravines 1972), but smaller sites, such as Coscori, Huanacane, Tala, and Cruz Laca, are known to have similar artistic forms (Aldenderfer 1998; Klarich in press; Watanabe 1990).

References

Aldenderfer, M. (1991) "Continuity and Change in Ceremonial Structures at Late Preceramic Asana, Southern Peru." *Latin American Antiquity* 2: 227–258.

Aldenderfer, M. (1998). *Montane Foragers: Asana and the South-Central Andean Archaic*. Iowa City: University of Iowa Press.

Aldenderfer, M. (1999). "Cronología y conneciones: La evidencia preceramica de Asana." In *El Periodo Arcaico en el Peru. Hacia una Definición de los Origenes*, ed. P. Kaulicke. Lima: Boletin de Arqueologia, Pontifica Universidad Catolica del Peru 3, 375–391.

Cardona, A. (1997). *Inventario Arequologico de las Zonas Altas: Cuenca del Rio Torata y la Quebrada Cocotea*. Moquegua: Asociación Contisuyo.

Cardona, A., and A. Oquiche (1994). *Inventario Arequologico de las Zonas Altas: Cuenca de la Quebrada Honda*. Moquegua: Asociación Contisuyo.

Klarich, E. (in press). "Camelid Depictions in the Rupestral Art of Quelcatani: Hunters or Herders?" In *Quelcatani: The Evolution of a Pastoral Lifeway*, ed. M. Aldenderfer. Washington, D.C.: Smithsonian Institution Press.

Ravines, R. (1972). "Secuencia y Cambios en los Artefactos Liticos del Sur del Peru." *Revista del Museo Nacional* 38: 133–184.

Santoro, C. (1989). "Antiguos cazadores de la puna." In *Culturas de Chile: Prehistoria*, ed. J. Hidalgo, V. Schiappacasse, H. Niemeyer, C. Aldunate, and I. Solimano. Santiago: Editorial Andres Bello, 33–56.

Watanabe, L. (1990). "Pintura Rupestre en Ccscocollo, Huacanane, y Cruz Laca, Moquegua." In *Trabajos Arqueologicos en Moquegua, Peru*. ed. L. Watanabe, M. Moseley, and F. Cabieses. Lima: Museo Peruano de Ciencias de la Salud, 105–138.

SITES

Asana

TIME PERIOD: 10,000–3500 B.P.

LOCATION: On the Rio Asana in the department of Moquegua, southern Peru.

DESCRIPTIVE SUMMARY

Local Environment

Asana is located on the Río Asana, a small tributary stream of the Rio Osmore, at an elevation of 3435 m above mean sea level. The site lies within the high sierra environmental zone, which is characterized by generally low primary productivity, a patchy distribution of resources that is tethered to water sources and small, widely dispersed *bofedales* (high-quality pasture), and very low rainfall that falls during a short rainy season from November through April. The site is found in a flat basin in the valley adjacent to a *bofedal*.

Physical Features

Asana is an open-air site found on the north bank of the Rio Asana. Buried by a landslide at some point within the past 500 years, the site was exposed in a cut bank of the river. Excavation has demonstrated a long sequence of occupation of the site; at least 36 distinct cultural layers are found in more than 80 natural stratigraphic levels. Thirty radiocarbon assays range in date from 9850–3650 B.P. The landslide debris has made it difficult to determine the size of the site, but it has been estimated to be no more than 0.25 ha in maximum extent.

Cultural Aspects

Asana is one of the most important sites in the south-central Andes because of its long occupation and the range of cultural materials found at the site (Aldenderfer 1990, 1998). Most levels contain domestic or residential architecture. The earliest houses, which date to 9850 B.P., are small (3.5 m^2) and circular, defined by a pattern of post molds. Through time, these floors of these houses are made of a prepared white clay and range in size from c. 4–6.5 m^2 (Aldenderfer 1988, 1998). Public architecture, consisting of a large, oval structure some 12 m^2 in size, appears first by 7100 B.P. and persists until 6500 B.P. Larger (8–10.5 m^2) residential structures appear around 4800 B.P., and these are accompanied by a complex of ceremonial structures with ritual features (Aldenderfer 1991). From 10,000–9400 B.P., the site was a short-term camp occupied by foragers practicing a coast-to-highlands mobility pattern. Hide working was an important activity at Asana, but declined in importance after 8000 B.P. After this, the site served as a residential base of increasingly long-term occupation for foragers who confined their mobility to the highlands of the region. Diet throughout the occupation of the site focused on camelids and deer and became increasingly reliant on wild plant foods, most importantly *Chenopodium*, after 6000 B.P.

References

Aldenderfer, M. (1988). "Middle Archaic Period Domestic Architecture from Southern Peru." *Science* 241: 1828–1830.

Aldenderfer, M. (1990). "Cronología y Definición de Fases Arcaicas de Asana, Sur del Peru." *Chungará* 22.

Aldenderfer, M. (1991). "Continuity and Change in Ceremonial Structures at Late Preceramic Asana, Southern Peru." *Latin American Antiquity* 2: 227–258.

Aldenderfer, M. (1998). *Montane Foragers: Asana and the South-Central Andean Archaic*. Iowa City: University of Iowa Press.

Chobshi Cave

TIME PERIOD: 10,000–7500 B.P.

LOCATION: On the Chobshi plain to the west of the Rio Santa Barbara in southern Ecuador (Lynch 1989).

DESCRIPTIVE SUMMARY

Local Environment

The site is located at an elevation of 2400 m in an environment characterized by generally moist, relatively warm conditions. The area surrounding the site, especially near the stream courses, is thick with vegetation. The site is only 20 km from the high *paramo* grasslands and 40 km west of the edge of the tropical forest environment of the Amazon basin. As Lynch (1989) notes, the site is found in the midst of significant modern environmental diversity.

Physical Features

Chobshi Cave is best characterized as a rock shelter rather than a cave and has a maximum floor area of 150 m^2. It has an excellent view of the plains looking to the north from the opening of the shelter. The archaeological deposit at the site has been wholly destroyed by looting and modern agricultural practice, and almost no part of the deposit remains intact.

Cultural Aspects

Despite the significant disturbance of the deposit, the site has yielded important data that speak to the process of adaptation to the lower highlands of southern Ecuador. One radiocarbon date suggests an occupation by 10,000 B.P but the majority of the others recovered from the site range from 8500–7500 B.P. Lynch (1989) characterizes the site as a short-term, seasonally occupied base camp of a small band of foragers. Although plant remains were not recovered, the faunal materials present suggest a focus on the hunting of whitetailed deer and *pudu*, a smaller deer native to this region. Small mammals, including rabbit, agouti, and tapir, were also hunted. Artifact types include point styles that show affinities to sites to the north as well as to Guitarrero Cave farther to the south. Lynch also sees similarities to point styles found on the north and central Peruvian coast, such as Paijan. Small quantities of obsidian were also recovered, and these appear to be from sources in northern Ecuador (Burger et al. 1989).

References

Burger, R., F. Asaro, and H. Michel (1989). The Sources of Obsidian for Artifacts at Chobshi Cave. *Andean Past* 2: 33–37.
Lynch, T. (1989). Chobshi Cave in Retrospect. *Andean Past* 2: 1–32.

Guitarrero Cave

TIME PERIOD: 10,000–4000 B.P.

LOCATION: In the Callejón de Huaylas in the department of Ancash, north-central Peru.

DESCRIPTIVE SUMMARY

Local Environment

The site is located at 2580 m approximately 150 m above the floodplain of the Rio Santa, the principal drainage of the Callejón (Lynch 1980). The environment is arid, and native vegetation is characterized as xerophytic. However, the river bottom below the site has significant botanical diversity and once included numerous edible plants, such as cacti (Smith 1980).

Physical Features

Guitarrero Cave is a relatively small cave with approximately 100 m^2 of floor space. Relatively wide and open at its mouth, it narrows significantly at the back of the cave. The deposit had suffered significant disturbance by looters, and this has caused some controversy in the interpretation of the dating of the cultivated plants found (Stothert and Quilter 1991). The deposit, very shallow in places, generally varies between 30 cm to over 1 m in depth. Lynch (1980) has defined four major stratigraphic complexes that are discontinuous across the extent of the site. The deposits at the site are very dry, and this has aided the preservation of plant remains as well as fiber nets and baskets.

Cultural Aspects

Guitarrero Cave has figured prominently in reconstructions of settlement patterns in this region of the Andes. For the period 8000–6000 B.P., Lynch (1971,

1980) suggests that the site was occupied for short periods during the wet season (November–April), when plants would have been more abundant. The hunter gatherers of the this portion of the valley would have practiced a form of seasonal transhumance that would have stretched to the *puna* rim some 30 km to the east as well as somewhat farther down valley. Animal species exploited were small mammals and deer, and in contrast to many other high-elevation sites, camelids are conspicuous by their relative scarcity. Among the plant foods encountered are wild species, including an impressive diversity of tubers, cactus fruits, and other plants. Possibly cultivated plants are beans (*Phaseolus vulgaris*), tubers (*Ullucus tuberosus* and *Oxalis* sp.), peppers (*aji, Capsicum* sp.), and squash (*Curcurbita*). These species, from Complex II (c. 10,000–7600 B.P.), continue to be found throughout the occupation of the site. Maize appears somewhat later in the deposit, in Complex III times, which appears, however, to be significantly disturbed by later cultural activities. However, the relatively early presence of cultivars of a variety of plants at the site is important, but has yet to be confirmed through excavations at other north-central Andean sites.

References

Lynch, T. (1971). "Prehistoric Transhumance in the Callejón de Huaylas, Peru." *American Antiquity* 36: 139–148.

Lynch, T. (1980). *Guitarrero Cave: Early Man in the Andes.* New York: Academic Press.

Smith, C. (1980). "Vegetation and Land Use near Guitarrero Cave." In *Guitarrero Cave: Early Man in the Andes*, ed. T. Lynch. New York: Academic Press, 65–86.

Stothert, K., and J. Quilter (1991). "Archaic Adaptations of the Andean Region 9000 to 5000 B.P." *Revista de Arqueología Americana* 4: 25–53.

Lauricocha

TIME PERIOD: 10,000–3000 B.P.

LOCATION: At the headwaters of the Rio Marañon near Lago Lauricocha in the department of Lima, central Peru.

DESCRIPTIVE SUMMARY

Local Environment

The Lauricocha sites are found in an elevation range from 3880–4100 m in what corresponds to the two distinct ecological zones: the high sierra, which is characterized by generally low primary productivity and a patchy distribution of resources that is tethered to water sources and the *puna*, which is characterized by relatively abundant, seasonal (November–March) rainfall, cool to cold temperatures, and high primary productivity of grasses palatable to the native Andean camelids, especially the vicuña.

Physical Features

The Lauricocha sites consist of a series of small cave and rockshelter sites found at varying elevations. Three important caves, L-1, L-2, and L-2, are found near one another in a folded bedrock outcrop at an elevation range from 3880–3950 m. These sites have an excellent view of the lake and the *pampa* that surrounds it. A fourth cave, U-1, is found slightly above these sites at an elevation of 4020 m (Cardich 1958). Each of these sites is relatively small, ranging from c. 25 m² to almost 50 m². U-1 and L-2 have very deep and well-stratified deposits reaching almost 4 m in depth.

Cultural Aspects

Although excavations have been conducted in most of these sites, L-2 and U-1 have the longest and most complete cultural sequences. Cardich (1959, 1964) has defined five major cultural horizons in the strata of these sites. Lauricocha I is the earliest of these and has been dated to 9525 B.P. Unfortunately, this complex does not have diagnostic cultural materials that can be easily compared to other sites, although it does contain unfacial scraping tools and some large bifaces (Lynch 1967). Lauricocha II, estimated to date between 8000–5000 B.P., is richer, containing abundant faunal remains (camelids, deer, and other high sierra and *puna* margin species), and projectile points typical of this time frame, including a variety of foliate forms. Scrapers and other tools forms are also common. Although the seasonality of site utilization is not known, the relatively low density of tools recovered suggests the sites were short-term camps or residential bases occupied only part of the year (Rick 1988: 36).

References

Cardich, A. (1958). *Los Yacimientos de Lauricocha.* Buenos Aires: Studia Praehistorica I.

Cardich, (1959). "Los Yacimientos de Lauricocha y la Nueva Interpretación de la Prehistoria Peruana." *Actas y Trabajos del II Congreso Nacional de Historia del Peru* 1: 93–106.

Cardich, A. (1964). *Lauricocha: Fundamentos para una Prehistoria de los Andes Centrales.* Buenos Aires: Studia Praehistorica III.

Lynch, T. (1967). *The Nature of the Central Andean Preceramic.* Pocatello: Occasional Papers of the Idaho State Museum 21.

Rick, J. (1988). "The Character and Context of Highland Preceramic Society." In *Peruvian Prehistory*, ed. R. Keatinge. Cambridge: Cambridge University Press, 3–40.

Pachamachay

TIME PERIOD: 11,000–2000 B.P.

LOCATION: On the Junin *puna* in the department of Junin, central Peru.

DESCRIPTIVE SUMMARY

Local environment

Pachamachay is found on the Junin puna at an elevation of 4300 m. The site is located within the wet *puna* environmental zone, which is characterized by relatively abundant, seasonal (November–March) rainfall, cool to cold temperatures, and high primary productivity of grasses palatable to the native Andean camelids, especially the vicuña.

Physical Features

Pachamachay is a large rock-shelter site found in a large bedrock outcrop overlooking the *puna* grasslands below it. The site has excellent stratigraphy, which reflects a long sequence of occupation.

Cultural Aspects

Pachamachay is a site with extraordinary artifact densities. Although only a relatively small area of the site has been excavated, artifact densities are extremely high; Rick (1988: 36) has estimated the tool density to be 1500/m^3. This is far greater than most contemporary sites in the Andean world. Bone densities are likewise high. These data, plus settlement pattern studies, have allowed Rick (1980, 1988) to construct a model of early sedentism in this high-elevation environment. Following an early logistical or short-term use of the site from 11,000–9000 B.P., Pachamachay was occupied by a small band of hunters who used it as a permanent residential base from 9000–7000 B.P. The hunters exploited the very dense populations of vicuña that are found on the Junin *puna*. Plant foods were relatively unimportant to the diet and were dominated by the use of wild chenopods. There are suggestions of residential structures built within the shelter at this time. Although camelids formed the basis of the diet, there is little evidence that these animals were husbanded or herded until after 4000 B.P. Projectile point styles recovered from the site include a well-stratified series of forms, including rhomboids, lanceolates, foliates, and stemmed forms. Because of the large quantities of points, a well-designed classification scheme, and good chronological control, the sequence at Pachamachay has served as a baseline of comparison for projectile point styles across the Andes.

References

Rick, J. (1980). *Prehistoric Hunters of the High Andes.* New York: Academic Press.

Rick, J. (1988). "The Character and Context of Highland Preceramic Society." In *Peruvian Prehistory*, ed. R. Keatinge. Cambridge: Cambridge University Press, 3–40.

Pikimachay

TIME PERIOD: 11,000–2000 B.P.

LOCATION: The site is located near the modern town of Ayacucho in the department of Ayacucho, central Peru.

DESCRIPTIVE SUMMARY

Local Environment

Pikimachay is found at an elevation of 2850 m on a low hill in the center of the Ayacucho valley. The site is found in a thorn forest scrub ecozone, which is characterized by low seasonal (October–March) rainfall, relatively mild temperatures, and moderate productivity of xerophytic species, including mesquite and cacti.

Physical Features

Pikimachay is a very large cave, with a maximum width of 50 m and depth of 20 m (MacNeish 1981: 28). Much of the floor area, however, is covered with massive roof fall. A conservative estimate of open space is approximately 200 m^2. The deposit of the site was highly complex and varied in depth from 40 cm to over 1.5 m. The stratigraphy revealed up to 16 major zones.

Cultural Aspects

Although MacNeish (1981) has argued that Pikimachay has a very early human presence (19,000–23,000 B.P.), most archaeologists working in the region are skeptical of these claims. There is little debate about the post-11,000 B.P. occupation of the site, however, and three of his phases (Jaywa, 9100–7800 B.P.; Piki, 7800–6400 B.P., and Chihua, 6400–5100 B.P.) are pertinent to this discussion. Although hunting was important in all three phases, there was a more intensive use of plants near the end of the Jaywa phase, a trend that continues into those that follow. The use of Pikimachay during this phase was a fall-winter camp of a small segment of the entire co-residential group. Although settlement was focused primarily upon the valley and its minor tributary streams, some logistical use of the nearby *puna* occurred. This pattern of wet season use continues into the Piki phase with continued short-term use. MacNeish (1983) argues that domesticated plants—*Chenopodium* sp. (*quinoa*), squash, and gourd—make their appearance in this phase. Gathered plants remain important. Finally, in Chihua times, although the use of the site remains the same, the season of its occupation shifts to the spring.

References

MacNeish, R. (1981). "The Stratigraphy of Pikimachay, Ac 100." In *Prehistory of the Ayacucho Basin, Peru. vol. II: Excavations and Chronology*, ed. R. MacNeish, A. Cook, L. Lumbreras, R. Vierra, and A. Nelken-Terner. Ann Arbor: University of Michigan Press, 19–56.

MacNeish, R. (1983). "The Ayacucho Preceramic as a Sequence of Cultural Energy-Flow Systems." In *Prehistory of the Ayacucho Basin, Peru. vol. IV: The Preceramic Way of Life*, ed. R. MacNeish, R. Vierra, A. Nelken-Terner, R. Lurie, and A. Cook. Ann Arbor: University of Michigan Press, 236–280.

Quelcatani

TIME PERIOD: 7500 B.P.–A.D. 1472.

LOCATION: Along the Rio Chila in the department of Puno, southern Peru.

DESCRIPTIVE SUMMARY

Local Environment

Quelcatani is found on the extreme southern margin of the Lake Titicaca basin on the north bank of the Rio Chila, a small tributary stream that flows into the Rio Chichillape. The site, at an elevation of 4420 m, is located within the dry *puna* environmental zone of the Andes and is characterized by relatively abundant, seasonal (November–March) rainfall, cool to cold temperatures, and high primary productivity of grasses palatable to the native Andean camelids, especially the vicuña.

Physical Features

Quelcatani is a large rock shelter with c. 200 m² of covered floor area beneath the dripline. The surface of the shelter is relatively flat, but in places is interrupted by massive rockfall from the walls, which in some places achieves a depth of over 5 m. The deposit of the site varies in depth from a minimum of 1 m to over 2 m, and within a series of over 60 natural soil layers are found 36 cultural strata that range in date from 7250 B.P. to recent times. The site lies approximately 5 m above the floor of the stream, which is itself surrounded by *bofedal*, a high-quality pasture that is capable of supporting high densities of wild as well as domesticated animals.

Cultural Aspects

Quelcatani was the first rock shelter in the southern Lake Titicaca basin to have been systematically excavated (Aldenderfer in press). The long sequence of occupation at the site has provided important insight into settlement dynamics and cultural change in the region. Moreover, the site has an extraordinary corpus of rupestral art comparable to that found at Toquepala and sites in northern Chile. Images include large numbers of camelids, deer, felines, native birds, anthropomorphic forms, and a diversity of geometrics (Aldenderfer 1987; Ravines 1986). Variation in the manner of execution of the camelid images in particular suggests that some images have been drawn by hunting peoples and others by herders (Klarich in press). These changes in the art are tracked by changes in other aspects of material culture. From 7500–4000 B.P., the inhabitants at Quelcatani were hunters who used the site on a seasonal basis. They constructed small shelters against the back wall of the cave, and their diet consisted mostly of camelids, but included some deer. Plant use was minimal, but did include wild forms of *Chenopodium* sp. After 3660 B.P., we see a shift toward a herding economy. Houses built within the shelter are more substantial, and the animal bone assemblage reflects patterns seen when camelids are herded. Ceramics and domesticated forms of chenopods are also found in the site, which was most likely occupied year-round. This pastoral lifeway continues, but with variation in the nature of external contacts, through the final abandonment of the site, which occurs some time during the 17th century A.D.

References

Aldenderfer, M. (1987). "Hunter-Gatherer Settlement Dynamics and Rupestral Art: Inferring Mobility and Aggregation in the South-Central Andes of Southern Peru." In *Actas del VIII Simposio Internacional De Arte Rupestre Americano*. Santo Domingo: Museo Del Hombre Dominicano, 373–403.

Aldenderfer, M. (in press). *Quelcatani: The Evolution of a Pastoral Lifeway*. Washington, D.C.: Smithsonian Institution Press.

Klarich, E. (in press). "Camelid Depictions in the Rupestral Art of Quelcatani: Hunters or Herders?" In *Quelcatani: The Evolution of a Pastoral Lifeway*, ed. M. Aldenderfer. Washington, D.C.: Smithsonian Institution Press.

Ravines, R. (1986). "Quelcatani." In *Arte Rupestre del Peru*, ed. R. Ravines. Lima: Instituto Nacional de Cultura, 51–52.

Telarmachay

TIME PERIOD: 9000–2000 B.P.

LOCATION: On the southern margin of the Junin *puna* in the department of Junin, central Peru.

DESCRIPTIVE SUMMARY

Local Environment

Telarmachay is found in the wet *puna* environmental zone of the Andes at an elevation of 4420 m. The site is located relatively near the headwaters of the Rio Shalka-Palcamayo, one of the valleys of the western flanks of the Andes. The wet *puna* is characterized by relatively abundant, seasonal (November–March) rainfall, cool to cold temperatures, and high primary productivity of grasses palatable to the native Andean camelids, especially the vicuña.

Physical Features

Telarmachay is a large rock shelter found in a series of eroding bedrock hills overlooking a large, open *pampa*. The area of the site within the drip line is relatively small, measuring no more than approximately 35 m². Disturbance was confined to an area adjacent to the back wall of the shelter. Excavations at the site have revealed a series of seven major strata, which contained nine distinct cultural levels. These levels were removed through a horizontal excavation strategy (*décapage*). The maximum depth of the undisturbed strata was just over 2 m.

Cultural Aspects

Unlike nearby Pachamachay, Telarmachay appears to have been used only during the wet season (December–April) over much of the occupation of the site (Lavallée 1987; Lavallée et al. 1982). It has been postulated that these hunter gatherers lived in the adjacent lower elevation valleys for the remainder of the year. The earliest inhabitants of the site practiced a form of mixed hunting, which included wild camelids (both the vicuña and the guanaco) and deer. During the period 7200–6000 B.P., the hunting strategy shifted to one in which the camelids were the primary focus of the diet. Between 6000–5500 B.P., the authors argue that an "alpaca-like" animal was herded, and that after 5000 B.P., the inhabitants of the shelter were full-time pastoralists. Throughout the occupation of the site, plant foods were relatively unimportant. Three burials were recovered from the site (all dating between 7200–6800 B.P.), and one of these, a female, was interred with a complete hide-working toolkit, which included bone needles and awls as well as stone knives and scrapers.

References

Lavallée, D. (1987). *Telarmachay: Chasseurs et Pasteurs Préhistoriques de Andes 1*. Paris: Institut Français d'Études Andines. Éditions Récherche sur les Civilisations.

Lavallée, D., M. Julien, and J. Wheeler (1982). "Telarmachay: Niveles Precerámicos de Ocupación." *Revista del Museo Nacional* 46: 55–133.

Toquepala

TIME PERIOD: 10,000–5000 B.P.

LOCATION: On the flanks of Cerro Huancanane in the department of Tacna, southern Peru.

DESCRIPTIVE SUMMARY

Local Environment

Toquepala is found in the lower high sierra environmental zone of the western flanks of the Andes at an elevation of approximately 2700 m. This zone is characterized by pervasive aridity and very low primary productivity. The site is located in a series of rock outcrops some 500 m above the floor of a small stream, which would have been the major source of water for the site in the past.

Physical Features

Toquepala consists of two parts: the cave (Ta 1-1) and the rockshelter (Ta 1-2), which is found to the east of the cave entrance. The cave has an interior floor space of some 50 m², with a maximum interior height of 3 m. Although the roof of the cave is irregular, its walls are relatively smooth. The rockshelter is somewhat smaller, measuring 40 m², with a maximum height of 4.6 m (Ravines 1986). Excavations within the cave defined a shallow deposit of varying depth; the rockshelter, in contrast, contained a series of at least five major strata in a depth of 0.65 m. Dates obtained from the rock shelter range from 9580–5160 B.P.

Cultural Aspects

Toquepala was one of the first cave and rockshelter sites to be systematically excavated in the south-central Andes (Ravines 1972). It provided the first approximation to understanding settlement dynamics as well as early cultural affiliations in the region. Moreover, the site has an extraordinary corpus of rupestral art in both the cave and rockshelter. Images depicted on the walls include hunting scenes, camelids, deer, humans, and geometric forms (Ravines 1986). Because the occupation of the site ends before the advent of pastoralism in the region, its art is an extraordinary record of hunting life. Despite the aridity of the region, the preservation of perishable artifacts of wood or fiber is very poor. What is known of diet suggests that hunting was of paramount importance. The site probably served as a short-term residential base or temporary camp throughout its period of use.

References

Ravines, R. (1972). "Secuencia y Cambios en los Artefactos Liticos del Sur del Peru." *Revista del Museo Nacional* 38: 133–184.

Ravines, R. (1986). "Toquepala." In *Arte Rupestre del Peru*, ed. R. Ravines. Lima: Instituto Nacional de Cultura, 57–86.

Viscachani

TIME PERIOD: 8000–5000 B.P.

LOCATION: The provincia of Sica Sica in the department of La Paz, west-central highlands of Bolivia.

DESCRIPTIVE SUMMARY

Local Environment

Viscachani is found on an ancient beach terrace above a small stream at an elevation of 3831 m. The site overlooks a large *pampa*, or grassland. The site is found in the wet puna (or altiplano) environmental zone, which is characterized by high primary productivity and marked seasonality of rainfall (November–April).

Physical Features

Viscachani is an open-air site, one of the few to be described for the Bolivian highlands. The site is said to be from 9–12 ha in size, but because it has not been systematically collected or mapped, it is difficult to verify this claim (Patterson and Heizer 1965). Wind erosion has exposed high concentrations of lithic materials across the surface of the site. Very limited test excavations have demonstrated the site has no stratigraphic integrity (Lynch 1967).

Cultural Aspects

Although the site has not been excavated or collected systematically, the evidence from the site, particularly that of projectile point form, has been of great importance in the development of chronologies for this region. The majority of the points are made of a local quartzite. The forms found at the site are typical of those of the period and include a range of stemmed forms, lanceolate, and foliate forms. Large numbers of reduction byproducts are also found at the site, including many broken and whole mid-to-late stage bifaces that have been labeled as "Viscachani foliates" (Ibarra Grasso 1954; Menghin 1955). Other stone tools said to have been recovered include unifacial scrapers and bifaces presumed to have been used as knives.

References

Ibarra Grasso, R. (1954). "Hallazgos de Puntas Paleolíticas en Bolivia." *Proceedings of the 31ˢᵗ International Congress of the Americas* 2: 561–568.

Lynch, T. (1967). *The Nature of the Central Andean Preceramic.* Pocatello: Occasional Papers of the Idaho State Museum 21.

Menghin, O. (1955). "Culturas Precerámicas en Bolivia." *Runa: Archivo para las Ciencias de Hombre* 6: 125–132.

Patterson, T., and R. Heizer (1965). "A Preceramic Stone Tool Collection from Viscachani, Bolivia." *Ñawpa Pacha* 3: 107–114.

MARK ALDENDERFER
Department of Anthropology
University of California
Santa Barbara, California
United States

Late Coastal Andean Formative

Early Horizon

ABSOLUTE TIME PERIOD: 3000–2200 B.P.

RELATIVE TIME PERIOD: Follows the Early Coastal Andean Formative tradition, precedes the Andean Regional Development tradition.

LOCATION: A narrow coastal desert strip 20–50 km wide running along the Pacific coast within the modern borders of Peru between La Leche valley in the north and the Nazca valley in the south.

DIAGNOSTIC MATERIAL ATTRIBUTES: Pottery on the north coast varies in thickness and is often decorated with incision, stamped circles and dots, textile and net impressions, or occasional painting. South coast pottery has incised designs associated with postfired polychrome painting as well as simpler prefired painting. Vessel shapes on the north coast include tall-neck bottles, thick stirrup spout vessels, neckless ollas, tall-neck and short-neck jars, large jars with everted rims, and open bowls, whereas the south coast vessel shapes are dominated by double-spout-and-bridge vessels and open bowls. Long, thin ground-slate projectile points are typical of the north coast. Woven cotton textiles with geometric designs occur on the north coast, whereas elaborate embroidered wool and cotton textiles typify the south coast. Copper and gold artifacts appear for the first time in this period. Houses are rectangular and irregular quandrangular structures with stone footings and cane

and/or wooden superstructures, and most are laid out in an irregular pattern. Settlement patterns are characterized by large communities of interconnected room complexes that incorporate low platforms.

REGIONAL SUBTRADITIONS: North Coast Late Formative, South Coast Late Formative.

IMPORTANT SITES: Chankillo, Kushipampa, Pampa Rosario, Paracas, San Diego.

CULTURAL SUMMARY

Environment

Climate. The Late Coastal Formative tradition evolved in a hyperarid desert environment that has changed little since the Pleistocene. The coast is a cool desert with relatively high humidity that ranges in temperature from about 60° F in the winter to about 80° F in the summer.

Topography. The Late Coastal Formative tradition is present within the confines of most major coastal river valleys as well as along the coastline adjacent to favorable places for fish and shellfish exploitation. Significant topographic changes include the aggradation of river valleys and the progradation of alluvial deposits at river mouths that eventually filled in most estuaries that once supplied ready sources of aquatic food.

Geology. The Late Coastal Formative region is characterized by numerous river valleys that descend down the western slopes of the Andes mountains, opening up to wider alluvial fan deposits within 30 km of the Pacific coastline. Feeding laterally into the main river channels are various colluvial channels that contain water and sediment only during rare El Niño rain events. Outside the river valleys are hyperarid zones characterized by bedrock overlain by eolian deposits of various ages. Granodiorite, andesite, and basalt are readily available in most areas for use in construction.

Biota. The Late Coastal Formative region is characterized by river valleys substantially altered by human intervention. Natural floodplains with associated vegetation are fairly narrow in most coastal valleys. Irrigation agriculture, which had been introduced in most valleys by 4000 B.P., quickly expanded cultivation zones out onto desert areas previously completely lacking in plant growth. This rapid expansion drastically reduced the area of natural vegetation, which included *algarrobo* trees and scrub bushes while also eliminating most of the edible land fauna such as whitetailed deer. During the Late Coastal Formative, animal protein was obtained from marine fish and shellfish as well as from domesticated terrestial species such as llamas and guinea pigs.

Settlements

Settlements System. Late Coastal Formative settlements seem to consist of five primary kinds of sites: (1) sizable urban settlements characterized by numerous courtyard-small platform-room complexes and deep midden deposits; (2) substantial sites dominated by one large compound; (3) fortified hilltop sites that may or may not be associated with substantial domestic components; (4) specialized elite cemeteries; and (5) small village sites. A partial settlement hierarchy exists in which larger sites are served by smaller ones, but no single site appears to dominate a single valleywide polity. The fortified portions of hilltop sites most likely served as places of refuge to fend off surprise attack. The number of fortified sites, especially along the north coast, suggest the existence of endemic intervalley and intravalley conflict among numerous small polities.

Community Organization. Sites typically do not show any degree of overall planning and appear to reflect accretional growth. The high quality of some pottery,

textiles, and metal artifacts suggests the existence of full-time specialists, but little hard evidence has been found of specialized areas for the production of these items.

Housing. Late Coastal Formative houses are small (2 × 4 m on a side), rectangular in shape, and were presumably used by nuclear families. Houses are above-ground or semisubterranean and made of quarried stone with cane or wooden superstructures covered with mud plaster.

Population, Health, and Disease. Larger sites probably housed about 1000–2000 people; smaller sites held only a few hundred individuals.

Economy

Subsistence. The Late Coastal Formative subsistence was based on permanent agriculture practiced within the irrigated coastal river valleys. Wild food resources came almost exclusively from the Pacific ocean.

Wild Foods. Almost no wild plant food sources were utilized or even available to the people of the Late Coastal Formative tradition. Fish and shellfish were gathered by inhabitants of coastal fishing villages, who exchanged these products for inland agricultural products. The marine products offered a stable year-round source of protein.

Domestic Foods. The vast majority of the food eaten by the people of this time period came from irrigation agriculture. The primary domesticates were maize, peanuts, common beans, lima beans, squash, potatoes, sweet potatoes, avocadoes, *lucuma*, guava, and *cansaboca*. Cotton and gourd were also grown for industrial purposes. Depending on the river valley, from one to three crops per year could be grown. Domesticated llamas and guinea pigs were also kept for use as food.

Industrial Arts. Late Coastal Formative technology was simple and generally available to everyone. Most items were probably manufactured by individuals within households, but the high quality of some textiles, ceramics, and gold objects suggests that the existence of some part-time or even full-time specialists.

Utensils. Primary utensils were (1) thin-walled pottery made from local soils; (2) scrapers and hoes made from large, locally available, marine shells; (3) pointed wooden digging sticks; and (4) ground-slate projectile points. Pottery forms include neckless ollas, short-necked and tall-necked jars, open bowls, bottles, stirrup spout vessels, and double spout and bridge vessels. Pottery decoration includes punctation, broad incision, zones of black graphite paint and red slip paint, appliqué bumps, fabric impressions, and circle-and-dot motifs.

Ornaments. Plain woven textiles are common at sites in the north. Elaborated embroidered textiles are typical of the south coast. Beads made of marine shell, bird bones, turquoise, and chrysocolla are the most common types of ornaments. Imported *Spondylus* shell from southern Ecuador occurs in small quantities at selected sites. On the south coast, gold nose ornaments and masks have been found in numerous mummy bundles. Other gold ornaments such as ear plugs are known, but these objects lack proper context, and their dating rests on somewhat shaky stylistic grounds. Red pigment is commonly found, some of which may have been used as body paint.

Trade. *Spondylus* shell, extant as whole shells or as worked ornaments, suggests long-distance trade with people along the southern coast of Ecuador. Occasional fragments of obsidian suggests long-distance trade with sources in the southern highlands of Peru. Such trade probably involved several parties in a down-the-line type of exchange system.

Division of Labor. Part-time or full-time specialists may have been present during this time period to produce ceramics, textiles, and gold ornaments, but no definite workshops have yet been reported.

Differential Access or Control of Resources. Elites appear to have controlled the production and distribution of food and some manufactured items as well as the distribution of irrigation water.

Sociopolitical Organization

Political Organization. Settlement patterns and artifact distributions suggest that small polities were organized around a single individual or small group of individuals. Site-size hierarchy suggests that two levels of authority existed in some places, representing a chiefdom of level organization. The modest size of the largest constructions of the time period suggests that the elites' power over labor was channeled into production of status artifacts such as fine pottery, textiles, and jewelry.

Conflict. The presence of numerous hilltop forts and fortified sites protected by walls and ditches indicates the presence or threat of conflict, both on an intravalley and intervalley level.

Religion and Expressive Culture

Religious Beliefs. Iconography suggests that religious beliefs involved a cosmology that included supernatural beings in the form of animals, humans, and combined human/animal creatures.

Ceremonies. Public ceremonies most likely took place in rectangular and square plazas and courtyards located within courtyard-small platform-room complexes. Iconographic depictions include San Pedro cactus, which was possibly used as a ritual hallucinogenic agent to enter the spirit world.

Arts. Inhabitants of this time period used a variety of media for art. Painted and plastic pottery decoration was rendered in both geometric and naturalistic styles. Unsurpassed embroidered textiles characterize the elite Paracas mummy bundles of the south coast of Peru. Designs consist of multicolored fantastic creatures with human and animal characteristics, which were embroidered on large mantles. Gold was rendered mostly into small jewelry items for facial, neck, and head decorations. A limited number of painted murals and possible friezes adorn some public buildings. Part-time or full-time specialists may have been needed to effect many of the more elaborate artistic accomplishments.

Death and Afterlife. Relatively few burials dating to this time period have been scientifically excavated. Elite grave goods sometimes consist of elaborate pottery vessels, some imported *Spondylus* shell, and small gold objects. Differential grave goods are more indicative of status differences than in the Early Coastal Formative tradition.

Suggested Readings

Burger, Richard L. (1992). *Chavin and the Origins of Andean Civilization*. London: Thames and Hudson.

Haas, Jonathan, Shelia, Pozorski, and Thomas Pozorski, eds. (1987). *The Origins and Development of the Andean State*. Cambridge: Cambridge University Press.

Keatinge, Richard, ed. (1988). *Peruvian Prehistory*. Cambridge: Cambridge University Press.

Moseley, Michael (1983). Central Andean Civilization. In *Ancient South Americans*, ed. J. Jennings. San Francisco: W. H. Freeman, 179–239.

Moseley, Michael (1992). *The Incas and Their Ancestors*. London: Thames and Hudson.

Paul, Anne, ed. (1991). *Paracas Art and Architecture: Object and Context in South Coastal Peru*. Iowa City: University of Iowa Press.

Pozorski, Shelia, and Thomas Pozorski (1987). *Early Settlement and Subsistence in the Casma Valley, Peru*. Iowa City: University of Iowa Press.

Pozorski, Shelia, and Thomas Pozorski (1992). "Early Civilization in the Casma Valley, Peru." *Antiquity* 66: 845–870.

Richardson, James (1994). *People of the Andes*. Washington, D.C.: Smithsonian Books.

Wilson, David (1988). *Prehispanic Settlement Patterns in the Lower Santa Valley, Peru*. Washington, D.C.: Smithsonian Institution Press.

SUBTRADITIONS

North Coast Late Coastal Formative

TIME PERIOD: 3000–2200 B.P.

LOCATION: A narrow coastal desert strip 20–50 km wide running along the Pacific coast between La Leche valley in the north and the Huarmey valley in the south.

DIAGNOSTIC MATERIAL ATTRIBUTES: Pottery varies in thickness, often decorated with incision, stamped circles and dots, textile and net impressions, or occasional painting. Vessel shapes include tall-neck bottles, thick stirrup spout vessels, neckless ollas, tall-neck and short-neck jars, large jars with everted rims, and open bowls. Long, thin slate projectile points are typical of the area. Woven cotton textiles with geometric designs are also present. Copper and gold artifacts appear for the first time in this period. Houses are rectangular and irregular quandrangular with stone footings and cane and/or wooden superstructures, and most are laid out in an irregular pattern. Settlement patterns include large, dense communities of interconnected room complexes that incorporate low platforms.

CULTURAL SUMMARY

Environment

The climate experienced by the people of this subtradition was cool and hyperarid, much like the modern climate. The topography of the area is characterized by a long, narrow coastal desert strip periodically cut by numerous river channels that descend the western slopes of the Andes mountains (Burger 1992; Richardson 1994). Vegetation, mostly confined to the narrow coastal river valleys, is present well beyond the confines of natural floodplains because of irrigation agriculture, which has supported coastal life for at least the last 4000 years (Moseley 1983, 1992). Most food consisted of domesticated plants grown in the river valleys. Animal protein came from marine fish and shellfish as well as from llamas and guinea pigs introduced from the highlands (Burger 1992; Moseley 1992).

Settlements

North Coast Late Coastal Formative settlements seem to consist of four primary kinds of sites: (1) sizable urban settlements characterized by numerous courtyard-small platform-room complexes and deep midden deposits, (2) substantial sites dominated by one large compound, (3) fortified hilltop sites that may or may not be associated with substantial domestic components, and (4) small village sites (Burger 1992; Daggett 1984, 1987; Pozorski 1987; S. Pozorski and T. Pozorski 1987, 1992; Wilson 1987, 1988). A partial settlement hierarchy exists in which larger sites are served by smaller ones, but no single site appears to dominate a single valley-wide polity. The fortified portions of hilltop sites most likely served as places of refuge to fend off surprise attack and suggest the existence of endemic intervalley and intravalley conflict among numerous small polities (Daggett 1984; Wilson 1988). Sites typically do not show overall planning and appear to reflect accretional growth. The high quality of some of the pottery, textiles, and metal artifacts suggests the existence of full-time specialists, but little hard evidence has been found of specialized areas for the production of these items. Houses are small (2–4 m on a side) and rectangular in shape, presumably for nuclear families. Houses are above-ground or semisubterranean and made of quarried stone with cane or wooden superstructures covered with mud plaster (S. Pozorski and T. Pozorski 1987). Larger sites probably housed about 1000–2000 people; smaller sites held only a few hundred individuals (Burger 1992; S. Pozorski and T. Pozorski 1987; Wilson 1988).

Economy

The people of the North Coast Late Coastal Formative relied almost exclusively on irrigation agriculture to grow a wide variety of plant foods, including maize, peanuts, common beans, lima beans, squash, potatoes, sweet potatoes, avocadoes, *lucuma*, guava, *cansaboca*, gourd, and cotton (Fung 1969; Pozorski 1987; S. Pozorski and T. Pozorski 1987). Fish and shellfish were gathered by inhabitants of coastal fishing villages who exchanged these products for inland agricultural products. Llamas and guinea pigs, introduced from the highlands during this time period, offered alternative animal protein resources to the stable marine faunal resources (Pozorski 1987; S. Pozorski and T. Pozorski 1987). Primary utensils were (1) thin-walled pottery vessels made from local soils; (2) scrapers and hoes made from large, locally available marine shells; (3) pointed wooden digging sticks; and (4) ground-slate projectile points (Daggett 1984; S. Pozorski and T. Pozorski 1987). Pottery forms include neckless ollas, short-necked and tall-necked jars, open bowls, bottles, and thick stirrup spout vessels. Pottery decoration includes punctation; broad incision; zones of black graphite paint, white paint, and red slip paint; appliqué bumps; fabric-impressions; and circle-and-dot motifs (Daggett 1984, 1987; Pozorski 1987; S. Pozorski and T. Pozorski 1987). Beads made of marine shell, bird bones, turquoise, and chrysocolla are the most common types of ornaments. Imported *Spondylus* shell, indicative of indirect or direct long-distance trade with southern Ecuador, occurs in small quantities at selected sites (S. Pozorski and T. Pozorski 1987). Occasional fragments of obsidian suggest trade connections with the southern highlands of Peru. The occasional gold ornaments encountered, such as ear plugs (Burger 1992), lack reliable contexts; therefore, the dating of these objects rests on somewhat shaky stylistic grounds. Red pigment is commonly found, some of which may have been used as body paint. Part-time or full-time specialists may have been present during this time period to produce ceramics, textiles, and gold ornaments, but no definite workshops have yet been reported. Elites appear to have controlled the production and distribution of food and some manufactured items as well as the distribution of irrigation water (S. Pozorski and T. Pozorski 1987).

Sociopolitical Organization

Settlement patterns and artifact distributions suggest that small polities were organized around a single individual or small group of individuals. Site-size hierarchy suggests two levels of authority existed in some places—representing a chiefdom level of organization (S. Pozorski and T. Pozorski 1987)—and perhaps three levels of authority existed in other places—representing an incipient state level of organization (Wilson 1988). The modest size of the largest constructions of the time period suggests that the elites' power over labor was channeled into production of status artifacts such as fine pottery, textiles, and jewelry. The presence of numerous hilltop forts and fortified sites protected by walls and ditches indicates the presence or threat of conflict, both on an intravalley and intervalley level (Daggett 1984, 1987; Wilson 1987, 1988).

Religion and Expressive Culture

Iconography suggests that religious beliefs involved a cosmology that included supernatural beings in the form of animals, humans, and combined human/animal creatures. Public ceremonies most likely took place in rectangular and square plazas and courtyards located within courtyard-small platform-room complexes (Burger 1992; Moseley 1992; Richardson 1994). Iconography includes depictions of San Pedro cactus, which was possibly used as a ritual hallucinogenic agent to enter the spirit world (Burger 1992). Inhabitants of this time period used a variety of media for art. Painted and plastic pottery decoration was rendered in both geometric and naturalistic styles. A limited amount of painted murals and possible friezes adorns some public buildings (Burger 1992; Richardson 1994). Part-time or full-time specialists may have been needed to effect many of the more elaborate artistic accomplishments. Relatively few burials dating to this time period have been scientifically excavated. Associated elite grave goods sometimes consist of elaborate pottery vessels, some imported *Spondylus* shell, and small gold objects (Burger 1992; Moseley 1992; Richardson 1994).

References

Burger, Richard L. (1992). *Chavin and the Origins of Andean Civilization*. London: Thames and Hudson.

Daggett, Richard (1984). "The Early Horizon Occupation of the Nepeña Valley, North Central Coast of Peru." Ph.D. diss., Department of Anthropology, University of Massachusetts, Amherst.

Daggett, Richard (1987). "Toward the Development of the State on the North Central Coast of Peru." In *The Origins and Development of the Andean State*, ed. J. Haas, S. Pozorski, and T. Pozorski. Cambridge: Cambridge University Press, 70–82.

Fung, Rosa (1969). "Las Aldas: Su ubicacion dentro del proceso historico del Peru antiguo." *Dedalo* : 5, 9–10: 1–208.

Moseley, Michael (1983) "Central Andean Civilization." In *Ancient South Americans*, ed. J. Jennings. San Francisco: W. H. Freeman, 179–239.

Moseley, Michael (1992). *The Incas and Their Ancestors*. London: Thames and Hudson.

Pozorski, Shelia (1987). "Theocracy vs. Militarism: The Significance of the Casma Valley in Understanding Early State Formation." In *The Origins and Development of the Andean State*, ed. J. Haas, S. Pozorski, and T. Pozorski. Cambridge: Cambridge University Press, 15–30.

Pozorski, Shelia, and Thomas Pozorski (1987). *Early Settlement and Subsistence in the Casma Valley, Peru*. Iowa City: University of Iowa Press.

Pozorski, Shelia, and Thomas Pozorski (1992). "Early Civilization in the Casma Valley, Peru." *Antiquity* 66: 845–870.

Richardson, James (1994). *People of the Andes*. Washington, D.C.: Smithsonian Books.

Wilson, David (1987). "Reconstructing Patterns of Early Warfare in the Lower Santa Valley: New Data on the Role of Conflict in the Origins of Complex North Coast Society." In *The Origins and Development of the Andean State*, ed. J. Haas, S. Pozorski, and T. Pozorski. Cambridge: Cambridge University Press, 56–69.

Wilson, David (1988). *Prehispanic Settlement Patterns in the Lower Santa Valley, Peru*. Washington, D.C.: Smithsonian Institution Press.

South Coast Late Coastal Formative

TIME PERIOD: 2800–2100 B.P.

LOCATION: A narrow coastal desert strip 20–40 km wide running along the Pacific coast between the Cañete valley in the north and the Nazca valley in the south.

DIAGNOSTIC MATERIAL ATTRIBUTES: Pottery varies in thickness, often decorated with incision, postfired polychrome resin painting, and negative painting. Vessel shapes include double-spout-and-bridge vessels, stirrup spout vessels, and open bowls. Elaborate embroidered textiles as well as plain woven textiles are present. Gold facial ornaments appear for the first time in this period. Subterranean tombs containing large mummy bundles represent the most significant features of this area.

CULTURAL SUMMARY

Environment

The climate was cool and hyperarid, much like the modern climate. The topography of the area is characterized by a long, narrow coastal desert strip periodically cut by numerous river channels that descend the western slopes of the Andes mountains (Burger 1992; Richardson 1994). Vegetation, mostly confined to the narrow coastal river valleys, is present well beyond the confines of natural floodplains because of irrigation agriculture, the which has supported coastal life for at least the last 4000 years (Moseley 1983, 1992). Most food consisted of domesticated plants grown in the river valleys. Animal protein came from marine fish and shellfish as well as from llamas and guinea pigs introduced from the highlands (Burger 1992; Moseley 1992; Richardson 1994).

Settlements

South Coast Late Coastal Formative settlements seem to consist of three primary kinds of sites: (1) sizable sites containing small mounds, compounds, and domestic dwellings; (2) elite cemeteries containing elaborate mummy bundles (Paul 1990, 1991a); and (3) small village sites associated with midden deposits (Massey 1991; Paul 1991a, 1991b, 1991c; Wallace 1986). The relative lack of systematic settlement pattern studies in the area has hampered identification of habitation sites pertaining to the Paracas culture, which remains the main culture that defines the South Coast Late Coastal Formative subtradition (Paul 1991b). The type site of Paracas on the Paracas peninsula still represents the main extant evidence of the Paracas culture. A small resident population occupied the type site, and the remaining known populations associated with this culture are located in small village sites in the nearby Canete, Pisco, Ica, and Nazca valleys (Silverman 1991; Wallace 1986). The high quality of some of the pottery, metal artifacts, and especially the embroidered textiles suggests the existence of full-time specialists, but little hard evidence has been found of specialized areas for the production of these items. House foundations are above-ground or semisubterranean and are made stone, adobe, wood or cane (Massey 1991; Wallace 1986).

Economy

The people of the South Coast Late Coastal Formative relied almost exclusively on irrigation agriculture to grow a wide variety of plant foods including maize, peanuts, common beans, lima beans, squash, potatoes, sweet potatoes, avocadoes, *lucuma*, guava *cansaboca*, gourd, and cotton (Moseley 1992; Richardson 1994; Silverman 1991). Fish and shellfish were gathered by inhabitants of coastal fishing villages who likely exchanged these products for inland agricultural products. Llamas and guinea pigs, introduced from the highlands during this time period, offered alternative animal protein resources to the stable marine animal resources (Moseley 1992; Richardson 1994; Silverman 1991). Primary utensils were (1) thin-walled pottery made from local soils; and (2) pointed wooden digging sticks (Paul 1991c). Pottery forms include open bowls, stirrup spout vessels, and double-spout-and-bridge vessels. Pottery decoration includes incision on postfired, polychrome resin-painted vessels as well as negative painted pottery (Silverman 1991; Tello 1959; Tello and Mejia Xesspe 1979). Some pottery designs appear to reflect influence of the Chavin culture centered in the north-central highlands of Peru (Burger 1992). Gold nose and facial ornaments often accompany bodies wrapped in hundreds of yards of exquisitely embroidered textiles (Paul 1991a; Tello 1959; Tello and Mejia Xesspe 1979). Part-time or full-time specialists may have been present during this time period to produce ceramics, textiles, and gold ornaments, but no definite workshops have yet been reported. Elites most likely controlled the production and distribution of food and the finer manufactured items as well as the distribution of irrigation water.

Sociopolitical Organization

The presence of the elite cemeteries at the site of Paracas suggests that Paracas society was organized around a single individual or small group of individuals. There may have been two levels of authority, perhaps representing a chiefdom level organization (Massey 1991; Silverman 1991; Wallace 1986). Elites presumably held power over labor that was mainly channeled into production of status artifacts such as elaborate embroidered textiles, fine pottery, and gold ornaments that were appear in mummy bundle burials of elite people (Paul 1991c; Tello 1959; Tello and Mejia Xesspe 1979).

Religion and Expressive Culture

Iconography suggests that religious beliefs involved a cosmology that included supernatural beings in the form of animals, humans, and combined human/animal creatures (Paul 1990, 1991c). Inhabitants of this time period rendered most of their art on embroidered textiles, pottery, and gold ornaments. Part-time or full-time specialists may have been needed to effect many of the more elaborate artistic accomplishments. Numerous burials, mainly mummy bundles consisting of flexed, seated individuals positioned within large baskets accompanied by pottery and gold ornaments and wrapped in several lengthy expanses of embroidered and plain textiles, have been scientifically excavated (Tello 1959; Tello and Mejia Xesspe 1979). The elaborate preparations and labor needed to produce these grave goods reflect the important social status of the individuals buried and a deep-seated belief in the afterlife.

References

Burger, Richard L. (1992). *Chavin and the Origins of Andean Civilization*. London: Thames and Hudson.

Massey, Sarah (1991). "Social and Political Leadership in the Lower Ica Valley: Ocucaje Phases 8 and 9." In *Paracas Art and Architecture: Object and Context in South Coastal Peru*, ed. A. Paul. Iowa City; University of Iowa Press, 315–348.

Moseley, Michael (1983). "Central Andean Civilization." In *Ancient South Americans*, ed. J. Jennings, San Francisco: W. H. Freeman, 179–239.

Moseley, Michael (1992). *The Incas and Their Ancestors*. London: Thames and Hudson.

Paul, Anne (1990). *Paracas Ritual Attire: Symbols of Authority in Ancient Peru*. Norman: University of Oklahoma Press.

Paul, Anne (1991a). "Paracas Necropolis Bundle 89: A Description and Discussion of Its Contents." In *Paracas Art and Architecture: Object and Context in South Coastal Peru*, ed. A. Paul. Iowa City: University of Iowa Press, 172–221.

Paul, Anne (1991b). "Paracas: An Ancient Cultural Tradition on the South Coast of Peru." In *Paracas Art and Architecture: Object and Context in South Coastal Peru*, ed. A. Paul. Iowa City: University of Iowa Press, 1–34.

Paul, Anne, ed. (1991c). *Paracas Art and Architecture: Object and Context in South Coastal Peru*. Iowa City: University of Iowa Press.

Richardson, James (1994). *People of the Andes*. Washington, D.C.: Smithsonian Books.

Silverman, Helaine (1991). "The Paracas Problem: Archaeological Perspectives." In *Paracas Art and Architecture: Object and Context in South Coastal Peru*, ed. A. Paul. Iowa City: University of Iowa Press, 349–415.

Tello, Julio (1959). *Paracas: Primera parte*. Lima: Empresa Grafica T. Scheuch S. A.

Tello, Julio, and Toribio Mejia Xesspe (1979). *Paracas, segunda parte: Cavernas y Necropolis*. Lima: Universidad Nacional Mayor de San Marcos and the Institute of Andean Research.

Wallace, Dwight (1986). "The Topara Tradition: An Overview." In *Perspectives on Andean Prehistory and Protohistory: Papers from the Third Annual Northeast Conference on Andean Archaeology and Ethnohistory*, ed. D. H. Sandweiss and D. P. Kvietok. Ithaca: Latin American Studies Program, Cornell University, 35–47.

SITES

Chankillo

TIME PERIOD: 2400–2200 B.P.

LOCATION: On the south side of the Casma branch of the Casma valley, Peru.

DESCRIPTIVE SUMMARY

Local Environment

Chankillo is located on a granitic hilltop and on a sandy *pampa* just south of modern cultivation in the lower Casma valley within a hyperarid desert environment (Pozorski and Pozorski 1987).

Physical Environment

The site of Chankillo covers some 50 ha and is made up of several stone constructions including a possible fortress, two multiroom compounds, several enclosures and plazas, and 13 enigmatic constructions known as the Thirteen Steps or Thirteen Towers. A substantial midden component also covers the *pampa* portion of the site among the structures there. The most notable construction is what most investigators have called the fortress, a hilltop structure that consists of three concentric elliptical walls that enclose two inner double-walled circular structures and a multiroom rectangular building. Passage through the encircling walls and within the enclosed structures is by way of baffled entrances that, in many cases, are still partially spanned by thick lintels of algarrobo wood. The tops of the elliptical encircling walls, which contain remnants of parapets, are reached by way of regularly spaced inset staircases on the walls' interior faces (Middendorf 1973; Pozorski and Pozorski 1987; Squier 1877). The Thirteen Steps consist of 13 towerlike constructions arranged in a line along a narrow ridgetop. Twelve of these have two sets of inset staircases—one ascending to and one descending from the summit of each structure. The 13th structure, located at the extreme end of the line of structures, has only one set of ascending steps leading to its summit (Kosok 1965; Pozorski and Pozorski 1987).

Cultural Aspects

Despite the presence of intrusive graffiti dating after 1000 B.P. (Fung and Pimentel 1973), limited investigation suggests that Chankillo dates near the end of the Late Coastal Formative (Pozorski and Pozorski 1987). Much work remains to be done to examine the many domestic and nondomestic components of the site. Best-known among the structures is what is often called the fortress. However, one feature that argues against interpretation of this part of Chankillo as a fortress is the presence of stone pins inset in small niches, which likely served as hinges for doors on the exterior faces of walls near entrances (Topic and Topic 1987). The Thirteen Steps may have had a ceremonial function, possibly connected with the lunar calendar (Kosok 1965).

References

Fung, Rosa, and Victor Pimentel (1973). "Chankillo." *Revista del Museo Nacional* 39: 71–80.

Kosok, Paul (1965). *Life, Land and Water in Ancient Peru.* New York: Long Island University Press.

Middendorf, Ernst (1973). *Peru, observaciones y estudios del país y sus habitantes durante una permanencia de 25 años*, 2. Lima: Universidad Nacional Mayor de San Marcos.

Pozorski, Shelia, and Thomas Pozorski (1987). *Early Settlement and Subsistence in the Casma Valley, Peru.* Iowa City: University of Iowa Press.

Squier, E. George (1877). *Peru: Incidents of Travel and Exploration in the Land of the Incas.* New York: Harper and Bros.

Topic, John, and Theresa Topic (1987). "The Archaeological Investigaiton of Andean Militarism: Some Cautionary Observations." In *The Origins and Development of the Andean State*, ed., J. Haas, S. Pozorski, and T. Pozorski. Cambridge: Cambridge University Press, 47–55.

Kushipampa

TIME PERIOD: 2400–2200 B.P.

LOCATION: On the south side of the upper Nepeña valley.

DESCRIPTIVE SUMMARY

Local Environment

Kushipampa is located within a hyperarid desert environment at an elevation of 480 m above sea level on a low plateau overlooking the south side of the upper Nepeña valley. Just north of the site is the Rio Salitre drainage that feeds into the main Nepeña river (Daggett 1987; Proulx 1968, 1973, 1985).

Physical Features

This site, covering about 35 ha, is dominated by an impressive compound measuring 420 by 120 m. The outer wall of the compound still stands up to 4 m high (Proulx 1985), but once probably stood over 6 m high (Squier 1877). This outer wall is made of large quarried stones carefully set in mud mortar. Finely polished granitic blocks make up the four sharply defined corners of the compound. The compound is subdivided into 10 courtyards of various sizes, one of which may contain a series of even smaller rooms. Access to the compound is restricted to two entrances: a southeast entrance that gives access to seven of the 10 courtyards and a northeast entrance that gives access to three courtyards located along the northeast side of the compound. Adjacent to the southeast entrance is a partially carved stone lintel reminiscent of carvings at Cerro Sechin in the Casma valley. Also found at the site are several small house foundations, a series of interconnected low-walled courtyards of a later date, and evidence of quarrying activities (Proulx 1985).

Cultural Aspects

No excavation has ever been carried out at Kushipampa; therefore, interpretations of the site are limited to surface evidence. The main types of decorated pottery found at the site are patterned burnished ware and postfired engraved ware (Daggett 1984, 1987; Proulx 1985). Both types have been tentatively dated to c. 2400–2200 B.P. in the Nepeña valley. The partially carved stone lintel is most likely a reused stone that dates substantially earlier than the site as a whole. The architecture and artifacts give few clues concerning the function of the main compound, but its overall size, finely cut stonework, and restricted access suggest that one of its main uses was for gatherings of special groups of people for religious and/or nonreligious public activities.

References

Daggett, Richard (1984). *The Early Horizon Occupation of the Nepeña Valley, North Central Coast of Peru*. Amherst: Department of Anthropology, University of Massachusetts.

Daggett, Richard (1987). "Toward the Development of the State on the North Central Coast of Peru." In *The Origins and Development of the Andean State*, ed. J. Haas, S. Pozorski, and T. Pozorski. Cambridge: Cambridge University Press, 70–82.

Proulx, Donald (1968). *An Archaeological Survey of the Nepeña Valley, Peru*. Amherst: Department of Anthropology, University of Massachusetts.

Proulx, Donald (1973). *Archaeological Investigations in the Nepeña Valley, Peru*. Research Report No. 13. Amherst: Department of Anthropology, University of Massachusetts.

Proulx, Donald (1985). *An Analysis of the Early Cultural Sequence in the Nepeña Valley, Peru*. Research Report No. 25. Amherst: Department of Anthropology, University of Massachusetts.

Squier, E. George (1877). *Peru: Incidents of Travel and Exploration in the land of the Incas*. New York: Harper and Bros.

Pampa Rosario

TIME PERIOD: 2800–2400 B.P.

LOCATION: On a flat plain between the Casma and Sechin branches of the Casma valley.

DESCRIPTIVE SUMMARY

Local Environment

Pampa Rosario is located on a flat colluvial plain set between the granitic foothills of the Andes mountains, all within a hyparid desert environment. To the north, south, and east lie modern cultivated fields of the Casma

and Sechin branches of the Casma valley (Pozorski and Pozorski 1987).

Physical Features

The site, some 40 ha in area, consists of a series of low, narrow platform mounds associated with small courts and other connected rooms. All visible early architecture is made of stone set in mud mortar. Each low platform is connected to a small court that is entered by way of a baffled entrance. Such platforms are similar to examples surveyed and excavated at the downvalley site of San Diego: the summit, which supports a row of posts or columns, is reached by way of a pair of ramps located at the opposite ends of one of the long sides of the platform. Midden up to 2 m deep is present over much of the site. Intrusive canals and much later structures of rectangular adobes or reutilized stone from the original occupation provide evidence of later prehistoric reuse of the site after 1400 B.P. Modern alteration of the site surface has resulted from the construction of gravel and dirt roads, a cement-lined canal, and a dirt landing strip.

Cultural Aspects

Pampa Rosario pertains to the same culture that produced the downvalley site of San Diego. Architectural, artifactual, and subsistence inventories of the two sites are virtually identical. The only significant difference is the presence of camelid remains (probably llama) among of the protein sources at Pampa Rosario (Pozorski 1987; Pozorski and Pozorski 1987). Artifactual evidence such as ceramic panpipes and polished slate points ties Pampa Rosario and San Diego to several sites in the Nepeña valley to the north (Daggett 1987). There is also some ceramic evidence of contact with the highland Chavin culture, but, for the most part, it would appear that developments in the lower Casma and Nepeña valleys remained largely autonomous with respect to the Chavin culture.

References

Daggett, Richard (1987). "Toward the Development of the State on the North Central Coast of Peru." In *The Origins and Development of the Andean state*, ed. J. Haas, S. Pozorski, and T. Pozorski. Cambridge: Cambridge University Press, 70–82.

Pozorski, Shelia (1987). "Theocracy vs. Militarism: The Significance of the Casma Valley in Understanding Early State Formation." In *The Origins and Development of the Andean State*, ed. J. Haas, S. Pozorski, and T. Pozorski. Cambridge: Cambridge University Press, 15–30.

Pozorski, Shelia, and Thomas Pozorski (1987). *Early Settlement and Subsistence in the Casma Valley, Peru.* Iowa City: University of Iowa Press.

Paracas

TIME PERIOD: 2800–2100 B.P.

LOCATION: On the Paracas peninsula 25 km south of the Pisco valley, Peru.

DESCRIPTIVE SUMMARY

Local Environment

Paracas is located on a rolling plain of rocky outcrops covered by eolian sand within a hyperarid desert environment. The Pacific ocean lies within 2 km of the site.

Physical Features

The site of Paracas consists of six different areas covering an expanse of at least 90 ha. These areas consist of cemetery, habitation, and refuse areas. The most important cemeteries areas are Cavernas and Wari Kayan Necropolis (Silverman 1991). Excavations carried out in these areas in the late 1920s by Julio Tello and Toribio Mejia Xesspe (Tello 1959; Tello and Mejia Xesspe 1979) uncovered hundreds of mummy bundles wrapped in spectacular textiles. In the Cavernas area of the site, over 70 tombs were explored. Many were intact, preserving their bottlelike form, called *cavernas* or caverns, based on how they were excavated into various hillside terraces. These tombs contained dozens of mummy bundles associated with fine woven textiles and two types of Paracas Cavernas pottery—postfired, polychrome resin-painted pottery and negative painted pottery (Silverman 1991; Tello 1959; Tello and Mejia Xesspe 1979). In the Wari Kayan Necropolis, excavations in two large subterranean tombs recovered 429 mummy bundles associated with spectacular embroidered textiles and a simple type of decorated pottery called Topara (Paul 1990, 1991; Silverman 1991; Tello 1959; Tello and Mejia Xesspe 1979).

Cultural Aspects

The site of Paracas served primarily as a special burial place for two sets of people who lived mainly in the Pisco, Chincha, and Cañete valleys north of the Paracas peninsula. One group of people produced the exquisite embroidered textiles and Topara pottery found in the Wari Kayan Necropolis portion of the site. A second group, who lived in the same neighboring valleys and may have been partially contemporary with the first group, buried their dead in the Cavernas portion of the site with woven textiles and Paracas pottery (Silverman 1991). Although the iconography of the Paracas pottery reflects some contact with the Chavin culture, both the Cavernas and Necropolis art styles were strictly regional phenomena of limited distribution (Burger 1992). Relatively little is known about the settlement patterns or lifestyles of the two groups responsible for the burials found at the Paracas site.

References

Burger, Richard (1992). *Chavin and the Origins of Andean Civilization.* London: Thames and Hudson.

Paul, Anne (1990). *Paracas Ritual Attire: Symbols of Authority in Ancient Peru.* Norman: University of Oklahoma Press.

Paul, Anne (1991). "Paracas Necropolis Bundle 89: A Description and Discussion of Its Contents." In *Paracas Art and Architecture: Object and Context in South Coastal Peru*, ed. A. Paul. Iowa City: University of Iowa Press, 172–221.

Silverman, Helaine (1991). "The Paracas Problem: Archaeological Perspectives." In *Paracas Art and Architecture: Object and Context in South Coastal Peru.* ed. A. Paul. Iowa City: University of Iowa Press, 349–415.

Tello, Julio (1959). *Paracas: Primera parte.* Lima: Empresa Grafica T. Scheuch S. A.

Tello, Julio, and Toribio Mejia Xesspe (1979). *Paracas, segunda parte: Cavernas y Necropolis.* Lima: Universidad Nacional Mayor de San Marcos and the Institute of Andean Research.

San Diego

TIME PERIOD: 2600–2300 B.P.

LOCATION: On the south side of the lower Casma valley, Peru.

DESCRIPTIVE SUMMARY

San Diego is located on a sandy plain bordered by low foothills of the Andes mountains within a hyperarid desert environment. The site is situated along the edge of a fossil bay and is some 5.5 km inland from the Pacific ocean (Pozorski 1987; Pozorski and Pozorski 1987).

Physical Features

The site, some 50 ha in area, consists of a series of interconnected stone architectural units including large and small rooms, corridors, plazas, courts, and small platform mounds. No single structure dominates the site. The most distinctive type of repetitive architectural unit is the low, narrow platform mound associated with a small court that is entered by way of a baffled entrance. The summit of each low platform is reached by means of a pair of ramps, located at opposite ends of one long side of the platform. Upon each platform summit, there are remains of a row of wooden posts or rectangular stone columns that once supported a roof. Much of the site contains midden deposits at least 2 m deep, and excavation revealed remains of small houses made of stone and cane (Pozorski 1987; Pozorski and Pozorski 1987).

Cultural Aspects

San Diego is the largest residential site in the valley for the Late Coastal Formative. Its overall layout represents a radical departure from Casma valley sites of the Early Coastal Formative, which all consist of structures oriented toward a central axis established by one or two very large platform mounds. At San Diego, typical associated ceramics are decorated with incision, zoned and unzoned punctation, textile and net impressions on vessel exteriors, and incision with zones of white painted designs. Circle-and-dot designs indicate some limited contact with the highland Chavin culture. Ceramic forms include neckless ollas, jars, bowls, vessels with thick stirrup spouts, and panpipes. Other typical artifacts include polished slate points and woven textiles decorated with blue geometric designs. The subsistence inventory consists of a wide variety of domesticated plants including maize (newly introduced to the Casma valley after 3000 B.P.) and various shellfish and fish species. The architectural features plus the artifacts and subsistence items are almost identical to those found at the inland Casma valley site of Pampa Rosario (Pozorski 1987; Pozorski and Pozorski 1987). The artifact inventory is also quite similar to materials found during surface survey of the neighboring Nepeña valley to the north (Daggett 1987).

References

Daggett, Richard (1987). "Toward the Development of the State on the North Central Coast of Peru." In *The Origins and Development of the Andean State*, ed. J. Haas, S. Pozorski, and T. Pozorski. Cambridge: Cambridge University Press, 70–82.

Pozorski, Shelia (1987). "Theocracy vs. Militarism: The Significance of the Casma Valley in Understanding Early State Formation." In *The Origins and Development of the Andean State*, ed. J. Haas, S. Pozorski, and T. Pozorski. Cambridge: Cambridge University Press, 15–30.

Shelia, and Thomas Pozorski (1987). *Early Settlement and Subsistence in the Casma Valley, Peru*. Iowa City: University of Iowa Press.

SHELIA AND THOMAS POZORSKI
Department of Psychology and Anthropology
University of Texas–Pan American
Edinburg, Texas
United States

Late East Brazilian Uplands

ABSOLUTE TIME PERIOD: 5000–50 B.P.

RELATIVE TIME PERIOD: Follows the Early Brazilian Uplands tradition, precedes the historic period.

LOCATION: Bordered on the west by the lowlands of the state of Matto Grosso and farther southwest by Bolivia, on the south by the lowlands of the southern half of the state of Rio Grande do Sul; on the east by the coastal plain and the north by the Amazon valley.

DIAGNOSTIC MATERIAL ATTRIBUTES: Ceramics are present. Many sites show evidence of horticulture, in particular, manioc. Most sites also have bola stones and plugs (*tembetas*).

REGIONAL SUBTRADITIONS: Casas Subterrâneas, Humaitá.

IMPORTANT SITES: Abrigo de Waldermar, Lagoa Sao Paulo, PR-FO-17, RS-SM-07, Três Vendas.

CULTURAL SUMMARY

Environment

The east Brazilian uplands are so vast, north and south, and have so much variation in altitude from the coastal range to the bottom of the river valleys that no single climatic pattern is universal. The interior on the west side is a tropical savanna. In the northwest, it is tropical and subtropical steppe.

The northern half of the highlands is always hot, and the southern half has hot summers and mild winters. Normal range in temperatures varies from 3°–36° C. There are three broad bands of vegetation, from north to south. On the north is the *caatinga*, an area of thorny xeophitica plants, such as giant cacti. In the midsection is the *cerrado*, with its forest of decidous trees and shrubs. From the southern half of the state of Paraná and south to the midsection of the state of Rio Grande do Sul are coniferous forests of Aurucanian pine.

Settlements

Some of the older settlements are located in rock shelters. Probably no more people than an extended family lived in these rock shelters. With the appearance of ceramic making and agricultural lifeways, open sites became more common. These sites have a circular village pattern with circular dwellings. Villages appear to have been relatively long term, with houses likely constructed of posts with thatched roofs.

Economy

The Late East Brazilian Uplands people were horticulturalists who supplemented their diet with hunted meat and collected plant foods. The bow and arrow and bola were used for hunting, but a spear and spear thrower might also be employed for larger game. The canoe was used for transportation.

Sociopolitical Organization

There is little formal evidence for social or political organization. On many sites, large circular dwellings suggest residences for extended families or larger kin groups. Some villages had 100 or more residents, and this suggests that some form of political structure, perhaps based on informal headmen or positions of kinship, was in place to maintain harmony in the community.

Suggested Readings

Bruhns, Karen (1994). *Ancient South America*. Cambridge: Cambridge University Press.

Bryan, Alan, and Ruth Gruhn (1993). *Brazilian Studies*. Corvallis: Center for the Study of the First Americans, Oregon State University.

Hurt, Wesley (1998). *Explorations in American Archaeology: Essays in Honor of Wesley R. Hurt*. Lanham, Md.: University Press of America.

Lothrop, S. K. (1946). "Indians of the Paraná and the La Plata Littoral." In *Handbook of South American Indians: The Marginal Tribes*, vol. 1. Washington, D.C.: Bureau of American Ethnology, Smithsonian Institutoion, Bulletin 142, 177–190.

Willey, Gordon R. (1971). *An Introduction to American Archaeology*, vol. 2: *South America*. Engelwood Cliffs NJ: Prentice Hall.

SUBTRADITIONS

Casas Subterrâneas

TIME PERIOD: c. 1200–250 B.P. Earliest dates are unknown but may begin as the same time as the Tupiguarani and last until the time of the conquest (Schmitz 1967: 11). This event occurred at 248 B.P. (Metraux 1948: 77). Chmyz estimates that the Catanduva variant of this subtradition in the Iguaçu river area of Paraná occurs between c. A.D. 820 and 1150 (1969: Fig. 9).

LOCATION: The sites are in the highlands of northern Rio Grande do Sul, the coast of this state, and the interior in the upper and middle Iguaçu river of the state of Paraná and the coast of Santa Catarina.

DIAGNOSTIC MATERIAL ATTRIBUTES: Pottery is simple and coarse tempered, compared with the painted and other highly decorated surfaces of Tupiguarani ceramics. Decorative techniques include red slipping. Surfaces are polished or semipolished. Rare are fingernail-impressed surface decorations. Shallow bowls, cylindrical jars, and short-necked jars. Lithic artifacts include pestles, polished axes, flaked axes, choppers, stemmed and unstemmed scrapers, pitted hammer stones, and bola stones.

CULTURAL SUMMARY

Environment

Because of the great difference in altitude of the highlands and coastal plain of the region, the climate varies considerably. In Paraná, the highlands are humid subtropical forests with four distinct seasons and no dry season. In contrast, the climate of the coast range is temperate with cool summers and cold winters. With this type of climate, a pit house is an ideal structure because of the insulating effect of the outside walls being covered by the ground. The highlands of northern Rio Grande do Sul and Santa Catarina, where the Casas Subterrâneas are located, are composed of basic rocks, Triassic in age, with an altitude between 700–900 m, and separated from the narrow coastal plain by a steep escarpment over 1000 m high which is difficult to traverse. These highlands in the east-west direction have a smooth inclination to the floodplains of major rivers such as the Pelotas and Antas. The vegetation of the highlands is predominately pine forests, but these are not present in the valleys of the large rivers. Below 500 m altitude, the vegetation changes to tropical rainforests, although between the valleys of the Antas and Pelotas rivers is open country of grasslands.

Settlements

Villages of the Casas Subterrâneas subtradition are composed of subterranean houses in open sites, although some of the sites are in rock shelters. The number of pit houses in a single village ranges from 4–10. Frequently a large house pit will be surrounded by several smaller ones. Size may range from 2–10 m in diameter. Floors may contain stone hearths, postholes, and stone artifacts. So steep and high are some of the walls of these pit houses that it is difficult to exit from them. Local people state that they have found in some of the sites a tunnel connecting one house with another. The houses are easy to find because they are often covered with a clump of bushes that contrasts with the much lower vegetation that surrounds them.

Villages are sometimes associated with small burial mounds (Miller 1971: 57). Burials are sometimes also found in rock shelters. The strata within the fill of the houses in one site show this pattern: below a thick layer of fill is a layer, 40–50 cm thick, of dark-colored containing hearths, charcoal, sherds, pestles, and other stone tools. Animal bones are absent because of the acid soil.

Economy

Subsistence in the Casas Subterrâneas subtradition was based on hunting, fishing, and gathering. Game animals taken were peccaries, armadillos, *capybaras*, anteaters, and monkeys. Fish taken included *surubis*, *dourados*, *pintados*, and *cascudos*. Plant material from *aurucaria* pines, *goiba serrana*, *guabiroba*, *ingá macaco*, *amora* preta, and *quaraesmeira* were all used (Miller 1971: 37–39).

Sociopolitical Organization

According to Soares de Souza (1938: 111), the Casas Subterrâneas subtradition existed at least until the 1868 entrance of Spanish missionaries. The present-day decendants of the prehistoric tribes are the Caingang, who now live in straw houses above ground (Metraux 1946: 453e and fig. 67).

References

Metraux, A. (1946). "The Caingang." In *Handbook of the South American Indians*, vol. 1, ed. T. Dale Stewart. Washington, D.C.: Smithsonian Institution Press, 445–475.

Metraux, A. (1948). "The Guaraní." In *Handbook of the South American Indians*, vol. 3, ed. T. Dale Stewart. Washington, D.C.: Smithsonian Institution Press, 65–94.

Miller, Eurico Th. (1971). "Pesquisas Arqueológicas Efetuadas no Planalto Meridional Rio Grande do Sul (Rios Uruguai, Pelotas e das Antas)." In *Programa Nacional de Pesquisas Arqueológicas, 4: Resultados Preliminares do Quarto Ano, 1968–1969*. Belem: Museu Paranense Emilio Goeldi, 37–71.

Saores de Souza, G. (1938). *Tratado Descriptivo do Brazil em 1587*. São Paulo: Companhia Editorial Nacional.

Schmitz, Pedro Ignacio (1967). *Archaeogia no Rio Grande do Sul*. Pesquisas, Antropologia, no. 16. Instituto Anchietano de Pesquisas. Rio Grande do Sul: Sao Leopoldo.

Humaitá

ABSOLUTE TIME PERIOD: 6865–2305 B.P. (Miller 1967). The Site Abrigo da Pedra Grande (RS-SM-07), which as been assigned to the Humaitá subtradition, has been dated by Goldmeier and Scmitz to 2795 B.P. (1987: 122). However, Ribeiro gives 910 B.P. as the terminal date (1983: 69).

LOCATION: This subtradition is spread over the vast area of the state of Paraná to the central depression of Rio Grande do Sul.

DIAGNOSTIC MATERIAL ATTRIBUTES: Both flake and core tools, with the former predominant. Choppers made of flakes with part of the cortex present were the major type of tools. Other common tool types include cores, worked flakes, semipolished and polished axes, pestles, manos, pitted hammer stones, drills, and polishing stones, flake side and end scrapers, and knives. These were made by direct percussion, and rare examples were pressure retouched. Raw material varies according to region, with chalcedony a favorite stone for flake tools. Miller (1967: 17–18) states that in the northeastern highlands of Rio Grande do Sul these tools were made from large chunks of basalt.

CULTURAL SUMMARY

Environment

Because the Humaitá subtradition covers such a wide area, from Paraná to Rio Grande Do Sul, there is a large variation in the type of local environment. The region of the northeast highlands of Rio Grande do Sul is characterized by navigable rivers with their sources in the basalt highlands. There are also large lakes in this region. The east slope of the highlands is abrupt and stepped and lies obliquely to the seacoast. The climate is wet subtropical without a dry season. Nevertheless, there are four distinct seasons. On the coast side of the highlands the maximum annual temperature is 40° C in the month of January, and the minimum is −2° C in July. On the highlands the maximum is 25° C and the minimum −9° C, with snow and sleet common. Precipitation is distributed uniformly over the winter months, with a mean annual amount of about 2000 mm for the highlands. At the time of the Portuguese conquest, the region was completely covered with a tropical forest. Along the rivers were mainly aurucarian pine. This region was formerly rich in game animals, fish, and edible vegetable products.

Settlements

In the northern part of the region of the Humaitá subtradition, the sites lie 60 m above the levels of the Rio Paraná but only 8 m above the Rio Capivara. Sites cover an eliptical area with a maximum size of 60 by 40 m (Chymz 1983: 11). In Rio Grande do Sul, the sites have an oval shape with a maximum of 250 sq m. The depth is rarely more than 15 cm.

References

Chymz, Igor (1983). *Séptimo Relatório Das Pesquisas Realizadas na área de Itaipu (1981/83)*. Paraná: Prjeto Arqueológico Itaipu, Curitiba.

Miller, Eurico Th. (1967). *Pesquisas arqueológicos efetuadas no nordest do Rio Rio Grande do Sul 15–38*. Programa Nacional de Pesquisas Arqueológicas, Resultados Preliminares do Primero Ano, 1965–1966, Publicaçoes Avulsas, No. 6. Belém, Pará: Museu Paraense Emílio Goeldi.

Miller, Eurico Th. (1987). *Pesquisas arqueológicas efetuadas no Rio Grande do Sul* (alto Uruguay, 33–54. Programa Nacional de Pesquisas Arqueológicas, Resultados Preliminares do Segundo Ano (1966–1967), Publicaçoes Avulsas, no. 10. Belém, Pará: Museu Paraense Emílio Goeldi.

SITES

Abrigo de Waldemar

TIME PERIOD: 3290–1170 B.P.

LOCATION: In a rock shelter in the limestone plateau about 8 km north of the city of Central, Municipio Central, state of Bahia.

DESCRIPTIVE SUMMARY

Local Environment

The area has a very dry hot climate, and since 1710 there have been droughts every 7–10 years. In 1983, when the site was excavated, there had been no rain for 5 years. Normally the dry season lasts about 7 months, from April through October. A long-term average of annual rainfall is 489 mm. In the summer, the average temperature is 40° C. In winter (May through August) the usual daytime temperature is between 20–25° C. The site lies in a cliff that is in the limestone ridge, called the "Serra Calcareo." This area has a *caatinga* type of xerophytic vegetation, which includes thorny types of low shrubs and trees and tall and small cacti. There are also deciduous trees such as the *gamileira* and trees such as the *umbu* and *caju*, which produce edible fruits. During prehistoric times, the region had animals such as jaguar, peccaries, marmosets and monkeys, armadillos, and birds, but the present-day inhabitants have over-hunted the area and these animals are rare or no longer exist. On the western border of the region is the river, the Rio Verde, which contains edible mussels and a few fish. Large edible gastropods, such as diprodon *Delodontus*, live on the land and are more numerous in wet areas.

Physical Features

The Abrigo de Waldemar lies under an overhang in a cliff and has a main chamber to the front and a smaller chamber in the interior. To one side of the interior chamber is an open area containing cultural deposits. At the front of the main chamber is a linear mound that prevents the entrance of water from the outside, although a small amount of water does enter the rock shelter by flowing down the escarpment. The strata in the rock shelter dip down toward the rear wall but not so steeply that people had problems living on the site. The uppermost material of the main chamber on the west consisted of gray ash; along the east side and in the rear chamber, there was a mixture of gray ash and red silt. Although the depths of the refuse strata varied slightly, in general the following stratigraphic units were present: *Unit 1*, 0–50 cm, unconsolidated gray/pink ash mixed with red silts and kitchen refuse such as mollusk shells, bones of birds and animals, and fire pits. Sherds were present only in the upper 0–20 cm deposits. The 10–20 cm level dates 1170 B.P.; the 20–30 cm level dated 1690 B.P. *Unit 2* had mottled red\gray deposits. No organic material such as bones or shells was present. Mixed in these deposits were calcium and iron concretions that increased in size and number the greater the depth. At the depth of 2 m, these concretions formed an almost solid impermeable floor. In fact, below the 30 cm level, the deposits were extremely difficult to remove with a pick. The 50–60 cm level had a radiocarbon date of 2420 B.P. and the 60–70 cm level, 3290 B.P. Artifacts were scarce below the 60 cm level, although a few were present in the 100 cm level. In stratigraphic Unit 2 were bone projectile points, chunks of red ocher, mussel shell scrapers, and tools of quartzite.

Cultural Aspects

Tools were placed against the rear wall, apparently to get them out of the habitation area of the main chamber, while others were placed in the small rear chamber, which seems not to have been a living area. There were two distinct ceramic complexes. Complex A was thick, undecorated, had rounded rims, and was almost if not identical to those in the Abrigo de Pilao (Bryan and Gruhn 1993: 79, 105–106). Ceramic Complex B items were better made and fired than those above. The mussels from the Rio Verde were eaten, and their shells were modified to make various types of scrapers. One type of tool was a mussel shell with a hole drilled in the center to make an arrow shaft straightener. Projectile points were fabricated from a split bird bone with a point cut at one end. Other tools included polished and grooved axes, mullers, and grinding stones made of quartzite and sandstone. These tools indicate a close relationship with the Serranópolis subtradition (Schmitz n.d.), while the ceramics level falls within the Brazilian Simple Ceramics subtradition.

References

Bryan, Alax, and Ruth Gruhn (1993). *Brizilian Studies*. Corvallis: Center for the study of the first Americans, Oregon State University.
Schmitz Pedro Ifnacio (n.d.). A Evoluçao da Cultura no Sudoeste de Gaias. Rio Grafarne do Sul: Institut de Pesquisas. Unisines.

Lagoa São Paulo

TIME PERIODA: c. 2500 B.P. (Pallestrini 1984: 381).

LOCATION: This shell mound is situated by the city of Presidente Epitácio, state of São Paulo.

DESCRIPTIVE SUMMARY

Local Environment

The site is located on the drainage of the extensive sedimentary basin of Paraná. The underlying formation of the site is the basaltic series called Grupo Bauru by some geologists and Caiuá by others. The whole area of the Município Epitácio is included in the Caiuá formation. In this formation are fine and medium-fine sandstones that have dark red color and represent aeolian deposits. The Sáo Paulo lake, which is near the site, is close to the left margin of the Paraná river, and, in addition, the tributary of this major river is the Bandeirantes river on whose right margin lies the archaeological site.

Physical Features

At the site are two terraces that correspond to two cycles of Quaternary sedimentation. The oldest, on which are situated three successive prehistoric occupations, are from 280–285 m above the level of the Bandeirantes river, and the most recent with the highest bed of this river. The three archaeological levels of the site are 6.8 m, 7.4 m, and 7.8 m above the bed of the river.

Cultural Aspects

Level I, between 0–40–50 cm, contained ceramics. Level 2, 40–45 cm, contained stone artifacts but no pottery; Level 3, 75–1.25 cm, contained charcoal and burned soil, which marked the existence of circular houses with diameters from 5–10 m. There were two basic types of pottery, decorated and undecorated. The undecorated types included smoothed surfaces on vases and plates of small and large sizes. The decorated types, which are Tupiguarani wares, included painted and plastic surfaces. Plastic types were corrugated, incised, and finger-impressed, and the painted types included rectangular and curvilinear forms in black and red. The levels with pottery contained the most fireplaces and burned soil, marking the presence of a village. Level 2 had pockets of flakes from a workshop. Each pocket contained between 15–30 flakes. These flakes were made mainly by percussion. The preferred raw material was quartzite and silicified sandstone. The lithic artifacts were well-made. Level 3 began between 80–85 cm and reached the depth of 110 cm. The raw material was quartzite, silicified sandstone, and quartz. Cores were present from which flakes were obtained by percussion. Scrapers were made with fine retouching.

References

Pallestrini, Luciana (1984). "Sítio Arqueológico da Lagoa São Paulo: Presidente Epitácio—SP. 381–410." *Revista de Pré-História*, vol. VI. Instituto de Préhistoria, São Paulo: Universidade de São Paulo.

PR-FO-17

TIME PERIOD: c. 3935 B.P.

LOCATION: This site is situated in the Município de Guaía, state of Paraná, at a distance of 200 km of the right bank of the Paraná river (Chymz 1983: 11–20, 100).

DESCRIPTIVE SUMMARY

Local Environment

The site occupies a gentle upland inclined toward the Rio Paraná. This site is 45 m above the water level of this river and 30 m above the level of the ancient channel. The Rio Paraná in this area has a series of rapids between its islands. Only along the Rio Paraná and the ancient channel are the remains of the prehistoric forest, which today has been largely removed by farming. The land is sandy with a light color, between outcrops of basalt. The forests in the area are the transition from the tropical rainforest and the subtropical humid forest.

Physical Features

The evidence of the site is scattered over an area with an elliptical form of 80 × 40 m, with the greatest dimension lying oblique to the Rio Paraná. The archaeological remains occurred from depths of 15–40 cm. The excavation trench revealed in the uppermost strata a light brown soil mixed with roots to the depths of 15 cm below surface. Under the depth of 30 cm, the stratum changed to a yellowish clay of decomposed basalt. From 30–40 cm, the strata became more friable. Below yellow-brown clay between 40–50 cm lay a compact layer of basalt.

Cultural Aspects

Only a small number of the lithics showed any signs of use or retouching. The largest number of this class were retouched flakes. The debitage consisted of 67.20 percent residual flakes and 3.62 percent spent cores. Among the raw materials utilized were quartz, basalt, silicified sandstone, limonite, and chert. The used and retouched tools consisted of side, pointed, circular, plano-convex, and double-sided scrapers. There were also blade tools such as side scrapers, an eliptical scraper, and a pointed scraper. Tools were made by direct percussion; only one was made by the bipolar technique. To finish the tools, pressure flaking was utilized. There was also a bifacial tool made of a retouched core and a chopper made of a retouched core.

References

Chymz, Igor Séptimo (1983). *Relatório das Pesquisas Realizadas na área de Itaip[u (1981/83).* Projeto Arqueológico Itaipu. Paraná: Curitiba.

RS-SM-07

TIME PERIOD: 2795–605 B.P.

LOCATION: The site is situated in the Município de Sao Pedro do Sul, state of Rio Grande do Sul.

DESCRIPTIVE SUMMARY

Local Environment

Site RS-SM-07 is situated in a rock shelter called O Abrigo de Pedra Grande, in a block of the Botucatu sandstone. The cliff in which the rock shelter is located is inclined to the east-northeast, and the face is slightly concave, forming a large rock shelter, 70 m wide, 2 m deep, and 8 m high. The base of the outcrop is 7 m above the level of the valley.

Physical Features

The strata with cultural remains were 140 cm deep against the rear walls and 60 cm at the entrance. Level 1, 4–5 cm thick, was dry and friable with a rose color, while all the other strata were darker brown or ash color. The rocks at the base were disintegrated sandstone or sterile sandstone, more or less compact.

Cultural Aspects

The artifacts, cores, and large flakes were concentrated outside the wall where there were fallen rocks while the small flakes were inside the rock shelter. It was evident that the inhabitants broke the raw material outside and retouched the artifacts inside. Very few finished artifacts occurred outside the rock shelter. There were concentrations of carbon and ash, indicating hearths. Remains of subsistence materials were rare and included bones of small animals, principally mammals, mollusk shells, and carbonized seeds of palm trees. The three radiocarbon dates, 2795 B.P., 800 B.P., and 605 B.P., do not indicate continuous occupation of the rock shelter, but three separate periods of habitation. The oldest occupation, assigned to the Humaitá subtradition, lacks projectile points; the second occupation had stemmed, barbed projectile points; and the last occupation in some parts of the site had axes with a polished cutting edge and is assigned to the Umbu subtradition. In some places, pottery of the Tupiguarani subtradition occurred to the depths of 60 cm and is related to the third period of occupation. This Tupiguarani occupation was a part of the Jesuit Sao José reduction (a concentration into certain villages) of 317–312 B.P. The artifacts were made of basalt, riolite, silicified sandstone, chalcedony, and quartz. Tools included large bifaces, small bifaces, drills, choppers, polished axes, hammer stones.

References

Goldmeier, Valter Augusto, and Pedro Ignácio Schmitz (1987). *O Artefatos Líticos do Abrigo da Pedra Grande (TS-SM-O&)*. Arquelogia, 121–147 do Rio Grande do Sul, Brasil. Documentos 01. Sao Leopoldo: Instituto Anchietano de Pesquisas—UNISINOS.

Três Vendas

TIME PERIOD:: 200–185 B.P.

LOCATION: The site is situated in Três, Município de Araruama, state of Rio de Janeiro.

DESCRIPTIVE SUMMARY

Local Environment

The climate of the area surrounding the site is hot and humid and without a pronounced winter. The summer has a marked rainy period. The site rests on the side of a hill 25 m above mean sea level and the base 10 m above sea level, indicating an ancient level of a now extinct river. The archaeological site Três Vendas is associated with Upper and Middle Holocene sandy deposits. A forest had originally grown in the region of the site, but agricultural activities in historic times destroyed most of the forest, and the site of Três Vendas at the time of excavation was covered with grass. The ancient forest furnished firewood, fruit, and material for subsistence and medicine. The local areas of water contained fish. Raw materials for making pottery and artifacts were abundant.

Physical Features

The site of Três Vendas was a prehistoric oval-shaped village of seven houses and a total population of approximately 150 persons. In size, the village was 120 by 100 m, while the houses varied from 10–20 m in diameter. The types of ceramics were those made by the Tupiguarani tribe, such as corrugated, painted, incised, punctated, finger impressed, and broad trailed. Human burials were placed in urns.

Cultural Aspects

Each house in the village likely held four or five nuclear families, and the village itself was politically independent. In addition to fishing, gathering of shell-fish, and a limited amount of hunting, subsistence was based on horticulture.

References

Kneip, Lina Maria, Antônio M. F. Monteiro, and Giralda Seyforth, (1980). "A Aldeia Préhistórica de Três Vendas Araruma, Estado do Rio de Janeiro." *Revista do Museu Paulista*, n.s. 27: 283–338.

WESLEY HURT (deceased)
compiled by PETER N. PEREGRINE
Department of Anthropology
Lawrence University
Appleton, Wisconsin
United States

Late Highland Andean Archaic

Late Preceramic, Terminal Late Archaic, Late Archaic, Transitional

ABSOLUTE TIME PERIOD: 4500–3800/3500 B.P.

RELATIVE TIME PERIOD: Follows the Early Highland Andean Archaic tradition, and precedes the Highland Andean Formative tradition.

LOCATION: Highlands of the western flanks of the Andes and adjacent high-altitude plains. The region is usefully divided into high sierras from 2500–3800 m, to altiplano (*puna*) from 3800–4500 m. The well-known regions consist of Peru, northern Chile, and northwestern Argentina.

DIAGNOSTIC MATERIAL ATTRIBUTES: A variety of projectile point styles including lanceolate, foliate, and triangular forms. In the central and south-central Andes, rare ceremonial sites consisting of rectangular/ovoid structures with central hearths and sometimes underground flues.

REGIONAL SUBTRADITIONS: Central Highland Andean (northern and central Peru), South-Central Highland Andean (southern Peru, northern Chile), and Salt Puna (North-Central Chile, southern Bolivia, and Northwest Argentina).

IMPORTANT SITES: Central Andean (Guitarrero Cave, Huaricoto, Jaywamachay, Kotosh, Lauricocha, Pacha-machay, Panalauca, Pikimachay, Puente, Telarmachay,

Tres Ventanas), South-Central Andean (Peru: Asana, Caru, Quelcatani, Toquepala, Chile: Hakenasa, Patap-atane, Tojo-tojones), Salt Puna (Chile: Chiu-chiu, Pu-ripica 1, Tulán 52, Argentina: Huachichocana, Inca Cueva 7, Quebrada Seca).

CULTURAL SUMMARY

Environment

Climate. The Terminal Late Archaic occurred during a period of environmental fluctuations that were part of a more general desiccation since the last glaciation 10,000 B.P. However, local conditions of latitude, air patterns, and topography complicate the picture, preventing easy generalizations for the region. Tentatively, many areas experience a warm/dry phase (hypsithermal) from about 6000–4000 B.P., after which there is a brief wet/cold phase until 3000 B.P., after which there is an increasingly dry pattern. Despite these fluctuations, essentially modern flora and fauna were in place after about 8000 B.P. Today the high sierras are characterized by low precipitation (usually below 500 mm per year), which falls seasonally from November to April. Temperatures are generally cool. The puna has higher precipitation (1200 mm or less) that falls between November and April and is characterized by cold temperatures and nightly frosts.

Topography. The region can be divided into two topographic zones, the high sierras and the *puna*. The high sierra is the mountainous zone from 2500–3800 m above mean sea level. This zone can be considered the Andes proper, consisting of massive mountains eroded from the uplifted volcanic bedrock. The high sierras are cut by west-flowing streams that form major river valleys to the Pacific coast. Terrain is very steep and rugged. The *puna* (or altiplano) is a high-altitude plateau that lies between 3800–4500 m above mean sea level. This plain is dotted by large marshes (*bofedales*), lakes, salt marshes (*salares*), and areas of vegetation along streams (*vegas*).

Geology. The region is dominated by the volcanic Andes mountains. The peaks of the Andes occur as two chains, or *cordillera*, between which lies the *puna*, or altiplano. Volcanoes and volcano cores are common. Glacial features are common in the *puna*, consisting of outwash plains and moraines. Much of the bedrock occurs as fine basalts such as rhyolite and andesite, both of which are suitable for chipped-stone tools. Also, obsidian occurs in certain locales.

Biota. The steep vertical gradient of the Andes forms a series of distinct biotic zones stratified by elevation. These vertical zones are crosscut by latitudinal variation based on decreasing rainfall from north to south. The high sierra receives low amounts of rainfall (500 mm per annum in the north to 1 mm per annum in the south), which generally supports scrub and thorn forests on the western flanks of the Andes. The few west-flowing streams and rivers that drain into the Pacific ocean present crucial resource zones and are for all practical purposes the only places human habitation is possible. The resources tightly tethered to these river valleys include *algorrobo* pods (*Prosopis* sp.), wild tubers, *Chenopodium* sp., and cactus fruits. The valleys are also about the only place where agriculture is possible. Today, and to an extent during the Terminal Late Archaic, domestic plants would include tubers such as potato (*Solanum tuberosum*), *oca* (*Oxalis tuberosa*), *ullucu* (*Ullucus tuberosum*), cereals such as maize (*Zea mays*), and quinoa (*Chenopodium quinoa*), pulses such as common and lima bean (*Phaseolus* sp.), and chile peppers (*Capsicum* sp.). Animal resources include the wild camelid guanaco (*Lama guanicoe*), Andean deer or *taruca* (*Hippocamelus antisensis*), and guinea pigs or *cuy* (*Cavia porcellus*).

The *puna*, with its frigid temperatures and difficulties in gas exchange, presents special problems for life. Few species of edible wild plants exist in the lower reaches of the *puna* such as hardy forms of wild potato and Chenopodium. Only a few hardy and only slightly productive domestic species such as special varieties of potato and Chenopodium can be grown. Consequently, human habitation depends on animal life in the *puna*. In lower areas of the *puna*, guanaco probably existed in the past. The primary wild mammal of the Andean *puna* is the vicuña (*Lama* or *Vicugna vicugna*), a small native camelid. Other animals would include. Andean deer or *taruca*, the *vizcacha* (*Lagidium* sp.), a large chinchilla-like animal, the *rhea* or *suri* (*Rhea americana*), an Andean ostrich, and *cuy*. Predators such as the puma (*Felis concolor*) and the condor (*Vultur gryphus*) also exist.

Settlements

Settlement System. The Terminal Late Archaic is important in the Andean highlands because it is during this time that evidence for increasing sedentarization begins to appear. Nonetheless, a variety of settlement systems exist, stratified by latitude and altitude. In the northern high sierra, habitation sites indicate seasonal occupations based on a wet season aggregation of forager/incipient horticulturalist bands and dry season dispersal of smaller units. However, there are also large ceremonial sites such as Huaricoto and Kotosh dating to c. 4000 B.P., which may have served as focal points in a regional settlement hierarchy. A similar system of seasonal mobility and limited transhumance up and down Andean valleys appears to be the case for the high sierras of the south-central Andes. Also, there is evidence that during the Terminal Late Archaic period, sites were inhabited for longer periods of time, tending toward a sedentary mobility system. The south-central Andean site of Asana also contains a ceremonial structure between 4800–4400 B.P. on a smaller scale than that seen in the later central Andean sites. In the salt *puna* regions of Chile, seasonal transhumance patterns occur in river valleys and centered on large *salares* that occupy a region between coastal ranges and the Andean mountain chain proper. As in the sierra sites to the north, increasing sedentism occurs, culminating in large sites of 30–50 semisubterranean stone-slab dwellings at Puripica 1 and Tulán 52 in Chile.

Puna settlement patterns are similar throughout the Andes during this time, with a logistical mobility system based on limited transhumance between higher *bofedales* and *vegas* and lower ones. Increasing sedentism is evident in increasing midden and refuse thicknesses and the construction of dwellings within rock shelters as at Pachamachay and Quelcatani in Peru. To date, no important site hierarchies or ceremonial centers have been discovered.

Community Organization. There is little evidence in habitation sites that permits detailed construction of social organization in either the high sierras or the *puna*. Owing to the small size of sites, band-level organization was likely throughout the *punas* and in the south-central and Salt Puna sierra zones. Salt Puna sites in the Chilean intermontane area such as Tulán 52 and Puripica 1 indicate that bands may have become increasingly large. There is circumstantial evidence for increasing social complexity in the central Andean sierras in the construction of elaborate ceremonial structures. At Kotosh, the large size and elaborate architecture of the site indicate that a larger polity may have organized the large amount of labor necessary for such construction. Here, a larger tribal or chiefly polity may have had some coercive power. The ceremonial site of Huaricoto required much less labor and was probably within the organizational abilities of a lineage headman or cargo holder.

Housing. Evidence for housing is variable. In the south-central and Salt Puna regions, stone-walled structures become evident during the Terminal Late Archaic. Salt Puna sites such as Tulán 52 and Puripica 1 have elaborate semisubterranean houses made by burying large stone slabs into the earth. Also, the south-central Andean sierra site of Asana has post-walled structures on cleaned sand floors. Because most sites investigated are rock shelters, dwellings are often minimal.

Population, Health and Disease. Given the small size and scattered nature of most sites, populations appear to be small in any one region. Given the paucity of burials from this period in the highlands, nothing can be said about health status.

Economy

Subsistence. Evidence of widespread, regular food production is equivocal during this period in the Andean highlands. This presents a particularly intriguing research problem for three reasons: (1) there are reputedly early dates for plant domestication in the central and salt *puna* zones; (2) reliance on domestic plants is clear for lower altitude zones at this time; (3) reliance on domestic plants and animals is clear during the succeeding Formative/Initial period. Unfortunately, evidence for reliance on domesticates is sporadic in the Andean highlands during the Terminal Late Archaic. It is likely

that mixed economies based on hunting and gathering, incipient horticulture, and camelid herding were interspersed in time and geography with more strictly forager economies at this time.

Wild Foods. Little evidence exists about the wild foods utilized by Terminal Late Archaic highlanders. Clearly, wild Chenopodium was used in the *puna* and sierras, as were tubers and cactus fruits.

Domestic Foods. Potatoes, *oca*, *ullucu*, beans, and chile peppers were purportedly domesticated during the Early Archaic in the central Andes and salt *puna* zones, based on evidence from Guitarrero Cave in Peru and Huachichocana in Argentina. However, virtually no evidence for these plants reappears in the archaeological record until the Terminal Late Archaic, indicating that these plants, even if early domesticated, were not regularly used by highlanders until much later. In addition to more regular appearances of these domesticates, new additions appear during the Terminal Late Archaic, such as maize and quinoa. The extent to which people relied on these domesticates during the Terminal Late Archaic is still unknown. Evidence for the widespread domestication of Andean camelids becomes more common during the Terminal Late Archaic. Evidence suggests that camelids were being herded in the Junin *puna* of the central Andes beginning around 6000 B.P., and evidence for incipient herding appears in the south-central Andes and the salt *puna* zone between 4500–3500 B.P.

Industrial Arts. The technology of the Terminal Late Archaic of the highlands, as with earlier periods, is based on chipped- and ground-stone, bone, and fiber tools.

Utensils. Chipped-stone tools include projectile points, scrapers, knives, and choppers. Ground-stone tools such as grinding stones and mortars become increasingly common during the Terminal Late Archaic at Pachamachay, Asana, and Puripica 1, indicating increased reliance on grains. Bone tools include awls, flakers, and weaving tools. Remains of wool cordage from both wild and possibly domestic camelids have also been found.

Trade. Local populations appear largely self-sufficient as far as their subsistence needs were concerned. However, there is evidence for the limited trade of fine lithic materials and for possible trade movements between the Argentine *puna* and Chilean sierra valleys. Also, movement of raw materials in valley systems may parallel trade in food items, as local economies specialize as seen in later periods.

Division of Labor. Not enough evidence is present to delineate a clear division of labor by sex in the archaeological record. However, arguing by analogy, it is likely that males were primarily responsible for hunting and pasturing animals, and females were primarily responsible for gathering and horticulture. No other evidence exists for societal divisions based on economic activity.

Sociopolitical Organization

Given the small size of nearly all Terminal Late Archaic sites and the lack of settlement hierarchies, sociopolitical organization was probably bandlike nearly everywhere, especially throughout the *punas*. Even where settlement hierarchies exist with the presence of regional ceremonial centers, the only evidence for social complexity above 2500 m is at Huaricoto where some lineage-based or rotational system allowed an individual or individuals to assemble a limited labor pool. In lower elevations, such as Kotosh, evidence exists for a more stratified and coercive political system. However, it should be stressed that these locations are the only evidence to date of social complexity in the entire Andean highlands.

Religion and Expressive Culture

Religious Beliefs. Religious beliefs, as evidenced by the sites of Huaricoto, Kotosh and Asana, appear to be centered on earth-reverence and burnt sacrifice. By analogy with modern Andean beliefs and consistent with interpretations of Formative/Initial period religion, it is likely that some Terminal Late Archaic people considered themselves interdependent with a supernatural aspect of the earth or fertility. Sacrifice of animals, and probably other items, was both a means of entreating the supernatural for continued fertility and abundance, and a necessary means of sustaining the health of the supernatural realm.

Ceremonies. Public ceremonial architecture is present at Asana, Huaricoto, and Kotosh. In all three cases, crematory hearths are part of rectangular/ovoid walled structures. The central hearths at these sites are furthermore walled in with stone or post construction, delineating a public/profane space versus private/sacred space, indicating that rituals may have been conducted by a small number of specialists on behalf of larger populations. Evidence suggests that blood sacrifices of animals were central to ceremonies as they are in modern Andean religion.

Art. Carved stone is present in a cross-armed figure on a wall at the central Andean Kotosh, in a possible bird carving at Asana in the south-central Andes, and in portable stone carvings of camelids at Puripica 1 in the Salt Puna. There is abundant rock painting on rock-shelter and cave walls, which likely dates to this period. The predominant motif is animal, and camelids are common, except in the Argentine salt *puna*. Animal paintings are possibly related to fertility rites designed to guarantee the maintenance of hunted wild and herded domestic camelid populations.

Death and Afterlife. Few burials date to this time period in the highlands. Grave goods of projectile points are found in a burial of the Chiu-chiu complex in the Salt Puna, indicating a belief in the afterlife. A burial in Ayacucho, Peru, had red ocher. Otherwise, burials are simple and of flexed form.

Suggested Readings

Aldenderfer, M. (1989). "The Archaic Period in the South-Central Andes." *Journal of World Prehistory* 3: 117–158.

Aldenderfer, M. (1998). *Montane Foragers: Asana and the South-Central Andean Archaic.* Ames: University of Iowa Press.

Aldenderfer, M. (in press). *Quelcatani: The Evolution of a Pastoral Lifeway.* Washington, D.C.: Smithsonian Institution Press.

Baied, C., and J. Wheeler (1993). "Evolution of High Andean Puna Ecosystems: Environment, Climate, and Culture Change over the Last 12,000 Years in the Central Andes." *Mountain Research and Development* 13: 145–156.

Browman, D. (1989). "Origins and Development of Andean Pastoralism: An Overview of the Past 6000 Years." In *The Walking Larder: Patterns of Domestication, Pastoralism, and Predation*, ed. J. Clutton-Brock. London: Unwin Hyman, 258–268.

Burger, Richard L., and Lucy Salazar Burger (1986). "Early Organizational Diversity in the Peruvian Highlands: Huaricoto and Kotosh." In *Andean Archaeology: Papers in Memory of Clifford Evans*, ed. R. Matos M., S. A. Turpin, and H. H. Eling Jr. Institute of Archaeology Monograph 27. Los Angeles: University of California, 65–82.

Kuznar, L. (2001). "An Introduction to Andean Religious Ethnoarchaeology: Preliminary Results and Future Directions". In *Ethnoarchaeology in Andean South America: Contributions to Archaeological Method and Theory*, ed. L. Kuznar. Ann Arbor: International Monographs in Prehistory, 38–66.

Lynch, T. (1980). *Guitarrero Cave: Early Man in the Andes.* New York: Academic Press.

Lynch, T. (1990). "Quaternary Climate, Environment, and the Human Occupation of the South-Central Andes." *Geoarchaeology* 5: 199–228.

MacNeish, R. S. (1983). "The Ayacucho Preceramic as a Sequence of Cultural Energy-Flow Systems." In *Prehistory of the Ayacucho Basin, Peru, vol. IV: The Preceramic Way of Life*, ed. T. S. MacNeish, R. Vierra, A. Nelken-Turner, R. Lurie, and A. Cook. Ann Arbor: University of Michigan Press, 236–280.

Markgraf, V. (1989). "Palaeoclimates in Central and South America since 18,000 B.P. Based on Pollen and Lake-Level Records." *Quaternary Science Reviews* 8: 1–24.

Molina, E., and A. Little (1981). "Geoecology of the Andes: The Natural Science Basis for Research Planning." *Mountain Research and Development* 1: 115–144.

Nuñez, Lautaro (1983). "Paleoindian and Archaic Cultural Periods in the Arid and Semiarid Regions of Northern Chile." *Advances in World Archaeology* 2: 161–203.

Olivera, D. (1998). "Cazadores y Pastores Tempranos de la Puna Argentina." In *Past and Present in Andean Prehistory and Early History*, ed. S. Ahlgren, A. Muñoz, S. Sjödin, and P. Stenborg. Göteborg, Sweden: Etnografiska Museet, 153–180.

Pearsall, D. (1992). "The Origins of Plant Cultivation in South America." In *The Origins of Agriculture: An International Perspective*, ed. C. W. Cowan and P. J. Watson. Washington D.C.: Smithsonian Institution Press, 173–205.

Quilter, J. (1991). "Late Preceramic Peru." *Journal of World Prehistory* 5: 387–438.

Rick, J. (1980). *Prehistoric Hunters of the High Andes*. New York: Academic Press.

Rick, J. (1988) "The Character and Context of Highland Preceramic Society." In *Peruvian Prehistory*, ed. R. Keatinge. Cambridge: Cambridge University Press, 3–40.

Santoro, Calagero M., and Lautaro Nuñez (1987). "Hunters of the Dry Puna and the Salt Puna in Northern Chile." *Andean Past* 1: 57–109.

SUBTRADITIONS

Central Highland Andean Terminal Late Archaic (Late Preceramic, Terminal Preceramic, Upper Archaic, Kotosh Religious Tradition, Central Andean Preceramic)

TIME PERIOD: 4500–3500 B.P.

LOCATION: Highlands above 2500 m, including the wet *puna* and the western flanks of the Andes from northern Peru to the southern reaches of Ayacucho, Peru. The highlands include intermontane highland valleys between the coast and Andean mountains proper, and the high plains of the wet *puna*, which have their own subregional traditions.

DIAGNOSTIC MATERIAL ATTRIBUTES: Small, leaf-shaped projectile points (Cardich 1964; MacNeish et al. 1980a; Rick 1988), Rectangular/ovoid ceremonial structures of Kotosh religious tradition (Burger 1995; Burger and Burger 1986).

CULTURAL SUMMARY

Environment

Sites of this tradition are found in the high sierras of the western flanks of the Andes above 2500 m up to the wet *punas* between 3800–4500 m above mean sea level Rick (1988) summarizes paleoclimate reconstructions from Guitarrero Cave, Ayacucho, Lauricocha, and Junin, and concludes that, although climate was not constant, no radical climatic changes occurred in the central Andes during the Late Archaic period. This is consistent with Markgraf's (1989) reconstruction of post-4000 B.P. highland climate as essentially modern, with human-influenced changes occurring after 2000 B.P. Rainfall levels drop from highs of 1200 mm in the north to 800 mm in the south, and rainfall is decidedly seasonal, falling from November to April, with lower precipitation levels in the sierras (Molina and Little 1981).

Most resources in the high sierras are restricted to watercourses in river valleys. Such resources include *algorrobo* pods (*Prosopis* sp.), various tubers such as potato, *oca*, and *ullucu*, grains such as quinoa, and pulses such as beans. The primary wild animal resources of this zone would include Andean deer, or *taruca* (*Hippocamelus antisensis*), guanaco (*Lama guanicoe*), and guinea pigs, or *cuy* (*Cavia porcellus*). Wet *puna* resources are less restricted, but still tethered to water sources, namely large *bofedales*, or vegetation-mat marshes where fine grasses and forbs grow. Such locations are the preferred habitat of the vicuña (*Lama*, or *Vicugna vicugna*) (Franklin 1982), and the Andean deer or *taruca* (*Hippocamelus antisensis*) (Roe and Rees 1976).

Settlements

A couple of distinct settlement systems are identified for this period. Economies rapidly change during this period from mobile foraging to more sedentary food producing. In the high sierras, a fusion/fission pattern of forager transhumance is replaced by a more sedentary system by 3500 B.P. (MacNeish 1983; MacNeish et al. 1975). Movements in this zone were largely restricted to river valleys and their flanks. During the wet season, large macrobands would gather in central locations, splitting into smaller family microbands during the dry season when people dispersed looking for increasingly scarce natural resources. By the end of the Terminal Late Archaic, a more sedentary system of settlement is present, based on permanent settlements and an overall restriction of mobility. Most sites pertaining to this time period are found in rock shelters, with the primary evidence offered for sedentism being increasing midden thickness and the presence of more elaborate structures and houses (MacNeish 1983; Rick 1988).

A notable exception to the small domestic sites of this period are the larger, architecturally elaborate ceremonial sites such as Huaricoto, Kotosh, Piruru, and the low sierra (1100 m) La Galgada (Burger 1995; Burger and Burger 1980). Although there is variability in the construction of these sites, they share the same settlement features, such as rectangular-ovoid walled structures with central hearths placed on low mounds. Whether Huaricoto and Kotosh in the highlands had permanent occupancy or were periodically visited for ceremonial activities is uncertain, although the low sierra La Galgada had domestic structures (Burger 1995).

The settlement system of the wet *puna* above 3800 m is simpler (Rick 1988). As with the high sierra sites, early sites indicate a mobility system within the zone based on the movements of foragers around water sources. However, the *puna* is a large plain, and mobility was more two-dimensional than that seen in the high sierras (Bocek and Rick 1984). By 4500 B.P., camelids had most likely been domesticated in the Junin *puna* (Browman 1989), so that the mobility pattern reflected not only movement from *bofedal* to *bofedal* in pursuit of wild camelids and deer, but also of domestic camelids from pasture to pasture. By 3500 B.P., *puna* settlements show evidence of increased sedentarization, such as stone houses (Rick 1980, 1988). Rick (1980, 1988) as well as MacNeish (1983) makes an argument that throughout this period, a *puna* settlement system, distinct from the high sierra system, was in place.

Economy

Two distinct economies were present in the central Andes during the Terminal Late Archaic: one in the high sierras, and one in the wet *puna*. Furthermore, changes occurred during this time period from a more foraging-oriented economy to a clearly horticultural/pastoral one. The early high sierra subsistence economy was based on hunting guanaco and *taruca* and on mixed plant gathering and potato/pepper horticulture (Lynch 1980; MacNeish 1983; Pearsall 1992). By the end of the Terminal Late Archaic, sedentary populations were growing potatoes (*Solanum* sp.), *oca* (*Oxalis tuberosa*), *ullucu* (*Ullucus tuberosus*), common beans (*Phaseolus vulgaris*), lima beans (*Phaseolus lunata*), peppers (*Capsicum* sp.), squash (*Curcubita* sp.), gourd (*Lagenaria* sp.), and quinoa (*Chenopodium quinoa*), and herding llamas (*Lama glama*) and raising guinea pigs (*Cavia porcellus*) (Cardich 1987; Kaplan and Lynch 1999; Lynch 1980; MacNeish 1983; Pearsall 1992; Quilter 1991; Wing 1972). Potatoes, *oca*, and chile peppers may have been cultivated since the Early Archaic, but more widespread evidence for them and new crops emerges during the terminal Late Archaic. From Ayacucho, there is evidence for domesticated maize (*Zea mays*), squash, and gourd by 3750 B.P. (MacNeish 1983), and in the Callejón de Huaylas, both the common bean (*Phaseolus vulgaris*) and lima bean (*Phaseolus lunata*) are clearly present by at least this time (Kaplan and Lynch 1999). Maize is present during the Terminal Late Archaic, but it does not appear to be a major constituent of the diet (Pearsall 1992; Quilter 1991). The possibility of high sierra camelid herding is raised at sites such as Kotosh, where a definite increase in the incidence of camelids indicates pastoralism, and the Ayacucho sites, where corrals appear between 5050–3700 B.P. (MacNeish and Vierra 1983a, 1983b; Quilter 1991; Rick 1988; Wing 1972).

A separate economic system developed in the wet *puna* where the focus of subsistence effort was clearly on camelids. Both the incidence of camelids remains as well as the percentage of neonate mortality increases dramatically during this period of time (Browman 1989; Wheeler 1984; Wheeler Pires Ferreira et al. 1976; Wing 1986). Evidence suggests that in the Junin Puna of the central Andes, domestication took place 6000 B.P., but that evidence rapidly accumulates during the Terminal Late Archaic, indicating that the process of domestication had become complete in the central Andes by this time. Pastoral groups appear to have been small and tethered to *bofedales*, which provide essential forage for animals. *Puna* herders also may have cultivated some crops, although the high altitude and frequent frosts make substantial agriculture infeasible. Nonetheless, there is evidence of incipient quinoa domestication (Pearsall 1980) and potato agriculture by 3600 B.P. in the *Puna* (Pearsall 1989).

Evidence of limited trade in obsidian is present for the southern part of the central Andes between highland and coastal populations (Quilter 1991).

Chipped-stone tool industries are dominated by small leaf-shaped projectile points, scrapers, and coarse choppers (Cardich 1964, 1987; MacNeish et al. 1980a,1980b; Rick 1980, 1988). Also, a variety of bone tools including awls, flakers, and fleshing tools are found (Cardich 1964, 1987; MacNeish and Nelken-Turner 1980; Rick 1988).

Sociopolitical Organization

Corresponding to the different economies and settlement histories of the *puna* and the sierra, different types of sociopolitical organization emerge. The sierra presents the most complex picture. In some regions, such as Ayacucho, sites appear small, with no more hierarchical organization than what appears to be the result of seasonal aggregations and dispersals of small horticultural/pastoral populations (MacNeish 1983; MacNeish et al. 1975). However, in some of the intermontane valleys, sites such as Kotosh present evidence of public architecture and sculpture that would have required large inputs of labor. Burger and Burger (1986; see also Burger 1995; Izumi and Terada 1972; Quilter 1991) interpret this as a higher level of sociopolitical integration involving an emerging elite. At the same time in the Callejón de Huaylas, ceremonial sites such as Huaricoto contain smaller, more easily constructed and maintained structures, indicating integrated communities with rotating headmanship or cargo systems managed not by polities, but by lineages (Burger and Burger 1986). The emergent complexity seen in some intermontane valleys is an important precursor to political and cultural elaborations that flourish during the following Formative or Initial periods in the Andean coast and sierra (Burger and Burger 1980).

A simpler sociopolitical situation is indicated in the *puna*, although the recent discovery of a ceremonial site at Piruru (3800 m) may challenge this inference (Burger 1995). In the *puna*, the main site hierarchy in the settlement pattern is a differentiation between permanent sedentary base camps that would have functioned as a focus of hunting and herding activities and smaller, temporary sites used for the grazing of animals in seasonal pastures or as hunting stands (Bocek and Rick 1984; Rick 1980, 1988).

Religion and Expressive Culture

As with earlier periods, rock art continues to be an important form of artistic expression. Motifs are almost always animal, with camelids dominating (Lavalée 1987; Rick 1980, 1988). Most authors assume that the art has ritual functions related to hunting and the fertility of herds. Sites throughout the region often contain exotic minerals, marine shell, and stones (Burger and Burger 1980; Quilter 1991; Rick 1980). In view of modern Andean ritual practices as well as abstract Andean religious principles, such artifacts provide evidence of the telluric, or earth-centered, principle essential to Andean religion today (Aldenderfer 1991; Kuznar 2001). Whether or not earth-related deities important today and through history such as *pachamama* existed during the Terminal Late Archaic is uncertain.

The major development in religion is the emergence of the Kotosh religious tradition. Burger and Burger (1980, 1986) stress that this was not a set of dogmatic ritual practice and belief, but rather a set of loosely shared ritual elements found in the sierras of the central Andes. The architectural elements of this tradition, along with associated remains, allow some inferences concerning religious practice and belief. All ceremonial structures are walled, delineating a sacred space, and all contain a central hearth where animal sacrifices took place. Burnt animal sacrifices are common offerings to deities today. People consider the sacrifices essential to the well-being of deities and especially for the continued fertility of the earth itself (Kuznar 1995, 2001). Further evidence for religious communication with the earth deity is found at Kotosh and Piruru, where many of the ceremonial structures contain an underground flue in their floors, reminiscent of the *sipapu* in modern Hopi and prehistoric Anasazi kivas. Although underground flues and exotic stone artifacts may indicate high regard for the earth as a supernatural entity, any number of aspects of deity could have been worshiped at these sites. There is also evidence in the presence of shells for the worship of the ocean or water deity at many central Andean sites. If this is the case, then the fundamental water and earth deities worshiped today and historically, and projected back to the Initial/Formative period by Lyon (1970), could very well have preceramic roots.

A secondary burial of a child, sprinkled with red ocher, was found in Ayacucho and dated to about 4600 B.P. (MacNeish and Vierra 1983a, 1983b).

References

Aldenderfer, M. (1991). "Continuity and Change in Ceremonial Structures at Late Preceramic Asana, Southern Peru." *Latin American Antiquity* 2: 227–258.

Bocek, B., and J. Rick (1984). "La Epoca Precerámica en la Puna de Junin." *Chungará* 13: 109–127.

Browman, D. (1989). "Origins and Development of Andean Pastoralism: An Overview of the Past 6000 Years." In *The Walking Larder: Patterns of Domestication, Pastoralism, and Predation*, ed. J. Clutton-Brock. London: Unwin Hyman, 258–268.

Burger, Richard (1995). *Chavin and the Origins of Andean Civilization*. London: Thames and Hudson.

Burger, Richard L., and Lucy Salazar Burger (1980). "Ritual and Religion at Huaricoto." *Archaeology* 33: 26–32.

Burger, Richard L., and Lucy Salazar Burger (1986). "Early Organizational Diversity in the Peruvian Highlands: Huaricoto and Kotosh." In *Andean Archaeology: Papers in Memory of Clifford Evans*, ed. R. Matos M., S. A. Turpin, and H. H. Eling Jr. Institute of Archaeology Monograph 27. Los Angeles: University of California, 65–82.

Cardich, A. (1964). *Lauricocha: Fundamentos para una Prehistoria de los Andes Centrales*. Buenos Aires: Centro Argentino de Estudios Prehistóricos.

Cardich, A. (1987). "Lauricocha: Asentamiento Preagrícolas, Recolección Vegetal e Inicios del Cultivo Altoandino." *Diálogo Andino* 6: 11–28.

Franklin, W. (1982). "Biology, Ecology, and Relationship to Man of the South American Camelids." In *Mammalian Biology in South America*, ed. M. A. Mares and H. H. Genoways. Pittsburgh: Special Publications Series Pymatuning Laboratory of Ecology, University of Pittsburgh. 457–489.

Izumi, S., and K. Terada (1972). *Andes 4: Excavations at Kotosh, Peru*. Tokyo: University of Tokyo Press.

Kaplan, L., and T. Lynch (1999). "Phaseolus (Fabaceae) in Archaeology: AMS Radiocarbon Dates and Their Significance for Pre-Columbian Agriculture." *Economic Botany* 53: 261–272.

Kuznar, L. (1995). *Awatimarka: The Ethnoarchaeology of an Andean Herding Community*. Fort Worth TX: Harcourt Brace.

Kuznar, L. (in press). 2001 "An Introduction to Andean Religious Ethnoarchaeology: Preliminary Results and Future Directions." In *Ethnoarchaeology in Andean South America: Contributions to Archaeological Method and Theory*, ed. L. Kuznar. Ann Arbor: International Monographs in Prehistory, 38–66.

Lavalée, D. (1987). *Telarmachay: Chasseurs et Pasteurs Préhistoriques de Andes I*. Paris: Institut Français d'Études Andines, Éditions Recherche sur les Civilisations.

Lynch, T. (1980). *Guitarrero Cave: Early Man in the Andes*. New York: Academic Press.

Lyon, P. (1970). "Female Supernaturals in Ancient Peru." *Ñawpa Pacha* 16: 95–140.

MacNeish, R. S. (1983). "The Ayacucho Preceramic as a Sequence of Cultural Energy-Flow Systems." In *Prehistory of the Ayacucho Basin, Peru, vol. IV: The Preceramic Way of Life*, ed. T. S. MacNeish, R. Vierra, A. Nelken-Turner, R. Lurie, and A. Cook. Ann Arbor: University of Michigan Press, 236–280.

MacNeish, R. S., and A. Nelken-Turner (1980). "Bone Tools." In *Prehistory of the Ayacucho Basin, Peru, vol. III: Nonceramic Artifacts*, ed. R. S. MacNeish, R. Vierra, A. Nelken-Turner, and C. Phagan. Ann Arbor: University of Michigan Press, 309–321.

MacNeish, R. S., and R. Vierra (1983a). "The Preceramic Way of Life in the Thorn Forest Riverine Ecozone." In *Prehistory of the Ayacucho Basin, Peru, vol. IV: The Preceramic Way of Life*, ed. T. S. MacNeish, R. Vierra, A. Nelken-Turner, R. Lurie, and A. Cook. Ann Arbor: University of Michigan Press, 48–129.

MacNeish, R. S., and R. Vierra (1983b). "The Preceramic Way of Life in the Puna Ecozone." In *Prehistory of the Ayacucho Basin, Peru, vol. IV: The Preceramic Way of Life*, ed. T. S. MacNeish, R. Vierra, A. Nelken-Turner, R. Lurie, and A. Cook. Ann Arbor: University of Michigan Press, 225–235.

MacNeish, R. S., T. Patterson, and D. Browman (1975). *The Central Peruvian Prehistoric Interaction Sphere*. Andover, MA: Papers of the R. S. Peabody Foundation for Archaeology.

MacNeish, R.S., R. Vierra, A. Nelken-Turner, and C. Phagan (1980a). "Haftable Pointed Bifaces." In *Prehistory of the Ayacucho Basin, Peru, Vol. III: Nonceramic Artifacts*, ed. R. S. MacNeish, R. Vierra, A. Nelken-Turner, and C. Phagan. Ann Arbor: University of Michigan Press, 35–95.

MacNeish, R.S., R. Vierra, A. Nelken-Turner, and C. Phagan (1980b). "Nonhaftable Pointed Bifaces." In *Prehistory of the Ayacucho Basin, Peru, Vol. III: Nonceramic Artifacts*, ed. R. S. MacNeish, R. Vierra, A. Nelken-Turner, and C. Phagan. Ann Arbor: University of Michigan Press, 119–175.

Markgraf, V. (1989). "Palaeoclimates in Central and South America since 18,000 B.P. Based on Pollen and Lake-Level Records." *Quaternary Science Reviews* 8: 1–24.

Molina, E., and A. Little (1981). "Geoecology of the Andes: The Natural Science Basis for Research Planning." *Mountain Research and Development* 1: 115–144.

Nuñez, Lautaro (1983). "Paleoindian and Archaic Cultural Periods in the Arid and Semiarid Regions of Northern Chile." *Advances in World Archaeology* 2: 161–203.

Pearsall, D. (1980). "Pachamachay Ethnobotanical Report: Plant Utilization at a Hunting Base Camp." In *Prehistoric Hunters of the High Andes*, ed. J. Rick. New York: Academic Press, 191–232.

Pearsall, D. (1989). "Adaptation of Prehistoric Hunter-Gatherers to the High Andes: The Changing Role of Plant Resources." In *Foraging and Farming: The Evolution of Plant Exploitation*, ed. D. Harris and G. Hillman. London: Unwin Hyman, 318–332.

Pearsall, D. (1992). "The Origins of Plant Cultivation in South America." In *The Origins of Agriculture: An International Perspective*, ed. C. W. Cowan and P. J. Watson. Washington D.C.: Smithsonian Institution Press, 173–205.

Pires-Ferreira Wheeler, Jane, E. Pires-Ferreira, and P. Kaulicke (1976). "Preceramic Animal Utilization in the Central Peruvian Andes." *Science* 194: 483–490.

Quilter, J. (1991). "Late Preceramic Peru." *Journal of World Prehistory* 5: 387–438.

Rick, J. (1980). *Prehistoric Hunters of the High Andes*. New York: Academic Press.

Rick, J. (1988). "The Character and Context of Highland Preceramic Society." In *Peruvian Prehistory*, ed. R. Keatinge. Cambridge: Cambridge University Press, 3–40.

Roe, Nicholas, and William Rees (1976). "Preliminary Observations of the Taruca (Hippocamelus antisensis: Cervidae) in Southern Peru." *Journal of Mammalogy* 57: 722–730.

Santoro, Calagero M., and Lautaro Nuñez (1987). "Hunters of the Dry Puna and the Salt Puna in Northern Chile." *Andean Past* 1: 57–109.

Wheeler, Jane (1984). "On the Origin and Development of Camelid Pastoralism in the Andes." In *Animals and Archaeology, vol 3: Early Herders and their Flocks*, ed. J. Clutton-Brock and C. Grigson. Oxford: BAR International Series 202, 395–410.

Wheeler Pires-Ferreira, Jane, E. Pires-Ferreria, and P. Kaulicke. (1976). "Preceramic Animal Utilization in the Central Andes." *Science* 194: 483–490

Wing, E. (1972). "Utilization of Animal Resources in the Peruvian Andes, Appendix IV." In *Andes 4: Excavations at Kotosh*, ed. S. Izumi and K. Terada. Tokyo: University of Tokyo Press, 327–351.

Wing, E. (1986). "Domestication of Andean Mammals." In *High Altitude Tropical Biogeography*, ed. F. Vuilleumier and M. Monasterio. Oxford: Oxford University Press, 246–264.

South-Central Highland Andean Terminal Late Archaic (Late Preceramic, Late Archaic, Transitional)

TIME PERIOD: 4500–3500 B.P.

LOCATION: Highlands above 2500 m, including the dry *puna* and the western flanks of the Andes from the southern half of the department of Arequipa, Peru, to extreme northern Chile. Within the highlands, *puna* and high sierra zones have their own regional traditions.

DIAGNOSTIC MATERIAL ATTRIBUTES: Small leaf-shaped projectile points (Aldenderfer 1989a, 1989b, 1998; Ravines 1972), small triangular projectile points (Santoro and Nuñez 1987).

CULTURAL SUMMARY

Environment

Sites of this subtradition are found in the high sierras of the western flanks of the Andes above 2500 m to the dry *punas* between 3800–4500 m above mean sea level. The climate of 4500–3500 B.P. appears to have been wet and cold, approaching more modern conditions, as reviewed by Kuznar (1989; see also Markgraf 1989; Nuñez 1983). Baied and Wheeler (1993), analyzing pollen from extreme northern Chile, note that a hypsithermal or dry period lasted from about 6500–5000 B.P., followed by a wet period from 5000–4000 B.P., at which time there is an increase in herbaceous taxa, indicating environmental desiccation and possibly human alteration of the flora by herding after 3000 B.P. Today, rainfall levels drop from highs of 800 mm in the north to 200 mm in Chile, and rainfall is decidedly seasonal, falling from November to April (Molina and Little 1981). Most resources in the high sierras are restricted to watercourses in river valleys. Such resources include *algorrobo* pods (*Prosopis* sp.), various tubers such as potato (*Solanum* sp.), *oca* (*Oxalis tuberosa*), and *ullucu* (*Ullucus tuberosus*), grains such as quinoa (*Chenopodium quinoa*), and pulses such as beans (*Phaseolus* sp.). The primary wild animal resources of this zone would include Andean deer, or *taruca* (*Hippocamelus antisensis*), guanaco (*Lama guanicoe*), and guinea pigs, or *cuy* (*Cavia porcellus*). Dry *puna* resources are also very restricted to water sources, namely large *bofedales*, or vegetation-mat marshes where fine grasses and forbs grow (Kuznar in press a). Such locations are the preferred habitat of the vicuña (*Lama* or *Vicugna vicugna*) (Franklin 1982), and the *taruca* (*Hippocamelus antisensis*) (Roe and Rees 1976).

Settlements

Two distinct settlement systems have been identified, one in the high sierra of the western flanks of the Andes, and one in the high altitude plains of the dry *puna*. High sierra settlement systems in the south-central Andean zone are characterized by seasonal transhumance up and down sierra valleys (Aldenderfer 1989a, 1989b, 1990, 1998; Nuñez 1983; Santoro and Chacama 1982; Santoro and Nuñez 1987). Most sites excavated are rock shelters (Nuñez 1983; Santoro and Chacama 1982; Santoro and Nuñez 1987), and the few excavated open-air sites are likewise small (Aldenderfer 1989a, 1990, 1998). Important surveys of surface sites likewise indicate small site size and therefore small population aggregations (Aldenderfer 1989c). An extensively excavated open-air site in the region, Asana in southern Peru, contains evidence for several post structures, domestic area cleaning, and systematic intrasite organization of hearths and refuse areas, indicating sedentary living between 4800–4400 B.P. (Aldenderfer 1989a, 1990, 1993, 1998). The structures increase in size through time from 8 m^2 to 10 m^2 during this phase of site occupation. The other striking settlement feature of Asana is a rectangular or U-shaped ceremonial structure made of rubble fill and covered with clay and small offertories. This structure, unfortunately half of which was destroyed by stream erosion, was further enclosed by a post structure encompassing at least 132 m^2 (Aldenderfer 1993, 1998). In the Asana valley of southern Peru at least, an abrupt change in settlement is indicated by the replacement of the sedentary site with a smaller pastoral camp. This camp is characterized by a single post dwelling set among several boulders, an outside hearth area, a human-made canal, and a probable corral area (Kuznar 1990, 1995). Aldenderfer (1998) has found evidence of other pastoral camps in the Asana valley, implying a new transhumance system based on the movements of herds sometime after 4400 B.P.

Puna settlement patterns are likewise based on small sites, although midden thicknesses and debris densities increase through time, indicating that occupations are becoming more sedentary (Aldenderfer 1989a, 1998; Kuznar 1989; Nuñez 1983; Santoro and Nuñez 1987). *Puna* sites are very much restricted to *bofedales* where animal resources can be procured or produced (Aldenderfer 1998; Kuznar 1989, in press b). At the site of Quelcatani in the southern Peruvian *puna*, the stone-walled dwellings of pastoralists become substantial during the Terminal Late Archaic, indicating more settled use of the site (Aldenderfer in press).

Economy

The Terminal Late Archaic is particularly important in the south-central Andes because a number of plant and animal domesticates first appear during this time. Nonetheless, hunting remains important. There is an emphasis on the use of camelids at many sites (Asana, Quelcatani, Tojo-tojone, Puxuma, Patapatane), but continued use of rodents and birds as well (Aldenderfer 1998, in press; Santoro and Nuñez 1987). Evidence that maize may have been domesticated by 4500 B.P. exists in the southern region of the south-central Andes at lower elevation sites such as Tarapaca 14-A and Tarapaca 12 in Chile (Pearsall 1992; Rivera 1991). Although maize is found in scattered locations throughout the Andes at this time, it is not widespread and does not appear to be a major component of the diet. No quinoa remains have been positively identified for the south-central Andean sierra at this time, but quinoa appears in the nearby Chilean coast (Zlatar 1983). Indirect evidence for cereal production occurs at Asana where, during the Qhuna phase (4800–4400 B.P.) levels of the site, many grinding stones were found (Aldenderfer 1989a, 1990, 1993, 1998). Interestingly, no potato remains have been found, although given the early occurrence of potato elsewhere in the Andes and its existence during the following Formative period (Browman 1989a), potatoes must have at least appeared in the south-central Andes during the Terminal Late Archaic. Other root crops such as *ullucu* (*Ullucus tuberosus*), *oca* (*Oxalis tuberosa*), and *isaño* (*Tropaeolum tuberosum*) date to Late Archaic levels of Patapatane in Chile (Santoro and Chacama 1982; Santoro and Nuñez 1987). Camelid herding is evidenced by the occurrence of a probable corral at Asana (Kuznar 1990, 1995). In contrast to the central Andean region, where evidence of herding occurs 6000 years ago, early dates for herding in the south-central Andes are later, between 4500 and 3500 years ago (Browman 1989b; Kuznar 1989, 1990). In summary, high sierra economy has shifted from a foraging economy to an incipient mixed horticultural/herding economy based on hunting, possible potato/quinoa agriculture, and llama herding by the Terminal Late Archaic.

Puna economic shifts similarly indicate a change from a foraging to an incipient food-producing econo-my during the Terminal Late Archaic. Sites like Quelcatani in Peru and Hakenasa in Chile indicate that people relied increasingly on camelids, which, based on mortality profiles and preserved dung caps in sites (corrals), appear to have been domesticated (Aldenderfer in press). In addition, Chenopodium becomes increasingly important at Quelcatani during this time, indicating possible trade with lower-altitude groups for this grain (Aldenderfer in press). Also, small storage facilities at Quelcatani, which appear during the Late Archaic, are interpreted as potato storage facilities by Aldenderfer (1989a).

There is limited evidence of trade with the presence of coastal shell at the site of Tojo-tojone in northern Chile, although whether the few fragments of shell were traded or directly collected is unclear (Santoro and Nuñez 1987). Aldenderer (1989b, 1998) reports that small amounts of highland lithic material are found at coastal sites in southern Peru and that this pattern increases throughout time. He infers that these small amounts of raw material are exchanged between the highlands and coast as tokens of reciprocal economic support to buffer uncertainties in resource availability.

Sociopolitical Organization

In contrast to the central Andean sierra, there is little evidence for complex sociopolitical integration during the Terminal Late Archaic of the south-central Andes. Sites tend to be small, and regional site hierarchies indicate seasonal fission/fusion patterns of small foraging or pastoral groups (Aldenderfer 1989a, 1989c, 1990; Nuñez 1983; Santoro and Nuñez 1987). The one possible exception would be the ceremonial site of Asana in southern Peru, which may have had a local significance as a religious site. However, whether the supernatural significance of this site had political implications is moot.

Religion and Expressive Culture

Rock art is common in highland rock shelters, and motifs center on animals, especially camelids and human lineups (Aldenderfer 1987; Ravines 1986; Santoro and Chacama 1982; Santoro and Nuñez 1987). Several sites contain coastal shell and exotic minerals, indicating a possible special reverence for a deified water/ocean and earth (Aldenderfer 1991; Kuznar 2001). However, Asana is the single site that offers the most insight on south-central Andean religious beliefs. A rectangular or U-shaped rubble fill mound occupying 132 m^2 and containing small, rock-lined offertories dates from

4800–4400 B.P. The mound is surrounded by crematory basins burnt red from intense fires and containing what is most likely powdered calcined bone. Outside these basins are the remains of a large post structure that would have enclosed the sacred interior. Outside the post structure are tiny post-mold patterns that appear to be the remains of miniature houses, about 10–20 cm in diameter (Aldenderfer 1993, 1998). This complex of features offers an intriguing glimpse into Terminal Late Archaic ritual. Aldenderfer (1991) has argued that this complex bears a striking resemblance to modern Aymara ritual sites. For instance, the important Andean ritual site, or *huaca*, of Cerro Baul in southern Peru contains a rubble structure similar in size to the one found at Asana, contains stone-lined offertories, is surrounded by crematory basin where animal sacrifices are made, and is further surrounded by small stone effigies of peoples' houses and fields (Kuznar 1995, 2001). A number of indigenous rituals take place at Cerro Baul, including offerings to the deified female earth principle, *pachamama*, and ceremonies entreating the god of luck, *eq'eq'o* (Aldenderfer 1991; Kuznar 1995). The parallels in structure and form with Asana are striking and have led both authors to argue by analogy that Asana is the earliest evidence of this highland Andean religious complex.

References

Aldenderfer, M. (1987). "Hunter-Gatherer Settlement Dynamics and Rupestral Art: Inferring Mobility and Aggregation in the South-Central Andes of Southern Peru." In *Actas del VIII Simposium Internacional de Arte Rupestre Americano*. Santo Domingo: Museo del Hombre Dominicano, 373–403.

Aldenderfer, M. (1989a). "The Archaic Period in the South-Central Andes." *Journal of World Prehistory* 3: 117–158.

Aldenderfer, M. (1989b). "Archaic Period "Complementarity" in the Osmore Drainage." In *Ecology, Settlement and History in the Osmore Drainage, Peru*, part i, ed. D. Rice, C. Stanish, and P. Scarr. Oxford: BAR International Series 545(i), 101–128.

Aldenderfer, M. (1989c). "Archaic Period Settlement Patterns in the High Sierra of the Osmore Basin." In *Ecology, Settlement and History in the Osmore Drainage, Peru*, part i, ed. D. Rice, C. Stanish, and P. Scarr. Oxford: BAR International Series 545(i), 129–166.

Aldenderfer, M. (1990). "Cronología y Definición de Fases Arcaicas de Asana, Sur de Peru." *Chungará* 24/25: 13–35.

Aldenderfer, Mark S. (1991). "Continuity and Change in Ceremonial Structures at Late Preceramic Asana, Southern Peru." *Latin American Antiquity* 2: 227–258.

Aldenderfer, M. (1993). "Domestic Space, Mobility, and Ecological Complementarity: The View from Asana." In *Domestic Architecture, Ethnicity, and Complementarity in the South-Central Andes*, ed. M. S. Aldenderfer. Iowa City: University of Iowa Press, 13–19.

Aldenderfer, M. (1998). *Montane Foragers: Asana and the South-Central Andean Archaic*. Ames: University of Iowa Press.

Aldenderfer, M. (in press). *Quelcatani: The Evolution of a Pastoral Lifeway*. Washington, D.C.: Smithsonian Institution Press.

Baied, C., and J. Wheeler (1993). "Evolution of High Andean Puna Ecosystems: Environment, Climate, and Culture Change over the Last 12,000 Years in the Central Andes." *Mountain Research and Development* 13: 145–156.

Browman, D. (1989a). "Chenopod Cultivation, Lacustrine Resources, and Fuel Use at Chiripa, Bolivia." *Missouri Archaeologist* 47: 137–172.

Browman, D. (1989b). "Origins and Development of Andean Pastoralism: An Overview of the Past 6000 Years." In *The Walking Larder: Patterns of Domestication, Pastoralism, and Predation*, ed. J. Clutton-Brock. London: Unwin Hyman, 258–268.

Franklin, W. (1982). "Biology, Ecology, and Relationship to Man of the South American Camelids." In *Mammalian Biology in South America*, ed. M. A. Mares and H. H. Genoways. Pittsburgh: Special Publications Series Pymatuning Laboratory of Ecology, University of Pittsburgh, 457–489.

Klarich, E. (in press). "Camelid Depictions in the Rupestral Art of Quelcatani: Hunters or Herders?" In *Quelcatani: The Evolution of a Pastoral Lifeway*. ed. M. Aldenderfer. Washington, D.C.: Smithsonian Institution Press.

Kuznar, L. (1989). "The Domestication of Camelids in Southern Peru: Models and Evidence." In *Ecology, Settlement and History in the Osmore Drainage, Peru*, part i, ed. D. Rice, C. Stanish, and P. Scarr. Oxford: BAR International Series 545(i), 101–128.

Kuznar, L. (1990). "Pastoralismo Temprano en la Sierra Alta del Departamento de Moquegua, Perú." *Chungará* 24/25: 53–68.

Kuznar, L. (1993). "Mutualism between Chenopodium, Herd Animals and Herders in the South Central Andes." *Mountain Research and Development* 13, 3: 257–265.

Kuznar, L. (1995). *Awatimarka: The Ethnoarchaeology of an Andean Herding Community*. Fort Worth: Harcourt Brace.

Kuznar, L. (in press). "Altiplano Human Ecology/Altiplano Past." In *Quelcatani: The Evolution of a Pastoral Lifeway*, ed. M. Aldenderfer. Washington, D.C.: Smithsonian Institution Press.

Kuznar, L. (2001). "An Introduction to Andean Religious Ethnoarchaeology: Preliminary Results and Future Directions." In *Ethnoarchaeology in Andean South America: Contributions to Archaeological Method and Theory*, ed. L. Kuznar. Ann Arbor: International Monographs in Prehistory, 38–66.

Markgraf, V. (1989). "Palaeoclimates in Central and South America since 18,000 B.P. Based on Pollen and Lake-Level Records." *Quaternary Science Reviews* 8: 1–24.

Molina, E., and A. Little (1981). "Geoecology of the Andes: The Natural Science Basis for Research Planning." *Mountain Research and Development* 1: 115–144.

Nuñez, Lautaro (1983). "Paleoindian and Archaic Cultural Periods in the Arid and Semiarid Regions of Northern Chile." *Advances in World Archaeology* 2: 161–203.

Pearsall, D. (1992). "The Origins of Plant Cultivation in South America." In *The Origins of Agriculture: An International Perspective*, ed. C. W. Cowan and P. J. Watson. Washington D.C.: Smithsonian Institution Press, 173–205.

Ravines, R. (1972). "Secuencia y Cambios en los Artefactos Liticos del Sur del Peru." *Revista del Museo Nacional, Lima* 38: 133–184.

Ravines, R. (1986). "Quelcatani." In *Arte Rupestre del Peru*, ed. R. Ravines. Lima: Instituto Nacional de Cultura, 51–52.

Rivera, M. (1991). "The Prehistory of Northern Chile: A Synthesis" *Journal of World Prehistory*. 511–547.

Roe, Nicholas, and William Rees (1976). "Preliminary Observations of the Taruca (Hippocamelus antisensis: Cervidae) in Southern Peru." *Journal of Mammology* 57: 722–730.

Santoro, C., and J. Chacama R. (1982). "Secuencia Cultural de las Tierras Altas del Area Centro Sur Andina." *Chungará* 9: 22–45.

Santoro, Calagero M., and Lautaro Nuñez (1987). "Hunters of the Dry Puna and the Salt Puna in Northern Chile." *Andean Past* 1: 57–109.

Zlatar, V. (1983). "Replanteamiento sobre el Problema Caleta Huelén 42." *Chungará* 10: 21–28.

Salt Puna Terminal Late Archaic (Late Archaic, Salt Puna Late Archaic, Arid North Late Archaic, Stage V. Puripica, Transitional)

TIME PERIOD: 4500–3500 B.P.

LOCATION: Highlands above 2500 m, including the salt *puna* of Chile, Bolivia, and northwestern Argentina. Subregional traditions in Chilean intermontane valleys and northwest Argentine salt *puna*.

DIAGNOSTIC MATERIAL ATTRIBUTES: Lanceolate, leaf-shaped, and small triangular projectile points (Nuñez 1983; Santoro and Chacama 1982; Santoro and Nuñez 1987).

CULTURAL SUMMARY

Environment

Sites of this subtradition are found in the salt *puna* of the Andes from 2500–4500 m above mean sea level. Markgraf (1989; also Nuñez 1983) notes an increase in precipitation levels at 4000 B.P. after a dry phase, or hypsithermal. After 3000 B.P., the climate becomes drier, and pollen evidence suggests that camelid pastoralism may have affected the flora of the region (Messerli et al. 1993). Lynch (1990), while pointing out that much regional variation exists in paleoenvironmental reconstructions, also notes that there is a trend toward increasing desiccation after the last glaciation in the salt *puna*, and that as time proceeds, precipitation levels become more and more similar to today's. Rainfall levels in this region are very low, varying from 1 mm per annum to 150 mm per annum depending on local conditions (Molina and Little 1981; Nuñez 1983). This precipitation is extremely seasonal, falling entirely during a wet season that lasts from November to April. Resources are extremely localized and tethered to water sources. Wild and domestic chenopodium, wood sources, and pastures are located along salt marshes and flats known as *salares*, and small areas of pasture along streams known as *vegas*. The primary wild animal resources of this zone would include Andean deer, or *taruca* (*Hippocamelus antisensis*) and camelids such as vicuña (*Lama* or *Vicugna vicugna*) and guanaco (*Lama guanicoe*) (Franklin 1982; Roe and Rees 1976).

Settlements

Two settlement patterns exist in these arid regions. The first is found in moderately high-altitude intermontane valleys between Chilean coastal ranges and the Andean mountain range proper near the Chilean border. Settlements in this intermontane region are mostly found near the shores of salt marshes and in valleys that lead up to the Andes proper. The Chilean sites of Tulán 52 and Puripica 1 exemplify this pattern. Both sites contain semisubterranean houses made from large stone slabs and are rather large, have about 30 and 50 dwellings, respectively, and contain substantial storage pits. Both sites are located near important resource locations such as major *salares* and *quebradas*. The settlement pattern of this region is also characterized by smaller, more temporary sites that probably function as seasonal or task specific camps (Aldenderfer 1989; Druss 1984a,1984b; Nuñez 1983; Santoro and Chacama 1982; Santoro and Nuñez 1987). So, by Terminal Late Archaic times, there is a definite pattern of sedentary or logistical mobility among the inhabitants of Chilean intermontane valleys.

A similar system of local sedentarization appears to be the case for salt *puna* sites near the Chilean/Bolivian border and in Northwest Argentina. Most sites are rock shelters, and so site area is restricted and the need for elaborate shelters within the sites is limited. However, midden thicknesses increase during this time, indicating an increase in site occupation length (Olivera 1998; Santoro and Nuñez 1987). Mobility is among *vegas* and *salares*, which often occur along long, broad valleys in the salt *puna*.

Economy

Hunting continues to be important and focused primarily on camelids, although birds and rodents were also hunted as found at Tulán 52, Puripica 1, and Chiu-chiu (Nuñez 1983). Evidence for early plant cultivation includes maize, quinoa, potato, beans, and gourds. At Huachichocana in Northwest Argentina, maize, common bean, and chile pepper were found during the Early Archaic (Pearsall 1992), presenting the possibility for very early domestication of these species as seen at Guitarrero Cave in the central Andes. However, evidence for domestication of these plants does not again reappear until the Terminal Late Archaic. In the intermontane valleys of Chile, maize appears at Tulán cave around 3760 B.P., and reappears at Huachichocana in the Argentine salt *puna* between 4500–2500 B.P. (Pearsall 1992); similar dates occur for quinoa (Nuñez 1983). Indirect evidence for grain production occurs in a sharp increase in grinding stones found at the Tulán sites during the Terminal Late Archaic, as seen at Asana in the south-central Andes (Nuñez 1983; Santoro and Nuñez 1987). Common bean, chile pepper, potato, and gourd appear around 4500 B.P. in Northwest Argentina as well (Pearsall 1992). Thus, a complex of incipient horticulture involving the cultivation of maize, potatoes, peppers, beans, gourd, and possibly quinoa emerges at least by the Terminal Late Archaic in the Salt Puna.

A more influential economic shift occurs with the domestication of camelids during this period in the Salt Puna. Data from both the intermontane valleys of Chile and the *punas* of northwest Argentina suggest that camelids were brought under human control during this time. Hesse (1982, see also Dransart 1991; Nuñez 1983), noticing increasing percentage of neonate mortality among camelids at Puripica 1, infers that camelids were probably domesticated between 4800–4000 B.P., and by 3700 B.P. at the nearby Tulán sites. Argentine researchers note that at the sites of Inca Cueva 7 (4080 B.P.), Quebrada Seca 3 (4930–4770 B.P.), and Huachichocana (3400 B.P.), osteometric data, wool fiber data, and the presence of dung indicate domestication of camelids during the Terminal Late Archaic (Elkin 1996; Olivera 1998; Olivera and Elkin 1994; Reigadas 1994). By the end of the Terminal Late Archaic, foraging subsistence economies had been transformed into foraging/pastoral economies supplemented with continued hunting and incipient horticulture in the salt *puna*.

Obsidian use increases at Tulán 52, and Santoro and Nuñez (1987) interpret this as direct procurement from *puna* source localities, not trade. Communication with the lowlands is evidenced by the presence of marine shell at Puripica 1 in the Chilean salt *puna*, and contact with other Chilean highland groups is evidenced by the presence of distinct lithic types (Chiu-chiu) and sandstones (Tulán) (Nuñez 1983).

Sociopolitical Organization

There is no evidence of complex social organization in the salt *puna* region. Site hierarchies, as with all *puna* sites of this time period, appear to relate to seasonal movements of forager and pastoral families or small groups (Nuñez 1983; Santoro and Nuñez 1987). However, some researchers point out that the shift from hunting camelids as prey to owning camelids as domestic animals represented a fundamental shift in human societies, which ultimately led to increased social complexity during the Formative period (Aschero 1996; Dransart 1991; Hesse 1982; Olivera 1998).

Religion and Expressive Culture

Rock art continues to be important in rock shelters and caves, with the main motifs being animals, especially camelids in the intermontane valleys of Chile, although camelid depictions are rare in the Argentine *puna* (Aschero 1996; Olivera 1998). There are also simple rock sculptures at Puripica 1 in Chile, depicting camelids (Dransart 1991). It is likely that all of this art is involved with rituals designed to ensure the fertility of animals, both wild and domestic (Aschero 1996). The possibility for a telluric/water orientation in religion is raised by the presence of copper ore, stone, and shell beads at Tulán 52 and shell at Puripica 1 in Chile (Nuñez 1983). A burial dating to the Terminal Late Archaic at Chiu-chiu Cemeterio, Chile, had annular cranial deformation and was associated with triangular projectile points (Jackson and Benavente 1994), indicating a belief in afterlife.

References

Aldenderfer, M. (1989). "The Archaic Period in the South-Central Andes." *Journal of World Prehistory* 3: 117–158.

Aschero, C. (1996). "Arte y Arqueología: Una Visión desde la Puna Argentina." *Chungará* 28: 175–197.

Dransart, Penny (1991). "Llamas, Herders and the Exploitation of Raw Materials in the Atacama Desert." *World Archaeology* 22: 304–319.

Druss, M. (1984a). "Environment, Subsistence Economy, and Settlement Patterns of the Chiuchiu Complex, Northern Chile." In *Archaeological Investigations in Chile: Selected Papers*, ed. M. Druss and B. Bittmann. Greeley: Occasional Publications in Anthropology Archaeology Series, no. 19, Museum of Anthropology, University of Northern Colorado, 1–7.

Druss, M. (1984b). "Computer Analysis of Chiuchiu Complex Settlement Patterns." In *Archaeological Investigations in Chile:*

Selected Papers, ed. M. Druss and B. Bittmann. Greeley: Occasional Publications in Anthropology Archaeology Series, no. 19, Museum of Anthropology, University of Northern Colorado, 8–30.

Elkin, D. (1996). "Arqueozoología de Quebrada Seca 3: Indicadores de Subsistencia Humana Temprana en la Puna Meridional Argentina." Ph.D. diss., Facultad de Filosofía y Letras, University of Buenos Aires.

Franklin, W. (1982). "Biology, Ecology, and Relationship to Man of the South American Camelids." In *Mammalian Biology in South America*, ed. M. A. Mares and H. H. Genoways. Pittsburgh: Special Publications Series Pymatuning Laboratory of Ecology, University of Pittsburgh, 457–489.

Hesse, Brian (1982). "Animal Domestication and Oscillating Climates." *Journal of Ethnobiology* 2: 1–15.

Jackson S., D., and A. Benavente A. (1994). "Secuencia, Cambios y Adaptación de los Cazadores-Recolectores de la Microcuenca de Chiu-chiu, Provincia del Loa." *Chungará* 26: 49–64.

Kuznar, L. (2001). "An Introduction to Andean Religious Ethnoarchaeology: Preliminary Results and Future Directions." In *Ethnoarchaeology in Andean South America: Contributions to Archaeological Method and Theory*, ed. L. Kuznar. Ann Arbor: International Monographs in Prehistory, 38–66.

Lynch, T. (1990). "Quaternary Climate, Environment, and the Human Occupation of the South-Central Andes." *Geoarchaeology* 5: 199–228.

Markgraf, V. (1989). "Palaeoclimates in Central and South America since 18,000 B.P. Based on Pollen and Lake-Level Records." *Quaternary Science Reviews* 8: 1–24.

Messerli, B., M. Grosjean, G. Bonani, A. Burgi, M.A. Geyh, K. Graf, K. Ramseyer, H. Romero, U. Schotterer, H. Schreier, and M. Vuille. (1993). "Climate Change and Natural Resource Dynamics of the Atacama Altiplano during the Last 18,000 Years: A Preliminary Synthesis." *Mountain Research and Development* 13: 117–127.

Molina, E., and A. Little (1981). "Geoecology of the Andes: The Natural Science Basis for Research Planning." *Mountain Research and Development* 1: 115–144.

Nuñez, Lautaro (1983). "Paleoindian and Archaic Cultural Periods in the Arid and Semiarid Regions of Northern Chile." *Advances in World Archaeology* 2: 161–203.

Olivera, D. (1998). "Cazadores y Pastores Tempranos de la Puna Argentina." In *Past and Present in Andean Prehistory and Early History*, ed. S. Ahlgren, A. Muñoz, S. Sjödin, and P. Stenborg. Göteborg, Sweden: Etnografiska Museet, 153–180.

Olivera D., and D. Elkin (1994). "De Cazadores y Pastores: El Proceso de Domesticación de Camélidos en la Puna Meridional Argentina." *Zooarqueología de Camélidos* 1: 95–124.

Pearsall, D. (1992). "The Origins of Plant Cultivation in South America." In *The Origins of Agriculture: An International Perspective*, ed. C. W. Cowan and P. J. Watson, Wahington D.C.: Smithsonian Institution Press, 173–205.

Reigadas, M. C. (1994). "Caracterización de Tipos de Camélidos Domesticos Actuales para el Estudio de Fibras Arqueológicas en Tiempos de Transición y Consolidación de la Domesticatión Animal." *Zooarqueología de Camélidos* 1: 125–155.

Roe, Nicholas, and William Rees (1976). "Preliminary Observations of the Taruca (Hippocamelus antisensis: Cervidae) in Southern Peru." *Journal of Mammology* 57: 722–730.

Santoro, C., and J. Chacama R. (1982). "Secuencia Cultural de las Tierras Altas del Area Centro Sur Andina." *Chungará* 9: 22–45.

Santoro, Calagero M., and Lautaro Nuñez (1987). "Hunters of the Dry Puna and the Salt Puna in Northern Chile." *Andean Past* 1: 57–109.

SITES

Asana

TIME PERIOD: 10,000–3500 B.P.

LOCATION: Along the Rio Asana, department of Moquegua, southern Peru.

DESCRIPTIVE SUMMARY

Local Environment

Asana is located on the Rio Asana, a tributary of the Rio Osmore, at an elevation of 3435 m above mean sea level. The site lies within the high sierra environmental zone, which is characterized by generally low primary productivity, resources concentrated near water sources, small, widely dispersed *bofedales* (marshes), and very low precipitation that falls during a short rainy season from November to April.

Physical Features

Asana is an open-air site on the bank of the Rio Asana. The site contains at least 36 distinct cultural layers in more than 80 natural stratigraphic levels, dating from 9850–3650 B.P. The site has been estimated to be no more than 0.25 ha in maximum extent (Aldenderfer 1998).

Cultural Aspects

Asana is a very important site for understanding the terminal Late Archaic of the south-central Andes. Not only is there evidence for the intensification of cereal use from 4600–4400 B.P., but an abrupt shift to a pastoral economy takes place around 3600 B.P. The Qhuna phase (4800–4400 B.P.) at Asana is characterized by domestic architecture, ceremonial structures, and an abundance of grinding stones (Aldenderfer 1989, 1990, 1991). Both Andean *taruca* deer and guanaco camelids were hunted at this time (Aldenderfer 1998). Unfortunately, no direct evidence of what was being ground at the site has been obtained. However, grinding becomes important after 4600 B.P. (Aldenderfer 1998). The most likely candidate for a grain would be *Chenopodium*, possibly even domesticated quinoa (Kuznar 1993). Rectangular to ovoid post houses increase in size during this phase from about 8 m^2 to 10 m^2, indicating an increase in site population and/or duration of site occupation (Aldenderfer 1993, 1998). Asana has the distinction of having some of the earliest ceremonial architecture in the Andean highlands. During the Qhuna phase, a rectangular or U-shaped rubble platform with small oval offertories occupied up to 132 m^2 of the site (Aldenderfer 1991, 1993, 1998). Larger pits surrounded the structure, which was also enclosed by a large post wall. Little material could be recovered from the pits, although extensive evidence of burning was present. Outside this walled area were many miniature postmold patterns. Also, a small stone carving, perhaps of a reclining bird, was recovered from the ceremonial area of the site. Both Aldenderfer (1998) and Kuznar (1995, 2001) have drawn parallels between these archaeological patterns and the material culture of contemporary Aymara ritual, especially the sacrifice of animals, and the *alasita* ceremony for good luck. An abrupt change in site use occurs during the Awati phase (c. 3650 B.P.) at the site. At this time, the site appears occupied by a family of llama herders who have a small post shelter (4.2 m^2), an adjacent area of possibly preserved llama dung, which may have served as a corral, and a canal that probably served to bring water closer to the domestic structure as well as to irrigate pasture (Kuznar 1990, 1995). Sometime after this occupation, a large landslide covered the site, destroying a portion, but preserving what was excavated (Aldenderfer 1998).

References

Aldenderfer, M. (1989). "The Archaic Period in the South-Central Andes". *Journal of World Prehistory* 3: 117–158.

Aldenderfer, M. (1990). "Cronología y Definición de Fases Arcaicas de Asana, Sur de Peru." *Chungará* 24/25: 13–35.

Aldenderfer, M. (1991). "Continuity and Change in Ceremonial Structures at Late Preceramic Asana, Southern Peru." *Latin American Antiquity* 2: 227–258.

Aldenderfer, M. (1993). "Domestic Space, Mobility, and Ecological Complementarity: The View from Asana." In *Domestic Architecture, Ethnicity, and Complementarity in the South-Central Andes*, ed. M. S. Aldenderfer. Iowa City: University of Iowa Press, 13–19.

Aldenderfer, M. (1998). *Montane Foragers: Asana and the South-Central Andean Archaic*. Ames: University of Iowa Press.

Kuznar, L. (1990). "Pastoralismo Temprano en la Sierra Alta del Departamento de Moquegua, Perú." *Chungará* 24/25: 53–68.

Kuznar, L. (1993). "Mutualism between Chenopodium, Herd Animals and Herders in the South Central Andes." *Mountain Research and Development* 13, 3: 257–265.

Kuznar, L. (1995). *Awatimarka: The Ethnoarchaeology of an Andean Herding Community*. Fort Worth: Harcourt Brace.

Kuznar, L. (2001). "An Introduction to Andean Religious Ethnoarchaeology: Preliminary Results and Future Directions." In *Ethnoarchaeology in Andean South America: Contributions to Archaeological Method and Theory*, ed. L. Kuznar. Ann Arbor: International Monographs in Prehistory.

Huaricoto

TIME PERIOD: 5300–2200 B.P.

LOCATION: Overlooking the central Callejón de Huaylas valley.

DESCRIPTIVE SUMMARY

Local Environment

Huaricoto overlooks a major river valley in north-central Peru at 2750 m above mean sea level. The location could be considered lower high sierra. Therefore, the site is located in a resource-rich area where wild animals and plants would flourish, as well as a region where agriculture would have been possible.

Physical Features

Huaricoto is a small artificial mound that sits on a terrace overlooking the river valley. Contained within this mound are 13 ceremonial structures dating from as early as 4260 B.P. to as late as 2200 B.P. (Burger and Burger 1980).

Cultural Aspects

Huaricoto is an important representative of what Burger and Burger (1980) call the Kotosh religious tradition. This is a complex in which rectangular or U-shaped rubble and wall structures containing central hearths, and sometimes underground flues, were used for making burnt offerings. Burger and Burger (1986) note that the structures at Huaricoto are smaller than those at lower altitude sites such as La Galgada and Kotosh and later sites such as Shillacoto and probably represent lineage or cargo ritual labor inputs. The hearths at Huaricoto are small (5m^2–24 m^2) and ovoid to rectangular in plan (Burger and Burger 1986). They contain central hearths that sometimes contain animal remains and quartz crystals, probably from sacrifices similar to those seen among Quechua and Aymara today (Kuznar 2001). The hearths seem to be oriented toward snow-capped peaks, a consideration of line of sight and mountain worship common ethnohistorically and today (Burger and Burger 1980; Kuznar 2001; Reinhard 1983).

References

Burger, Richard L., and Lucy Salazar Burger (1980). "Ritual and Religion at Huaricoto." *Archaeology* 33: 26–32.

Burger, Richard L., and Lucy Salazar Burger (1986). "Early Organizational Diversity in the Peruvian Highlands: Huaricoto and Kotosh." In *Andean Archaeology: Papers in Memory of Clifford Evans*, ed. R. Matos M., S. A. Turpin, and H. H. Eling Jr. Los Angeles: Institute of Archaeology Monograph 27, University of California, 65–82.

Kuznar, L. (2001). "An Introduction to Andean Religious Ethnoarchaeology: Preliminary Results and Future Directions." In *Ethnoarchaeology in Andean South America: Contributions to Archaeological Method and Theory*, ed. L. Kuznar. Ann Arbor: International Monographs in Prehistory.

Reinhard, Johann (1983). "Las Montañas Sagradas: Un Estudio Etnoarqueologico de Ruinas en las Altas Cumbres Andinas." *Cuadernos de Historia 3*: 27–62.

Pachamachay

TIME PERIOD: 11,000–2000 B.P.

LOCATION: In the *puna* of the Department of Junin, central Peru.

DESCRIPTIVE SUMMARY

Local Environment

Pachamachay is found in the wet *puna* at an elevation of 4300 m. The wet *puna* is characterized by relatively abundant, seasonal (November–March) rainfall, cool to cold temperatures, and high primary productivity of grasses palatable to the native Andean camelids, especially the vicuña.

Physical Features

Pachamachay is a rock shelter found in a large bedrock outcrop overlooking grasslands.

Cultural Aspects

Pachamachay contains important information on early herding in the Andes. As seen at Asana, grinding implements become common at the site during terminal Late Archaic times after 4500 B.P. (Rick 1980). Minerals such as mica and quartz crystals are also present in preceramic levels (Rick 1980), indicating religious activity as minerals are indispensable to contemporary Andean rituals (Kuznar 2001). Pearsall (1980) points out that while Chenopodium seeds are present throughout the site's occupation, they increase in size during the transition from the preceramic to ceramic periods (Levels 18–12), possibly indicating initial domestication of *Chenopodium quinoa*. Pachamachay became a sedentary, intensively used base camp during the Late Archaic with stone-walled domestic structures and at the end of this period (3600–3500 B.P.) was probably a pastoral camp (Rick 1980).

References

Kuznar, L. (2001). "An Introduction to Andean Religious Ethnoarchaeology: Preliminary Results and Future Directions." In *Ethnoarchaeology in Andean South America: Contributions to Archaeological Method and Theory*, ed. L. Kuznar. Ann Arbor: International Monographs in Prehistory.

Pearsall, D. (1980). "Pachamachay Ethnobotanical Report: Plant Utilization at a Hunting Base Camp." In *Prehistoric Hunters of the High Andes*, ed. J. Rick. New York: Academic Press, 191–232.

Rick, J. (1980). *Prehistoric Hunters of the High Andes*. New York: Academic Press.

Puripica 1

TIME PERIOD: 4800–4000 B.P.

LOCATION: Overlooking the Rio Puripica, Salar de Atacama, northern Chile.

DESCRIPTIVE SUMMARY

Local Environment

Puripica 1 is on a high promontory overlooking the Rio Puripica at 3200 m above mean sea level, above the Salar de Atacama. Vicuña and guanaco are available along these watercourses, along with a variety of plants.

Physical Features

Puripica 1 is an open-air site on a high promontory. It contains some 40–50 habitations and features radiocarbon dated at 4815–4050 B.P. (Nuñez 1983).

Cultural Aspects

Puripica 1 is important as it contains evidence of early domestication of camelids in the Salt Puna. The site was likely a sedentary community of some size given its numerous semisubterranean dwellings (Nuñez 1983).

The site resembles Tulán 52 in this regard. However, Puripica 1 is unique in that it contains an unusually high percentage of juvenile large camelid remains, evidence Hesse (1982) argues for llama domestication. Nuñez (1983; Santoro and Nuñez 1987) notes that the lithic assemblage more resembles a butchering/hide processing site and less a hunting station, in concert with the pastoral hypothesis.

References

Hesse, Brian (1982). "Animal Domestication and Oscillating Climates." *Journal of Ethnobiology* 2: 1–15.

Nuñez, Lautaro (1983). "Paleoindian and Archaic Cultural Periods in the Arid and Semiarid Regions of Northern Chile." *Advances in World Archaeology* 2: 161–203.

Santoro, Calagero M., and Lautaro Nuñez (1987). "Hunters of the Dry Puna and the Salt Puna in Northern Chile." *Andean Past* 1: 57–109.

Quelcatani

TIME PERIOD: 7500 B.P.–A.D. 1472

LOCATION: On the Rio Chila in the department of Puno, southern Peru.

DESCRIPTIVE SUMMARY

Local Environment

Quelcatani is located near the border of the western flank of the Andes, and the Titicaca basin on the north bank of the Rio Chila, which ultimately drains into lake Titicaca. The site sits at 4420 m above mean sea level. The biotic province of this site is considered dry *puna* and is characterized by seasonal (November–March) rainfall, cool to cold temperatures, and high primary productivity of grasses palatable to native Andean camelids, especially the vicuña (Kuznar in press).

Physical Features

Quelcatani is a large rock shelter containing c. 200 m² of covered floor area. Thirty-six cultural strata varying in date from 7250 B.P. to A.D. 1472 are found in 1m–2 m of deposit. The site lies along a high productive *bofedal*, which provides high-quality pasture for vicuña and domestic camelids (Kuznar in press).

Cultural Aspects

Although the analysis of Quelcatani is not yet complete, this site will be extremely important to the understanding of the high Andean Late Archaic. It contains a near-continuous occupation from Middle Archaic through Inca (Late Horizon) times, with outstanding preservation and copious rock art (Aldenderfer in press). After 3660 B.P., there is a shift toward a herding economy (Aldenderfer in press). Earlier Archaic inhabitants constructed stone houses, but those of pastoralists become more substantial (Aldenderfer 1987). Also, there is an increase in the percentage of young camelids, indicating domestication. Chenopodium becomes increasingly important, indicating possible domestication during the Late Archaic (Aldenderfer in press). Finally, variation in the depictions of camelids indicates that artistic representations of herding also became prevalent after earlier periods of the site's occupation (Aldenderfer 1987; Klarich in press; Ravines 1986).

References

Aldenderfer, M. (1987). "Hunter-Gatherer Settlement Dynamics and Rupestral Art: Inferring Mobility and Aggregation in the South-Central Andes of Southern Peru." In *Actas del VIII Simposium Internacional de Arte Rupestre Americano.* Santo Domingo: Museo del Hombre Dominicano, 373–403.

Aldenderfer, M. (in press). *Quelcatani: The Evolution of a Pastoral Lifeway.* Washington, D.C.: Smithsonian Institution Press.

Klarich, E. (in press). "Camelid Depictions in the Rupestral Art of Quelcatani: Hunters or Herders?" In *Quelcatani: The Evolution of a Pastoral Lifeway,* ed. M. Aldenderfer. Washington, D.C.: Smithsonian Institution Press.

Kuznar, L. (in press). "Altiplano Human Ecology/Altiplano Past." In *Quelcatani: The Evolution of a Pastoral Lifeway,* ed. M. Aldenderfer. Washington, D.C.: Smithsonian Institution Press.

Ravines, R. (1986). "Quelcatani." In *Arte Rupestre del Peru,* ed. R. Ravines. Lima: Instituto Nacional de Cultura, 51–52.

Tulán 52

TIME PERIOD: c. 4300 B.P.

LOCATION: Along Quebrada Tulán, Salar de Atacama, northern Chile.

DESCRIPTIVE SUMMARY

Local Environment

The Tulán sites are located in the extremely dry salt *puna* of northern Chile. Being located along a tributary of the large salt marsh of the Salar de Atacama, inhabitants would have been able to exploit populations of wild camelids such as vicuñas and perhaps manage some agriculture.

Physical Features

The Tulán sites are mostly open-air lithic workshops, although Tulán 52 is notable for having substantial domestic structures and refuse and occurs as a low mound of accreted refuse. The site lies at 2925 m above mean sea level and is dated at 4340–4270 B.P.

Cultural Aspects

Tulán 52 provides a view of increasing sedentarization and intensification of subsistence activity in the terminal Late Archaic. The dwellings consist of about 30 structures made from large vertical slabs of stone placed in circular plans to form semisubterranean houses (Nuñez 1983). The structures contained storage pits in their floors and niches in their walls. The bones of camelids, probably both vicuña and guanaco, are found at the site, and the relatively low incidence of juvenile animals indicates a hunting economy (Hesse 1982). The notable economic feature of the site is its abundant grinding stones (Nuñez 1983; Santoro and Nuñez 1987).

What food was being ground is not certain, but this is evidence for increasing intensification of gathering if not incipient agriculture, possibly quinoa. Yarns made from wild camelid wool have been recovered from the site as well (Dransart 1991). Also, exotic materials such as copper ore, stone beads, and shell beads occur at the site (Nuñez 1983).

References

Dransart, Penny (1991). "Llamas, Herders and the Exploitation of Raw Materials in the Atacama Desert." *World Archaeology* 22: 304–319.

Hesse, Brian (1982). "Animal Domestication and Oscillating Climates." *Journal of Ethnobiology* 2: 1–15.

Nuñez, Lautaro (1983). "Paleoindian and Archaic Cultural Periods in the Arid and Semiarid Regions of Northern Chile." *Advances in World Archaeology* 2: 161–203.

Santoro, Calogero M., and Lautaro Nuñez (1987). "Hunters of the Dry Puna and the Salt Puna in Northern Chile." *Andean Past* 1: 57–109.

LAWRENCE KUZNAR
Department of Sociology and Anthropology
Indiana-Purdue University
Fort Wayne, Indiana
United States

Late Parana-Pampean

ABSOLUTE TIME PERIOD: 1500–500 B.P.

RELATIVE TIME PERIOD: Follows the Early Parana-Pampean tradition and precedes the historic period.

LOCATION: Parana-Pampas region.

DIAGNOSTIC MATERIAL ATTRIBUTES: The presence of ceramics is the primary diagnostic feature of this tradition. Small, triangular projectile points are also diagnostic.

CULTURAL SUMMARY

Environment

Three major environments are included within the Parana-Pampas region. These include the northern river lowlands and alluvial plains, the flat grasslands of the Pampas proper, and the southern arid flatlands of northern and eastern Patagonia. Thus flat grassland topography dominates the region. Large rivers flow west-to-east across these flatlands at rather wide intervals. Game animals such as the guanaco and rhea were plentiful on these grasslands, as were fish in the rivers.

Settlements

A wide variety of Late Parana-Pampean settlements have been found, from cave sites to large villages. All seem to have access to water and tend to be located near major river valleys. Dwellings, where found, appear to be of two major styles, round or rectangular, but are only large enough to house a single family. They are made from either stone or adobe, with adobe dwellings sometimes having a stone foundation. Communities seem to vary in size from small hamlets of perhaps only a few related families to villages of perhaps 300 or more people.

Economy

The Late Parana-Pampas people were primarily hunter gatherers, but some groups, particularly in the river valleys in the northern range of the tradition, may have supplemented their diet with domesticated plant foods. Animals such as the guanaco and deer were hunted with the bolas and bow and arrow. Arrows were armed with small, triangular arrow points manufactured from chipped stone. Ground-stone implements included bolas stones and a variety of hammer and grinding stones. Bone was used for a variety of tools, including awls, fishhooks, and arrow points.

Ceramics were manufactured by the Late Parana-Pampean peoples. These ceramics were red-brown wares in a variety of forms, with bowls predominating. Some were decorated with geometric designs, often using a stab-and-drag technique. In the northwestern range of the tradition, influences from the Andes lead to a greater diversity of ceramic styles and forms, which included the use of polychrome decoration.

Sociopolitical Organization

Little is formally known about the sociopolitical organization of the Late Parana-Pampean peoples. Burials do not appear to show differences in social or political status, and there are few other indicators of social differentiation, suggesting they were egalitarian. It seems likely, however, that larger settlements would have had some form of leaders to keep order. The nature of political organization in these larger communities is, however, unknown.

Religion and Expressive Culture

Burials were placed in refuse mounds along with red ocher and small offerings of food and tools, suggesting a belief in the afterlife.

Suggested Readings

Bennett, Wendell C., Everett F. Bleilber, and Frank H. Sommer (1948). *Northwest Argentine Archaeology*. New Haven: Yale University Press.
Howard, George D., and Gordon R. Willey (1948). *Lowland Argentine Archaeology*. New Haven: Yale University Press.
Mazzanti, Diana L. (1996). "An Archaeological Sequence of Hunter-Gatherers in the Tandilia Range: Cueva Tixi, Buenos Aires, Argentina." *Antiquity* 70: 450–452.
Nami, Hugo G. (1995). "Archaeological Research in the Argentinean Rio Chico Basin." *Current Anthropology* 36: 661–664.
Willey, Gordon R. (1971). *An Introduction to American Archaeology, vol. Two: South America*. Engelwood Cliffs, NJ: Prentice-Hall.

PETER N. PEREGRINE
Department of Anthropology
Lawrence University
Appleton, Wisconsin
United States

Magellan-Fuegian

ABSOLUTE TIME PERIOD: 6300–50 B.P.

RELATIVE TIME PERIOD: This is the only native cultural tradition definable in the area, although there is an earlier record of the occasional presence of small groups of another, still culturally undetermined, tradition.

LOCATION: The southern and western Patagonian coasts, from the Golfo de Corcovado (44° S) in the north, to Cape Horn (56° S) in the south and Bahía Sloggett (66° W) to the southeast.

DIAGNOSTIC MATERIAL ATTRIBUTES: Bark or plank canoes. Two types of dwellings: dome-shaped huts (of branches and leaves) and conical huts (of poles). Bone tools are very abundant but do not outnumber the lithic ones. Most diagnostics are two harpoon classes (detachable point with one or two barbs and fix-to-handle multibarbed ones). Lithic tools are very abundant, little varied and, except for the weapon points, they are poorly specialized in function.

REGIONAL SUBTRADITIONS: Beagle Channel-Cape Horn, and western Magellan-Otway. In the last centuries, this differentiation was more noticeable in languages and in ethnic self-identification than in the material culture.

IMPORTANT SITES: Bahía Buena (Strait of Magellan), Englefield, Lancha Packewaia, Shamakush I, Túnel I, Túnel VII, Punta Baja, Bahía Colorada (Otway Sound), Lanashuaia (Beagle Channel).

CULTURAL SUMMARY

Environment

Climate. Although cold, rainy, and very windy, the climate it is highly oceanic, with very slight seasonal differences. Summers are cool (average temperatures: from 8°–12° C), and winters are cold without extremely low temperatures (average temperatures from 1–7° C). In the coastal regions, the rain and snowfall oscillate from some 500 to more than 5000 mm per year.

Topography. The area is a longitudinal contact zone of the Andes mountain range with the sea; therefore, the coasts are very broken by fjords and bays. There are many islands of different sizes, often just emerging mountain tops separated from the continent and one another by channels, narrows, and straits. The slopes are steep, and the landscape is, as a rule, very rough. There is scarce intraareal variation.

Geology. Metamorphic rocks prevail, whereas volcanic rocks are less frequent. During the Pleistocene, there was strong glacial activity. Today soils are podzolic, brown forest, or peaty. There are few mineral resources that may have been of use for the natives. The raising of the coastlines in the whole area by isostatic and tectonic processes should be remembered in considering the nowadays above-sea-level heights mentioned for the different sites. For pre-5500 B.P. occupations, the eustatic variation should also be taken into consideration. Consequently, there is an abundance of raised paleobeaches in all the area.

Biota. Plentiful rains permit the area to be covered by dense forests of tall trees. The species diversity, however, is low. Prevailing trees are the *Nothofagus*: the evergreen *N. betuloides* (*coihue*) and the broad-leaved *N. pumilio* (*lenga*). There are also *Drimys winteri* (winter's bark), *N. antarctica* (*ñire* or Antarctic beech), *Maytenus magellanica* (*leña dura*), and *Pilgerodendron uvifera* (Guaytecas cypress), the latter only in the area's northwestern portion. Shrubs of various species occupy the forest margins. Toward the southeast, the proportion of open surface increases to some extent and is very often occupied by peat bogs and small meadows. The forests provide abundant wood for fuel but harbor a very scarce animal population; in winter *Lama guanicoe* (guanaco) approaches the coast in the southeastern portion of the area as does *Hippocamelus bisulcus* (*huemul*) in the northwestern sector. In contrast, the littoral fauna is very rich: pinnipeds (*Arctocephalus australis* and *Otaria flavescens*), a diversity of marine and coastal birds, shellfish, and other seafood. In ancient times, large whales approached the coasts with more frequency than at present. The fishing on species that live at a low depth (down to 3–4 m) was prominantly seasonal. The biota variation within the area seems to have had a limited influence on the native lifestyle. The palynological profiles do not indicate important variations since before 5500 B.P., and the archaeofaunal data do not suggest major changes in the species availability before the exploitation of the European and American sealers and whalers.

Settlements

Settlement System. Nomadism; camp shiftings were very frequent. This has been attributed many times to a supposed environmental poverty of nutritional resources. On the contrary, it has been recently shown that the abundance of resources and their nonpatched distribution better explain the almost continual shifting. The peopling of the area could be successful because of the concurrence of four main factors: (1) a rich littoral biomass was available everywhere; (2) tall trees were available to provide raw material for canoes and

harpoon handles; (3) the area was already forested, thus providing large quantities of low cost wood for fuel; and (4) waters relatively protected from the excessive surge of the open oceans by outer islands. The outward islands tended be visited only for specific purposes, although some were visited very often. There was an almost excluding link with the coasts. Natives rarely went inland because of the difficulty of traveling over the rough terrain covered with dense and muddy forest down to the sea edge, and because all the essential resources were available near the littoral. The general settlement pattern in the area was decentralization: huts tended to be isolated except in exceptional circumstances. They were not grouped in villages, the settlement locations were not ordered in a hierarchic system, and there was little encampment specialization.

Housing. According to the ethnographic information, there were two types of huts, both of circular base: (1) dome-shaped, made of bent thin branches and covered with boughs, leafage, and skins, more frequent in the west and southwest; and (2) conical, made of straight logs of the thickness of an arm or less, more frequent in the southeast. As a rule, in each hut lived only one family. Huts built for more than one family were exceptional, although under certain circumstances more than one family could share one hut. There were also larger special huts intended for group ceremonies. There are numerous archaeological findings that match the characteristics of the one-family huts, although some of them suggest the early existence of windbreakers. A characteristic feature of the housing was the mainly culinary waste accumulations in the huts' periphery, forming archaeologically visible mounds that are spread along the coasts with but a few discontinuities.

Population, Health and Disease. Ancient DNA analyses yield two of the four classes determined for Amerindian populations lacking the special mitochondrial indicator of the South Pacific peoples, so that peopling from this area is denied. Estimates of population for the Beagle Channel-Cape Horn region's population toward 1860 are of 2500–3000 people. For the same period, the estimates for the Pacific coast differ from 1000–3500 persons. Although the linear distribution along the coasts hinders density calculations, the demography would have been 30–40 times superior to that assignable to the neighboring peoples in the Patagonian and Pampa plains. This datum may be considered an evidence of the wealth that resources offered along coastal environment. Some people reached 60 years of age. It is presumed that infant mortality would have been high. There is no demographic information for previous times. After 1880, these groups underwent a great mortality because of the spread of tuberculosis and of diseases of European origin: in 20 years, some 85 or perhaps 93 percent of the original population disappeared.

Economy

Subsistence. The native subsistence was founded on hunting, gathering, and fishing. Food storage was practiced to a minimal extent (cetacean blubber, fungi). There were gender differences in the food search: the men hunted pinnipeds, guanacos, and birds, while women fished and gathered seafood. Other tasks (such as the gathering of fungi, berries, and eggs) were carried out by either sex according to the circumstances. There was food exchange among neighbors, relatives, and guests, but not true trade.

Wild Foods. Until the arrival of Europeans, all nourishment of these natives was wild in origin. The supply of nutritional vegetables was and is very scarce, there being only fungi, berries, and a few roots of low caloric value. Therefore, nearly the whole subsistence was of animal origin. Archaeological data show that the most important staple was pinnipeds, mainly the southern fur seal (*Arctocephalus australis*). These mammals have a thick fat layer, which was an abundant source of calories for humans. Another advantage was that, outside of the breeding season, they are very mobile and may feed on vast extensions of open sea. The natives predated on individuals that entered the interior channels; therefore it was difficult to cause overexploitation. The seasonal use of pinnipeds varied according to whether mating and breeding rookeries were included in the catchment ranges of the different human group settlements.

The second rank staple was shellfish and, in the eastern portion of the Beagle channel, the guanacos. The latter are large land mammals, but their meat is lean, especially in winter. The costs of their search and capture are higher than that of the pinnipeds, and their presence along the coast is mainly during this season. The caloric yield of mussels is insufficient to satisfy the daily human metabolic requirements. Nevertheless, they occupy fixed locations, are available year-round, and are easy to gather by almost any person, with no special ability or technology being necessary. Therefore, mussels were a complementary but important food for they functioned as an economic "safety valve," enabling the people to sustain themselves during the days when no other more substantial prey was available. Limpets, whelks, crabs, and sea urchins were also consumed in smaller quantities.

Dolphins seem to have been captured with little frequency. Whales were not actively hunted. They were used only when beached or when approached and killed while moribund, although on these occasions they provided huge quantities of meat and blubber that justified the natives gathering together during weeks or even longer periods. Penguins, cormorants, wild geese, and other birds were hunted in large quantities, but their small body size did not provide a substantive caloric contribution. The same occurred with fish: as a rule they were small, laborious to obtain, and scarce in winter and spring, although abundant in summer and autumn. Occasionally, in the latter seasons, large aggregations of fish pass through the channels and were easily obtained.

Domestic Foods. The natives of the area did not cultivate the land and had no domestic animals. Although still under discussion, it is probable that their first dogs came from European navigators. Anyway, dogs were not eaten, and their role as hunting auxiliaries was limited.

Industrial Arts. The principal staple of the natives of the area, the pinnipeds, could be obtained at their breeding and reproductive colonies during only 2 summer months. During the rest of the year, it was more practical to search and capture them in the water. On land, a simple club was sufficient; in the sea, the use of both items that characterize the tradition was necessary: canoes and toggling or detachable-head harpoons. In most of the area, canoes were made with bark slabs supported by a framework of wood rods sewn with fibers of whale baleen, plaited tendons, leather strips, etc. The preferred bark was that of *Nothofagus betuloides*. The oars were short and also made of wood of that tree. In the 19th century, from the strait of Magellan northward, some plank canoes were seen, perhaps imitating the Mapuche model. Only after the European arrival, the dugout canoes were known in the area.

Harpoons had wood handles and a detachable single-barbed head made of whalebone. More rarely and probably in a very late period, these harpoon heads had two symmetrical barbs. The harpoon head separated itself from the handle on striking the animal, but remained attached to it by a short leather strap. In the first millennium of the tradition, the basal portions of these harpoon heads had a cross-shaped form, doubtless to secure the strap that joined it to the handle. In more recent times, that shape was replaced by a one-sided tenon. The handle was made of *Nothofagus* wood or, along the west coast, of *Pilgerodendron*. In the 19th century, the handles were 3–4 m long. Another class of harpoons, called spears by other authors, had a fixed multibarbed bone head and a smaller handle. They were used to hunt birds and to spear medium-sized fish. The natives also had bows and arrows with flaked stone points, slings of leather and plaited tendons, snares for bird hunting made with whalebone and leather straps, wooden forks to gather crabs and sea urchins, wood spatulae to pry off limpets and mussels, bone chisels, etc. Birds were also hunted with clubs (especially penguins) and, sometimes, with the aid of torches (especially cormorants). The fishing lines had no fishhook: a loop made with a feather *raquis* supported the bait in the end of a line made of kelp or leather strips and/or plaited tendons. There are records of fish traps, but it seems that they were seldom us. There are no archaeological or ethnographical data on atlatls in the area, nor is there information on nets for fishing. The data on bolas are extremely scarce.

Utensils. Ethnographical sources suggest that there was little use of stone except for arrowheads, but archaeological data show a wide utilization of side scrapers and cutting flakes; end scrapers were less abundant. With some frequency, objects with their surfaces totally or partially pecked are found. Wedges made with whale bone and chisels of pinniped bone (to split wood?) were common; bark strippers and flakers of guanaco bone and bird bone awls were also used. Baskets of several classes were made with rushes. The ethnographical information indicates the use of skins for cloaks and for strap making; small containers were of leather or bark. The gullets, stomachs, intestines, and bladders of pinnipeds were used as waterproof bags for various objects. There was a wide range of applications for whalebone, plaited tendons, and some vegetable fibers. Ceramics and metallurgy were unknown.

Ornaments. Beads for necklaces were made of limpet shells or segments of avian long bones. The ethnographical data suggest intense use of facial and corporal painting in black, white, and red. These colors were obtained respectively from charred wood, a clay, and ferruginous concretions. Leather wristlets and anklets were commonly used. Headbands made of bird skin, feathers, and down were used on special occasions. Personal painting seems to have fulfilled an important function in social communication; some authors say that there were special designs for situations such as mourning or blood revenge and that some forms of headbands were reserved for the medicine men. They did not ornament their housings; only the ceremonial huts were decorated for the occasion.

Trade. Sharing of hunted or gathered products existed on a neighborhood scale. A few archaeological findings suggest that some objects could have travelled long distances. Ethnohistorical sources asserted that the iron pyrite used throughout the Beagle channel-cape Horn region was received by bartering from a single source on Isla Capitán Aracena, near the strait of Magellan. However, a formalized exchange system or market did not exist.

Division of Labor. Aside from the hunt, the men occupied themselves in butchering the large prey, turning down trees, cutting wood, extracting bark for the canoes, and making canoes, oars, weapons, leather straps, and a variety of tools. Besides fishing and gathering seafood, the women were occupied in rowing, mooring, casting off, and caring for the canoes, transporting water, preparing food, and making baskets, fishing lines, and ornaments such as necklaces, wristlets, anklets. The girls helped much more than the boys in their own gender adult tasks. There were no full-time specialists. Someone could be more skilled than another in a certain activity, but all were capable of carrying out any necessary duties in a higher or lesser degree.

Differential Access or Control of Resources. This does not seem to have exist. Nearly all the resources need for their life could be individually found by the natives along the coast sections that they could travel in less than a day, either walking or by canoe. Even so, the comparative costs of search and procurement differed in different localities.

Sociopolitical Organization

Social Organization. Society organization was almost exclusively based on nuclear families without more complex levels. Much dispersion prevailed: the gathering of more than two or three families during several days was not common. There was a very loose link among the families that shared the same territory. Polygamy was frequent. Consanguinity was a matrimonial impediment, at least for cousins. There were neither differences of social range nor acquisition of status through birth or marriage. There were no formal chiefs. Social relationships depended on randomly available special resources (e.g., stranded whales), which could support a somewhat extensive group during a certain time in a location without the need to wander around in search for food. Collective ceremonies were held on such occasions, so that they were not strictly periodical. During these, a local group would impart to the adolescents ethical and practical teachings as preparation for adult life.

Religion and Expressive Culture

Religious Beliefs. The 19th-century observers agreed that these societies had no notion of a god, although there was a dread of spirits (usually malevolent) and a belief in other mythical beings. Certain prohibitions of ritual character were individually respected by the natives. In the 1920s, Gusinde claimed to have proven their belief in a supreme God, but it should be remembered that by then the natives of the area had been submitted to intensive acculturative influences for 50 years and, in the Beagle channel region, to missionary teaching.

Religious Practitioners. There were no priests or religious ceremonies. The men participated in ceremonies (forbidden to the women) in which ancestral myths were transmitted. One legend asserted the ancient social supremacy of the women, later assumed by the men.

Arts. Other than personal ornament and the decoration of some mobile and utilitarian objects, there were no developed arts.

Death and Afterlife. Mourning was expressed with facial painting, cutting of hair, and or injuring themselves on faces and bodies. There were various ways to dispose of the corpse: burial or cremation in the south and diverse forms on the west coast, which included the deposit in caves. The belongings of the deceased were not inherited: they were destroyed or distributed.

Suggested Readings

Emperaire, Joseph (1955). *Les Nomades de la mer.* L' Espèce Humaine. Paris: Gallimard.

Gusinde, Martín (1937). *Die Yamana.* Die Feuerland-Indianer. II Mödling: Verlag St. Gabriel.

Gusinde, Martín (1974). *Die Halakwulup.* Die Feuerland-Indianer, III/1. Mödling: Verlag St. Gabriel.

Hyades, Paul Daniel Jules, and Deniker J. (1891). "Anthropologie, Ethnographie." In *Mission Scientifique du Cap Horn 1882–1883*, ed. Gauthier-Villars and son. Paris: Ministères de la Marine et d'Instruction Publique.

Lalueza, Carlos, A. Pérez-Pérez, E. Prats, P. Moreno, J. Pons, and D. Turbón (1993). "Ausencia de la delección 9B.P. COII/t RNA lyc en aborígenes de Tierra del Fuego-patagonia mediante el análisis de DNA antiguo." *Anales del Institutode la Patagonia* 22: 181–191.

Lalueza, Carlos, A. Pérez-Pérez, E. Prats, and D. Turbón (1995). "Linajes mitocondriales de los aborígenes de Tierra del Fuego y Patagonia." *Anales del Instituto de la Patagonia* 23: 175–186.

Legoupil, Dominique (1989). *Ethno-archéologie dans les archipels de Patagonie: Les Nomades marines de Punta Baja.* Paris: Éditions Recherche sur les Civilisations.

Legoupil, Dominique (1992). "Une Méthode d'interpretation etno-archéologique en deux temps: Un Modèle culturel, sur 6000 ans, chez les nomades marins de Patagonie." In *Ethnoarchéologie: Justification, problémes, limites.* XII° Rencontres Internationales d'Archaeologie et d'Histoire d' Antibes. Juan-les-Pins: APDCA, 357–375.

Orquera, Luis Abel (1987). "Advances in the Archaeology of the Pampa and Patagonia." *Journal of World Prehistory* 1, 4: 333–413.

Orquera, Luis Abel, and Ernesto Luis Piana (1995). "Túnel VII en la secuencia arqueológica del canal Beagle: Hipótesis y expectativas de los investigadores argentinos." In *Treballs d' Etnoarqueologia: Encuentros en los conchales fueguinos*, ed. J. Estévez E. and A. Vila Mitja. 1 Madrid-Barcelona: CSIC Universidad Autónoma de Barcelona, 25–45.

Orquera, Luis Abel, and Ernesto Luis Piana (in press). "Arqueología de la región del canal Beagle (Tierra del Fuego, República Argentina)." *Bullettino di Paletnologia Italiana* 87.

Orquera, Luis Abel, Arturo E. Sala, Ernesto Luis Piana, and Alicia H. Tapia (1978). *Lancha Packewaia: Arqueología de los canales fueguinos.* Buenos Aires: Editorial Huemul SA.

Piana, Ernesto Luis (1984). "Arrinconamiento o adaptación en Tierra del Fuego." In *Antropología Argentina1984*, ed. Premios Coca-Cola en las Artes y las Ciencias. Buenos Aires: Universidad de Belgrano, 9–110.

SUBTRADITIONS

Beagle Channel-Cape Horn

In the 19th century, this subtradition's people called themselves Yamana, although they are more widely known as Yahgan. The latter denomination was given to them by Bridges (1880). Of course, none of these two terms should be applied to pre-17th-century times.

TIME PERIOD: 6300–50 B.P.

LOCATION: These people ranged from the southern coast of the Isla Grande de Tierra del Fuego (from near Brecknock peninsula to Bahía Sloggett) southward to cape Horn. In the 19th century, the southwestern fringe of that region was occupied by the Alacaluf, the last remnant of the Western Magellan-Otway subtradition, but archaeologically it is still not possible to differentiate them.

DIAGNOSTIC MATERIAL ATTRIBUTES: The bone tools are abundant and varied. Most outstanding are the single-barbed detachable harpoon heads and multibarbed harpoon heads. Lithic tools are also abundant but little specialized, except for arrowheads (and/or dagger points?) of different types. Annular patterned shell middens are diagnostic. At least from 1620–1880 (and probably earlier), there were also bark canoes and dome-shaped and conical huts.

CULTURAL SUMMARY

Environment

The climate is cold, rainy, very windy, and highly oceanic, with small seasonal variations. The average winter temperature ranges from 1–2° C, the average summer temperatures around 9° C. The annual precipitation is from 500–1200 mm, being higher to the westward, including winter snowfalls (Iturraspe et al. 1989). During the 6000–100 B.P. period, the surface sea temperature was very stable although reflecting the Medieval Optimum Climaticum and the Little Ice Age (Obelic et al. 1997). It is an archipelago environment. From at least before 5500 B.P., the dominant vegetation has been the forest, with few species diversity (Heusser 1984: 66, 1989), which grows on little developed soils. To the west, the evergreen *Nothofagus betuloides* prevails, and to the eastward there is an increase in the deciduous *N. pumilio* (Moore 1983; Pisano Valdés 1977; Richter and Frangi 1992; Tuhkanen 1992). In both types of forest, there is little animal life. Toward the east, open spaces, where it was possible to find guanacos especially in winter, are more frequent. The interisland waters supported many pinnipeds; even today it is possible to find an abundance of bird life, mussels, and other seafood. The fish obtainable in superficial to subsuperficial seawater are generally small, and the seasonal migrations of some of them restrict their abundance to summer and autumn. Whales are occasionally seen, although in ancient times they stranded with a random frequency.

Settlements

The ethnohistorical data record very frequent location movements within small spatial ranges. The archaeological data coincide with this movement frequency but are still unable to determine the spatial ranges. The natives occupied only the coasts and did not venture into the interior of the larger islands because of travelling difficulties over the rough terrain and the lack of resources unavailable near the coast. Along the coasts, there is a great density of archaeological sites. According to survey analysis, criteria such as snow cover, exposure to the wind, the surge, the sun, or the availability of fresh water were apparently not determinant in the selection of the encampent locations. Most important criteria seem to have been the coastal landing facilities and the possibility to stay near shore.

The volume of refuse accumulations and the extensions covered by shell middens and their stratigraphies indicate that within a site the same spots were occupied again and again. This phenomenon may have been due to the microtopographic features raised up by the residue accumulations themselves (Orquera and Piana 1992). There is both archaeological and ethnographical evidence of the fact that the occupation of those different spots was not simultaneous. Although the largest aggregations of annular shell middens surpass 100, a settlement was restricted to one or very few dwelling units at a time, not to villages. The 19th-century observers indicate that the huts were equally dome-shaped and conical (Hyades and Deniker 1891: 342–343); both ethnographical and archaeological data show that their bases were nearly round with a diameter of 3 m or slightly more. In spite of a great deal of claims, the floor was not dug, or, at most, the deepening did not surpass a few centimeters (Orquera and Piana 1991). By 1860–1880, the population of the region was estimated at 3,000 persons (Bridges 1880: 74). Between that date and 1900, infectious diseases of European origin reduced the native population by 92–94% (Gusinde 1937: 219–223; Lawrence 1899: 217).

Economy

Along the Beagle channel coast, a continuous sequence of occupational events denoting a high adjustment to the exploitation of littoral resources is register, giving the impression of great cultural stability throughout a long period. From 6300 B.P. until the 19th century, subsistence was based on predation in flexible proportions of pinnipeds, guanacos, small and large cetaceans, birds, and mollusks. Preserved fish remains are scarce except in the most recent records. In summer and autumn, there was a greater diversity of resources than in winter, although in the latter prey of greater caloric yield was available. Therefore, in spite of the writings of different voyagers and chroniclers (e.g., Darwin 1839; Fitz-Roy 1839), there were no real periodical shortage lapses. However, adverse weather conditions could prevent the people from leaving the encampment in search of food for a few successive days.

Simply made or expeditive artifacts found are the majority, but detachable harpoon heads denote an advanced functional adjustment to the hunting of pinnipeds in the water. This gave them the ability to hunt pinnipeds year round. In most of the archaeological collections, the proportion of artifacts made with bone is fairly high. Typical of this subtradition is the presence, from the very beginning, of cross-based detachable bone harpoon heads with two small parallel teeth and/or incised curvilinear decoration. The presence of pecked-stone mauls and pecked, polished, and even bored lithic artifacts, some of them decorated by incision or careful pecking, is tantalizing for this type of adaptative process. A general review of stone pecking in the study area and surroundings is given by Mansur-Franchomme et al. (1989).

The most ancient record of this way of life is the Túnel I Second Component (6300–4500 B.P.: Orquera and Piana 1988b, in press; Piana 1984: 49–64). Among the alimentary remains preserved, the most important are the pinnipeds (Schiavini 1993). At that time, some sort of navigation craftsmanship had to be in use in the region (Piana 1984), enabling the natives to reach the southern shores of Isla Navarino (Legoupil 1993–1995). Later on, modifications of the artifacts were produced in the region but more of a stylistic than functional nature. The exceptions are the presence of large flaked-stone points (supposedly spearheads) in the Lancha Packe-waia Ancient Component of 4000 B.P. (Piana 1984: 66–70; Orquera et al. 1978: 115–150) and of small points, probably arrowheads, from 2700 B.P. onward (Orquera y Piana 1988b: 232). Within our era, the cross-based detachable harpoon heads were replaced by the also detachable simple-tenon ones (different shapes for the same function; the latter required less effort in construction). On the contrary, as time pass, other features disappeared, such as the incised decoration of the bone equipment. Sites later than 1700 B.P. are included in the Recent phase of the Beagle channel. In it, the Recent component of Lancha Packewaia has a very similar technology and fauna exploitation to that of Túnel I Second Component, 4000–6000 years older. However, in other sites of the same phase, the topographic dissimilarities produced differential cost in the access to the same general resources; for instance, at Shamakush I and X, it was easier to capture guanacos (Orquera and Piana 1997). It is reasonable to think that, among other artifacts, bark canoes and rush baskets were in use during all the tradition.

The long-lasting economic patterns plus the paucity of meaningful changes in the material culture of these people have been interpreted as a product of (a) little diversity and homogeneous distribution of the natural resources (nonpatched or showing intraregional differences in density); (b) great stability of the environment throughout the last 6000–5000 years; (c) the comparatively high culling rates supportable by pinnipeds without being overexploited; and (d) the lack of external human pressures (Orquera and Piana 1996, in press). Using the same arguments, it seems probable that the lack of data indicating craft specialists, massive redistributions, or economic stratification would reflect a real situation present from the beginning

of the tradition, not only as a product of insufficient research.

After crosschecking archaeological and historical data, it seems possible (1) that after A.D. 1850 there was less use of bows and arrows, and (2) that about 1880 the drastic reduction of the pinniped stocks caused by European and American sealers almost certainly forced a major readjustment of the native subsistence, which the spread of foreign infectious diseases did not permit to develop (Orquera and Piana in press; Orquera and Piana 1995).

Sociopolitical Organization

According to 19th-century ethnographical data, the society was organized only as nuclear families, at times with the addition of few relatives. There was polygamy, most commonly of two wives, although there were cases of up to four wives. The sorority and levirate were optative, and there was no polyandry. The husband had some authority and frequently mistreat his wife, but women enjoyed great economic and personal independence. The inequality among husband and wives was much smaller that among other hunters and gatherers. Kinship was recognized along paternal and maternal lines alike. There was marriage among cousins or more distant consanguineus relations. Patrilocality or matrilocality could occur, but it seems that neolocality was more frequent. To become adults, adolescents of both sexes had to undergo collective ceremonies in which ethical and practical teachings were transmitted to them. There were no political authorities or centralization of wealth. Aged people and medicine men were usually treated with respect, but no true power was acknowledged to them. Social control was informal and diffuse. Quarrels and blood revenge were frequent among the natives, but there were no internal or external wars (Gusinde 1937; Hyades and Deniker 1891).

Religion and Expressive Culture

The ethnographical data of the 19th century given above for the general tradition are also relevant for this subtradition: belief in spirits and mythical beings (the introduction of some cultural goods was attributed to a triad of brothers) and secret ceremonies (intended to uphold masculine supremacy). Priests and truly religious ceremonies did not exist. It is unlikely that they had a belief in a single supreme god. The medicine men fulfilled some shamanlike functions, but, if successful, prestige was their only reward. The only artistic expressions were very schematic painting (anciently also incised) and decoration of mobile artifacts. Death was accompanied by lamentations and external mourning manifestations. The dead were cremated or buried. The belongings of the dead were distributed or destroyed, to pronounce their name was forbidden, and the survivors did not return to the burial place for several years. In spite of this, the dead were sorrowfully remembered for a long time, and commemorative meetings could be held, but worship was not rendered to them. The natives did not seem to have had any belief in a future life or, at least, in postmortem punishments or rewards. Yet they feared that medicine men might return after death as malevolent spirits (Gusinde 1937; Hyades and Deniker 1891).

References

Bridges, Thomas (1880). "Appeal for a Church and Schools for Ooshooia, Tierra del Fuego." *South American Missionary Magazine* 14: 74–77.

Darwin, Charles (1839). "Journal and Remarks (1832–1836)." *Narrative of the Surveying Voyages of His Majesty's Ships Adventure and Beagle between the Years 1826 and 1836*, ed. H. Colburn. London.

Fitz-Roy, Robert (1839). *Proceedings of the Second Expedition (1831–1836) under the Command of Captain Robert Fitz-Roy (R.N.): Narrative of the Surveying Voyages of His Majesty's Ships Adventure and Beagle between the Years 1826 and 1836*, ed. H. Colburn. London.

Gusinde, Martín (1937). *Die Yamana. Die Feuerland-Indianer*, 2. Mödling.

Heusser, Calvin J. (1984). "Late Quaternary Climates of Chile." In *Late Cainozoic Paleoclimates of the Southern Hemisphere*, ed. J. C. Vogel. Rotterdam-Boston: A. A. Balkema, 59–83.

Heusser, Calvin J. (1989). "Climate and Chronology of Antarctica and Adjacent South America over the Past 30000 Yr." *Palaeography, Palaeoclimatology, Palaeoecology* 76: 31–37.

Hyades, Paul Daniel Jules, and J. Deniker (1891). "Anthropologie, Ethnographie." In *Mission Scientifique du Cap Horn 1882–1883*. ed. Gauthier-Villars and son. Paris: Ministères de la Marine et d'Instruccion Publique.

Iturraspe, Rodolfo, Roberto Sottini, Carlos Schroder, and Julio Escobar (1989). *Hidrología y variables climáticas del territorio de Tierra del Fuego: Información básica*. Contribución Científica. 7. Ushuaia: CADIC.

Lawrence John (1899). "Untitled Report." *South American Missionary Magazine* 33: 214–218.

Legoupil, Dominique (1993). "El archipiélago del Cabo de Hornos y la costa Sur de la Isla Navarino: Poblamiento y modelos económicos." *Anales del Instituto de la Patagonia* 22: 101–121.

Legoupil, Dominique (1995). "Des indigènes Cap Horn: Conquête d'un territoire et modèle de peuplement aux confins du continent sud-américain." *Journal de la Société des Américanistes* 81: 9–45.

Moore, David M. (1983). *Flora of Tierra del Fuego*. Oswestry, England: Anthony Nelson.

Obelic, Bogomil, Aureli Alvarez, Judit Argullós, and Ernesto L. Piana (1997). "Determination of Water Palaeotemperature in the Beagle Channel (Argentina) during the Last 6000 Years through Stable Isotope Composition of Mytilus Edulis Shells." *Quaternary of South America and Antarctic Peninsula* 11: 49–73.

Orquera, Luis Abel, and Ernesto Luis Piana (1988a). "Human Littoral Adaptation in the Beagle Channel Region: The Maximum Possible Age." *Quaternary of South America and Antarctic Peninsula* 5: 133–162.

Orquera, Luis Abel, and Ernesto Luis Piana (1988b). "Composición tipológica y datos tecnomorfológicos y tecnofuncionales de los conjuntos arqueológicos del sitio Túnel I (Tierra del Fuego, República Argentina)." *Relaciones* n.s. 17, 2: 201–239.

Orquera, Luis Abel, and Ernesto Luis Piana (1991). "La formación de los montículos arqueológicos de la región del canal Beagle." *Runa* 19: XIX 59–82.

Orquera, Luis Abel, and Ernesto Luis Piana (1992). "Un paso hacia la resolución del palimpsesto." In *Análisis espacial en la arqueología patagónica*, ed. L. A. Borrero and J. L. Lanata. Buenos Aires: Ayllu SRL, 21–52.

Orquera, Luis Abel, and Ernesto Luis Piana (1995). "Túnel VII en la secuencia arqueológica del canal Beagle: Hipótesis y expectativas de los investigadores argentinos." In *Treballs d' Etnoarqueologia*: *Encuentros en los conchales fueguinos*, ed. J. Estévez E. and A. Vila Mitja. Madrid-Barcelona: CSIC and Universidad Autónoma de Barcelona, 25–45.

Orquera, Luis Abel, and Ernesto Luis Piana (1996). "La imagen de los canoeros magallánico-fueguinos: Conceptos y tendencias." *Runa* 22: 187–245.

Orquera, Luis Abel, and Ernesto Luis Piana (1997). "El sitio Shamakush I (Tierra del Fuego, República Argentina)." *Relaciones* n.s. 21: 215–265.

Orquera, Luis Abel, and Ernesto Luis Piana (in press). "Arqueología de la región del canal Beagle (Tierra del Fuego, República Argentina)." *Bullettino di Paletnologia Italiana* 87.

Orquera Luis Abel, Arturo E. Sala, Ernesto Luis Piana, and Alicia H. Tapia (1978). *Lancha Packewaia: Arqueología de los canales fueguinos*. Buenos Aires: Editorial Huemul SA.

Piana, Ernesto Luis (1984). "Arrinconamiento o adaptación en Tierra del Fuego." In *Antropología Argentina 1984*, ed. Premios Coca-Cola en las Artes y las Ciencias. Buenos Aires: Universidad de Belgrano, 9–110.

Pisano, Valdés, Emundo (1977). "Fisiografía de Fuego-Patagonia Chilena, I: Comunidades vegetales entre las latitudes 52 y 56° S." *Anales del Instituto de la Patagonia*. 8: 121–250.

Richter, Laura L., and Jorge Luis Frangi (1992). "Bases ecológicas para el manejo del bosque de *Nothofagus pumilio* de Tierra del Fuego." *Revista de la Facultad de Agronomía*. 68: 35–52.

Schiavini, Adrián Carlos Miguel (1993). "Los lobos marinos como recurso para cazadores-recolectores marinos: El caso de Tierra del Fuego." *Latin American Antiquity* 4: 346–366.

Tuhkanen, Sakari (1992). "The Climate of Tierra del Fuego from a Vegetation Geographical Point of View and its Ecoclimatic Counterparts Elsewhere." *Acta Botanica Fennica* 145: 1–64.

Western Magellan-Otway

The Europeans gave the name "Alacaluf" to the latest ethnos of this subtradition. This is probably a deformation of a term applicable only to the southern natives (Fitz-Roy 1839). The natives of Isla Wellington call themselves Kaweskar (Emperaire 1955), but this name should not be extend to all the epigonal groups of this subtradition. Likewise, these ethnic names should not be used for pre-17th-century times.

TIME PERIOD: 6000–50 B.P.

LOCATION: Southern South American Pacific coast, from Golfo de Corcovado to Paso Brecknock, perhaps as far as Christmas sound.

DIAGNOSTIC MATERIAL ATTRIBUTES: Abundant although not dominant bone industry and abundant but little specialized stone tools (although in the 6th millennium B.P. there were a slightly greater specialization than in the other subtradition). Harpoons with single-barbed detachable heads and fixed multibarbed are present. The shell middens are nonannular. The natives of the 19th century used canoes either of bark or planks. Huts were dome-shaped.

CULTURAL SUMMARY

Environment

Cold, rainy, and very windy. Very oceanic, with no very marked seasonal differences. The average winter temperatures are within 1–7° C, the average summer temperature from 8–12° C. The rain and snowfalls vary from 800–3500 mm per year, although there are places where only 450 mm falls and others, on the outer coast, with over 5000 mm per year (Zamora and Santana 1979). The Andes mountain range almost parallels the sea and is partially submerged in it. As a consequence, there is an abundance of islands separated from the continent by narrow channels, beaches are very short and narrow, and slopes are very abrupt. The dominant vegetation is the forest of *Nothofagus betuloides*, with other trees such as *Maytenus magellanica* (*maitén*) and *Pilgerodendron uvifera* (Guayteca's cypress) and shrubs (Moore 1953; Pisano Valdés 1977; Tuhkanen 1992). These forests harbor a very scarce terrestrial animal life, although in ancient times the small deerlike *Hippocamelus bisulcus* (*huemul*) descended in winter from the highlands to the coast. On the other hand, the coastal waters provided abundant pinnipeds, birds, mussels, and other seafood. Fish obtainable at less than 4 m depth are small, although in summer time migrations from offshore made them

plentiful. Whale stranding is thought to have been in ancient times fairly similar to that of the more southern region.

Settlements

The rough and steep terrain and the distribution of resources favored an occupation restricted to the coasts, with preference (but not exclusively) for places shielded from the ocean by outer islands. Natives were nomads, and according to ethnographical data, group mobility was very frequent. Huts were dome-shaped, built with bent branches and leaves on a rounded base some 3 m in diameter (Emperaire 1955: 125–132). Archaeological shell middens are very abundant, and known population estimations for c. 1880 vary from 1000–2000 to 3500–4000 people. By 1900, only 200–500 people survived (Martinic 1989).

Economy

The lives of these people depended of the exploitation of littoral resources. There is abundant archaeological information for the early and late periods of this subtradition, but there is almost none for the period 5000–300 B.P. Nevertheless, at the present state of knowledge, it is more reasonable to presuppose a population continuity and a cultural stability similar to that described for the Beagle Channel-Cape Horn subtradition than early extinctions or adaptive or population shifts. The available data underline the importance of pinnipeds, complemented by whales, *huemuls*, guanacos, birds, fish, mussels, and other seafood (Emperaire and Laming 1961: 17–18; Legoupil 1992a).

From a technological standpoint, the Englefield, Bahía Buena, Punta Santa Ana, and Bahía Colorada archaeological records, dated from 6000–5000 B.P. (Emperaire and Laming 1961; Legoupil 1992b; Ortiz Troncoso 1980), show a greater variety of specialized types of flaked stone (weapon points, borers) than those of their contemporaries of the Beagle Channel-Cape Horn region. Flaked stone points were stemless with lanceolate or subtriangular shapes. The known bone industry is somewhat less abundant than in the other subtradition sites; even so crossshaped detachable harpoon heads and multibarbed ones are represented. Sometimes the former have rectilinear incised decoration, although at present instances of two small parallel barbs or curvilinear decorations are not known. The Marazzi site and some levels of the Ponsonby site probably are remains of foot hunters of the northeastern plains. Only the two upper levels of the second site should be included in this subtradition. The Ponsonby site's Level B (c. 3700 B.P.) yielded large lanceolate flaked points (Laming-Emperaire 1968) resembling very much those of the Lancha Packewaia ancient component (c. 4000 B.P.) (Orquera et al. 1978). Clement's (1980–1981) assignation of subspheroids to bolas is not convincing; they probably were fishline sinkers (Mansur-Franchomme et al. 1989). Of the late sites, Punta Baja is the only important one that has been radiocarbon-dated. The stone flaked points, believed to be arrowheads, are generally (although not exclusively) stemmed with a triangular blade and eventually microlithic (Legoupil 1989: 127–149). The late detachable harpoon heads known archaeologically have a single tenon and a single lateral barb. Nevertheless, some recorded ethnographically have double tenons and two opposite lateral barbs. Through all the sequence, lithic side scrapers and cutting flakes and bone wedges and awls abound (Emperaire and Laming 1961: 63–73; Legoupil 1989: 127–169; Ortiz Troncoso 1980). From ethnographical data, canoes and rush baskets must be added to this subtradition as important items. The former, made of bark or planks, were larger than those of the Beagle channel, ranging from 7–10 m in length (Cooper 1917: 197–198).

Sociopolitical Organization

For the subject, there is little pre-20th-century information for this region. It seems certain that polygamy was practiced and that there were puberty-initiation ceremonies. Commonly no more than two or three families camped together. There was no formal chiefmanship, legal or political structures, or even persons who concentrated wealth.

Religion and Expressive Culture

As in the previous section, a warning about little information must be made. The data of the 19th century indicate a belief in spirits (generally malignant, although some were benevolent). There were no priests or religious ceremonies, but the natives accomplished secret men meetings in which the ancestral myths were revealed to the youths. The dead could be (1) buried; (2) deposited in the forest, covered with branches and/or stones; (3) deposited in caves; (4) abandoned on top of a tree; (5) placed in a small funeral hut; or (6) thrown into the sea (Cooper 1917; Emperaire 1955; Gusinde 1974).

References

Clément, Georges (1981). "Typologie d'une collection des bolas provenant de Ponsonby (Chili austral)." *Journal de la Société des Américanistes* 47 (1980–1981): 49–68.

Cooper, John Montgomery (1917). "Analytical and Critical Bibliography of the Tribes of Tierra del Fuego and Adjacent Territory." *Bulletins of the Smithsonian Institution, Bureau of American Ethnology* 63: 233.

Emperaire Joseph (1955). *Les Nomades de la mer.* L'Espèce Humaine. Paris: Gallimard.

Emperaire, Joseph, and Annette Laming (1961). "Les Gisements des îles Englefield et Vivian dans la mer d'Otway (Patagonie australe)." *Journal de la Société des Américanistes* 50: 7–77.

Fitz-Roy, Robert (1839). *Proceedings of the Second Expedition (1831–1836) under the Command of Captain Robert Fitz-Roy (R.N.): Narrative of the Surveying Voyages of His Majesty's Ships Adventure and Beagle between the Years 1826 and 1836.* ed. H. Colburn. London.

Laming-Emperaire, Annette (1968). "Missions archéologiques françaises Chili austral et au Brésil méridional: Datations de quelques sites par le radiocarbone." *Journal de la Société des Américanistes* 57: 77–99.

Legoupil, Dominique (1989). *Ethno-archéologie dans les archipels de Patagonie: Les nomades marines de Punta Baja.* Paris: Éditons Recherche sur les Civilisations.

Legoupil, Dominique (1992a). "La Vie animale dans la mer d'Otway (Patagonia australe) depuis 6000 ans: Faunes archéologiques et données ecologiques." In *Archaeology and Environment in Latin America,* ed. O. R. Ortiz Troncoso and T. van der Hammen. Amsterdam: Amsterdam University, Instituut voor Pre- en Protohistorische Archeologie Albert Egges van Giffen, 283–293.

Legoupil, Dominique (1992b). "Une Méthode d'interpretation etno-archéologique en deux temps: Un Modèle culturel, sur 6000 ans, chez les nomades marins de Patagonie." *Ethnoarchéologie: justification, problèmes, limites.* Juan-les-Pins: XIIº Rencontres Internationales d'Archaeologie et d'Histoire d' Antibes, 357–375.

Mansur-Franchomme, María Estela, Luis Abel Orquera, and Ernesto Luis Piana (1989). "El alisamiento de la pira entre cazadores-recolectores: El caso de Tierra del Fuego." *Runa* 17–18: 111–206.

Martinic Beros, Mateo (1989). "Los canoeros de la Patagonia meridional: Población histórica y distribución geográfica (siglos XIX y XX): El fin de una etnia." *Journal de la Société des Américanistes.* 75: 35–61.

Moore, David M. (1953). *Flora of Tierra del Fuego* London: Anthony Nelson.

Orquera, Luis Abel, Arturo E. Sala, Ernesto Luis Piana, and Alicia H. Tapia (1978). *Lancha Packewaia: Arqueología de los canales fueguinos.* Buenos Aires: Editorial Huemul SA.

Ortiz Troncoso, Omar R. (1980). "Punta Santa Ana et Bahia Buena: Deux gisements sur une ancienne ligne de rivage dans le Détroit de Magellan." *Journal de la Société des Américanistes.* 67: 133–204.

Pisano Valdés, Edmundo (1977). "Fisiografía de Fuego-Patagonia Chilena, I: Comunidades vegetales entre las latitudes 52° y 56° S." *Anales del Instituto de la Patagonia* 8: 121–250.

Tuhkanen, Sakari (1992). "The Climate of Tierra del Fuego from a Vegetation Geographical Point of View and Its Ecoclimatic Counterparts Elsewhere." *Acta Botanica Fennica* 145: 1–64.

Zamora, Enrique, and Ariel Santana (1979). "Características climáticas de la costa occidental de la Patagonia entre las latitudes 46° 40' y 56° 30' (S)." *Anales del Instituto de la Patagonia* 10: 109–144.

SITES

Bahía Buena-Punta Santa Ana

TIME PERIOD: 5900–5210 B.P. Dates of 6410 and 5620 B.P. were obtained for Punta Santa Ana by radiocarbon analysis on seashells; so they have to be correct by the reservoir effect, and therefore these two last radiocarbon dates have to be some centuries more recent.

LOCATION: Continental coast of the strait of Magellan on Brunswick peninsula.

DESCRIPTIVE SUMMARY

Local Environment

It is a cold and windy locality at the limit between the evergreen woods and the Patagonian mixed wood. Precipitations amount to some 600 mm per year (Legoupil 1989: 21).

Physical Features

These nearby sites are located on a terrace at some 12 m above sea level. In both sites, the middle levels are shell middens including sand lenses, pebbles, reddish soil, sea urchin remains; the lowest levels are dark silts. The Bahía Buena diggings covered 32 m^2, while at Punta Santa Ana 27 m^2 were excavated.

Cultural Aspects

The recovered artifacts were more abundant at Bahía Buena than at Punta Santa Ana. Lithic industry is similar to that of Englefield, including bifacially flaked lanceolate stemless points of green obsidian and end and side scrapers of the same and other raw materials. There were some pebbles with pecked grooves or knapped notches. The bone industry encompassed detachable single-barbed harpoon heads with a cross-shaped base, multibarbed harpoon heads and wedges (all made of cetacean bone) and awls (made of bird long bones). Decoration of bone tools is sporadic (Ortiz Troncoso 1975, 1980). The existence of mollusk, fish, and marine mammal remains was mentioned by Ortiz Troncoso, but there is no published analysis of them. Within the avian food remains, penguins and cormorants are dominant; when used as raw material for awls, the species represented are somehow more varied and balanced

(Lefevre 1989). An important find at Punta Santa Ana is a human skeleton buried in a flexed position and partially covered with stones (Ortiz Troncoso 1980).

References

Lefevre, Christine (1989). "L'avifaune de Patagonie Australe et ses relations avec l'homme au cours des six derniers millenaires." Ph.D. diss., Université de Paris (Pantheon-Sorbonne).

Legoupil, Dominique (1989). *Punta Baja: Ethno-archéologie dans les archipels de Patagonie: Les nomades marins de Punta Baja.* Mémoire 84. Paris: Editions Recherche sur les Civilisations.

Ortiz Troncoso, Omar R. (1975). "Los yacimientos de Punta Santa Ana y Bahía Buena (Patagonia Austral): Excavaciones y fechados radiocarbónicos." *Anales del Instituto de la Patagonia* 6: 94–122.

Ortiz Troncoso, Omar R. (1980). "Punta Santa Ana et Bahia Buena: Deux gisements sur une ancienne ligne de rivage dans le Détroit de Magellan." *Journal de la Société des Américanistes* 66: 133–204.

Englefield

TIME PERIOD: The Englefield site was the first to prove that littoral adaptation was of great antiquity in the area. The first studies dated the site in 8450–9250 B.P. (Emperaire and Laming 1961: 16–17) but were later changed to 3915 B.P. (Ortiz Troncoso 1979). More recently, Legoupil (1988) obtained a date of 6100 B.P., which seems more reliable.

LOCATION: Englefield island at Otway sound.

DESCRIPTIVE SUMMARY

Local Environment

The site is on a small island, formerly forested, in Otway sound, an almost closed sea extension although is connected with open sea at both extremes. Rain and snowfall reach some 700 mm per year (Zamora et al., in Legoupil 1989: fig. 3). Some 30 km eastward of Englefield, the continental plains begin, and the vegetation changes.

Physical Features

Englefield shell midden is on a terraced level. Its altitude above present sea level was first estimated at 25–27 m and is now amended to 15–17 m (Legoupil 1988). The excavation covered some 250 m^2, and no internal stratification of the shell midden was recognized (Laming-Emperaire 1961: 12–15). The archaeological record was considered to be a homogeneous cultural manifestation, and no internal differences were looked for.

Cultural Aspects

Englefield site yielded very abundant flaked stone tools—over 1200 pieces. The most frequent raw materials used were greenish obsidian and beach pebbles (sandstone, quartzite, schist, and basalt). The former was preferred for bifacial flaking, for the lengthened shape of the cores allow the extraction of bladelike blanks (actually not true blades). Weapon points were abundant, mainly lanceolate (with a convex base) and elongated triangular (with a straight base shape). No single shoulder or fluted points were found. Many bifacial scrapers ("knives"), end scrapers (including thumbnail ones) and borers (that would be better catalogued as "becs") were found. Side scrapers and some end scrapers were made with pebble flakes. Also, many objects were found with their surfaces totally or partially pecked: an ax and pebbles with rustic notches or perimetrical grooves. Probably they were sinkers for fishing lines, but it is unlikely that they were net sinkers as suggested by Emperaire and Laming. The bone equipment (9 percent of all instruments) includes detachable cross-based harpoon heads, multibarbed ones, and wedges (all of whale bone), awls made with avian long-bone fragments and so-called chisels (*huemul* horns beveled by polishing). On the detachable harpoon heads, incised decoration with rectilinear motives is frequent, but curvilinear designs have never been found (Emperaire and Laming 1961: 18–42). The researchers found bones of pinnipeds, whales, birds, and fish (Emperaire and Laming 1961: 17–18) but did not made any special study of them; guanaco and *huemul* remains would have been very few. Later test pits rendered high amounts of bird remains (Lefevre 1989). Legoupil (1989: 30) suggests that the nearby site of Bahía Colorada would be very similar to Englefield.

References

Laming-Emperaire, Annette (1968). "Missions archéologiques françaises Chili austral et au Brésil méridional: Datations de quelques sites par le radiocarbone." *Journal de la Société des Américanistes* 57: 77–99.

Lefevre, Christine (1989). "L'Avifaune de Patagonie Australe et ses relations avec l'homme au cours des six derniers millenaires." Ph.D. diss., Université de Paris (Pantheon-Sorbonne).

Legoupil, Dominique (1988). "Ultimas consideraciones sobre las dataciones del sitio de Isla Englefield (Seno de Otway)." *Anales del Instituto de la Patagonia.* 18: 95–98.

Legoupil, Dominique (1989). *Ethno-archéologie dans les archipels de Patagonie: Les nomades marines de Punta Baja.* Mémoire 84. Paris: Éditions Recherche sur les Civilisations.

Ortiz Troncoso, Omar R. (1979). "Nuevo fechado radiocarbónico para la isla Englefield (seno Otway, Patagonia austral)." *Relaciones de la Sociedad Argentina de Antropología* n.s. 12: 243–444.

Lancha Packewaia

TIME PERIOD: 4000–280 B.P.

LOCATION: North coast of the Beagle channel.

DESCRIPTIVE SUMMARY

Local Environment

The site is locaton a small terrace level within a small creek downslope to the sea. The lateral walls and the surrounding mixed forest of *Nothofagus betuloides-N. pumilio* protect it from the prevailing winds.

Physical Features

The site covers some 2000 m^2. The base of the fertile layers is 6–7 m above sea level. There are several shell midden layers, each some decimeters thick, interbedded with thin soil layers that also contain archaeological remains.

Cultural Aspects

The stratigraphy and the technological differences between records enabled us to distinguish two components: the ancient (c. 4000 B.P.) and the recent (1590–280 B.P.). Each component is formed by many single occupational events, but each one represents general activity encampments. The ancient component is characterized by large lanceolate or biacuminate spear heads (12–17 cm long and 45–60 g in weight) or their fragments. They were knapped by bifacial flaking reduction of large corelike blanks of basaltic-andesitic vulcanite. At present, the only known morphological parallel in the area is the lithic points found in Ponsonby's B level, which are attributed to the Western Magellan-Otway subtradition. Other tools are side scrapers, end scrapers, and expeditive ones made of metamorphized rhyolite, a detachable cross-shaped base harpoon head and several wedges of whalebone, avian long-bone awls, chisels made of pinniped's radii, (Orquera and Piana 1995a: 331–338; Orquera et al. 1978: 115–150; Piana 1984: 65–70). The archaeofaunal remains have permitted us to infer a diet composed of 53 percent of its caloric value by pinnipeds, 37 percent by guanacos, 6 percent by mussels and 4 percent by birds (Orquera and Piana 1995: 339–352; Saxon 1978). On the other hand, the recent component is characterized by (1) quite smaller lithic points, made from much smaller metamorphized rhyolite or shale slablike blanks, and (2) detachable harpoon heads with a single barb and simple-tenon bases (Orquera and Piana 1995a: 331–338; Orquera et al. 1978: 51–72; Piana 1984: 75–79). Other findings are side scrapers, wedges, awls, chisels, similar to the ones described for different layers of Túnel I site. In this component, the objects of pecked stone and those for ornament are scarce. The faunal remains indicate that 66 percent of the calories ingested in the site came from pinnipeds, only 12 percent from guanacos, 18 percent from mussels, and just 4 percent from birds (Orquera and Piana 1995a: 339–352; Saxon 1978). In both components, the pinnipeds remains show a sex-and age-pattern very similar to that of Túnel I second component.

References

Orquera, Luis Abel, and Ernesto Luis Piana (1995). "Lancha Packewaia: Actualización y rectificaciones." *Relaciones* n.s. 19: 325–362.

Orquera, Luis Abel, Arturo E. Sala, Ernesto Luis Piana, and Alicia H. Tapia (1978). *Lancha Packewaia: Arqueología de los canales fueguinos.* Buenos Aires: Editorial Huemul S.A.

Piana, Ernesto Luis (1984). "Arrinconamiento o adaptación en Tierra del Fuego." In *Antropología Argentina 1984*, ed. Premios Coca-Cola en las Artes y las Ciencias. Buenos Aires: Universidad de Belgrano, 9–110.

Saxon, Earl C. (1978). "Natural Prehistory: The Archaeology of Fuego-Patagonian Ecology." *Quaternaria* 21: 329–356.

Shamakush I

TIME PERIOD: 1000–900 B.P.

LOCATION: North coast of the Beagle channel.

DESCRIPTIVE SUMMARY

Local Environment

The site is located on a plain of some 80 ha crossed by the Río Remolino. The plain is an ancient sandy marine beach with a very thin soil developed on top. Never forested, it is grass-covered, and the comparatively easy pass inland through the river valley made it a favorable location for encountering guanaco. On the other hand, the kelp fringe is little developed because of a lack of a firm substratum, so the associated fish and mollusk fauna is not rich. In turn, pinnipeds do not frequently visit the location, and marine birds are not abundant. The *Nothofagus* forest is some 500 m away, offering plenty of wood for fuel and raw material.

Physical Features

The archaeological site extends for some 1500 m^2. Nearly half of it is covered by a cluster of annular shell middens that reach 80 cm in height above the surrounding soil. Many reoccupations of the same spot built up each of these. In their interior, there are shell midden lenses of different thicknesses interbedded with thinner layers of soil or eolic sand.

Cultural Aspects

Arctifactual and faunal remain densities are low when compared with the findings of the other sites of the subtradition. The foreseen bias of the site toward the guanaco encounter is reflected in the preserved faunal remains—these animals probably provided up to two-thirds of the calories ingested at the site by the human occupants, much more than that of pinnipeds and mussels. This correlates with the recovered artifacts: flaked-stone tools include projectile points with and without stems, side scrapers, many small and microlithic end scrapers, and so on. The prevailing raw material is metamorphized rhyolite. Also metamorphized cinerite and some schists were us. Bone tools recorded are few, and no harpoon heads were found. Even so, Shamakush I was not a guanaco-hunting specialized encampment; different daily activities were carried out on the spot; the presence of women was inferred; the settlement pattern was determined by the dependence on the littoral environment rather on guanaco hunting (Orquera and Piana 1997). Several decades ago, not referring to this site in particular but to all the annular shell middens, Bird (1938) and Menghin (1956) dissented on whether the natives huts of this region were pit houses with their floors intentionally dug several decimeters deep. In Shamakush I, as also in Shamakush X, Túnel VII, and Lanashuaia sites, our studies proved that such intentional deepening did not exist, or that at the most it did not exceed a few centimeters. Being on sand or pebbles, such a shallow pit could be made just by use and transit, not necessarily implying intentional deepening. The refuse accumulations raised the flat soil surrounding the huts, eventually forming annular structures (Orquera and Piana 1991).

References

Bird, Junius (1938). "Antiquity and Migrations of the Early Inhabitants of Patagonia." *Geographical Review* 28, 2: 250–275.

Menghin, Osvaldo F. A. (1956). "Existe en Tierra del Fuego la auténtica casa-pozo?" *Runa* 7, 1: 107–112.

Orquera, Luis Abel, and Ernesto Luis Piana (1991). "La formación de los montículos arqueológicos de la región del canal Beagle." *Runa* 19: 59–82.

Orquera, Luis Abel, and Ernesto Luis Piana (1997). "El sitio Shamakush I (Tierra del Fuego, República Argentina)." *Relaciones* n.s. 21: 215–265.

Túnel I

TIME PERIOD: 7000–450 B.P.

LOCATION: North coast of the Beagle channel.

DESCRIPTIVE SUMMARY

Local Environment

The Túnel I site lies on a slope made of redeposited moraine sediments that interrupt the generally steep coast. The climate is cold and windy; the annual average precipitation is 550 mm. The surroundings are covered by a mixed forest of *Nothofagus betuloides* and *N. pumilio*.

Physical Features

The archaeological site covers some 250 m². The fertile layers are 13–16 m above sea level. The site is formed by several shell midden lenses (Alpha, ß, Gamma, D), interbedded soil layers (A, C), a silt with little pebbles (E), and light brown and black silts with volcanic ashes (F, G). Shell midden D is the thickest layer, up to 2 m high (Orquera and Piana 1988a: 137–143, 1988b; Piana 1984: 31–34). It is not an annular-type mound but primarily a refuse landfill. The D layer internal stratification enabled us to differentiate eight successive formation phases and even to suggest the location of the huts and their displacements within the site (Orquera and Piana 1992: 33–43 and 47–50).

Cultural Aspects

The stratigraphy and the differences in the recovered items enabled us to group the findings into six components and to recognize evidence of other smaller occupations. In all cases, the data suggest general-activities encampments, not specialized settlements. The first component (6680 or 6980 B.P.) involves the evidence preserved in the lower part of the F silt layer. This has been interpreted as a very short occupation of hunters. Nothing suggests fitness to the littoral environment (Orquera and Piana 1988b: 226; Piana 1984: 39–47); therefore, this component must not be included in the general tradition.

The second component encompasses the upper F layer portion and the layers E and D. As 21 radiocarbon dates indicate, it covers the period c. 6300–4600 B.P. Archaeofaunal remains as well as technological ones clearly indicate a fully integrated and successful human adaptation to the littoral environment. The present hypothesis, based on environmental factors unrelated to sea level rise, consider it unlikely that much older manifestations of adaptation to the littoral could be found in the Beagle channel region (Orquera and Piana 1988a: 150–157). Therefore, the adaptation process must have begun in some other region.

In the excavated portion of the site (150 m²), more than 80,000 pinniped bones and fragments were recovered from this component. They belonged to a minimum of 340 individuals. Of these, 94 percent were *Arctocephalus australis*, 86.5 percent being males. Although animals of all ages were hunt, 69 percent of the *Arctocephalus* males and 37 percent of the females were under reproductive age. There were no remains of newborns, and the bones of less than 1-year-old pups were very scarce. From the study of thin cuts of canine teeth, 90 percent of these animals died between March and September. These data enable us to deduce that hunting was performed primarily in the water, far from the mating and breeding rookeries (Schiavini 1993).

More than 6000 bones and splinters were recovered, belonging to a minimum of 22 guanacos (probably quite more). Thirty-five different bird species were represented by some 36,000 bones including those of some 300 cormorants and some 50 penguins. Nearly 860 cetacean bones or fragments evidence that at least 21 dolphins and an indeterminable number of whales were utilized. A low figure of 2600 fish bones indicates a low contribution to the diet (Orquera and Piana in press). Extrapolation on column samples indicates that in the excavated portion of the site were heaped shells of 5.5×10^6 mussels of edible size, that is to say 98–99 percent of all the mollusks consumed (Orquera in press). Although the archaeofaunal analysis is not yet finish, it can be provisionally and conservatively estimated that the pinnipeds would have provided more than 60 percent of the calories ingested at the site by its human visitors. Within D layer, a nongeneral tendency toward increase in the rate of smaller size pinnipeds can be seen. In the upper formation phases of that layer, the number of guanaco remains increased (Orquera and Piana in press). The size of the mussels gathered is 26 percent smaller than the ones that can be found today, but there is no evidence that they were overexploited (Orquera and Piana 1992).

The bone equipment is very abundant: it includes harpoon heads with cross-shaped bases (often with two small parallel barbs and/or incise curvilinear decoration), multibarbed harpoon heads, avian bone awls, whalebone wedges, chisels made with pinniped ulnae, decorated bone artifacts of unknown use. There are more than 1000 flaked-stone tools; many side scrapers and cutting flakes were found, but few end scrapers and only one borer. The only weapon point found is made of allochthonous green obsidian that appears in the western mouth of the strait of Magellan (its type and raw material are common in Englefield site). The prevailing raw materials are metamorphized rhyolite and cinerite. In much smaller proportion, shales and basalt are found. In this context, the finding of a quantity of objects of pecked stone, including mauls, probably hafted and used to strike on bone wedges (Mansur-Franchomme et al. 1989: 142–146) and spheroids supposed to be fishing line sinkers, should be remarked.

Ornamental items are also plentiful: necklace beads made with *Fissurella* shell fragments or bird long bone segments, pendants of faunal teeth. (Orquera and Piana 1988b: 227–230 and tables II–VIII, in press; Piana 1984: 53–63).

The third component of Túnel I (c. 4300 B.P.) was recovered from the C layer, without an associated shell midden. The percentage of guanaco remains continued the increasing tendency found in upper D formation phases. The other archaeofaunal data, the tools typology, and the percentages of different classes of artifacts do not significantly differ from those of the second component. Toward 2700 B.P., the shell midden Alpha was formed, and the associated remains constitute the fourth component. It is distinguished by an enigmatical large quantity of microlithic end scrapers made of quartz (114 in total, 80 of them found in only 4 m^2). The oldest points assignable to arrows of this subtradition were found in this component. The fifth component is an occupation floor with few associated shells and is dated around the beginning of our era. The sixth component, in the lens ß, included a lithic bifacial knapping accumulation associated with a shell midden dated in 450 or 670 B.P. Flaked-stone points with very short stems and large expanded barbs were found. In all of these late occupations appeared a greater or smaller quantity of food remains of the species above mentioned, preserving their comparative ranks of importance (Orquera and Piana 1988b: 230–232, 1997).

References

Mansur-Franchomme, María Estela, Luis Abel Orquera, and Ernesto Luis Piana (1989). "El alisamiento de la piedra entre cazadores-recolectores: El caso de Tierra del Fuego." *Runa* 17–18: 111–206.

Orquera, Luis Abel (in press). "Análisis de conchales fueguinos y de la distribución espacial interna del sitio Túnel VII." In *XII Congreso Nacional de Antropología Argentina 1997*, La Plata.

Orquera, Luis Abel, and Ernesto Luis Piana (1988a). "Human Littoral Adaptation in the Beagle Channel Region: The Maximum Possible Age." In *Quaternary of South America and Antarctic Peninsula*, 5: 133–162.

Orquera, Luis Abel, and Ernesto Luis Piana (1988b). "Composición tipológica y datos tecnomorfológicos y tecnofuncionales de los conjuntos arqueológicos del sitio Túnel I (Tierra del Fuego, República Argentina)." *Relaciones* n.s. 17, 2: 201–239.

Orquera, Luis Abel, and Ernesto Luis Piana (1992). "Un paso hacia la resolución del palimpsesto." In *Análisis espacial en la arqueología patagónica*, ed. L. A. Borrero and J. L. Lanata. Buenos Aires: Ayllu SRL, 21–52.

Orquera, Luis Abel, and Ernesto Luis Piana (in press). "Arqueología de la región del canal Beagle (Tierra del Fuego, República Argentina)." *Bullettino di Paletnologia Italiana* 87:

Piana, Ernesto Luis (1984). "Arrinconamiento o adaptación en Tierra del Fuego." In *Antropología Argentina 1984*, ed. Premios Coca-Cola en las Artes y las Ciencias. Buenos Aires: Universidad de Belgrano, 9–110.

Schiavini, Adrián Carlos Miguel (1993). "Los lobos marinos como recurso para cazadores-recolectores marinos: El caso de Tierra del Fuego." *Latin American Antiquity* 4: 346–366.

Túnel VII

TIME PERIOD: 100 B.P., coterminous with the ethnographic information.

LOCATION: North coast of the Beagle channel.

DESCRIPTIVE SUMMARY

Local Environment

Túnel VII is on a marine terrace at 2–3 m above sea level. Being almost rounded by a small cliff, it is exposed only to the dominant southwestern winds. The coast is open with no inlet protection. The shores are good for mollusk gathering. As the kelp fringe is abundant and near the coast, fish and their predators (birds and pinnipeds) gather there. On the other hand, because of the steep slope of the locality, guanaco encounters would not be expect. Also, the abrupt coastline is not a good place for whale stranding. Woods were very near the encampent. No year-round freshwater source other than temporary streams or small pools existed near the site.

Physical Features

The site is a shell midden up to 90 cm thick on a plaeobeach. It is covered by a thick soil layer that contains remains of both native and recent sawmill activities.

Cultural Aspects

The stratigraphy, dating, and lack of technological differences indicate that it is a single-component site raised up by many different occupational events (Orquera 1995). Various daily activities were accomplished in the location. A dwelling unit and its surroundings were excavated, and in its central depression there was a sequence of 10 superposed hearths (Orquera and Piana 1995b). In the basal portion, the remains of a consumed whale were found (Estévez et al. 1995). In Túnel VII, there was a notorious increase in fish consumption, including several events of sardine stranding (Estévez et al. 1995). Pinniped was still an important staple, while guanaco remains are minimal. Radiocarbon dating was confirmed by the finding of cutting traces on bone made with metal edges and, although very scanty, remains of fauna European in origin (Piana and Estévez 1995).

The artifacts found in the site match the known ones for the recent phase of the Beagle channel and, with the adition of a high and varied presence of arrowheads, end scrapers, and expeditive tools such as cutting flakes, with the ones registered by chroniclers and ethnographers. The lithic raw material is that available in the immediate surroundings (Vila et al. 1995).

References

Estévez Escalera, Jordi, Nuria Juan-Muns Plans, Jorge Martínez Moreno, Raquel Piqué Huerta, and Adrián Schiavini (1995). "Zooarqueología y antracología: estrategias de aprovechameinto de los recursos animales y vegetales en Túnel VII." In *Treballs d' Etnoarqueologia: Encuentros en los conchales fueguinos*, ed. J. Estévez E. and A. Vila Mitja. Madrid-Barcelona: CSIC—Universidad Autónoma de Barcelona, 143–238.

Orquera, Luis Abel (1995). "Túnel VII: La estratigrafía." In *Treballs d' Etnoarqueologia: Encuentros en los conchales fueguinos*, ed. J. Estévez E. and A. Vila Mitja. Madrid-Barcelona: CSIC—Universidad Autónoma de Barcelona, 83–104.

Orquera, Luis Abel, and Ernesto Luis Piana (1995a). "Túnel VII: la excavación." In *Treballs d' Etnoarqueologia: Encuentros en los conchales fueguinos*, ed. J. Estévez E. and A. Vila Mitja. Madrid-Barcelona: CSIC—Universidad Autónoma de Barcelona, 47–82.

Orquera, Luis Abel, and Ernesto Luis Piana (1995b). "Túnel VII en la secuencia arqueológica del canal Beagle: Hipótesis y expectativas de los investigadores argentinos." In *Treballs d' Etnoarqueologia: Encuentros en los conchales fueguinos*, ed. J. Estévez E. and A. Vila Mitja. Madrid-Barcelona: CSIC—Universidad Autónoma de Barcelona, 25–45.

Piana, Ernesto Luis, and Jordi Estévez Escalera (1995). "Confección y significación de las industrias ósea y malacológica en Túnel VII." In *Treballs d' Etnoarqueologia. Encuentros en los conchales fueguinos*, ed. J. Estévez E. and A. Vila Mitja. Madrid-Barcelona: CSIC—Universidad Autónoma de Barcelona, 239–260.

Vila Mitja, Assumció, Xavier Terradas, Ignacio Clemente, and María Estela Mansur (1995). "La larga marcha: De roca a instrumento." In *Treballs d' Etnoarqueologia: Encuentros en los conchales fueguinos*, ed. J. Estévez E. and A. Vila Mitja. Madrid-Barcelona: CSIC—Universidad Autónoma de Barcelona, 261–274.

Punta Baja 1

TIME PERIOD: c. 270 B.P.

LOCATION: South coast of the Otway sound (northwest coast of Brunswick peninsula). This site is located next to the entry of the deep Silva Palma fjord, some 15 km southward from Isla Englefield.

DESCRIPTIVE SUMMARY

Local Environment

Rugged (mountains up to 1000 m in height) with impenetrable, abrupt, and rocky coasts. Cold and windy climate (mean temperatures: 0° C in July and 9–10° C in January). The precipitation reaches some 800 mm per year. The surroundings, although perhaps not exactly the site, were covered by *Nothofagus betuloides* and associated species forest. In the proximity there are favorable places for pinniped encounters. However, some 20 km to the east, the landscape turns flatter, drier, and with a more open vegetation transitional to steppe, where it is possible to find guanacos. To the same distance toward the west, the annual rainfall amounts to some 1500 mm per year.

Physical Features

The site is on a peninsula or tombolo of some 600 × 165 m, on the lowest of three terraced levels (2–3 m above sea level) and is protected from the prevailing winds by a rocky knob that forms small shelters. Fertile layers extend on the flatter portion of the palaeobeach close to the knob. They were 20–50 cm thick, some meters wide, and included discontinuous shell accumulations. Some 900 m² were excavated.

Cultural Aspects

The site has only one cultural component. Legoupil (1986, 1989, 1992) gave much importance to the analysis of the faunal remains. The predominance in quantity of specimens as well as in nutritional values belongs to the pinnipeds, for they would have provided 95 percent of the calories ingested by the natives at the site. The remains of 70 pinnipeds were found, of which 68 were *Otaria flavescens*; 44 percent were pups of less than a year in age, 23 percent were yearlings (with a prominance of females), and 23 percent adult females. At least most of the pops were killed in autumn. This suggests hunting at some nearby rookery when the mating and breeding season had already ended but the pups and their mothers had stayed at the locality. Today there still are rookeries not far from Punta Baja, although Legoupil considers the exploitation of a pinniped hauling-out area at the opposite extreme of the peninsula more probable (Legoupil 1989: 55–80 and table 33, 1992). The sample of bird bones recovered is large, and cormorants dominate in it; some of them are young ones, implying for the occupation the same season as that of the pinnipeds (Lefevre 1989). Minor quantities of dolphin, otter, and *huemul* bones were recover. An estimated 115,000 individual mollusks were found; limpets are predominant, while mussels make up less than 5 percent. Fish remains were few (Legoupil 1989: 80–123, 1992).

Many bifacially chipped-stone points of medium and small sizes were found. Nearly all of them are of obsidian, stemmed and with triangular blades. They are presumed to have been arrowheads. Legoupil identified several concentrations of bifacial reduction flakes. The rest of the flaked tools are coarse. There are few retouched scraping tools, suggesting to the describer that the natives would have had metallic implements of European origin; in fact, some fragments of the latter were found (Legoupil 1989: 127–153 and 224). The bone equipment includes the characteristic detachable single-barbed harpoon heads with a single-tenon base made of whale bone, beveled rods of the same material, and awls of bird bone. No multibarbed harpoon heads were found (Legoupil 1989: 153–167).

Bason the artifact and faunal dispersion, Legoupil presumed the existence of four different hut locations around repeatedly lighted hearths (Legoupil 1989: 181–204). Encampments would have been of short duration, but they would have been repeatedly reoccupied. Notwithstanding the possibility of a pinniped rookery exploitation and apparently seasonal occupation, Punta Baja 1 encampments were not devoted only to the hunting of these animals; the abundance of arrowheads and, to a lesser degree, the composition of the rest of the instruments suggest that other activities would have been fulfilled in the place.

References

Lefevre, Christine (1989). "L'Avifaune de Patagonie Australe et ses relations avec l'homme cours des six derniers millenaires." Ph.D. diss., Université de Paris (Pantheon-Sorbonne).

Legoupil, Dominique (1986). "Los indios de los archipiélagos de la Patagonia: Un caso de adaptación a un ambiente adverso." *Anales del Instituto de la Patagonia* 16: 45–52.

Legoupil, Dominique (1989). *Ethno-archéologie dans les archipels de Patagonie: Les nomades marines de Punta Baja*. Mémoire 84. Paris: Éditions Recherche sur les Civilisations.

Legoupil, Dominique (1992). "La Vie animale dans la mer d'Otway (Patagonia australe) depuis 6000 ans: Faunes archéologiques et données ecologiques." In *Archaeology and Environment in Latin America*, ed. O. R. Ortiz Troncoso and T. van der Hammen. Amsterdam: Amsterdam University, Instituut voor Pre- en Protohistorische Archeologie Albert Egges van Giffen, 283–293.

Ernesto Luis Piana
CADIC-CONICET
Malvinas Argentinas s/n
Tierra del Fuego
Argentina

Moche

Mochica, Early Chimú

ABSOLUTE TIME PERIOD: 1950–1200 B.P.

RELATIVE TIME PERIOD: Follows the Andean Regional Development tradition and precedes the Wari tradition. Encompasses the 6 last centuries of the Early Intermediate period and the first 2 centuries of the Middle Horizon.

LOCATION: The northern coast of Peru, between the Pacific ocean in the west and the Andean piedmont in the east, extends from the valley of the Piura in the north to that of the Huarmey in the south.

DIAGNOSTIC MATERIAL ATTRIBUTES: Ceramics with black paste and, especially, orange or red paste with bi- or trichromatic (red, white, black) painting, or with decoration in relief, produced by molding, stamping, or surface additions. Ornaments of gold, silver, copper, or alloys, manufactured by a variety of methods including lost wax casting. Camelid wool or cotton textiles with polychrome decoration made on rudimentary looms. Wattle-and-daub or adobe houses with packed earthen floors. Monumental public architecture, called *huacas*, built out of adobe and consisting of platforms, terraces, and ramps. Polychrome murals.

REGIONAL SUBTRADITIONS: Northern Moche, Southern Moche.

IMPORTANT SITES: Galindo, Moche, Pacatnamú, Pampa Grande, Pañamarca, Sipán.

CULTURAL SUMMARY

Environment

Climate. The Moche territory was periodically subjected to major climatic variations. Its subtropical climate is marked by two seasons: a dry summer, from December to March, and a relatively wet winter, from April to November. Except for the extreme wetter north, it is relatively arid toward the south with the presence of the Sechura desert. The annual average temperature is maintained between 15° and 18° C, and precipitation is sparse and generally comes in the form of drizzles (the *garúa*) and fogs bringing less than 30 mm of water annually. The winds are sometimes violent. The El Niño phenomenon occasionally breaks this climatic rhythm. Occurring on a 5- to 15-year cycle and lasting on average from 12 to 18 months, El Niño results in abundant precipitation that can cause devastating floods. Between 1500 and 1400 B.P., the Moche territory experienced an unusually severe El Niño, following a drought that lasted more than 30 years.

272

Topography. The Moche environment presents a corrugated relief marked by dunes and strewn with a dozen rivers running out from the Andes and flowing into the Pacific. These rivers create valley-oases where the majority of the Moche communities were concentrated, the remainder living especially on the edge of the coast. Occasionally, the Moche territory underwent harmful environmental disturbances, such as earthquakes, which sometimes modified the topography substantially.

Geology. The Moche territory is formed by the broad tertiary basin of Sechura, which presents a rock substrate of batholithic granite and dioritie covered by marl deposits, gypsum, limestone, and sand, as well as loess in the river plains. At the time the Moche inhabited the region, communications appear to have been more difficult to maintain between the parts north and south of the Moche territory because of the presence of the Pampa of Paiján, a desert zone of approximately 60 km in width, located between the valleys of the Jequetepeque and the Chicama. Among the natural resources offered by the basement geology and exploited by the Moche peoples were copper, gold, and silver, as well as salt and clay, but these resources are very unequally distributed inside the Moche territory.

Biota. The Peruvian northern littoral is characterized by arid regions, shrubby steppes called *lomas*, and by the Pacific ocean, which constituted, for the Moche peoples, a practically inexhaustible reservoir of exploitable resources, both plant (trees, cacti, etc.) and animal (terrestrial and marine mammals, freshwater and saltwater fish, shellfish, and birds). Periodically, several of these resources could be decimated during the climatic changes caused by El Niño or drought, causing substantial reduction in the food resources available.

Settlements

Settlement System. Moche settlements take five forms: (1) urban centers, places where political, economic, and religious activities were concentrated by the Moche elite and which sometimes contained populations of several thousand inhabitants; these centers were organized in a hierarchical way, and most occupied the lower or middle sections of river valleys, near arable lands; (2) agglomerations of several hundreds of inhabitants, located in the middle and lower parts of river valleys, with the houses around only one *huaca*; these settlements were where bureaucrats of less importance resided; (3) villages and hamlets of a few dozen or even a hundred farmers, located on the desert margins and with access to cultivable land; (4) villages or hamlets of fishermen, with around 100–200 people, dispersed along the coast on the edge of the Pacific ocean; (5) fortresses and bastions, generally arranged in the high parts of valleys. These various establishments each played a role in the local and regional economy and were connected by a network of roads, sometimes marked, arranged inside and between the valleys. Certain sites were also accessible by inland waterways or by sea. These transportation and communication channels allowed trade between the establishments located along a valley, or between one valley and another, but also to the whole of the Moche territory and with the neighboring areas of the Pacific littoral and the Andean highlands.

Community Organization. The Moche settled in places with easy access to important natural resources, especially along the river valleys where there is cultivable soil, and in certain points along the Pacific coast; some communities lived near the marshes in the margins of certain rivers or close to water sources located in the more desert zones between river valleys. In the sites of average or major importance, the inhabitants lived in residential sectors in the periphery of one or more structures of ceremonial use called *huacas* (platforms staged with approach ramps, terraces, and platforms); the largest residences and best made were built close to these public structures. The largest sites had varied public architecture: *huacas*, palaces, markets, cemeteries, open places for public rites or trade, workshops for products of ritual consumption and objects of prestige (ceramic *chicha*, objects of metal, etc.), storage buildings, llama enclosures, aqueducts, or reservoirs. The public buildings were sometimes built in multiple stages, suggesting that more or less frequent maintenance and periodic rebuilding took place. They are indexes revealing an organized division of labor, which probably required the participation of specialized groups taken from the local communities. This transfer of labor achieved the tasks required in the form of corvée and in a context of reciprocity between the leading elite, redistribution of certain essential resources, and the local population.

Housing. Generally less than 15 sq m, the Moche house is of rectangular form, without predetermined plan, and only large enough for a nuclear family. The basic residential unit is divided into three separated but adjacent areas: (1) an area for cooking and other domestic activities, (2) an area for the storage of food, and (3) a sleeping area. This domestic architecture is made from light and perishable materials; the framework is wooden, the walls and roof are made from woven rushes and/or wattle and daub, and the floor is packed earth. There are significant differences between urban and rural communities in regard to the style of construction, the locations of the residences, their number, size, elaborations, and contents. Located close to the public structures and sometimes among other domestic residences, in separate areas, certain dwellings have several rooms, with walls constructed out of adobe bricks and set on a stone foundation. Some houses even have stone walls supported by wood beams and covered with plaster. Some of these houses have more than one level, with steps connecting them. Certain areas are used as storerooms and have trunks, benches, and niches to store various, sometimes exotic, goods. The most sophisticated residences are even protected by an enclosing wall. These differences and variability mark a hierarchy in the domestic structures, which reflects the Moche social hierarchy and the relative richness of its members.

Population, Health, and Disease. In spite of a rate of death that is relatively high at low age, the demographic growth is apparently constant in the whole of the territory during the first centuries of Moche history, but the difficult environmental conditions during the century after 1500 B.P. involved a substantial demographic fall, with a resumption of growth thereafter. At its apogee, the Moche territory contained a population of several tens of thousand of individuals, and sites like Moche, and later Pampa Grande, each had at least a few thousand inhabitants. Recent studies have shown that with an average adult height of 1.58 m for men and 1.47 m for women, the Moche peoples presented few physical deficiencies because they were in general well fed and in good health. Women lived generally longer than men, on average 5 year more, and several lived past 50 years, regardless of their social status. But the diet of the Moche, rich in soft food and carbohydrates, made dental problems common, in particular, decay and loss of teeth. Because of their active lifestyle in spite of sedentism, Moche men and women also suffered from certain forms of arthritis. Moche iconography suggests that skin diseases (such as leishmaniasis), malformities (such as dwarfism), and handicaps (like blindness) were not rare in the population.

Economy

Subsistence. The Moche were primarily sedentary. Irrigation agriculture formed the basis for food production. Farmers used simple tools—the hoe and the digging stick—as well as guano for manure to permanently maintain fields in cultivation. To increase crop yields as well as to provide drinking water to the larger towns, an effective system of irrigation canals was deployed in several valleys, sometimes supplemented by an aqueduct or a reservoir. Other more rudimentary, and sometimes provisional, means, of water collecting existed, in particular in the *lomas*, the lake zones, or by using ground water close to the surface. In periods of dryness, certain communities supplied themselves with water and other food products by means of the system of redistribution under control of the Moche authorities. Freshwater fishing, gathering of shells and mollusks, as well as animal husbandry were also practised on a regular basis, providing a substantial supplement to the diet of the Moche peoples. Fishing was practised close to the shore using a line and hook, or in deep water by means of nets of various types or harpoons projected out of reed boats. Hunting for small and big game animals (both marine and terrestrial mammals, birds, and reptiles) was done using spears, atlatls, nets, or blowpipes. Certain hunting activities were reserved for the Moche elite. According to iconographic data, men were apparently more likely than women to take part in these various subsistence activities, but it is more probable to think that at the base it was families—men and women, young and old—who jointly achieved the various tasks of food collection and preparation. In the urban sites, food production intended for the elite seems to have been supervised by appointed people. The apparent intensification of food production during the course of the Moche tradition could support the increased complexity of the administrative machinery, and the networks of exchange under control of the Moche elite could be expanded between the coastal valleys and even between the northern littoral and outlying areas in order to acquire specific exotic products. Around 1400 B.P., the intensified operation of the systems of supply water and irrigation set up by the Moche peoples seems to have accelerated the degradation of the architectural structures, while causing a pronounced imbalance in the food chain, apparently creating great economic instability and significant social disorder.

Wild Foods. In addition to domesticated foods, the Moche peoples collected many plants and wild roots, including coca, the cactus San Pedro, the fruit of the *ulluchu*, and the seed of the *espingo*, among others, but these were used especially for ritual or medicinal ends. The Moche peoples hunted game (stag, fox, lizard, birds) in the *lomas*, the alluvial plains, and the hills at the top of the valleys, as well as sea animals (otters, sea lions, penguins). Among the fish species exploited by the Moche peoples, the most important appear to have been bonito, anchovy, catfish, mullet, barracuda, and ray. They also collected shellfish (crab, lobster) as well as mollusks. The availability of these various resources fluctuated greatly according to the environmental modifications generated by the periodic passage of El Niño, in particular because of its duration and its intensity, causing an imbalance more or less pronounced in the food chain.

Domestic Foods. Moche farmers produced a wide range of cultigens, including the lima bean and the common broad bean, gourd, squash, corn, potato, cotton, papaya, and peanut. Certain processed products, like *chicha*—fermented beer containing corn—were produced on a large scale for domestic use and sometimes for ritual. For meat, the Moche peoples bred llama in enclosures, as well as muscovy duck and guinea pig. The dog was also a domestic animal among the Moche elite, but it is difficult to say if they consumed its meat. Several studies have suggested that the yield of harvests was unequal from one year to another and sometimes even insufficient to support the dependent communities, thus causing shortages, even famines. This was particularly the case between 1438 and 1406 B.P., when the cultivated fields and irrigation canals of Moche underwent repeated silting, which significantly damaged crop production.

Industrial Arts. Moche craft specialists, several types of whom labored in workshops located in the significant centers, made a wide range of objects, both utility and ritual. Moche ceramists produced two classes of pottery. The first, of higher quality, was reserved mainly for ceremonial and funerary uses; objects produced according to rudimentary techniques (including modeling, molding, and stamping) included figurines, musical instruments and different standard forms of containers, including restricted-neck bottles, handled bottles, handled vases, high-collared jars, and bowls. The paste was made of a good-quality clay and sand tempering, and smoothed with a stone; the paste was covered with a slip, decorated, polished, and finally fired in a well-oxygenated kiln. The second class, of poorer quality, consisted of utility wares, generally without any decoration, whose types (bowls and earthenware jars) remained unchanged throughout Moche history. These were used for food preparation and storage.

Metallurgists used gold, copper, silver, or an alloy of these various metals through the addition of arsenic to produce utensils, figurines, and ornaments according to varied techniques (hammering, lost wax casting, gilding,

etc.). Other materials, such as wood, mother of pearl, coral, bone, turquoise, and lapis lazuli, were employed in the decoration of ustensils or ornaments. Other craftsmen specialized in the manufacture of Moche armament (club, spear, and atlatl, sling, shield, helmet). Moche textile production was done apparently almost completely by female specialists who manufactured fabrics with cotton and/or camelid wool (llama, alpaca); the fibres were treated beforehand with various vegetable dyes, carded, spun, then woven on a rudimentary loom.

Moche monumental art includes polychrome murals, sometimes in relief, which where typically cream-colored white, red, yellow, black, and blue. These works, often wrongly described as frescos, were initially traced by incision or stamping on wet clay, then painted with mineral pigments of various colors. These pigments, mixed with juice of cactus (of the *Trichocereus* variety) or gum of the zapote (*Capparis angulata*) as binder, were applied using brushes.

Utensils. In regard to food, the Moche peoples used plates for solid food and bowls for liquids, sometimes manufactured from gourds, and wooden serving spoons. They ate, however, with their fingers. For food storage, they used large earthenware jars, whereas for cooking, they used smaller pots; during the preparation, certain food was cut using a knife of bone or, more simply, shell with a sharp edge. For making clothes, they used needles of fish bone, borers of bird bone, and carding brushes of llama bone, as well as spindles made out of wood with clay weights.

Ornaments. In architecture, the roofs of certain Moche public buildings were sometimes surmounted by a series of ceramic sculptures of animals or objects, whereas the walls might be ornamented with friezes or polychrome murals. In clothing, men's or women's clothes manufactured out of cotton or camelid wool were sometimes decorated with feathers and metal items. Moche iconography suggests that the costume and body ornamentation of men were more varied than those of women, especially among the members of the elite and certain groups of specialists. The basic costume of men was a loincloth and shirt with or without arms; several items supplemented this costume: a tunic with long sleeves, a short skirt (resembling the Scottish kilt) and apron, and, for the head, a headband or turban. Political and religious dignitaries, as well as warriors, had hair ornaments of metal, leather, and fabric, which, along with their clothing, generally included raised metal ornaments or feathers (collars, bracelets, armbands, etc.), which were more or less elaborate according to the individual's social status. Unlike men, women wore a simple costume made up of a long dress, often tied with a broad belt, and a shawl covering the shoulders and sometimes attached in front with a pin; in certain cases, women covered their heads with a veil. Moche women seldom wore personal ornaments, only earrings or a necklace. It seems that tattooing or face painting was a common practice among the Moche, particularly among men. In general, Moche apparel reflects stature, social position, and the public role of each individual, but can also underline membership in a community or a group (household, lineage) or even evoke the context of social action in which one participated.

Trade. Among the Moche peoples, trade was probably ensured by specialized merchants who already maintained active networks of exchange before the Moche time; as there did not exist any currency of exchange, commercial transactions were done by barter. For ground transport, the llama constituted, along with humans, effective means for the transport of goods. Products were thus conveyed by means of a system of roads connecting the valleys, in particular, urban sites. At sea or on rivers, Moche merchants would employ boats made out of reeds or balsa and could thus transport varied cargoes from one valley to another or leave the Moche territory altogether. Recent work has showed that the Moche developed a system of redistribution of cultivated products, placed under administrative control, which at the same time allowed centralized accumulation of surplus and the potential to meet the needs of more than one community. One can think that the majority of the villages of importance as well as the great sites had a market, making it possible for local and regional populations to supply themselves with basic commodities.

Division of Labor. Recent research reveals that each Moche community constituted an autonomous unit of labor force marked by family ties and, therefore, by common ancestors. Each community, consisting of one or more villages or hamlets, was probably organized, at the local level, according to principles similar to the Incan *ayllu*, but in a less elaborate form. According to these principles, the members of the community, men and women, together had the responsibility to help one another while collectively subjecting themselves to daily work (maintenance of cultivated fields, fishing, caring for animals, etc.) and season or annual chores (e.g., cleaning irrigation canals of silt) and stock management; in return, they were to share in the various products thus

produced, at least of a minimal part. In various valleys of the Moche territory, goods and labor could be exploited periodically by a centralized authority, thanks in particular to ideological means strategically used. However, the Moche leading elite does not seem to have been strongly implicated in the current management of basic consumer goods inside the communities that depended on its administration. Elites apparently acted as planners, organizers of community work, and agents of social cohesion. In major Moche centers, which contained workshops of specialized production, the craftsmen were divided on the basis of their qualifications and skills and thus fitted into a hierarchy of functions: master craftsmen, assistants, and apprentices. Moreover, certain specializations seem to have been reserved for one sex, for example, metallurgy for men and weaving for women. It is plausible to that there were "noble trades," like ceramic production, which conferred more social status than others. For the repair and refitting of public buildings, the material indexes indicate the existence of a principle of organization of segmented work, requiring the participation of varied groups from local communities. This form of corvée labor achieved the tasks required in a context of reciprocity between the leading elite, redistribution of certain basic resources, and surrounding communities.

Differential Access or Control of Resources. At several important Moche sites, one finds places of storage for both subsistence goods (cotton, wool, food) and luxury goods (in particular, worked metals, textiles, and exotic ceramic objects), which allowed the Moche authorities to control the production and distribution of certain items and also to have a privileged access. These surpluses made it possible on the one hand to meet more adequately the urgent needs for the population in the event of shortage or to nourish the workers engaged in corvée labor, but also to be able to make use of it easily at the time of public festivals and ceremonies, such as feasts. It made it possible in addition for the members of the elite to accumulate and hoard personal wealth, which they then carried with them into the tomb. However, it seems that Moche administrators did not exert an absolute control over the reciprocity in goods and services, except perhaps at the time of community activities. In addition, the management of certain natural resources, like copper and iron mines, or salt and clay sources, and the ability to acquire certain exotic raw material (shells from Ecuador, lapiz lazuli from Chile, animals from the Amazon), must have constituted for the Moche elite a considerable economic advantage, which must have reinforced or increased the network of exchange between the various Moche communities and between the elites and others in the local community.

Sociopolitical Organization

Social Organization. Moche society as a whole had an uneven hierarchical structure, with elite leaders and other members of the nobility at the node of the social pyramid—men and women, apparently linked by family ties and holding many administrative, legal, and religious capacities. In their entourage lived the bureaucrats, soldiers, tradesmen, and craftsmen, the other servile groups (farmers, fishermen, collectors), and perhaps also slaves. Among the elite Moche, descent appears to have been important, in particular, among leaders who seem to have legitimized their authority based on heredity, transmitting their political, economic, and religious capacities from generation to generation. It is possible that in this context they practiced endogamy. For the remainder of the Moche people, members of each community were registered in lineages and thus linked by family ties through common ancestors. Among communal obligations, it seems that the worship of the ancestors was very respected, whatever the position of the community and its status in the sociopolitical organization. This worship was articulated around various private and public rites. The data are, however, insufficient to know exactly how the rules of filiation and marriage were exercised in these communities and how collective rights and liabilities were transmitted from one generation to another.

Political Organization. For a long time, it was believed that the Moche constituted a single state, theocratic and expansionist, which had succeeded in imposing, thanks to a powerful and disciplined army, hegemony over a wide area. In fact, recent excavations suggest a much more complex situation. Two areas, one in north and the other in the south, separated by the Pampa de Paiján, developed by initially incorporating separate kingdoms or complex chiefdoms, then developing into autonomous states. In these two areas, each valley had one or more royal lineages, which preserved a sovereign authority over the local communities, but whose members perhaps had very few contacts with the rest of society. Certain major sites, like Moche or Pampa Grande, constituted major poles of political and economic control, their influence overflowing the borders and their authority extending across more than one valley. Sepulchral and iconographic data reveal that certain people, both men and women, held positions of supreme authority at the local or regional level. Their

capacity probably rested on hereditary status and personal wealth; these would have been useful of tools of ideological conviction, such as the display of the material symbols underlining their higher position (even quasisupernatural), their privileges, and their social obligations (such as control of principal public rituals like human sacrifice and agrarian rites).

Social Control. Several researchers estimate that the military apparatus was not sufficient for the establishment and maintenance of Moche polities during their history and could not have played a coercive role in creating and maintaining structures of authority of these polities. It seems, however, that the polities spread out over the Moche territory remained welded by common religious ideology, that the supreme representatives were linked by bonds of kinship, and that the majority of the population agreed to share basic cultural concepts suitable for the Moche tradition. The recurrence of iconographic topics in religious matter over the territory, like the broad diffusion of certain elements of material culture (furniture and architecture) or the wide sharing of some ritual practices (funerary rites, sacrifices), represents major indexes suggesting that the Moche leaders could effectively exploit labor forces available to them and that they probably deployed an effective administrative organization. It is possible that among the requirements of the Moche political participation, in addition to those of religious nature (respect of the crowned institutions) or to communal obligations (corvée), there was imposed on local communities within the Moche polity payment of tribute to guarantee the continuation of the political system and the correct operation of the administrative machinery.

Conflict. In periods of social stress or in conflict situations between various Moche polities, there was probably an army, but it is at present difficult to establish whether standing armies or full-time soldiers existed. However, the military installations—fortresses and bastions—concentrated in the buffer zone between the highlands and lowlands in the north of Peru reveal that there were periodically, in particular, during the ends of both centuries of their history, marked tensions between the Moche peoples and neighboring communities of the Andean highlands, especially those of Cajamarca and Huamachuco. Certain researchers also think that in spite of their relative autonomy, certain Moche polities sometimes made strategic alliances or even constituted themselves in confederation, to conquer new grounds and thus to extend their hegemony or to defend themselves against too quarrelsome neighbors.

In addition, among the factors used to explain the abrupt end of Moche political institutions, it seems that certain local communities revolted against the leading authorities.

Religion and Expressive Culture

Religious Beliefs. Iconographic analyses have revealed the existence of a rich pantheon that, like Moche society itself, was arranged hierarchically. The dominant deity in this pantheon is a male with wrinkled face and catlike mouth, wearing a belt and earrings in the form of a snake. Among the other members of this pantheon are deities with evocative names and forms. These supernatural beings appear to have lived in a universe familiar to the Moche: the sea, the desert, or the mountains, but also the sky and the underworld. Their actions seem to refer to the maintenance of a fragile balance of the environment, symbolized by antagonistic forces in perpetual comfort, and undoubtedly found their correspondence in the many rites practiced by the Moche peoples. The mythical origins and spiritual development of the Moche, in particular, those of its dignitaries, appear closely associated with emergence with the these supreme gods and their dualistic confrontation for the cosmic maintenance of law and order.

Religious Practitioners. Some researchers have argued that there was a hierarchical arrangement of religious personnel in Moche society, living in the entourage of the leading elite, and probably acting like priests at the time of public ceremonies. Important male or female priests seem to have held a quasi divine status because they are depicted with distinctive attributes associated with the principal actors of the Moche pantheon. The remainder of the sacred personnel was composed of men and women, sometimes handicapped, who formed groups specialized for the achievement of specific ritual practices, like preparing funerary offerings or taking care of future victims of sacrifice. The iconography also evokes the existence of male and female shamans who would have filled various magicoreligious functions, such as those of healers, fortunetellers, and sorcerers, some with apparently dangerous capacities. Researchers have proposed that the leaders were perceived as shamans because of the control a shaman could exert on the supernatural powers for the general well-being of society.

Ceremonies. According to several scholars, Moche public rites, several of which followed a set religious calendar whereas others were held on occasionally, such as death or natural catastrophe, called on one or more groups of priests and were carried out in cities either on or near the *huacas*, or in special locations in nature (mountain peaks, deserts, islands). The Moche peoples practiced varied funeral rites, agrarian rites, warlike rites intended for the capture of future sacrificial victims, human sacrifices, sacrifices of animals or objects, as well as feasts, dances, and ritual songs. Among the private rites that could be performed by shamans or lineage or household heads, the iconography suggests propitiatory and expiatory rites, rites of cure, and rites of reproduction, as well as rites related to the worship of the ancestors, the majority being able to be practiced within homes.

Arts. Visual arts, generally carrying elite or religious iconography, constitute, for researchers, the most accessible form today, but other forms of art (dance, song, poetry) undoubtedly were also practiced in Moche communities, often linked with the religious rites. Most iconography is found on ceramics, but objects of metal, wood, stone, or shell, textiles as well as monumental architecture were used to convey iconographic messages and thus to spread religious and ideological content to the whole of Moche territory. Used in an ostentatious way at the time of public ceremonies, modeled, engraved, painted, or woven artistic objects constituted a powerful instrument in the symbolic system of valorization and legitimation of Moche political and religious authorities.

Death and Afterlife. Moche iconography illustrates animated beings with skeletal features engaged in varied actions (dances, sex acts) and sometimes in exchanges with living peoples. This world of death was apparently treated on a hierarchical basis, reproducing in a simplified allegorical form the social reality of the Moche peoples. The Moche tradition was, by all appearances, characterized by an extremely developed worship of ancestors and elaborate funerary practices. Cemeteries were arranged either inside or near the *huacas* or on the slopes of valleys at the borders between residential sites, on arable lands and uninhabited desert zones; sometimes individuals were also buried under dwellings or in garbage middens. The Moche peoples developed seven distinct modes for the processing and deposition of corpses, the labor involved in internment, and the contents of the burials, corresponding to the status, sex, age, and family origin of the deceased. Moreover, individuals (men, women, and children) and some animals were sacrificed to accompany the body of high-ranking political or religious leaders into the tomb.

Suggested Readings

Alva, Walter, and C. B. Donnan (1993). *Royal Tombs of Sipán*. Fowler Museum of Natural History, Los Angeles: University of California.

Arsenault, D. (1995). "Balance de los estudios mochicas (1970–1994): Primera parte: Los estudios iconográficos." *Revista Andina* 13, 1: 237–270.

Arsenault, D. (1995). "Balance de los estudios mochicas (1970–1994): Segunda parte: Los trabajos arqueologicos." *Revista Andina* 13, 2: 443–480.

Bawden, G. (1996). *The Moche*. Oxford: Blackwell.

Berezkin, Y. E. (1983). *Mochika*. Leningrad: Academy of Sciences of USSR.

Campana, Cristobal (1994). *La Cultura Mochica*. Lima: Consejo Nacional de Ciencia y Tecnología.

Donnan, C. B. (1979). *Moche Art of Peru*. Los Angeles: Museum of Cultural History, University of California.

Donnan, C. B. (1995). "Moche Funerary Practice." In *Tombs for the Living: Andean Mortuary Practices*, ed. T. D. Dillehay. Washington D.C: Dumbarton Oaks, 111–160.

Donnan, C. B., and G. A. Cock, ed. (1997). *The Pacatnamu Papers, vol 2: The Moche Occupation*. University of Cultural History, Los Angeles: University of California.

Donnan, C. B., and D. McClelland (1999). *Moche Fineline Painting: Its Evolution and Its Artists*. University of Cultural History, Los Angeles: University of California.

Hocquenghem, A.-M. (1987). *Iconografía Mochica*. Lima: Fondo Editorial de la Pontificia Universidad Católica del Perú.

Lavalle, J. A. de (1989). *Culturas Precolombinas: Moche*. Lima: Banco de Credito del Perú en la Cultura, Colección Arte y Tesoros del Perú.

Shimada, I. (1994). *Pampa Grande and the Mochica Culture*. Austin: University of Texas Press.

Uceda, S., and E. Mujica, ed. (1994). *Moche: Propuestas y Perspectivas*. Lima: Universidad Nacional de la Libertad, Institut français d'Études andin and Asociación Peruana para el Fomento de las Ciencias Sociales.

DANIEL ARSENAULT
Département d'histoire
Université Laval
Québec
Canada

Nasca (Nazca)

ABSOLUTE TIME PERIOD: 2200–1300 B.P.

RELATIVE TIME PERIOD: Precedes the Huari tradition and follows the Late Coastal Andean Formative tradition. Corresponds to the Early Intermediate Period in the Peruvian chronological sequence; follows the Early Horizon Paracas culture and precedes the Middle Horizon Huari (Wari) culture.

LOCATION: Nasca was centered in the Río Grande de Nasca drainage and in the Ica valley of the south coast of Peru, with influences affecting the Pisco, Cañete, Acarí, and Yauca coastal valleys and Ayacucho in the highlands. Recently, Nasca cultural materials have been found in cemeteries at Ocoña, Camaná, and in the Sihuas valley in the department of Arequipa, but this material may represent trade items, not necessarily a Nasca occupation or colonization of this peripheral region.

DIAGNOSTIC MATERIAL ATTRIBUTES: Polychrome pottery painted in up to 15 colors with complex mythical as well as naturalistic motifs; evidence of warfare and the ritual use of human trophy heads; large ground drawings (geoglyphs) etched on the surface of the desert in the form of lines, geometric forms, and naturalistic figures; settlements small to moderate in size, constructed of irregular fieldstone (where available) or adobe; ceremonial centers consisting of modified natural hills forming pyramidal structures.

IMPORTANT SITES: Cahuachi, Pampa de San José, Ventilla, Majoro Chico, Ocongalla, Aja, Cantayo, Huayurí, Paradones, and Huaca del Loro (all in the Río Grande de Nasca drainage); Ocucaje, Santiago, Cerro Soldado (in the Ica valley); Tambo Viejo (Acarí valley).

CULTURAL SUMMARY

Environment

Climate. The Nasca tradition was centered in a subtropical desert environment, which had an annual precipitation ranging from 0–25 millimeters. The temperature ranges between 10–32° C, with an annual average temperature of 21° C. During the winter months, fog banks extend inland from the ocean, helping to hold temperatures down. Summers are sunny, dry, and very hot. Agriculture was possible only through irrigation fed by water emptying into the river tributaries during the summer rainy season in the highlands (January–March). Beginning around A.D. 500, because of severe drought conditions, wells (*pukios*) were dug to tap underground aquifers to supplement the surface water sources.

Topography. The Nasca people occupied a series of tributary rivers separated by stretches of mountain ranges or deserts lying mostly between sea level and

600 m, a zone referred to as the *chala* or coastal region. Fewer settlements are located in the *yunga* zone above 600 m, but Nasca influence eventually reached Ayacucho in the highlands at 2440 m. The Río Grande de Nasca is considered the heartland of the Nasca culture and consists of nine separate tributaries covering an area of 10,750 sq km. These rivers originate in the highlands from the summer rains that fall at those higher elevations and make their way into the drainage. The other major valley with abundant Nasca occupation, the Ica, is unusual in having no tributaries and flowing in a north–south direction.

Geology. A series of river valleys carrying water from the high Andes cuts across the arid coastal strip emptying into the Pacific ocean. All habitation is restricted to these oases. The soils of the Nasca region are composed of Quaternary sedimentary rock formations that are primarily riverine and riverine-alluvial.

Biota. The Nasca lived in a dry, desert environment with a minimal amount of naturally occurring xerophytic vegetation, such as cacti and the scrubby *huarango* tree.

Settlements

Settlement System. Nasca settlements were of two major types: (1) ceremonial centers, such as Cahuachi, with artificial and semiartificial platform mounds and cemeteries that served as pilgrimage centers for the populace, and (2) habitation sites of varying size. Early Nasca habitation sites were generally small villages scattered near the edges of the valleys off the floodplain, or on hills or other topographic features unsuitable for agriculture. Increasing drought conditions forced a change in settlement patterns in Middle Nasca times, culminating in the abandonment of many small villages and the concentration of the population in a few large population centers.

Monumental architecture is surprisingly absent in the Nasca cultural tradition. The mounds at Cahuachi are for the most part modified natural hills, which required much less labor output than the contemporary adobe pyramids of the Moche culture on the north coast.

Cemeteries, often containing hundreds of graves, are usually isolated from the habitation areas. Many are located on the sandy flanks of the valleys or on the slopes of hills bordering areas of cultivation. No superficial architecture or other markings were used to distinguish these burial places.

Community Organization. Knowledge of Nasca settlement planning is in its infancy and is based on surface survey rather than excavation. Nasca communities vary in size, but most are well under 4 ha in size. The vast majority of these sites are internally and functionally undifferentiated, suggesting that political organization was not at the level of a state where one would expect to find sites of varying size arranged in a hierarchy.

Housing. Nasca habitations were commonly constructed of wattle and daub—a framework of poles and intertwined branches covered with a clay plaster, often erected on a foundation of fieldstones. Houses varied in form and had a single entry. A fire pit was sometimes located in the center of the structure. Sites with monumental architecture, like the ceremonial center of Cahuachi, utilized adobe for wall construction. A variety of adobe shapes were present, including conical, rectangular, and oval.

Population, Health, and Disease. Silverman estimates a population for the Nasca valley drainage of between 15,000–22,000 individuals. Adding another 10,000 people for the Ica valley and other peripheral settlement areas in Pisco and Acarí, a total population of 30,000 for this culture seems reasonable. Allison and his colleagues have found that respiratory disease was the leading cause of death among ancient Peruvians. Also present were chronic infectious diseases such as tuberculosis, blastomycosis, bronchopneumonia, lobar pneumonia, in addition to malaria, intestinal parasites, and syphilis. Fifty percent of all children died before the age of 15 years; however, children living on the coast benefited from a high-protein diet of fish and shellfish. Although average life expectancy was about 40 years in the Nasca culture, about 27 percent of the population lived beyond the age of 40, and women lived longer than men.

Economy

Subsistence. The Nasca people were intensive agriculturalists dependent on irrigation and wells for water. The rich maritime resources of the Pacific also were an important part of their diet. Domestic animals included llamas and alpacas (exploited for their meat and wool but also used for ritual purposes) and guinea pigs. Some hunting of wild camelids and smaller creatures such as the fox is represented in the ceramic iconography. Utilitarian plants, such as cotton, were used as a raw material for textiles; gourds served as containers and fishnet floats.

Wild Foods. The cold waters of the Pacific ocean provided the Nasca people with fish, mollusks, crustaceans, and sea mammals. Included in this category is a wide range of shellfish including *Chromytilus chorus*, *Aulacomya ater*, *Mulinia edulis*, and *Crepipatella* spp., whose remains have been found at the inland site of Cahuachi. María del Carmen Rodríguez de Sandweiss has identified several species of fish, also excavated by Helaine Silverman at Cahuachi. Included on this list is a fish known locally as a *Anaque* or *Cachema* (*Cynoscion analis*), the popular *corvina* (*Sciaena gilberti*), and the *Coco* (*Paralonchurus peruanus*), along with other members of the families *Sciaenidae* and *Clupeidaie*.

Domestic Foods. Nasca domesticated agricultural plants include corn (*Zea mays*); the common bean (*Phaseolus vulgaris*); lima beans (*Phaseolus lunatus*); manioc (*Manihot esculenta*); potato (*Solanum* spp.); sweet potato (*Iopmoea batatas*); Achira (*Canna* spp.); squash (*Cucurbita maxima*); peanuts (*Arachis hypogaea*); Lúcuma (*Lucuma bifera*); Guayaba (*Psidium guajava*); Pacae (*Inga feuillei*); Palta (*Persae americana*); Jíquima (*Pachrrhizus tuberosus*); and peppers (*Capsicum* spp.).

Nonedible utilitarian plants included cotton (*Gossypium barbadense*); Totora (*Typha* spp.); Junco (*Cyperaceae* spp.); Caña brava (*Gynerium sagittatum*); gourd (*Lagenaria* spp.); and others.

Industrial Arts. The Nasca produced some of the finest polychrome pottery in the world, decorated with slip paints obtained from mineral sources. Elaborate textiles, including many decorated with finely embroidered mythical figures, were prominent in the earliest phases of the culture, but were soon replaced by ceramics as the main medium of artistic expression. Metallurgy was restricted to gold facial masks and ornaments used by the elite in ritual ceremonies. Some copper was used for utilitarian purposes, but metals in general were rare in this tradition. Other crafts include pyroengraved gourds, feather work, and the working of shell, bone, and stone. Clay panpipes were a major component of religious rituals. Their manufacture involved technical skills in slip casting, with precise measurements needed to obtain the range of tones required.

Utensils. Primary utensils are (1) sand-tempered pottery, manufactured from locally available clays and fired in a pit or over an open fire; (2) gourd containers, sometimes decorated with pyroengraved designs; (3) bags, constructed either of cloth or cotton netting; (4) weapons consisting of spears, sometimes tipped with obsidian points, spear throwers (or atlatls), slings, and stone-headed clubs. Characteristic pottery was thin walled and formed in a variety of closed and open vessel shapes, including a distinctive double-spout and bridge bottle, bowls, cups, vases, plates, and various effigy forms. Most were decorated with naturalistic or mythical polychrome designs, but cooking vessels were undecorated. Stone (such as obsidian), rather than metal, was used for tools and weapons.

Ornaments. The elite or religious practitioners in Nasca society wore mouth masks, nose ornaments, and hair bangles constructed of beaten sheets of gold with raised or repoussée designs, along with necklaces made of imported *Spondylus* shell. Tattooing of the arms and genital areas as well as facial painting was common, as evidenced archaeologically on preserved mummies as well as in the iconography of the pottery. Hair was sometimes braided or tied on the top of the head in large knots. Cranial deformation was commonly practiced, especially among the elite. Many individuals carried small woven bags containing coca leaves. Males wore breech cloths and a T-shirt garment on the upper body; Women wore ankle-length dresses and covered their upper bodies with mantles for added warmth. A variety of headgear was present, including turbanlike wrappings for men and conical woven hats for farmers. Sandals made of leather or woven from fibers have been preserved as well. Brightly colored feathers, some perhaps imported from the jungle area, were woven onto clothing or used in headdresses.

Trade. Long-range trade for ritual and luxury items was present in the Nasca economy. The thorny oyster shell (*Spondylus principens*), symbolizing water and blood, was an important sacred commodity used in rituals and for ornament. Found only in the warm waters off the Ecuadorian coast some 1900 km (1140 m) to the north, *Spondylus* shells were imported to the south coast where they were fashioned into pendants and necklaces. Obsidian, or volcanic glass, was imported from the central highlands to form the blades of knives used for trephination and for ritual decapitation. Monkeys and the feathers of tropical birds were traded from the jungles to the east or from Ecuador to the north. Contact with the powerful Moche state, located on the north coast of Peru, took place during the latter half of the Nasca sequence, introducing new ideological traits that are portrayed in the ceramic iconography.

Division of Labor. As is true in most societies, certain occupations were gender related in Nasca society. Women apparently were the primary weavers, judging from the contents of their graves, which often included implements of this trade; men were the primary officiants in warfare and ritual activities. Craft specialization was likely present in the manufacture of fine polychrome pottery, the production of the most elaborate textiles, feather work, and metallurgy. There is no evidence for a market system, and exchange took place between individuals at the local level, with long-range trade perhaps being controlled by the elite.

Differential Access or Control of Resources. The elite appear to have controlled access to water and the manufacture and trade of prestige goods.

Sociopolitical Organization

Social Organization. In later Andean societies like the Incas, the basic social unit was the *ayllu*, an endogamous group claiming descent from a common ancestor. Some scholars believe that the *ayllu* was present in Nasca society and was represented archaeologically by the multiple mounds or temples at the ceremonial site of Cahuachi, each built and maintained by an individual *ayllu*. Carmichael has argued that Nasca society was ranked, not stratified, meaning that the position of individuals in the society is based on a continuum, not separated into distinct classes, as would be true in a state. Using mortuary data, Carmichael attempted to demonstrate that there are no exclusive or absolute differences in the types of graves for any individuals in Nasca society. Unless and until distinct elite tombs are found in the future, Carmichael's model appears to be valid.

Political Organization. Recent evidence suggests that the Nasca political realm consisted of a number of local chiefdoms united by a common religion and symbolic system. Although archaeological evidence is still being evaluated, each tributary of the Nasca drainage may have had its own center of power and leadership, as was the case in the other valley systems sharing the Nasca tradition. From time to time, there may have been consolidation of some of these local chiefdoms into larger entities, but the notion of a singe central government with Cahuachi as its capital now has been discounted.

The leaders of Nasca society had dual functions as religious leaders (shamans) and secular warriors. The role of warrior-chief seems to have become more important in Phases 5, 6 and 7, although religion remained an important function of the leadership.

Conflict. There is ample archaeological evidence for warfare in Nasca society. Nasca ceramics frequently depict warriors, battle scenes, weapons, and trophy heads. Preserved slings, spear throwers (atlatls), clubs with star-shaped stone heads, and obsidian knives are commonly found in graves. Skulls exhibiting primitive skull surgery (trephination) attest to the frequency of battle wounds to the heads. Decapitated human heads, taken in battle, were used for ritualistic purposes. Some scholars have argued that warfare took place for entirely ritualistic purposes; however it is more likely that the leaders of the various chiefdoms were attempting to gain territory and power for themselves, especially in the middle and late Nasca phases. The evidence points to intracultural warfare. No Nasca sites are fortified, and the iconography does not indicate physical or cultural differences in the combatants.

Religion and Expressive Culture

Religious Beliefs. Nasca religion centered on agricultural fertility, especially the unpredictability of water in their harsh environment. The taking of human heads in battle and the use of these trophy heads in rituals were the primary means of propitiating the gods. The Nascans worshiped a wide variety of mythical creatures that represented the most powerful elements of nature. They are represented in the art as anthropomorphic figures composed of symbolic elements of felines, killer whales, condors and falcons, and snakes.

Religious Practitioners. Religious leaders, or shamans, were major figures in Nasca society. These individuals sometimes dressed in the form of the mythical creatures or gods, wearing golden mouth masks and forehead ornaments with feline attributes, animal headdresses or capes, *Spondylus* shell necklaces, and bangles in their hair.

Ceremonies. Among the rituals represented on the pottery are those connected with agriculture, warfare, the ritual entombment of trophy heads, and the burial of individuals. Music was an essential part of such ceremonies and included the playing of panpipes, drums, rattles, and flutes, along with the ritual drinking of hallucinogenic drugs obtained from the San Pedro cactus. Pilgrimages to sacred centers like Cahuachi, and the ritual burial of offerings at such locations, was also important.

Among the most notable achievements of the Nascans was the construction of geoglyphs (gigantic lines, geometric patterns, and naturalistic figures) etched onto the surface of the desert. Known popularly as the Nasca Lines, these designs were constructed by removing the layer of dark pebbles, which covered the surface of the desert, exposing the lighter sand beneath, thus forming patterns that endured through the ages. The hummingbird, monkey, killer whale, and other figural motifs are identical to the designs on Nasca pottery and are thought to have been constructed as sacred symbols of their mythical creatures or gods. The linear patterns, once thought to be oriented toward astronomical phenomenan, may have been used by pilgrims as ritual pathways to sacred sites.

Arts. The Nascans used a variety of media for art, including textiles, ceramics, shell, gold, copper, wood, and feathers. Motifs include naturalistic, geometric motifs as well as a wide variety of mythical figures.

Death and Afterlife. The Nasca buried their dead in a seated position with the bodied dressed in typical clothing. The graves consisted of pits excavated into the sandy flanks of the river valleys up to a depth of about 6–10 feet. Pottery containers (numbering from a single vessel to 15 or more) were placed with the body and often held food and drink for the corpse. Other grave goods included weapons, spinning implements, gourd containers, baskets, llama hooves, and supplementary textiles. The grave pit was often roofed over with log beams. Judging from the ceramic iconography, elaborate rituals took place at the burial, including masked officients, music, and ritual drinking.

Suggested Readings

Allison, Marvin (1979). "Paleopathology in Peru." *Natural History* 88, 2: 74–82.

Aveni, Anthony, ed. (1990). *The Lines of Nazca.* Philadelphia: American Philosophical Society.

Blasco Bosqued, Concepcion, and Luis Javier Ramos Gomez (1980). *Cerámica Nazca.* Valladolid: Seminario Americanista de la Universidad de Valladolid.

Browne, David, Helaine Silverman, and Rubén García (1993). "A Cache of 48 Nasca Trophy Heads from Cerro Carapo, Peru." *Latin American Antiquity* 4, 3: 274–294.

Carmichael, Patrick (1988). "Nasca Mortuary Customs: Death and Ancient Society on the South Coast of Peru." Ph.D. diss., Department of Archaeology, University of Calgary, Alberta.

De Lavalle, José Antonio (1986). *Culturas Precolombinas: Nazca, Colección Arte y Tesoros del Perú.* Lima: Banco del Crédito del Perú.

Gayton Anna, and Alfred Kroeber (1927). *The Uhle Pottery Collections from Nazca.* University of California Publications in American Archaeology and Ethnology 24, 1: 1–46. Berkeley and Los Angeles: University of California Press.

Hadingham, Evan (1987). *Lines to the Mountain Gods.* New York: Random House.

Orefici, Giuseppe (1993). *Nasca: Arte e Societa del Popolo dei Geoglifi.* Milan: Jaca Book.

Proulx, Donald A. (1968). *Local Differences and Time Differences in Nasca Pottery.* University of California Publications in Anthropology, vol. 5. Berkeley and Los Angeles: University of California Press.

Proulx, Donald A. (1983). "The Nasca Style." In *Art of the Andes: Pre-Columbian Sculptured and Painted Ceramics from the Arthur M. Sackler Collections,* ed. L. Katz. Washington, D.C.: AMS Foundation, 87–105.

Proulx, Donald A. (1989). "Nasca Trophy Heads: Victims of Warfare or Ritual Sacrifice?" In *Cultures in Conflic: Current Archaeological Perspectives, Proceedings of the 20th Annual Chacmool Conference,* ed. D. Tkaczuk and B. Vivian. Calgary: The Archaeological Association of the University of Calgary, 73–85.

Schreiber, Katharina, and Josué Lancho Rojas (1995). "The Puquios of Nasca." *Latin American Antiquity* 6, 3: 229–254.

Seler, Eduard (1923). "Die buntbemalten Gefässe von Nazca in sudlichen Peru und ihre Hauptelemente ihrer Verzierund." In *Gesammelte Abhandlungen zur amerikanischen Sprach und Altertumskunde,* ed. E. Seler. Berlin: Verlag Behrend, 160–438.

Silverman, Helaine (1990). "Beyond the Pampa: The Geoglyphs in the Valleys of Nazca." *National Geographic Research* 435–456.

Silverman, Helaine (1993). *Cahuachi in the Ancient Nasca World.* Iowa City: University of Iowa Press.

Silverman, Helaine, and Donald Proulx (in press). *The Nasea (The People of American Series).* Cambridge MA: Blackwell.

SITES

Cahuachi

TIME PERIOD: 2200–1200 B.P.

LOCATION: On the southern bank of the Rio Nasca, south coastal Peru.

DESCRIPTIVE SUMMARY

Local Environment

Cahuachi is situated at an elevation of 365 m above sea level on a series of ancient river terraces facing the Pampa de San José to the north and the Pampa de Atarco to the south. Fierce winds, known locally as Paracas, frequently produce sandstorms that blow across the site, making life here somewhat unpleasant. The water table is shallow in the vicinity of the site, with permanent seepage just above the river. Undoubtedly this feature was an important factor in determining the location of this site (Silverman 1993: 11–12).

Physical Features

Cahuachi covers an area of 150 ha, but its monumental architecture is concentrated in an area of 25 ha located near the center of the site (Silverman 1993: 57).

Some 40 mounds make up the core of the site along with three- and four-sided enclosures. The mounds were fashioned by modifying natural hills found on the ancient terraces; few were augmented or enlarged with artificial adobe construction. All mounds were truncated or had platforms on their summits. There were several forms: single mounds (a spatial feature without smaller component parts); composite mounds (a mound with component spatial features); or mound complexes (where two or more mounds were in direct association with one another) (Silverman 1993: 89). Some mounds were used for burials, while others supported construction that had a ritual function. The areas between the mounds consisted of bounded open spaces referred to by Silverman as *kanchas* (1993: 89).

Cultural Aspects

Cahuachi was once thought to be a major urban center, the capital of a primitive regional state (Proulx 1968; Rowe 1963; Strong 1957). Recent excavations by Silverman (1993) and Orefici (1993) have demonstrated that the site was an empty ceremonial center, which apparently served as a place of pilgrimage and burial until Nasca Phase 5, after which it became a mortuary area and place of offerings. Silverman (1990) has argued that some of the "Nasca Lines" or geoglyphs in the Pampa de San José may connect Cahuachi to the urban settlement of Ventilla in the Ingenio tributary. Ritual offerings, such as those found in the "room of the posts" by Silverman (1987), suggest a long usage of the site with continuation of burials into the Middle Horizon Nasca Phase 8. Orefici (1997) has also traced the beginnings of occupation at the site to the late Paracas Phase 10 and early Nasca Phase 1 periods.

References

Orefici, Giuseppe (1993). *Nasca: Arte e Societa del Popolo dei Geoglifi*. Milan: Jaca Book.

Orefici, Giuseppe (1997). "Nuevos Enfoques Sobre la Transición Paracas-Nasca en Cahuachi (Peru)." In *Andes MAA: Boletin de Mission Arqueológica Andino de la Universidad Varsovia*. Varsovia: 173–198.

Proulx, Donald A. (1968). *Local Differences and Time Differences in Nasca Pottery*. University of California Publications in Anthropology, vol. 5. Berkeley and Los Angeles: University of California Press.

Rowe, John H. (1963). "Urban Settlements in Ancient Peru." *Ñawpa Pacha* 1: 1–28.

Silverman, Helaine (1987). "A Nasca 8 Occupation at an Early Nasca Site: The Room of the Posts at Cahuachi." *Andean Past* 1: 5–55.

Silverman, Helaine (1990). "Beyond the Pampa: The Geoglyphs in the Valleys of Nazca." *National Geographic Research* 435–456.

Silverman, Helaine (1993). *Cahuachi in the Ancient Nasca World*. Iowa City: University of Iowa Press.

Strong, William Duncan (1957). *Paracas, Nazca, and Tiahuanacoid Cultural Relationships in South Coastal Peru*. Salt Lake City: Memoirs of the Society for American Archaeology, no. 13.

Pampa de San José

TIME PERIOD: 2000–1000 B.P.

LOCATION: Pampa de San José is situated between the Nazca and Ingenio rivers of the Río Grande de Nazca drainage on the south coast of Peru some 400 km south of Lima, 50 km from the Pacific ocean at an elevation of 500 m above sea level (Aveni 1990: 3).

DESCRIPTIVE SUMMARY

Local Environment

This elevated dry plain—called a *pampa* by the local Peruvians—is triangular in shape, covering an area of 220 sq km (Aveni 1990). In this rainless desert environment, the *pampa* has stabilized, and there has been little erosion either by wind or water over the past 2000 years. The surface of the *pampa* is covered by a desert varnish—a dark layer of pebbles composed of manganese and iron oxides (Dorn and Oberlander 1981).

Physical Features

In 1927, Peruvian archaeologist Toribio Mejía Xesspe was excavating in the Nazca drainage when he climbed a hill adjacent to the Pampa de San José and looking down on the *pampa* was the first to discover a maze of lines and figures etched into the surface of the desert (Silverman 1990a). Additional investigation revealed a whole series of furrows of varying widths running for miles across the landscape. These markings, known as geoglyphs, were produced by the ancient inhabitants of the valley by clearing or sweeping away the small dark pebbles on the surface, revealing the lighter, unoxidized sand beneath. The material removed from the surface was used as a border for the geoglyphs.

Geoglyphs can be divided into two major categories. The majority consist of straight lines, trapezoids, triangles, rectangles, spirals, and zigzags numbering in the thousands. Many of the straight lines emanate from "line centers" where several lines radiate out from a central hub, often located on a small hill or rise. Aveni (1990) has counted over 62 of these line centers. Many of these lines run perfectly straight over several kilometers across the *pampa*. Several lines of evidence, including broken pottery offerings in association with these lines, suggest that they were constructed over a long time by peoples of several cultures (Clarkson 1990).

Other geoglyphs can be categorized as biomorphs or life forms. Maria Reiche (1968; Kern and Reiche 1974) has cataloged most of these. There are over 18 birds including cormorant, pelican, and hummingbirds, killer whales, a spider, lizard, plants, and other forms. All of these correspond to identical motifs on Nasca ceramic vessels, and there can be no doubt that they were constructed by people of this culture.

Cultural Aspects

The lines of Nasca have been variously interpreted as roadways (Mejía 1940), an ancient calendar system (Kosok 1965; Reiche 1968), indicators of ancient water sources in the mountains (Hadingham 1987; Reinhart 1983), pathways for pilgrimages (Silverman 1990b), pathways connecting shrines (Morrison 1978), and various eccentric theories too numerous to list. The biomorphs are thought by some to be representations of Nasca spirits drawn on a gigantic scale.

There is probably no single explanation for the function of the geoglyphs, because they were constructed over a time period of over 1200 years. The astronomical theory has been largely discounted (Aveni 1990; Hawkins 1969). Silverman's theory that some of the lines served as ritual pathways for pilgrimage seems to have some merit, yet other lines (and many more have been found outside the *pampa* in remote areas of the drainage) seem to be oriented to sources of water (see Johnson 1997). Additional research is needed to answer these questions.

References

Aveni, Anthony, ed. (1990). *The Lines of Nazca*. Philadelphia: American Philosophical Society.

Aveni, Anthony (2000). *Between the Lines*. Austin: University of Texas Press.

Clarkson, Persis (1990). "The Archaeology of the Nazca Pampa, Peru: Environmental and Cultural Parameters." In *The Lines of Nasca*, ed. A. Aveni. Philadelphia: American Philosophical Society, 115–172.

Dorn, R., and T. Oberlander (1981). "Microbial Origin of Desert Varnish." *Science* 213: 1245–1247.

Hadingham, Evan (1987). *Lines to the Mountain Gods*. New York: Random House.

Hawkins, Gerald S. (1969). *Ancient Lines in the Peruvian Desert—Final Scientific Report for the National Geographic Society*. Cambridge: Smithsonian Astrophysical Observatory.

Johnson, David (1997). "The Relationship between the Lines of Nasca and Water Sources." Paper presented at the 16th Annual Northeast Conference on Andean Archaeology and Ethnohistory, Orono, Maine.

Kern, H., and Maria Reiche (1974). *Peruvian Ground Drawings*. Munich: Kunstraum München E.V.

Kosok, Paul (1965). *Life, Land and Water in Ancient Peru*. Brooklyn: Long Island University Press.

Mejía Xesspe, Toribio (1940) [1927]. "Acueductos y Caminos Antiguos de la Hoya del Río Grande de Nasca." In *Actas y Trabajos Científicos, XXVII International Congress of Americanists, Lima (1939), 1.* Lima, pp., 559–569.

Morrison, Tony (1978). *Pathways to the Gods*. New York: Harper and Row.

Reiche, Maria (1968). *Mystery on the Desert*. Stuttgart: Heinrich Fink GmbH.

Reinhard, Johann (1983). "Las Líneas de Nazca: Montañas y Fertilidad." *Boletín de Lima* 2: 29–49.

Silverman, Helaine (1990a). "Beyond the Pampa: The Geoglyphs in the Valleys of Nazca." *National Geographic Research* 435–456.

Silverman, Helaine (1990b). "The Early Nasca Pilgrimage Center of Cahuachi and the Nasca Lines: Anthropological and Archaeological Perspectives." In *The Lines of Nasca*, ed. A. Aveni. Philadelphia: American Philosophical Society, 207–244.

Ocucaje (Cerro Max Uhle)

TIME PERIOD: 2200–1700 B.P.

LOCATION: In the lower Ica valley on the south coast of Peru.

DESCRIPTIVE SUMMARY

Local Environment

The Hacienda Ocucaje is situated on the western bank of the Ica river in a basin formed by the river as it emerges from a narrow channel. The climate is dry and rainless, with agriculture conducted by means of irrigation and wells. The major natural vegetation consists of *huarango* trees, which have deep roots and thrive in the desert environment.

Physical Features

Ocucaje is the name of a former hacienda whose roots go back to Colonial times. Famous for its vineyards, the hacienda is located entirely within a large basin just below the main section of the Ica valley and separated from it by a group of dry hills through which the river has cut a narrow passage. The basin is bordered on the west side by a line of chalk hills called Cerro Blanco, and to the east is a rolling sandy plain. The floor of the basin is flat, but is broken by two natural eminences. The larger is a short range of dry hills divided by a saddle into two sections, one called Cerro de la Cruz because it had a wooden cross on top, the other now known as Cerro Max Uhle in honor of the German-born archaeologist who first discovered Nasca pottery in situ here on the south coast of Peru in 1901 (Proulx 1970; Uhle 1913). Another sandy hill lies between these two and Cerro Blanco and is known as El Tambo.

Cultural Aspects

In 1901, Uhle discovered six separate cemeteries on this hacienda, which he lettered A through E. Cemeteries A, B, C, and F contained Nasca graves, with Site F containing the majority. Uhle, who was under contract to the University of California, excavated a total of 32 Nasca graves, which yielded 146 pottery vessels (Proulx 1970). His excavation methods were advanced for the time, and Uhle carefully noted the context and content of each grave. These gravelots became the earliest documented burials from the south coast, and, along with graves of other periods he excavated in the Ica valley, allowed Uhle to establish the first regional chronology for the area (Rowe 1954, 1956; Uhle 1924). His gravelots dated to the earlier phases of the Nasca sequence and have served as a valuable resource for archaeologists to the present day.

References

Proulx, Donald A. (1970). *Nasca Gravelots in the Uhle Collection from the Ica Valley, Peru*. Amherst: Department of Anthropology, University of Massachusetts.

Rowe, John H. (1954). *Max Uhle, 1856–1944: A Memoir of the Father of Peruvian Archaeology*. University of California Publications in American Archaeology and Ethnology 46, 1. Berkeley and Los Angeles: University of California Press.

Rowe, John H. (1956). "Archaeological Explorations in Southern Peru, 1954–1955: Preliminary Report on the Fourth University of California Archaeological Expedition to Peru." *American Antiquity* 22, 2: 199–226.

Uhle, Max (1913). "Zur Chronologie der alten Culturen von Ica." *Journal de la Société des Américanistes de Paris* ns. 10, 2: 341–367.

Uhle, Max (1924). "Ancient Civilizations of Ica Valley." In *The Uhle Pottery Collections From Ica*, eds. A. Kroeber and W. D. Strong. University of California Publications in American Archaeology and Ethnology 21, 2. Berkeley and Los Angeles: University of California Press, 128–132.

Ventilla

TIME PERIOD: 2000–1600 B.P.

LOCATION: On the south side of the Rio Ingenio tributary in the Río Grande de Nazca drainage on the south coast of Peru and directly north of the ceremonial site of Cahuachi.

DESCRIPTIVE SUMMARY

Local Environment

Like many Nasca habitation sites, Ventilla is situated on the dry desert margin of an irrigated river valley overlooking a broad expanse of agricultural land.

Physical Features

Ventilla is a large Nasca habitation site first occupied during Phase 1 of the sequence and reaching its apogee in Phases 3 and 5 (Silverman 1990: 439). The site consists of hundreds of habitation terraces containing the remains of densely agglutinated houses, along with several large enclosures, and a few artificial mounds. Although the site is rapidly being encroached on by agricultural activities, it originally stretched along the flank of the valley for a distance of 2–4 km and covered an area of more than 200 ha, making it the largest known Nasca site, even larger than Cahuachi (Silverman 1993: 324).

Cultural Aspects

Ventilla was connected to the ceremonial site of Cahuachi by a major linear geoglyph running across the *pampa* linking the sites. This geoglyph may have served as a ceremonial road for pilgrimages leading from Ventilla to Cahuachi. Helaine Silverman (1990: 439) suggests that perhaps the urban population not found at Cahuachi was centered here. She believes that Ventilla and Cahuachi may have served as "dual capitals of early Nasca society" (Silverman 1993: 326), with Cahuachi acting as the religious capital and Ventilla as the urban capital. However, she concludes that the Nasca was not a true state-level society, partly because Nasca sites show no hierarchical arrangement—they are internally and functionally undifferentiated (1993).

References

Silverman, Helaine (1990). "Beyond the Pampa: The Geoglyphs in the Valleys of Nazca." *National Geographic Research* 435–456.

Silverman, Helaine (1993). *Cahuachi in the Ancient Nasca World*. Iowa City: University of Iowa Press.

DONALD PROULX
Department of Anthropology
University of Massachusetts
Amherst, Massachusetts
United States

Old Amazonian Collecting-Hunting

ABSOLUTE TIME PERIOD: 11,000–7000 B.P. Dates between 11,200–10,200 B.P. (c.13,200–12,500 cal B.P.) were obtained for the Paleoindian subtradition from 56 radiocarbon samples of tropical fruits, nuts, and wood, three OSL dates on sediment, and 10 thermoluminescence dates on burned lithic artifacts. Five dates on charcoal from hearths give the Archaic subtradition a range of about 8000–7000 B.P.

RELATIVE TIME PERIOD: Begins the known human occupation of the Amazon; precedes the Early Amazonian tradition.

LOCATION: The Paleoindian subtradition occurs in the tropical rainforest along the main floodplains of the lower Amazon, and the Archaic subtradition occurs in the tropical forest-savanna transition zone of the Carajas region of southeastern Amazonia, both in Para state. Only two sites have been extensively excavated and reported, so that the pattern of expansions and contractions is not known.

DIAGNOSTIC MATERIAL ATTRIBUTES: Nomadic collector hunters with a focus on tropical forest nuts and fruits, fish, shellfish, and smaller game. These people were rock artists and makers of a wide range of flaked-stone tools. The Paleoindian subtradition was first recognized in surface finds of finely flaked triangular, stemmed, or hollow-based projectile points of hyaline quartz or chalcedony. When finally excavated, the projectile points were found with a variety of other tools, including unifacial gravers, slug-shaped scrapers (limaces), blades, and flake scrapers. The projectile points were made of hyaline quartz and chalcedony. Larger, coarser tools with fewer flake removals were made of quartz breccia. The Paleoindian subtradition is similar to the earliest accepted Paleoindian culture of central and southern Brazil, first described at Lagoa Santa, Minas Gerais state, and of the Itaparica culture of Goias. The Archaic tradition is characterized by percussion-flaked hyaline quartz lithics lacking bifacial projectile points.

CULTURAL SUMMARY

Environment

Although scholars had hypothesized that the Amazon had been a cold savanna during the late glacial maximum and a very moist forest in the early Holocene, the paleoecological and archaeological environmental evidence does not support this idea for the Amazon. The flora and fauna recovered from the archaeological sites are all humid tropical species, not temperate or cold climate species. The highly negative stable carbon isotope ratios of the late Pleistocene-dated wood and seeds and the lack of any grasses along the Amazon mainstream at Monte Alegre indicate a habitat of closed tropical rainforest. In comparison, the isotope ratios of early Holocene Carajas are less negative by 5–10 points per mil, which indicate a more open tropical rainforest there, compared with the mainstream Amazon. Paleoecological data from the Manaus region, upstream, in Amazonas state, also shows a wetter and slightly cooler tropical rainforest with only traces of grasses. Although a moderate abundance of Podocarp pollen at Manaus had been interpreted at first as evidence of extreme cooling and drying, Podocarps are humid tropical species highly intolerant of drought. They are a common, commercially valuable tree found both at sea level and at moderate elevations in many areas of South and central America, except where logged out. They are accompanied in the cores by abundant tropical flora vulnerable to cold. Given the great abundance of airborne pollen production in Podocarps compared with the mostly faunal pollinated tropical rainforest species, the pollen record suggests a dominance of the latter at the time in Manaus. According to all these data, in all three regions the ancient forests were wetter and more dense than the highly human-affected and sometimes rather open, forest-savanna mosaic vegetation of the region today.

The terrain of the mainstream Amazon has near sea level elevations for the most part, with sporadic hill ranges reaching up to about 300 m. Carajas is characterized by hilly terrain between 100–1000 m above sea level. The mainstream Amazon has primarily sandstone, limestone, and volcanic rock dikes exposed at the surface in the uplands and extensive hydromorphic sediments in river terraces and floodplains. In the late Pleistocene, the Amazon cut deeply because of lower sea levels and thus lacked such extensive floodplains. In the early Holocene, high sea levels led to the development of flooded coastal plains and more extensive swampy areas. Carajas is dominated by lateritic crusts developed from volcanic rocks, but there are some limestone areas and river floodplains and terraces. The mostly underground Precambrian rock in both areas is dominated by acid crystalline gneisses and granites. Of the lithic raw materials used by people at Monte Alegre, only the hyaline quartz is commonly locally

available. Chalcedony and quartz breccia desposits are not located in the Monte Alegre hills and must have been brought in.

The biological remains collected by fine screening at Pedra Pintada and by coarse screening at Caverna do Gaviao include only humid tropical taxa. There are no megafauna from the sites and no remains of temperate or desert plant species. The common plants are fruits and wood of palms and broad-leafed evergreen trees. Plants common in savannas, such as grass, were nonexistent at Pedra Pintada and very rare at Caverna do Gaviao. Common animals are fish, shellfish, water turtles, land tortoises, medium-sized rodents, lizards, snakes, frogs, etc. Larger species, of sizes such as deer, tapir, or peccary, are extremely rare, and many of the small species were present in juvenile forms. Fish and shellfish are most available during the dry season in Amazonia, when water bodies shrink, but some fish make annual migrations in the early rainy season and can be caught in large numbers at that time. Most of the fishes in the cave were small individuals, but there were several examples of individuals, over a 1.5 m long. Game is available year-round.

Settlements

The Old Amazonian tradition Paleoindian subtradition has been excavated only at Caverna da Pedra Pintada near Monte Alegre, Para state. At this site, a roughly 30-cm layer of stratified black soil midden rich in food remains, red iron oxide pigment, stone artifacts, and chipping debris lay under a sterile layer that was superimposed by material from later ceramic cultures. The excavations were placed under a painted ceiling to trace in which layers paint drops fell. The earliest levels of the preceramic deposit had most of the paint drops in them, suggesting that people brought the tradition of rock painting with them. There were 24 formal lithic artifacts and c. 30,000 debris flakes. The artifacts included rare broken projectile points, unifacial limaces (slug-shaped scrapers), a graver, blades, and flake scrapers. The hyaline quartz and chalcedony tools were made by percussion followed by pressure flaking. Some limaces and flake tools were percussion flaked of quartz breccia. Features were limited to broad, poorly defined, shallow hearths. There were no postholes, and the refuse areas associated with the successive occupations were of small extent, less than 10 sq m. The lack of structural remains would fit a settlement pattern of recurrent but relatively brief occupations. The lack of raw material pieces, the rarity of cortical flakes, and the abundance of finishing flakes in the lithic assemblage suggest that people must have visited quarries elsewhere and made preforms to bring to the cave for shaping and finishing. The food remains show that people must have descended from the hills to the adjacent Amazon lakes and floodplains to collect fauna.

Economy

The subsistence of the Old Amazonian tradition appears to be broad-spectrum forest and riverine gathering and hunting. Most of the numerous food remains were cracked and burned nut shells and fruit pits of tropical rainforest trees, whose stable carbon isotope ratio range of $-26o/oo$ to $-37o/oo$ (normalized to wood values) matches those of closed canopy tropical rainforest vegetation much denser than the secondary forest and cattle pasture found in the region today. Also present were numerous carbonized fragmentary bones of small fish and small fauna, such as turtles, lizards, and rodents. Most fishes were small individuals, but several individuals would have been about 1.5 m long. Large land fauna was extremely rare. Only three fragments of larger land fauna were encountered.

Sociopolitical Organization

The small-use areas in the upland caves suggest that people visited in small groups, but floodplain locations could in principle have supported larger groups at lakes and rivers in the dry season, although this is speculation. The lack of discrete hearths and post structures in the site fits the idea of a nomadic settlement pattern. Although some archaeologists have modeled ancient cave painting as an exclusive male activity, the rock art in the Monte Alegre hills has hand prints of all sizes and ages, including babies'. In addition, the fact that the food remains were dominated by fish, shellfish, small animals, juvenile animals, and plant products suggests an importance of women and children in subsistence, because they tend to be responsible for bringing those kinds of foods in, while men tend to carry out the hunting of larger game. Thus, two bodies of independent evidence suggest that the cave was occupied by family groups, not just by men on hunting trips. Perhaps 5–10 people made up the group.

Religion and Expressive Culture

The iconography of the rock art includes images of possible suns, moons, stars, comets, and eclipses, suggesting an interest in and knowledge of astronomy. Human stick figures are common but not as common as animals and not as intricately represented as animals. Humans are, however, often larger than animals. Humans are shown mainly just standing, but there are rare images of women giving birth. There are also images with human stance, hands, and feet, but animal torsos and head. One of these is an insect. Animal images include fish, birds, rabbits, manatee, or dolphin. The large size of many images, c. 1 m in diameter, and the location of painted panels looking out from heights over wide open spaces, suggests that people felt that it was important that the art be visible over large distances, perhaps by spirits in the heavens above.

Suggested Readings

Colinvaux, Paul A., Paulo E. Oliveira, P. E. Moreno, M. C. Miller, and Mark B. Bush (1996). "A Long Pollen Record from Lowland Amazonia: Forest and Cooling in Glacial Times." *Science* 274: 85–88.

Imazio da Silveira, Maura (1994). "Estudo sobre estrategias de subsistencia de cacadores-coletores prehistoricos do sitio Gruta do Gaviao, Carajas, Brazil." M.A. thesis, Department of Archaeology, University of São Paulo.

Magalhaes, Marcos (1994). *Archaeology of Carajas: The Pre-historic Presence of Man in Amazonia*. Rio de Janeiro: Companhia Valle do Rio Doce.

Roosevelt, A. C. (1998). "Amazonian Hunter-gatherers." In *Advances in Historical Ecology*, ed. W. Balee. New York: Columbia University Press, 190–212.

Roosevelt, A. C. (1998). "Paleoindian and Archaic Occupations in the Lower Amazon: A Summary and Comparison." In *Explorations in American Archaeology: Essays in Honor of Wesley R. Hurt*, ed. M. G. Plew Lanham, MD: University Press of America, 165–191.

Roosevelt, A. C. (1999) "Twelve Thousand Years of Human-Environment Interaction in the Amazon floodplain." In *Diversity, Development, and Conservation in Amazonia's Whitewater Floodplains*, eds. C. Paroch, J. M. Ayres, M. Pinedo-Vasquez, and A. Henderson. Advances in Economic Botany 13: 371–392. New York: New York Boranical Garden.

Roosevelt, A. C. (1999) "Ancient Hunter-gatherers of South America." In *Cambridge University Encyclopedia of Hunter-gatherers*, eds. R. Lee and R. Daly, Cambridge. Cambridge University Press, 86–92.

Roosevelt, A. C. (1999) Dating the Rock Art at Monte Alegre, Brazil." In *Dating and the Earliest Known Rock Art*, eds. M. Strecker and P. Bahn. Oxford: Oxbow Books, 35–41.

Roosevelt, A. C. (in press). "Amazonia, A Dynamic Human Habitat." In *Pre-Columbian New World Ecosystems*, ed. D. Lentz. New York: Columbia University Press.

Roosevelt, A. C., Linda Brown, John Douglas, Matthew O'Connell, Ellen Quinn, and Judy Kemp (1997). "Dating a Paleoindian Site in the Amazon in Comparison with Clovis Culture: Technical Comments." *Science* 275: 1950–1952.

Roosevelt, A. C., M. Lima da Costa, C. Lopes Machado, M. Michab, N. Mercier, H. Valladas, J. Feathers, W. Barnett, M. Imazio da Silveira, A. Henderson, J. Sliva, B. Chernoff, D. S. Reese, J. A. Holman, N. Toth, and K. Schick (1996). "Paleoindian Cave Dwellers in the Americas: The Peopling of the Americas." *Science* 272: 373–384.

Roosevelt, A. C., Rupert Housley, Maura Imazio da Silveira, Silvia Maranca, and Richard Johnson (1991). "Eighth Millennium Pottery from Prehistoric Shell Midden in the Brazilian Amazon." *Science* 254: 1621–1624.

ANNA ROOSEVELT
Department of Anthropology
The Field Museum
and
Department of Anthropology
University of Illinois
Chicago, Illinois
United States

Old South American Hunting-Collecting

ABSOLUTE TIME PERIOD: 15,000–13,000?–10,000 B.P.

RELATIVE TIME PERIOD: The first cultural tradition in Andean South America; it precedes the Late Andean Hunting-Collecting tradition.

LOCATION: The Andean mountain chain from Colombia to Chile, the eastern tropical lowlands of Brazil, and the Pampa and Patagonian grasslands of the southern cone.

DIAGNOSTIC MATERIAL ATTRIBUTES: Various kinds of bifacial and unifacial stone tool technologies, features such as hearths and small storage pits, and quarry, camp, and kill sites.

REGIONAL SUBTRADITIONS: Flake Tool, Stemmed Point, and Leaf-Shaped Point.

IMPORTANT SITES: Tequendama, Tibitó, and Suave in Colombia; Taima-Taima in Venezuela; El Inga and Ilaló in Ecuador; Cupisnique Quebrada sites in Peru; Panalauca, Uchumachay, and Telarmachay in Peru; Grande Abrigo da Santana do Riacho, Lapa Dos Bichos, Lapa La Boquete, and Pedra Furada in Brazil; various Tandalia Hill sites in the Argentina Pampa; Fell's Cave, Palli Aike, Mylodon Cave, Cueva del Medio, and Tres Arroyos in southern Patagonia; Monte Verde, Quereo, and Tagua-Tagua in Chile.

CULTURAL SUMMARY

Environment

Climate. The Old South American Hunting-Collecting tradition is associated with the late Pleistocene period. Between 15,000–11,000 B.P., increased aridity and deglaciation occurred, with great vegetation and climatic changes in the high altitudes and high latitudes. The Pacific and Atlantic coastlines were stabilized, and rich resource zones, such as bays and deltas, were formed.

Geology. The geological eras in most regions of South America are comparable to the North American glacial sequence. Most of the southern hemisphere was not glaciated in the late Pleistocene, in spite of significant temperature fluctuations. Therefore, associating sites with worldwide Pleistocene divisions, except on a gross scale, is very difficult. Glaciation occurred only in high altitude and high latitude zones such as the Andean

293

mountains and southern Patagonia. The topographic geology is highly varied, from the rugged Andean mountains in the west to the low tropical forests of Brazil and the arid grasslands of Argentina to the east. Important geological resources were chippable rocks for making stone tools.

Biota. Although climatic conditions were variable in the late Pleistocene, the changes in vegetation that took place seem to have been relatively modest in many areas: a shifting of the boundaries of various types of forests, parklands, and savannas. These shifts would have had a far-reaching effect on the fauna and vegetation and on the foraging behavior of early hunter-gatherer groups, especially in the high Andes and in tropical areas. The continent is characterized by extensive grasslands in Patagonia, tropical and semitropical forests in the Amazon basin, arid grasslands and desert plains along the coast of Peru and Chile, and variable forests and grasslands in the Andes.

Settlements

Settlement System. Sites are mainly campgrounds, quarry stations, and kill localities situated on the high terraces of large rivers, bays, and old glacial lakes. Although the majority of early sites are caves and rock shelters, a few open-air sites are known. During the height of the glacial period, populations might have preferred to live in lowland environments, making only seasonal excursions into the mountains for fauna, such as guanaco and deer. As the sea level rose gradually between 12,000–11,000 B.P., populations augmented their subsistence base by increased access to resources from the Pacific and Atlantic oceans, with a greatly expanded coastline, but there is no direct evidence of such marine adaptations until the end of the Pleistocene period.

Housing. Many rock shelters and caves have so far been discovered. Cave sites in general may have allowed for a larger local group, but most South American caves excavated so far provided only restricted areas and appear to have been the dwellings of small families at best. Thus, the scanty evidence for housing points to temporary shelters and to small foraging groups. Although people still lived in caves, the proportion of open sites increased after 10,000 B.P., and caves began to decline as major places of community activity.

Population, Health, and Disease. As for the health and disease of these people, no reliable human skeletal remains have been found, and little can be said about these aspects of their lives. However, indirect evidence of disease from Monte Verde is available. Several species of medicinal plants have been found at the site, suggesting that they might have been used to treat stomach and pulmonary ailments.

Economy

Subsistence. All of the evidence points to opportunistic exploitation of a wide variety of environmental zones and to an Archaic-like broad-spectrum economy, regardless of the time depth in the late Pleistocene.

Wild Foods. Little is known of the subsistence base except for the faunal component, and it is not wise to assume that all bones found on sites represent animals eaten by the human inhabitants. However, animal bones are the primary evidence for hunting, especially when they bear traces of butchering. The most likely animal food sources include various mastodon, ground sloth, native American horse, camelid, deer, and giant armadillo. Many sites on large rivers and on the coasts were situated to take advantage of fish and marine resources. Sites such as Quebrada Tacahuay and Quebrada Jaguay in southern coastal Peru were located to exploit marine resources. Examples of other wild foods are the thousands of snails recovered from Paiján sites on the coast of Peru; the variety of seeds, nuts, soft leafy plants, tubers, and seaweeds recovered from residential floors at Monte Verde; and the abundant remains of palm nuts and other plant types found at caves in eastern Brazil dating between 11,500–10,000 B.P.

A gradual change in food sources is apparent in archeological deposits dated to about 11,000 B.P. This change consisted of a significant broadening of the subsistence base to include progressively greater amounts of fish, land snails, birds, and plants. The hunting of large game remained a major subsistence activity, but the addition of smaller animals, birds, aquatic creatures, and invertebrates was a precursor of a major change in lifestyle. This broadened diet allowed people to remain in one location longer and led to the development of local traditions of technology. Being in one place for a longer time allowed people to develop nonportable equipment, such as heavy ground-stone tools, elaborate dwellings, and a means of storing food. The transition to a broad base of subsistence resources was crucial to later cultural developments. People who viewed almost all living organisms as potential sources of food and were willing to organize their activities to collect them would have been developing an awareness and organizational system potentially receptive to the collection and eventual domestication of wild plants. Many of the cultural advances made by hunters and gatherers at the end of the Pleistocene became more important and widespread with the succeeding cultures in both the Andean region and the tropical lowlands to the east.

Domestic Foods. The cultigens discovered in early sites in the highlands and on the coast of Peru and Ecuador and dated 9000–7000 B.P. have generally implied an origin elsewhere, because most of the plants are lowland or tropical species. Their adaptation to drier and seasonally cooler, higher altitude climates must therefore reflect an earlier domestication in their original environments. Large, seemingly semi-permanent base camps, limited storage facilities, and food-processing equipment were present by 10,000–9000 B.P. It is in the remains of intensive food collectors and camelid pastoralism that archaeologists find the evidence for the birth of South American village life between 8000–6000 B.P. with all of its technological and organizational implications.

Industrial Arts. The early stone tool industries of South America are classified into traditions based on their size, shape, and methods of manufacture. These traditions are broadly divided into bifacial and unifacial industries. South America contains a wide variety of bifaces, including projectile points, heavier cutting and chopping artifacts, and parallel-sided blades. Unifacial tools often are simpler and involve fewer manufacturing steps than bifaces, but they perform many of the same functions.

Utensils. The primary utensils were chipped- and ground-stone tools, although scant evidence of wood and bone tools also occurs. South America also contains sling stone and grooved bola stone industries, which represent a grinding- and pecking-tool tradition. Direct evidence of other technologies is very sparse, but not completely absent. At Monte Verde and Guitarrero Cave, wooden artifacts and cordage are preserved. Pieces of animal hide, tied reed, and wooden timbers and poles at Monte Verde remain from a long tent structure that housed at least 20 people. Hearths and pits at the site reflect the extensive use of fire and perhaps the need to store food and other items. The important point, however, is that whenever organic remains are preserved, a broad-spectrum economy is always documented.

Ornaments. Very few decorative devices have been found in late Pleistocene sites. The notable exception is a piece of mastodon ivory with etched geometric designs from the Tagua-Tagua site in Chile.

Trade. Large-scale exchange networks are not present in South America. Most stone raw materials are local; only in later times do we see the exchange or direct procurement of exotics, such as obsidian in the Peruvian highlands, and even then from no more than 200 km away. Still, the similarity in the form of fishtail, Ayampitín, highland triangular points and unifacial tools in South America and the styles of rock art across the continent suggest that even if goods did not travel, ideas and cultural styles traversed vast distances.

Division of Labor. In modern-day hunting and gathering groups, the young and middle-aged men do the hunting, whereas the women, children, and elderly collect and prepare other sources of food. In light of this model, the broad-spectrum collecting pattern of early South America may be an indication of more participation by women in the subsistence activities of the community. Many ethnographic communities reveal that it is the women and so-called less mobile members of a community who bring in most of the food, especially when game is unavailable. Because prehistoric women may have collected a wide variety of small animals, invertebrates, and plant foods, they may have been instrumental in effecting the recognition of these resources as edible substances. Such recognition was a change in the information content of the culture, which in turn altered the information flow among members of the society—changes typical of those that contributed to the introduction of agriculture several thousand years later. Thus it may have been women who primarily prompted the reorganization of activities necessary for a food-producing economy.

Differential Access or Control of Resources. Seasonal scheduling of movement was undoubtedly very important to these people. In the temperate forests of eastern Brazil, for example, they learned to exploit a widening spectrum of resources with ever-increasing skill. As people seasonally harvested wild palm nuts, fruits, and other vegetable foods, they continuously hunted. By 11,000 B.P., they employed a local diversity of unifacial and bifacial stone tools. The variety of plant and animal species taken increased continuously as the centuries passed, and there was a multiplication of specialized tools of every sort; technological skill also increased. The rise of cultural diversity in most regions between 11,000–10,500 B.P. points to increased innovation by local peoples and to culture diffusion from elsewhere.

Sociopolitical Organization

Early cultural development required adaptations to new situations, including new social environments created by exploration: it must have depended on the existence of a home territory and a way of keeping contacts among independent groups frequent and stable. With strong group and family ties came another cultural development vital for society's growth: the idea of a home base. At the outset of movement into new landscapes, splintering subgroups of hunters and gatherers would have been isolated from the main group for a time or perhaps permanently. Constant association as a group would not have been possible for people whose foragers ranged far and wide. The solution was a place or home territory probably organized around kinship ties.

Religion and Expressive Culture

Religious Beliefs. Every society has a system of shared beliefs, a cosmology, or worldview that expresses its answers to profound questions. Most worldviews offer a view of the nature of the present world, its origins, and the role and destiny of humans. In many living hunter and gatherer societies, activities related to land and territory involved in hunting are a part of a religious way of life. We can presuppose that people's religious experiences and beliefs in late Pleistocene times resembled those of aboriginal peoples today. This is very difficult to demonstrate archaeologically, although such an experience is certainly plausible as a motivating force for some of the symbolic rock art found in the early caves of the Andes.

Art. South America is rich in rock art. Rock art is difficult to date. Several archaeologists believe that they can assign it a late Pleistocene age based on the presence of pigment spalls in the deeper levels of caves, but these could have migrated down from upper levels and are dated only as they appear stratigraphically. In the early Archaic period, however, caves and rock shelters begin to show a distinctive form of rock art. Many rock shelters have been decorated with single scenes or figures. Animals—camelids, felines, deer, birds, snakes, and capybara—are the most frequent subjects, either alone or in larger groups such as herds or in hunting scenes. The stylized figures are full of life and action. People are sometimes shown with bows and arrows and spears. Other subjects include anthropomorphic figures, heavily stylized human figures, and geometric designs, but these probably date to the late Archaic period.

Suggested Readings

Ardila, G., and G. Politis (1989). "Nuevos datos para un viejo problema: Investigación y discusión en torno del poblamiento de América del Sur." *Revista del Museo del Oro* 23: 3–45.

Bryan, A. L. (1973). "Paleoenvironments and Cultural Diversity in Late Pleistocene South America." *Quaternary* 3: 237–256.

Bryan, A. L. (1991). "The Fluted Point Tradition in the Americas—One of Several Adaptations to Late Pleistocene Environments." In *Clovis: Origins and Adaptations*, ed. R. Bonnischen and K. Turnmire. Corvallis: Center for the Study of the First Americans, 15–33.

Cann, R. L. (1994). "MtDNA and Native Americans: A Southern Perspective." In *American Journal of Human Genetics* 55: 256–258.

Clapperton, M. (1993). *Quaternary Geology and Geomorphology of South America*. Amsterdam: Elsevier.

Dillehay, T. D. (1997). *Monte Verde: A Late Pleistocene Settlement in Chile*, vol. 2: *The Archaeological Context*. Washington D.C.: Smithsonian Institution Press.

Dillehay, T. D. (2000). *The Settlement of the Americas: A New Prehistory*. New York: Basic Books.

Dillehay, T. D., G. Ardila, G. Politis, and M. C. Beltrão (1992). "Earliest Hunters and Gatherers of South America." *Journal of World Prehistory* 6: 145–204.

Fagan, B. (1989). *The Great Journey: The Peopling of Ancient America*. New York: Thames and Hudson.

Hyslop, J. ed. (1988). *Travels and Archaeology in South Chile*. Ames: University of Iowa Press.

Meltzer, D. (1993). *Search for the First Americans*. New York: St. Remy Press.

Meltzer, D. (1997). "Monte Verde and the Pleistocene Peopling of the Americas." *Science* 276: 754–755.

Nichols, J. (1995). *Linguistic Diversity and the Peopling of the Americas*. Berkeley: University of California Press.

Willey, G. (1971). *An Introduction to American Archaeology, vol. 2: South America*. Englewood Cliffs, NJ: Prentice-Hall.

SUBTRADITIONS

Flake Tool

TIME PERIOD: 15,000–10,000 B.P.

LOCATION: The eastern tropical lowlands from Brazil to the north and central Andes. This subtradition is not present in the Pampa and Patagonia grasslands of Argentina and Chile.

DIAGNOSTIC MATERIAL ATTRIBUTES: Edge-trimmed unifacial stone tools, including scrapers, wedges, spoke shaves, drills, burins, and other tools. Small grinding-stone slabs and manos are occasionally present. Often associated with a plant-collecting economy in vegetated areas (Bryan 1986; Dillehay 2000; Richardson 1978; Willey 1971).

CULTURAL SUMMARY

Environment

The climate occupied by the Flake Tool inhabitants varied from the high Andes of the Sabana de Bogotá in Colombia where cold conditions existed to the arid grassland semidesert coast of Peru and to the semitropical to tropical forest, parklands, and savannas of eastern Brazil (Van der Hammen 1974). The tropical and deciduous forests of Brazil contained a wide variety of plant and animal food. The Andean mountains and desert Pacific coasts provided a more limited array of waterfowl, fish, shellfish, and small to large game animals.

Settlements

Communities of the Flake Tool subtradition were residing in caves and rock shelters situated in proximity to lakes, rivers, deltas, and bays, and other wetlands to take advantage of aquatic resources as well as access to a multitude of other environments (Ardila and Politis 1989; Dillehay et al. 1992).

Economy

These people were generalized hunters and collectors exploiting riverine and marshland areas. The primary utensils were scrapers, spoke shaves, burins, slugs, wedges, and drills. Most tools are manufactured from local quartzites, quartzes, basalts, and cherts. Bifacial implements are rare occurrences. The presence of grinding-stone slabs and small manos suggests widespread manipulation of wild plants from various ecological zones.

Sociopolitical Organization

A band-level organization is frequently hypothesized for late Pleistocene groups in general, although the South American data show considerable complexity. However, a few South American sites imply that they were created by large aggregates of people. Although the extensive open-air sites of Monte Verde in Chile and El Inga in Ecuador are possible exceptions, it remains to be seen whether they represent multiple occupations or synchronous gatherings. The scanty evidence points to minimal bands, even family groups, as the social units that occupied most of the sites.

References

Ardila G., and G. Politis (1989). "Nuevos datos para un viejo problema: Investigación y discusión en torno del poblamiento de América del Sur." *Revista del Museo del Oro* 23: 3–45.

Bryan, L. (1986). "Paleoamerican Prehistory as Seen from South America." In *New Evidence for the Pleistocene Peopling of the Americas*, ed. A. L. Bryan. Orono: Center for the Study of Early Man, University of Maine, 1–14.

Dillehay, T. D. (2000). *The Settlement of the Americas: A New Prehistory*. New York: Basic Books.

Dillehay, T. D., G. Ardila, G. Politis, and M. C. Beltrão (1992). "Earliest Hunters and Gatherers of South America." *Journal of World Prehistory* 6: 145–204.

Richardson, J. B., III, (1978). "Early Man on the Peruvian North Coast, Early Maritime Exploitation and the Pleistocene and Holocene Environment." In *Early Man in America from a Circum-Pacific Perspective*, ed. A. L. Bryan. Edmonton: Department of Anthropology, University of Alberta.

Van der Hammen, T. (1974). "The Pleistocene Changes of Vegetation and Climate in Tropical South America." *Journal of Biogeography* 1: 3–26.

Willey, G. (1971). *An Introduction to American Archaeology, vol. 2: South America*. Englewood Cliffs, NJ: Prentice-Hall.

Leaf-Shaped Projectile Point

TIME PERIOD: 13,000–12,000–9500 B.P.

LOCATION: Andean region from western Venezuela and Colombia to southern Chile.

DIAGNOSTIC MATERIAL ATTRIBUTES: Bipointed willowleaf- and laurel-leaf-shaped projectile points associated with a wide array of drills, scrapers, wedges, and other stone tools.

CULTURAL SUMMARY

Environment

This subtradition is affiliated with the onset of deglaciation and the end of the Pleistocene period. This subtradition was spread across the widest variety possible of climates in South America, from the high tundra grasslands of the Andes to the Pacific desert coast to the tropical forest along the western and eastern slopes of portions of Andes. Paleocamelid, jaguar, deer, native American horse were exploited as well as plants in wetlands.

Settlements

Most sites are caves and rock shelters located in the high puna and altiplano environments of the Andes stretching from northern Ecuador to southern Chile. The bipointed leaf-shaped points at Taima-Taima in Venezuela and at Monte Verde in Chile occur at open-air sites in low altitude, forested environments.

Economy

Most sites reflect game hunting, but plant exploitation was practiced as well. The projectile points were manufactured from locally available and high-quality imported cherts and quartzites using standard flaking techniques. Bone and shell tools are often found in sites (e.g., Lavalleé et al. 1995; Lynch 1980, 1983; Rick 1980; Willey 1971). The Monte Verde site represents a generalized hunter and gatherer economy (Dillehay 1997).

Sociopolitical Organization

Groups were probably organized in small to large bands of families that moved from local environment to local environment depending on the availability of resources. The inhabitants of Monte Verde probably lived year-round at the site as suggested by plants that mature during all seasons of the year.

References

Dillehay, T. D. (1997). *Monte Verde: A Late Pleistocene Settlement in Chile, vol. 2: The Archaeological Context.* Washington D.C.: Smithsonian Institution Press.

Lavalleé, M. Julien, J. Wheeler, and C. Karlin (1995). *Telarmachay: Cazadores y Pastores de los Andes.* Lima: Instituto Francés de Estudios Andinos.

Lynch, T. F. (1983). "The Paleo-Indians." In *Ancient South Americans,* ed. J. D. Jennings. New York: W. H. Freeman, 87–137.

Lynch, T. F. (1980). *Guitarrero Cave: Early Man in the Andes.* New York: Academic Press.

Rick, J. W. (1980). *Prehistoric Hunters of the High Andes.* New York: Academic Press.

Willey, G. (1971). *An Introduction to American Archaeology, vol. 2: South America.* Englewood Cliffs, NJ: Prentice-Hall.

Stemmed Projectile Point

TIME PERIOD: 11,000–10,000 B.P.

LOCATION: The fishtail or Magallanes stemmed point is the only horizon-like style in late Pleistocene South America. It is found throughout the Andean region from Colombia to Tierra del Fuego and in Panama, Argentina, and parts of southern Brazil. Other stemmed types are found regionally, such as the Paiján point in highland Ecuador and coastal Peru, the tanged point of southern Brazil and Uruguay, the Restrepo point of highland Colombia, and a wide variety of weakly shouldered contracting stem types scattered across the continent.

DIAGNOSTIC MATERIAL ATTRIBUTES: Weakly shouldered projectile points with waisted stems and possible fluting on the fishtail points and weakly shouldered and long or short contracting stems on other styles found in the highlands and puna grasslands of the central Andes (Bird 1938; Lynch 1983; Mayer-Oakes 1986; Politis 1991). Both types are associated with a wide variety of burins, scrapers, and at times slugs. Fishtail points are often associated with the bone remains of extinct animals such as giant ground sloth, mastodons, and paleocamelids.

CULTURAL SUMMARY

Environment

The climate during the 11,000–10,000 B.P. period was generally arid and warm. Most stemmed point sites are located in open grasslands in both high and low altitude zones and associated with rock shelters and caves. The few exceptions, such as the Tagua-Tagua site in central Chile, is located next to an old pluvial lake (Montane 1976; Núñez et al. 1994). A few localities are situated in semiforested to forested areas. More may exist but because of poor archaeological visibility in forests, especially the Amazon basin, sites are difficult to locate.

Settlements

Most sites are caves and rock shelters located in proximity to water sources and with good vistas overlooking waterholes and grassy plains where large game aggregated. Quarry and kill sites are also typical of this subtradition. These localities are generally located in proximity to the habitation sites. In the high-altitude grasslands of Peru, Chile, and Argentina, most sites are caves and rock shelters that have a commanding view of open plains and lagoons below where guanacos and other wild game reside.

Economy

The evidence suggests that most stemmed point cultures were hunters, although the record may be skewed by preservation of bones. Fishtail points are usually associated with mastodon, giant ground sloth, and paleocamelid sites. Chauchat (1975) believes that the Paiján culture of the north desert coast of Peru is primarily associated with the exploitation of fish and other maritime resources. The subsistence pattern of other stemmed cultures is not well known because of poor preservation of organic remains. The presence of grinding stones in several sites suggests that these people also gathered wild plants. In the high grassy plains of the central Andes and of the southern extremes of the continent, guanaco, rhea (the South American ostrich and native horse were hunted regularly, with plant species and probably shellfish and fish being supplementary foods.

Sociopolitical Organization

These people were probably living in small bands and involved in seasonal transhumance between high and low elevated environmental zones in the Andes and perhaps elsewhere.

Religion and Expressive Culture

The few human burials of this time period reveal no discernible mortuary pattern or ornaments buried with the bodies. The only expressive culture is a fragment of a mastodon tusk that has etched geometric designs from the site of Tagua-Tagua in Chile, which dates between 11,200 and 10,000 years ago.

References

Bird, J. (1938). "Antiquity and Migrations of the Early Inhabitants of Patagonia." *Geographical Review* 1, 6: 250–275.

Chauchat. (1975). "The Paijan Complex, Pampa de Cupisnique, Perú." *Nawpa Pacha* 17: 143–146.

Lynch, T. F. (1983). "The Paleo-Indians." In *Ancient South Americans*, ed. J. D. Jennings. New York: W. H. Freeman, 87–137.

Mayer-Oakes, W. J. (1986). "El Inga: A Paleo-Indian Site in the Sierra of Northern Ecuador." *Transactions of the American Philosophical Society D*, 76, 4: 1–663.

Montane, J. (1976). "El Paleoindio en Chile." In *Actas del 41o. Congreso Internacional de Americanistas, Tomo III*, México City: 492–503.

Núñez, L. et al., (1994). "Cuenca de Tagua-Tagua en Chile: El Ambiente del Pleistoceno y ocupaciones humanas." *Revista Chilena de Historia Natural* 67, 4: 503–519.

Politis, G. (1991). "Fishtail Projectile Points in the Southern Cone of South America." In *Clovis: Origins and Adaptations*, eds. R. Bonnischen and K. Turnmire. Corvallis: Center for the Study of the First Americans.

SITES

Itaparita Phase Sites in Eastern Brazil

TIME PERIOD: c. 11,500–10,000 B.P.

LOCATION: Eastern and Central Brazil.

DESCRIPTIVE SUMMARY

Local Environment

Arid to tropical environments in low hilly country.

Physical Features

Grande Abrigo da Santana do Riacho, Lapa dos Bichos, and Lapa do Boquete in the state of Minas Gerais are rock shelters with good preservation and well-stratified cultural deposits (Prous 1996; Schmitz 1987).

Cultural Aspects

These sites are primarily unifacial sites, although a few rare projectile points are found at Grande Abrigo da Santana do Riacho. Lapa do Boquete has produced stone artifacts in the lower levels typical of the Paranaiba phase of the Goias state, which are dated between 12,070–9000 B.P. Use-wear studies of the edges of the tools suggest they were used to work plants and wood. Flaked unifaces and cores made of chert, quartzite, and limestone were abundant. Also found were small bifacial thinning flakes and the tip of a projectile point and thick elongated, plano-convex tools or limaces, many retouched or utilized flakes, charred palm nuts, and several nutcrackers for breaking open palm nuts or seeds. A broad-spectrum foraging economy associated with deer and small game (armadillo, rodent, fish, lizard) is represented at Lapa do Boquete. The Grande Abrigo da Santana do Riacho is dated between 9460–7900 B.P. and is associated with human skeletons. A deeper level is dated at 11,960 B.P. and is associated with a hearth and exotic flakes of rock crystal, all in stratigraphic and chronological order. Several flakes, hearths, and pigment fragments were also recovered in the deeper levels of the rock shelter. The context of the deeper level has not been studied extensively enough to confirm the presence of humans around 12,000 B.P. At Lapa Vermelha IV, archeologists found a simple flake and core tool industry associated with ground sloth bone dated between 10,200–9580 B.P. Also reported is a possible human occupation dated between 25,000–15,300 B.P. and associated with quartz cores and flakes and unifacial scrapers in the deepest level. Exotic quartz flakes were later excavated from the deeper levels of the site and dated between 15,300–11,680 B.P. A human skeleton was found in a stratum dating between 11,960–10,200 B.P.

References

Schmitz, P. I. (1987). "Prehistoric Hunters and Gatherers of Brazil." *Journal of World Prehistory* 1 1: 126.

Prous, (1996). "L'Archéologie au Brésil: 300 siècles d'occupation humaine." *L'Anthropologie* 90: 257–306.

Monte Verde

TIME PERIOD: Monte Verde is characterized by two layers. Monte Verde II dated around 12,500 years ago, and Monte Verde I, a possibly older culture, dated around 33,000 years ago.

LOCATION: Site is located on a small tributary of the Maullin river in southern Chile.

DESCRIPTIVE SUMMARY

The Monte Verde II site is an extremely well-preserved domestic locality defined by the remains of a long tentlike structure associated with impressions of human footprints, hearths, clusters of animal and plant foods, and a wide variety of stone, bone, and wood tools.

Local Environment

The paleoecological evidence for the Monte Verde I and II periods suggests warming trends characterized by colonizing beech forests and moors.

Physical Features

Monte Verde II is an open-air settlement on the banks of a small freshwater creek, surrounded by sandy knolls and by a cool, damp forest that has existed there since late Pleistocene times. A bog later developed in the creek basin to bury and preserve the abandoned settlement under a layer of peat. At the site, a community of perhaps 20 to 30 people built a 20-m long tentlike structure made of wood and animal hides and a smaller hut nearby (Dillehay 1989, 1997).

Cultural Aspects

The frame of the long tent structure was constructed of logs and planks anchored by stakes, and the walls were of poles covered with animal hides. Several pieces of cordage and string made of junco reed were wrapped around wooden posts and around wooden stakes recovered among the architectural remains. Inside the tent were individual living spaces divided by planks and poles. On the floors of each living space were brazier pits lined with clay, stone tools, and the remains of edible seeds, nuts, and berries. Outside the tent were two large communal hearths, a store of firewood, wooden mortars with their grinding stones, and even three human footprints in the clay near a large hearth. All these remains indicate a wide range of domestic tasks, primarily food preparation and consumption, tool production and maintenance, and the construction of shelters. In the second structure, wishbone-shaped in ground plan and made of wooden uprights set into a foundation of sand and gravel hardened with animal fat, mastodon carcasses had been butchered, hides prepared, tools manufactured, and possibly healing carried out with the aid of medicinal plants. These combined activities suggest a public nonresidential area instead of the living area associated with the long tent.

The remains of a wide variety of edible plants, along with mastodon, paleo-llama, small animals, and freshwater mollusks were recovered from the hearths, living floors, and small pits. Aquatic plants from the freshwater marshes, bogs, and lagoons of the floodplain and from brackish marshes of the river delta provided the greatest variety and, along with meat, the bulk of the diet. Most of these ecological zones are located far away along the Pacific shoreline and in the Andean mountains. The presence of salt, beach-rolled pebbles used as tools, and bitumen at the site also shows that coastal habitats provided important nonfood items to the Monte Verde II economy. This means that the Monte Verdeans either regularly traveled to distant environments or they were part of a web of social and exchange relationships. Many of the artifacts excavated at Monte Verde II are of wood, including possible digging sticks, mortars, fragments of two lances, stakes, and poles used to lay out the architectural spaces. Bone artifacts consist of a baton for striking flakes off stones, gouges made of mastodon tusks, and digging and prying tools.

Three different stone tool technologies exist at the site. Some stones were bifaces (projectile points and knives) made by percussion. Others were "bola" or sling stones formed by pecking or grinding, with results similar to bolas and grinding stones found at other early sites in South America. The third type of stone tool is fractured, edge-trimmed pebbles with one or more sharp edges, which the Monte Verdeans found on distant beaches and in nearby creek beds. Some of these latter artifacts show minimal modification by humans prior to use. Sophisticated knowledge and a division of labor were probably required to use the wide range of resources. This is suggested by the separation of the residential from nonresidential areas and by the association of distinct activity areas and living spaces with different tool types and food remains. The discrete living structures, features, and concentrations of specific materials suggest that the occupation was continuous and that portions of the site were used more intensively than others. Analysis of the stone tools, bone, plant, and other artifact collections suggests a mixed hunting and gathering economy focused on many different ecological zones.

In the deepest levels of Monte Verde, separated from the later settlement by over 1.2 m of sediment and buried in a different area of the site, there is a possible earlier occupation, Monte Verde I, with 26 unifacial and battered stone tools and three burned clay features. The burned features were possibly made by humans. Of the 26 fractured stones, 7 of them were clearly flaked by humans. The archeological data from this deeper level remain inconclusive.

References

Dillehay, T. D. (1989). *Monte Verde: A Late Pleistocene Settlement in Chile*, vol. 1: *Paleoenvironmental and Site Context*. Washington D.C.: Smithsonian Institution Press.

Dillehay, T. D. (1997). *Monte Verde: A Late Pleistocene Settlement in Chile*, vol. 2: *The Archaeological Context*. Washington D.C.: Smithsonian Institution Press.

Patagonian Complex

TIME PERIOD: 11,000–10,000 B.P.

LOCATION: Southern regions of Chile and Argentina.

DESCRIPTIVE SUMMARY

Local Environment

Various types of arid grasslands and adjacent mountains.

Physical Features

Sites are caves and rock shelters overlooking grasslands and pluvial lakes. They contain early remains of extinct animals associated with fishtail points and unifacial tools (Bird 1938: Borrero 1988; Cardich and Miotti 1983; Hyslop 1988; Massone et al. 1997; Miotti and Caltaneo 1997; Nami 1987).

Cultural Aspects

At Fell's Cave, underlying a layer of roof fall, were fishtail points, associated with the bones of horse, giant ground sloth, and camel. Radiocarbon dates on charcoal from the deepest levels were about 11,000 and 10,720 B.P. The Fell's Cave industry has a large number of small flakes, small scrapers, gravers, and notched pieces. Local quartzite was unsuitable for making such small delicate tools, and finer grain materials were carefully sought and collected. The Fell's Cave people hunted guanaco more than other game. Plant food was probably collected but either not preserved or not found. At Tres Arroyos Cave, the human sequence extends back to between 10,280 and possibly 11,880 B.P. The deepest level yielded dates on charcoal from four human hearths. The oldest date was 12,400 B.P., but its context is questionable. Cueva del Medio site is in the same area. The deepest levels yielded two complete fishtail points, numerous other stone tools, and the abundant bone remains of the American horse as well as evidence of ground sloth, deer, feline, canid, and guanaco. Associated with these remains was a hearth. Two dates on charcoal from the hearth were processed at 12,390 and 10,550 B.P.

References

Bird, J. (1938). "Antiquity and Migrations of the Early Inhabitants of Patagonia." *Geographical Review* 1, 6: 250–275.

Borrero, L. A. (1988). "Problemas con la definición arqueológica de sistemas adaptativos." In *Arqueología de las Américas, 45o. Congreso Internacional de Americanistas*. Bogotà: Fondo de Promoción de la Cultura, Banco Popular, 247–262.

Cardich, and L. Miotti, (1983). "Recursos Faunísticos en la Economía de los Cazadores-Recolectores de Los Toldos (Provincia de Santa Cruz, Argentina)." *Relaciones de la Sociedad Argentina de Antropología* 15: 145–157.

Hyslop, J. ed. (1988). *Travels and Archaeology in South Chile*. Ames: University of Iowa Press.

Massone, M. et al., (1997). "Los Cazadores Tempranos y sus Fogatas: Una Nueva Historia para la Cueva de Tres Arroyos 1, Tierra del Fuego." *Boletín de la Sociedad Chilena de Arqueología* 26: 11–18.

Miotti, L., and R. Cattaneo (1997). "Bifacial/Unifacial Technology c. 13.000 Years Ago in Southern Patagonia." *Current Research in the Pleistocene* 14: 60–61.

Nami, H. (1987). "Cueva del Medio: A Significant Paleoindian Site in Southern South America." *Current Research in the Pleistocene* 4: 157–159.

Tagua-Tagua

TIME PERIOD: Two localities at the site contain cultural materials and are known to have been mastodon kill and butchering sites: TT-1 and TT-2. The first dates between 11,400 and 11,000 B.P. The second is dated between 10,190 and 9700 B.P.

LOCATION: Tagua-Tagua is located at the edge of an old lake in the central valley of chile, some 120 km south of Santiago (Montane 1976; Núñez et al. 1994).

DESCRIPTIVE SUMMARY

Local Environment

The climate at the time of site use was dry and hot.

Physical Features

Both localities at Tagua-Tagua are represented by several major concentrations of stone tools and other artifacts occurring in buried areas that formerly bordered a small lake. The places most favored for the animal kills were either on beaches of low promontories that jutted out into the lake or on patches of sand that generally occurred in the channels of seasonal streams draining into the lake. Although the campsites of the hunters associated with these two episodes were not found in the vicinity of the site, it is suspected that they are located nearby, probably situated on a low hill or knoll within a few hundred meters or a few kilometers of the lake where it could have been monitored for animal activity.

Cultural Aspects

In 1969, when the site was first excavated, a cultural occupation layer buried approximately 2.5 m below the present-day surface yielded about 50 stone and bone artifacts in association with the remains of horse, deer, both a juvenile and an adult mastodon, and plentiful bones of birds, frogs, fish, and other small animals. It was first thought that the stone tool collection was unifacial because the excavators recovered well-made scrapers and flake tools made of basalt, chalcedony, and obsidian. Several possible tools are made of flaked mastodon tusk and horse bones. Subsequent excava-tions recovered an abundance of mastodon bones and stone artifacts, including fishtail projectile points and a tusk fragment with etched geometric designs. The tusk fragment represents the earliest "art work" discovered in South America. Judging from the bone evidence at both localities, portions of the butchered animals were carried to nearby campsites. Bones remaining in the site are mainly of the pelvises, skull, feet, and vertebrae sections of the body. Those probably taken to distant campsites are ribs, vertebrae, femur, tusks, and other long bones. At each Tagua-Tagua locality, the skeletons are disarranged as if they had been tugged and hacked apart. Lying among the bones are discarded choppers and other stone tools, including points, that apparently did the butchering. Butchering also is suggested by a few possible cut marks on bones, but many marks can also be attributed to trampling scars produced by animals watering at the hole when the bones were evidently exposed on the surface.

References

Montane, J. (1976). "El Paleoindio en Chile." In *Actas del 41o. Congreso Internacional de Americanistas. Tomo III*. México City: 492–503.

Núñez, L. et al., (1994). "Cuenca de Tagua-Tagua en Chile: El Ambiente del Pleistoceno y ocupaciones humanas." *Revista Chilena de Historia Natural* 67, 4: 503–519.

Tequendama

TIME PERIOD: Charcoal from two hearths in the deepest levels were dated between 12,500 and 10,100 B.P.

LOCATION: Tequendama is a rock shelter located at the edge of a savanna, at 2570 m above sea level, in a valley that links the Magdelena river and the highlands of Bogotá, Colombia.

DESCRIPTIVE SUMMARY

Local Environment

Beginning around 12,500 B.P., the climate in the site area began to resemble that of today, becoming much wetter and more temperate. By 12,000 B.P., the area was forested. At 11,000–10,000 B.P., as the climate grew colder again, the forest became more open and thus more favorable for deer, other game, and people.

During this wet period, Tequendama was located in an open woodland and mountainous terrain.

Physical Features

The shelter is a large sandstone boulder having about 30 sq m of floor space and early deposits, and it contains an occupational deposit varying in depth from 1.5 to over 3 m.

Cultural Aspects

The early deposits have been divided into two major stone tool industries spanning the late Pleistocene and early Holocene periods. The earliest of the stone industries in the deeper Zone I indicates that it was a crude flake industry, called Tequendamiense, which was followed by a culture of the Abriense industry. These remains are characterized by carefully prepared, mainly pressure flaked, "edge-trimmed" unifacial tools with fine retouch along the used edges. The inhabitants of the site imported stones of lidite, basalt, quartzite, and diorite, found in the upper reaches of the nearby Magdelena valley. Although few in number, the unifaces are dominated by convex flake scrapers thought to have been used to work plants and wood. Also among these tools are flaked cobbles of quartzite, limestone, or chert that could have been used for battering and chopping and simple tools made of flakes that might have been used for cutting various foods. Typically in some early sites, a few bifaces are present, and these are found in the Tequendamiense levels. The most noteworthy pieces are a possibly reworked point fragment and two crudely shaped bifacial blades. Associated with the stone tools were the bone remains primarily of deer and secondarily of mouse, rabbit, armadillo, kinkajou, and guinea pig. All of these remains were concentrated in small workshop areas and around two hearths. In addition to edge-trimmed tools, the lowest levels contained battered cobble stones, sling stones, and other flake tools. The deposits in the next or younger level, Zone II containing the Abriense industry, extend from the terminal Pleistocene to the historic period, with the earliest dates centered between 10,000–8500 B.P. This zone contains only percussion flaked tools. No formal unifacial or bifacial tools were recovered from this zone. Instead, a flake struck from locally available pebbles or chunks of raw material and with small flakes removed from the edges to produce sharp usable edges characterizes the tools . The edge-trimmed tools of the Abriense tradition are also thought to reflect woodworking and processing of vegetal matter (Correal and Van der Hammen 1977).

Reference

Correal Urrego, G., and T. Van der Hammen (1997). *Investigaciones arqueológicas en los abrigos rocosos de Tequendama*. Bogotá: Biblioteca del Banco Popular, Premios de Arqueología, 1.

TOM DILLEHAY
Department of Anthropology
University of Kentucky
Lexington, Kentucky
United States

Sambaqui

ABSOLUTE TIME PERIOD: 7000–650 B.P.

RELATIVE TIME PERIOD: Overlaps with the Early East Brasilian Uplands and Late East Brasilian Uplands traditions in coastal areas, precedes the historic period.

LOCATION: The entire length of the Brazilian coastal plain south of the mouth of the Amazon river.

DIAGNOSTIC MATERIAL ATTRIBUTES: The major diagnostic trait is the presence of *sambaquis* or shell mounds. These mounds consist of mollusk shell mixed with windblown and water-born deposits. Some mounds are refuse mounds, and other served as platforms for habitation structures. Burials may occur in both types of mounds. Also diagnostic are bone and shell fishhooks and an economy based on mollusks and wild nuts and fruits.

REGIONAL SUBTRADITIONS: Itarare (Atlantic Coast Village), Nitoroi (Refuse Mound), Paranagua (Platform Mound), Brazilian Simple Ceramics.

IMPORTANT SITES: Pantano do Sul, Praia da Tapera, Sambaqui da Caieira, Sambaqui de Camboinhas, Sambaqui da Carnica, Sambaqui at Forte Marechal Luz, Sambaqui da Pedra Oca, Sambaqui da Piçaguera, Sambaquis de Ponta das Almas, Sambaqui do Rio Sao Joao.

CULTURAL SUMMARY

Environment

The climate along the Brazilian coast is subtropical and humid, with rainfall throughout most of the year. The coast itself is rocky with Quartenary alluvial and marine deposits. There is often a series of dunes paralleling the water, which were formed by oscillating levels of the ocean during the Holocene. Mangrove swamps, lagoon forests, and dune forests grew along the coast, while tropical rainforests grew farther inland. There were many palm trees with edible nuts and fruits. Many of the other trees in these forests were great value also for nuts, fruits, material for baskets, firewood, making bows and arrows and canoes, and fiber for textiles and fishnets and medicine. The mollusks of various kinds, including snails, oysters, and mussels, were plentiful. Common fauna on the coast and adjacent waters included fish of various types, peccarys, tapir, deer, jaguar, racoon, capybara, *paca*, agouti, whale, turtle, cayman, and dolphin.

Settlements

Postholes for house walls have been found in some of the *sambaquis*. Houses were circular, roughly 5–6 m in diameter, and had a compacted and depressed floor. Hearths were located within the houses and were

304

composed of layers of ash and charcoal mixed with granite and quartz debris. Villages may have had up to 30 or 40 houses. Associated with houses were cemeteries, usually located toward the ocean.

Economy

The economy of the Sambaqui peoples was based on collecting marine resources, fishing, and hunting animals in the inland tropical rainforests. Projectiles armed with bone points were used to hunt anteater, capybara, deer, peccary, marmoset, *paca*, and armadillo. Nets were used for fishing. To collect mollusks, pebbles and choppers were used to free them from the tree roots and rocks and to break them open. Wild fruits and nuts formed a secondary source of food.

Tools manufactured by the Sambaqui peoples included pitted hammer stones for breaking open nuts and perhaps shellfish, flat and semipolished axes, net weights, and hook weights. Flaked-stone tools included burins, denticulates, knives, drills, flake axes, retouched flakes, projectile points, scrapers, and utilized pebbles. The projectile points had a rough triangular shape with a straight or rounded base. Some specimens were retouched on only one face and others on both faces. There was also a considerable bone industry. Bone artifacts included simple and double ended projectile points, fishhooks of catfish spine, beads made of perforated teeth of sharks and fish bones.

Sociopolitical Organization

The scant available evidence suggests that extended families or family groups formed the basis of Sambaqui social and political organization. Sambaqui society was egalitarian, and social control was based on informal mechanisms.

Religion and Expressive Culture

One outstanding artistic achievement of the Sambaqui peoples was the polished stone artifacts known as zooliths. These artifacts had in their center a bowl-shaped depression while the overall shape was that of a cross, fish, or a wild animal.

Suggested Readings

Bruhns, Karen (1994). *Ancient South America*. Cambridge: Cambridge University Press.
Hurt, Wesley (1998). *Explorations in American Archaeology: Essays in Honor of Wesley R. Hurt*. Lanham, Md.: University Press of America.
Menghin, O. F. A. (1962). "Los Sambaquis de la Costa Atlantica del Brasil Meridional." *Amerindia* 1: 53–81.
Willey, Gordon R. (1971). *An Introduction to American Archaeology, vol. 2: South America*. Engelwood Cliffs, NJ: Prentice Hall.

SUBTRADITIONS

Itarare (Atlantic Coast Village)

TIME PERIOD: 1200–600 B.P.

LOCATION: Atlantic coast of Brazil, primarily in Santa Catarina.

DIAGNOSTIC MATERIAL ATTRIBUTES: The lack of raised *sambaquis* and the presence of large village sites are key diagnostic features. Both flakes and cores were used for the lithics. Core tools included choppers, anvil stones, axes, grooved net weights, scrapers, wedges, pitted hammer stones (*quebracocos*), and pestles. There were also quartz prisms, some with grooves. Projectile points were made from a vertically cut section of a mammal or bird long bone. These projectile points are commonly barbed. Beads were made of shells or animal teeth. Both simple and more complex Tupiguarani ceramics were made.

CULTURAL SUMMARY

Environment

Coastal areas are the same as those described for the other subtraditions. Santa Catarina island itself is humid in summer and drier in the winter. The winters are relatively cold, accompanied by frosts in the interior of the island. In the summer, the temperatures oscillates between 18–31° C, and the annual precipitation is about 2000 mm. The island is separated from the continent by three straits that form two bays. This island is surrounded by extensive sandy beaches, alternating with spits, meanders, dykes, and rocky points. In the interior are two groups of mountains separated by a sandy sedimentary plain. The vegetation on interior is the tropical rainforest; on the coast the vegetation varies from mangrove swamp, sandy coast, dunes, shoals, and reefs. The shoals have many varieties of edible fruits such as *pitanga* and *pitagoa*. Animal bones encounted in the sites include anteater, whale, porpoise, coati, peccary, capybara, seal, jaguar, armadillo, *paca*, and deer, lizards, turtles. There were also many different types of fish and shellfish.

Settlements

Although sites of the Itarare subtradition are located on the Brazilian coast and contain a thin layer, no more than 50 cm, of shellfish shell, they should not be considered as *sambaquis*. The archaeological material in a village site does not exceed 100 cm in thickness. They are primarily villages. Evidence of houses is indicated by the postholes of walls. Hearths are present within the houses and are composed of ash, charcoal, granite, and quartz. Villages may have as much as 37 houses (Rohr 1990: 186–188). The circular-walled houses may have a diameter of as much as 5.8 m. Associated with houses were cemeteries, usually located toward the ocean. Sites of this tradition contained a great variety of artifacts made of many different types of material and manufactured with varied techniques.

Economy

The Itarare peoples subsisted on the various wild resources of the areas surrounding the sites. A basic economic activity was the hunting of terrestrial animals that lived in the tropical rainforests. Projectiles armed with bone points were used to hunt anteater, capybara, deer, peccary, marmoset, *paca*, and armadillo. Nets were used for fishing. To collect mollusks, pebbles and choppers could be used to free them from the tree roots and rocks. Wild fruits and nuts formed a secondary source of food.

Rohr (1990: 53–55) describes four types of Itarare ceramics, based on color: red, dull red, brown, and black. All were sand tempered. Surfaces were polished or smoothed. Surface is usually undecorated, but there are rare examples of pinched and punctated ware. There was a great variety of vessel shapes, some being very shallow bowls, others of intermediate depth, still others being deep bowls. There was also a great variety of rim shapes from those with thin to thickened lips (Rohr 1990: figs. 1–7).

Tools used by the Itararé peoples indicate that they were primarily hunters and gatherers. Axes may have been used for clearing horticultural fields, but they were certainly used for gathering firewood, making dugout canoes, and gathering shellfish. They also had smoothing stones for making stone, bone, and shell tools. Pestles were used for preparation of vegetable foods or pulverizing minerals. Bone artifacts most common were projectile points and net weights used for fishing. Other bone and stone artifacts were scrapers of several types. For self-decoration, beads were made of animal teeth and perforated shells and bone.

Religion and Expressive Culture

Many human skeletons were buried with useful items, such as lithic tools, polished axes, pitted hammer stones, and projectile points, indicating a belief in afterlife of the deceased person.

References

Rohr, Joao Alfredo (1990). *Exvaço Arqueológicas do PE: Joao Alfredo Rohr, S.J., O sitio Arqueológico da Praira da Tapera: Um Assentamento Itararé e Tupiguarani, in Pesquisas*. Sao Leopoldo, Rio Grande do Sul: Antropologia, no. 45, Instituto Anchietano de Pesquisas.

Nitoroi (Refuse Mound)

TIME PERIOD: c. 8000–850 B.P.

LOCATION: Coastal plains from north of Rio de Janeriro southward to Santa Catarina.

DIAGNOSTIC MATERIAL ATTRIBUTES: The major trait is that the *sambaquis* of this subtradition are composed of refuse in contrast to the sites of the Paraguana (Platform Mound) subtradition, which are platform mounds. They tend to be spread out horizontally rather than accumulated to heights less than 10 m, for there is no purpose in climbing up a mound any higher than this to toss a basket of refuse. The strata of the refuse mounds tend to be dark in color from the charcoal and burnt bones remaining from the kitchen. These refuse sites, however, share many traits in common with the platform sites, including layers of kitchen midden, such as abandoned mollusks, shells, fish and sea mammal bones of whales and porposes. Most of both types of mounds have fire hearths and human burials. Because the refuse *sambaquis* extend over such a long period of time, the oldest lack ceramics that are present in the most recent. Again, two ceramic complexes are represented. One is Tupiguarani types, which tend to be more recent in time and have many different kinds of surface decorations, including painted designs on a white slip. The other type lacks the painted designs and has a lesser number of other types of decoration. These two ceramic complexes are also represented on sites of the interior highlands, where their beginning was earlier than on the coast, evidence of migration to the latter area. Because of the great area and time expanse, the diagnostic artifacts vary greatly from one site to another. Through time, polished and pressure-flaked lithic instruments increase. as does the presence of ornaments such as lip plugs and bone and stone beads. Projectile points made of stone and bone remain about the same in numbers.

CULTURAL SUMMARY

Environment

The climate of the region is hot and humid, with a mean annual temperature above 20° C and a mean annual precipitation above 2000 mm. The local coastal plain, on which the shell mounds are located, is complex, with many valleys and rocky outcrops. Vegetation is varied, from the mangroves swamps and dune forests of the coastal plain proper to tropical forests farther inland. At present, most of the vegetation is secondary type because the original forests were destroyed by agriculture in the historic period.

Settlements

Because these sites are refuse mounds and the surrounding areas have not been excavated (at least no publications exist that describe them), the settlement pattern is unknown.

Economy

Like the Paranagua (Platform Mound) subtradition, the peoples of the Nitoroi subtradition relied on mollusks for a major part of their diet. Mollusks were supplemented by fish and gathered plant foods.

Choppers are the most common artifact and may be finely flaked. Axes may be semipolished or manufactured only by flaking. Scrapers may be rectangular and made of a hard raw material such as basalt. Projectile points occur but not in the earliest strata of the *sambaquis*. They may be made of quartz by pressure flaking. Some may have a single barb. The stem is constricted and may be one-third of the length. Lance points may be larger and have a shorter stem. Hammer stones and pestles are made of quartzite pebbles. Scrapers are made of flakes. Rounded pebbles may be used for grinding and crushing. Knives are long and narrow, with edges flaked or semipolished. Some mollusk shell tools seem to be projectile points. They are long and have a single barb and a stem for attaching to a narrow shaft. Other shell tools were end scrapers. Projectile points were also made of bone. Beads were made by perforated fish vertebrae. Perforated jaguar and peccary teeth were used for necklaces. Perforated disks of whalebone are present. Artifacts were usually not associated with human burials, but one burial was accompanied by two stone pendants, a chipped ax, one semipolished ax, and a large hammer stone.

References

Rauth, Jose Wilson (1967). *Nota prévia sôbre a excavaçao do sambaqui do Pôrto Mauricio.* Programa Nacional de Pesquisas Arqueológicas, Resultados Preliminares do Pimero Ano, 1965–1966. Publicaçoes Avulsas, no. 6. 47–79. Belém, Pará: Museu Paraense Emílio Goeldi.

Rauth, Jose Wilson (1969), *Nota Prévia sôbre a excavaçao do sambaqui do Rio Sao Joao.* Programa Nacional de Pesquisas Arqueológicas, 2, Resultados Preliminares do Segundo Ano, 1966–1967. Publicaçoes Avulsas, no. 10, 75–95. Belém, Pará: Museu Paraense Emílio Goeldi.

Paranagua (Platform Mound)

ABSOLUTE TIME PERIOD: 4887–710 B.P. (Hurt 1974: Fig. 1).

LOCATION: The Atlantic coast from the state of Pernambuco on the north to Rio Grande do Sul on the south.

DIAGNOSTIC FEATURES: The major diagnostic feature was the construction of the *sambaqui* as a platform for structures such as houses. This contrasts to the *sambaquis* of the Nitoroi subtradition, which were refuse mounds ("kitchen middens"). The Paranagua platform mounds generally have evidence of their function in the presence of post molds for the walls of circular houses, also marked by signs of concave floors revealed by a thin layer of red ocher from the trait of face painting. The floors are also marked by a layer of lithic, bone, and shell artifacts. Human burials are generally present in the platform mounds. Generally the preceramic platform mounds are earlier in age than those with potsherds, but the beginning of strictly refuse mounds preceded the platform *sambaquis*. Lithic tools were made by both percussion and pressure flaking. Axes may be polished or semipolished. Axes are manufactured from cores by flaking pebbles. Some scrapers have a slight stem. Pitted hammer stones for cracking coconuts are present as are perforated disks. Shell beads and bone artifacts are rare. Other lithics include choppers, unifacial or bifacial scrapers, hammer stones, and knives. Single-shouldered stone projectile points are also present. Both fully flexed and extended burials are present.

CULTURAL SUMMARY

Environment

Major features of the environment are revealed in the changes of the sea level and its relation to a relatively stable coast. During the "Older Peron High" (dated 4800–4100 B.P.) and the "Younger Peron High" (4100–3400 B.P.), the sea level rose to 2.5–3 m higher than today, and as a result the shoreline was much farther to the interior than at present. Because the higher sea level was apparently the result of there being less ice and snow than present, it can be postulated that the climate from this period was also warmer than today. After this high, the sea fell to more than 2 m below its present level in the "Crane Key" and "Pelham Bay" periods. It is thought this sea level fall was the result of there being more ice and snow on the continents and hence a colder climate. This was a major time of initial construction of the *sambaquis*. Once again, the sea rose about 1.3 m during the "Abrolhos High" (2600–2000 B.P.) This was also a time period when older shell mounds continued to be constructed. After the seas reached their present level, sometime prior to 700 B.P., ceramic-making peoples moved to the coast, and some of them lived on top of the older shell mounds, such as the Sambaqui da Caieiera (SCLL-29).

Settlements

Most platform *sambaquis* probably began as campsite refuse mounds with such material as mollusk shells, charcoal, and ashes. As refuse accumulated and possibly as sea levels rose, the tops of the mounds began to be used as platforms for circular house structures. Several houses, each 5 or 6 m in diameter and with a central hearth, might be present on the top of a single mound. Occupation of these mounds appears to have been intermittent but long-term. Some mounds were clearly constructed solely as platforms and never served as refuse mounds.

Economy

The main economic activity of the Paranagua peoples was the collecting of mollusks, followed by fishing, and hunting in the tropical rainforests. A secondary economic activity was the harvesting of plant materials such as coconuts. Stone artifacts included hammer stones, axes, choppers, and grinding stones. Flaked-stone tools included scrapers, knives, and used flakes and projectile points. Bone tools were comparatively rare but included projectile points and bone drills or perforators. Well-fired but simple pottery was made.

References

Hurt, Wesley R. (1974). *The Interrelationships between the Natural Environment and Four Sambaquis, Coast of Santa Catarina, Brazil.* Occasional Papers and Monographs, no. 1. Bloomington: Indiana University Museum.

SITES

Pantano do Sul

TIME PERIOD: 4515–c. 4400 B.P.

LOCATION: The site is situated on the southeast of the island of Santa Catarina and extends for 400 m along the beach. The *sambaqui* is located on the hill on the east side and on a level area below this hill.

DESCRIPTIVE SUMMARY

Local Environment

Summers are warm and humid; winters are relatively cold. Frost occurs in the interior of the island. In the summer, the temperatures vary from 18–31° C. Santa Catarina island has on the interior two mountain ranges and is separated from the mainland by a narrow strait and two bays. The island is bordered by extensive sandy beaches. The rivers, Rio Taveras, Raztones, and Rio Papacoara, plus several lagoons, had in prehistoric times many fish that were gathered with nets with stone net weights. The coastal area is composed mainly of mangrove swamp. The most common mollusks are *Anomalocadrdia brasiliana Ghemnitz* and the type that live on tree trunks, *Ostrea arborea Chemnitz*. Common animals in prehistoric times, judging by the bones encountered in the site, were the porpoise, *paca*, capybara, coati, seal, deer, sea lion, jaguar, and the *jaguartirica*.

Physical Features

The part of the site that lies on top of the hill has the characteristics of a *sambaqui*, while the portion on the level land below is an open site. The highest part of the hill on which the *sambaqui* lies is 4.5 m above mean sea level. The cultural level of the *sambaqui* was Level 2. It was 90–100 cm thick and contained numerous bones of fish, birds, and mammals such as whales and porpoises, lithic and bone artifacts, hearths, and human burials. Charcoal from this level had an age of 4515 years. Rohr (1977: 93) believes that the site was abandoned only a few years later.

Cultural Aspects

The economy of the people living at Pantano do Sul was based on the gathering of shellfish and fishing with nets and hooks. Hunting of local mammals was a minor activity. In the refuse of the site, there were also bones of whales and porpoises. The presence of a pitted hammer stone indicates the gathering of nuts and coconuts. Other stone artifacts included axes that were flat and semipolished with a square shape, hammer stones, net weights, and hook weights. Bone artifacts included simple and double-ended projectile points, fishhooks of catfish spine, beads made of perforated teeth of sharks and fish bones. The outstanding stone artifacts were the zooliths. These artifacts had in their center a bowl-shaped depression, while the overall shape was that of a cross, fish, or a wild animal. These lithic artifacts represent the highest art among the *sambaqui* dwellers. Four human burials were also encountered in the excavations.

References

Rohr, Joao Alfredo (1977). *O Sítio Arqueológico do Pântano do Sul SC-F-10*, Florianodrais, SC: Governor do Estado de Santa Catarina.

Praia da Tapera

TIME PERIOD: c. 1200 B.P. for the lower strata and 600 B.P. for the upper strata.

LOCATION: Santa Catarina island in the state of Santa Catarina.

DESCRIPTIVE SUMMARY

Local Environment

Santa Catarina island is separated from the mainland by two straits that form two bays, the Bahia Sul and the Bahia Norte. The site is on the Bahia Sul. The island itself is surrounded by extensive sandy beaches, spits, dykes, rocky points, and mangrove swamps. Inland and coastal forests offered the largest number of animals important to the subsistence of the prehistoric peoples. Faunal remains from the excavations suggest that there were many animals used, including the anteater, coati whale, porpoise, capybara, seal, marmoset, jaguar, *paca*, peccary, armadillo, and deer, as well as reptiles such as lizards and turtles. There was also a great variety of mollusks and fishes and crabs taken. Nets were used for fishes, axes to free mollusks from their resting places, and bows and arrows to kill the land and sea mammals.

Physical Features

The site is located a few meters from the ocean's edge on well-drained, almost flat ground. The northeast side borders a small stream, the Rio da Era, which brings potable water to the site. The stratigraphy of the areas of the site with mollusk shells showed an upper stratum of sand and humus covered with shells, an intermediate stratum of shells, principally of oysters and terrestrial gastropods, mixed with fish, mammal, and bird bones, and a lower stratum of dark sand mixed with broken shell and very few artifacts and likely associated with the intermediate stratum. The upper stratum had artifacts and sherds of the Tupiguarani tradition; the middle stratum contained ceramics of the Itararé types; and the lower stratum contained human burials, in addition to hearths with pebbles, bones of birds, fish, and small mammals and charcoal. In this stratum were postholes of house walls. These holes had a diameter of 8–12 cm, and were between 60–85 cm below the ground surface. The total thickness of the archaeological strata was generally not over 100 cm.

Cultural Aspects

The first group of people of the Itararé subtradition who arrived at the beach of Tapera constructed three small houses parallel to the beach. The houses had a circular shape. Human burials were made within the houses. These people lived at the Tapera beach for perhaps a few dozen years. The second group of people of Itararé subtradition came and occupied the same site for more than a half century. The Tupiguarani arrived c. 600 B.P. in the same area. Their village was located more to the interior than the older Itararé houses. These Tupiguarani were horticulturists.

References

Rohr, Pe. Joao S. J. et al. (1990). *Excavaçoes Arqueológicas do Pe. Alfredo Rohr. Jr. O Siio Arquelógico da Praira da Tapera: Um Assento Itararé and Tupiguarani*. Pesquisas, Antropologia, no. 45. Sao Lepoldo, Rio Grande do Sul: Instituto Anchietano de Pesquisas.

Sambaqui da Caieira (SCLL.12)

TIME PERIOD: 3230–710 B.P.

LOCATION: The site lies on the side of the El Morro da Gloria, a rocky headland, at a distance of c. 88 m from the town of Laguna, Santa Catarina, and 375 m east of the Atlantic ocean (Hurt 1974: 11–12).

DESCRIPTIVE SUMMARY

Local Environment

The driest months in the area of the Sambaqui da Caieira are June, July, and August, and the mean annual temperature is 19.6° C. Precipitation varies from 1500–2000 mm per year. The Morro da Gloria, on which the *sambaqui* lies, was once one of a chain of offshore islands, formed during the major period of faulting of the Precambrian basement rocks of the southern Brazil coast. After barrier bars linked these islands together, they became a peninsula projecting from the mainland in the vicinity of the hamlet of Marim. At the time when the site was occupied, it fronted on a long, narrow inlet that is now completely infilled with sediments over which are superimposed row of sand dunes and beach ridges.

Physical Features

The refuse layers of the mound are parallel and conform to the diagonal slant of the hill. The lower-most layers of refuse lie on a layer of sand rather than directly on the hill. Judging by the radiocarbon dates, the construction of the mound began when the sea level was 1–1.5 m below present. After the initial abandonment of the site, sand was blown on top of the shell mound. As this layer was being formed, the site was reoccupied by ceramic-making peoples. From the point of view of the prehistoric inhabitants, the most important biota were the small shellfish, *Anamolacardia brasiliana*, oysters, and fish that lived in the nearest mangroves.

Cultural Aspects

The Sambaqui da Caieira is one of the important sites along the Brazilian coast, which contains definite evidence that it was a platform mound constructed to form a base for habitations. This is evident in the presence of postholes for circular structures that had concave floors covered with flecks of red ocher that accidently fell during face painting. Human skeletons were also present, for the site was also a burial mound. The site did not have the typical dome, but rather it had the form of diagonally inclined refuse layers that conformed to the sloping sides of the Morro da Gloria. Artifacts in the site are typical of other *sambaquis* of the southern Brazilian coast, such as shell fishhooks, scrapers, knives, and pestles. Burials were covered with intervertebral disks of whales.

References

Bigarella, Joan José (1964). "Variaçoes Climáticas no Quaternário e sus Impliçoes no revistimentico florístico Paraná." In *Boletim da Universidade do Paranáe Conselho Nacional Paraná*. Curitiba.

Hurt, Wesley R. (1974). *The Interrelationships between the Natural Environment and Four Sambaquis, Coast of Santa Catarina, Brazil*. Occasional Papers and Monographs, no. 1. Bloomington: Indiana University Museum.

Sambaqui de Camboinhas

TIME PERIOD: 7958–1410 B.P.

LOCATION: The site lies on the side of the Lagoa de Itaipu, Niterói, state of Rio de Janeiro.

DESCRIPTIVE SUMMARY

Local Environment

The climate has monsoonal rains, with a short dry season, but with enough rain to support a tropical rainforest. The area has a crystalline rocky coast with Quartenary alluvial and marine deposits. In the immediate area of the *sambaqui* are dunes closing the entrance the ancient lagoon of Itaipu, and these dunes now separate this body of water from the Atlantic ocean. These dunes were formed by oscillating levels of the ocean during the Holocene. Originally the entire area was a series of islands composed of gneiss. The interior side of the lagoon of Itaipu was bordered by a rocky hill, formerly an island, and now called the "Morro das Andrinbas." The Sambaqui de Comboinhas lies within one of the fossil dunes at the heights of 7–8 m above mean sea level, which represents the level of the ocean at the time that this structure was first accumulated (Cunha and Francisco 1981: 15–24). During the Holocene, the level of the coast, buried in these dunes, varied in altitude with the regressions and invasions of the sea. In the 16th century, a dense tropical rainforest covered 70 percent of the area, but it no longer exists because of clearing by the European settlers for agricultural purposes (Araujo and Vilança 1981: 27–46). However, there were various types of forests, coastal, growing at a higher altitude, lagoon forests and dune forests, and forests in the nearby Rio Paraíba. There were many palm trees with edible nuts and fruits. Many of the other trees in these forests were also of great value for nuts, fruits, material for baskets, firewood, making bows and arrows, and canoes, and fiber for textiles and fishnets and medicine.

Physical Features

In this *sambaqui*, the different strata were observable by the bands of the shellfish, *Anomalocardia braziliana*, by dark-colored sediments, with small pockets of dark sand and ash. The lowermost level revealed in the north excavation face was dated 7958 B.P.; the 1.10-m layer was dated 2562 B.P.; and the 0.75-m-level was dated 1410 B.P. The east face had the date of 4475 B.P. at the 1-m depth, and the 0.30-m level was dated 2328 B.P. Because of the location of the shell mound on a dune-covered beach between an inland lagoon and the ocean, a large variety of bones of fish, turtles, sea mammals such as whales and porposes, rays, and sharks was encountered in the refuse (Cunha and Francisco 1981: 155–153).

Cultural Aspects

The Comboinhas *sambaqui* was a refuse mound left by a group of individuals who lived in adjacent area where they collected shellfish, fish, and local mammals for food, and who used tools made from local materials (Kneip and Pallestrini 1981: 57–64). About 90 percent of the artifacts were made of quartz, which is a common mineral in this region (Pallestrini and Chiara 1981: 71–95). Others were fabricated of gneiss, basalt, and quartzite. The quartz was obtained from veins in local basalt. The lithic raw material was represented in cores. Tools included burins, denticulates, knives, drills, flake axes, retouched flakes, projectile points, scrapers, and utilized pebbles. The projectile points had a rough triangular shape with a straight or rounded base. Some specimens were retouched on only one face and others on both faces. There was also a considerable bone industry. The artifacts made of fishbone are perforated and sometimes polished to make beads. A perforated Y-shaped bone of a *Seláquio* was represented but of unknown use. Other artifacts were fish spines with one perforated end, also of unknown use. A rare object was a monkey's tooth that had a perforated root. A single projectile point made of an unidentified bone had a triangular shape and a convex-concave crosssection.

References

Araujo, Dorothy Sue Dunn, and Aparecida Maria Neiva Vilança (1981). "Avaliaçao da Coberatura Vegetal Remanescente de Itaipu." In *Pesquisas Arqueológicas no litoral de Itaipu, Nitorói, RJ*. Rio de Janeiro: Editorial Gráfica Luna.

Cuhna, Fausto L. de Souza, and Benedicto H. Rodrigues Francisco (1981). "Geologia de Itaipu." In *Pesquisas Arqueológicas, Niterói, RJ*. Rio de Janeiro: Editorial Gráfica Luna.

Kneip, Lina Maria (1981). "O Material ósseo." In *Pesquisas Arqueológicas, no litoral de Itaipu, Niterói, RJ*. Rio de Janeiro: Editorial Gráfica Luna.

Kneip, Lina Maria, and Luciana Palestrini (1981). "Escavçao and Estrtigrafia." In *Pesquisas Arqueológicas no litoral de Itaipu, RJ*. Rio de Janeiro: Editorial Gráfica Luna.

Paloestrini, Luciana, and Philamena Ciara (1981). "O Material Litíca." In *Pesquisas Arqueológicas mo Litoral de Itaipu, Niterói, RJ*. Rio de Janeiro: Editorial Gráfica Luna.

Sambaqui da Carniça

TIME PERIOD: c. 2550 B.P.

LOCATION: The shell mound is situated on an island about 5 km south of the town of Laguna.

DESCRIPTIVE SUMMARY

Local Environment

The climate is humid and subtropical, with rainfall throughout most of the year. The shell mound lies on the side of a dune that crisscrosses an ancient beach ridge. The base of the shell mound lies 5.57 m above the ancient sea level.

Physical Features

Pimenta (1958), who measured the mound before commercial operations to obtain mollusk shell for making lime had destroyed a large part of the *sambaqui*, estimated that the height of the site was 50 m. According to Leonardos (1938: 78–79), this *sambaqui* measured 400 m in circumference, 120 m in diameter, and 20 m in height in 1938. Evidently, the workers destroying the mound to obtain calcium had much reduced the height when Leonardos visited the site. The mound was composed of layers of shellfish, predominately *Anomalocardia Brasiliana*, although there were many mangrove oysters and mussels. The shells of the former mollusk formed the thickest strata in the mound and were "clean," that is, this stratum was composed almost entirely of this shellfish. Other strata of this mollusk were "dirty," that is, the white shells were mixed with charcoal and other types of dark refuse. The presence of the "clean" stratum indicated that it was a deliberate creation, most likely done over a very short time period to add to the mound's height as a platform, while the "dirty" strata represented kitchen refuse.

A short distance to the east was another much smaller *sambaqui* (Carniça 1A) that lay on top of a ancient beach ridge, approximately 150 cm above present mean sea level. Judging by the radiocarbon dates, 3350–3275 B.P., this *sambaqui* was occupied during the same time that Carniça 1 was being constructed. On the same island are many large *sambaquis*, some of which have a dome shape, and others are shaped like a loaf of bread. None of these other *sambaquis* was excavated, and their relation to the *sambaquis* of Carniça 1 and Carniça 1A is unknown. They testify, however, to the abundance of the food supply on and near the island.

Cultural Aspects

The *sambaqui* was both a place to dump kitchen refuse and a platform mound used as an elevated site for houses at different time periods. There were circular depressions of house floors in some of the strata. Cut into the underlying dune beneath the central portion of the *sambaqui* was a unique feature not present in other excavated shell mounds. This was a large sun-dried clay coffin containing a dozen adult human skeletons. The upper surface and sides of the coffin were a crosshatched series of red ocher in the pattern of the weave of a basket. Because of the absence of this feature in other described *sambaquis*, the coffin probably contained the remains of very important individuals.

References

Hurt, Wesley R. (1974). *The Interrelationships between the Natural Environment and Four Sambaquis, Coast of Santa, Brazil.* Occasional Papers and Monographs, no. 1. Bloomington: Indiana University Museum.

Leonardos, Othon Henry (1938). *Concheiros e Sambaquis.* Rio de Janeiro: Departamento Nacional da Produçao Mineral, Vulso, no. 32.

Pimenta, Jean (1958). "A faixa costeira meridional de Santa Catarina." *Boletim no. 176*, Rio de Janeiro: Divisao de Geologia e Mineralogia do DNPM.

Sambaqui at Forte Marechal Luz

TIME PERIOD: 4350–650 B.P.

LOCATION: The site is located at the northern end of the island of Sao Francisco do Sul, Santa Catarina, about 20 km south of the border with the state of Parana. (Bryan 1993).

DESCRIPTIVE SUMMARY

Local Environment

The Sambaqui de Forte Marechal Luz site is situated by a small, shallow bay overlooking in the mangrove swamps that outline the sandy shores of Babitonga bay to the west. It lies over bedrock on a hillside between 19–36 m above sea level. The hill on which the site lies is composed of quartz-diorite hill. On the hill is a series of three wave-cut terraces. The local area has a humid subtropical climate, with rainfall throughout most of year. At one time, a dense rainforest must have covered the island. The predominant mollusks that served as food for humans were *Anomalocardi brasiliana*, mangrove oysters, and mussels. Common fauna on the island and adjacent waters included fish, peccary, tapir, deer, jaguar, raccoon, capybara, *paca*, agouti, whale, turtle, cayman, and dolphin. Also various seeds and fruits of various trees and palms were present in the mound, indicating that they were major items of the diet of the inhabitants.

Physical Features

The site lay on a hillside. Occupation I was a campsite beginning at 2400 B.C. On top of this camp, a shell mound was accumulated, forming Occupation II (2000–1 B.C.). In Occupation III (A.D. 1), more refuse was deposited. This kitchen refuse continued to be thrown on the shell mound in Occupations IV and V during the years A.D. 1–1100. On top of this *sambaqui* was refuse of a ceramic-making people, Occupations VI–VII (A.D. 1100–1350). These new people were closely related to the ones in the interior of the highlands of the Simple Ceramic subtradition.

Cultural Aspects

Because the *sambaqui* was 20 m high, it must have been a series of platform mounds for habitation rather than a simple refuse mound. There would have been no purpose in climbing up a mound this high to deposit a basket of kitchen refuse. No signs of structures, however, were noted by the excavators of this shell mound. The economy of the *sambaqui*'s inhabitants was based on the hunting and gathering of the natural resources of the island. The first human burials appear in Occupation IV. Stone artifacts were most abundant in the upper occupations area (IV–VII). Lithic tools included axes with ground bits, flaked axes, discoidal pebbles, grooved pebbles, ground plumets, pitted hammer stones for breaking coconuts, and hammer stones. Bone tools included whale phalanges used for chopping blocks. There were also perforated whalebones, perforated fish vertebrae, projectile points made of bone and ray spines, fishhooks, bead made of teeth, beads of the columella of mollusks.

References

Bryan, Alan L. (1993). *The Sambaqui at Forete Marechal Luz, State of Santa Cataina, Brazil*. Brazilian Studies, ix–114. Corvallis: Center for the Study of the First Americans, Oregon State University.

Sambaqui da Pedra Oca

TIME PERIOD: c. 2000–1500 B.P.

LOCATION: The Sambaqui da Pedra Oca is located in the Municipio de Periperi, state of Bahia, on the side of the bay of Todos os Santos at its junction with the Atlantic ocean.

DESCRIPTIVE SUMMARY

Local Environment

The climate is a tropical savanna. The geological structure of the hill on which the *sambaqui* is located is composed of large beds of shale alternating with thinner strata of sand that is being eroded by high tides, resulting in the formation of the bay, Todos Os Santos. These high tides have removed a large portion of the Sambaquid da Pedra Oca.

Physical Features

The hill on which the *sambaqui* lies was at one time a beach, now extinct. The site is now 200 m above mean sea level. This extinct beach was probably formed by the invasion of the sea over the local coastal area at c. 2000 B.P. A study of the types of mollusks encountered in the excavations of Calderon showed these major types: *Ostrea arborea, anomalocardia brasialiana Gemlin, Lucina pectinata Gmelin, Venus* sp. *Strombus pugilis Linn* (Calderon 1964: 74–75). Terrestial gastrods, such as *Strophocheilus oblongus*, were less frequent.

Cultural Aspects

Sambaqui da Pedra Oca began as a campsite with refuse such as mollusk shells, charcoal, and ashes. As the refuse accumulated, it became a platform for crude house structures, as indicated by ash-filled postholes. Over these structures, refuse continued to be accumulated. Occupation, as shown by sterile zones, indicated intermittent but long-time occupation. A single human burial in a flexed position was encountered in Stratum III. As erosion continued to remove part of the site, campsites were made away from the main portion of the shell mound.

The main economic activity was the collecting of mollusks, followed by fishing. Another secondary economic activity was the harvesting of coconuts, as indicated by the *quebracocos*, pitted hammer stones used to crack nuts. Only three bone projectile points were excavated, indicating that hunting was a minor activity. Another type of projectile used was the stone throwing bow, evidence of which is small rounded pebbles. Other stone artifacts included hand axes, stone files, grinding stones, and bone drills or perforators.

Well-fired but simple pottery was made. According to Calderon (1964: 88), the absence of chipped-stone axes as well as knives and scrapers, typical of most *sambaqui* cultures, makes the Sambaqui da Pedra Oca unique.

References

Calderón, Valentin (1964). *Osambaqui da Pedra Oca*. Salvador: *Instituto de Ciências Sociais*, Universidade Federal da Bahia.

Sambaqui da Piaçaguera (Garcia and Uchôa 1980)

ABSOLUTE TIME PERIOD: 4930–4890 B.P.

LOCATION: The *sambaqui* was situated on the hill of Tapera, in the Município de Cubatao, state of Sao Paulo.

DESCRIPTIVE SUMMARY

Local Environment

The climate of the region is hot and humid, with a mean annual temperature above 20° C, with a maximum of 38° C, and a minimum of below 10° C, and mean annual precipitation of 2000–2500 mm. The rainy season is concentrated from January–March, and the least rain in July–August. The local coastal plain on which the shell mound is located has valleys and crystalline outcrops. Vegetation is varied, from that of the mangroves, dunes, and sandbars, coastal plain, and the sides of the coast range. At present, most of the vegetation is secondary types because the original forests were destroyed by agriculture in the historic period.

Physical Features

The shell mound covered approximately 850 sq m, with the lowest part inclined toward an inlet of the sea. The lowest part of the site was 10 m above sea level, and the highest part, 12.30 m. About 150 m from the site was a mangrove swamp. The rivers nearest to the site were Rio Quilombo and Rio Mogi. There were three stratigraphic units in the site. The lowermost stratum (III), 40 cm thick, was composed mainly of large oysters, a large quantity of fishbone, and crustaceans. It also contained concretions, formed by the precipitation of calcium carbonate. Stratum II, c. 0.95 cm thick, was more compact, containing the shells of *Mytella* sp. and remains of fish and crustaceans. This strata had a color varying from light yellow to ash color. Human burials were concentrated in this stratum. Stratum I, 0.25 m thick, was the uppermost deposit and was composed of remains of oysters and altered bones, with a large amount of humus that resulted in a dark color.

Cultural Aspects

In the shell mound were encountered the skeletons of 87 individuals. They were buried in a flexed position and lay on their sides. Burials were often accompanied by *Olivella* shell beads and other types of ornaments. Raw material used for lithic artifacts included basic rocks such as diabase. Other materials included granite, gneiss, quartz, quartzite, and anphibolite. Tools included rectangular axes with parts of the cortex present made of pebble cores. These had a rough groove, and none was completely polished. There were hammer stones and pitted hammer stones, chisels, lance points, spatulas made of whale and mammal bone, spheres made of tympanic bones of whales, perforated animal teeth, scrapers made of mollusk shells, and shell beads. Projectile points were made of bird bones and stingray spines. Artifacts made of the teeth of peccary, porpoise, capybara, coati, and alligator were used for decoration. Subsistence was based on the collecting of shellfish, fish, fruits, nuts, and the hunting small and medium-sized mammals. There seems to have been no gap in the occupation of this site, and the abandonment was probably the result of overharvest of shellfish.

Reference

Garcia, Caio del Rio, and Dorath Pinto Uchôa (1980). "Um Sambaqui do Litoral del Estado de Sao Paulo, Brasil." *Revista de Préhistória* 2.

Sambaquis de Ponta das Almas (SC-LL-17) (Hurt 1974; Piazza 1966)

TIME PERIOD: 4289–3690 B.P.

LOCATION: The *sambaquis* of Ponta das Almas lie on a small peninsula that projects from the west bank into the lake called the Lagôa da Conceiçao, on the island of Santa Catarina, 14 km northeast of the capital city of Florianópolis. The island lies offshore from the midpoint of the Santa Catarina coast and is separated from the mainland by a narrow channel.

DESCRIPTIVE SUMMARY

Local Environment

At present, the region of the *sambaquis* falls within the zone of the southeast trade winds and has a mean average rainfall from a minimum of 1000 mm to a maximum of 3000 mm. The winter is relatively dry and cool. Temperatures are ameliorated by the northward-trending Falkland current. In the warmer areas of Santa Catarina, the bays are bordered by mangrove swamps, but in the area of the *sambaquis* da Ponta das Almas, the bay is bordered by salt marshes. The upper sand deposits of the coast area rest on basal rocks such as granite. The beach ridges of the region lie both below and above present sea levels because of past oscillations in sea levels.

Physical Features

The *sambaquis* de Ponta das Almas rest on top of a large group of boulders that at one time were located offshore. Later they became joined to the lake by a sandbar. Once this landmass was formed, sand dunes accumulated on it, so that the surface rose above the maximum high tide level of the lagoon. The archaeological site itself was once an interlocked series of *sambaquis* that lay on top of the end of the peninsula. At present, the channel that serves as an exit to the sea of the Lagôa da Conciêç is so shallow that dredging is necessary for small boats to enter the lagoon. After the archaeological site was abandoned, windblown deposits almost completely filled in not only the exit of the lagoon but also the lee side of the peninsula. This infilling almost buried the boulders that formed the habitat of the mussel (*Mytilus*) and the rock oyster (*Ostrea stetina tayraudeau*), two major sources for food for the prehistoric inhabitants of these *sambaquis*. Excavations were conducted in Sambaquin A by Piazzi (1966) and the main shell mound, Sambaqui B, by Hurt (1974). Excavation across the latter *sambaqui* revealed that there was an area of dry land between the shell mound and the shoreline.

Cultural Aspects

Once humans moved to Ponta das Almas, their kitchen refuse formed the Sambaqui A. The site was abandoned when the refuse extended over the ancient beach for c. 5 m. The site was probably abandoned first during the "Pelham Bay Low" at 2800 B.P., when the sea was 2.5 m below present levels. This fall of sea level would have isolated Sambaqui A too far from the shoreline of the diminished lagoon with little fish and mollusks remaining. After a few hundred years, the sea level began rising and reached a height about 2 m above present and the fish and mollusks became abundant once more. As a result, the peninsula of Ponta das Almas was reoccupied by humans, and their kitchen formed Sambaqui B. In time, this refuse extended over Sambaqui A, forming a single saddle-shaped shell mound. A radiocarbon sample obtained by Piazza (1966: 19) from the Sambaqui A was dated at 2400 B.P., which gives a minimum date of the reoccupation of this shell mound.

References

Hurt, Wesley R. (1974). *The Interrelationships between the Natural Environment and Four Sambaquis, Coast of Santa Catarina, Brazil.* Bloomington: University of Indiana.

Piazza, Walter F. (1966). "O Sambaqui de Ponta das Almas." In *Estudos de Sambaquis (Nota Pfrevia), Sírie Arqueologia 2,* Florianópolis: Universidade Federal de Santa Catarina.

Sambaqui do Rio Sao Joao

TIME PERIOD: 4487–4960 B.P.

LOCATION: The *sambaqui* is situated within the floodplain about 200 m from the right bank of the Sao Joao river, to the west of the bay of Antonina, state of Paraná (Rauth 1969).

DESCRIPTIVE SUMMARY

Local Environment

The shell mound is situated on a rocky crystalline outcrop that at one time was a reef. It is surrounded by the floodplain of the now infilled bay of Nundiquara and is 2000 m from the Nundiquara river. To the northwest is the Rio Sao Joao, and the site is also 1 km from the Pinho river in which high tides enter. The beach ridge under the *sambaqui* was formed when the sea was about 2 m higher than present.

Physical Features

The refuse mound was ovoid, 30 by 35 m. Sterile soil occurs at the depth of 2.5 m. The strata are refuse from the kitchen and are composed mainly of oyster shells with local concentrations of *Modiolus brasilienas*. Few fish and animal bones were encountered in the excavations of the mound. A dark layer, composed of clay and ash with a small amount of mollusk shells, was present in the 50–75 mm depths and appears to represent temporary abandonment of the site. Twenty-five of the 27 human burials were in this layer. Position was either completely flexed or with legs extended. One burial was covered with pebbles, ash, and shell. Artifacts rarely accompanied the burials, but one had two pendants, two axes (one flaked and the other semipolished), and a large polishing stone.

Cultural Aspects

Artifacts in the upper stratum were percussion or pressure flaked from diabase. Three axes showed slight polishing, and three stone pendants were polished. Other tools included choppers, unifacial and bifacial scrapers, hammer stones, knives, and single-shouldered projectile points. The only bone artifacts were a perforated disk of a whale and a small projectile point. Artifacts from the lower level show rougher flaking. They included unifacial choppers, hammer stones, a pitted hammer stone, and unshaped flakes. Perforated shell beads were also present. All these characteristics indicate that the Sambaqui do Sao Joao is part of the Nitoroi subtradition.

References

Fairbridge, R. W. (1961). "Conference on Evidence on Climatic Change and Ice Ages." *Annals of New York Academy of Science* 5: 95–542.

Rauth, José Wilson (1969). *Nota Prévia sôbre a escavaçao do sambaqui do rio Sao Joao*. Programa Nacional de Pesquisas Arqueológicas, Resultados Preliminares do Segundo, 1966–1967. Publicaçoes Avulsas, no. 10. Belém, Pará: Museu Eímilio Goeldi.

WESLEY HURT (deceased)
compiled by
PETER N. PEREGRINE
Department of Anthropology
Lawrence University
Appleton, Wisconsin
United States

South Andean Ceramic

ABSOLUTE TIME PERIOD: C. 2500–500 B.P.

RELATIVE TIME PERIOD: Follows the Highland Andean Formative and precedes the historic period. The Incas strongly influenced the region prior to the Spanish conquest.

LOCATION: Southern Andes from Bolivia through central Chile.

DIAGNOSTIC MATERIAL ATTRIBUTES: Agricultural villages with ceramics.

CULTURAL SUMMARY

Environment

The southern Andes create one of the most varied environments in the world. The coast begins as a sandy beach but quickly rises onto the western slopes the mountains—uplifted limestone ridges and volcanic cones rising to over 6500 m. Steep alluvial valleys bisect these ridges and provide highly fertile soils even at high altitudes. Above 4000 m, the steep mountain slopes give way to gently rolling glacial grassland interspersed with lakes. The eastern side of the mountains, like the west, are steep slopes with dissected river valleys descending into Patagonia and the pampas.

Climate varies by elevation. The coast is mild, with average daily temperatures about 20° C. The highlands are, by comparison, quite cool, with average daily temperatures only 12° C in upland valleys. Rainfall follows a similar pattern. On the coast rain is rare, while higher elevations get 500 mm a year or more. Above 4000 m, snowfall is common. Biota varies by elevation as well. Fish, shellfish, and marine mammals are plentiful in the waters of the coast. Inland, both plants and animals are sparse except in the alluvial valleys, where grasses, shrubs, and, as elevation increases, bushes, and trees become plentiful. Deer were present in these upland environments, as were the unique Andean camelids, particularly the guanaco. Small mammals and birds were plentiful throughout the region.

Settlements

South Andean settlements tended to be along major river valleys. Settlements varied in size from small villages to large fortified towns. Dwellings were small and rectangular, typically built on terraces, with walls made from stone, adobe, or woven cane. Larger dwellings were also present, as were large, multistructure compounds at some sites. These compounds may have been for elites and would have contained special-purpose rooms for storage and administrative duties.

Most communities were not internally organized, but were more of an "agglutination" of dwellings and compounds.

Economy

The South Andean economy was primarily agricultural, but was supplemented by fishing, hunting, and collecting. Irrigation was used in many places, and crops were diverse. Domestic plants included corn, potatoes, manioc, legumes, squash, and chili pepper. Domesticated animals included the llama, guinea pig, and Muscovy duck.

Tools used by the South Andean peoples included chipped-stone hoes, knives, and arrows. Bone was used for tools as well. Textiles included bolas, fishing lines, and nets. A wide variety of ceramics was also employed by the South Andean peoples. All were handmade, and early forms lacked decoration. Forms included bowls, globular storage jars, cups and beakers, and urns, among others. Later ceramics were more often decorated than earlier ones, often adopting styles from the northern Andes.

Sociopolitical Organization

Large residential compounds in some communities suggest the presence of elites, and the overall scale of society with large communities, irrigation, and the like, suggests the presence of formal political leaders. Neighboring regions to the north were, of course, developing large states and empires, and it is reasonable to think that parallel processes were underway farther south. Thus, we can envision emergent leaders in the South Andes combining elements political, economic, religious, and military authority.

Religion and Expressive Culture

Like many other traits, religious beliefs seem to have diffused to the South Andes from the north. Effigy ceramic vessels, carved wooden trays, stone sculptures, and the like suggest an elaborate iconography with strong ties to the northern Andes.

Suggested Readings

Bennett, Wendell C., Everett F. Bleiler, and Frank H. Sommer (1948). *Northwest Argentine Archaeology.* Publications in Anthropology, no. 38. New Haven: Yale University Press.

Bruhns, Karen Olsen (1994). *Ancient South America.* Cambridge: Cambridge University Press.

Cassman, Vicki (1997). "A Reconsideration of Prehistoric Ethnicity and Status in Northern Chile: The Textile Evidence." Ph.D. diss., Department of Anthropology, Arizona State University, Tempe.

Rivera, M. (1991). "The Prehistory of Northern Chile: A Synthesis." *Journal of World Prehistory* 5: 1–47.

Santoro Vargas, Calogero Mauricio (1995). "Late Prehistoric Regional Interaction and Social Change in a Coastal Valley of Northern Chile." Ph.D. diss., Department of Anthropology, University of Pittsburgh.

Willey, Gordon R. (1971). *Introduction to American Archaeology, vol. 2: South America.* Engelwood Cliffs, NJ: Prentice-Hall.

Peter N. Peregrine
Department of Anthropology
Lawrence University
Appleton, Wisconsin
United States

Tiwanaku

Tiahuanaco

ABSOLUTE TIME PERIOD: c. 1600–900 B.P.

RELATIVE TIME PERIOD: Follows the Andean Regional Development tradition and precedes the Aymara Kingdoms and Andean Regional States traditions. In the terminology of the Tiwanaku region, the tradition includes the terminal "Early Intermediate Period" and "Middle Horizon" and precedes the "Late Intermediate Period."

LOCATION: The south-central Andes. The Tiahuanaco type site is at an elevation of 3800 m, in the southern lake Titicaca basin of Bolivia. The Tiwanaku Core Region extends through most of the Peruvian and Bolivian *altiplano*. The Tiwanaku peripheries include lowland regions of southern Peru, northern Chile, and eastern Bolivia.

DIAGNOSTIC MATERIAL ATTRIBUTES: Stone sculptural traditions of anthropomorphic stelae and low relief carvings. Cut-stone public architecture including sunken rectangular courts and pyramidal or stepped platform mounds. Settlement pattern hierarchy with large urban site, secondary centers, and farmsteads with raised-field agricultural systems in highlands. Serving and ceremonial pottery including *kero* drinking goblets, anthropomorphic and zoomorphic vessels, polychromes typically red-slipped with motifs in black, white, orange, and blue-gray. Characteristic utilitarian plain-ware pottery.

Camelid wool and cotton textiles including polychrome striped warp-faced plain weaves and figural tunics of interlocked tapestry technique, both with loop stitch embroidery. Bronze, gold, and silver metallurgy, diverse lithic and lapidary industries.

REGIONAL SUBTRADITIONS: Azapa Tiwanaku (Loreto Viejo/Cabuza), Cochabamba Tiwanaku, Moquegua Tiwanaku, San Pedro de Atacama Tiwanaku, Tiwanaku Core Region.

IMPORTANT SITES: Tiahuanaco, Lukurmata, Pajchiri, Iwawe, Omo, Azapa AZ-83, Piñami, San Pedro de Atacama.

CULTURAL SUMMARY

Environment

Climate. Climate in the *altiplano* Tiwanaku Region exemplifies extreme high altitude at a tropical latitude, with an annual mean temperature of 9° C and diurnal variation of up to 15° C because of extreme solar radiation. Night frosts are a significant limiting factor. *Altiplano* rainy season is from November through March, with a mean annual precipitation approaching 700 mm. Tiwanaku's hyperarid western peripheries in Peru and Chile enjoy mild temperatures year-round, but are climatically constrained by the near-total rain shadow of the Pacific coast. Periodic El Niño southern oscillation (ENSO) events disrupt these normal patterns with highland droughts and coastal floods.

Long-term trends suggested by glacial ice cores correlate the Tiwanaku tradition with two relatively wet periods from 1340–1300 B.P. and 1190–910 B.P. Decreasing rainfall inferred after 910 B.P., culminating in severe drought and low lake levels from 705–640 B.P., have been implicated by Kolata et al. in the Tiwanaku collapse. However, Erickson argues that most Tiwanaku site abandonment took place 100–200 years before the onset of this drought. Major flood events in Moquegua, dated by Magilligan et al. to 1290 B.P. and 620 B.P., indicate that extreme ENSO cycles occurred during the Tiwanaku era.

Topography. The Tiwanaku Core Region is in the *altiplano*, a flat depression that runs 800 km north to south between the Eastern and Western Cordilleras of the southern Andes. The Tiahuanaco site is located in an 11-km-wide valley formed between the east–west running Kimsachatta and Achuta ranges. Elevations above 3800 m for Tiahuanaco and nearby sites by the shores of lake Titicaca make the Tiwanaku Core Region the world's highest ancient civilization center. Tiwanaku settlements are also found at lower elevations in the Pacific-draining river valleys of Tambo, Moquegua, Locumba, Sama, Caplina, Lluta, and Azapa in the coastal desert of Peru and Chile. No sites have been found on the Pacific littoral, with colonial settlement concentrating inland in these oasis valleys. Variants of the Tiwanaku tradition also appear in the wetter Amazon-draining eastern slope valleys of Cochabamba, Mizque, and Capinota in Bolivia.

Geology. The south-central Andes are a tectonically active region, where uplift and volcanic activity are caused by the collision and subduction of the eastward-moving Nazca plate with the South American continent. The geology of the south-central Andes is highly variable, but might be typified as uplifted Pre-Cambrian conglomerate formations mixed with metamorphic and igneous rocks created by intrusive volcanics. There are a number of historically active volcanoes in the region, and significant mineral deposits of tin, silver, copper, gypsum, and salt are found in the southern Bolivian *altiplano*, northern Chile, and southern Peru. The *altiplano* of the Tiwanaku Core Region was formed by conglomerate and sandstone sediments deposited in the depression formed by the uplift of the Eastern Cordillera. Subsequent Early and Late Pleistocene lakes,

known as Ballivian and Tauca, respectively, covered the *altiplano* to a level 50 m above the current level of Titicaca, leaving stranded terraces now visible in the Taraco peninsula. Evaporation and sedimentation through the Holocene have left salt flats covering much of the southern *altiplano* and continue to decrease the levels of lake Titicaca and the increasingly saline lake Poopo.

Biota. The Tiwanaku Core Region includes as many as seven microenvironmental zones, including marshes and periodically inundated lands in the Titicaca basin, extensive flat and rolling grasslands, foothills, alluvial terraces, and colluvium. Predominant flora consists of *stipa ichu* and a variety of other grass species, the lake reed *totora*, and deciduous bushes such as *thola* and *khoa*. Indigenous fauna include the domesticated and wild camelid species (llama, alpaca, guanaco, and vicuña), rodents such as guinea pigs and viscacha, a wide variety of birds including hawks, condors and owls, rhea, flamingoes, ducks, and other waterfowl, and freshwater fish.

Settlements

Settlement System. The first-order site of Tiahuanaco, at least 420 ha in area with a population approaching 40,000, dominated the Tiwanaku Core Region settlement pattern. Interpretations differ on the systemic integration of second-order sites like Lukurmata, Pajchiri, Khonko Wankane, Chiripa, Iwawe, and Omo, few of which exceeded 10,000 in population. Ponce Sangines and Kolata describe them as secondary centers in a highly hierarchical four-level Tiwanaku settlement system corresponding to state agricultural investment and administrative functions. McAndrews et al.'s recent rank-size and cluster analyses of Tiwanaku Core Region settlement pattern data suggest a less-integrated arrangement in which the second-order sites were the centers of autonomous subsystems. A similar range of interpretations exists for settlement systems of the Tiwanaku peripheries. In Moquegua, Goldstein notes the sudden appearance of four large Tiwanaku towns, agricultural works, and specialized facilities for regional provincial administration. In contrast, Higueras notes virtually no change from preexisting local settlement pattern in the Mizque and Capinota valleys of Cochabamba with the advent of Tiwanaku material culture.

Community Organization. The Tiahuanaco site's ceremonial, administrative and residential palace precincts were laid out on a cardinal orientation and surrounded by a moat to separate them from the rest of the city. Elite residential complexes have been identified on the summit of the Akapana pyramid and in the Putuni palace, and it is likely that the monumental center was reserved for royal or high-status residents. The 4 sq km of surrounding nonelite residential sectors at Tiahuanaco maintained the same cardinal orientation as the monumental center. Residential groups were bounded by perimeter walls into socially or functionally differentiated barrios, which in turn were subdivided into patio groups. These are believed to represent social units corresponding to *ayllus* or kin groups within the city. Similar community segmentation appears to be the case in other Core Region settlements like Lukurmata.

In Moquegua, desert preservation permits the exposure of entire Tiwanaku town plans, including extensive residential districts and ceremonial/administrative structures. Omo phase occupations at the Omo site, dated to 1350–1200 B.P., consisted of freestanding multiroom buildings, arrayed around three large plazas. These plaza-centered residential groups appear to correspond to intentionally segregated *ayllu* communities.

Housing. Tiwanaku Core Region domestic structures were constructed of adobe over stone foundations, with packed earth floors and informal hearths in each habitation room. Although circular structures are reported in later levels at Lukurmata, rectangular structures predominated. Dispersed single-structure household units were typical of earlier occupations. Walled compounds appear within Tiahuanaco's Akapana East residential center after 1350 B.P., and similar compact patio groups, consisting of two domestic structures, a storage building, and subfloor burials, appear at Lukurmata between 1200–1100 B.P. In both cases, it is believed that the reorganization from a minimal household plan into larger compounds corresponds to a coalesced family structure that maximized household production in the period of maximum state tribute.

Lowland Tiwanaku settlers used cane wall and timber post construction rather than adobe in most domestic architecture. Early household units at Omo did not have independent patios or storage facilities. As in the Core Region, autonomous patio groups with contiguous roofed rooms, open patios, and storage units (mud-plastered stone cists or rectangular cribs) appeared after 1200 B.P., and may indicate changes in household organization, size, and production in later settlements. In the later phases, steeper domestic sites were terraced for occupation with stone retaining walls.

Population, Health, and Disease. A comprehensive study of nonmetric traits by Blom found no significant biological distance among skeletal populations of Tiahuanaco, Lukurmata, and rural sites of the Tiwanaku valley and the Katari basin. This indicates relatively open migration and marriage among Core Region majority populations. Small groups from the Akapana East and Mollo Kontu sectors at Tiahuanaco, who exhibit different mortuary practices and possibly biological distinction, could represent enclaved foreign populations within the city. The Tiwanaku population of the Chen Chen site of the Moquegua valley was far closer genetically to that of the Tiwanaku Core Region than to non-Tiwanaku peoples of Moquegua, confirming that peripheral settlements were peopled by colonists and their descendents, and not acculturated local populations.

Most Tiwanaku populations practiced intentional cranial deformation, using annular binding or devices that produced variations of frontooccipital flattening and parietal widening. Tiwanaku cranial modification styles correlated with regional, ethnic, or clan affiliations rather than status, and stylistic variation has been noted among regions and among individual cemeteries. As might be expected for a cosmopolitan city, the Tiahuanaco site displays the greatest heterogeneity of styles.

Tiwanaku health was generally good, and no major epidemics or violent episodes have been identified. Child and infant mortality was relatively high, in keeping with other pre-Columbian societies. Periostosis and porotic hyperostosis suggest that Tiwanaku peoples suffered from moderate rates of anemia and systemic infections, perhaps more severely in lowland areas. Dietary differences may account for higher rates of caries in the lowlands and more extreme tooth wear in the Core Region.

Economy

Subsistence. Tiwanaku's Core Region depended primarily on the large-scale herding of the domesticated camelids llama and alpaca and the cultivation of specialized frost-resistant crops in labor-intensive raised field systems. Raised field systems covering over 120,000 ha in the *altiplano* were the principal staple subsistence base for the Tiwanaku Core. Raised fields mitigated nightly frosts by storing solar energy in the water-filled swales between fields, managed drainage, and permitted fertilization of crops with organic materials dredged up in canal maintenance. Experiments by Erickson and Kolata's teams suggest that these advantages can dramatically decrease failure risk and increase yield over flatland agriculture in the *altiplano*.

Lacustrine and some terrestrial wild foods, hunted with small reed watercraft, snares, bow and arrow, darts, slings, and bolas, played a significant supplementary role in Tiwanaku diet. Husbandry of the lacustrine flora and fauna may have been a by-product of the extensive artificial wetlands created in the swales of the raised field systems.

Tiwanaku agriculture in the temperate lowlands of the Pacific slope concentrated on irrigation near the floodplains of the riverine oases. In Moquegua, Tiwanaku farmers modified the landscape to reclaim extensive areas of desert through the construction of laterally extended canal systems. A single preserved canal and field system investigated by Williams at the Chen Chen site alone irrigated over 90 ha, and comparable systems may be assumed at other sites in the valley. Unlike Wari, Late Intermediate, and Inca agriculturists in the same region, the Tiwanaku seldom resorted to terracing of steep terrain, preferring to extend canals to relatively flat areas.

Marine resources, such as mollusks, seaweed, bird guano fertilizer, seabirds, fish, and sea mammals, were utilized in lowland Tiwanaku settlements. These were probably obtained through occasional foraging trips or exchange with maritime specialists, as no Tiwanaku colonies have been identified on the littoral, and there is no evidence of any Tiwanaku maritime technology.

Wild Foods. Waterbirds composed a significant dietary contribution in the Tiwanaku Core Region, and freshwater fish and amphibians are also well represented in the faunal record. Reed plants were harvested for industrial purposes. Deer, the wild camelid species of vicuña and guanaco, and small rodents and amphibians were also consumed. *Choromytilus*, other sea mollusks, river crustaceans, and possibly fish, seabirds, and sea mammals were consumed in the Moquegua and Azapa peripheries.

Domestic Foods. Agriculture in the Tiwanaku Core Region relied on a complex of frost-resistant tubers including potatoes, *oca*, *olluco*, and *mashua* and chenopod grains such as *quinoa*. A freeze-drying process utilizing sunlight and frosts permitted the preparation and long-term storage of tuber crops in a dehydrated form late- known as *chuño*. Because of high-altitude frost, maize could not be a significant staple cultigen in the *altiplano*, although it may have grown in protected areas near lake Titicaca.

Maize was nonetheless extremely significant as the source of *chicha*, or maize beer, which ceramic evidence suggests was consumed in quantity in throughout the Tiwanaku tradition. Maize, along with hot peppers, coca leaf, peanuts, and beans, was cultivated at low-elevation Tiwanaku settlements in the eastern and western Andean slopes. Sandness's isotope analysis of human remains from the Omo site suggests that lowland Tiwanaku colonists consumed significant quantities of maize.

Domesticated food animals included llamas, (also used as pack animals), alpacas (valued for wool), guinea pigs, and probably ducks and other waterfowl.

Utensils. Pottery production, despite considerable regional variation, can be considered a single technological tradition. Both Tiwanaku fine serving wares and utilitarian plain-ware pottery were dense, moderately hard, low-fired terracottas, their principal differences being varieties, amounts, and sizes of sand temper, vessel thickness, and quality of burnishing and surface treatment. Most fine serving vessels were red-slipped, often with polychrome decoration with principal motifs in black and subsidiary decoration in somewhat translucent white, orange, and blue-gray mineral pigments. Plain and decorated wares at Chiji Jawira, a potter's barrio at Tiwanaku, were fired in open pits, using camelid dung and grass for fuel. Elsewhere, however, a burnished black serving ware was produced through smudging or reduction firing that may have required different firing conditions or fuels.

Ceramic serving vessels included *keros* or drinking goblets, *tazones* or flaring sided bowls, basins, small pitchers, and modeled anthropomorphic and zoomorphic drinking vessels. These vessels also appear in wood and metal. Ceramic ceremonial burners were used to burn llama fat or other offerings. Utilitarian plainware pottery, which accounts for roughly 90 percent of sherds in domestic and midden contexts, included several sizes of globular *ollas*, cooking vessels with vertical rim-strap handles, and cylindrical neck *tinajas*, storage and brewing vessels with vertical body handles. Full-sized flat handle wooden spoons, often decorated with a llama silhouette or geometric motif, were commonly used with *tazones* for eating.

Spinning was done on drop spindles with wooden shafts and whorls made of wood, drilled sherds, or specially made pottery whorls used for finer thread. Weaving tools such as picks or shuttles were typically made of camelid limb bones. Most Tiwanaku textiles were probably made on staked looms, although backstrap looms may have been used as well. As in most Andean cultures, textiles were used as woven or as two joined panels, and never cut or tailored.

Because of poor highland preservation, Tiwanaku textiles are best known from desert sites in Chile and Peru. Plainweave all-cotton textiles, found in domestic middens at the Omo site, bore no decoration, were never included in tombs, and appear to have been of utilitarian function. Tiwanaku-contemporary cotton textiles have also been reported by Oakland in the Cochabamba region. Most decorated textiles were of camelid wool or occasionally cotton-wool composite, either in natural colors or dyed red, blue, purple, green, yellow, and white. Warp-faced plain-weave tunics and blankets were most commonly decorated with warp stripes. Supplementary warp decoration does appear, although it appears to be more popular in post-Tiwanaku cultures. A characteristic loop stitch embroidery of geometric or figural motifs was used to finish selvages and edges. The most labor-intensive textiles were interlocked tapestry tunics with figures depicting mythical themes. These are rare and usually associated with elite contexts.

Bone and stone tool industries provided most utensils in daily use. Bermann and Janusek have documented specialized workshops at Lukurmata that produced bone pan pipes and a characteristic hafted utensil made from the snapped mandible of a camelid. Musical instruments also included ceramic whistles and cane and bone flutes.

Tiwanaku ground-stone utensils included bowls and palettes, mortars and pestles, manos and metates and some very large rocker grinders in Moquegua probably used for maize. Chipped-stone flake tools and hoes were casually made from chert, basalt, or volcanic stone in very large numbers.

Tiwanaku hunters and warriors used wooden bows and wood or cane arrows with narrow-stemmed points and double fletching with feathers. Atlatls with darts and pecked sling stones, woven slings, and grooved bola stones were also used. Characteristic to Tiwanaku are *trompos*, top-like conical or cylindroconical pecked stone or wooden objects of unknown function.

Bundles or kits related to hallucinogenic drug use have been found in elite Tiwanaku burial contexts and occasionally in middens. These include decorated textile bags, wood, stone, or bone snuff tablets, and small bone spoons, brushes, tubes, and containers. Larger rectangular bags, carrying cloths, and cordage were used to wrap coca leaves for practical purposes and for offering bundles.

Ornaments. Tiwanaku stonemasons produced some of the finest monuments in the Andes. Cut prismatic blocks were precisely fitted to face the sunken court temples, enclosures, and terraces of large pyramid structures at Tiahuanaco and Core Region sites. Figural stone carving included low relief decoration and three-dimensional sculpture that developed out of previous *altiplano* sculptural traditions of Pukara, Chiripa, and other sites. Massive humanoid stelae, including the 7-m Bennett monolith, the largest stone sculpture in the New World, were carved from local sandstones with stone and bronze tools. Like lintels, jambs, and other architectural elements, the classic Tiwanaku stelae were decorated in low relief with figures of deities and geometrics that may represent tapestry tunics, tattoos, or face paint.

Tiwanaku metallurgy was advanced, including gold, silver, and copper, and bronze alloys of copper-arsenic-nickel, copper-tin, and copper-arsenic, but was largely limited to ornamental purposes. Metal joining techniques did not attain the complexity achieved in the northern Andes, and most small tools and ornaments such as pins, needles, axes, and small figures were formed and hammered in one piece. The most common technique for decoration of metalwork was repoussé, used on thin beaten sheet ornaments, headdresses, and vessels. Bronze architectural cramps were cast and hammered into carved depressions in cut stones to join architectural elements of monumental buildings. Some gold decorative elements may have been added to stonework in a similar fashion.

Clothing, headgear, jewelry, and body decoration marked Tiwanaku social and status identities. Both males and females wore sleeveless rectangular tunics and blankets, which women fastened with metal or cactus spine pins. Undecorated cotton plain weaves may have served as everyday clothing or underwear. Tapestry tunics, the most elaborately decorated and labor-intensive textile, were rare. Their representation in low relief carving on Tiohuanaco's major stelae, supports that they were reserved for elites. Ceramic portrait head vessels depict often-mustachioed males with complex facial painting, wearing large cylindrical ear spools, lip plugs, four-pointed hats, or turbans. Wooden and ceramic pigment kits containing red and yellow ochers have been found in the Azapa and Moquegua valleys. Specialized workshops at Tiahuanaco and in Moquegua worked in rare and imported lapidary materials, producing metal headdress ornaments, pendants, *tupus*, or cloak or turban pins, and drilled beads and inlay pieces of lapis lazuli, malachite, sharks' teeth, and seashell, including *Oliva Peruvianus*, *Choromytilus Choro*, and occasionally *Spondylus*. Flamingo and other feathers found in domestic and midden contexts were probably used ornamentally as well.

Trade. It is generally accepted that Tiwanaku did not have a developed entrepreneurial market system, and that most trade involved either reciprocal relations among kin and affines or state-sponsored exchange. Llama caravans and human transport linked the Tiwanaku Core Region with the eastern and western peripheries. Except for lake Titicaca, where water transport is possible, Andean terrain and the caloric requirements of llamas probably made bulk long-distance transport of staples impractical. Exceptions would have been lowland crops such as maize, coca, and hot peppers, which were highly valued in the Core Region for ceremonial use or as condiments.

Long-distance exchange either through traders or intermediaries obtained exotic raw materials such as *Spondylus* shell from the Ecuadorian coast, obsidian from sources in the Colca valley near Arequipa, Peru, lapis lazuli and copper from northern Chile, and perhaps medicinal plants, hallucinogens, bird feathers, and exotic wildlife from the Amazonian lowlands. Tiwanaku sumptuary objects such as snuff kits and tapestry tunics, often bearing complex Tiwanaku iconography, were traded to non-Tiwanaku elites in San Pedro de Atacama in Chile and perhaps as far as Northwest Argentina. Exotic pottery found at Tiahuanaco suggests trade or resident foreigners from several eastern Bolivian regions.

Division of Labor. Tiwanaku crafts were produced both by individual households and by specialists. Simple bone and ground-stone tools, flake implements, and stone hoes were probably made casually by their users, and most plain textile spinning and weaving also took place in the household. It has not been possible to identify gender-specific production activities except from iconography and grave goods, which suggest male rulers, priests, and curers, and female weavers.

Production of more elaborate crafts was by corporate specialist groups residing in urban barrios or rural settlements. Pottery production was specialized to workshop groups like the Ch'iji Jawira barrio at Tiahuanaco, which oversaw all phases of production and maintained distinctive substyles. Janusek suggests that such coresidential crafts specialists may have corresponded to descent or ethnic groups, or *ayllus*, embedded in Tiwanaku's social substructure. Nonetheless, elite-attached specialists are also probable for highly skilled, sumptuary crafts like tapestry weaving, fine lithic production, bronze, gold, and silver metallurgy, and lapidary industries. Workshop evidence in Moquegua suggests that stemmed chert projectile points were produced as preforms near the point of quarrying

and transported to other locations for finishing, and lapidary work was specialized as well.

Differential Access or Control of Resources. It may be assumed that pasture and farmlands were held by households or corporate groups like *ayllus*, and it is likely that differential access to prime lands and herds among these groups was the basis for social stratification within Tiwanaku society. Ready access to labor for the construction and upkeep of public works and the collection of surplus to support the urban elite and their retainers would have been critical for maintaining political power. Tiahuanaco's ruling elites lived in palaces within the monumental center and enjoyed preferred access to labor-intensive sumptuary goods and those of exotic raw materials. Few intact elite tombs have been recorded by archaeologists in the Core Region; however, museum and private collections reflect looted elite burials with offerings of numerous metal objects. Provincial Tiwanaku sites have not revealed elite residences, although some residential sectors enjoyed preferred access to elaborate pottery. Elite burials in Cochabamba and Moquegua also suggest differential access to metal objects, beads, and tapestry tunics.

Sociopolitical Organization

Social Organization. The Tiwanaku-period Titicaca basin encompassed diverse ethnic communities, and these were probably also subdivided structurally at several levels. Kolata argues that a social hierarchy grew out of a coalition of proto-Aymara herders who formed Tiwanaku's elite with lower status Pukina agriculturists and Uru aquatic specialists. Spatial variations of ceramic style and household ritual between *barrios* within Tiahuanaco are seen by Janusek to represent diverse social segments subsumed within the hierarchy of the Tiwanaku polity. Similar spatial division into socially constituted sectors has also been noted by Goldstein in lowland Tiwanaku habitation sites. Most scholars believe that the fundamental social unit was the *ayllu*, a descent-based group that pooled labor and resources above the level of the household.

Political Organization. Recent fieldwork in the Tiwanaku Core Region has engendered debate on the strength and centricity of the Tiahuanaco site as the capital of a bureaucratic and hierarchical state. Analysts focusing on the Tiahuanaco type tend to emphasize the centripetal nature of the capital city and a strongly centralized Tiwanaku state. Researchers focusing on smaller sites of Tiwanaku's Core Region have emphasized more segmentary interpretations of Tiwanaku as a loose ethnic confederacy of politically autonomous communities that shared only cultural and ceremonial ties to the capital.

Social Control. State or elite sponsorship of festivals, performance of ritual obligations, effective redistribution of surplus, and elaborate gift giving may have been critical for maintaining political power. In exchange, the Tiwanaku populace contributed labor for public works and surplus to support elites and specialists. There is relatively little evidence for coercive social control, and much of this relationship may have been consensual. Most evidence suggests social controls dedicated to maintaining distinctions among Tiwanaku's component ethnic or social groups, which were separated by walls or moats within Tiahuanaco, and identified with specific styles of dress, material culture, and cranial deformation.

Conflict. Relatively little direct evidence of external warfare has been demonstrated for Tiwanaku. Evidence of possible human sacrifice on the Akapana pyramid, reworked cranea curated in Tiahuanaco domestic contexts, and *chachapuma* stone sculptures that depict decapitator feline figures may point to sanctioned violence in Tiwanaku. However, iconographic evidence for organized combat, sacrifice, or the taking of trophy heads is far rarer than in comparable Peruvian cultures like Moche and Nasca. Core Region Tiwanaku sites were not walled or defensibly located, and no correlation of Tiwanaku culture change with incidence of skeletal trauma, site burning, or increased presence of weapons has been observed. Peripheral Tiwanaku settlement patterns suggest competition with the contemporary Wavi cultures, but there is no direct evidence of conflict. Deliberate site destruction does accompany the abandonment of residential and ceremonial sites in Moquegua c. 1000 B.P. and may indicate a generalized rebellion or attack by outsiders. The peripheral Tiwanaku collapse was followed by a transfer of settlement to walled and defensible hilltop sites.

Religion and Expressive Culture

Religious Beliefs. Tiwanaku textile, stone, and ceramic iconography suggests a set of state deities associated with the Staff or Gateway God, a frontal figure depicted wearing an elaborate headdress and holding a puma-headed staff in either hand. The Staff God and a variable group of winged figures that accompany him on Tiahuanaco's archetypal "Gateway of the Sun" and numerous other carved architectural elements have been interpreted as a pantheon of sky, weather, mountain, or cosmic deities, possibly ancestral to the ethnohistorically known deities Viracocha and Illapa. Portable depictions of the Staff God on pottery, textiles, and other media accompanied Tiwanaku long-distance exchange and the colonization of new territories, but disappeared from the tradition at the time of societal collapse, supporting the god's association with the power of the Tiwanaku state.

Beyond state ideologies, the Tiwanaku tradition also encompassed enduring religious practices on the household and community levels. These included the sacrifice of pottery, jewelry, and animals to dedicate homes, temples, and fields. These offering traditions strongly resemble ethnographically recorded Aymara rituals dedicated to local mountain, earth, and landscape deities.

Ceremonies. It is believed that Tiahuanaco became an important center for pilgrimage, as well as a capital, and the city's monumental core is famous for terraced pyramids, platforms, enclosures, and sunken courts where religious ceremonies took place. Both at Tiahuanaco and at other Tiwanaku tradition sites, Conklin proposes that the architectural plan of temple structures suggests processional paths from public spaces through narrow doorways and staircases to progressively more restrictive sanctuaries. The inner temple complexes, typically walled sunken courts, were the location of the most exclusive ceremonies and housed the most elaborate stone sculptures or other sacred objects. Hallucinogenic drug use, probably restricted to ritual specialists in private contexts, played a role in prognostication, propitiation, or curing ceremonies. Both religious and mundane buildings were consecrated with buried offerings of young or fetal camelids, ritually killed pottery, metal pins and other artifacts, amulets including architectural models, seashells, and bundled coca leaves, and by ritual burning of llama fat in ceramic censors. One mass human interment excavated by Manzanilla on the Akapana pyramid may represent a human sacrifice to dedicate the pyramid's construction or to commemorate an event.

Ceramic evidence throughout the Tiwanaku tradition and analogy to Inca practices suggest that popular celebrations involved politically sponsored feasting and mass consumption of maize beer in civic, household, or rural contexts. Beer-drinking paraphernalia such as *kero* goblets are found in domestic middens throughout the Tiwanaku tradition, but also occur in concentration in Moquegua in particular households that may have been ceremonial *chicherias*, near public plazas, and outside settlements on promontories with views of temples or important landscape features. It is possible that ceremonies may have been celebrated simultaneously in sunken courts out of sight at the top of artificial pyramids on platforms that were visible from below.

Arts. Complex figural iconography, such as portrayals of the Staff or Gateway God, appears on only a small proportion of Tiwanaku works in architectural stone, textile, metal, and ceramic media. Although temples and palaces were stuccoed and painted in solid red, green, and yellow pigments, no Tiwanaku mural painting has yet been found. Cut-stone architecture was commonly ornamented with recessed jambs and lintels and deep carvings of crosses, step motifs, or other motifs. When figures were carved, usually in low relief on stone architraves, there is no use of perspective, and it is difficult to decipher any narrative or thematic organization of scenes. The same would apply to figures depicted on tapestry textiles and pottery.

In painted pottery and wood vessels, geometric motifs predominate, the most common being opposed step-stair designs that may represent terraced pyramids or mountains with cosmological embellishments. Spiral, volute, and cross motifs are also common. Painted and wood-carved representations of llamas, felines, flamingos, and humans are less common and tend to be highly abstracted or rectangularized to fit panels.

In-the-round stone sculptures were highly stylized, and most analysis has focused on the representation of the humanoid stelae figures' dress, adornment, and utensils such as *keros* lime dippers and hallucinogenic snuff tablets and the knives and decapitated heads held by feline figures known as *chachapumas*. In contrast, many modeled ceramic vessels depicting human heads, full-body llamas, felines, and ducks and the heads of felines and eagles often displayed great sensitivity and realism. It appears that at least some human representations on drinking vessels are true portraits of individuals. Relatively crude plain-ware figurines of females with long braids and deformed crania are also found.

There is good evidence that Tiahuanaco curated stone sculpture of ancient and foreign styles, perhaps by practicing *huaca* capture, the imprisonment of revered idols of subjugated peoples. Kolata argues that sculpture collections of varied styles depicting diverse costumes, such as the group of stelae and tenon heads collected at Tiahuanaco's Semisubterranean Temple, may have been assembled as microcosmic social maps of the Tiwanaku world.

Death and Afterlife. Most Tiwanaku burials were individual primary interments, buried with offerings in simple pits, or stone-lined cylindrical cists. Individuals were wrapped in one or more tunics or blankets, tightly bound with cordage, and interred in a seated, flexed position with offering objects, which typically included one or more *keros*, *tazones*, or other serving vessel, small plain ollas, and wooden spoons. Less commonly, jewelry items, weaving implements, pigment boxes, musical instruments, and drug paraphernalia were included. An east-facing orientation was customary in Tiwanaku interments in Moquegua, Lukurmata, and the Coyo Oriental and Quitor cemeteries of San Pedro de Atacama. In the Tiwanaku Core Region, burials were placed either within household units or in separate cemeteries, while in the peripheries of Moquegua, Azapa, and San Pedro, burials were segregated to nearby cemetery areas and tombs were marked with wooden posts. The proximity of the interred to domestic space and the marking and probable maintenance of many tombs suggest a concept of the afterlife in which ancestors played important roles in the affairs of the living.

Suggested Readings

Albarracin-Jordan, J. (1996). "Tiwanaku Settlement Systems: The Integration of Nested Hierarchies in the Lower Tiwanaku Valley." *Latin American Antiquity* 3, 3: 183–210.

Bennett, W. C. (1934). "Excavations at Tiahuanaco." *Anthropological Papers of the American Museum of Natural History* 34, 3: 361–493.

Bennett, W. C. (1936). "Excavations in Bolivia." *Anthropological Papers of the American Museum of Natural History* 35, 4: 329–508.

Berenguer, J. R., and Percy Dauelsberg H. (1989). "El Norte Grande en la órbita de Tiwanaku (400 a 1,200 d.C.)." In *Culturas de Chile, Prehistoria Desde sus Orígenes Hasta los Albores de la Conquista*, ed. J. Hidalgo L., V. Schiappacasse F., H. Niemeyer F., C. Aldunate, and I. Solimano R. Santiago: Editorial Andrés Bello, 129–180.

Bermann, M. P. (1994). *Lukurmata: Household Archaeology in Prehispanic Bolivia*. Princeton: Princeton University Press.

Blom, D. (1999). *Tiwanaku and the Moquegua Settlements: A Bioarchaeological Approach*. Ph.D. diss., University of Chicago.

Browman, D. L. (1985). "Cultural Primacy of Tiwanaku in the Development of Later Peruvian States." *Diálogo Andino* 4 (La problematica Tiwanaku Huari en el contexto panandino del desarollo cultural, ed. M. Rivera): 59–72.

Browman, D. L. (1997). "Political Institutional Factors Contributing to the Integration of the Tiwanaku state." In *Emergence and Change in Early Urban Societies*, ed. L. Manzanilla. New York: Plenum, 229–243.

Chavez, S. J. (1976). "The Arapa Thunderbolt Stelae: A Case of Stylistic Identity with Implications for Pucara Influences in the Area of Tiahuanaco." *Nawpa Pacha* 13: 3–25.

Conklin, W. (1991). "Tiwanaku and Huari: Architectural Comparisons and Interpretations." In *Huari Administrative Structure: Prehistoric Monumental Architecture and State Government*, ed. W. Isbell and G. McEwan. Washington, D.C.: Dumbarton Oaks, 281–292.

Eisleb, D., and Renate Strelow (1980). *Altperuanische Kulturen III: Tiahuanaco*. Berlin: Museum für Völkerkunde.

Erickson, C. L. (1999). "Neo-environmental Determinism and Agrarian 'Collapse' in Andean Prehistory." *Antiquity* 73: 634–642.

Goldstein, P. S. (1993). "Tiwanaku Temples and State Expansion: A Tiwanaku Sunken Court Temple in Moquegua, Peru." *Latin American Antiquity* 4, 3: 22–47.

Goldstein, P. S. (1996). "Tiwanaku Settlement Patterns of the Azapa Valley, Chile—New Data, and the Legacy of Percy Dauelsberg." *Dialogo Andino* 14/15 (Special issue Prehistoria del Norte de Chile y del Desierto de Atacama: Simposio Homenaje a Percy Dauelsberg Hahmann): 57–73.

Janusek, J. W. (1999). "Craft and Local Power: Embedded Specialization in Tiwanaku Cities." *Latin American Antiquity* 10, 2: 107–131.

Kolata, A. L. (1986). "The Agricultural Foundations of the Tiwanaku State: A View from the Heartland." *American Antiquity* 51: 748–762.

Kolata, A. L. (1992). "Economy, Ideology and Imperialism in the South-Central Andes." In *Ideology and Pre-Columbian Civilizations*, ed. A. A. Demarest and G. W. Conrad. Santa Fe: School of American Research Press, 65–87.

Kolata, A. L. (1993). *The Tiwanaku: Portrait of an Andean Civilization*. Cambridge, MA: Blackwell.

Kolata, A. L. ed. (1996). *Tiwanaku and its Hinterland: Archaeology and Paleoecology of an Andean Civilization*. Washington, D.C.: Smithsonian Institution Press.

Lechtman, H. (1997). "El Bronce Arsenical y el Horizonte Medio." In *Arqueologia, Antropología e História en los Andes: Homenaje a Maria Rostworowski*, ed. R. Varón G. and J. Flores E. Lima: Instituto de Estudios Peruanos, Banco Central de Reserva del Perú, 153–186.

Llagostera, A. (1996). "San Pedro de Atacama: Nodo de complementariedad reticular." In *La Integracion Surandina Cinco Siglos Despues*, ed. X. Albó, M. Arratia, J. Hidalgo, L. Nuñez, A. Llagostera, M. Remy, and B. Revesz. Cusco and Antofagasta: Centro de Estudios Regionales Andinos Bartolomé de Las Casas, and Universidad Católica del Norte, 17–42.

Manzanilla, L. (1992). *Akapana: Una Pirámide en el Centro del Mundo*. Mexico City: Universidad Nacional Autónoma de México, Instituto de Investigaciones Antropológicas.

Moseley, M. E. (1992). *The Incas and their Ancestors: The Archaeology of Peru*. New York: Thames and Hudson.

Moseley, M. E., Robert A. Feldman, Paul S. Goldstein, and Luis Watanabe M. (1991). "Colonies and Conquest: Tiahuanaco and Huari in Moquegua." In *Huari Administrative Structure: Prehistoric Monumental Architecture and State Government*, ed. W. G. M. Isbell. Washington, D.C.: Dumbarton Oaks, 91–103.

Mujica B., E. (1996). "La Integración Surandina durante el periódo Tiwanaku." In *La Integracion Surandina Cinco Siglos Despues*, ed. X. Albó, M. Arratia, J. Hidalgo, L. Nuñez, A. Llagostera, M. Remy, and B. Revesz. Cusco and Antofagasta: Centro de Estudios Regionales Andinos Bartolomé de Las Casas, and Universidad Católica del Norte. 81–116.

Muñoz Ovalle, I. (1996). "Integración y Complementaridad en las Sociedades Prehispanicas en el Extremo Norte de Chile: Hipótesis de Trabajo." In *La Integracion Surandina cinco Siglos Despues*, ed. X. Albó, M. Arratia, J Hidalgo, L. Nuñez, A. Llagostera, M. Remy, and B. Revesz. Cusco and Antofagasta: Centro de Estudios Regionales Andinos Bartolomé de Las Casas and Universidad Católica del Norte, 117–134.

Oakland Rodman, A. (1992). "Textiles and Ethnicity: Tiwanaku in San Pedro de Atacama, North Chile." *Latin American Antiquity* 3, 4: 316–340.

Ponce Sangines, C. (1969). "Tiwanaku: Descripcion Sumaria del Templete Semisubterraneo." *Academia Nacional de Ciencias de Bolivia* 20.

Ponce Sangines, C. (1972). *Tiwanaku: Espacio Tiempo y Cultura*. Academia Nacional de Ciencias de Bolivia. La Paz.

Ponce Sangines, C. (1989). *Arqueología de Lukurmata* 1. La Paz: INAR.

Reinhard, J. (1985). "Chavín and Tiahuanaco: A New Look at Two Andean Ceremonial Centers." *National Geographic Research* 1: 395–422.

Rivera Diaz, M. A. (1991). "The Prehistory of Northern Chile: A Synthesis." *Journal of World Prehistory* 5, 1: 1–48.

Rivera Sundt, O. (1989). "Resultados de la excavación en el centro ceremonial de Lukurmata." In *Arqueología de Lukurmata*, vol. 2, ed. A. L. Kolata. La Paz: INAR, 59–89.

Stanish, C. (1992). *Ancient Andean Political Economy*. Austin: University of Texas Press.

SUBTRADITIONS

Azapa Tiwanaku (Loreto Viejo/ Cabuza)

TIME PERIOD: 1550–950 B.P.

LOCATION: The Azapa Tiwanaku subtradition (Loreto Viejo/Cabuza) is found in the Pacific-draining Azapa valley of northern Chile, in the Chaca and Camarones valleys to the south, and the Lluta valley of Chile and the Sama and Caplina valleys of southern Peru to the north, all approximately 300 km west of the site of Tiahuanaco at elevations from 0 to 1000 m.

DIAGNOSTIC MATERIAL ATTRIBUTES: Azapa Tiwanaku pottery (also known as the Loreto Viejo style) corresponds closely to Tiwanaku IV and V in the Core Region and the Omo and Chen Chen styles of Moquegua Tiwanaku. Azapa Tiwanaku polychrome *keros*, *tazones*, and small pitchers appear at mortuary sites in Azapa, and wooden spoons and serving vessels are also found. Tiwanaku utilitarian olla and *tinaja* forms are found at a few habitation sites. Azapa Tiwanaku textiles include a limited number of polychrome interlocked tapestry tunics bearing complex iconography of elaborately adorned supernatural figures similar to low relief carvings at Tiahuanaco (Conklin 1983: 8–11). These and warp striped plain-weave tunics, *mantas*, and bags and knotted four-pointed hats were woven of two-ply Z-spun s-plied camelid wool fibers (Frame 1990; Oakland Rodman 1985, 1992). Hallucinogenic snuff kits of Tiwanaku style are relatively rare in Azapa Tiwanaku (Focacci 1993: 81). Carved wooden vessels, flat handled decorated spoons (Espouyes 1976), and narrow-stemmed white chert arrow points are more commonly found.

The few known Tiwanaku-contemporary habitation sites consisted of perishable structures, some with stone foundations. Azapa Tiwanaku cemeteries consisted of seated flexed burials in pits and cists with ceramic and other offerings. One elite above-ground stone cemetery structure has been discovered. Extensive hillside geoglyphs and petroglyphs in Azapa probably date to both Tiwanaku and later traditions.

Ceramics of the Cabuza style, a contemporary local style, emulated Tiwanaku *keros* and other forms in local pastes, with decoration in black over a purplish-red slip. The Cabuza tradition is also characterized by seated flexed cist burials. Cabuza textiles include plain weave and floating warp decorated tunics, long belts, and four-pointed hats (Ulloa 1982). Part of the subsequent Maitas-Chiribaya polychrome pottery style may also overlap with the Azapa Tiwanaku (Loreto Viejo) tradition (Focacci 1983, 1993; Mujica 1985, 1996; Muñoz 1996a, 1996b; Rivera 1991, 1996).

CULTURAL SUMMARY

Environment

Climate in the Azapa valley region is temperate and hyperarid, with virtually no precipitation. The absence of any biota outside the river valleys has limited human occupation to the immediate area of the floodplains.

Settlements

Systematic full coverage survey of the middle Azapa valley by Goldstein (1996) found 54 sites with Azapa Tiwanaku or Cabuza sherds. Of these, 15 produced both styles, 27 produced only Cabuza, and 12 produced only Azapa Tiwanaku fragments. The distribution of Azapa Tiwanaku cemetery and settlement sites closely parallels that of their Cabuza contemporaries, with a marked avoidance of coastal settlement (Bird 1943) and the incised upper sectors of the valley. Both Azapa Tiwanaku and Cabuza sites were found below km 24 of the Azapa highway, concentrated at locations overlooking open river floodplain, particularly near natural springs at Las Riberas, Alto Ramirez, and Saucache, suggesting a preference for zones optimal for irrigated cultivation. There were only three confirmed habitation sites with Tiwanaku household material culture predominant, with an aggregate area of under 5 ha.

Cabuza and Tiwanaku-contemporary dwellings were built of ephemeral materials such as cane, and little surface-visible architecture other than structural platforms or stone terrace facings remains (Muñoz 1986: 315; Muñoz and Focacci 1985). At 3 ha the largest Tiwanaku habitation site was AZ-83, located in the Pampa Alto Ramirez. Salvage excavations conducted before the sites' bulldozing in 1974 revealed circular and rectangular stone foundations, Cabuza and Azapa Tiwanaku ceramics and textiles, and two C14 dates of 560 +/− 110 and 760 +/− 70, which place it within the Cabuza/Tiwanaku chronological range (Rivera 1987: 12). The site was also centrally located among three Tiwanaku cemeteries (AZ-9, AZ-14, and AZ-19).

Economy

The Tiwanaku and Cabuza economies were essentially agricultural, with sites clustering in optimal irrigable zones and little presence on the Pacific littoral. Greater settlement has been associated with "sweet water" (less mineralized) valleys like the lower Azapa valley of the San Jose river and particularly locations near natural springs. Cultigens included maize, beans, fruits, and coca, which has been identified in Azapa only after the Tiwanaku arrival. Coca, perhaps of a variety cultivated only in the dry western valleys (Molina et al. 1989: 47), could have been a significant economic attraction for the Tiwanaku presence. Other potential trade items for export to the Tiwanaku Core Region would have included mineral ores and fish and shellfish from the Pacific coast.

Tiwanaku-style crafts do not appear in Azapa in sufficient numbers to confirm local production, and no textile or ceramic workshops have been identified. Pottery of the locally made Cabuza tradition may appear in Azapa as early as A.D. 380, predating the arrival of the Tiwanaku-style ceramics (Berenguer and Dauelsberg 1989: 147–148; Dauelsberg 1985), although most absolute dates place Cabuza somewhat later (e.g., Focacci 1987; Muñoz 1983b; Schiappacase et al. 1991: 52). Stylistically similar kero-using ceramic styles in southern Peru seldom date before A.D. 900 and are considered products of local craftsmen heavily influenced by Tiwanaku precedents (Bermann et al. 1989; Goldstein 1989; Owen 1993).

Sociopolitical Organization

Most Tiwanaku sites in the Azapa valley are small components of multicomponent cemeteries or habitation sites, suggesting segregated islands in a sea of denser Cabuza settlement. The most likely explanation of Azapa Tiwanaku occupation is that small enclaves of colonists from the Tiwanaku Core Region coexisted with a larger local population who emulated the Tiwanaku tradition in the Cabuza style. Interpretations of this coexistence have ranged from a "symbiosis" of ethnic groups (Rivera 1985: 17) to a vision of marked social stratification, with the Loreto Viejo ceramic tradition representing a "cupula dirigente de las colonias costeras de Tiwanaku" (Berenguer and Dauelsberg 1989: 151). This conception, of enclaves of a Tiwanaku "ruling elite" imposed on a Cabuza substrate, assumes higher status for Tiwanaku individuals based on the quality of Azapa Tiwanaku pottery and textiles and the presence of snuff tablets, spoons, and four-pointed hats of elite Tiwanaku style associations (Berenguer and Dauelsberg 1989: 151; Focacci 1981: 70). However, one recent examination of skeletal remains from Azapa sites has failed to isolate *altiplano* individuals from Azapa valley residents on biological grounds (Richard Sutter 2000).

Religion and Expressive Culture

Azapa Tiwanaku burials were seated flexed individual interments in either pits or stone-lined cist tombs, originally marked with wooden poles. Cemeteries were typified by offerings of Tiwanaku or mixed Cabuza and Tiwanaku ceramic and textile styles. Focacci (1983: 112) discovered at least one looted burial with entirely "Classic" Tiwanaku offerings at the AZ-75 cemetery site at San Lorenzo, dated to 1390 B.P.; another cemetery, Atoca I, with its above-ground stone structures, figurine and jewelry fragments, and Tiwanaku, Cabuza, and imported Chakipampa Wari pottery vessels, also appears to be of elite affiliation (Goldstein 1996: 65; Muñoz 1986: 314). Cabuza and later Chiribaya-Maytas burials often included offerings of paws, heads, or ears of camelids, entire guinea pigs, coca, textiles, feathers, or wool (Focacci 1993:76), but these are uncommon in Tiwanaku tombs. Tiwanaku offerings were also placed at locally sacred sites, including pre-Tiwanaku *tumulo* mound burials, Cabuza cemeteries, and rocky hillside prominences (Focacci, personal communication; Goldstein 1996; Muñoz 1996: 253).

References

Berenguer, J. R., and Percy Dauelsberg H. (1989). "El Norte Grande en la órbita de Tiwanaku (400 a 1200 d.C.)." In *Culturas de Chile, Prehistoria Desde sus Orígenes Hasta los Albores de la Conquista*, ed. J. Hidalgo L., V. Schiappacasse F., H. Niemeyer F., C. Aldunate, and I. Solimano R. Santiago: Editorial Andrés Bello, 129–180.

Bermann, M., P. Goldstein, C. Stanish, and L. Watanabe M. (1989). "The Collapse of the Tiwanaku State: A View from the Osmore Drainage." In *Settlement, History and Ecology in the Osmore Drainage, Southern Peru*, ed. D. S. Rice and C. Stanish. Oxford: British Archaeological Reports 545, International Series, 269–286.

Bird, J. (1943). "Excavations in Northern Chile." *Anthropological Papers of the American Museum of Natural History* 38, 4: 173–318.

Conklin, W. (1983). "Pucara and Tiahuanaco Tapestry: Time and Style in a Sierra Weaving Tradition." *Nawpa Pacha* 21: 1–44.

Dauelsberg, P. (1985). "Desarollo regional en los valles costeros del norte de Chile." *Diálogo Andino* 4 (La problematica Tiwanaku Huari en el contexto panandino del desarrollo cultural, ed. M. Rivera): 277–287.

Espouyes, O. (1976). "Tipificacion de Keros de Madera de Arica." *Chungará* 4: 39–54.

Focacci Aste, G. (1981). "Nuevos fechados para la epoca del Tiahuanaco en la arqueologia del norte de Chile." *Chungara* 8: 63–77.

Focacci Aste, G. (1983). "El Tiwanaku Clasico en el valle de Azapa." In *Asentamientos Aldeanos en los Valles Costeros de Arica, Documentos de Trabajo*. vol. 3. Arica: Instituto de Antropologia y Arqueología, Universidad de Tarapacá.

Focacci Aste, G. (1993). "Excavaciones Arqueológicas en el Cementerio AZ-6, Valle de Azapa." *Chungara* 24/25: 69–124.

Focacci Aste, G., and Sergio Erices (1971). "Excavaciónes en lus Túmulos de San Miguel de Azapa (Arica, Chile)." *Actas del VI Congreso Nacional de Arqueología Chilena*.

Frame, M. (1990). "Andean Four-Cornered Hats: Ancient Volumes." In *Exhibit from the Collection of Arthur Bullowa, Organized by Julie Jones*. New York: Metropolitan Museum of Art.

Goldstein, P. S. (1989). "Omo, a Tiwanaku Provincial Center in Moquegua, Peru." Ph.D. diss., Anthropology, University of Chicago.

Goldstein, P. S. (1996). "Tiwanaku Settlement Patterns of the Azapa Valley, Chile—New Data, and the Legacy of Percy Dauelsberg." *Dialogo Andino* 14/15 (Special issue Prehistoria del Norte de Chile y del Desierto de Atacama: Simposio Homenaje a Percy Dauelsberg Hahmann): 57–73.

Molina, Y., Tatiana Torres, Eliana Belmonte, and Calogero Santoro (1989). "Uso y posible cultivo de coca (*erythroxylum spp.*) en Epocas Prehispánicas en los Valles de Arica." *Chungara* 23: 37–49.

Mujica B., E. (1996). "La Integración Surandina durante el periódo Tiwanaku." In *La Integracion Surandina Cinco Siglos Despues*, ed. X. Albó, M. Arratia, J. Hidalgo, L. Nuñez, A. Llagostera, M. Remy, and B. Revesz. Cusco and Antofagasta: Centro de Estudios Regionales Andinos Bartolomé de Las Casas, and Universidad Católica del Norte, 81–116.

Muñoz Ovalle, I. (1986). "Aportes a la Reconstitucion Historica del Poblamiento Aldeano en el Valle de Azapa (Arica—Chile)." *Chungara* 16/17: 307–322.

Muñoz Ovalle, I. (1988). "Analisis de dos fases culturales de los valles costeros del extremo norte de Chile, en el periodo de influencia Tiwanaku (300 D.C.–900 D.C.)."

Muñoz Ovalle, I. (1996a). "Integración y Complementaridad en las Sociedades Prehispanicas en el Extremo Norte de Chile: Hipøtesis de Trabajo." In *La Integracion Surandina cinco Siglos Despues*, ed. X. Albó, M. Arratia, J Hidalgo, L. Nuñez, A. Llagostera, M. Remy, and B. Revesz. Cusco and Antofagasta: Centro de Estudios Regionales Andinos Bartolomé de Las Casas and Universidad Católica del Norte, 117–134.

Muñoz Ovalle, I. (1996b). "Poblamiento Humano y Relaciones Interculturales en el Valle de Azapa: Nuevos Hallazgos en torno al Periodo Formativo y Tiwanaku." *Dialogo Andino* 14/15 (Special issue Prehistoria del Norte de Chile y del Desierto de Atacama. Simposio Homenaje a Percy Dauelsberg Hahmann): 241–278.

Muñoz Ovalle, I., and Guillermo Focacci (1985). "San Lorenzo: Testimonio de una comunidad de agricultores y pescadores Postiwanaku en el valle de Azapa (Arica—Chile)." *Chungará* 15: 7–30.

Nuñez A., L. (1965). "Desarrollo cultural Prehispanico del Norte de Chile." *Estudios Arqueologicos* 12.

Oakland, A. (1985). "Tiwanaku Textile Style from the South Central Andes." Ph.D. diss., University of Texas.

Oakland Rodman, A. (1992). "Textiles and Ethnicity: Tiwanaku in San Pedro de Atacama, North Chile." *Latin American Antiquity* 3, 4: 316–340.

Owen, B. D. (1993). "A Model of Multiethnicity: State Collapse, Competition, and Social Complexity from Tiwanaku to Chiribaya in the Osmore Valley, Perú." Ph.D. diss., University of California, Los Angeles.

Rivera Diaz, M. A. (1985). "Alto Ramirez y Tiwanaku, un caso de interpretación simbólica a través de datos arqueológicos en el área de los valles occidentales, Sur del Peru y Norte de Chile." *Diálogo Andino* 4 (La problematica Tiwanaku Huari en el contexto panandino del desarrollo cultural): 39–58.

Rivera Diaz, M. A. (1987). "Tres Fechados Radiométricos de Pampa Alto de Ramírez, Norte de Chile." *Chungara* 18: 7–14.

Rivera Diaz, M. A. (1991). "The Prehistory of Northern Chile: A Synthesis." *Journal of World Prehistory* 5, 1: 1–48.

Santoro, C. (1980). "Estratigrafia y secuencia cultural funeraria: Fase Azapa, Alto Ramirez y Tiwanaku." *Chungara* 6.

Sutter, Richard C. (2000). "Prehistoric Genetic and Culture Change: A Bioarchaeological Search for Pre-Inka Altiplano Colonies in the Coastal Valleys of Moquegua Valley, Peroe, and Azapa, Chile." *Latin American Antiquity* (11(1):43–70.

Trimborn, H. (1973). "Investigaciones arqueologicos en el Departamento de Tacna." Paper presented at the Atti del XL Congreso Internazionale Degle Americanisti, Genoa.

Ulloa, L. (1982). "Estilos decorativos y formas textiles de poblaciones agromarítimas en el extremo norte de Chile." *Chungara* 8: 109–136.

Vela Velarde, C. (1992). "Tiwanaku en el Valle de Caplina (Tacna)." *Pumapunku* (*new series*) 1, 3: 31–45.

Cochabamba Tiwanaku

TIME PERIOD: 1550–950 B.P.

LOCATION: The Cochabamba Tiwanaku subtradition is found in the intermontane Mizque, Capinota, Santivañez, Sacaba, Valle Alto, and central Cochabamba valleys of eastern Bolivia, approximately 400–600 km southeast of the site of Tiahuanaco, at elevations from 1800–2800 m.

DIAGNOSTIC MATERIAL ATTRIBUTES: Cochabamba Tiwanaku polychrome pottery has been described as a "derived" style of Tiwanaku Core Region serving wares, although vessels of classic Tiwanaku style are also found. Tiwanaku also influenced the contemporary regional pottery styles of Omereque (also known as Mizque and Nazcoide), Yampara, and Mojocoyo.

Tiwanaku-style wool tapestry tunics and bags appear in association with Tiwanaku pottery, wooden spoons, snuff tablets, and other objects in mortuary contexts. Cochabamba Tiwanaku peoples constructed rectangular domestic structures with stone foundations and stone-lined circular storage pits, and practiced seated flexed burials in caves and bark-lined cist tombs.

CULTURAL SUMMARY

Environment

Climate variation within the Cochabamba region is largely altitude-determined, with mean annual temperatures between 6–18° C at elevations from 1800–2800 m and seasonal precipitation (November–March) ranging from 300–1000 mm. Natural biota include arid xerofitic, humid and subspinous vegetation (Higueras 1996). Rainfall agriculture of maize, potatoes, legumes, and fruits is possible in most of the mesothermal valley bottoms, while upland slopes are used for pasture. The region overall is considered extremely fertile and was a major area of colonization for agricultural production under Inca control.

Settlements

To date, there is little excavation-based information on Cochabamba Tiwanaku habitation sites. Bennett found the remains of rectangular domestic structures with stone foundations and stone-lined circular storage pits at Arani (1936: 341). Céspedes reports over 300 Tiwanaku-affiliated sites in the region, including a major mortuary center at Piñami in Quillacollo and administrative centers at Jarka Pata in the Pocona valley and Caraparial in Omereque (Céspedes Paz 1982, 1993: 65). From a 10 percent survey sample of the Capinota and Mizque valleys, Higueras estimates aggregate Middle Horizon occupations of 159.9 ± 99.7 ha for Capinota and 365.9 ± 259 for Mizque, but failed to detect any change in site location from pre-Tiwanaku settlement patterns or any settlement preference for the more fertile Mizque valley in the Middle Horizon (Higueras 1996).

Economy

Tiwanaku-contemporary subsistence in Cochabamba presumably relied on rainfall and irrigated cultivation of maize, potatoes, legumes, and fruits and the herding of camelids. Excavation of habitation midden at Arani found rocker-grinding stones and stone-lined cylindrical storage cists for processing and storing crops. Deer antler and bone projectile points, grooved axes, and bola stones suggest supplementary hunting (Bennett 1936: 341, 350).

Cochabamba Tiwanaku pottery has been defined as "Derived Tiahuanaco," a style of local manufacture, distinguishable from the Core Region serving wares by restricted-base *keros*, different hues of polychrome pigments, the greater use of panels on the upper vessel for painted iconography, and an idiosyncratic selection of design motifs (Bennett 1936: 402–403; Browman 1997: 231; Byrne de Caballero 1984: 70; Higueras 1996; Ibarra Grasso 1986; Rydén 1947, 1959). Distance from the Core Region and petrography also suggest that most of this pottery was made locally; however, many vessels follow Tiwanaku archetypes very closely, and the Tiwanaku-style ceramic collections in Cochabamba are very similar overall to those of the Tiwanaku Core Region and Moquegua (Goldstein 1989: 238; Janusek 1994: 127; Kolata 1993: 270). Recent analyses found Illataco and Piñami phase vessels excavated in the Central Cochabamba valley to correspond to Tiwanaku IV and V in the Core Region (Anderson et al. 1998).

Cochabamba Tiwanaku pottery coexisted with contemporary regional styles. The Omereque style (also known as Mizque and Nazcoide) is a polychrome with unusually opaque and colorful pigments and local forms such as tripod vessels (Anderson 1997). Later Omereque pottery displays strong Tiwanaku influence (Bennett 1936: 387, 403; Byrne de Caballero 1984). Other local styles include Yampara in the southern valleys and Mojocoyo in the east (Browman 1997:231; Ibarra Grasso 1984). Omereque and gray ware local pottery is commonly found in association with Tiwanaku wares in the Capinota and Mizque valleys (Higueras 1996). Further research is required on the relative frequency of Tiwanaku serving wares, utilitarian plain wares, and local vessels at Cochabamba domestic sites. Trade pottery of Cochabamba's Omereque and Yampara styles appears in low frequency in the Tiwanaku Core Region at the Lukurmata and Tiahuanaco sites (Janusek 1993: 16; 1994: 127; 1999: 122–123).

Oakland reports that an identifiable Tiwanaku style predominated in textile bags and bands from Manzanani, Omereque, and Perez, which were found in burial association with Tiwanaku pottery (1986: 246). Other Tiwanaku-style textiles may have been provincial imitations using local coloring and materials, while local-style cotton garments continued in use as well. However, the frequencies and contextual relation of these categories have not been quantified (Oakland 1985: 233, 248).

Tiwanaku tapestry textile tunics and bags of highland manufacture have been found in dry cave burial contexts in Cochabamba such as Niño Korin (Wassen 1972).

In the absence of household excavations, it is unclear whether the economic relation of Cochabamba to the Tiwanaku Core Region was one of direct administration, colonization, or hegemony over local populations through religious proselytizing or long-distance trade. The low frequency and association with local contexts of sumptuary Tiwanaku goods like tapestry tunics and snuff kits suggest that those were long-distance trade imports for local elites (Browman 1997: 232; Oakland 1985: 245). On the other hand, Bennett noted that the burial offerings of ceramic *keros* and *tazones* at the Arani site were of exclusively Tiwanaku style (1936: 353), as are the grave offerings at Piñami in Quillacollo (Céspedes Paz 1993: 65). Oakland reports that Tiwanaku textile bags and bands from Manzanani, Omereque, and Perez were found in burial association with Tiwanaku pottery (1985: 246). The absence of local materials suggests some interments by culturally Tiwanaku people, either colonists or fully acculturated local populations.

Sociopolitical Organization

Interpretations differ on the intensity of Tiwanaku exploitation and integration of Cochabamba. Céspedes, citing the overwhelming adoption of Tiwanaku stylistic elements, the sheer quantity of Tiwanaku material culture, and the construction of administrative centers, suggests that direct Tiwanaku expansion began as early as 1650 B.P., and was followed by full provincial incorporation after 1200 B.P. (Anderson et al. 1998; Céspedes Paz 1993: 65). Others point to continuity in local settlement pattern, Cochabamba Tiwanaku's "derived" pottery style, and the prevalence of Tiwanaku materials in mortuary rather than domestic contexts to support an interpretation of indirect trade, elite clientage and stylistic emulation of Tiwanaku by the region's preexisting societies (Browman 1997: 231; Higueras 1996; Oakland 1985: 246). This would suggest the emulation of Tiwanaku styles and practices within the context of locally based chiefdoms. This debate may be clarified with full coverage survey, household archaeology, and comparative examination of domestic material culture from Tiwanaku-contemporary sites in the region.

Religion and Expressive Culture

Cochabamba Tiwanaku burials at the Arani site were stone covered, bark-lined cist tombs, typified by ceramic offerings of exclusively Tiwanaku style (Bennett 1936: 353). The cist burials represented a marked departure from pre-Tiwanaku burials, which were typically in ceramic urns. This, plus the prevalence of tombs with exclusively Tiwanaku offerings, rather than mixed local and Tiwanaku contexts, suggests major culture change and the adoption of highland mortuary practice, rather than the incorporation of Tiwanaku trade goods into existing traditions.

References

Anderson, K. (1997). "Omereque: A Middle Horizon Ceramic Style of Central Bolivia." M.A. thesis, University of California at Santa Barbara.

Anderson, K., Ricardo Céspedes, and R. Sanzetenea (1998). "Tiwanaku and the Local Effects of Contact: The Late Formative to Middle Horizon Transition in Cochabamba, Bolivia." Paper presented at the 63rd annual meeting of the Society of American Archaeology, Seattle.

Bennett, W. (1936). "Excavations in Bolivia." *Anthropological Papers of the American Museum of Natural History* 35, 4: 329–508.

Browman, D. L. (1997). "Political Institutional Factors Contributing to the Integration of the Tiwanaku state." In *Emergence and Change in Early Urban Societies*, ed. L. Manzanilla. New York: Plenum, 229–243.

Byrne de Caballero, G. (1984). "El Tiwanaku en Cochabamba." *Arqueología Boliviana* 1: 67–72.

Céspedes Paz, R. (1982). *Mapa Arqueológico de Cochabamba*. Cochabamba: Instituto de Investigaciones Antropologicas, Universidad Mayor de San Simón/Banco Boliviano Americano.

Céspedes Paz, R. (1993). "Tiwanaku y los Valles Subtropicales de los Andes." *Análisis Cultural, Revista de la Sociedad de Geografia, História y Estudios Geopolíticos de Cochabamba* 2: 63–66.

Goldstein, P. S. (1989). "The Tiwanaku Occupation of Moquegua." In *Ecology, Settlement and History in the Osmore Drainage, Peru*, ed. D. S. Rice, C. Stanish, and P. Scarr. BAR International Series 545(i). Oxford: British Archaeological Reports, 219–256.

Higueras, A. (1996). "Prehispanic Settlement and Land Use in Cochabamba, Bolivia." Ph.D. diss., University of Pittsburgh.

Ibarra Grasso, D. E., and R. Querejazu Lewis (1986). 30,000 Años de Prehistoria en Bolivia. La Paz: Los Amigos del Libro.

Janusek, J. (1993). "Nuevos Datos sobre el Significativo de la Producción y Uso de Instrumentos m Musicales en el Estado de Tiwanaku." *Pumapunku* 2, 4: 9–47.

Janusek, J. W. (1994). "State and Local Power in a Prehispanic Andean Polity: Changing Patterns of Urban Residence in Tiwanaku and Lukurmata." Ph.D. diss., University of Chicago.

Janusek, J. W. (1999). "Craft and Local Power: Embedded Specialization in Tiwanaku Cities." *Latin American Antiquity* 10, 2: 107–131.

Kolata, A. L. (1993). The Tiwanaku: Portrait of an Andean Civilization. Cambridge, MA: Blackwell.

Oakland, A. (1985). "Tiwanaku Textile Style from the South Central Andes." Ph.D. diss., University of Texas.

Rydén, S. (1947). *Archaeological Researches in the Highlands of Bolivia*. Göteborg: Elanders Boktryckeri Aktiebolag.

Ryden, S. (1959). *Andean Excavations Vol. II*. The Etnographical Museum of Sweden, Stockholm.

Wassen, S. H. (1972). "A Medicine-Man's Implements and Plants in a Tiahuanacoid Tomb in Highland Bolivia." *Etnologiska Studier* 32.

Moquegua Tiwanaku

TIME PERIOD: 1350–950 B.P.

LOCATION: The Moquegua Tiwanaku subtradition is found in the Pacific-draining Moquegua (also known as Middle Osmore) valley of southern Peru, approximately 300 km west of the site of Tiahuanaco, at elevations between 900–2000 m. Post-collapse Tiwanaku-derived ceramic styles appear near Ilo, on the Pacific coast.

DIAGNOSTIC MATERIAL ATTRIBUTES: The Omo and Chen Chen ceramic styles of Moquegua Tiwanaku correspond to late Tiwanaku IV and V pottery in the Tiwanaku Core Region, respectively, and to the Loreto Viejo style of the Azapa Tiwanaku subtradition. Fine serving vessels, principally polychrome *keros*, *tazones*, small pitchers, with some portrait vessels, zoomorphic censers, and jars, are found in all Tiwanaku cemeteries and most habitation sites. Most fine wares were red slipped, with polychrome painting in black, white, orange, and gray-blue. Reduced black ware pottery composes up to 40 percent of the fine serving vessels in the Omo style, but is not found in the Chen Chen assemblage (Goldstein 1989a; 1990). Wooden *keros* and other serving vessels are also found in domestic and mortuary contexts. Standard Tiwanaku utilitarian forms prevail in all household contexts at Moquegua Tiwanaku habitation sites (Goldstein 1989a; 1993a). The Tumilaca and Chiribaya styles, local pottery that emulated Tiwanaku forms and decoration, may overlap temporally with the Chen Chen style, but are believed to postdate the Tiwanaku state collapse (Bawden 1989; Goldstein 1989a, 1989b; Owen 1993).

The only known Moquegua Tiwanaku monumental construction is a stepped adobe platform mound built on Core Region patterns, with a cut-stone sunken rectangular court (Goldstein 1993b). Most vernacular architecture was of mud-covered cane or post-supported organic material, although some stone and adobe structures are known.

Stone sculpture consists of rustic versions of Tiwanaku anthropomorphic stelae and statuary and architectural models carved of local volcanic tuff (Goldstein 1993a, 1993b). Lithic industries produced large ground-stone *metates* and *manos*, casually chipped basalt hoes, and finely chipped narrow-stemmed white chert projectile points. Bronze and silver pins and other jewelry and tools have been found in mortuary, ceremonial, and habitation contexts. Also present are *trompos*, toplike conical or cylindroconical pecked-stone or wooden objects of unknown function.

Most decorated textiles were of camelid wool or occasionally cotton-wool composite, either in natural colors or dyed red, blue, purple, green, yellow, and white. Plain-weave tunics and blankets were typically decorated with warp stripes. Supplemental warp decoration appears to be more popular in postcollapse contexts. A characteristic loop stitch embroidery of geometric or figural motifs was used to finish selvages and edges (Oakland Rodman 1987). The most labor-intensive textiles were interlocked tapestry tunics with figures depicting mythical themes. Fragments of these are rare and usually associated with elite contexts. Undecorated plain-weave cotton textiles and cordage appear in domestic middens, but were never included in tombs and appear to have been of exclusively utilitarian function.

Complete hallucinogenic snuff tablet kits have not been found in Moquegua Tiwanaku, although related decorated tubes have been found.

CULTURAL SUMMARY

Environment

Climate in the middle altitude Moquegua valley region is hyperarid and temperate. Moquegua mean annual precipitation resembles the 5.3 mm measured for the nearby coastal port of Ilo. Rainfall increases with altitude, approaching 500 mm in the valley headwaters above 4800 m. Greatest precipitation totals are registered in the summer months of December through March (Rice et al. 1989: 20). Below 2000 m, the absence of biota outside the immediate valley bottom limits human occupation to the river valley floodplains. The region is considered optimal for irrigated cultivation of maize, fruits, and legumes.

Major flood events in Moquegua, dated to 1290 B.P. and 620 B.P., indicate that extreme El Niño Southern Oscillation (ENSO) cycles occurred during the Tiwanaku era (Magilligan and Goldstein 2000).

Settlements

Systematic full coverage survey of the middle Moquegua valley found an aggregate Tiwanaku occupation of over 126 ha (Goldstein 1996). Omo style pottery is found at 15 site components covering 28.7 ha. Chen chen style pottery is found at 54.6 ha of habitation and 10.4 ha of cemeteries. Moquegua Tiwanaku settlement clustered at four large towns of Chen Chen, Omo, Rio Muerto, and Cerro Echenique, with few smaller settlements and no fortified sites. The principal towns were located near large artificially irrigated pampas (Williams 1997: 90) or productive natural springs (Goldstein 1989a), indicating a preference for large agglutinated settlements adjacent to optimal zones for irrigated cultivation. Smaller, fortified and defensible settlements only appear in postcollapse sites with Tumilaca-style ceramics (Bawden 1989; Bermann et al. 1989). The Tumilaca settlement appears to have migrated away from the previous mid-valley focus, with increased settlement in the tributaries of the upper Osmore valley (Owen 1995; Stanish 1985, 1992) and the coastal or lower Osmore valley (Owen 1993).

Well-preserved Moquegua Tiwanaku towns include extensive residential districts, plazas, spatially distinct cemeteries, and some ceremonial/administrative structures. Occupation at the Omo M12 site consisted of freestanding multiroom buildings, arrayed around three large plazas. These plaza-centered residential groups appear to correspond to intentionally segregated *ayllu* communities.

Early household units at Omo did not have independent patios or storage facilities. As in the Tiwanaku Core Region, autonomous patio groups with contiguous roofed rooms, open patios, and storage units (mud-plastered stone cists or rectangular cribs) appeared after 1200 B.P., and may indicate changes in household organization, size, and production in later settlements. In the later postcollapse Tumilaca phase, defensible hilltop habitation sites were terraced for occupation with stone retaining walls.

Economy

Tiwanaku agriculture in Moquegua concentrated on irrigation near the floodplains of the riverine oases. Moquegua Tiwanaku farmers modified the landscape to reclaim extensive areas of desert through the construction of laterally extended canal systems. Unlike Wari, Late Intermediate, and Inca agriculturists in the same region, the Tiwanaku seldom terraced steep terrain for cultivation, preferring to extend canals to relatively flat areas. A single preserved canal and field system at the Chen Chen site irrigated over 90 ha (Williams 1997: 90), and comparable systems may be assumed at other sites in the valley. A study of carbon and nitrogen isotope content of Moquegua Tiwanaku human skeletal samples suggests a diet consisting of high levels of carbon four plants such as maize, with less substantial consumption of carbon three plants and meat (Sandness 1991). This contrasts sharply with the more diverse diet suggested by analysis of pre-Tiwanaku samples.

Marine resources, such as mollusks, seaweed, bird guano fertilizer, seabirds, fish, and sea mammals, were utilized in Moquegua Tiwanaku settlements for food, ritual offering, and ornaments. These were probably obtained through foraging trips or exchange with maritime specialists, as no Tiwanaku colonies have been identified on the littoral, and there is no evidence of Tiwanaku maritime technology.

Craft production of most textiles and cruder implements took place in the household, although specialized lithic and lapidary work areas have been investigated at Omo and Rio Muerto. No ceramic or metallurgical workshops have been identified in Moquegua. Although many vessels may have been imported, much of the ceramic production was probably local, but adhered strictly to Core Region archetypes.

Long-distance exchange either through traders or intermediaries obtained exotic raw materials such as *Spondylus* shell from the Ecuadorian coast, lapis lazuli and copper from northern Chile. The localization of the source of most of Moquegua's scant obsidian to sources in the Colca valley near Arequipa, Peru, suggests some form of contact through Wari intermediaries, as Wari appears to have controlled that source. Short-distance trade networks provided sharks' teeth, *Oliva peruvianus*, *Choromytilus*, and other seashell for jewelry production.

Sociopolitical Organization

The Moquegua Tiwanaku occupation is the best and clearest case for large colonies of settlers from the Tiwanaku Core Region in lowland regions. Unlike the contemporary settlements of Cochabamba and Azapa, the Moquegua enclaves were neither of or among a larger local population of Tiwanaku-acculturated peoples. Biological distance studies indicate that the Tiwanaku population of the Chen Chen site was far closer genetically to that of the Tiwanaku Core Region than to non-Tiwanaku peoples of Moquegua, confirming that peripheral settlements were peopled by colonists and their descendants, not acculturated local populations (Blom et al. 1998).

Also unique is the construction of a temple center at Omo, which suggests the replication of Core Region monumental architecture for public ceremonial and administrative functions (Goldstein 1993b). Some degree of social stratification is indicated by the range of tomb elaboration from simple pits to stone-lined cists.

There is one example of a complex stone mausoleum with offerings of tapestry tunics, thousands of beads, and other sumptuary regalia. Differential surface frequencies of elaborate ceramics suggest social distinctions among residential sectors.

Tiwanaku's relation with the near-contemporary Wari occupation of Cerro Baul in the upper Osmore drainage, and with indigenous peoples of the middle Moquegua valley is unclear. Despite the distance of under 20 km between the Wari and Tiwanaku enclaves, Wari and Tiwanaku ceramic interchange, as measured in large systematic collections, is practically nil.

Religion and Expressive Culture

Iconography on some elite Moquegua Tiwanaku ceramic *keros* represents the face and headdress of the Staff or Gateway God of Tiahuanaco in a simplified masklike form that is known from Tiwanaku (Goldstein 1985, 1990; Ponce Sangines 1947). The Staff God and the winged figures that accompany him on Tiahuanaco's archetypal "Gateway of the Sun" also appear on tapestry tunics found in elite contexts in Moquegua and are considered to be associated with the power of the Tiwanaku state. Representations of the Staff God disappeared from Tumilaca-style ceramics, which appear after the time of state collapse.

The architectural plan of the Omo temple structure suggests the Core Region pattern of processional paths from public spaces through narrow doorways and staircases to progressively more restrictive sanctuaries (Conklin 1991; Goldstein 1993b). The temple was consecrated with buried offerings of young or fetal camelids and a starfish, and by ritual burning of llama fat in zoomorphic ceramic censors.

Ceramic evidence in Moquegua indicates that popular celebrations involved politically sponsored feasting and mass consumption of maize beer in civic, household, or rural contexts. Beer-drinking paraphernalia such as *askero* goblets are found in domestic middens throughout the Tiwanaku tradition, but also occur in concentration in Moquegua in particular households that may have been ceremonial *chicherias*, near public plazas, and outside settlements on promontories with views of temples or important landscape features. It is possible that public ceremonies may have been celebrated simultaneously by placing sunken courts out of sight at the top of artificial pyramids or platforms that were visible from below.

Beyond state ideologies, the Moquegua Tiwanaku subtradition shared most Tiwanaku Core Region religious practices on the household and community levels. These included the sacrifice of pottery, metal *tupu* pins, seashell, and young or fetal camelids as offerings to dedicate homes, temples, and fields. These offering traditions strongly resemble ethnographically recorded Aymara rituals dedicated to local mountain, earth, and landscape deities.

Moquegua Tiwanaku burials were individual primary interments, buried with offerings in simple pits or stone-lined cylindrical cists. Individuals were wrapped in one or more tunics or blankets, tightly bound with cordage, and interred in a seated, flexed position with offering objects that typically included one or more *keros, tazones,* or other serving vessel, small plain ollas, and wooden spoons. Less commonly, jewelry items, weaving implements, pigment boxes, musical instruments, and drug paraphernalia were included. An east-facing orientation was customary. All interments were in separate cemetery areas adjacent to habitation sites, and tombs were marked with wooden posts. The proximity of the interred to domestic space and the marking and maintenance of tombs suggest a concept of the afterlife in which ancestors played important roles in the affairs of the living (Buikstra 1995; Goldstein 1989a,1989b).

References

Bawden, G. (1989). "The Tumilaca Site and Post-Tiahuanaco Occupational Stratigraphy in the Moquegua Drainage." In *Settlement, History and Ecology in the Osmore Drainage, Southern Peru,* ed. D. S. Rice, C. Stanish, and P. Scarr. Oxford: British Archaeological Reports, vol. 545, International Series, 287–302.

Bermann, M., P. Goldstein, C. Stanish, and L. Watanabe M. (1989). "The Collapse of the Tiwanaku State: A View from the Osmore Drainage." In *Settlement, History and Ecology in the Osmore Drainage, Southern Peru,* ed. D. S. Rice and C. Stanish. Oxford: British Archaeological Reports, vol. 545, International Series, 269–286.

Blom, D., Benedikt Hallgrímsson, Linda Keng, Maria C. Lozada C., and Jane E. Buikstra (1998). "Tiwanaku State Colonization: Bioarchaeological Evidence of Migration in the Moquegua Valley, Perú." *World Archaeology* 30, 2: 238–261.

Buikstra, J. (1995). "Tombs for the Living or for the Dead: The Osmore Ancestors." In *Tombs for the Living: Andean Mortuary Practices,* ed. T. D. Dillehay. Washington, D.C.: Dumbarton Oaks, 229–280.

Conklin, W. (1991). "Tiwanaku and Huari: Architectural Comparisons and Interpretations." In *Huari Administrative Structure: Prehistoric Monumental Architecture and State Government,* ed. W. Isbell and G. McEwan. Washington, D.C.: Dumbarton Oaks, 281–292.

Goldstein, P. S. (1985). "Tiwanaku Ceramics of the Moquegua Valley, Peru." M.A. thesis, University of Chicago.

Goldstein, P. S. (1989a). "Omo, a Tiwanaku Provincial Center in Moquegua, Peru." Ph.D. diss., Anthropology, University of Chicago.

Goldstein, P. S. (1989b). "The Tiwanaku Occupation of Moquegua." In *Ecology, Settlement and History in the Osmore Drainage, Peru,* ed.

D. S. Rice, C. Stanish, and P. Scarr. Oxford: BAR International Series 545(i), British Archaeological Reports, 219–256.

Goldstein, P. S. (1990). "La Ocupacion Tiwanaku en Moquegua." *Gaceta Arqueológica Andina* 5, 18/19: 75–104.

Goldstein, P. S. (1993a). "House, Community and State in the Earliest Tiwanaku Colony: Domestic Patterns and State Integration at Omo M12, Moquegua." In *Domestic Architecture, Ethnicity, and Complementarity in the South-Central Andes,* ed. M. Aldenderfer. University of Iowa Press, 25–41.

Goldstein, P. S. (1993b). "Tiwanaku Temples and State Expansion: A Tiwanaku Sunken Court Temple in Moquegua, Peru." *Latin American Antiquity* 4, 3: 22–47.

Goldstein, P. S. (1996). "Tiwanaku Settlement Patterns of the Azapa Valley, Chile—New Data, and the Legacy of Percy Dauelsberg." *Dialogo Andino* 14/15 (Special issue Prehistoria del Norte de Chile y del Desierto de Atacama. Simposio Homenaje a Percy Dauelsberg Hahmann): 57–73.

Magilligan, F. J., and Paul S. Goldstein (2000). "A Late Holocene and Modern El Niño Flood History for the Mid-valley Rio Moquegua, Southern Peru." Paper presented at the annual meeting of the Assocation of American Geographers, Pittsburgh, April.

Oakland Rodman, A. (1987). "Tiwanaku Textiles of the Omo Site, Moquegua, Peru." Unpublished manuscript, Notes on file, Proyecto Omo.

Owen, B. D. (1993). "A Model of Multiethnicity: State Collapse, Competition, and Social Complexity from Tiwanaku to Chiribaya in the Osmore Valley, Perú." Ph.D. diss., University of California, Los Angeles.

Owen, B., D (1995). "Warfare and Engineering, Ostentation and Social Status in the Late Intermediate Period Osmore Drainage." Paper presented at the Society for American Archaeology 60th annual meeting, Minneapolis.

Ponce Sangines, C. (1947). "Ceramica Tiwanacota." *Revista Geografica Americana* 28: 204–214.

Rice, D. S., C. Stanish, and P. R. Scarr (1989). *Ecology, Settlement and History in the Osmore Drainage, Peru.* Oxford: British Archaeological Reports International Series 545.

Sandness, K. (1992). "Temporal and Spatial Dietary Variability in the Osmore Drainage, Southern Peru: The Isotope Evidence." M.A. thesis, University of Nebraska.

Stanish, C. (1985). "Post Tiwanaku Regional Economics in the Otora Valley, Southern Peru." Ph.D. diss., The University of Chicago.

Stanish, C. (1992). *Ancient Andean Political Economy.* Austin: University of Texas Press.

Williams, P. R. (1997). "The Role of Disaster in the Development of Agriculture and the Evolution of Social Complexity in the South-Central Andean Sierra." Ph.D. diss., University of Florida.

San Pedro de Atacama Tiwanaku

TIME PERIOD: 1550–950 B.P.

LOCATION: The San Pedro de Atacama Tiwanaku sub-tradition is found near the desert town of San Pedro in the Atacama desert, 105 km northeast of the modern city of Calama, Chile, at an altitude of 2430 m. San Pedro is approximately 800 km south of the Tiahuanaco site. Tiwanaku material has been found in cemeteries in San Pedro's 13 small agricultural oases, which are locally known as ayllus.

DIAGNOSTIC MATERIAL ATTRIBUTES: Very little Tiwanaku pottery has been found in San Pedro de Atacama. The few Tiwanaku vessels in museum collections are polychrome *keros*, *tazones*, and small pitchers that correspond to Tiwanaku IV and V in the Core Region, the Omo and Chen Chen styles of Moquegua Tiwanaku, and Loreto Viejo or Azapa Tiwanaku polychromes. There appears to be a high rate of repair. No Tiwanaku utilitarian pottery is found in San Pedro.

The vast majority of ceramics are of the local San Pedro tradition. In the San Pedro III or Quitor Phase (1550–1250 B.P.), these are dominated by local forms such as face-neck bottles and incurving bowls in the black polished (*negra pulida*) ware that accounts for roughly 82 percent of the total funerary pottery in San Pedro (Tarrago 1976: 61). *Negra pulida* may have some relation to Tiwanaku black ware (Browman 1980: 117; Tarrago 1984; Thomas et al. 1985). In the later Coyo phase (1250–950 B.P.), the San Pedro tradition emulated Tiwanaku *keros* and other forms in local red-slipped or black *casi pulida* wares (Berenguer and Dauelsberg 1989: 160). Trade pieces of the Isla tricolor and black-on-red style of Northwest Argentina have been identified in the Quitor 5, Quitor 6, and Tchecar Sur cemeteries, and isolated examples of unidentified other styles are also found (Tarrago 1977: 56–62).

Tiwanaku textiles from San Pedro include polychrome interlocked tapestry tunics and *mantas* and warp striped plain-weave wool tunics, *mantas*, and bags, and four pointed hats (Conklin 1983; Frame 1990; Oakland 1985). These appear only in a small minority of burial contexts, the most frequent occurrence being six tapestry pieces found in 216 excavated burials in the Coyo Oriental cemetery (Oakland Rodman 1992: 321). These Tiwanaku textiles have been associated with the distinctive "group B" of local headdresses and garments. The majority "group A" of local styles seldom co-occurs with Tiwanaku elements.

Elaborately carved wooden snuff tablets, engraved bone tubes, and other paraphernalia associated with the use of hallucinogenic drugs are found in approximately 15 percent of San Pedro burials (Berenguer and Dauelsberg 1989:155; Torres 1984, 1985). The majority of snuff tablets and kits are of local style; only a small proportion bears Tiwanaku iconography (Torres 1987).

There is no habitation or ceremonial architecture in San Pedro associated with any Tiwanaku occupation. Burials with Tiwanaku offerings are typically seated flexed interments in unlined pit tombs, as are burials with only local offerings.

CULTURAL SUMMARY

Environment

San Pedro is situated near the northern edge of the Salar of Atacama, in the foothills of the Andes near the northernmost Chilean pass to the Salta region of Argentina. Intermittent rivers that water this part of the Atacama desert provided the basis for the very limited cultivation of grain crops in both historic and pre-Hispanic periods (Hidalgo 1984: 424, 1989; Orellana 1985: 243). The region is highly volcanic and is rich in minerals, notably copper ores.

Settlements

Most investigation of San Pedro Tiwanaku has focused on over 3000 burials excavated in 47 cemeteries by Father Gustavo LePaige (1964) and subsequent mortuary archaeology. Tiwanaku tradition material culture appears only in funerary context as one of several foreign minority styles of imports. There are no known Tiwanaku residential sites in San Pedro or any examples of Tiwanaku domestic pottery or utensils (Mujica 1996: 93). Even small-scale Tiwanaku settlement in San Pedro is yet to be demonstrated.

Economy

Irrigation from San Pedro's two intermittent rivers permits limited cultivation of fruits, legumes, and maize in the 13 small oases known as ayllus. Compared to the oasis valleys of Moquegua and Azapa, the amount of irrigable land available in San Pedro is minimal and would not have been a significant resource for Tiwanaku or have supported a very large population.

Mineral resources from the Atacama region and beyond may have been of some importance to Tiwanaku. Rich copper ore deposits and semiprecious stones are found in the region and were mined in the pre-Columbian era (Bird 1979; Graffam et al. 1996).

The long round trip from Tiwanaku to San Pedro would have made transport of bulky or fragile commodities like foodstuffs or pottery impractical. Neither imported Tiwanaku pottery nor the exact local replicas that might be preferred by Core Region Tiwanaku colonists are numerous in San Pedro. The high incidence of repairs among the few genuine Tiwanaku vessels attests to their rarity and high value there.

There is general agreement that exchange with the Tiwanaku Core Region was limited to portable, iconographically charged sumptuary goods used as status signifiers and for ritual activities (Browman 1985: 64, 1987; Mujica 1985: 116, 1989: 97; Torres 1984, 1986). Imports included labor-intensive tapestry textiles and four-pointed hats, hallucinogenic snuff tablets, some of which had inlay of exotic semiprecious stones or *Spondylus* shell from the Ecuadorian coast, and carved wooden and gold drinking vessels. A high proportion of the Tiwanaku tradition imports in San Pedro bore iconographic elements of the Staff God of Tiahuanaco and his entourage, believed to be the deities associated with the Tiwanaku state (Berenguer et al. 1989: 159; Torres 1987).

It has been suggested that individuals buried in the ayllus of Larrache, Quitor, and Solcor enjoyed preferential access to Tiwanaku ceramics and gold artifacts (LePaige 1964; Llagostera 1996: 32; Orellana 1985: 250), while Oakland Rodman has noted an elevated incidence of imported Tiwanaku textiles at Coyo Oriental (1992). This implies that Tiwanaku agents had different exchange relationships with the various San Pedro ayllus and may have fostered competition among them as clients vying for Tiwanaku patronage.

Finds of Tiwanaku gold vessels in the Doncellas river valley of Jujuy and a Tiwanaku influence on the forms and designs of the Isla ceramic tradition of Northwest Argentina indicate the exchange of Tiwanaku goods and concepts with regions accessible via San Pedro (DeBenedetti 1911; Tarrago 1977: 61). However, the appearance of pre-Tiwanaku San Pedro black polished pottery in Northwest Argentina indicates that this trade route antedated the appearance of Tiwanaku traits (Tarrago 1976: 62). The presence of Argentine Isla style and other non-Tiwanaku trade ceramics in San Pedro tomb lots suggests that San Pedro was a terminal port of trade that indirectly linked Tiwanaku with other regional traditions (Gonzalez 1963; Tarrago 1977: 62). Although Tiwanaku probably had a hegemonic effect on this elite exchange network for a time, it probably was controlled by local elites and both predated Tiwanaku and survived the Tiwanaku collapse (Llagostera 1996: 37).

Sociopolitical Organization

The most likely explanation of the Tiwanaku presence in San Pedro de Atacama is one of elite-level alliances between the Tiwanaku Core Region and the chiefs of local lineages. Better understanding of the sociopolitical organization of indigenous San Pedro society will be critical to understanding Tiwanaku's influence there. Orellana (1985: 249) suggests a situation close to a centralized government on the threshold of a theocratic state. Most, however, consider a segmentary political organization and a climate of shifting power relations among various *ayllus* or lineages to be more likely (Thomas et al. 1985: 268). Seeking foreign alliances and patronage and trading for status-affirming sumptuary goods would have been key competitive strategies for such lineage factions.

Nonelite San Pedro populations also emulated some aspects of the Tiwanaku tradition in the Coyo phase of San Pedro pottery and textiles (Berenguer and Dauelsberg 1989: 155). There is no evidence on whether Tiwanaku influences changed local settlement patterns or household productive patterns.

Oakland, privileging textile style in tomb lots as an ethnic marker, distinguishes a "group B" in the cemetery of Coyo Oriental from the majority San Pedro "group A" by associating the few highland-style Tiwanaku tapestry pieces with unique local furry hat headgear, warp faced plain-weave tunics with embroidered selvages and checkered neck plaques, tie-dyed tunics with lozenge designs, and hafted stone hammers (Oakland Rodman 1992), as well as a higher frequency of snuff trays bearing Tiwanaku iconography and a lower incidence of cranial deformation (Llagostera 1996: 34). Oakland argues that the group B textiles marked an ethnic enclave of Bolivian Tiwanaku colonists who deliberately maintained a minority identity through dress (Kolata 1993: 277; Oakland Rodman 1992: 336). Another plausible reconstruction might consider the group A and B ensembles as the distinctive dress of two local lineages, one of which enjoyed preferred access to Tiwanaku trade goods. A temporal sequencing has also been proposed (Llagostera 1996: 35).

Religion and Expressive Culture

San Pedro is known for a regional cult centered on the use of hallucinogenic snuff. Elaborately carved wooden snuff tablets, engraved bone tubes, and other paraphernalia associated with the use of hallucinogens are found in approximately 15 percent of San Pedro burials (Berenguer and Dauelsberg 1989:155; Torres 1984, 1987). This snuff complex, which appears to have concentrated on derivatives of *Anadenthera*, certainly predates Tiwanaku influence in San Pedro (Llagostera et al. 1989), and only a small percentage of snuff tablets bear Tiwanaku iconography.

Ongoing information exchange and perhaps religious proselytizing between elites may explain the incorporation of Tiwanaku icons and ideology into the San Pedro hallucinogen complex in the Coyo phase (Berenguer and Dauelsberg 1989: 155; Browman 1980, 1997; Oakland Rodman 1992; Torres 1985, 1987). Although few wooden snuff tablets are preserved in the highlands, surviving stone snuff tablets and imagery of tablets on stone stelae indicate that the hallucinogen complex also appeared in the Tiwanaku Core Region at approximately the same time (Berenguer 1985).

References

Berenguer, J. R. (1985). "Evidencias de inhalación de alucinogenos en esculturas Tiwanaku." *Chungara* 14: 61–70.

Berenguer, J. R., and Percy Dauelsberg H. (1989). "El Norte Grande en la órbita de Tiwanaku (400 a 1,200 d.C.)." In *Culturas de Chile, Prehistoria Desde sus Orígenes Hasta los Albores de la Conquista*, ed. J. Hidalgo L., V. Schiappacasse F., H Niemeyer F., C. Aldunate Del Solar, and I. Solimano R. Santiago: Editorial Andrés Bello, 129–180.

Bird, J. B. (1979). "The "Copper Man": A Prehistoric Miner and His Tools from Northern Chile." In *Pre-Columbian Metallurgy of South America*, ed. E. P. Benson. Washington, D.C.: Dumbarton Oaks Conference on Pre-Columbian Metallurgy of South America. Dumbarton Oaks, 105–132.

Browman, D. (1980). "Tiwanaku Expansion and Altiplano Economic Patterns." *Estudios Arqueológicos* 5: 107–120.

Browman, D. (1984a). "Prehistoric Aymara Expansion, the Southern Altiplano and San Pedro de Atacama." *Estudios Atacameños* 7: 236–252.

Browman, D. (1984b). "Tiwanaku: Development of Interzonal Trade and Economic Expansion in the Altiplano." In *Social and Economic Organization in the Prehispanic Andes*, ed. D. Browman, R. Burger, and M. Rivera. International Series 194. Oxford: British Archaeological Reports, 117–142.

Browman, D. L. (1997). "Political Institutional Factors Contributing to the Integration of the Tiwanaku State." In *Emergence and Change in Early Urban Societies*, ed. L. Manzanilla. New York: Plenum, 229–243.

Conklin, W. (1983). "Pucara and Tiahuanaco Tapestry: Time and Style in a Sierra Weaving Tradition." *Nawpa Pacha* 21: 1–44.

DeBenedetti, S. (1911). "Influencias de la cultura de Tiahuanaco en la región del Noroeste Argentino." *Revista de la Universidad de Buenos Aires* 17: 326–348.

Frame, M. (1990). "Andean Four-Cornered Hats: Ancient Volumes." In *Exhibit from the Collection of Arthur Bullowa, Organized by Julie Jones*. New York: Metropolitan Museum of Art.

Gonzalez, A. R. (1963). "Cultural Development in Northwestern Argentina." In *Aboriginal Cultural Development in Latin America*, ed. B. J. Meggars and C. Evans. Washington, D.C.: Smithsonian Miscellaneous Collection, vol. 146.

Graffam, G., Mario Rivera, and Alvaro Carevic (1996). "Ancient Metallurgy in the Atacama: Evidence for Copper Smelting during Chile's Early Ceramic Period." *Latin American Antiquity* 7, 2: 101–113.

Hidalgo Lehuedé, J. (1996). "Relaciones protohistóricas interétnicas entre las poblaciones locales y altiplánicas en Arica." In *La Integracion Surandina Cinco Siglos Despues*, ed. X. Albó, M. Arratia, J. Hidalgo, L. Nuñez, A. Llagostera, M. Remy, and B. Revesz. Cusco and Antofagasta: Centro de Estudios Regionales Andinos Bartolomé de Las Casas, and Universidad Católica del Norte, 161–174.

Kolata, A. L. (1993). *The Tiwanaku: Portrait of an Andean Civilization*. Cambridge, MA: Blackwell.

LePaige, G. (1964). "El Preceramico en la cordillera Atacameña y los cementerios del periodo agroalfarero de San Pedro de Atacama." *Anales de la Universidad del Norte* 3.

Llagostera, A. (1996). "San Pedro de Atacama: Nodo de complementariedad reticular." In *La Integracion Surandina Cinco Siglos Despues*, ed. X. Albó, M. Arratia, J. Hidalgo, L. Nuñez, A. Llagostera, M. Remy, and B. Revesz. Cusco and Antofagasta: Centro de Estudios Regionales Andinos Bartolomé de Las Casas, and Universidad Católica del Norte, 17–42.

Llagostera, A., Manuel Constantino Torres, and Maria A. Costa (1988). "El complejo psicotrópico en Solcor-3 (San Pedro de Atacama)." *Estudios Atacameños* 9: 61–98.

Mujica B., E. (1985). "Altiplano-coast Relationships in the South Central Andes: From Indirect to Direct Complementarity." In *Andean Ecology and Civilization*, ed. S. Masuda, I. Shimada, and C. Morris. Tokyo: University of Tokyo Press, 103–140.

Mujica B., E. (1996). "La Integración Surandina durante el periódo Tiwanaku." In *La Integracion Surandina Cinco Siglos Despues*, ed. X. Albó, M. Arratia, J. Hidalgo, L. Nuñez, A. Llagostera, M. Remy, and B. Revesz. Cusco and Antofagasta: Centro de Estudios Regionales Andinos Bartolomé de Las Casas, and Universidad Católica del Norte, 81–116.

Oakland, A. (1985). "Tiwanaku Textile Style from the South Central Andes." Ph.D. diss., University of Texas.

Oakland Rodman, A. (1992). "Textiles and Ethnicity: Tiwanaku in San Pedro de Atacama, North Chile." *Latin American Antiquity* 3, 4: 316–340.

Orellana R., M. (1985). "Relaciónes culturales entre Tiwanaku y San Pedro de Atacama." *Diálogo Andino* 4 (La problematica Tiwanaku Huari en el contexto panandino del desarrollo cultural, ed. M. Rivera): 247–258.

Tarrago, M. N. (1976). "Alfareria tipica de San Pedro de Atacama." *Estudios Atacameños* 4: 37–64.

Tarrago, M. N. (1977). "Relaciones prehispanicas entre San Pedro de Atacama (Norte de Chile) y regiones aledanas: La quebrada de Humahuaca." *Estudios Atacameños* 5: 50–63.

Tarrago, M. N. (1984). "La historia de los pueblos circumpuneños en relacion con el atltiplano y los Andes Meridionales." *Estudios Atacameños* 7: 116–132.

Thomas, C., Maria Benavente, and Claudio Massone (1985). "Algunos Efectos de Tiwanaku en la Cultura de San Pedro de Atacama." *Diálogo Andino* 4 (La problematica Tiwanaku Huari en el contexto panandino del desarrollo cultural, ed. M. Rivera): 259–276.

Torres, C. M. (1984). "Tabletas para alucinogenos de San Pedro de Atacama: Estilo e iconografia." In *Tesoros de San Pedro de Atacama*. Santiago: Museo Chileno de Arte Precolombino, Banco O'Higgins, 23–36.

Torres, C. M. (1985). "Estilo y iconografía Tiwanaku en la cultura de San Pedro de Atacama." In *La problematica Tiwanaku Huari en el contexto panandino del desarrollo cultural*, ed. M. Rivera. Diálogo Andino 4. Arica: Universidad de Tarapacá, 247–259.

Torres, M. C. (1987). "The Iconography of Prehispanic Snuff Trays from San Pedro de Atacama." *Andean Past* 1: 191–245.

Tiwanaku Core Region

TIME PERIOD: 1575–950 B.P.

LOCATION: The Tiwanaku Core Region extends throughout the Bolivian southern lake Titicaca basin and as far north as Puno in the Peruvian Titicaca basin, regions at elevations above 3800 m.

DIAGNOSTIC MATERIAL ATTRIBUTES: Stone sculptural traditions of anthropomorphic stelae and low relief carvings. Cut-stone public architecture including sunken rectangular courts and pyramidal or stepped platform mounds. Settlement pattern hierarchy with large urban site, secondary centers, and farmsteads with raised field agricultural systems. Serving and ceremonial pottery including *kero* drinking goblets, anthropomorphic and zoomorphic vessels, polychromes typically red-slipped with motifs in black, white, orange, and blue-gray. Characteristic utilitarian plainware pottery. Bronze, gold, and silver metallurgy, diverse lithic and lapidary industries.

CULTURAL SUMMARY

Environment

Climate in the *altiplano* Tiwanaku Core Region exemplifies extreme high altitude at a tropical latitude, with an annual mean temperature of 9° C and diurnal variation of up to 15° C because of extreme solar radiation. Night frosts are a significant limiting factor. *Altiplano* rainy season is from November through March, with a mean annual precipitation approaching 700 mm.

Long-term trends suggested by glacial ice cores correlate the Tiwanaku tradition with two relatively wet periods from 1340–1300 B.P. and 1190–910 B.P. Decreasing rainfall inferred after 910 B.P., culminating in severe drought and low lake levels from 705–640 B.P., have been implicated by Kolata et al. in the Tiwanaku collapse (Ortloff and Kolata 1993: 199–200; Kolata and Ortloff 1996: 183–186). However, Erickson argues that most Tiwanaku site abandonment took place 100–200 years before the onset of this drought (Erickson 1999: 635).

Settlements

The first-order site of Tiahuanaco, with its extensive monumental center of cut-stone temples, enclosures and platform pyramids and at least 420 ha in urban area, dominates the Tiwanaku Core Region settlement pattern. The Tiahuanaco site's ceremonial, administrative, and residential palace precincts were laid out on a cardinal orientation and surrounded by a moat to separate them from the rest of the city (Kolata 1993: 90). Elite residential complexes have been identified on the summit of the massive Akapana pyramid (Manzanilla 1992) and in the Putuni palace, and it is likely that the monumental center was reserved for royal or high-status residents. The 4 sq km of surrounding nonelite residential sectors at Tiahuanaco maintained the same cardinal orientation as the monumental center. Residential groups were bounded by perimeter walls into socially or functionally differentiated barrios, which in turn were subdivided into patio groups. These are believed to represent social units corresponding to *ayllus* or kin groups within the city. Similar community segmentation appears to be the case in other Core Region settlements like Lukurmata (Janusek 1999).

Interpretations differ on the systemic integration of second-order sites like Lukurmata, Pajchiri, Khonko Wankané, Chiripa, and Iwawe, all of which have extensive domestic areas and temple structures or some other form of public cut-stone architecture. Ponce Sangines (1972, 1989) and Kolata (1982, 1985, 1986, 1993) describe a highly hierarchical four-level Tiwanaku settlement system corresponding to state agricultural investment and a quadripartite division of administrative and production functions. Tiwanaku Core Region settlement does correspond closely to raised field areas, and Tiwanaku sites are seldom fortified (Stanish and Steadman 1994: 10). Although this could indicate centralized coordination of agricultural activity and adjudication of land disputes, recent rank-size and cluster analyses of systematic settlement pattern data for the Core Region suggest a less-integrated arrangement of autonomous subsystems, focused at each of the regional centers (Albarracin-Jordan 1996; McAndrews et al. 1997).

Economy

Tiwanaku's Core Region depended primarily on the large-scale herding of domesticated camelids (Browman 1974, 1980, 1984; Kolata 1993; Lynch 1983; Webster 1993) and the cultivation of frost-resistant crops in over 120,000 ha of labor-intensive raised fields (Denevan 1970, 1980; Erickson 1984, 1987, 1999; Graffam 1988; Kolata 1982, 1983, 1986, 1992; Lennon 1982; Mathews 1989; Ortloff and Kolata 1993). Providing the principal staple subsistence base for the Tiwanaku Core, raised fields managed drainage, mitigated nightly frosts by storing solar energy in the water-filled swales between fields, and helped to fertilize crops with organic material dredged up in canal maintenance. Experiments suggest that these advantages can dramatically decrease failure risk and increase yield over flatland agriculture in the *altiplano* (Carney et al. 1993; Erickson 1985; Kolata and Ortloff 1989, 1996). Lacustrine waterbirds, freshwater fish, and amphibians were hunted with small reed watercraft, snares, bow and arrow, darts, slings, and bolas and played a significant supplementary role in Tiwanaku diet. Deer, the wild camelid species of vicuña and guanaco, and small mammals were also consumed. Increased exploitation of the lacustrine flora and fauna may have been a by-product of the extensive artificial wetlands created in the swales of the raised field systems.

Tiwanaku crafts were produced both by individual households and by corporate coresidential specialist groups living in urban barrios or rural settlements. These craft groups may have corresponded to descent or ethnic groups, like *ayllus* embedded in Tiwanaku's diverse social substructure (Albarracin-Jordan 1996; Janusek 1999). Nonetheless, elite-attached specialists may be assumed for highly skilled or sumptuary crafts like fine lithic production with imported obsidian (Brooks et al. 1997), bronze, gold, and silver metallurgy, and lapidary industries that required imported raw materials.

Tiwanaku and Lukurmata have produced metal objects of gold, silver and copper and bronze alloys of copper-arsenic-nickel, copper-tin, and copper-arsenic (Lechtman 1997:158). Most small tools and ornaments such as pins, needles, small figures, and axes were cast and hammered or repoussé decorated on thin beaten sheets. Bronze T-shaped architectural cramps at Tiahuanaco's Pumapunku and other monumental buildings were cast in situ to join cut-stone architectural elements, and some gold decorative elements may have been added to stonework in a similar fashion.

Sociopolitical Organization

Recent fieldwork in the Tiwanaku Core Region has engendered debate on the strength and centricity of the Tiahuanaco site as the capital of a bureaucratic and hierarchical state. Analysts focusing on the Tiahuanaco type tend to emphasize the centripetal nature of the capital city and a strongly centralized Tiwanaku state (Kolata 1982, 1985, 1986, 1993, 1996). Researchers focusing on regional settlement patterns and local approaches to smaller sites of Tiwanaku's Core Region have emphasized more segmentary interpretations of Tiwanaku as a loose

ethnic confederacy of politically autonomous communities that shared only cultural and ceremonial ties to the capital (Albarracin-Jordan 1996; Bermann 1994, 1997). A similar interpretation, citing the segmentary ethnographic concept of the *ayllu*, has also been applied to barrios within the urban Tiahuanaco site (Janusek 1999).

Kolata argues that a social hierarchy grew out of a coalition of proto-Aymara herders with lower-status Pukina agriculturists and Uru aquatic specialists (Kolata 1993: 101). Dualistic readings of Aymara categories of cosmos, landscape, ecology, and social organization are interpreted to explain the architectural division of ritual space between Tiwanaku's Akapana and Pumapunku monuments (1993: 98). Spatial variations of ceramic style and household ritual found in domestic excavations within the Tiwanaku urban site have been seen to represent diverse social segments subsumed within the hierarchy of the Tiwanaku polity (Janusek 1994). The Tiwanaku-period Titicaca basin encompassed diverse ethnic communities, and these were subdivided structurally at several levels.

A comprehensive study of nonmetric traits by Blom (1998; Blom et al. 1998) found no significant biological distance among skeletal populations of Tiahuanaco, Lukurmata, and rural sites of the Tiwanaku valley and the Katari basin. This indicates relatively open migration and marriage among fairly homogeneous Core Region majority populations. Nonetheless, Tiwanaku cranial modification styles may have correlated with regional, ethnic, or clan affiliations, with annular types predominating in the Katari basin contrasting with the frontooccipital types dominating in the Moquegua subtradition. As might be expected for a cosmopolitan city, the Tiahuanaco site displays the greatest heterogeneity of styles (Blom 1998: 250). Small groups from the Akapana East and Mollo Kontu sectors at Tiahuanaco, which exhibit different mortuary practices and possibly biological distinction, could represent enclaved foreign populations within the city.

Religion and Expressive Culture

Tiwanaku stone iconography suggests a set of state deities associated with the Staff or Gateway God, a frontal figure depicted wearing an elaborate headdress and holding a puma-headed staff in either hand. The Staff God and a variable group of winged figures that accompany him on the Tiahuanaco site's archetypal "Gateway of the Sun," have been interpreted as a pantheon of sky, weather, or cosmic deities, possibly ancestral to the ethnohistorically known deities Viracocha and Illapa.

Other figures in monolithic stone sculpture may represent human political or religious elites (Cook 1983; Demarest 1981; Isbell 1983; Kolata 1992, 1993).

It is believed that Tiahuanaco became an important center for pilgrimage, as well as a capital. The city's monumental core is famous for terraced pyramids, platforms, enclosures, and sunken courts where religious ceremonies took place. Both at Tiahuanaco and at other Tiwanaku Core Region centers, the architectural plan of temple structures suggests processional paths from public spaces through narrow doorways and staircases to progressively more restrictive sanctuaries (Conklin 1991; Goldstein 1993). The inner temple complexes, typically walled sunken courts, were the location of the most exclusive ceremonies and housed the most elaborate stone sculptures or other sacred objects. Hallucinogenic drug use, probably restricted to ritual specialists in private contexts, played a role in prognostication, propitiation, or curing ceremonies.

Beyond state ideologies, the Tiwanaku tradition also encompassed enduring religious practices on the household and community levels. These included the sacrifice of pottery, jewelry, and animals to dedicate homes, temples, and fields. These offering traditions strongly resemble ethnographically recorded Aymara rituals dedicated to local mountain, earth, and landscape deities. Both religious and mundane buildings were consecrated with buried offerings of young or fetal camelids, seashells, bundled coca leaves, ritually killed pottery, metal *tupu* pins, amulets, architectural models, and other artifacts. Ceramic sherds in temple contexts indicate the ritual burning of llama fat in ceramic censors. One mass human interment excavated on the Akapana pyramid may represent a human sacrifice to dedicate the pyramid's construction or to commemorate an event (Manzanilla 1992; Manzanilla and Woodard 1990).

Ceramic evidence throughout the Tiwanaku tradition and analogy to Inca practices suggest that popular celebrations involved politically sponsored feasting and mass consumption of maize beer in civic, household, or rural contexts. It is possible that restrictive and public ceremonies may have been celebrated simultaneously by placing sunken courts out of sight at the top of artificial pyramids or platforms that were visible from below.

References

Albarracin-Jordan, J. (1996). "Tiwanaku Settlement Systems: The Integration of Nested Hierarchies in the Lower Tiwanaku Valley." *Latin American Antiquity* 3, 3: 183–210.

Bermann, M. P. (1994). *Lukurmata: Household Archaeology in Prehispanic Bolivia.* Princeton: Princeton University Press.

Bermann, M. P. (1997). "Domestic Life and Vertical Integration in the Tiwanaku Heartland." *Latin American Antiquity* 8, 2: 93–112.

Blom, D. (1998). "Tiwanaku and the Moquegua Settlements: A Bioarchaeological Approach." Ph.D. diss., University of Chicago.

Blom, D., Benedikt Hallgrímsson, Linda Keng, Maria C. Lozada C., and Jane E. Buikstra (1998). "Tiwanaku State Colonization: Bioarchaeological Evidence of Migration in the Moquegua Valley, Perú." *World Archaeology* 30, 2: 238–261.

Brooks, S., Michael D. Glascock, and Martin Giesso (1997). "Source of Volcanic Glass for Ancient Andean Tools." *Nature* 386, 3: 449–450.

Browman, D. (1974). "Pastoral Nomadism in the Andes." *Current Anthropology* 15: 188–196.

Browman, D. (1980). "New Light on Andean Tiwanaku." *American Scientist* 69: 408–419.

Browman, D. (1984). "Prehistoric Aymara Expansion, the Southern Altiplano and San Pedro de Atacama." *Estudios Atacameños* 7: 236–252.

Carney, H. J., Michael W. Binford, Alan L. Kolata, Ruben R. Marin, and Charles R. Goldman (1993). "Nutrient and Sediment Retention in Andean Raised-field Agriculture." *Nature* 364: 131–133.

Conklin, W. (1991). "Tiwanaku and Huari: Architectural Comparisons and Interpretations." In *Huari Administrative Structure: Prehistoric Monumental Architecture and State Government*, ed. W. Isbell and G. McEwan. Washington, D.C.: Dumbarton Oaks, 281–292.

Cook, A. G. (1983). "Aspects of State Ideology in Huari and Tiwanaku Iconography: The Central Deity and the Sacrificer." In *Investigations of the Andean Past*, ed. D. Sandweiss. Ithaca: Cornell University, 161–185.

Demarest, A. A. (1981). *Viracocha, The Nature and Antiquity of the Andean High God.* Cambridge, MA: Peabody Museum Monographs.

Denevan, W. (1970). "Aboriginal Drained Field Cultivation in the Americas." *Science* 169: 647–654.

Denevan, W. (1980). "Latin America." In *World Systems of Traditional Resource Management*, ed. G. Klee. New York: Hasted Press, 217–244.

Erickson, C. L. (1984). "Waru Waru: Una tecnologia agricola del Altiplano pre-hispanico." *Boletin del Instituto de Estudios Aymaras* 2, 18: 4–37.

Erickson, C. L. (1985). "Applications of Prehistoric Andean Technology: Experiments in Raised Field Agriculture." In *Prehistoric Intensive Agriculture in the Tropics*, ed. I. F. Farrington. Oxford: British Archaeological Reports, International Series, 209–232.

Erickson, C. L. (1987). "The Dating of Raised-Field Agriculture in the Lake Titicaca Basin, Peru." In *Pre-Hispanic Agricultural Fields in the Andean Region Part II*, ed. W. Denevan, K. Mathewson, and G. Knapp. Oxford: British Archaeological Reports, International Series, 373–384.

Erickson, C. L. (1999). "Neo-environmental Determinism and Agrarian 'Collapse' in Andean Prehistory." *Antiquity* 73: 634–642.

Goldstein, P. S. (1993). "Tiwanaku Temples and State Expansion: A Tiwanaku Sunken Court Temple in Moquegua, Peru." *Latin American Antiquity* 4, 3: 22–47.

Graffam, G. C. (1988). "Back across the Great Divide: The Pakaq Senorio and Raised Field Agriculture." In *Multidisciplinary Studies in Andean Anthropology*, ed. V. J. Vitzthum. Ann Arbor: Michigan Discussions in Anthropology.

Isbell, W. (1983). "Shared Ideology and Parallel Political Development: Huari and Tiwanaku." In *Investigations of the Andean Past*, ed. D. Sandweiss. Ithaca: Cornell University, 186–208.

Janusek, J. W. (1994). "State and Local Power in a Prehispanic Andean Polity: Changing Paterns of Urban Residence in Tiwanaku and Lukurmata." Ph.D. diss., University of Chicago.

Janusek, J. W. (1999). "Craft and Local Power: Embedded Specialization in Tiwanaku Cities." *Latin American Antiquity* 10, 2: 107–131.

Kolata, A. L. (1982). "Tiwanaku: Portrait of an Andean Civilization." *Field Museum of Natural History Bulletin* 53, 8: 13–18, 23–28.

Kolata, A. L. (1983). "The South Andes." In *Ancient South Americans*, ed. J. Jennings. San Francisco: W.H. Freeman, 241–285.

Kolata, A. L. (1985). "El papel de la agricultura intensiva en la economia politica del estado Tiwanaku." *Diálogo Andino* 4 (La problematica Tiwanaku Huari en el contexto panandino del desarrollo cultural): 11–38.

Kolata, A. L. (1986). "The Agricultural Foundations of the Tiwanaku State: A View from the Heartland." *American Antiquity* 51: 748–762.

Kolata, A. L. ed. (1989). *Arqueología de Lukurmata*. 2. La Paz: INAR.

Kolata, A. L. (1992). "Economy, Ideology and Imperialism in the South-Central Andes." In *Ideology and Pre-Columbian Civilizations*, ed. A. A. Demarest and G. W. Conrad. Santa Fe: School of American Research Press, 65–87.

Kolata, A. L. (1993). *The Tiwanaku: Portrait of an Andean Civilization*. Cambridge, MA: Blackwell.

Kolata, A. L. ed. (1996). *Tiwanaku and its Hinterland: Archaeology and Paleoecology of an Andean Civilization*. Washington, D.C.: Smithsonian Institution Press.

Kolata, A. L., and C. Ortloff (1996). "Agroecological Perspectives on the Decline of the Tiwanaku State." In *Tiwanaku and its Hinterland: Archaeology and Paleoecology of an Andean Civilization*, ed. A. L. Kolata. Washington, D.C.: Smithsonian Institution Press, 181–202.

Lechtman, H. (1997). "El Bronce Arsenical y el Horizonte Medio." In *Arqueologia, Antropología e História en los Andes: Homenaje a Maria Rostworowski*, ed. R. Varón G. and Javier Flores E. Lima: Instituto de Estudios Peruanos, Banco Central de Reserva del Perú, 153–186.

Lennon, T. J. (1982). "Raised Fields of Lake Titicaca, Peru: A Pre-Hispanic Water Management System." Ph.D. diss., University of Colorado.

Lynch, T. F. (1983). "Camelid Pastoralism and the Emergence of Tiwanaku Civilization in the South-Central Andes." *World Archaeology* 15: 1–14.

Manzanilla, L. (1992). *Akapana: Una Pirámide en el Centro del Mundo*. Mexico City: Universidad Nacional Autónoma de México, Instituto de Investigaciones Antropológicas.

Manzanilla, L., and E. Woodard (1990). "Restos humanos asociados a la pirámide de Akapana (Tiwanaku, Bolivia)." *Latin American Antiquity* 1: 133–149.

Mathews, J. (1989). "Preliminary Investigations of Prehistoric Raised Fields in the Tiwanaku Mid-Valley, Tiwanaku, Bolivia." Paper presented at the 17th annual midwest conference on Andean and Amazonian archaeology and ethnohistory, Mt. Pleasant, Michigan.

McAndrews, T., Juan Albarracin-Jordan, and Marc Bermann (1997). "Regional Settlement Patterns of the Tiwanaku Valley of Bolivia." *Journal of Field Archaeology* 24: 67–83.

Ponce Sangines, C. (1972). *Tiwanaku: Espacio Tiempo y Cultura*. La Paz: Academia Nacional de Ciencias de Bolivia.

Ponce Sangines, C. (1989). *Arqueología de Lukurmata* 1. La Paz: INAR.

Stanish, C., and L. Steadman (1994). *Archaeological Research at Tumatumani, Juli, Peru*. Fieldiana Anthropology, New Series 23. Chicago: Field Museum of Natural History.

Webster, A. D. (1993). "The Role of the South American Camelid in the Development of the Tiwanaku State." Ph.D. diss., University of Chicago.

PAUL GOLDSTEIN
Department of Anthropology
University of California, San Diego
San Diego, California
United States

Tupi

The term may be applied to (a) speakers of the Tupían languages (Tupían linguistic families): (1) Tupi-Guarani (including Tupinambá and Guarani), (2) Ari-kém, (3) Juruna, (4) Mondé, (5) Munduruku, (6) Ramaráma, (7) Tupari. Tupían isolated languages: (1) Puruborá, (2) Aweti, (3) Mawé; (b) Tupi archaeological cultures (Guarani and Tupinambá); (c) Tupi ethnohistoric and ethnographic cultures (Guarani, Tupinambá, and all other speakers of the languages of the linguistic families listed above in (a) whose archaeological past is not known). There is evidence that the Guarani and Tupinambá ethnohistoric and ethnographic cultures (c) were those that left the Guarani and Tupinambá archaeological cultures (b) and that both spoke languages of the Tupi-Guarani family of the Tupi stock (a); therefore, they partake of the archaeological, ethnohistoric, ethnographic, and linguistic data.

ABSOLUTE TIME PERIOD: c. 1500–150 B.P. Tupían languages were spoken from 5000 B.P. (that is the glotochronological estimate for the origin of the Tupi proto-language), to the present. Around 120 radiocarbon assays (Carbon 14) date the archaeological Tupi ceramics (Guarani and Tupinambá) from 1800–300 B.P. Tupi ethnohistoric cultures were known from 450 B.P. to the present.

RELATIVE TIME PERIOD: Follows the Sambaqui/Umbu tradition, precedes the historic period.

LOCATION: (a) The Tupían linguistic stock includes about 41 languages divided into seven linguistic families, which spread throughout an enormous area of South America, including parts of the basins of the Amazon (Madeira, Guaporé, Tapajós, Xingu), Paraguai, Paraná, Uruguai, and São Francisco, as well as parts of the Chaco and Eastern Brazil. Tupían speech communities once covered a north-south distance of almost 4500 km between French Guiana and the Río de La Plata estuary, and a east-west distance of around 3500 km from the mouth of the Amazon to the Upper Napo. (b) Guarani subtradition sites have been found in an area forming a massive block between the Atlantic coast and the Paraguay river, stretching from the tropic of Capricorn to the Río de La Plata. In that area, as many as 900 archaeological sites have been surveyed. Tupinambá subtradition sites have been found in a strip 200–700 km in width bordering the Atlantic coast from Maranhão in the north to the tropic of Capricorn, with an extension on the headwaters of the Araguaia. In that large area, only around 150 archaeological sites have been so far surveyed. The areas now occupied by the rest of the speakers of the seven Tupían linguistic families have never been surveyed and are not known archeologically. (c) Most Guarani speakers lived and still live inland on the watersheds of the Paraná, Paraguay and Uruguay, but their territory extended to the adjoining stretch of the coast to the south. The speakers of Tupinambá lived mainly along the coast from the Río Pará, just south of the mouth of the Amazon, to the tropic of Capricorn, but their territory extended some distance inland as well.

DIAGNOSTIC MATERIAL ATTRIBUTES: (b and c). For both the Guarani and the Tupinambá, a sand-tempered pottery sometimes decorated by elaborate polychrome painting in red and/or black or brown on a white slip. In the case of the Guarani, the coiled technique of vessel forming has not been often obliterated externally (corrugated), whereas in the case of the Tupinambá it has been smoothed (plain); moreover, vessel forms are completely different in the two subtraditions. Decorated techniques include also nail incisions. Lithic instruments are small polished stone axheads (celts); stone pendants; quartz T-shaped labrets; bipolar flaked chert tools and massive bifaced choppers. Wooden houses were elongated or rounded and often arranged linearly or in a circle around a plaza.

REGIONAL SUBTRADITIONS: Guarani and Tupinambá. (The postulated succession of painted, corrugated, and brushed subtraditions was only an artifact of the way the frequency of pottery sherds with different surface finishings was quantified in different regions.)

IMPORTANT SITES: Almeida, Arroyo Malo, Fazenda Soares, São Miguel I.

CULTURAL SUMMARY

Environment

Climate. Guarani subtradition: Humid, mesothermal, or subtropical, characterized by mean monthly temperatures between 14–24°, from 1000 mm to more than 2,000 mm of rain, and no dry season. At the lower elevations and along the coast, summers are hot (Cfa); at the top of the uplands, the climate is characterized by cool summers and relatively cold winters (Cfb). Tupinambá subtradition: Because the sites are found over all the coastal area from the tropic of Capricorn to the mouth of the Amazon with extensions westward to the São Francisco river basin, they occupied tropical climates ranging from humid (Af, Ams') on the eastern coast to dry and semiarid (Aw, Bsh) on the interior of northeastern Brazil.

Topography. Guarani: Major river valleys up to 400–800 m elevation, lowlands, and coastal lacustrine environments. Tupinambá: Ranging from coastal lacustrine environments at the back of mangrove swamps and the major river valleys at lower elevations to the mountains of southeastern Brazil up to 800 m elevation.

Geology. Guarani: Habitat characterized by river valleys dissecting the eruptive rocks of the southern *planalto*, the granite (metamorphic rocks of the East Brazilian) shield and its peripheral areas, and the adjoining sand plains of the Atlantic coast. Basalt, sandstones, and quartz (crystalline rocks) were employed for the stone tools. Tupinambá: Sand plains of the Atlantic coast (*restinga* formations), low areas on the interior of northeastern Brazil, and the granite of the mountainous areas along the coast.

Biota. Guarani: Occupation restricted to forested areas: tropical semideciduous forests, gallery forests, and riverine or lacustrine coastal environments. Rich diversity of plant and animal life. Tupinambá: Occupation ranging from the riverine or lacustrine environments, mangrove swamps, and tropical evergreen forests along the coast, to the gallery forests going into the tropical savannas and the subhumid forests (*agreste*) in northeastern Brazil. Rich diversity of plant and animal life. Fishing and mollusk collecting were very important.

Settlements

Settlement System. Guarani and Tupinambá: In the historic period there were (1) hamlets of only one or two houses; (2) small villages of up to 15 houses (some of these villages were fortified with palisades); (3) permanent campsites for agriculture, fishing, and gathering; and (4) seasonal campsites for hunting, fishing, and gathering, sometimes related to shell middens.

Community Organization. Guarani and Tupinambá: Communities seem to have been located to have access to: (1) good soils for slash-and-burn horticulture, (2) water resources for drinking, fishing, and canoeing, (3) hunting grounds, (4) mineral (clay and stone) resources. In the historic period, communities were organized in webs capable of expanding and contracting according to environmental and political circumstances. Four major activity areas have been suggested for the villages: (1) communal square for public activities, (2) domestic front for public activities, (3) domestic back for private and "messy" activities, and (4) communal back for "messy" activities.

Housing. Guarani and Tupinambá: Darkened soil and concentrations of sherds indicate circular plans 2–10 m in diameter and elongated forms 20 m long by 10 m wide. In the historical period, houses were oval, rectangular, or circular in plan. Longhouses measured from 5–100 m in length and from 2–20 m in width. Rounded ones were up to 15 m in diameter. They were covered with palm leaves, grass, or bark and had ogival roof walls. Some of them were said to house up to 600 people. No Guarani or Tupinambá house has been completely excavated.

Population, Health, and Disease. In the historical period, sources indicate villages with up to 3000 inhabitants for the Guarani and up to 6000 people for the Tupinambá, but most of them had from 650–850 people, and some less than a hundred. Archaeological villages appear to be much smaller, because those larger ones are today under main cities. Excavated urn burials suggest a high juvenile death rate.

Economy

Subsistence. Known almost only from historical sources. Based almost equally in horticulture, hunting, fishing, and collecting.

Wild Foods. Hundreds of species of fruits, palm nuts, roots, and seeds, as well as fungi, were collected, some from managed stands. The hunting and trapping strategies included big and small game animals and birds. Fishing was very important in rivers, lagoons, and the sea. Shellfish collecting was important for the Tupinambá. Insects and honey were also collected. Wild-food collecting was a year-round activity.

Domestic Foods. Around 50 species of plants were domesticated, among them maize, manioc, sweet potato, beans, cucurbit, pepper, peanut, yam, yambean, taro, amaranth, chenopodian, *urucu*, *genipa*, papaya, pineapple, passion flower, tobacco, cotton, and gourd. In most cases, all these were intercropped. We could consider also as domesticates and semidomesticates the managed stands of fruit trees such as palm trees (*Bactris*, *Butia*, *Euterpe*), cashew, *araucária*, ilex, and some species of fruit trees. There were many domesticated animals, but they were not eaten.

Industrial Arts. Tupi technology was simple and available to everyone. Most technological items were manufactured by the individuals or households who used them. Archaeological finds are constituted by pottery, stone, bone, antler, and shell utensils, but in the historic period the material culture included also utensils made of wood, gourds, cotton, wild and cultivated fibers (cotton), seeds, plumes, leather, wax, and resins. Guarani: Foodstuffs were preferably stewed; little or no salt and pepper were used. Tupinambá: Foodstuffs were preferably roasted, toasted, or smoked; salt and pepper were widely used. In both cases, archaeological vessel forms indicate cooking preferences.

Utensils. Archaeological utensils included (1) sand-tempered pottery, fashioned by coiling from locally available clays and fired over an open fire. The characteristic functional forms are, for the Guarani, (a) inflected cooking pots, (b) large deep conical bowls also for cooking, (c) simple bowls for eating, and (d) simple, (e) inflected, or (f) complex (carinated) bowls for drinking, and (g) large inflected or complex carinated jars for storing water or brewing and serving alcoholic beverages; Most vessels have conical bases and were finished by a kind of complex corrugation. The drinking bowls (d–f) and the serving jars (g) are often elaborately painted on the outside. Other kinds of surface finishing are smoothing, nail incising, pinching, rim nicking, punctations, and brushing. For the Tupinambá, (a) large deep complex (carinated) cauldrons were used for roasting manioc flour as well as for brewing alcoholic beverages; (b) large or medium-sized basins with thickened rims were used for serving food. Sometimes (c) large restricted ovoid jars or (d) inflected or complex (carinated) jars were used for storing water or brewing and serving alcoholic beverages. Flat plates to roast *beiju* are rare (e). Most vessels have flat bases and are plain. Basins for serving food (b) are sometimes elaborately painted in the inside and on the thickened rims, and most of these are oval or squarish in plan. Other kinds of surface finishing are nail incising, rim nicking, grooving, and corrugation.

(2) Lithic instruments included polished-stone axes (celts) made of basalt, diabase, melafire, and rarely gneiss; chipped-stone tools; ground or polished palm-nut breakers; slab abraders of sandstone and other abrasive rocks. In the historic period, there were many (3) wooden implements such as bows and arrows, clubs, knives, pounders, troughs, roasting paddles, and carved stools, some of the latter zoomorphic; (4) basketry containers and mats; (5) gourd recipients, spoons, and ladles; (6) shell scrapers, fishhooks, spoons, and ladles; (7) bone tools; (8) nets and hammocks; (9) textile bands and clothing such as loincloths and "shirts" were apparently used only by the Guarani. There were also many kinds of traps for terrestrial or aquatic animals and three types of watercraft: dugouts, bark canoes, and rafts. Archaeological utensils do not show a pattern of change through time. Tupinambá archaeology is less well known than that of the Guarani.

Ornaments. (1) Lip plugs of polished stones (usually quartz), resins, or bone; (2) polished stone pendants; (3) necklaces of shells and animal teeth. In the historic period, there were many (4) plume adornments such as headgear, capes, necklaces, belts, and arm or ankle rings, sometimes combining vegetable fibers and shells. Plumes could also be glued to the body. (5) Body painting in black (*Genipa*) and red (*Bixa*) was common.

Trade. Rocks for lithic instruments and clays for white slip, which were not found everywhere, would have been traded. In historic times, there was mention of short- and long-distance trade of rocks for lip plugs and axes, plumes, decorated gourds, textiles, pottery, and in the case of the Guarani, bits of silver and gold. Redistribution was part of the reciprocity system.

Division of Labor. In historic times, labor activities followed the lines of age and gender. Many of them were collectively done.

Differential Access or Control of Resources. In historic times, there were hints about differential access or control of such resources as fishing in prime locations.

Sociopolitical Organization

Social Organization. In historic times, the social organization was based in undifferentiated lineal descent. There were no lineage or clan systems. Tupi and Guarani kinship structures were *sui generis* and cannot be compared with the paradigmatic ones. The linearity was based in a kindred system. Marriage depended on social position. Polygamy was restricted to chiefs and warriors. Extended families were the rule.

Political Organization. In historic periods, there was a vertical organization for political authority, constituted by the chiefs of extended families, the village, and the region. Villages were related by kinship and alliances and participated in the same rituals, defense of territory, and raiding warfare. Chiefdom was gained through personal prestige; the better hunter, warrior, and orator, generous with his wealth. Chiefs represented the extended families, coordinated, hunting, fishing and house building, and in the past waged war, but did not have coercive power. Actual chiefs wished to maintain power in their families. Sometimes political and religious power was vested in the same individual.

Social Control. Social control was based solely on tradition.

Conflict. In historic times, domestic conflict was handled by the chief of the extended family and intravillage conflict by the village chief. External warfare was endemic and engaged for (1) revenge, usually in response to the seizing of women, (2) gaining prestige, and (3) economic advantages in terms of access to prime agricultural lands. An important motif for warfare was obtaining prisoners to be sacrificed in anthropophagic rituals. Every man was a warrior, and success in war was a source of status and the usual means to attain chiefdom. Some of the larger villages were palisaded. Long wooden trumpets terminated by a conch shell or gourd were used in combat.

Religion and Expressive Culture

Religious Beliefs. The Guarani had an imposing mythology with series of powerful gods inhabiting a multilayered cosmos. Gods created and will destroy the world. Spirits were masters of animals, plants, and places. Supernatural relations were surmised between animals and plants and men. Shamanic practices and witchcraft were very common. Messianic and revivalistic movements were common in historic times. The Guarani had gods, spirits and ghosts. The Tupinambá had mostly harmful ghosts. The power of speech was central for the Tupi cultures.

Religious Practitioners. In historic times, there was a horizontal organization for religious authority. Shamans were born. Among the Guarani, they had different functions: "suckers" attended to natural illnesses, and "blowers" to religious problems. Shamans wore ritual sticks. The bones of great shamans were kept in adorned hammocks hung in special huts and worshiped and consulted for oracles.

Ceremonies. Drinking bouts celebrated the mayor events of life. Maize, manioc, yams, sweet potatoes, all fruits, and honey were brewed in beverages with variable alcohol content. All praying was done through dancing accompanied by sacred religious instruments: the gourd rattle for men and the stamping tube for women. Guarani: *maté* (*Illex paraguayensis*) and tobacco seen to have been taken mostly by shamans in religious rituals. Archaeological clay pipes were straight. Nowadays, wooden and clay pipes are elbowed. Tupinambá: Tobacco was smoked by everyone in huge cigars. Tubular cane pipes were used only by shamans.

Arts. Ornaments and the motifs displayed on them, like the motifs painted on vessels, gourds for drinking, and on textiles or woven in baskets, could be regarded as true artistic manifestations whatever their functional meaning. The motifs in pottery painting and in basketry could be described as geometric. Modern basketry still has woven motifs. Flutes were made from the long bones of slain enemies. In the historic period, the most important expressive art seens to be oratory.

Death and Afterlife. Some people were interred in primary or secondary burials inside ceramic vessels; in the case of the Guarani, these were the larger jars for serving drinks, and in the case of the Tupinambá, the larger basins used for serving food. Anthropophagic rituals were focal for both the Guarani and the Tupinambá religion and societies. Prisoners of war were clubbed to death and ritually eaten in well-attended eating and drinking bouts.

Suggested Readings

Brochado, José Proenza (1984). "An Ecological Model of the Spread of Pottery and Agriculture into Eastern South America." Ph.D. diss., Department of Anthropology, University of Illinois, Urbana-Champaign.

Brochado, José Proenza (1989). "A expansão dos Tupi e da cerâmica da tradição policrômica amazônica." *Dédalo, Revista do Museu de Arqueologia e Etnologia* 27: 65–82.

Métraux, Alfred (1928). *La Civilisation matérielle des tribus Tupi-Guaraní*. Paris: Librarie Orientaliste.

Métraux, Alfred (1948). "The Guarani." In *Handbook of South American Indians*, vol. 3, ed. J. H. Steward. Washington, D.C.: Smithsonian Institution, Bulletin 143, Bureau of American Ethnology, 69–94.

Métraux, Alfred (1948). "The Tupinambá." In *Handbook of South American Indians*, vol. 3, ed. J. H. Steward. Washington, D.C.: Smithsonian Institution, Bulletin 143, Bureau of American Ethnology, 95–133.

Noelli, Francisco S. (1993). "Sem Tekohá não há Tekó (em busca de um modelo etnoarqueológico da subsistência e da aldeia Guarani aplicado a uma área de domínio no delta do Jacuí-RS)." M.A. thesis, Instituto de Filosofia e Ciências Humanas, Pontifícia Universidade Católica do Rio Grande do Sul, Porto Alegre.

Noelli, Francisco S. (1998). "The Tupi: Explaining Origin and Expansions in Terms of Archaeology and of Historical Linguistics." *Antiquity* 72: 648–663.

Prous, André (1992). *A arqueologia brasileira*. Brasília: Editora da Universidade Nacional de Brasília.

Rodrigues, Aryon D. (1964). "A classificação do tronco lingüístico Tupi." *Revista de Antropologia* 12: 99–104.

Rodrigues, Aryon D. (1984–1985). "Relações internas na família lingüística Tupi-guarani." *Revista de Antropologia* 27–28: 33–53.

Viveiros De Castro, Eduardo B. (1992). *From the Enemy's Point of View: Humanity and Divinity in Amazonian Society*. Chicago: University of Chicago Press.

Wagley, Charles (1977). *Welcome of Tears*. Prospect Heights: Waveland Press.

SUBTRADITIONS

Guarani

The term may be applied to (a) speakers of the Guarani language, (b) the Guarani archaeological culture, and (c) the ethnohistoric and ethnographic culture of the Guarani. There is evidence that (c) were those that left (b) and that they spoke a language of the Tupi-Guarani family of the Tupi stock (a); therefore they partake of the archaeological, ethnohistoric, ethnographic, and linguistic data (Brochado 1984; Noelli 1998).

TIME PERIOD: Guarani was spoken from 2500 B.P. (that is the glotochronological estimate for the origin of proto-Guarani), around 100 radiocarbon assays (Carbon 14) suggest that the Guarani occupied the area beginning 1800 B.P. and the ethnohistoric Guarani were known from the beginning of the historic period (450 B.P.). Classical pottery was discontinued about 300 B.P., but the Guarani language is still spoken and part of their culture is still extant (Brochado 1984, 1989; Montoya 1876a, 1876b; Noelli 1998).

LOCATION: (a) Guarani subtradition sites have been found in an area forming a massive block between the Atlantic coast and the Paraguay river, stretching from the tropic of Capricorn to the Río de La Plata. In that area, as many as 900 archaeological sites have been surveyed. (b) Most Guarani speakers lived and still live inland on the watersheds of the Paraná, Paraguay and Uruguay, but their territory extended to the adjoining stretch of the coast to the south (Brochado 1984, 1989; Métraux 1928a, 1948; Noelli 1993, 1998; Susnik 1975). Since the Guarani material culture, in what can be ascertained archaeologically (painted pottery and vessel forms), is at least 2 millenia earlier in Amazonia, it is believed that the Guarani spread from north to south by the way of the rivers that connect the basins of the Amazon and the Paraná, but by exactly what rivers has not been ascertained yet (Brochado and Lathrap 1982). Around 100 radiocarbon assays suggest that the Guarani occupied the area beginning 2000 B.P. The process included a very rapid initial spread over all the core area, along the major rivers, followed by a more gradual occupation climbing the lesser rivers up to the southern highlands. Only after 950 B.P., the Guarani attained their historic southern and eastern boundaries on the Rio de La Plata and the Atlantic coast (Brochado 1984, 1989; Noelli 1993, 1998).

DIAGNOSTIC MATERIAL ATTRIBUTES: Archaeological utensils were (1) sand-tempered pottery, fashioned by coiling from local available clays and fired over an open fire. The characteristic functional forms are (a) inflected cooking pots, (b) large deep conical bowls also for cooking, (c) simple bowls for eating, and (d) simple, (e) inflected, or (f) complex (carinated) bowls for drinking, and (g) large inflected or complex (carinated) jars for storing water or brewing and serving alcoholic beverages. Most vessels have conical bases. The coiled technique of vessel forming has not been often obliterated externally; therefore most vessels were finished by a kind of complex corrugation. Some vessels have white or red slip, and others show an elaborated polychrome painting in red and/or black or brown on a white slip. Polychrome painting is found inside the simple drinking bowls (d) and on the outside of the complex (carinated) bowls for drinking (f) and the inflected and complex serving jars (g). Other kinds of surface finishing are smoothing, nail incising, pinching, rim nicking, punctations, and brushing. (2) Lithic instruments included polished stone axes (celts) made of basalt, diabase, melafire, and rarely gneiss; stone pendants; slender T-shaped labrets made of quartz, up to 8 cm long; bipolar flaked chert tools and massive bifaced choppers; ground or polished palm-nut breakers; slab abraders of sandstone and other abrasive rocks (Brochado 1984, 1989; Brochado et al. 1990; Landa 1995; LaSalvia and Brochado 1989; Lothrop 1932; Métraux 1928a, 1948; Montoya 1876a, 1876b; Noelli 1993, 1998; Scattamacchia 1981, 1990; Schmitz 1991; Susnik 1982, 1983, 1984). Archaeological utensils do not show a pattern of change through time. Seriated sequences of the frequency of sherds with different surface finishing techniques built around about 100 radiocarbon assays (Carbon 14) do not show trends through time but rather oscillations around a means (Brochado 1984). In the historic period, there were many (3) wooden implements such as bows and arrows, clubs, knifes, pounders, troughs, roasting paddles, and carved stools, some of the latter zoomorphic; (4) basketry containers and mats; (5) gourd recipients, spoons, and ladles; (6) shell scrappers, fishhooks, spoons, and ladles; (7) bone tools; (8) textile bands and clothing such as loincloths and "shirts"; (9) nets and hammocks. There were also many kinds of traps for terrestrial or aquatic animals and three types of watercraft: dugouts, bark canoes, and rafts (Landa, 1995; Métraux 1928a, 1948; Montoya 1876a, 1876b; Müller 1934–1935, 1989; Noelli 1993; Scattamacchia 1981, 1990; Susnik 1982, 1983, 1984). In the historic period (17th–19th centuries), the Guarani were gathered in Catholic missions, and their pottery changed radically, assuming European characteristics.

CULTURAL SUMMARY

Environment

Climate is humid, mesothermal, or subtropical, characterized by mean monthly temperatures between 14–24°, from 1000 mm to more than 2000 mm of rain, and no dry season. At the lower elevations and along the coast, summers are hot (Cfa). At the top of the uplands, the climate is characterized by cool summers and relatively cold winters (Cfb). Winter temperature around 0° C on a few days and summer around 30° C. They occupied the major river valleys up to 400–800 m elevation, lowlands, and coastal lacustrine environments. Their habitat was characterized by river valleys dissecting the effusive rocks of the southern *planalto*, the granite (metamorphic rocks of the East Brazilian) sheeld and its peripheral areas, and the adjoining sand plains of the Atlantic coast. Basalt, sandstones, and quartz (crystalline rocks) were employed for the stone tools. The Guarani occupation was restricted to forested areas: tropical semideciduous forests, gallery forests, and riverine or lacustrine coastal environments. Rich diversity of plant and animal life (Brochado 1984; Métraux 1928a; Montoya 1876a, 1876b; Müller 1934–1935, 1989).

Settlements

Darkened soil and concentrations of sherds where houses are thought to have been are circular, measuring up to 10 m in diameter, or elongated, measuring 20 by 10 m. The thickness of the archaeological deposits is generally only 15–20 cm and does not exceed 30–40 cm (Brochado 1984; Noelli 1993; Scattamacchia 1981, 1990). In the historic period, there were (1) hamlets of only one or two houses, (2) small villages of up to 8 houses, often arranged linearly or in circle around a plaza (some of these villages were fortified with palisades), (3) permanent campsites for agriculture, fishing, and gathering, and (4) seasonal campsites for hunting, fishing, and gathering, sometimes related to shell middens. Wooden houses were oval, rectangular with rounded ends or circular in plan, measuring up to 50 m; they were covered with palm leaves, grass or bark and had ogival roof walls (Métraux 1928a, 1948; Montoya 1876a, 1876b; Müller 1934–1935, 1989; Susnik 1975, 1982, 1983, 1984). Communities seen to have been located to have access to (1) good soils for slash-and-burn horticulture, (2) water resources for drinking, fishing, and canoeing, (3) hunting grounds, (4) mineral (clay and stone) resources. In the historic period, communities were organized in webs capable of expanding and contracting according to environmental and political circumstances (Montoya 1876a, 1876b; Noelli 1993, 1998).

Sociopolitical Organization

Preferred marriages were between cross-cousins. Polygyny was a mark of prestige and a source of wealth. Each communal house had a headman and each village its own chief. Some chiefs extended their power over a whole district and commanded a great many villages. Rank was determined by war prowess, magic power, oratorical gifts, and wealth (Métraux 1928a, 1928b; 1948; Montoya 1876a, 1876b; Schaden 1974; Soares 1997). Four major activity areas have been suggested for the historic period and present villages: (1) communal square for public activities, (2) domestic front for public activities, (3) domestic back for private and "messy" activities, and (4) communal back for "messy" activities (Noelli 1993).

Religion and Expressive Culture

The Guarani still have an imposing mythology with series of powerful gods inhabiting a multilayered cosmos. Gods created and will destroy the world. Spirits are masters of animals, plants, and places. Supernatural relations are surmised between animals and plants and men. Shamanic practices and witchcraft were very common. Messianic and revivalistic movements were common in historic times. They had gods, spirits, and ghosts. In historic times, there was a horizontal organization for religious authority. Shamans were born, and they had different functions: "suckers" attended to natural illnesses and "blowers" to religious problems. Shamans wore ritual sticks. The bones of great shamans were kept in adorned hammocks hung in special huts and worshiped and consulted for oracles. Drinking bouts celebrated the major events of life. Maize, manioc, yam, sweet potato, all fruits, and honey were brewed in beverages with variable alcohol content. All praying was done through dancing accompanied by the sacred religious instruments: the gourd rattle for men and the stamping tube for women. Maté (*Illex paraguayensis*) and tobacco seem to have been taken mostly by shamans in religious rituals. Archaeological clay pipes were straight. Nowadays, wooden and clay pipes are elbowed.

Ornaments and the motifs displayed on them, like the motifs painted on archaeological vessels, gourds for drinking and on textiles or woven in baskets, could be regarded as true artistic manifestations regardless of their functional meaning. The motifs in pottery painting and in basketry could be described as geometric. Modern basketry still has woven motifs. Flutes were made from the long bones of slain enemies. In the historic period, the most important expressive art seened to be oratory. Some people were interred in primary or secondary burials inside ceramic vessels of different sizes, most of then in the large painted jars for serving drinks. Anthropophagic rituals were focal for religion and society. Prisoners of war were clubbed to death and ritually eaten in well-attended eating and drinking bouts (Landa, 1995; Lothrop 1932; Métraux 1928a, 1928b, 1948; Montoya 1876a, 1876b; Noelli and Brochado 1998; Schaden 1974; Soares 1997; Susnik 1975, 1982, 1983, 1984).

References

Brochado, José P. (1984). "An Ecological Model of the Spread of Pottery and Agriculture into Eastern South America." Ph.D. diss., University of Illinois, Urbana-Champaign.

Brochado, José P., and Donald W. Lathrap (1982). "Amazonia." Unpublished manuscript, Department of Anthropology, University of Illinois, Urbana-Campaign.

Brochado, José P., and Gislene Monticelli (1994). "Regras práticas na reconstrução gráfica das vasilhas cerâmicas Guarani a partir dos fragmentos." *Estudos Ibero-Americanos* 20, 2: 107–118.

Brochado, José P., Gislene Monticelli, and E. Neumann (1990). "Analogia etnográfica na reconstrução gráfica das vasilhas Guarani arqueológicas." *Veritas* 35, 140: 727–743.

Landa, Beatriz (1995). "A mulher Guarani: Atividades e cultura material." M.A. thesis, Pontifícia Universidade Católica do Rio Grande do Sul, Porto Alegre.

La Salva, Fernando, and José P. Brochado (1989). *Cerâmica Guarani.* Porto Alegre: Posenato Arte e Cultura.

Lothrop, Samuel K. (1932). "Indians of the Paraná Delta, Argentina." *Annals of the New York Academy of Science* 32: 77–232.

Métraux, Alfred (1928a). *La Civilisation materiélle des tribus Tupi-guarani.* Paris: Librarie Orientaliste.

Métraux, Alfred (1928b). *La Réligion des Tupinambá et ses rapports avec celle des autres tribus Tupí-guarani.* Paris: Bibliothèque de l'École des Hautes Études, vol. 15.

Métraux, Alfred (1948). "The Guarani." In *Handbook of South American Indians*, vol. 3, ed. J. H. Steward. Washington, D.C.: Smithsonian Instituition, Bulletin 143, Bureau of American Ethnology, 69–94.

Montoya, Antonio Ruiz de (1876a). *Arte Bocabvlario, Tesoro y Catesismo de la lengva Gvarani, por Antonio Ruiz de Montoya, publicado nuevamente sin alteración alguna por Júlio Platzmann*, 4 vols, Leipzig: Julio Platzmann, B. G. Teubner.

Montoya, Antonio Ruiz de (1876b). *Arte de la lengua guarani, ó mas bien tupi.* Vienna: Faesy y Frick; Paris: Maisonneuve y Cia.

Müller, Franz (1934–1935). "Beiträge zur Ethnographie der Guaraní-Indianer im östlichen Waldgebiet von Paraguay." *Anthropos* 29–30.

Müller, Franz (1989). *Etnografía de los Guaraní del Alto Paraná.* Rosario: Colegio Salesiano San José.

Noelli, Francisco S. (1993). "Sem Tekohá não há Tekó (em busca de um modelo etnoarqueológico da subsistência e da aldeia Guarani aplicado a uma área de domínio no delta do Jacuí-RS)." M.A.

thesis, Pontifícia Universidade Católica do Rio Grande do Sul, Porto Alegre.

Noelli, Francisco S. (1998). "The Tupi: Explaining Origin and Expansions in Terms of Archaeology and of Historical Linguistics." *Antiquity* 72: 648–663.

Noelli, Francisco S., and José P. Brochado (1998). "O cauim e as beberagens dos Guarani e Tupinambá: Equipamentos, técnicas de preparação e consumo." *Revista do Museu de Arqueologia e Etnologia* 8.

Scattamacchia, M. C. T. (1981). "Tentativa de caracterização da tradição Tupiguarani." M.A. essay, Universidade de São Paulo, SAB.

Scattamacchia, M. C. T. (1990). "A Tradição Policrômica no Leste da América do Sul evidenciada pela ocupação Guarani e Tupinambá: Fontes arqueológicas e etnohistóricas." Ph.D. diss., Universidade de São Paulo.

Schaden, Egon (1974). *Aspectos fundamentais da cultura Guarani.* São Paulo: Editora da USP.

Schmitz, Pedro Inácio (1991). "Migrantes da Amazônia: A Tradição Tupiguarani." In *Arqueologia pré-histórica do Rio Grande do Sul,* ed. A. A. Kern. Porto Alegre: Mercado Aberto (Série Documenta/RS).

Soares, André Luis R. (1997). *Guarani: Organização social e arqueologia.* Porto Alegre: EDIPUCRS, Coleção Arqueologia 4.

Susnik, Branislava (1975). *Dispersión Tupi-Guaraní prehistórica: Ensayo analítico.* Asunción: Museo Etnográfico "Andrés Barbero."

Susnik, Branislava (1982, 1983, 1984). *Los aborígenes del Paraguay, IV: Cultura material, V: Ciclo vital y estructura social, VI: Aproximación a las creencias de los indígenas.* Asunción: Museu Etnográfico "Andrés Barbero."

Tupinambá

The term may be applied to (a) speakers of the Tupinambá language; (b) the Tupinambá archaeological culture; and (c) the ethnohistoric and ethnographic culture of the Tupinambá. There is evidence that (c) were those that left (b) and that they spoke a language of the Tupi-Guarani family of the Tupi stock (a); therefore they partake of the archaeological, ethnohistoric, ethnographic, and linguistic data (Brochado 1984, 1989; Fausto 1992; Fernandes 1963, 1970; Martin 1996: 169–182; Noelli 1998).

TIME PERIOD: Tupinambá was spoken from 2500 B.P. (that is the glotochronological estimate for the origin of the proto-Tupinambá); around 20 radiocarbon assays (Carbon 14) suggest that the Tupinambá occupied the area beginning 2000 B.P.; and the ethnohistoric Tupinambá were known from the beginning of the historic period (500 B.P.), but all of them had disappeared by the middle of the 19th century (150 B.P.) (Brochado 1984; Noelli 1998).

LOCATION: (b) Tupinambá subtradition sites have been found in a strip 200–700 km in width, bordering the Atlantic coast from Maranhão in the north to the tropic of Capricorn, with an extension on the headwaters of the Araguaia. In that large area, only around 150 archaeological sites have been so far surveyed. (c) The speakers of Tupinambá lived mainly along the coast from the Río Pará, just south of the mouth of the Amazon, to the tropic of Capricorn, but their territory extended some distance inland as well (Brochado 1984, 1989; Fausto 1992; Fernandes 1963, 1970; Martin 1996; Métraux 1928a, 1948; Pinto 1935, 1938; Scattamacchia 1981, 1990). Since the Tupinambá material culture, in what can be ascertained archaeologically (painted pottery, some vessel forms such as reinforced rims) is at least 2 millenia earlier in Amazonia (Brochado and Lathrap 1982), it is believed that the Tupinambá spread from north to south along the Atlantic coast. The process of occupation cannot be ascertained because of the lack of field research and absolute or relative dating (Brochado 1984; Noelli 1998).

DIAGNOSTIC MATERIAL ATTRIBUTES: Archaeological utensils were (1) sand-tempered pottery, fashioned by coiling from local available clays and fired over an open fire. The characteristic functional forms are (a) large deep complex (carinated) cauldrons used for roasting manioc flour as well as for brewing alcoholic beverages and (b) large or medium-sized basins with thickened rims for serving food. Sometimes (c) large restricted ovoid jars or (d) inflected or complex (carinated) jars were used for storing water or brewing and serving alcoholic beverages. Flat plates to roast *beiju* are rare (e). Most vessels have flat bases and are plain. The large basins for serving food (b) are usually elaborately painted on the inside and on the thickened rims with lines in red and/or black or brown on a white slip, and most of these are oval or squarish in shape. Other kinds of surface finishing are nail incising, rim nicking, grooving, and corrugation. (2) Lithic instruments included polished stone axheads (celts) made of basalt, diabase, melafire, quartzite, and rarely gneiss; stone pendants; lip plugs generally made of well-polished green stones such as amazonite, jadeite, green quartz, alabaster, and white quartz, in at least four distinguishable forms: cuneiform, straight, and conical; nail-shaped with a flat round head; thick and short, shaped like bottle stoppers, large buttons, or disks; or T-shaped, but with a thicker, conical or wedge-shaped foot; they measured up to 4 cm long and 25 mm in diameter. There are also ground or polished palm-nut breakers; chipped-stone tools; slab abraders of sandstone and other abrasive rocks (Brochado 1984, 1989, 1991; Fausto 1992; Martin 1996; Métraux 1928a, 1948; Noelli and Brochado 1998; Pinto 1935, 1938; Scattamacchia 1981, 1990). In the historic period, there were many (3) wooden implements such as bows and arrows, clubs, knives, pounders, troughs, roasting paddles, and carved stools, some of the latter zoomorphic; (4) basketry containers and mats; (5) gourd recipients, spoons, and ladles; (6) shell scrapers, fishhooks, spoons, and ladles; (7) bone tools; (8) nets and hammocks; (9) feather ornaments. There were also many kinds of traps for terrestrial or aquatic animals and three types of watercraft: dugouts, bark canoes, and rafts (Baldus 1970; Fausto 1992; Métraux 1928a, 1948; Pinto 1935, 1938). Archaeological utensils do not show a pattern of change through time. Seriated sequences of the frequency of sherds with different surface finishing techniques built around about 20 radiocarbon assays (Carbon 14) do not show trends through time but rather oscillations around a means (Brochado 1984).

CULTURAL SUMMARY

Environment

Tupinambá subtradition sites are found over all the coastal area from the tropic of Capricorn to the mouth of the Amazon with extensions westward to the São Francisco river basin; they occupied tropical climates ranging from humid (Af, Ams') on the eastern coast to dry and semiarid (Bsh) on the interior of northeastern Brazil. They ranged from coastal lacustrine environments at the back of mangrove swamps and the major river valleys at lower elevations to the mountains of southeastern Brazil up to 800 m elevation. Their habitat was characterized by the *restinga* formations in the sand plains of the Atlantic coast, low areas on the interior of northeastern Brazil, and the granite of the mountainous areas along the coast. Tupinambá occupation ranged from the riverine or lacustrine environments, mangrove swamps and tropical evergreen forests along the coast, to the gallery forests going into the tropical savannas and the subhumid forests (*agreste*) in northeastern Brazil (Brochado 1984, 1989; Fernandes 1963; Scattamacchia 1981, 1990). Rich diversity of plant and animal life. Fishing and mollusk collecting were very important (Métraux 1928a, 1948; Pinto 1935, 1938).

Settlements

Darkened soil and concentrations of sherds where houses are thought to have been are circular, measuring from 12–20 m in diameter. The thickness of the archaeological deposits does not exceed 40 cm (Martin 1996; Pallestrini 1975). In the historic period, there were (1) hamlets of only one or two houses, (2) small villages of up to 8 houses often arranged linearly or in a circle around a plaza (some of these villages were fortified with palisades), (3) permanent campsites for agriculture, fishing, and gathering, and (4) seasonal campsites for hunting, fishing, and gathering, sometimes related to shell middens. Wooden houses were rectangular in plan, measuring from 15 m to as much as 150 m in length by 9–15 m in width. The average house sheltered more than 100 people, and some are said to house up to 200 people. They were covered with palm leaves and had ogival roof walls. Communities seen to have been located to have access to (1) good soils for slash-and-burn horticulture, (2) water resources for drinking, fishing, and canoeing, (3) hunting grounds, (4) mineral (clay and stone) resources. In the historic period, communities were organized in webs capable of expanding and contracting according to environmental and political circumstances (Fausto 1992; Fernandes 1963, 1970; Métraux 1928a, 1948; Pinto 1935, 1938). No Tupinambá house has been completely excavated.

Sociopolitical Organization

Preferred marriages were between cross-cousins. Polygyny was a mark of prestige and a source of wealth. Each communal house had a headman, and each village its own chief. Some chiefs extended their power over a whole district and commanded a great many villages. Rank was determined by war prowess, magic power, oratorical gifts, and wealth. Guests were greeted with tears (Baldus 1970; Fausto 1992; Fernandes 1963, 1970; Métraux 1928a, 1928b, 1948; Pinto 1935, 1938).

Religion and Expressive Culture

Gods created and will destroy the world. Spirits were masters of animals, plants, and places. Supernatural relations are surmised between animals and plants and men. Shamanic practices and witchcraft were very common. Messianic and revivalistic movements were common in historic times. They had mostly harmful ghosts. The power of speech is central for the Tupi cultures. In historic times, there was a horizontal organization for religious authority. Shamans were born, and they had different functions: suckers attend to natural illnesses and blowers to religious problems. Shamans were ritual sticks. Drinking bouts celebrated the major events of life. Maize, manioc, yam, sweet potato, all fruits, and honey were brewed in beverages with variable alcohol content. All praying was done through dancing accompanied by the sacred religious instruments: the gourd rattle for men and the stamping tube for women. Tobacco seemed to have been taken mostly by shamans in religious rituals and was smoked by everyone in huge cigars. Tubular cane pipes were used only by shamans. Ornaments and the motifs displayed on them, like the motifs painted on archaeological vessels, gourds for drinking, and on textiles, or woven in baskets, could be regarded as true artistic manifestations whatever their functional meaning. The motifs in pottery painting could be described as geometric. Flutes were made from the long bones of slain enemies. Some people were interred in primary or secondary burials inside ceramic vessels, such as the large bowls used for serving food. Anthropophagic rituals were focal for religion and societies. Prisoners of war were clubbed to death and ritually eaten in well-attended eating and drinking bouts (Baldus 1970; Brochado 1991; Fausto 1992; Métraux 1928a, 1928b, 1948; Noelli and Brochado 1998; Pinto 1935, 1938).

References

Baldus, Herbert (1970). *Tapirapé, tribo Tupi no Brasil Central*. São Paulo: Companhia Editora Nacional.

Brochado, José Proenza (1984). "An Ecological Model of the Spread of Pottery and Agriculture into Eastern South America." Ph.D. diss., Department of Anthropology, University of Illinois, Urbana-Champaign.

Brochado, José Proenza (1989). "A expansão dos Tupi e da cerâmica da tradição policrômica amazônica." *Dédalo, Revista do Museu de Arqueologia e Etnologia* 27: 65–82.

Brochado, José Proenza (1991). "What Did the Tupinambá Cook in their Vessels?" *Revista de Arqueologia* 6: 40–89.

Brochado, José P., and Donald W. Lathrap (1982). "Amazonia." Unpublished manuscript, Department of Anthropology, University of Illinois, Urbana-Campaign.

Fausto, Carlos (1992). "Fragmentos de história e cultura Tupinambá: Da etnologia como instrumento crítico do conhecimento etnohistórico." In *História dos índios no Brazil*, ed. M.C. da Cunha. São Paulo: SMC/FAPESP/Companhia das Letras, 381–396.

Fernandes, Florestan (1963). *A Organização social dos Tupinambá*. São Paulo.

Fernandes, Florestan (1970). *A importância social da guerra na sociedade Tupinambá*. São Paulo: Editora da USP.

Métraux, Alfred (1928a). *La Civilisation matériélle des tribus Tupí-Guaraní*. Paris: Librarie Orientaliste.

Métraux, Alfred (1928b). "La Rél* avec celle des autres Tribus Tupi-Guarani." Paris: Bibliothèque de l'École des Hautes Études, vol. 15.

Métraux, Alfred (1948). "The Tupinambá." In *Handbook of South American Indians*, vol. 3, ed. J. H. Steward. Washington, D.C.: Smithsonian Institution, Bulletin 143, Bureau of American Ethnology, 95–133.

Noelli, Francisco S. (1993). "Sem Tekohá não há Tekó (em busca de um modelo etnoarqueológico da subsistência e da aldeia Guarani aplicado a uma área de domínio no delta do Jacuí-RS)." M.A. thesis, Pontifícia Universidade Católica do Rio Grande do Sul, Porto Alegre.

Noelli, Francisco S. (1998). "The Tupi: Explaining Origin and Expansions in Terms of Archaeology and of Historical Linguistics." *Antiquity* 72: 648–663.

Noelli, Francisco S., and José Proenza Brochado (1998). "O Cauim e as Beberagens dos Guarani e Tupinambá: Equipamentos, técnicas de preparação e consumo." *Revista do Museu de Arqueologia e Etnologia* 8.

Pinto, Estevão (1935, 1938). *Os indígenas do Nordeste*. São Paulo: Companhia Editora Nacional, Biblioteca Pedagógica Brasileira, ser. 5a., Brasiliana, vols. 44 and 112.

Scattamacchia, M. C. T. (1981). "Tentativa de caracterização da tradição Tupiguarani." M.A. diss., Universidade de São Paulo, SAB.

Scattamacchia, M. C. T. (1990). "A Tradição Policrômica no Leste da América do Sul evidenciada pela ocupação Guarani e Tupinambá: Fontes arqueológicas e etnohistóricas." Ph.D. diss., Universidade de São Paulo.

SITES

Almeida

TIME PERIOD: Ceramic level: 560–470 B.P. (thermoluminescence) (lithic level: 3600–930 B.P. (thermoluminescence and Carbon 14).

LOCATION: Near Tejupá, São Paulo, Brazil.

DESCRIPTIVE SUMMARY

Local Environment

Almeida is located on a low hill of sandstone, with outcrops of silicified sandstone on its west side. The area was covered by subtropical forest and drained by small streams.

Physical Features

The site covers 120 by 90 m. Ceramic is found to a depth of about 40 m, and down to 1.50 m there are only lithic artifacts and debris. Only two wares were described: plain and painted polychrome (red and black lines on a white slip). Lithic artifacts are described as polished axes, scrapers, knives, hammers, polishing stones, stone chips, and nuclei, in silicified sandstone.

Cultural Aspects

Almeida was a small village and contains nine areas of darkened soil described as houses, most of them disposed in one line oriented approximately east–west. Houses were circular and measured between 12–20 m.

The pottery as described appears to be from the Tupinambá subtradition.

References

Palestrini, Luciana (1975). "Interpretação das estruturas arqueológicas em sítios do Estado de São Paulo." *Coleção do Museu Paulista, Série Arqueologia* 1: 1–206.

Arroyo Malo

TIME PERIOD: Historic.

LOCATION: Near Buenos Aires, Argentina.

DESCRIPTIVE SUMMARY

Local Environment

Level ground, often inundated, along the Arroyo Malo, an affluent of the río Luján, which enters the río de La Plata estuary.

Physical Features

Two areas were excavated along the Arroyo Malo; one 143 m long and 2–21 m in width and another 27 m long and 2–13 m in width. Occupation was only 20–30 cm deep in very damp soil.

Cultural Aspects

Campsite and burial ground. Excavated five groups of urn burials, in each one vessel—often covered with an inverted bowl—contained human bones, and from two to three others contained food and red paint. Also 12 "sherd-burials" consisting of large fragments of pottery, food, red paint, clay firedogs, polished axes, hammers, bolas, and polishing stones, stone chips, and nuclei, associated with complete skeletons or scattered human bones. Vessel shapes were compared with Guarani pottery elsewhere. Four kinds of wares were described: corrugated, nail incised, red slipped, and polychrome (black-line geometric panels placed between red bands on a light gray background). Glass beads and potsherds of Spanish origin date the site in the historic period.

References

Lothrop, Samuel K. (1932). "Indians of the Paraná Delta, Argentina." *Annals of the New York Academy of Science* 33: 77–232.

Fazenda Soares

TIME PERIOD: Carbon 14 dates 580 B.P., 510 B.P.

LOCATION: Near Rio Grande, Rio Grande do Sul, Brazil.

DESCRIPTIVE SUMMARY

Local Environment

Level ground 1.5 km from Patos Lagoon, near sedimentary deposits of a coastal plain, 10 m above sea level.

Physical Features

Systematic surface collections over 650 m^2. Excavated areas: 250 m^2 by artificial levels of 5 cm, a trench 10 m long, 1 m wide, and 1.6 m deep, and 10 1 m^2 test pits. Occupation was 30–50 cm deep in a paleosoil overlaying the last marine transgression (Barreira – Lagunar III) composed of dark brown sandy wind deposits, humid and compact, indicating a climate warmer and more humid than now.

Cultural Aspects

There was uncovered one hearth with pottery vessel in situ and four postholes 30 cm in diameter and depths up to 1.20 m, aligned aproximately east–west, near charcoal, shellfish, crustacea, and mammal and bird bones. More than 12,000 pottery sherds: corrugated, plain, painted, and nail incised, sherd and sand tempered. Painted pottery was white slipped or polychrome (black and/or red lines or bands on white slip) forming geometric designs. Found also 229 lithics. Hamlet of at least one house oriented east–west; discard areas outside it. Urn burial with child near the house.

References

Brochado, José Proenza, and Klaus Hilbert (1999). "Os construtores de aterros na pré-história do Rio Grande do Sul. Uma revisão das evidências: o sítio Guarani da Fazenda Soares." Unpublished manuscript, Porto Alegre CEPA, IFCH, Pontifícia Universidade Católica do Rio Grande do Sul, Brazil.
Costa, Cristiane, and Mirian Carle, (1998). "Análise do material cerâmico Guarani de Povo Novo, Rio Grande, RS." *Histórica* 3.

São Miguel del Itaiacecó (Pedra Grande)

TIME PERIOD: Historic, A.D. 1628–1632.

LOCATION: Near São Pedro do Sul, Rio Grande do Sul, Brazil.

DESCRIPTIVE SUMMARY

Local Environment

Slightly slopping ground next to a huge sandstone block forming a shelter, on which wall there are petroglyphs engraved.

Physical Features

Scatered sherds over about 3 ha of sandy soil with some darkened spots about 100 by 70 m. Excavated 110 m^2 to a depth of 30–40 cm. Uncovered one house 8 by 4 m outlined by 10 postholes 30 cm in depth and 20–30 cm in diameter and one hearth inside it.

Cultural Aspects

One glass bead and two potsherds of Spanish origin, 2 iron knives, 6 iron nails, and 1 brass nail date the site in the historic period. Some of the Guarani vessels show European forms (flat-based bowls and dishes) and are painted red.

References

Brochado, José Proenza, and Klaus Hilbert (1999). "Pedra Grande, São Pedro do Sul, São Miguel do Itaiacecó." Unpublished manuscript, CEPA, IFCH, Pontifícia Universidade Católica do Rio Grande do Sul, Brazil.

Brochado, José Proenza, and Pedro Ignácio Schmitz (1976). "Petroglifos do estilo de pisadas no Rio Grande do Sul." *Estudos Íbero-Americanos* 2, 1: 93–145.

Hilbert, Klaus, and José Proenza Brochado (1997). "São Miguel de Itaiacecó: Uma redução do primeiro período no Rio Grande do Sul." *Congresso do Sociedade de Arqueologia Brasileira.*

Schmitz, Pedro Ignácio, and José Proenza Brochado (1982). "Petroglifos no estilo de pisadas no centro do Rio Grande do Sul." *Pesquisas. Antropologia* 34: 1–47.

JOSE PROENZA BROCHADO
CEPA, IFCH
Pontifica Universidade Catolica do RGS
Rio Grande del Sul
Brazil

Index